The New Antiquity

Series Editor
Matthew S. Santirocco
New York University
New York, USA

Over the past two decades, our understanding of the ancient world has been dramatically transformed as classicists and other scholars of antiquity have moved beyond traditional geographical, chronological, and methodological boundaries to focus on new topics and different questions. By providing a major venue for further cutting-edge scholarship, *The New Antiquity* will reflect, shape, and participate in this transformation. The series will focus on the literature, history, thought, and material culture of not only ancient Europe, but also Egypt, the Middle East, and the Far East. With an emphasis also on the reception of the ancient world into later periods, *The New Antiquity* will reveal how present concerns can be brilliantly illuminated by this new understanding of the past.

Del A. Maticic • Jordan Rogers
Editors

Working Lives in Ancient Rome

palgrave
macmillan

Editors
Del A. Maticic
Vassar College
Poughkeepsie, USA

Jordan Rogers
North Carolina State University
Raleigh, USA

ISSN 2946-3017 ISSN 2946-3025 (electronic)
The New Antiquity
ISBN 978-3-031-61233-6 ISBN 978-3-031-61234-3 (eBook)
https://doi.org/10.1007/978-3-031-61234-3

Cover illustration: Artefact / Alamy Stock Photo

This Palgrave Macmillan imprint is published by the registered company Springer Nature Switzerland AG.
The registered company address is: Gewerbestrasse 11, 6330 Cham, Switzerland

Craig Lanier Allen
Raffaella Cribiore
James Dryden
Gadget
Luann Gaffney
David Konstan
Eric Littmann
Vania Pittioni
Caroline Porter
James Elbert Rivers
Ashley Simone

Preface

In the summer of 2018, after a hard day's work excavating in the Roman colony of Cosa, we were sitting on the balcony of our hotel under the Tuscan twilight engaged in a spirited discussion about the unspeakable nature of the academic job. At the time, both of us were still graduate students, and even in that pre-pandemic world were both living in a state of irresolvable anxiety about our professional futures. Would there be jobs? Would we be good enough (and lucky enough) to get those jobs? What even *were* the jobs we wanted so badly?

It was immediately apparent that this set of questions was no less relevant in an ancient Roman context than it was in the present. How, in short, did the ancient Roman conceive of the relationship between their labor and their lives? What is the relationship between knowledge and practice in Roman professional settings? To what extent are ancient professions "describable," and what do the limits of those descriptions reveal about different forms of Roman agency? Does ancient evidence reify the familiar categories of "elite" vs. "non-elite" work, or do these distinctions get blurred and confused through various forms of collaboration and comparison? To what extent do ancient Roman discourses on jobs and professions enable us to think differently about our own categories of work and labor?

We decided in Cosa that we wanted to work together to organize a conference on these questions, and upon returning from the field we began to plan the series of meetings and presentations that ultimately culminated in this volume. But the path to this end was circuitous, and the onset of the pandemic demanded we adjust. Embracing our new working lives, conducted entirely via the computer screen, we invited a dozen specialists in various sub-disciplines of Roman studies to offer papers in a digital workshop series that spanned the 2020–21 academic year, titled *Work/Life: Institutions, Subjectivities, and Human Resources in the Roman World*. While these workshops were designed initially to facilitate interdisciplinary discussions on the nature of Roman work/life, they were also welcome reminders of the human contact that made our own work matter in our own lives. Given the success of the digital workshop series, we invited the speakers to participate in the annual Ranieri Colloquium held at NYU, to which we also lent the same title. This, too, was held entirely online over the course of three days in Fall 2021, from October 13 to October 15.

This volume began as a means of grappling with the difficulties of our working lives during a pandemic that forced many to reconsider what constituted "work" and "life" in the first place, especially as homes were transformed into offices, schools, and daycares all at once. It was also a way for two young academics facing the impending vagaries of a brutal and often dehumanizing job market, to guide their work/life anxieties in a productive direction. It has, despite a challenge, been a labor of love that both of us look back upon fondly. We hope that the papers collected here spark some insights, crack some smiles, and inspire intellectual and emotional solidarity across disciplinary and professional boundaries.

Poughkeepsie, NY, USA — Del A. Maticic
Raleigh, NC, USA — Jordan Rogers

Acknowledgments

Our gratitude is due first and foremost to Matthew Santirocco, who from the earliest days has been an ardent supporter of this project. When Del first awkwardly explained the idea to him in the spring of 2018, he immediately said that if we put a volume together on the topic, he would consider it for the *The New Antiquity* book series. Now here we are. He lent the imprimatur of the NYU Center for Ancient Studies to our year-long workshop series and gave us the distinct honor of the first graduate students to organize the annual Ranieri Colloquium of the Center. This project simply would not have existed without him, and we are both lucky to have learned from his unmatched leadership and intellectual generativity.

This has been a highly collaborative project, and many people have contributed to its outcomes. The inimitable Maura Pollard provided administrative support for many years and events and made our lives immeasurably easier as a result. In addition to those who contributed chapters, many others have contributed to different phases. Joe Howley contributed both a workshop and a conference paper but was prevented by work/life from submitting a chapter. But his influence on the volume is felt throughout. Astrid Van Oyen presented a paper at the workshop and acted as a panel moderator at the conference. Emilia Barbiero, Dan-el Padilla Peralta, Nandini Pandey, and Lauren Hackworth Petersen also served as conference panel moderators, richly adding to the discussion. Dozens of others were faithful supporters of the conference as audience members of the conference, the workshops, and a conference paper delivered by Jordan at the 2019 Annual Meeting of CAMWS. We could never produce a complete list of these work/lifers who attended our workshop, but they include Emily French, Ian Goh, David Levene, Mark Letteney, Rhiannon Pare, Marcie Persyn, Mike Peachin, Brent Shaw, Irene Soto Marín, and many more. Finally, at its earliest stage, we recall with warmth and gratitude the discussions about work/life during the 2018 season of the Cosa Excavations, where we both met many great friends and collaborators.

Many friends and family members have supported both editors in this process. Special thanks is due to Cherihan and Cara, for putting up with our chatty enthusiasm for this collaboration. In addition, Del is grateful to Ben Nikota, Figen Geerts, Josh Ziesel, Chase Mizzell, and his brother Eric for reading drafts and for the intellectual and personal conversation about living and working. Jordan bears eternal gratitude toward his parents, Maria and Dean Rogers, whose own working lives, arduous as they at times were, allowed them to nourish his curiosities and support him in his pursuit of a work/life in the academy.

Though this book is about life, it came to be in a period of time filled with profound loss. Many of those involved in this project lost loved ones during this project's lifespan. It is to them, in loving memory, that we dedicate this volume.

Contents

Notes on Contributors

John Bodel is W. Duncan MacMillan II Professor of Classics and Professor of History at Brown University. He writes about ancient Roman history and religion, epigraphy, and Latin literature, especially of the Roman Empire, and he has broad comparative interests in slavery, funerals and burial customs, and ancient writing systems. Since 1995 he has directed the U.S. Epigraphy Project, the purpose of which is to gather and share information about ancient Greek and Latin inscriptions in American collections.

Caroline Cheung is Assistant Professor of Classics at Princeton University. She works on the socio-economic history, material culture, and archeology of the Roman Empire. To study groups in history that are often invisible, muted, and silent, she works across disciplinary boundaries using a variety of sources, and her interests inhabit overlapping areas of the field of classics, spanning from the material to the textual. Her scholarship to date explores ancient agriculture and food; technology, craft production, and labor; and urban and rural relations. Her works have been published in the *American Journal of Philology*, *Archaeometry*, *Quaternary International*, *Bulletin of the American Society of Papyrologists*, and *Oxyrhynchus Papyri* as well as several edited volumes. [She received her PhD in Ancient History and Mediterranean Archaeology from the University of Berkeley, California, an MA in Classical Archaeology from the Florida State University, and a post-baccalaureate certificate in Classics, BA in Classical Civilization, and BS in Biochemistry from the University of California, Los Angeles.]

Marco Formisano is Professor of Latin Literature at Ghent University (Belgium). He has written extensively on late antique literature as well as on early Christian martyr acts (in particular Perpetua and Polycarp). Other research interests include ancient technical texts, Ovid's *Metamorphoses*, and Classical reception in film and literature. He is editor of the series "sera tela. Studies in Late Antique Literature and its Reception" (Bloomsbury) and "The Library of the Other Antiquity" (Universitätsverlag Winter, Heidelberg) and he is the Principal Investigator of the research project "Coming After. Late Antique Ecopoetics," funded by FWO, Research Foundation Flanders.

Tom Geue teaches Latin at the Australian National University. He has written about Roman satire, anonymous Roman literature, and the repressions of slavery in Virgil's Georgics. His 2019 book, *Author Unknown*, proposed some new ways of working with anonymous authorship; the next installment will hopefully treat the ultimate anonymous author, the enslaved amanuensis co-authoring alongside Virgils and Horaces. In the meantime, he's writing something between intellectual history and classical scholarship, called *Major Corrections: The Materialist Philology of Sebastiano Timpanaro* (forthcoming with Verso). It seeks to show technical philology and militant Marxism working together toward a future of full human flourishing.

Nicole J. Giannella is Assistant Professor of Classics at Cornell University. Her research focuses on understandings of slavery, freedom, and ownership in Roman legal, literary, and philosophical texts. She is working on a book on slavery and the limits of ownership in Roman society and law. She has a PhD from the University of Southern California and a BA from Vassar College.

Claire Holleran is Associate Professor in Classics and Ancient History at the University of Exeter. Her research focuses on Roman social and economic history, particularly the Roman economy, ancient retail, and human mobility. She is the author of *Shopping in Ancient Rome: The Retail Trade in the Late Republic and the Principate* (OUP, 2012), and co-editor of *Demography and the Greco-Roman World* (CUP, 2011), *A Companion to the City of Rome* (Wiley-Blackwell, 2018), and *A Handbook to Diet and Nutrition in the Roman World* (Routledge, 2018).

Ann Kuttner is Associate Professor in History of Art at the University of Pennsylvania and was trained at Bryn Mawr and UC Berkeley; she works in Hellenistic, Roman, and Late Antique interdisciplinary studies of western Eurasia and northern Africa. Her publications engage multiple media and spectacles of display, public and domestic, taking in images, architecture, and landscape architecture. Material subjects range from the monumental domain to small portable things. Political and social contexts of decor are an abiding interest. She also works on ancient Greek and Latin texts that engage visual and material culture.

Del A. Maticic is the Blegen Research Fellow in Greek and Roman Studies at Vassar College. He writes about Latin literature and its reception and is interested especially in how Latin authors draw connections between literature, the built environment, and the natural world. His current book project, *The Invention of Metal in Latin Literature* is a study of *metalla*—mines, quarries, and the substances obtained from them—in Latin literature. Beyond this he is also interested in globalizing approaches to Classics and the ethical stakes of philology.

Jordan Rogers received his Ph.D. in Ancient History from the University of Pennsylvania, USA, and is currently an Assistant Professor in the Department of History at North Carolina State University. His research concerns Roman social and cultural history, especially the sociology of small communities in urban environments. His current monograph project, *Making Neighbors: Neighborhoods, Neighborliness, and Urban Community in Republican Rome*, explores the social production of neighborhood spaces and the norms that governed everyday life in the city of Rome.

Jane Sancinito is Assistant Professor of History at the University of Massachusetts Lowell. Her first book, *The Reputation of the Roman Merchant* (University of Michigan Press, 2024), addresses the institutional power of social ties in the Roman economy. She is also pursuing research on the history of greed in the Mediterranean and the coinage of the third century CE.

Rebecca Sausville's research interests include urbanism and civic identity in imperial Greece and Anatolia, skilled labor, and ancient education. She has taught at Brandeis University, NYU, and the University of Kentucky, and conducted fieldwork and research across Greece, Sicily, and Cyprus. Sausville has an abiding interest in supporting doctoral students as they navigate professional life within, adjacent to, and beyond academia, and currently works in graduate student professional development at Princeton University.

Abbreviations of Ancient Sources and Corpora

Abbreviations of ancient authors and texts follow the conventions set out by *Oxford Classical Dictionary*, 4th ed. (https://oxfordre.com/classics/fileasset/images/ORECLA/OCD.ABBREVIATIONS.pdf).

Abbreviations of corpora for inscriptions of the Greek language follow the conventions set out by the International Association for Greek and Latin Epigraphy, AIEGL (https://www.aiegl.org/grepiabbr.html). Those for inscriptions of the Latin language follow the conventions described by the Epigraphik-Datenbank Clauss/Slaby (https://db.edcs.eu/epigr/hinweise/abkuerz.html).

References to papyri or ostraca follow the abbreviations described in the checklist available on papyri.info (https://papyri.info/docs/checklist).

List of Figures

PART I

Getting Up, Brushing Up, and Going In

CHAPTER 1

Structuring Subjects: Weaving the Web of Work/Life

Del A. Maticic and Jordan Rogers

Studs Terkel opens his classic 1974 oral history of labor, *Working*, by remarking that "[t]his book, being about work, is, by its very nature, also about violence—to the spirit as well as to the body."[1] Work, along the lines sketched in the book, constitutes above all the soul-crushing drudgery of daily toil, the control exerted by employers over their laborers' very lives, and the physical dangers posed by the work itself. This picture of labor is all too recognizable in the wake of the epoch-defining COVID-19 pandemic in the United States and worldwide, a moment in which pundits

We extend our thanks to Kim Bowes and to the anonymous reviewers for their criticisms and suggestions in improving this piece.

D. A. Maticic (✉)
Vassar College, Poughkeepsie, NY, USA
e-mail: dmaticic@vassar.edu

J. Rogers (✉)
North Carolina State University, Raleigh, USA
e-mail: jrroger7@ncsu.edu

D. A. Maticic, J. Rogers (eds.), *Working Lives in Ancient Rome*, The New Antiquity,
https://doi.org/10.1007/978-3-031-61234-3_1

and bad-faith politicians have framed the decision to commute to work or to remain home as a binary one. According to this false dichotomy, one must either contribute virtuously to the economic machine or acquiesce lazily to the dissolution of the civilized world.[2] This type of fallacious reasoning has only exacerbated how acutely many have come to feel the innate violence of labor, as Terkel remarked almost fifty years ago.[3] The condition of the laboring body in the system of capitalism has no less been a subject of Marxist criticism.[4] But such a pessimistic take as this is not merely the product of a modern capitalist economic model; the notion that work is inherently violent in fact has deep roots in antiquity. There is perhaps no articulation of this sinister view of work more famous for scholars of the Greco-Roman world than Vergil's first *Georgic*. There, the poet's ambivalent claim that "outrageous labor conquers all things" (*labor omnia uincit/improbus*, *Geo.* 1.145–6) is taken to be either a lament about how fallen man is doomed to toil to stay alive or a celebration of the power of human striving to dominate the natural world.[5] In each interpretation, *labor* is considered a type of punishment, either for the one toiling or for the raw materials that such toil transforms. *Labor*, then, can only consist in either enduring or meting out a violence that is stitched into the very nature of things.[6]

This, in a sense, paradoxical connection of work to both violence against life and order within the universe is illustrated nowhere more succinctly than in the anonymous *Moretum*, which Tom Geue studies in depth in the opening chapter of this volume. Already in the 1990s, William Fitzgerald recognized in the short poem crucial evidence for labor and the low-status laborer in Latin verse.[7] But what has been fully appreciated more recently is the extent to which the poem blends the banal morning toiling of an agricultural laborer with the lofty cosmological structures of popular Empedocleanism.[8] Through an evocative comparison of the round bread and ball of pesto to the cosmos itself, the poet subtly compares the lowly peasant Simulus to a demiurge crafting the world, bearing marked similarities to the accounts of creationist cosmogony detailed from Plato to Ovid.[9] By inviting us to conceive of the demiurgic activity of worldmaking not as a one-off event but as a daily routine or "grind," the poem insists upon a point that is essential to this volume: work is not only a cosmological principle in an abstract, metaphorical sense. It is through our actions and *labores* that the world and its various forms keeps from falling apart.[10]

Nor is this just the realm of the literary imaginary. Among ancient historians no less than anonymous poets, the notion that work is bound up in violence holds considerable sway in contemporary theorizations of the ancient Roman economy and of the contours of professional life in the ancient world. Examining work and *labor* in much of Roman Studies since Moses Finley's seminal 1973 monograph, *The Ancient Economy*, has involved studying the powerful institutional and ideological forces, exerted from the top-down, that structure subjective experience and impose ranks and gradations among working people.[11] Until relatively recently, for instance, the predominant interpretation of Roman professional identities took at face value Cicero's infamous and oft-quoted aside in *de Officiis* (1.150–1), in which the orator offers his thoughts concerning which occupations befitted the honorable man's life and which occupations were considered sordid.[12] Unsurprisingly, trades occupied by the lower classes in this Ciceronian picture—the butcher, the fishmonger, the carpenter—rank lowest; teachers and doctors, given their more useful knowledge, are accounted a measure of respect; and atop the hierarchy are the individuals whose profits from Mediterranean trade are funneled into the ownership and cultivation of land.[13] To this we might compare a similar scholarly impulse in the past decades to focus on institutions and impersonal forces governing the Roman economy, under the ever-widening umbrella of New Institutional Economics.[14] In doing so, such efforts, rather than focusing on the cultural consequences of a dominant ideology as Finley did, have tended toward an elaboration of systems and their effects, prompting some historians of the ancient world to attempt to quantify the economic productivity of those systems and to interpret such results in broad comparative analyses with other historical economies.[15] The goal of such analyses has been, by and large, to identify the existence (or not) of economic growth in the ancient economy and the institutional frameworks which fostered such growth. While certainly helpful for revealing how institutions—understood broadly—shaped macro-economic behaviors, these studies nevertheless have almost entirely effaced the individual and the sub-elite in their desire to fully explicate an abstract concept of the economy and to rationalize economic behavior in a way unfamiliar to many of those whose lives they aim to illuminate.[16] As one criticism of such approaches to the study of ancient labor and work contends, these models not only misconstrue the complexity of ancient valuations of labor, but in many instances ignore them in favor of quantifying *per capita* economic growth or, in the more measured instances, at least the *possibility* for growth and the institutions that made it possible.[17]

In light of this overwhelming emphasis on how the lives of individual Roman subjects were structured by institutional, ideological, or even cosmic forces, this volume aims instead to contribute to the growing literature seeking to illuminate other facets of ancient economic life, in particular by considering the many ways in which individual agency and subjectivity exerted their own forces on the economic, ideological, or cosmic structures within which individuals lived and worked. The title of this chapter, "Structuring Subjects," is a purposely ambiguous reference to this dialectical process, in which individuals appear as both subjects and as the subjected, as both structuring agents themselves and passive adherents to, or victims of, the overarching structures of society (be they economic institutions, cosmic orderings, status hierarchies, etc.). Research undertaken by both anthropologists and sociologists has long acknowledged the fundamental importance of the individual agent in contributing to, manipulating, or outright resisting social structures, and the consequential alterations to these structures such individual reactions produce.[18] In the study of the ancient Mediterranean, the direct application of similar approaches to the agency of the individual has yielded simultaneously complex and analytically bountiful interpretations of subjects ranging from the dynamic nature of communal life in rural settlements in Late Antiquity to the social negotiation of ideas of violence in the Egyptian legal papyri.[19] Alongside the present volume, there is currently also a concerted attempt to bring similar frameworks of analysis to bear on work, labor, and the ancient economy more generally.[20] These studies are most welcome, as scholarly output concerning labor and work from the perspective of the individual or the communal group has been vastly outpaced in the past two decades by the studies of economic institutions or quantification of the economy already mentioned.

One means by which the individual's relationship to both self and labor is evoked throughout this volume is through the familiar modern phrase "work/life," which is reformulated in the title of this volume as "Working Lives." This collocation should raise for many the specter of the surely countless correspondences from Human Resources departments encouraging, for example, a healthy "work/life" balance for their employees, often for not entirely altruistic reasons. Or perhaps some will be reminded of the burgeoning industry of self-help publications, digital and analogue, that promise to unlock the secret to the perfect "work/life" balance and, therefore, to a blissful state of existence. Yet while the modern understanding of such a phrase encourages an easy separation of these two spheres of existence in our own thinking—where "work" becomes time commoditized, "life" time wasted; "work" something performed in particular spaces, "life" lived in those domestic—we would do well to remind ourselves that such lines are not easily demarcated or even for that matter essential. What division between work and life, we might ask, did the Pompeiian *tabernarius* actually experience in their daily existence, where the spaces of both were in fact the same? In the case of occupational inscriptions, in which individuals identify themselves both in life and death by the labor they performed, can any division of work and life truly be discerned for those memorializing themselves as *pistor*, *faber*, or *tonsor*? To what extent is the fictional peasant Simulus' life anything but work, or his work anything but life? How are Claire Holleran's itinerant doctors entirely subsumed by their medicinal working identity? Or, as Del Maticic explores in his chapter, how do we separate the "work" and "life" of a poet like Vergil, whose biographies in the ancient world were shaped by the reception of his works?[21]

In one sense, such questions are entirely unanswerable given the evidence available to us; yet they still are valuable in demonstrating that the relationship between work and life, then as now, is a historically contingent one that merits investigation on its own terms and within its immediate context. The phrase "working lives," then, is intended to denote two discrete modes of inquiry found within this volume. On the one hand, we intend this volume to make new inroads into the study of the practical realities of many different jobs and careers from across the spatiotemporal span of Roman history. We are, like many others, concerned also with the typologies of professional identities and the way they, sometimes stable and sometimes fluid and hybridized, constellate and organize individuals.[22] But this volume's focus on working lives and the life of work, above all, moves past the limiting focus on forms of work and forms of meaning that derive from it and considers what is lively and lifelike about *labor* in the first instance: its flexibility, its contingency, and its constant oscillation between the mundane and the sublime, between the individual and the cosmic. Ultimately, this volume claims that the laboring subject, in this way, can and did exert structuring power over their conditions of life.

It is fortunate, then, that recent engagements with how Romans constructed and responded to ideologies of labor have become not only more disciplined in critically interpreting Roman sources but have also begun questioning the analytical value of typical twentieth-century reconstruction of ancient notions of work, workers, and working. For instance, many of the essays in Verboven and Laes' 2017 edited volume, *Work, Labour, and Professions in the Roman World*, build on the work of Sandra Joshel and Paul Veyne to offer convincing revisions to the status-based model of the Roman economy described in Finley's *The Ancient Economy* without veering into the territory of measuring economic growth or, for that matter, the nature of economic institutions.[23] Recent elaborations of the ancient agricultural economy, for instance, have jettisoned this tendency toward construing all economic change in terms of growth, opting instead to view the Greco-Roman economy as both a dynamic system and one interdependent on other economies of the Mediterranean basin.[24] Considerations of the economics of individuals, as well—from pay rates in Roman Egypt to individual rates of consumption in Pompeii—have shed light on the small-scale realities of participating in broader economic systems.[25] Several monographs and volumes published in the past decade have also begun reframing the discussion of Roman labor entirely, placing less emphasis on its quantitative economic value and, in many cases, overlooking the dismissive attitude toward labor found in many of our literary sources. They do so in favor of exploring how the cultural discourse of work,[26] the identification, definition, and articulation of skill and professional duty in both literature and art,[27] and the organization of labor practices and workshops, both rural and urban, indelibly affected other aspects of Roman society,[28] including the cultural, aesthetic, and social realms of Roman life. Our own Tom Geue's damning study of the slaver's ideology of the *Georgics*, for instance, has reminded us that plenty of Romans were not conquered by labor themselves but instead leached happily off that of others.[29] Similar examinations of the "work that work-words do"[30] in shaping hierarchies of labor and producing work in their own right have shed significant light, for example, on the texts of the Roman agronomists.[31] What many of these studies share is a simple shift in perspective; it may have been the case that the literature-producing aristocracy of the Roman empire disparaged labor and those performing it, but that was clearly not an opinion shared by the lower or even perpetually difficult, if impossible (or unhelpful), to define "middle-class," who, it is apparent, identified with and took pride in their occupations, to say nothing of the vastly complex economic lives of the lower classes and the impoverished.[32] Such a shift in perspective is a reminder that the diverse forms that labor assumed in Rome must be studied together not as disparate ranks in a status hierarchy, as Cicero contends, but as scattered nodes caught in a dense web of interrelation.

This volume, then, is concerned less with how powerful external forces imposed structures of labor upon living than in how life itself, in all its messy contingencies, inconsistencies, and contradictions, shaped forms and structures of work on its own terms. In other words, our approach to the ancient evidence is to toggle dialectically between the macro and micro to capture more faithfully the variegated experiences of working lives in the Roman world, following the example of other labor historians and practitioners of "bottom up" history.[33] Doing so requires the acknowledgment of the complex interplay between agency and structure—a methodological stance that Magalhães de Oliveira and Courier, in a recent collected volume, have described as requiring historians to recognize the "limitations imposed on the choices and actions of the sub-altern" as they reconstruct the motivations and behaviors of the sub-elite in navigating whatever choices were afforded or available to them.[34] The introductory chapter to that volume, "Ancient History from Below," is an especially useful overview of how "bottom-up" history has developed over the course of the twentieth and twenty-first centuries, in both ancient and non-ancient contexts. While the authors persuasively connect those occupying the "below" status within Roman society to Spivak's notion of the "subaltern," it is important nevertheless to identify and reconstruct the gradations of difference within such broad categories, both in terms of agency and experience, and in regard to how various relationships of domination manifested even within so-called sub-altern groups. This latter point is especially apparent in E.P. Thompson's *Customs in Common*, where the popular culture of rural villages—as adduced, for example, in the public shaming of individuals for perceived domestic misbehavior—while certainly produced by the non-elite, nevertheless in turn created striations of experience as a result of such localized structures of power and control.[35]

Many of the case studies in this project, from the diachronic development of the responsibilities of the *praefica* in the lived experience of Roman dying (Bodel), to the mundane activities of an imagined farmer's morning routine (Geue), testify to the variegated reality of Roman working lives across the status spectrum. Essays by Rogers, Kuttner, and Sancinito consider how the individual relationships within and shared priorities of communities of craftsmen and professionals both shaped the forms work could take and asserted novel ideals related to the laboring body, in spite of the powerful ideological structures of labor that persisted. Itinerancy and mobility are also key themes, as different chapters follow skilled craftsmen (Cheung, Holleran), doctors (Sausville, Holleran), and writers (Maticic) across the Mediterranean world in search of opportunities for new work and new lives. In doing so, these professionals both participated in existing networks of labor mobility and (re)shaped those networks through their own participation. Finally, by exploring Ciceronian dramas of re-enslavement, Giannella explores the means by which economic systems of power and control in the Roman world often attempted but failed to contain and erase individual wills and agencies.

To illustrate the power of this hermeneutic shift, it is informative to compare for a moment two different animals used to very different purposes in Roman analogies of labor: the bee and the spider. For an emblem of structured subjectivity, we may look no further than Vergil's famous bees in *Georgics* 4 and *Aeneid* 1, who stand as exemplary models for so much of Roman professional life. The entirety of the hive is organized around the seemingly teleological toil of the warrior class. Here, work does not conquer all but rather unites all in a common purpose: among the hive, Vergil writes in *Georgics* 4, there is "one labor for all" (*labor omnibus unus*, *Geo.* 4.184). The bee is goal-directed and knows its place. There are, of course, the freeloading drones—but they are at best foils for the orderliness and industry of the rest. The top-down organization of the hive keeps in line the Cicero-style *gradus dignitatis* into which its members are arranged. The individual bee is either an extension of functionally the same agency, or will, in contradistinction to that common impulse. As an alternative to the established notion of the Roman worker as bustling bee, we offer the model of the industrious spider, considered at length in Marco Formisano's study of Arachne in this volume. Individual and not part of a collective, the spider deals in webs rather than hierarchies. The web-like nature of the spider's work extends to function and not just form, as it must take into account the agency of non-spiders and (literally) enmesh them within the product of the spider's labor. Thus, the world of the spider is, like the violent cosmos represented on Arachne's tapestry in Book 6 of the *Metamorphoses* (*Met.* 6.103–128), a chaotic one in which the antagonisms inherent in the very relationalities organizing the relationships between different groups of agents are reified by the webs made from raw materials that emanate entirely from the spider's body.

While these creatures emphasize two discrete notions of the relationship between an individual, their labor, and society, they are nevertheless both evocative of a similar stance toward the subject-position of the laborer as marginalized. The figure of the *vilicus*, for example, provides a non-fictional accounting of the hierarchies of status and labor implied by the productive organization of the beehive and the autonomous (if unconscious) laboring of the spider. As both a slave and an overseer of slaves, the *uilicus* has posed a category problem in traditional understandings of the Roman world, the likes of which contradicts the convenient categories proposed by Cicero in *de Officiis*. Butting up against what Joseph Howley calls the "epistemic firewall" of Roman agronomic knowledge, the *uilicus* embodied the contradictions and compromises necessary to maintain the web of relations that constituted the world of Roman work.[36] Giannella's consideration in this volume of Tiro, whose (coerced) literary work on behalf of his former *dominus* is mentioned in a number of Cicero's letters, raises a number of similar questions about the nature of subjectivity and agency in the work of literary production among the elite.

Structuring Studies

This volume is the product of a workshop series and conference, both titled *Work/Life: Institutions, Subjectivities, and Human Resources in the Roman World* and held over the course of a year, from Oct. 2020 to Oct. 2021.[37] Like the workshops and conference that preceded it, the present volume explores the "work/life" of Romans of every stripe, from agricultural laborers to merchants, from craftsmen to poets, and from the enslaved to emperors. The papers in the study are eclectic in their source material, covering Latin poetry (Geue, Formisano, Maticic), legal and rhetorical prose (Sancinito, Giannella), Imperial literature and epigraphy in the Greek East (Sausville) and across the Roman world (Holleran), visual art (Kuttner, Rogers), antiquarian musings (Bodel), and archaeology (Cheung). They are also chronologically expansive in scope, ranging from mid-Republican cultural history through the art and literature of the late empire and to medieval and early modern receptions. This range of methodology, evidence, and chronology is purposeful; from its outset, the project has sought not only to claim interdisciplinarity in outlook but also to embody it in practice, in order to provide genuine opportunities for productive discussions not typically found in studies of Greco-Roman labor. Relatedly, we do not purport to offer a singular model for interpreting ancient labor, nor do we presume that superstructures of labor either prompted a unified experience of work among the non-elite. Nor do we imagine that they were consistently applied in the first instance. Again, this approach—the acknowledgment that a "bottom-up" approach to historical reconstruction must also engage with abstracting frameworks of analysis, as uneven as their results might be—locates analytical value in the toggling between web (structure) and spider (individual).

The following chapters, therefore, explore the nature of "work" in numerous interconnected forms. In both Latin and English, the words for "work" mostly have a similar double meaning as either a verbal action or the tangible product of that action. Our volume takes this semantic fact seriously and accepts the invitation implicit in it to critically consider the relationship between workings and works in the ancient world and more generally—including our own intellectual work as Romanists. As such, the "subjects" of our title refer not just to Roman workers who were construed as laborers in their contemporary contexts but also to the subject matter of the collective research program contained in this volume. Such scope has enabled the contributors to this volume to interrogate what is common, for instance, between handicraft, agricultural administration, funerary service, and poetic production in a more expansively interdisciplinary manner. It has also fostered an intellectual space in which the contributors have been capable of reflecting meaningfully on the nature of their own work, research methods, and positionalities in the different forms that structure our work. As a result, we invited participants during the conference proceedings to consider how studying the concept of work/life in the Roman world could possibly lead to new understandings of configurations of labor and the self in the contemporary academy. Rather than being simply an exercise in self-reflection, these meditations were both highly provocative and, in some instances, subversive. Inspired by a number of contemporary theoretical reflections on the nature of scholarly work in the humanities, this volume promises to invite readers to think not only about ancient labor but also about how it impinges upon our own conceptions of work in the academy. It also promises to bridge conversations present in a wide array of subdisciplines of Roman Studies with current theoretical and philosophical debates about the forms and formlessness of knowledge.[38]

One way in which we have grappled with such conversations in the humanities is to contemplate critically how the very form of the edited volume in Roman Studies can be exercised and innovated upon. Taking our cue from the different studies conducted here, the arrangement of the chapters in this book endeavors to be more arachnoid than apiary. Rather than adopt a more typical organizational structure, in which chapters are arranged into sections based on the methodologies they employ, the types of evidence analyzed or the nature of their subject matter, our organization is instead intended loosely to evoke the narrative of a "normal" work-day. As in our own work/lives, so typified by the 9-to-5 structure of the work-day, positing the notion of a normal working day would seem to exert a unified form of labor upon those experiencing it. In reality, beyond a general subjection to the ontology of capitalist time[39]—what might be profitably compared to the realities of Roman imperial/institutional power and its influence in the ancient world—those whose working lives take place within the 9-to-5 structure experience radically different working environments, relationships to power and authority, and even the amount of social satisfaction derived from their labor. Such a choice to employ a similar metaphor of daily, laboring time in the ancient world is borne not only of a desire to create more informative and productive connections between the contributions within this volume; it is also meant to raise a modest critique of those typical organizational structures employed by historians of ancient laboring and of the ancient economy.

What might appear at first blush as a merely descriptive organizational schema, for example, in the 2020 volume *Capital, Investment, and Innovation in the Roman World*—"Investment and Innovation," "Capital and Investment in the Rural Economy," and "Human Capital, Financial Capital, and Credit Markets"—in fact reveals an argument regarding the nature of the ancient economy in itself, one that the editors defend at lengths as appropriate in their introduction.[40] A glance at the organization of *The Cambridge Economic History of the Greco-Roman World*, published in 2007 and now largely considered to reflect *communis opinio*, reveals a similar understanding of the economy, as various "Determinants of Economic Performance" precede sections arranged geographically, where those determinants are explored in further depth.[41] Similar exercises in the organization of knowledge undertaken by editors of other volumes are also revealing, even when their analytical approaches to the evidence differ drastically.[42] Such categorizations as these, based on an acknowledgment of the fundamental importance of institutions, structures, or forms, are increasingly the norm. The point here is not to claim that the examples cited above are methodologically similar in their reconstruction of the ancient economy—and this is certainly not the case—or even to discount their conclusions but to demonstrate how the manner in which we structure our presentation of historical data about the ancient economy must be confronted as an analytical argument in itself.

Acknowledging this reality, our examination of work is categorized as an individual laborer might have experienced it—waking up, getting ready, going in, doing work, and coming home. In some senses, then, the organization of this volume is an experiment and a provocation, one that seeks to ask whether the structuring of our own academic subjects can be approached with both more sensitivity and more creativity, and whether this approach, as a result, can reveal novel avenues of investigation in the future. Here we draw from James Ker's exploration of the "ordered day," which he has explored in its chronological and socio-cultural dimensions.[43] Daily time, as Ker demonstrates, acted as the interface between both individual and community, and nature and culture—as such, the Roman day "shapes and is shaped by the social order" of Roman society. A day's work, therefore, is a unifying form within which individual experience—whether through the repair of a *dolium*, the making of furniture, or the performance of funeral rites—could vary wildly. Still, it must be admitted that the conceit of the "working day" to some extent flattens what were essential discrepancies in status and obligation. The working day of the enslaved agricultural laborer, for instance, was categorically different from Cicero's, especially as regards the level of coercion involved. These realities are explored to some extent in each of the contributions to this volume. Even so, our use of the metaphor of the working day is by no means meant to signal an exhaustive treatment of the subject; rather, it leaves open the possibility of further analyses of the ancient economy through the lens of those whose work kept it running.

The remaining chapters in Part I, "Getting Up, Going In, and Brushing Up," each consider different preparatory and educational activities that precede and underlie acts of laboring, whether those be rising from bed, learning the tricks (and metaphors) of a trade, or relocating for work. In the first chapter, we awaken with the literary peasant Simulus in Tom Geue's reading of power imbalances inherent in the metaphors of work peppering the poem *Moretum*. Claire Holleran then reconsiders different kinds of evidence for and the practical and social consequences of itinerant labor in the Roman world, focusing in particular on the networks of migrant doctors and construction workers that stretched across the Mediterranean. Chapter 3 considers education in relation to agronomic regimes, with Caroline Cheung drawing from pottery remains new insights into the contexts and practices of learning how to repair and maintain the cargo containers of the ancient world, *dolia*.

The chapters in Part II, "Showing Up," explore different aspects of the relationship between work and representation, both in word and image. In a sweeping survey of the iconography of labor and laboring from across the Roman empire, Ann Kuttner documents the emergence and embrace of what she calls "cultures of competency"; both workers and those for whom they labored participated in this visual discourse, as demonstrated competencies—both of the processes and products of laboring—served to assert social legitimacy. Jane Sancinito and Rebecca Sausville then consider the different ways in which Roman workers themselves first articulate and then express their own and others' professional identities. Through a focus on merchants and their stereotypes, Sancinito explores how both individual traders and groups of merchants responded to such stereotypes through concerted efforts of positive self-representation. With Sausville, our narrative travels to the cities of Roman Anatolia, where public intellectuals similarly engaged in acts of self-representation to assert their importance to their community and, in the best cases, to receive special dispensations from the State. Rounding out the work-day, Jordan Rogers closely examines one image in particular, the so-called *fabri tignarii* relief, and considers the individual and communal agencies that underlie its representation of laboring as a sacred act performed for the benefit of both the Gods and society at large.

Finally, Part III collectively considers what comes after work and the work that comes after. Nicole Giannella explores the dramatic Ciceronian accounts of the fugitive freedman, Chrysippus, and the famous Tiro, and examines the relationship between how these literary servants navigated their legal and professional duties as literary experts and their personal responsibilities and obligations to their master. Marco Formisano then turns us from history to myth through his consideration of a different laborious encounter across power hierarchies—that of Ovid's tale of Arachne in the *Metamorphoses*. By drawing on Hannah Arendt's contrast between work and labor, Formisano reveals the contours of the poet's own attitudes toward labor through the metaphorical "death" of the laboring Arachne and transformation into the working spider. He argues that Minerva's punishment of Arachne collapses the metaphor of work and labor, forcing her against her will to identify with her work. Chapters 11 and 12 then turn to the work of death and the afterlife of Roman works. John Bodel rewrites the history of the Roman funerary worker and hired mourner, known as the *praefica*, accounting for the position's slow but steady transition from a hired professional responsible for giving public praise and leading funeral dirges, to its relegation to managing the mourning of enslaved household members. As Bodel argues, this transition is reflective of broader changes in gender roles and the private-public interface in Roman funerary rites. Finally, Del Maticic considers how Vergil's *Eclogues* and their reception in ancient lives of the poet draw on the growth of plants to bring life to bucolic and biographical forms, retooling a tradition of reception and imitation as a living literary lineage.

As we escape from the pandemic and emerge like Arachne into metamorphosized worlds of work and life, we hope this volume sparks new discussions about the interrelation between different elements of Roman culture across the wide spans of space and time covered by its individual chapters. We also are hopeful that the critical examination of our own working processes, during a time of general societal reckoning as regards the relationship between work and life, and the impacts those processes have on our understanding of what we *do* as scholars of the past will, if nothing else, be a breath of clean, fresh air for those of us who have found it so difficult to catch our breath these past few years. In short, however readers engage with the chapters, whether read sequentially or cherry-picked to suit particular research needs, we hope that the volume's patterning will evoke the effect of an enmeshed interrelation of peoples, places, and things, at once chaotically arranged and governed by forces and orders, like Darwin's tangled bank or the web engineered to catch flies in the tangled understories of Roman Studies.

Notes

1. Terkel 1974: xiii.
2. See, for example, Harold Pollack's *Washington Post* article from March 27, 2020, entitled "Who lives, who dies, who decides."
3. Or, alternatively, to feel like our jobs are, in the words of Graeber 2018, "bullshit" no matter the environments in which they are performed. Such a condition is rendered admirably by the recent HBO series *Severance*, which toys with the thought experiment of what would happen if our work-lives were completely severed cognitively from our non-work selves. While we do not engage substantively with Graeber's category of the bullshit job here, it is nevertheless a useful concept with which to think, especially in connection with the mechanisms of control that we see, for

instance, prescribed by agronomic writers in connection to managing the *vilicus*.

4. See, for instance, Jameson 2013 on the realist novel and Geue 2018 on the *Georgics*.
5. On *labor* in the *Georgics*, see Gale 2000: 143–195. The concept is one of the most intensively studied in Vergil's works. See esp. Allen 2010, Goins 1992–3, Jenkyns 1993, and Stachniw 1973–4.
6. We see this phenomenon alive today in the use of the word "work" in physics to denote the exertion of energy systems.
7. Fitzgerald 1996.
8. See Farrell 2014. Henderson 2004 reads a similar cosmic tendency in Columella, Virgil, Pliny, and Palladius.
9. On Ovidian receptions of Platonic creationism, see Kelly 2020. On ancient creationism more broadly, see Sedley 2008. Cf. also the notion of the text as cosmos, as in Gee 2001.
10. This notion, entangled in literature and lived experience, is explored poignantly in the HBO Max series *Station Eleven* and the 2014 novel by Emily St. John Mandel of the same name on which it is based. In the imaginary world of these works, a traveling troupe of actors uses Shakespearean works to cope with and reorganize, mentally and in their own social structures, the world that was destroyed by an almost world-ending plague.
11. Finley 1973.
12. See Laes 2011; Verboven and Laes 2017 for bibliography. Both advocate for a more nuanced and complex understanding of work, labor, and status as understood by those living in the ancient Mediterranean basin, one that focuses in particular on laborers and their own conceptions of work.
13. While the Aristotelian pedigree of Cicero's denigration of banausic labor is evident (see, e.g., Arist. *Pol.* 1260b1: ὁ γὰρ βάναυσος τεχνίτης ἀφωρισμένην τινὰ ἔχει δουλείαν, "For the Baunasic artisan endures a sort of delimited slavery"), it must be remarked that several other competing discourses of work/labor can be adduced. The embrace of work as being what's "better for you" (τὸ ἐργάζεσθαι ἄμεινον), no matter one's lot, can be found as early as Hesiod's *Works and Days* (here 314). A similar notion of the importance of agricultural laboring, especially, can be found in Xen. *Oec.* 11, as espoused by Socrates' interlocutor, Ischomachus—though it should be noted that the figure of Ischomachus likely mocks the faux "laboring" done by the Athenian καλοὶ κάγαθοί, cf. Kronenberg 2010. An entirely different notion of work as futile or meaningless is also evident in Ecclesiastes 1.3–4 and in the numerous inscriptions that idolize the hedonistic pleasures of Roman life, for example, *CIL* VI 15258.

14. Scheidel et al. 2007; Frier and Kehoe 2007; Harris 2008; Bang 2009; Temin 2012; Erdkamp et al. 2015, 2020; Erdkamp and Verboven 2015; Droß-Krüpe et al. 2016; Wilson and Bowman 2018.
15. See Noreña 2022: 530, for remarks on how this "mildly developmental" interpretation of the Roman economy, found both in New Institutional Economics (NIE) oriented studies of the economy as well as the Oxford Roman Economy Project, can be traced to the quantitative modeling of Keith Hopkins. Cf. Bowman and Wilson 2009: 11–12: "The overarching aim here, then, is a series of studies which will suggest how we might identify major structural features, behaviour, and performance of the Mediterranean economy over 450 years of Roman domination, which can be compared with other periods and areas, by collecting and analysing quantifiable documentary and archaeological evidence for key areas and economic activities." While the authors pronounce their skepticism of the NIE approaches prominent in *CEHGRW*, they nevertheless share the general acceptance of quantification and analysis of large datasets as their preferred method of inquiry. It is striking that in Wilson and Bowman 2018, their focus is principally on the State institutions that set the parameters for long-distance trade in the Roman empire.
16. See Bowes 2021a for an extensive bibliography.
17. Bowes 2021a.
18. Bourdieu 1977; De Certeau 1984; Raud 2016; Lundgreen 2017.
19. Grey 2011; Bryen 2013.
20. Hawkins 2016; Venticinque 2016; Bowes 2021b; Courrier and Magalhães de Oliveira 2022; Sancinito 2024.
21. See also Kearey 2018 on this problem.
22. Here we have been inspired by theories of the job description as articulated in Industrial/Organizational Psychology. On this, see Brannick et al. 2007. Recent attempts, for example, Stewart et al. 2020, to identify and label "professions" as opposed to "occupations" have encountered the same issues of definition that have long plagued historians of ancient labor. We do not deign to assume that such neat distinctions are either possible to make or heuristically valuable.
23. Joshel 1992; Veyne 2000; Verboven and Laes 2017.
24. Lerouxel and Zurbach 2020.
25. On wage labor in Roman Egypt, see most recently Freu 2022 and Bernard 2023. See Bowes 2021c for a discussion of five graffiti lists from Pompeii, with relevant bibliography.
26. Verboven and Laes 2017; Hochscheid and Russell 2021; Flohr and Bowes 2024.
27. Ruffing 2008; Stewart et al. 2020; Monteix and Tran 2020.

28. Droß-Krüpe 2011; Flohr 2013; Bond 2016; Wilson and Flohr 2016; Flohr and Wilson 2017; Wagner-Hasel and Nosch 2019; Flohr 2020; Groen-Vallinga 2022; Murphy Forthcoming.
29. Geue 2018.
30. Vanhaegendoren 2007; Marcone 2016.
31. Reay 2005; Howley Forthcoming.
32. Mayer 2014. Collins et al. 2009 demonstrates the complexity of the economic lives of the "poor" in modern India, Bangladesh, and Africa.
33. Esp. Thompson 1963: 9, referencing Marx's dialectic of historical materialism as first articulated in *The German Ideology* and the *18th Brumaire of Louis Bonaparte*. Cf. Hobsbawm 1998.
34. Courrier and Magalhães de Oliveira 2022: 15.
35. Thompson 1993: 467–538.
36. Howley Forthcoming.
37. We are grateful for the contributions of Astrid Van Oyen, who spoke during the workshop and moderated a panel at the conference. For her work on the tools of a rural blacksmith in Marzuolo, Italy, see Van Oyen et al. 2022.
38. Arendt 1958, here, is foundational. For more recent work, see Kramnick 2021 on critical methodology. Postcritical methodologies like those pioneered in Felski 2015 are important to bring to bear here as well.
39. Adams 2020 on the ontology of capitalism.
40. Erdkamp et al. 2020.
41. Scheidel et al. 2007.
42. Wilson and Bowman 2018 ("Institutions and the State," "Trade Within the Empire," "Trade Beyond the Frontiers"); Bowman and Wilson 2009 ("Approaches," "Urbanization," "Field Survey and Demography," "Agriculture," "Trade," "Coinage," "Prices, Earnings, and Standards of Living"); etc.
43. Ker 2023.

Bibliography

Adams, Z. 2020. *Labour and the Wage: A Critical Perspective*. Oxford University Press.

Allen, A. 2010. "Virgil's Acquisitive Bees." *Classical Quarterly* 60.1: 258–61.

Arendt, H. 1958. *The Human Condition*. University of Chicago Press.

Bang, P. 2009. *The Roman Bazaar: A Comparative Study of Trade and Markets in a Tributary Empire*. Cambridge University Press.

Bernard, S. 2023. "The Premium for Skilled Labor in the Roman World." *Explorations in Economic History*. https://doi.org/10.1016/j.eeh.2023.101516.

Bond, S. E. 2016. *Trade and taboo: Disreputable professions in the Roman Mediterranean*. University of Michigan Press.
Bourdieu, P. 1977. *Outline of a Theory of Practice*. Translated by Richard Nice. Cambridge University Press.
Bowes, K. 2021a. "When Kuznets Went to Rome: Roman Economic Well-Being and the Reframing of Roman History." *Capitalism* 2.1: 7–40.
Bowes, K.. ed. 2021b. *The Roman Peasant Project 2009–2014: Excavating the Rural Poor*. University of Pennsylvania Press.
Bowes, K.. ed. 2021c. "Tracking Consumption at Pompeii: The Graffiti Lists." *JRA* 34.2: 552–84.
Bowman, A. and Wilson, A., eds. 2009. *Quantifying the Roman Economy: Methods and Problems*. Oxford University Press.
Brannick, M. T., Levine, E.L., and Morgenson, F. P. 2007. *Job and Work Analysis: Methods, Research, and Applications for Human Resource Management*. Sage Publishing.
Bryen, A. 2013. *Violence in Roman Egypt: a Study in Legal Interpretation*. University of Pennsylvania Press.
de Certeau, M. 1984. *The Practice of Everyday Life*. University of California Press.
Collins, D., Morduch, J., Rutherford, S. and Ruthven, O. 2009. *Portfolios of the Poor: How the World's Poor Live on $2 a Day*. Princeton University Press.
Courrier, C. and Magalhães de Oliveira, J.C. eds. 2022. *Ancient History from Below: Subaltern Experiences and Actions in Context*. Routledge.
Droß-Krüpe, K. 2011. *Wolle—Weber—Wirtschaft: die Textilproduktion der römischen Kaiserzeit im Spiegel der papyrologischen Überlieferung*. Harrassowitz.
Droß-Krüpe, K., Föllinger, S. and Ruffing, K., eds. 2016. *Antike Wirtschaft und ihre kulturelle Prägung—The Cultural Shaping of the Ancient Economy*. Harassowitz.
Erdkamp, P. and Verboven, K., eds. 2015. *Structure and Performance in the Roman Economy: Models, Methods, and Case Studies*. Latomus.
Erdkamp, P., Verboven, K., and Zuiderhoek, A., eds. 2020. *Capital, Investment, and Innovation in the Roman World*. Oxford University Press.
Erdkamp, P., Verboven, K., and Zuiderhoek, A., eds. 2015. *Ownership and Exploitation of Land and Natural Resources in the Roman World*. Oxford University Press.
Farrell, J. 2014. "Looking for Empedocles in Latin Poetry: A Skeptical Approach." *Dictynna* 11: np. https://journals.openedition.org/dictynna/1063.
Felski, R. 2015. *The Limits of Critique*. University of Chicago Press.
Finley, M. 1973. *The Ancient Economy*. University of California Press.
Fitzgerald, W. 1996. "Labor and laborer in Latin poetry: the case of the Moretum." *Arethusa* 29.3: 389–418.
Flohr, M. 2020. *Urban Space and Urban History in the Roman World*. Routledge.

Flohr, M. 2013. *The World of the Fullo: Work, Economy, and Society in Roman Italy.* Oxford University Press.

Flohr, M. & Bowes, K., eds. 2024. *Valuing Labor in Antiquity.* Brill.

Flohr, M. and Wilson, A. eds. 2017. *The Economy of Pompeii.* Oxford University Press.

Freu, C. 2022. *Les salariés de l'Égypt romano-byzantine. Essai d'histoire économique.* StudPAP 3.

Frier, B. and Kehoe, D. 2007. "Law and Economic Institutions." In Scheidel, W., Morris, I., and Saller, P., eds. *The Cambridge Economic History of the Greco-Roman World,* 113–43.

Gale, M. 2000. *Virgil on the Nature of Things: The Georgics, Lucretius and the Didactic Tradition.* Cambridge University Press.

Gee, E. 2001. "Cicero's Astronomy," *CQ* 51.2: 520–536.

Geue, T. 2018. "Soft Hands, Hard Power: Sponging off the Empire of Leisure (Virgil, *Georgics* 4)." *JRS* 108: 115–40.

Goins, S. E. 1992. "Two aspects of Vergil's use of *labor* in the *Aeneid.*" *Classical Journal* 88: 375–84.

Grey, C. 2011. *Constructing Communities in the Late Roman Countryside.* Cambridge University Press.

Groen-Vallinga, M. J. 2022. *Work and Labour in the Cities of Roman Italy.* Liverpool University Press.

Harris, W, ed. 2008. *The Monetary Systems of the Greeks and Romans.* Oxford University Press.

Hawkins, C. 2016. *Roman Artisans and the Urban Economy.* Cambridge University Press.

Henderson, J. 2004. *Hortus: The Roman Book of Gardening.* Routledge.

Hobsbawm, E. 1998. *On History.* The New Press.

Hochscheid, H. & Russell, B., eds. 2021. *The Value of Making.* Brepols.

Howley, Joseph. Forthcoming. *Slavery and the Roman Book.* (Geue).

Jameson, F. 2013. *The Antimonies of Realism.* Verso.

Jenkyns, R. 1993. "*Labor improbus.*" *Classical Quarterly* 43: 243–8.

Joshel, S. 1992. *Work, Identity, and Legal Status in Rome: A Study of the Occupational Inscriptions.* University of Oklahoma Press.

Kearey, T. 2018. *The Poet at Work: Concepts of Authorship in the Ancient Receptions of Virgil.* Ph.D. Dissertation. Clare College, Cambridge.

Kelly, P. 2020. "Crafting Chaos: Intelligent Design in Ovid, *Metamorphoses* book 1 and Plato's *Timaeus.*" *Classical Quarterly* 70: 734–48.

Ker, J. 2023. *The Ordered Day: Quotidian Time and Forms of Life in Ancient Rome.* Johns Hopkins University Press.

Kramnick, J. 2021. "Criticism and Truth." *Critical Inquiry* 48.2: 218–40.

Kronenberg, L. 2010. *Allegories of Farming from Greece and Rome: Philosophical Satire in Xenophon, Varro, and Virgil.* Cambridge University Press.

Laes, C. 2011. *Children in the Roman Empire: Outsiders Within.* Cambridge University Press.

Lerouxel, F. and Zurbach, J. eds. 2020. *Le changement dans les économies antiques.* Ausonius.

Lundgreen, C. 2017. "Norme, loi, règle, coutume, tradition: Terminologie antique et perspectives modernes." In Itgenshorst, T. and Le Doze, P. eds. *La norme sous la République et le Haut-Empire romains: élaboration, diffusion et contournements.* 17–33. Ausonius.

Marcone, A., ed. 2016. *Storia del lavoro in Italia. L'età Romana. Liberi, semiliberi e schiavi in una società moderna.* Roma.

Mayer, E. 2014. *The Ancient Middle Classes: Urban Life and Aesthetics in the Roman Empire, 100 BCE–250 CE.* Harvard University Press.

Monteix, N. and Tran, N. eds. 2020. *Les savoirs professionnels des gens de métier: études sur le monde du travail dans les sociétés urbaines de l'Empire romain.* Centre Jean Bérard.

Murphy, E. A. Forthcoming. *Crafting Community: Potters of the Roman East.*

Noreña, C. 2022. "From Wigwams to Worlds: on the Work of Keith Hopkins." *JRA* 35.1: 524–39.

Raud, R. 2016. *Meaning in Action: Outline of an Integral Theory of Culture.* Polity Press.

Reay, B. 2005. "Agriculture, Writing, and Cato's Aristocratic Self-Fashioning." *ClAnt* 24.2: 331–61.

Ruffing, K. 2008. *Die berufliche Spezialisierung in Handel und Handwerk: Untersuchungen zu ihrer Entwicklung und zu ihren Bedingungen in der römischen Kaiserzeit im östlichen Mittelmeerraum auf der Grundlage griechischer Inschriften und Papyri.* Leidorf.

Sancinito, J. 2024. *The Reputation of the Roman Merchant.* University of Michigan Press.

Scheidel, W. Morris, I., and Saller, W., eds. 2007. *The Cambridge Economic History of the Greco-Roman World.* Cambridge University Press.

Sedley, D. 2008. *Creationism and its Critics in Antiquity.* University of California Press.

Stachniw, J. M. 1973. "*Labor* as key to the *Aeneid.*" *Classical Bulletin* L: 49–53.

Stewart, E., Harris, E., and Lewis, D., eds. 2020. *Skilled Labour and Professionalism in Ancient Greece and Rome.* Cambridge University Press.

Temin, P. 2012. *The Roman Market Economy.* Princeton University Press.

Terkel, S. 1974. *Working: People Talk about What They Do All Day and How They Feel about What They Do.* Ballantine Books.

Thompson, E. P. 1993. *Customs in Common: Studies in Traditional Popular Culture.* The New Press.

Thompson, E. P. 1963. *The Making of the English Working Class.* Victor Gollancz.

Vanhaegendoren, K. 2007. "Travail et loisir en Grèce ancienne: à propos de la complémentarité des activités du citoyen." *Ancient Society* 37: 1–35.

Van Oyen, A., Tol, G.W., Vennarucci, R.G., Agostini, A., Serneels, V., Mercury, A.M., Rattighieri, E. and Benatti, A. 2022. "Forging the Roman rural economy: A blacksmithing workshop and its toolset at Marzuolo (Tuscany)." *American Journal of Archaeology* 126.1: 53–77.

Venticinque, P.F. 2016. *Honor Among Thieves: Craftsmen, Merchants, and Associations in Roman and Late Roman Egypt*. University of Michigan Press.

Verboven, K. and Laes, C., eds. 2017. *Work, Labour, and Professions in the Roman World. Impact of Empire, 23*. Brill.

Veyne, P. 2000. "La "plèbe moyenne" sous le Haut-Empire romain." *Annales* 55–6: 1169–99.

Wagner-Hasel, B. and Nosch, M., eds. 2019. *Gaben, Waren und Tribute: Stoffkreisläufe und antike Textilökonomie: Akten eines Symposiums (9./10. Juni 2016 in Hannover)*. Steiner.

Wilson, A. and Flohr, M., eds. 2016. *Urban Craftsmen and Traders in the Roman World, Oxford Studies on the Roman Economy*. Oxford University Press.

Wilson, A. and Bowman, A. eds. 2018. *Trade, Commerce, and the State in the Roman World*. Oxford University Press.

CHAPTER 2

The Politics of Pesto: Making Metaphor Work (Moretum)

Tom Geue

Women and men writers can lyrically exalt these triumphs because they never or rarely do housework. Done every day, this work becomes monotonous and mechanical.
—de Beauvoir *(2011: 481; quoted in* Kadue *2021: 13)*

The housekeeper's immediate goals are only means, not real ends … and they reflect no more than anonymous projects.
—de Beauvoir *(2011: 481; quoted in* Kadue *2021: 161)*

When Ev'ning does approach, we homeward hie,
And our domestic Toils incessant ply:
Against your coming Home prepare to get
Our Work all done, our House in order set;
Bacon and Dumpling in the Pot we boil,
Our Beds we make, our Swine we feed the while;

T. Geue (✉)
Centre for Classical Studies, The Australian National University, Canberra, ACT, Australia
e-mail: Tom.Geue@anu.edu.au

D. A. Maticic, J. Rogers (eds.), *Working Lives in Ancient Rome*, The New Antiquity,
https://doi.org/10.1007/978-3-031-61234-3_2

Then wait at Door to see you coming Home,
And set the Table out against you come:
Early next Morning we on you attend;
Our Children dress and feed, their Cloaths we mend;
And in the Field our daily Task renew,
Soon as the rising Sun has dry'd the Dew.
—Mary Collier, *The Woman's Labour, 74–85; quoted in* Kadue *(2021: 153)*

For most of us knowledge workers doing our thing in exploitative institutions, work is far from a metaphor: it is a painful, literal reality. Just because we work mostly by pumping thoughts through our brains, extending and reformulating those thoughts with students and colleagues, then punching those thoughts into word documents, polishing them into slides and chiselling them into emails, it doesn't make the work any less work. Does it? Perhaps the recent Covid-19 pandemic has revealed more than ever the shakiness of professional class attempts to identify our work as essential labor through resorting to the sleight of hand that is metaphor ("polishing," "chiselling"—come on). And even as we academics struggle for better working conditions, for an end to casualization, for a turnaround in precarity, a corrosive hum of white-collar guilt plagues our inner ears. Is the work of the computer really equivalent to the work of the cleaner? When I say I am "working," am I really using a metaphor? Am I really committing a theft, in language, to equate two things which should not be equated?

It's these different kinds of work, and the work of metaphor connecting them, which I'd like to talk about in this chapter, apropos of this promised Latin poem, the *Moretum*. The core questions are these: what kinds of "real work," which I cheekily and unprofessionally use in its commonsense meaning of "domestic or manual labor," can be turned, through the magic of metaphor, into aesthetic work, the work of art? And what kinds of "real work" *can't* be metaphorized so easily from the mundane to the celestial? And what might all this tell us about the relationship between the cleaner and the poet. Or better yet, what does it tell us about Roman work, and our work, if any such relationship is denied?[1]

Katie Kadue has written brilliantly of late on what she calls the "domestic georgic": the tendency of many mainstream male authors of the early modern period to plunder metaphors for their own creative process from the typically feminized household tasks of pickling, preserving, caring, and supporting.[2] Such historically unglamorous and classically unremunerated forms of domestic labor, far from being invisible in high-brow male authors (as the charge often goes), actually turn out to hold a surprising purchase on the imaginations of such writers—even if only at particular historical moments. In this chapter, I want to talk about a similar fusion of different sorts of domestic labor with poetry—though as we shall see, it is only really the male version of such labor which is allowed to pass as (partially) assimilable into the hexametric mode. But it is worth raising from the very beginning the general question of how these metaphorical transitions and overlaps may *work*. When high poets, who are definitively not cleaners or laborers, mine "mundane" work as metaphors for their creative process, are they playing a conceit, performatively slumming it, talking street but really walking the leafier neighborhoods? Or as Kadue goes some way to suggesting, do some of these metaphors actually work because they rest on a genuine likeness between the repetitive and preservative qualities of literary-scholarly-critical labor, and the same such qualities in care and housework?[3] Perhaps part of the problem is that we—especially we snobby classicists—tend to picture poetry as a special, set-apart, transcendent form of "work," when really it is just material work like any other—boring, frustrating, inherently collaborative, mechanistic, and slightly unpredictable at one and the same time. As the *Moretum* will show us, the distribution of metaphors *can* work overtime in snobby ways: to keep work and "work" distinct. In Arendt's terms, helpfully recalled by Marco Formisano in this volume, the *Moretum* goes to great strides to separate drudging and constrained "labor" from the more creative and autonomous "work."[4] But metaphors, of course, also connect and convert. And if they can transform labor into work, they can also show that work is just labor dressed up. That, too, is the work of poetry.[5]

Divisions of Labor

The *Moretum* is a gem of a poem: an anonymous 122-hexameter poem bundled up in the *Appendix Vergiliana*, it treats the early morning breakfast prep of the peasant Simulus and his enslaved companion Scybale, in the bleary sliver of day between waking and plowing. A "domestic georgic," if ever there was one. The action is simple: Simulus gets up, makes bread, digs in the garden for herbs and garlic, whacks them in the mortar, just adds olive oil, and bingo, you have yourself a perfectly acceptable pesto to line the stomach for a hard day out in the fields. What is not simple is the mode in which this humble activity—perhaps the longest and most focused treatment of peasant activity to survive from antiquity, in fact[6]—is treated. The poem's tone is notoriously tough to nail, exacerbated by the gaping void in authorship,[7] the sort of basic orientation which might usually guide our rough assessment (or constraining labelling) of a poem's politics. Is it that rarest of artisanal objects from antiquity: a genuine, sympathetic, honest, and kind treatment of the hard life of the rural poor?[8] Or is it rather a satire, through *reductio ad absurdum*, on the way elite hexameter writers—for example, Virgil, or perhaps other alexandrianizing/neotericizing poets—tend to lionize humility in their verse?[9] Or is the core work of the poem—making pesto, the eponymous *moretum*—actually about something else entirely—making poetry, as William Fitzgerald has shown;[10] or demiurging the cosmos;[11] or perhaps sublimating a sexual relationship between the two protagonists, as Francesca Bellei has spotted?[12] Is there work in this work, or is it, as usual in Latin poetry, instantly spirited away into "work"?

Joe Howley—friend of the Work/Life gang and expert on the ideology of enslaved labor—has cooked up the very helpful concept of the "epistemic firewall" set up to silo different forms of work from each other and to keep certain human beings excluded from certain kinds of knowledge and labor.[13] Joe has shown brilliantly how hard enslavers fight to keep white- (or purple-) collar and blue-collar work quarantined from each other in their management of enslaved agricultural staff: there are distinct limits set on the cognitive and epistemic capacities of the slave, and these boundaries are policed with particularly intense intellectual tasers precisely at the moment where an enslaved figure threatens to cross the boundary from body to mind, as happens with the *vilicus*, the slave entrusted with the management of the enslaver's estate when he (as usual) is away carousing in the big smoke.[14] What I would like to show in these next pages is this: that the *Moretum*'s remarkable dynamism as a poem stems partly from its erection of not one but two epistemic firewalls across both intra- and extra-diegetic relationships. Broadly speaking, the first, a firewall of the hearth, is the gendered break between Simulus and Scybale: the former is allowed to pass over, through metaphor, into the world of what Fitzgerald calls the "high mimetic," or the epic mode, and is allowed to have artwork made of his labor; the latter, Scybale, is completely denied the boosting capacity of metaphor to allow a "redemptive" crossover between social realms. So much for firewall 1.[15]

The second firewall stands between Simulus and the poet: for though Simulus is permitted the baby steps of the artist, it is clear that he does not see his work as art. For that transmutation to take place, the luxury subjectivity of the poet—Unacknowledged Minter of Metaphorical Currency!—is necessary. So really, there are three stages in a hierarchy delimited by heavily tended firewalls: Scybale, who is condemned to remain in a world without metaphor; Simulus, who can be metaphorized but cannot use metaphors himself; and the poet, who is gifted the power of hanging back and turning work into "work." Reformulated in the key term of this volume, we might call this a hierarchy of subjectivity: Scybale, all straight object, untransformable through metaphor; Simulus, inchoate subjectivity, subject to the metaphor-transformations of *another* subjectivity; and the poet, subjectivity par excellence, gifted the capacity to transform the world with the work of words.

In the first airing of this material, I committed the rookie error of putting too much Quintilian in. In the second, I more or less took him out. Now I reinsert him—with this minor potted history designed merely as performative testimony to the repetitive and sometimes futile nature of the intellectual labor done by us all. Circles of indecision aside, the following passage is what got my mind originally racing on these questions, because it is about the class connotations of using metaphor in language and how the transformative resources of metaphor are actually rooted in a material base. In book 8 of the *Institutio Oratoria*, our oratory Prof extraordinaire gives an interesting account of what metaphor is and how it works, as part of a long section of the treatise devoted to unpacking all the manifold tropes at the orator's disposal. Quintilian kicks off with metaphor, Latin *translatio*, because it's the most commonly deployed and "most beautiful" (*pulcherrimus*) of all the tropes. Here is how it starts. Forgive the long quote, but hopefully the investment will be repaid:

> *Incipiamus igitur ab eo qui cum frequentissimus est tum longe pulcherrimus, tralatione dico, quae* μεταφορά *Graece vocatur. Quae quidem cum ita est ab ipsa nobis concessa natura ut indocti quoque ac non sentientes ea frequenter utantur, tum ita iucunda atque nitida ut in oratione quamlibet clara proprio tamen lumine eluceat. Neque enim vulgaris esse neque humilis nec insuavis haec recte modo adscita potest. Copiam quoque sermonis auget permutando aut mutuando quae non habet, quodque est difficillimum, praestat ne ulli rei nomen deesse videatur. Transfertur ergo nomen aut verbum ex eo loco in quo proprium est in eum in quo aut proprium deest aut tralatum proprio melius*

est. Id facimus aut quia necesse est aut quia significantius est aut, ut dixi, quia decentius. Ubi nihil horum praestabit quod transferetur, inproprium erit. Necessitate rustici 'gemmam' in vitibus (quid enim dicerent aliud?) et 'sitire segetes' et 'fructus laborare', necessitate nos 'durum hominem' aut 'asperum': non enim proprium erat quod daremus his adfectibus nomen. Iam 'incensum ira' et 'inflammatum cupiditate' et 'lapsum errore' significandi gratia: nihil enim horum suis verbis quam his arcessitis magis proprium erit. Illa ad ornatum, 'lumen orationis' et 'generis claritatem' et 'contionum procellas' et 'eloquentiae fulmina', ut Cicero pro Milone Clodium 'fontem gloriae eius' vocat et alio loco 'segetem ac materiem'. Quaedam etiam parum speciosa dictu per hanc explicantur:

hoc faciunt nimio ne luxu obtunsior usus
sit genitali arvo et sulcos oblimet inertes. [Virgil *Georgics* 3.135–6] (Quintilian *Insitutio Oratoria* 8.6.4–8)

Let's start then with the most common and by some way the most beautiful trope, i.e. *translatio* (μεταφορά in Greek). On the one hand, this is something given to us by nature, so that even the uneducated and unconscious use it; on the other, it's so nice and elegant that it shines by its own light, however bright the speech around it. If it's done right, it can't be vulgar or lowly or inelegant. It increases the wealth of language by exchange or borrowing, to furnish what it doesn't have; hardest of all, it guarantees that everything gets a name. A noun or verb is transferred from the place where it's "proper" to a place where either there is no "proper" word, or where the transferred word is better than the "proper" one. We do this either from necessity, or because it's more meaningful, or (as I said) because it's more fitting. When the transfer secures none of that, it will be "improper". Peasants call a vinebud a "gem" by necessity—what else could they say?—and talk of crops as "thirsty" or the harvest as "struggling"; by necessity we too talk of a "hard" or "prickly" man—because there isn't a "proper" term to give these qualities. Next, metaphor for the sake of meaning: "blazing with anger", "aflame with desire", "fallen into error"—none of these will be more "proper" by its own words than by the imports from outside. But then there's metaphor for beautification: "light of speech", "brilliance of birth", "storms of assemblies", "bolts of eloquence", as Cicero in the *Pro Milone* calls Clodius either the "font", or elsewhere the "crop and staple" of Milo's glory. Even things which are less nice to talk about can be explained via metaphor:

They do it to stop luxury living dull the generative field, and to stop it sliming up unused furrows. [Virgil *Georgics* 3.135–6]

What I am interested in here, no prizes for guessing, is the class distribution of differing capacities for metaphor. Quintilian starts by rooting metaphor in nature, thus making it the property, too, of beings who are *indocti* or *non sentientes.* But that does not mean that metaphor is a lowly enterprise—*vulgaris*, *humilis*, *insuavis.* Oh no. It actually *cannot* be those things (as long as it is used properly, *recte*). The basic thing that metaphor does here, you could say, is enrich and expand: it increases the *copia* of language by exchange and borrowing, it gives impoverished *sermo* what it does not have, and makes sure that everything has the resource of a name granted it. Metaphor—ironically, "metaphorically"—is a matter of property: it is about moving a term from its own proper place to a place where there is no proper term, or the transferred term works better than the proper term. In some ways, this is settler colonial thinking: as a proprietor of language, you move one verbal pawn into a new area where supposedly no one is living; you expand, and you claim, and eventually that becomes your property too.

Of course, not all metaphorists are equal; only some can manage linguistic property in the best way. Note how Quintilian assigns metaphorical rights in accordance with social class, on a spectrum from bare necessity to lavish luxury. At the lower end, "natural" metaphors are used *even* by *rustici*, who elevate their vinebud into a precious *gemma*, or talk of their thirsty fields, *only* because that is the only option available. Their creativity is firmly capped at what is already baked into the language as a norm. At the highest end, by contrast, ornamental metaphors are the most valuable precisely because they are the most gratuitous; they are the luxury products of Roman geniuses living a long way above linguistic subsistence levels. Note how the examples from Cicero culminate in an agricultural metaphor, which makes sense as the apex of the Roman landowner's view of endlessly generative crops of glory grown in the field. Cicero might be making the high-brow low-brow, the ideal material, by bringing the material world of an agricultural field to the high abstraction of "glory." But the real summit of the list goes in the other direction, bringing the low high. As Quintilian says, metaphor is also good for *euphemism*: explaining things which are not so nice to talk about, and lifting those things up in the process. Virgil pulls this move off with aplomb in the quoted *Georgics* passage, which talks of horse sex in the language of agricultural fertility. In fact, this elevation through metaphor is the sort of thing Virgil does the whole of the *Georgics*, and especially book 3 of it; he relentlessly "dignifies" country living by using metaphors from epic and the language of noble Roman values, sometimes to the point where we forget we are hanging out with a bunch of sheep and goats (e.g., from 3.284). All those metaphors generate a surplus which does not square with the straitened conditions of slave production, the ultimate tenor to all these fancy vehicles (or perhaps I mean that the other way around). It is this process of bringing *high* through metaphor—but also, on the other hand, keeping low by literalism—that characterizes the work of the *Moretum*.

To demonstrate what I mean, let us compare a few moments where Simulus and Scybale appear side by side. (Here I am very much reheating and adding condiments to William Fitzgerald's classic 1996 article, *Labor and Laborer in Latin Poetry*, which talks at length about the entry of the hero Simulus into the "high mimetic" being dependent on the mundane labor of the enslaved Scybale.)[16] I would like to pay attention particularly to what we might call the skewed distribution of metaphorical wealth between the protagonists. Perhaps the clearest example of this falls early in the poem, at the moment Scybale is first introduced. Simulus has woken up, fumbled for the fire, swept off the mill, and now he's setting about making the bread. Check out how the discourse changes when the focus moves from "hero" Simulus to housemaid Scybale:

> *advocat inde manus operi, partitus utroque:*
> *laeva ministerio, dextra est intenta labori.*
> *haec rotat adsiduum gyris et concitat orbem*
> *(tunsa Ceres silicum rapido decurrit ab ictu),*
> *interdum fessae succedit laeva sorori*
> *alternatque vices. modo rustica carmina cantat*
> *agrestique suum solatur voce laborem,*
> *interdum clamat Scybalen. erat unica custos,*
> *Afra genus, tota patriam testante figura,*
> *torta comam labroque tumens et fusca colore,*
> *pectore lata, iacens mammis, compressior alvo,*
> *cruribus exilis, spatiosa prodiga planta.*
> *hanc vocat atque arsura focis imponere ligna*
> *imperat et flamma gelidos adolere liquores.* (*Moretum* 24–37)

After that Simulus calls up his hands for the work, distributing them both sides: the left tasked to play helper, the right tasked for the labor itself. The right hand turns and drives the wheel, round and round in circles (the grain runs through, thumped by the stones' quick punches); on and off, the left hand takes over from her slumped sister, switching places. Now he rattles off

> some country tunes and eases the labor with his down to earth voice; occasionally he yells at Scybale. She was his sole house help, of African origin, her entire figure testifying as much: she had curly hair, large lips, dark skin, flat breasts, a tight stomach, thin legs, big broad feet. He calls her and directs her to put fuel to burn on the fireplace, and to boil cold water on the flames.

Simulus' body is here turned into a multiply staffed organization headed by Simulus himself: the arrangement between his individual hands in fact reflects the division of labor which we will see in his own relationship with Scybale—one hand, the slightly icky left hand, charged with the supplementary devalued task of the "help," *ministerio*, the other, the heroic right, given the "real work" of driving the mill. Metaphor and metonymy expand the operation: this grain is not just grain, it is Ceres, a cereal version of the goddess herself; and the hands themselves become personified, that is, "sisters" helping each other out. It seems that everything around Simulus is enjoying an aesthetic promotion, a metaphorical nudge up a notch on the *scala naturae* (grain to goddess, body part to family member). Even the man himself is allowed the first fruits of poetic production, singing his rustic songs, using verse to lighten his load, *suum solatur … laborem*—which is a version of what the poet is doing to him. For Simulus, aesthetic work—even in rudimentary form—is allowed to soften and solace the work of the hands; and such lightening is mirrored in the promotional metaphors applied by the poet, to make the tasks heroic, to make work "work."

But then, suddenly, the register shifts, and the metaphors screech to a halt. Simulus had been doing "real art"—making bread, singing along the way—until he is shunted back to the realm of the literal by yelling an *order* to Scybale. There is nothing more literal than the imperative mood.[17] Cue now the famous description of Scybale—a very rare detailed depiction of an enslaved North-African person—which some used to think an exoticizing stereotype, until Shelley Haley stepped in and showed us that often it is the translator who is exoticizing, not the poet. She is right.[18] I am deeply indebted to Haley for pointing out white scholars' tendency to make Scybale's situation look worse than it actually is, and Francesca Bellei has recently built even more on Haley's redemptive reading partly by calling out the "white male gaze fixation with Scybale's oppression."[19] So I am worried I am taking things backward here, but humbly, hesitantly, I am not sure I would go so far as Haley to reinject black pride into the language here: the bodily description of Scybale seems to be quite flat, anatomizing, more scientific than sexualizing.[20] Perhaps not as bad as translators have made it, but perhaps not quite a monument to ancient respect for people of color either. And I think this shift in tone is precisely the point. While Simulus' body is exaggerated in the most over-the-top fashion, his hands suddenly sprouting bodies all their own and becoming additional women workers in his very own production team, Scybale is parcelled into bits of body that are *just that*, nothing more; they are denied the promotion of metaphor, denied the animation of anthropomorphosis.[21] In fact, Scybale is stuck fast in the realm of the literal: her whole figure screams her birthplace in Africa. Indeed, as a limited racial signifier, she cannot but be anything else. Just as, in William Fitzgerald's terms, she is not allowed to enter the realm of the high mimetic,[22] so also is she unable to break through to the "value-added" world of metaphor. She looks like an African woman, and her body parts do not get to be anything but body parts. What you see, allegedly, is what you get.

Throughout the poem, this dialectic between expansion and contraction (or stagnation), raising and keeping in place, metaphor and its denial, sticks to Simulus and Scybale, even in moments where it feels a little gratuitous. And it becomes clearer that these unequal rights to metaphor map quite neatly onto the division of labor I hinted at above. Take the moment where Simulus plies the finishing touches to the bread and pops it in the oven:

> *iamque subactum*
> *levat opus palmisque suum dilatat in orbem*
> *et notat impressis aequo discrimine quadris.*
> *infert inde foco (Scybale mundaverat aptum*
> *ante locum) testisque tegit, super aggerat ignes.*
> *dumque suas peragit Volcanus Vestaque partes,*
> *Simulus interea vacua non cessat in hora,*
> *verum aliam sibi quaerit opem, neu sola palate*
> *sit non grata Ceres, quas iungat comparat escas.* (46–54)

Now he lifts the kneaded work and stretches it in a circle with his palms, and marks quadrants engraved symmetrically. He then lays it on the hearth (Scybale had already cleaned a good spot for it), buries it with bricks, and piles the fire on top. While Vulcan and Vesta do their part, in the meantime Simulus keeps working through the break, and looks for further help, lest neat Ceres be hard on his palate, and gathers some extras to add to it.

Again, this workaday task of Simulus becomes—in the poet's charitable hands—high-level work: dubbed opus—a word which gets a real workout in the poem to refer to Simulus' menial projects[23]—this work is also a work of marking tantamount to writing (*notat*). Simulus adds value—*infert, super aggerat ignes*;[24] indeed, his work of spicing up the bread is pictured as aesthetic or gourmet surplus, adding flavor (*aliam … opem*; cf. the redux of *aliam … opem* at 59) to the basic necessities. Again, metonymy offers some help, with Vulcan and Vesta doing their bit, even Ceres making another cameo. In fact, while the former gods are busy performing *their* role of cook, Simulus busies himself with other tasks; it is almost as if they are all, Vulcan, Vesta, and Ceres, part of the same plane of household operation, and all employed under Simulus (cf. Ceres and the hand sisters above). Metaphorically speaking, Simulus is blessed with a big staff and a full kit of divine equipment. But Scybale? She gets barely a line, parenthetically inserted: *Scybale mundaverat aptum/ante locum*. This is exactly the kind of flat epexegetic insertion that could be written off as an interpolation—and incidentally, the interpolator is the lowliest vagrant on the boundary of scholarly/creative labor—were it not completely necessary to the politics I am trying to tease out. For the point is, again, that the moment Scybale steps on stage, the curtain of aestheticizing metaphor slips; straight descriptive statement comes back; and we get verbs like *mundaverat* spoiling the fun (*mundare* is rare but attested elsewhere only in prose;[25] cf. the slightly more dignified and rarefied collocation *emundata Ceres* 42,[26] when Simulus gets to purify the grain. Scybale cleans, but Simulus "cleans").[27] This task of place-clearing is also shunted into the pluperfect, drained of its color and rendered pure incidental pre-game next to Simulus' more lively actions in the present. By contrast, let's remember that *Simulus*' tasks of cleaning grain, kneading and dividing dough, putting it in the oven, even letting it cook—all of that can be flung to the heights via metaphor (38–50 is crawling with them). The person who does not respond to metaphor, or more accurately, the person who doesn't even receive the call-up to be metaphorized, is the enslaved woman called Scybale—quite literally, bluntly, "piece of shit."[28] With a nominal brand like that on her, Scybale bears the stigma of being mimetically, metaphorically, unassimilable, and indigestible—lumped with the existential weight of being the matter out of place she herself clears, and *is*, alone.

You Can't Take the Labor Out of Laborer

There is thus a clear metaphorical division of labor assigned to both these workers: Scybale inhabits a "non-poetic," straight-talking realm shorn of the "adornments" of metaphor; Simulus is granted the right to access, or at least be represented with, the first touches of aesthetic surplus. Interestingly, the next scene of the couple's interaction replays the dynamic, but its overhauling of a very similar vignette earlier in the poem clues us into the idea that this binary of unmetaphorizable and metaphorizable goes beyond the two separate characters. Indeed, the split regime of representation also abides, in a sense, in Simulus himself. I said above that Simulus' hands plying the mill to grind the grain are anthropomorphized into a whole collective staff—and that the structure of this collective is governed by the very same distribution (and redescription) of work given to Scybale and Simulus: *laeva ministerio, dextra est intenta labori* (25). The left hand is assigned the task of "helper," that is, the subordinate job of "merely" supplying the grain; the right hand is privileged with the "real work" of powering the mill. The feminine labor of support earmarked for the unlucky side; the masculine and metaphorizable proper labor given to the flagship right. But notice how this pattern is retained when the hands move from mill to mortar:

> *haec ubi collegit, laetum considit ad ignem*
> *et clara famulam poscit mortaria voce.*
> *singula tum capitum nodoso corpore nudat*
> *et summis spoliat coriis contemptaque passim*
> *spargit humi atque abicit; servatum gramine bulbum*
> *tinguit aqua lapidisque cavum demittit in orbem.*
> *his salis inspergit micas, sale durus adeso*
> *caseus adicitur, lectas super ingerit herbas,*
> *et laeva testam saetosa sub inguina fulcit,*
> *dextera pistillo primum fragrantia mollit*
> *alia, tum pariter mixto terit omnia suco.* (90–100)

> When done collecting, he settles by the nice fire and calls the maid for the pestle and mortar in a loud voice. Then he strips each head of its knotty shell, pillages their outer skins, scatters the offcuts here and there on the ground, tosses them away; he keeps the bulb along with the leaves, moistens it, and throws it into the hollow ring of the stone mortar. On this he sprinkles a pinch of salt, adds a hard cheese eaten away by salt, piles on that the

> herbs he's picked, and with his left hand props the mortar in his hairy groin, with his right first breaks in the stinking garlic with his pestle, then grinds it all evenly into a mixed paste.

Once the garden ingredients are hoovered up, Simulus sets about crushing the actual paste—a task supplied with a repertoire of epic and cosmic imagery that will only get more overblown as the poem climaxes in a pungent whiff of herbs and garlic. Scybale's presence is again subtle, straight, completely no-frills: Simulus once more addresses her without beating about the bush, *clara … poscit … voce*, as if Scybale lives in a world which cannot be seasoned with any linguistic salsa beyond the barest minimum of a loud, sharp imperative.[29] Her job, again, is a supporting role, an instrument for furnishing the crucial piece of tech to enable the next phase of the recipe: the mortar and pestle themselves (*mortaria*). My central point here is that the relationship of unglamorous support labor to aestheticized "work" *again* seems to break out in Simulus' left-right hand arrangement; but this time, expanding on the *laeva ministerio* … line above, the division is roughly coordinated with a distinct representational regime. The left-hand work of propping the mortar in his lap—*fulcio* as a crucial catchword of subordinate domestic labor, the work of "support," "stabilization," "securing"—is tied to the jolting demystification of Simulus as animalistic laboring body with a hairy groin (*saetosa sub inguina*). The right hand, however, is allotted the more glamorous, or at least more heroic, beat of "softening" the reeking garlic, squashing it into compliance. The two hands almost carry with them, each their own, the dual modes of the poem—low comic realism and high epic inflation—until the pestle and mortar do the job of clumping everything together into a coarse, uneasy unity. This division of labor is modal, too—and the end-product is meant as a blend.[30]

Up to that last paragraph, I had been drawing a fairly cut and dried distinction between the modes of labor and representation permitted to Scybale and Simulus; but more accurately, as the poetics of the pestle processor whizz ever more vigorously, we could say that these different modes are contained within Simulus himself. It is not just that our "hero's" body inhabits two worlds simultaneously, dipping his left hand into the unmetaphorizable dirt, and raising his right to the aesthetically workable levelling--up—a walking ambassador for work staying work, but also becoming "work," in the very same frame. It is also that Simulus, like Scybale, often seems to get *dragged back* to the world of the literal, even at the moment of highest metaphorical flight; he becomes a figure for the imprisoning stasis of poverty. Immediately chasing the description of the mixed pesto—famous for equipping the United States of America with its tag of either idealized melting pot or crushing vessel of assimilation[31]—we find yet another piece of literalism punching Simulus right back down to ground:

> *it manus in gyrum: paulatim singula vires*
> *deperdunt proprias, color est e pluribus unus,*
> *nec totus viridis, quia lactea frusta repugnant,*
> *nec de lacte nitens, quia tot variatur ab herbis.*
> *saepe viri nares acer iaculatur apertas*
> *spiritus et simo damnat sua prandia vultu,*
> *saepe manu summa lacrimantia lumina terget*
> *immeritoque furens dicit convicia fumo.* (101–8)

> His hand rolls round: gradually the individual ingredients lose their strength, one color emerges from many, but the mixture isn't wholly green, since milky bits put up a fight, nor is it a shiny milk-white, since it's flecked by so many herbs. The sharp aroma often spears the man's nostrils and he swears at the lunch through his snub-nosed face, and often wipes his teary eyes with the back of his hand, and angrily hurls abuse at the smoke, which did nothing to deserve it.

None of this work is done particularly willingly or easily, which certainly puts the *Moretum* a cut above the worst cases of naïve ruling-class idealization: just like the white ingredients pushing back against their lot of intermingling, so Simulus winces and carps at the unpleasantness of his work—which he can do, we might surmise, precisely because he has had a taste of more aesthetically rewarding ways of working. But this moment of bodily recoil from foul-smelling labor—perhaps confusable for the snobby turn-up of the nose one might imagine from an elite bystander reading the scene—does not quite haul Simulus from his peasant world. Instead, ironically, it restores him to it by a kind of over-literal nominative determinism:[32] Simulus, the "little snub-nosed," in this context reveals he is actually, literally, snub-nosed. As with Scybale's horrific brand (probably assigned by her enslaver), so with Simulus' milder mocking nomenclature: he is what he says on the tin. Here, in his essence, Simulus is denied the aesthetic redemption of vehicle separating from tenor. If he approaches hero through the liberation of metaphor, he remains stuck as a peasant through literalism, a static convergence of name and thing.

Digging Out/Sinking In

We have only just scratched the surface on metaphor in the *Moretum*, but I want to move toward the end with a passage that complicates further what I have been arguing or perhaps points to a different dimension to it. So far, I have tried to show how uneven clusters of metaphor—a trope which is the poetic sign of aesthetic valuation par excellence—are matched with the way certain work and workers are valued in this poem. Simulus' bread-making but also his other activities which we have not gone into as much—gardening and pesto-making—can be raised through metaphor; but then again, Simulus always seems to harbor a part of himself which stays deep in the weeds, which keeps flat, literal, unreceptive to such value-adding. In this scheme, the unequal distribution of metaphor is clustered quite clearly across Simulus (metaphor-heavy) and Scybale (metaphor-zero), but also within Simulus himself—an entity rent between two worlds, working with different sized hands, a peasant-poet occupying the threshold between work and "work." The last lines of the poem, however, seem to move us back to a stance of full separation between the flattened domestic labor of Scybalian "support," and the aesthetically transformable process of Simulan work. Except this time, everyone gets a metaphor.

While I said the poet is always the one doing the metaphorizing—herein lies the second firewall, and more on this subjectivity in a second—there are a few hints over the course of the poem that our primitivized peasant is also starting to *think*. This is something I think I underplayed in the first version of this chapter. As we saw, Simulus can sing poetry to lighten the load of work (29–30—more on this briefly); he is capable of showing off artistic knowledge in the garden, "knowing" how to arrange the plants properly (*varias disponere plantas/norat* 68–9); and he can also think and plan, *tum quoque tale aliquid meditans* (85). *Meditor* is the kind of casual mental activity you need to compose poetry (cf. Horace *Sat.* 1.9.2, *nescioquid meditans*), even if Simulus' *aliquid* might implicitly consist of thoughts about vegetables he wants from the garden. Perhaps I am underestimating Simulus by putting thoughts in his head here—David Ross thinks *tum quoque tale aliquid meditans* means that the previous lines' slight romanticization of rustic self-sufficiency is actually being attributed to Simulus himself.[33] In any case, however we pitch the poet's estimation of Simulus' creative capacities here, there are *at least* entry-level signs of an inchoate subjectivity and interiority. Scybale, on the other hand, is rendered in two dimensions: she is pure physical appearance and manual action without interiority. I think this dynamic kicks into gear again during the duo's final interaction, right at the end of the poem:

> *Eruit interea Scybale quoque sedula panem,*
> *quem laetus recipit manibus, pulsoque timore*
> *iam famis inque diem securus Simulus illam*
> *ambit crura ocreis paribus tectusque galero*
> *sub iuga parentis cogit lorata iuvencos*
> *atque agit in segetes et terrae condit aratrum.* (117–22)

> In the meantime, as well, the trusty Scybale digs out the bread, which Simulus happily takes in his hands—with the fear of hunger now chased away, unworried for the rest of that day, he wraps a pair of greaves round his legs, and donning a cap, forces his obedient cattle under their leather yokes, and drives them into the fields, and sinks his plow in the ground.

All-told, this is a nicer, less gruff encounter between the two characters than in other parts of the poem. Smiling, bread in hand, his basic material requirements met, Simulus can now leap up a rung on the pyramid of human needs, and the poem concomitantly steps it up a level: now he gets a full-on arming scene, kitted out like an epic warrior, dominating his beasts, entering the plowing register of Virgil *Georgics* book 1.[34] Again, surprise surprise, the man gets promoted for doing nothing. But what I want to point out is the very subtle counterpose between two words for earthwork, a.k.a two metaphors: *eruit* and *condit*. *Eruo* is to "dig something out," and it is Scybale's task to "dig out" the bread, just as she cleaned space for it before. But in this act of digging, she both takes Simulus' place—when he was in the garden just now, the peasant hero had literally got his hands dirty digging up garlic and herbs (86)—and yet does not *quite* manage to take his place. You should not have to "dig" bread—digging is a lower-order activity in the *scala naturae* of this little country paradise. So, the only metaphor Scybale is really allowed in the poem actually does an inverse operation on her: it brings her low, it makes the neutral and relatively simple activity of removing the bread from the oven into something *dirtier* than it needs to be. Simulus, on the other hand, gets the five-star *condit*—the opposite ground-level activity, of burying something in it rather than removing something from it, of sowing, planting, founding—and also seasoning and preserving. I do not need to tell you it is one of the buzzwords for Aeneas' ktistic miracle in the *Aeneid*, indeed also the last verb of that poem[35] (and *eruo* can be used of razing cities to the ground rather than founding them—a hint of feminized destruction here too then? The true antonym for the foundational and preservative *condo*?). So, while Scybale is finally allowed to enter the world of (very subtle) metaphor, it is a metaphor that brings the low lower; Simulus, lucky guy, is raised higher than ever, to Aenean proportions; and their drifting apart is cleverly inscribed through metaphors staking different relationships to the earth, digging out and/or razing versus sinking in and building.

Background Work

This Working Lives project is keen to reintroduce human subjectivity into accounts of work, and injections of subjectivity are precisely what poetry is good for. I have touched on this issue already in the tripartite hierarchy of metaphor-worker at the beginning: if Scybale gets no real hint of subjectivity or interiority, Simulus is granted the limited first lineaments of it, but at the "top" lies the *Moretum*-maker themselves, the poet, equipped with the skill of lifting low to high like the best luxury metaphorizer of Quintilian's scheme. But what kind of subject position might this programmatically mysterious poet represent? This is an important question, even if I have taught myself (as a fan of the anonymous) to repress it. As our De Beauvoir epigraph shows, our notion of the poet's subjectivity colors our reading of the poem's tone, and vice versa: the aestheticization of labor is often performed by those who have no direct experience of its drudgery, and it is also often performed for members of that class with a thirst for the entertainment value of the impoverished, as Ann Kutner reminds us in this volume.[36] All of this is infinitely annoying, not to say offensive. So is our poet just another one of these pesky, cynical aestheticizers? Is this idealization *from above* the *Moretum*'s task, its stance?

Let me end—genuinely end—by offering another version of how the poet fits into all this; a version which pivots around a shift in my thinking on this poem, and ancient authorship in general, arising from the various strata of work in giving this paper at the first Work/Life workshop, and then again at UCLA a few months later, and then again at the second Work/Life conference, and in general, from sitting on many a panel with Joe Howley and Candida Moss over the years (this, once more, a small attempt to weave the work of collaboration onto my sleeve, into the main text, not just let it lie fallow in the acknowledgments). In this earlier version, I assumed—for reasons of an inherent and impoverishing classism, perhaps—that the ideological stance of the *Moretum* poet was more or less aligned with the slave-owning Roman elite. Hence, my strand of thought in this chapter about how metaphor acts as the extra-diegetic firewall in the poem: high-brow poet can make lovely metaphors, beautifully and self-consciously, whereas Simulus is blissfully unaware that the pesto he is smashing together is anything close to high art (rather than daily grind). Now, I am not so sure this account is up to the job. So, I leave you with an alternative thought experiment. What if we made use of the poem's anonymity to take it in the other direction entirely? What if we imagined it as the work not of the usual slave-owning, hexameter-crafting elite, but of someone—perhaps a grammarian or similar—who had themselves experienced transplantation and enslavement, like our good Scybale? We know that there were lots of hyper-literate, and hyper-literary, enslaved people and freedmen filling out secretarial (and other) duties in upper-class Roman houses. Joe Howley's forthcoming classic will shine the spotlight on them,[37] as does Nicole Giannella's chapter in this volume. Some of these could well have been behind the bits and bobs of *pseudepigrapha* and *adespota* that eventually got folded under daddy Virgil's wing.[38] So what if our pesto poem was the product of someone with direct experience (a) of being themselves subaltern and (b) of seeing up close the annoying posh Roman habit of aestheticizing the life of the poor?

Let us work this out. A further singular trait of the *Moretum*—related to the combination of realism and idealism mentioned above—is that it plants quite subtle hints of what we might call the "material realities" of Simulus' economic position right next door to the wishful thinking of a standard elite portrait of the peasant's blessed condition.[39] In this way, it almost smooshes together an implicit poetic subjectivity that is *both* idealizing *and* hard-nosed about rural poverty at one and the same time.[40] A good clue here might lie in the initial description of Simulus' garden, which is a strange mix of rosy self-sufficiency and realistic embedding in a market economy. First, an odd detail is nested in the picture of absolute vegetal abundance:

Hortus erat iunctus casulae, quem vimina pauca
et calamo rediviva levi munibat harundo,
exiguus spatio, variis sed fertilis herbis.
nil illi deerat quod pauperis exigit usus;
interdum locuples a paupere plura petebat.
nec sumptus ullius erat, sed recula curae:

si quando vacuum casula pluviaeve tenebant
festave lux, si forte labor cessabat aratri,
horti opus illud erat. (60–68)

Next to the little hut was a garden, which a few osiers and repurposed reed was fortifying with its delicate stalks; it was small-sized, but abundant in its range of herbs. It had everything a poor man's need calls for; and sometimes a rich man would even ask more from this peasant. It didn't cost him anything except a bit of labor: if rain or a holiday ever gave him free time in the house, if perhaps the work of the plow was paused, the garden became the task at hand.

In a passage that steals liberally from the playbook of the locus classicus of garden excess, the Corycian gardener of *Georgics* 4.116–48,[41] we have a strange addition: apparently Simulus' garden is so productive, it is often raided by rich people looking for "more." Could this be an inchoate allegory of exploitation—a quick, winking meta-signal that this poet knows how posh writers tend to "make use" of the poor in idealizing hexameters, to take from their gardens, to make a dent in the poor's "surplus" and appropriate them for their own poetic purposes into the high mimetic? William Fitzgerald, as usual, already hit the nut: "In fact, what the rich need from Simulus, in addition to his produce, is the fantasy of independence from the city that his imagined life provides them."[42] A similar touch of the realist puncturing the idealist occurs soon after, when again the poet spells out, this time more extensively, that this crop of garden vegetables is not actually *for* the people who grow them:

verum hic non domini (quis enim contractior illo?)
sed populi proventus erat, nonisque diebus
venalis umero fasces portabat in urbem.
inde domum cervice levis, gravis aere redibat
vix umquam urbani comitatus merce macelli:
cepa rubens sectique famem domat area porri
quaeque trahunt acri vultus nasturtia morsu
intibaque et Venerem revocans eruca morantem. (78–84)

Yet this haul was marked not for the owner (who had a tighter-belt than he?) but for the people; every ninth day he'd lug his packets into town on his shoulders, putting them up for sale. From there he'd come home with a lighter neck and heavier pockets—rarely if ever kept company by goods from market. Red onion brought his hunger to heel, and his plot of chives, and watercress—it makes you wince with its sharp taste—and endive, and rocket, which gets a sluggish Venus going again.

Simulus produces for market: he heads into town with neck laden, comes back with pockets loaded. The luxury goods—that is, the more substantial vegetables like asparagus or gourds in 71–76—are not bound for his belly; rather, he must make do with the light stuff, onion, chives, watercress (contorting the face with a flash forward to our snub-nose wrinkling later on), rocket. So, on the one hand, we have a discourse of the wonderful autonomy of the peasant smallholder; on the other, an up-front nod to the pressing limits of that autonomy. Why is Simulus selling so much stuff if he is so self-sufficient? Why does he need cash—for rent?[43] Or to buy his freedom, if he is in fact a slave, as the quick doff to Tityrus in Virgil *Eclogue* 1 suggests (*gravis aere*: cf. Virgil *Eclogue* 1.35, *non umquam gravis aere domum mihi dextra redibat*).[44] These are "reality effect" details that did not have to go in. And they somehow magnetize the subjectivity behind the *Moretum*, bring it more toward the perspective of someone who *knows*—who understands deeply the cracks and contradictions of elite rusticating discourse. Someone, perhaps, who sees themselves in Simulus' position, forced to port product, to traffic between two worlds, to save money for a rainy day? Or someone who has been close to being the Scybale in the partnership?

Let us honor the circular motion[45] of the *Moretum* by revisiting our first passage—where again, I would say, there could be a hint of the poet's sub-elite subjectivity poking through. Here we are on terra markedly less firma, but let us avail ourselves of the carnival space of conclusion and go out on a long limb. If this *Moretum* poet, like many producers of parodic or pseudepigraphic works in Rome, were a *grammaticus* or *notarius* import, originally enslaved in the home of a wealthy enslaver,[46] chances are they would have had some direct experience performing literary labor for the master.[47] If we bear that possible arrangement in mind, could we not see Simulus' initial encounter with Scybale as a kind of rustic refraction of a certain enslaver-enslaved dynamic of which the poet may have been on the constant front-line, namely, dictation?

modo rustica carmina cantat
agrestique suum solatur voce laborem,
interdum clamat Scybalen. (29–31)

Now he sings rustic songs, and with rude strains solaces his toil; at times he shouts to Scybale.

Simulus barking out the song, punctuating the poetry only with rude commands to his helper? That looks close enough to, or perhaps a rustic version of, how it might have felt to be on the receiving end of the imperative of someone who fancied himself the sole generator of the song you were co-creating. In this moment where part of Simulus escapes into the land of poetry, even as his hands remain busy at the mill, we see the continuing gruff speech acts as foundational to the escape. The yells at Scybale are not just co-extensive or simultaneous with the poetry. They *are* the poetry. For this is precisely how poetry at Rome is made: through screaming at a slave. The work is the "work" … is the work.

If these hunches were true, we could see the *Moretum* as an incredibly sharp hatchet job, not necessarily buying into this discourse of aestheticization, but perhaps exposing it for the puffed up, patronizing bollocks it is. More in the line of David Ross' argument that the poem parodies the Hellenistic and neoteric habit of bringing low matter into high contexts;[48] and something akin to the satire Francesca Bellei has brilliantly tracked across it;[49] but encapsulating the subjectivity of someone who had been at the pointy end of the elite tendency to conflate work and "work." For in the end, *Moretum* is the only ancient poem I know to show how art in a slave society is a zero-sum game. Elite ideology may strive to suppress it, but in giving airtime to the asymmetric symbiosis (or parasitism) of peasant and slave, the *Moretum* pitches a square truth: that the elevation of one humble being into the high register is completely dependent on the subjugation and maintenance of another humble being in the low register. You cannot have a Simulus cooking up miracles without a Scybale cleaning up his shit—nor can you have the work of poetry without the work of the enslaved on which it ultimately depends.

Notes

1. For a fascinating attempt to approach our own thinking about work through the Ovidian fable of full work-worker identification, cf. Formisano in this volume.
2. Kadue 2021.
3. Or at least a kind of isomorphy: as Kadue 2021: 4 says, her authors describe their literary labors as work that "formally resembles the mundane mainte-

nance work of housewives and domestic laborers rather than the trailblazing feats of modern and modernizing heroes."

4. Verboven and Laes 2017: 5.
5. Cf. Fitzgerald 1996: 391: "the laborious preparations of Simulus described by the poet serve to materialize the otherwise invisible work of writing poetry."
6. Cf. Fitzgerald 1996: 390: 411–12.
7. The poem comes down under Virgil's brand, but unlike, say, the *Culex*, makes no explicit pseudepigraphic attempt to fold itself into his career; and if dating by allusion is secure enough, it's probably post-Ovidian (Kenney 1984). Other than that, anyone's guess.
8. Cf. Heinze 1960: 404–16.
9. Cf. Ross 1975, Kenney 1984, Bellei 2024.
10. Fitzgerald 1996: 414.
11. See Gowers 2021: 253–4, and introduction to this volume.
12. Bellei 2024.
13. Howley Forthcoming; but this kind of firewalling is also common to gendered work: see, for example, Kadue 2021: 3.
14. Howley Forthcoming.
15. For a similar binary in a very different context, cf. Formisano's comments on the distinction between Arachne and the spider into which she is transformed in Ovid's *Met.*: Arachne's human identity allows her some distance between herself and her work, a distance which collapses when she becomes the mechanically producing spider. In a sense, Simulus in my scheme is permitted the artistic autonomy of Arachne pre-transformation; Scybale, on the other hand, is reduced to pure identification with her work.
16. Fitzgerald 1996.
17. Cf. Formisano in this volume on Arachne self-silencing to let her work speak for itself.
18. Haley 1993: 42.
19. Bellei 2024
20. See also Fitzgerald 1996: 404, who sees the descriptive step change slightly differently here: it marks Scybale as foreign, unfamiliar, unassimilable into the high mimetic.
21. Although, since reading Gowers 2021: 252–3, I realize I may be even more guilty of flattening this description in its metaphorical link with the garden vegetables of 71–77.
22. Fitzgerald 1996: 404–5.
23. *Opus* as task of grinding (24, 38), dough (47), garden (68), pestling (109), and the pesto itself (113)—alternating, as the word likes to do in both English and Latin, between process and product (cf. introduction to this volume).

24. Cf. the acts of heaping and addition at 96–7, 111–2.
25. The *OLD* (*mundo*) cites only two other instances: Columella 12.3.8 and Petronius 47.8. The editors rightly point me to the cosmogonic valence of *mundaverat* (> *mundus*)—so perhaps the word has as much of the sublime as it does of the mundane, and my reading of Scybale's language risks being over-impoverished.
26. See Ross 1975: 257–8 on this first use of *emundata* in Latin; and its appearance in context of the slightly OTT tendency of the *Moretum* toward verbs with dignifiying and intensifying prefixes (e.g., *perverrit* 23, *transversat* 45, *dilatat* 47)—although I would not agree that these verbs also "trivialize" Simulus' activity.
27. On the racial politics of the *Moretum*'s language of purification and filtration, see Gowers 2021: 260.
28. With overtones, too, of food waste, "leavings": see Gowers 2021: 251 on the connotations of Scybale's and Simulus' names.
29. On the *figura etymologica* here—"clarifying" the origins of the word *moretum*—see Gowers 2021: 256.
30. For this combination of idealism and realism in the artistic representation of lower status figures, cf. Kuttner (this volume).
31. See Fitzgerald 1996: 416; Gowers 2021: 259–60.
32. Ross 1975: 260. There are in fact several acts of punning etymologization in these lines—see Gowers 2021: 256.
33. Ross 1975: 259.
34. Höschele 2005: 225–9; Gowers 2021: 251.
35. Fitzgerald 1996: 401; Gowers 2021: 251.
36. See Kuttner (this volume) on peasants as household entertainment.
37. Howley Forthcoming.
38. Certainly in the case of the *Culex*—more explicitly pseudepigraphic—it is conceivable that the work could come from the pen of one of Virgil's slaves or freedmen; this inference on the analogies of other (ex)slaves tasked with labors of "completion," whether editorial (e.g., Tiro after Cicero's death) or more authorial (e.g., Cornelius Epicadius, freedman of Sulla, completing the last book of Sulla's autobiography after his death—see Suetonius *De Grammaticis* 12).
39. It is notable that the poem does this regularly at the linguistic level throughout, with bubbles of high-sounding diction popped by the vulgar or the workaday—see Ross 1975: 255–8.
40. Fitzgerald 1996: 397 is again helpful here, on Simulus' burning himself at the beginning of the poem: "On the one hand, the life of Simulus needs to be shielded from ridicule to become the object of high cultural attention, and in this context the decorum of the language attempts to tune out the 'noise' that interferes with its being recognized as life. On the other hand,

the life of Simulus can only truly appear in what resists incorporation into the high cultural style, and is indirectly present in the cry or curse that we hear under the elegance of language."

41. Cf. Gowers 2021: 251 on this section as "a miniature of the postponed gardening poem" in *Georgics* 4.
42. Fitzgerald 1996: 406.
43. If Simulus were pictured as a poor subsistence farmer rather than enslaved, he would probably be subject to rent, and so needing to sell crops for cash (Verboven and Laes 2017: 10, 15).
44. Kenney 1984.
45. On the cosmic ring of which: Gowers 2021: 254.
46. It is striking how many of the prominent grammarians fleshed out by Suetonius in *De Grammaticis* were freedmen: Q. Caecilius Epirota (DG 16), M. Verrius Flaccus (DG 17), Lucius Crassicius (DG 18), Modestus (DG 20); and stories were going round that Valerius Cato was a freedman too (DG 11). See also Howley Forthcoming.
47. Howley Forthcoming.
48. Ross 1975: 261–2. On the poem's line of parody toward Latin literature's overuse of Empedocles, see the brief hint in Farrell 2014 n.47 and brief remarks in Maticic and Rogers in this volume (p. 4).
49. Bellei 2024.

Bibliography

Bellei, Francesca. 2024. "The Nose at the Crossroads: An Intersectional Reading of the Pseudo-Virgilian *Moretum*." *TAPA* 154.1: 213–250.

Farrell, J. 2014. "Looking for Empedocles in Latin Poetry: A Skeptical Approach." *Dictynna* 11: np. https://journals.openedition.org/dictynna/1063.

Fitzgerald, W. 1996. "Labor and Laborer in Latin Poetry: the Case of the *Moretum*." *Arethusa* 29.3: 389–418.

Gowers, E. 2021. "Pun-Fried Concoctions: Wor(l)d-Blending in the Roman Kitchen." In Morales, H., Fantuzzi, M., and Whitmarsh, T. eds. *Reception in the Greco-Roman World: Literary Studies in Theory and Practice*. 241–65. Cambridge University Press.

Haley, S. P. 1993. "Black Feminist Thought and Classics: Re-Membering, Re-Claiming, Re-Empowering." In *Feminist Theory and the Classics*, edited by Nancy Sorkin Rabinowitz and Amy Richlin, 23–43. Routledge.

Heinze, R. 1960. *Vom Geist des Römertums*. Teubner.

Höschele, R. 2005. "Moreto-Poetik: das Moretum als Intertextuelles Mischgericht." In Holzberg, N., ed. *Die « Appendix Vergiliana »: Pseudepigraphen im Literarischen Kontext*. 244–69. Narr.

Howley, Joseph. Forthcoming. *Slavery and the Roman Book*.

Kadue, K. 2021. *Domestic Georgic: Labors of Preservation from Rabelais to Milton.* University of Chicago Press.

Kenney, E. J., ed. 1984. *Moretum. The Ploughman's Lunch, a Poem Ascribed to Virgil.* Bristol Classical Press.

Ross, D. O. 1975. "The *Culex* and *Moretum* as Post-Augustan Literary Parodies." *Harvard Studies in Classical Philology* LXXIX: 235–63.

Verboven, K. and Laes, C., eds. 2017. *Work, Labour, and Professions in the Roman World. Impact of Empire, 23.* Brill.

CHAPTER 3

Wandering Workers: Mobility and Skills in the Roman World

Claire Holleran

These men are invited all over the boundless earth.
—Hom. Od. *17. 386* (Loeb 105, *translated* A. T. Murray, *revised* George E. Dimock, *1919)*

In the *Odyssey*, τέκτονες (*tektones* or skilled artisans) appear among Eumaeus' list of strangers who might reasonably be invited into a different city, alongside seers, doctors, and singers. While Homer's world may be

My thanks to Paul Erdkamp, Rebecca Flemming, Jordan Rogers, and Ben Russell for their thoughtful comments on earlier drafts of this chapter, as well as the audiences at the "Work/Life: Institutions, Subjectivities, and Human Resources in the Roman World" workshop in New York and at the Durham Department of Classics and Ancient History research seminar. All remaining errors of fact or argument are my own.

C. Holleran (✉)
University of Exeter, Exeter, UK
e-mail: c.holleran@exeter.ac.uk

D. A. Maticic, J. Rogers (eds.), *Working Lives in Ancient Rome*, The New Antiquity,
https://doi.org/10.1007/978-3-031-61234-3_3

one of heroes, Eumaeus is here likely reflecting a social reality in which the mobility of skilled workers was a recognizable trend.[1] In fact, this practice has a long history, and there is evidence of artisanal mobility in the Mediterranean going back at least as far as the Bronze Age.[2] Skilled workers were not evenly distributed and neither was access to training. Nor was there necessarily a consistent demand for particular skills in a single place. Skilled work on building projects, for example, is, for the most part, temporary, and once completed, workers must look for a new project, potentially in a different location. For skilled workers such as doctors, demand for their services may have been greater in the wealthier urban centers, but it was relatively consistent across geographical areas. Yet mobility enabled doctors not only to improve their training and develop their expertise but also to increase their profit and enhance their standing and prestige. Therefore, although military mobility and in particular the enforced relocation of millions of enslaved people—many of whom were themselves highly skilled—were undoubtedly the most significant examples of human movement in the ancient world, legally free skilled workers could also be mobile, moving to take account of when and where their skills might be most in demand or where they could gain the most profit and prestige.

The amount of movement, its geographical extent, and its structure and organization, however, will surely have varied over time and place, and both within and between economic sectors, as it does in other periods. In the later Middle Ages and early modern period, for example, economic mobility among skilled workers is relatively well documented.[3] Craftsmen who had completed an apprenticeship often travelled for several years as journeymen in order to gain experience in their chosen field before they became masters, a tradition continued by the so-called *Wandergesellen* of Europe; many others remained itinerant journeymen for longer periods, making use of journeymen networks that linked dispersed skilled labor with local employers.[4] This system of organized—and perhaps even more significantly "un-organized"—tramping developed over the fourteenth and fifteenth centuries and became an actual requirement for many craft guilds by the late sixteenth or early seventeenth centuries, so much so that markets in itinerant skilled labor have been described as "a fundamental feature of pre-modern European crafts."[5] This comparative material from a better-documented period indicates that even within the same economic sector, there were varied patterns of movement, and typically the more specialized a craft, the further workers moved. Within construction, for instance, some workers were more-or-less constantly itinerant over a relatively small geographic area, undertaking small building jobs and repairs as they moved seasonally. Other more specialized or highly skilled builders worked on major building projects for longer periods of time, often moving further but only intermittently.[6] The type of work and the nature of the project were also of important considerations here, as some specialized workers may have been required on a site for longer than others.

Though several contributions in this volume consider the mobility of workers to some extent—including Cheung's ceramicists, Sancinito's merchants, and Sausville's doctors—this chapter focuses explicitly on the structural underpinnings of skilled mobility in the Roman world. Taking medicine and the construction industry as case studies, it asks three fundamental questions about the mobility of skilled workers within these two economic sectors, focusing principally on the Roman imperial period. It asks who moved ("The Movers"), how this movement was structured and organized ("The Organization"), and how skilled workers demonstrated their competence and professional ability ("Getting Established"). As is typically the case with the ancient world, our evidence is partial and answers to some of these questions prove more elusive than others, but we can at least go some way toward building a picture of the mobility of skilled workers in the Roman world. In doing so, this chapter reinforces the importance to the Roman economy of the movement of goods, information, and people, supported by a network of connectivity across the provinces.

Medical Practitioners

The Movers

Medical practitioners are among the best-documented and most mobile skilled professionals in the ancient world. They travelled for training and the accrual of knowledge and experience, but also to improve their standing, increase their potential for profit, and, as Sausville demonstrates in this volume, enhance the possibility for public prestige and honors.[7] Already in the archaic period in Greece, medical practitioners were moving around. According to the account of Herodotus (3.125; 3.129–137), Democedes, the most skilled physician of his time, came from Croton in Southern Italy but worked in Aegina, then Athens, then Samos; he was later captured and taken to the court of Darius I, from where he escaped and returned to Croton. Although his initial move to Aegina was undertaken in order to get away from a violent father, he was able to establish quickly such a reputation for himself that by the second year, the Aeginetans paid him a talent to be their public physician. He then moved to Athens for a higher salary and to Samos where he was paid two talents (Hdt. 3.131); his willingness to move clearly increased both his profit and prestige.[8] His fame and reputation was such that it established Croton as a center of medical excellence, with medical practitioners from Croton at that time being regarded as the best in Greece. All this relied on connectivity and the spread of information between communities and individuals.

Medicine remained a mobile profession into the Roman period, both within the Greek world and in the western provinces. A doctor from Nicaea in Bithynia, for example, died in Perrhaebia in Thessaly and his tombstone proudly declared that he had "wandered much over land and sea" (*IG* 9^2 1276).[9] A recently excavated skeleton of a man found buried with two wooden boxes filled with medical tools, discovered near Jászberény to the east of Budapest in Hungary, has been interpreted as that of an itinerant Roman doctor dating to the first century CE.[10] Perhaps unsurprisingly, the imperial city of Rome drew in medical practitioners from all over the Mediterranean, but particularly from the Greek world. Pliny the Elder (*HN* 29.12) claims on the authority of Cassius Hemina that the very first *medicus* in Rome was Archagathus, who came from the Peloponnese in 219 BCE; presumably, he does not mean that he was the very first doctor in Rome, but that he was the first Greek doctor who was publicly endorsed and funded by the Roman state.[11] Certainly it seems unlikely that there were no doctors in Rome before 219 BCE, but his purported origins set the scene for centuries of Greek dominance of Roman medicine, even if Archagathus himself was nicknamed "executioner" (*carnifex*: Plin. *HN* 29.13). In fact, Pliny claims that because of him, doctors became objects of loathing, but if this were true, it does not appear to have deterred other Greek doctors from coming to the city subsequently. Literature records many other examples, such as Asclepiades from Bithynia, active in Rome in the second century BCE.[12] From Pliny (*HN* 29.5.8–11), we learn of a series of popular doctors making huge profits in first-century CE Rome, including Crinas and Charmis from Marseille, and Thessalus from Tralles, while a number of imperial doctors in the first and second centuries came from the Greek world, such as Stertinius Xenophon from Cos (Tac. *Ann.* 12.61; 67; Plin. *HN* 29.5.7), Andromachus from Crete (Galen, K14.2), and Statilius Crito and Statilius

Attalus from Caria (Mart. 11.60.6; Galen, K10.909–16; K12.455). Soranus, the author of numerous medical treatises, came from Ephesus, most likely studied in Alexandria, and displayed knowledge of Rome in his writings. He notes, for instance, the number of bow-legged children in Rome, claiming that this is because they are encouraged to walk on the hard paving from a young age, the water is cold, and (presumably displaying a Greek prejudice) their mothers take less care of them than Greek mothers (Sor. *Gyn.* 2.44).[13] Most famously, Galen came from Pergamum to Rome in the 160s CE, having already travelled to Smyrna, Corinth, and Alexandria for further training and research.[14]

The medical practitioners recorded in literature are typically the most renowned, with the most famous patients, but a number of inscriptions indicate the presence of less well-known doctors from the Greek world in Rome. Squeezed on the bottom of a tombstone recording the deaths of Castor and Dionysia, a freedman and a freedwoman of Munatius Plancus, for example, is the name of Sosicrates, a freeborn *medicus* from Nicaea, who must have been active in Rome in the early years of the first century CE (EDCS-64800454).[15] Roughly contemporary with Galen was T. Flavius Coelius Severus, a *medicus* from Side (*CIL* VI 9680; EDCS-19301123). Not all, however, came from Greece. From less further afield (and not from the east, despite his Greek cognomen) came Marcus Licinius Philomusus, who is described as a *medicus Pollentinus*, or a doctor from Pollentia in the far north of Italy (*CIL* VI 9587; EDCS-19301130). In the later fourth century, Rapetiga's tombstone records his origin in Hispania (*CIL* VI 9597; EDCS-19301140).

These inscriptions were all in Latin, but many other medical practitioners in Rome chose to use Greek in their inscriptions. Some of these explicitly record an origin in the Greek-speaking world, such as C. Iulius Themison, an ἰατρὸς (*iatros)* from Tralles, active in Rome in the first century CE (*IGUR* 607), or the ἰατροί (*iatroi*) Claudius Zosimus from Ephesus (*IGUR* 682) and Q. Aelius Archelaus from Nicomedia (*IGUR* 299).[16] For others, it is probable that they came from the East, but their exact origins are unclear. Patron, for example, erected a tomb for himself and his family between the Via Latina and the Via Appia in Augustan Rome.[17] This was excavated in the first half of the nineteenth century and fragments of the wall paintings from the burial chamber are now in the collection of the Louvre, together with some of the Greek-language inscriptions (*IG* XIV 1934; *IGUR* III 1303a–k). These inscriptions record Patron's profession as a doctor or ἰατρὸς (*iatros*) (*IGUR* III 1303d) and also include a dedication by his daughter, Appoleia (*IGUR* III 1303f). Another inscription from the tomb looks to have originally recorded details of Patron's origin, but this is fragmentary and can no longer be read (*IGUR* III 1303e). Based on his daughter Appoleia's gentilicium, however, it has been suggested that Patron came from Pergamum and received Roman citizenship from Sextus Appuleius, proconsul of Asia 23–22 BCE.[18] The dedication by his daughter, as well as her inclusion—and that of his wife, Atheno—among the labelled figures in the funeral procession depicted in the tomb paintings would suggest that both Patron and his family had settled in Rome. A century or so later, Claudius Agathemerus and his wife Myrtale also left an impressive funerary monument in Rome, noting that he was a "swift healer of disease."[19] These people were clearly successful and moved for the long term, bringing their families with them or establishing them once they had moved.

In fact, over 90% of the names of doctors recorded on inscriptions in imperial Rome are Greek, and around the same percentage of Greek names is found on inscriptions recording names of medical practitioners across the Roman empire in the first century CE.[20] In Chester in Northwest England, for example, an altar inscribed in Greek records a dedication by one Hermogenes, a doctor (*RIB* 461; see also *RIB* 3151). Hermogenes was probably an army doctor, although overall Latin names predominate among army doctors and many were freeborn citizens; this can be explained by the fact that many of these doctors were also soldiers and so had to abide by the usual rules of military recruitment.[21] Of course, when it comes to Greek names, some of these may not have been genuinely "Greek" but may have simply adopted a Greek name in order to meet the expectation that doctors came from the Greek-speaking world (see below). Furthermore, a Greek name in itself need not mean that an individual actually came from that region. Bader, for example, points to the example of Marcus Rubrius Zosimus, a doctor stationed with an auxiliary unit in Germania (*CIL* XIII 6621). Although his *cognomen* is Greek, he was a Roman citizen from Ostia and undertook his medical training locally in the vicinity of Rome.[22] His name may perhaps indicate servile origins but, as Lavan has demonstrated, the assumption that an individual with a Greek name must be freed is debatable.[23]

These people were successful enough in their profession to leave funerary monuments, some of which were lavish, but Juvenal's inclusion of *medicus* among his (albeit satirical) list of professions undertaken by the "hungry Greekling" (*Graeculus esuriens*) in Rome suggests at least a popular association between Greeks and the medical profession, not necessarily confined to the elite (Juv. *Sat.* 3.77). Further down the social scale, we might also think of more itinerant medical practitioners, who moved around rural areas and between towns. Cicero (*Clu.* 40), for example, claimed that Oppianicus' father paid an itinerant medicine seller (*pharmacopola cicrumforaneus*) 2000 sesterces for drugs to kill his mother-in-law; the pharmacist in question—Lucius Clodius of Ancona—happened to be passing through Larinum on his way to many other towns (*fora multa*). While for medical practitioners at the top level, mobility was central to the development of a career, enabling training and facilitating the development of a reputation and access to more lucrative economic opportunities, for those at the lower levels, mobility was often a simple necessity, with such practitioners moving in search of patients to treat and clients to serve, and perhaps also to escape bad reputations earned elsewhere.

The Organization

The mobility of medical practitioners was officially encouraged at the highest levels. Archagathus, supposedly the first doctor to come to Rome from Greece in 219 BCE, was awarded citizenship and given a *taberna* to work in at public expense (Plin. *HN* 29.12–13); this was located at the *Compitum Acili*, a central location on the south west slopes of the Oppian hill, an area which continued to be associated with medicine for centuries.[24] He was almost certainly an officially appointed doctor, and although we do not know precisely how he was selected for the role, Nutton suggests that Rome was acting in a similar way to contemporary Greek cities.[25] Here the formation of centers of medical excellence such as Cos, together with established networks of information about medical practitioners, helped cities to select publicly appointed doctors. Sometimes a city might approach a center such as Cos requesting a doctor, who was then selected on their behalf, as happened with Hermias who was sent from Cos to Gortyn on Crete around 217 BCE (*I. Creticae* IV, 168 and I, 8.7). Other times, cities knew exactly whom they would like and sent embassies or letters of invitation directly, as with the town of Gytheion in Laconia, who requested a doctor directly from Sparta (*IG* 5, 1, 1145). Whether he was chosen directly by Rome or was suggested for them, Archagathus must already have established a strong reputation to be selected as the first publicly sponsored doctor in Rome; perhaps he was even supported by the *gens Acilia* given the location of his *taberna*, although any direct link must remain conjecture.[26]

A hundred and fifty years later, Caesar granted citizenship to practitioners of medicine (and teachers) to encourage them to remain in Rome, as well as to attract others to the city (Suet. *Caes.* 42).[27] Augustus also exempted the same groups from a general expulsion of *peregrini* from Rome during a period of grain shortage in 6 CE, indicating both the perceived value of doctors to the city and the understanding that many of these would be from elsewhere (Suet. *Aug.* 42). At other times, we hear of doctors moving in order to treat specific ailments or patients. Under Claudius, for example, Pliny notes that a new skin infection began to circulate in Italy, apparently introduced from Asia Minor and especially prevalent among the elite due to their habit of greeting each other with a kiss (Plin. *HN* 26.2–4). Doctors from Egypt who specialized in the treatment of this infection came to Italy, encouraged by the large sums that some were willing to pay for treatment. When Cossinus, an equestrian friend of Nero, was infected, the emperor himself called in a doctor from Egypt; this proved to be a mistake as the doctor's treatment of Cossinus with *cantharis* or Spanish fly crushed in a drink killed him (Plin. *HN* 29.93).

We can also see the official encouragement of a wider mobility of doctors between towns within Italy and in the provinces. In a world of intercivic rivalry, having the best doctors was an important marker of civic status and pride, leading to town councils granting tax immunity to doctors, as well as to philosophers and grammarians (see Sausville, Chap. 7). Antoninus Pius set the number of doctors to whom these privileges could be granted at between five and ten, depending on the size of the city.[28] Beyond this, the evidence for the organization of the movement of medical practitioners is limited, although again we can suppose some continuation of the practices already established in the cities of Classical and Hellenistic Greece, with the centers of medical excellence playing a role in the (re)distribution of doctors. It might be possible that *collegia* or associations of medical practitioners were also involved in this practice, although the evidence for medical associations in the Roman world is relatively limited.[29] Moreover, the increased connectivity of the Roman period may have increased knowledge and awareness of certain sects, doctors, and medical practices, helping facilitate the movement of individual doctors.

Itinerant doctors most likely moved along familiar circuits, returning to particular places where they were known, or following market schedules, as we have already seen with Lucius Clodius moving from forum to forum

(Cic. *Clu.* 40). As such movement followed relatively predictable rhythms and was comparatively limited in its geographical scope, these people may have maintained a base in a fixed location where their families lived. Other movement will have been more controlled, including the enforced movement of enslaved medical practitioners. The army too must have played a significant role in the movement of doctors and the diffusion of medical knowledge across the Roman world, as potentially did other occupational groups, such as mining corporations.[30] Marcus Aerarius Telemachus, for example, was a freedman *medicus* linked to a *soc(ietas) aerar(iarum fodinarum)* in Corduba, a group who presumably controlled the rights to copper mining in the region in the first century CE (*HEpOnl* 3914).[31] In the case of the army and mining corporations, these groups were often located in relatively remote places or were on the move and required their own medical staff to ensure the health of those working within these often dangerous occupations.

Getting Established

For those medical practitioners expressly invited to come to a particular place or to treat a specific patient or ailment, their reputation clearly preceded them. Others were directly recommended to friends, family, or acquaintances. Cicero, for example, recommended one Asclapo, a Greek *medicus* from Patrae, to Servius Sulpicius Rufus by letter (*Ad Fam.* 13.20). This is taking place at the highest level, but we can suppose that similar recommendations were going on lower down the social scale. Word of mouth was surely important in the establishment of a reputation.[32]

For those without recommendations or an established reputation, a professed adherence to a particular medical sect, a link to a known center of medical excellence, or an association with a particularly famous doctor may have acted as a shorthand indicator of a certain level of skill or professionalism; this would be particularly important in a world without official training schools or medical licenses, in which anybody could call themselves a doctor.[33] Although outside of our period, the process of public appointment of doctors (and architects) in Classical Athens described by Plato (*Grg.* 514a-e) and Xenophon (*Mem.* 4.2.5) is revealing.[34] Candidates gave a speech in the Assembly, describing their training and career to date, with an emphasis placed not only on their experience but also on their teacher, who should be "good and reputable" (*agathos kai ellogimos*: Pl. *Grg.* 514c). As Massar notes, a Hellenistic decree from Halasarna recording honors granted to a certain Onasander, a doctor, followed a similar pattern, noting his training with one Antipater, and then describing his career and experience to date in order to demonstrate that he was worthy of the honors granted to him. Witnesses could offer testimony and support the account given, and doctors could give public lectures or demonstrations.[35] Having previously held a public post elsewhere and perhaps even having been granted honors by public decree—a copy of which could be carried around and shown—could also help establish a reputation.[36] Similar practices were still ongoing in the Roman period.[37]

As we have seen, there was a clear link between "Greekness" and medicine in the Roman world, with the vast majority of doctors attested in both literature and epigraphy having either a Greek origin or at the very least, a Greek name. Greek names also dominate on the so-called oculist or Collyrium stamps that have been found in their hundreds in Gaul, Britain, and Germany.[38] These incised stone stamps were used to mark blocks of eye ointment (*collyrium*) with names, usually in the genitive case and indicating either the owner of the medicament and therefore the practitioner, or perhaps in some cases, the inventor or manufacturer of the particular ointment, as well as details of the remedy and its uses.[39] Twenty blocks of *collyrium* were found preserved in a grave of a late second- or early third-century CE date in Lyon in the 1980s.[40] The imprint of stamps were still (partially) legible on eight of these *collyria*, mostly written in Greek language and script; these include (in Latin) a remedy for dim vision (*ad caliginem*) and (in Greek) others labelled "soldierly" (*stratiôtikon*; Flemming suggests "hardworking"), frankincense-based (*dialibanou*), saffron-remedy (*krokôdês*), and olive oil-based (*diaelaiou*).[41] The stamps on at least six of these blocks also included the name Zmaragdos, probably the Greek name of the oculist.[42]

Zmaragdos' *collyria* were found stored in a small metal box. A circular indentation on one side of the box was most likely intended to prepare the medicaments before application. A small cylindrical brass carrying case holding three bronze surgical tools that could be used for the process of mixing and application—and perhaps also for minor eye surgery—was also found.[43] The carrying of such kit could in itself potentially act as a marker of medical competence. It is recommended in the Hippocratic corpus that a doctor carry a methodically arranged case (*Decorum* VIII), and as medical equipment became more standardized across the Roman world by the late first century CE, perhaps the carrying of a particular core set of instruments in a relatively standardized rectangular or cylindrical storage case was as reassuringly recognizable as the doctor's bag of the nineteenth and twentieth centuries.[44] Furthermore, the *collyrium* blocks and their storage box were clearly intended to be transportable, and their very presence implies the mobility of the medical practitioners who carried them. They also point to the potential specialization of roles within ancient medicine.

Elsewhere in the northwest provinces, *collyrium* labels are more commonly found in Latin, even if they are sometimes rendering Greek terms.[45] The names of the practitioners, however, are typically Greek. In some circumstances, this sense of "Greekness"—whether it be in language, names, or medicines—may have been enough to establish some level of medical competence (although consultations of Latin-speaking patients by Greek doctors may have been problematic on occasion). A link to the Greek world seems to have been expected for those working in medicine and to carry with it a certain amount of cachet (Plin. *HN* 29.8.17), even if in some cases, a link may well have been fabricated.[46] Indeed, while all these particular markers were intended to assert medical authority and provide an outward and easily recognizable sign that these people were to be trusted, they were also part of self-promotion and advertising. Ultimately, there may have been a certain amount of misrepresentation and outright fakery at work here. As Bader notes, however, "it would be a mistake to rely entirely on the origin of a doctor to determine their level of training and skills"; he is referring here to the mistakes of researchers, but the warning may equally apply to potential patients in the Roman world.[47]

This kind of fraudulence is clearly illustrated in a scene described by Galen himself.[48] In this anecdote, a doctor is attempting to establish a reputation for himself through a public demonstration of his skill in the center of Rome, a practice that we can imagine to have been commonplace in the city. As Sancinito shows in the case of merchants in the Roman world, reputation was a highly sought after and guarded currency in the world of business. Like the work of merchants, much of Roman medicine was public in nature, practiced in marketplaces, central squares, and in *tabernae* or workshops, with their wide entranceways that maximized the visibility of the interior. Medical practices deliberately drew in observers and onlookers (e.g., Plut. *How to tell a Flatterer from a Friend* [*Mor.* 71A]); doctor's surgeries (*tabernae medicorum*) were notorious places of gossip (Jer. *Ep.* 50.5.1).[49] A competent consultation, a successful treatment, or an impressive anatomical dissection could then be publicized quickly and easily, although, of course, this also holds for less positive outcomes, as we see in this particular doctor's encounter with Galen. The doctor begins his medical demonstration by introducing himself to onlookers as being from Aleppo, with his professed Syrian origins perhaps intended to establish his credibility from the outset. He goes on to claim that he had studied with Galen himself, before beginning to treat his patient for toothache, getting the onlookers to close their eyes while he plants a worm in the patient's molars that he then removes as the source of the pain. Galen observes the treatment, and then at the end, reveals himself to both the doctor and the crowd, denouncing the Syrian as a swindler. He hands him over to the authorities in Rome for punishment, although Nutton notes that as his crime is not immediately clear, the fact that he was flogged may have more to do with Galen's position in the city than with legal liability per se.[50] Nevertheless, the anecdote points to the public nature of ancient medicine and some of the ways in which a newcomer might have sought to establish a reputation for themselves, as well as the need for caution in selecting a doctor.

The Construction Industry: Architects and Artisans

The Movers

Skilled workers within construction—and its various linked professions—can offer another useful case study for thinking about patterns of skilled mobility in the Roman world, albeit somewhat different in nature. The movement of architects, for instance, is well known. At the top levels at least, this would seem analogous to doctors, in that this movement was as much (and in many cases more) about prestige as economic necessity. Apollodorus of Damascus is perhaps the most famous example from the imperial period; after serving with Trajan in the Dacian campaigns, he moved to Rome to design his forum and baths, as well as to renovate Domitian's Odeon (Cass. Dio 69.4).[51] Outside of these elite imperial circles, one Gaius Sevius Lupus, an architect originally from Aeminium in Lusitania dedicated an altar to Augustan Mars around 105km away in Brigantium in Tarraconensis (*HEpOnl* 8369).[52] In Olbia in modern-day Ukraine, a fragmentary building dedication from the late second or early third century CE commemorates the architect who presumably designed the building; his name is lost but he was a citizen of both Nicomedia and Tomis.[53]

Beyond architects, there is evidence that other skilled workers linked to construction were moving around to wherever their skills were in demand; some were in search of prosperity, others were simply in search of work. Work on construction projects is by its nature finite and episodic and very often seasonal, which will have encouraged mobility among workers whose skills were only required on a project for a relatively short period. Although outside of our period, this is especially well-illustrated by construction records at Greek sanctuaries, such as the Erechtheion accounts of the early fifth century BCE, or the Eleusinian accounts of the mid-fourth century BCE.[54] Mobility appears to be particularly well documented among artisans such as sculptors and stonemasons, while we hear little of unskilled laborers on the move. In part, this could be down to our surviving sources, as skilled workers are more visible in ancient literature and within the epigraphic record, but it is probable that this is also a reflection of reality, with unskilled workers recruited locally, while the skilled moved. Certainly when Pliny the Younger writes to Trajan to ask for assistance with the construction of a canal near Nicomedia, he expressly notes that the necessary unskilled labor was readily available locally but that he needed help with the recruitment of skilled labor for the project (Plin, *Ep.* 10.41.3; see below).[55] In Jerusalem in the 60s CE also, the completion of work on the temple apparently resulted in the unemployment of over 18,000 workers, presumably local laborers (Joseph. *AJ* 20.219).

Already in the sixth century BCE, Pliny the Elder (*HN* 35.157) and Plutarch (*Poplicola* 13) claim that the artisan Vulca was brought from Veii to sculpt terracotta statues on commission in Rome.[56] Pliny (*HN* 12.5) even attributes the Gallic invasion of 390 BCE to a Helvetian artisan named Helico, who was at Rome because of his skills (*fabrilem ob artem*, possibly a sculptor?); he took dried figs and grapes back to Gaul, triggering an attack. Whether or not these stories are true, the fact that they were (re)told by Roman authors in the first and second centuries CE indicates an understanding of the mobility of artisans. As late as the fifth century, such stories continued. Constantius, for example, writes in his hagiography of Germanus of Auxerre that when Germanus crossed over from Gaul to Italy in early summer, he met a party of workmen (*artifices*) on their way back to Italy after a period of working for hire in Gaul (Constantius, *Vita S. Germani* 31). Hawkins suggests that these were builders, possibly on their way back to farms for the harvest after a spell of hired work in the spring, although if this were the case, it is probably not typical, as this was quite early in the year and would have been a short commission.[57]

The material evidence, particularly inscriptions, provides further support for these written accounts of mobility. One Zenon, for example, erected a monument in Rome in the mid-second century CE for his young son, also called Zenon, his wife Clytine, and himself, who died aged 70. The inscription specifically records that he sculpted the monument with his very own hands. It also notes that he was originally from Aphrodisias, but that faith in his skills had taken him through many cities before reaching Rome (*IGUR* 1222).[58] The manufacture of his own monument in Rome indicates that he had settled there permanently, but we do not know at what age; this makes it difficult to determine whether he brought his family with him or whether he started a family once he had settled in the city. Rome, however, must have offered a large enough market for sculptors and stoneworkers that Zenon made it his home. The market in other large cities may also have been significant enough for permanent settlement, although in smaller urban centers, work may have been more episodic and workers correspondingly more transient.[59]

A number of other sculptors in the imperial period recorded their place of origin as Aphrodisias, which seems to have become a significant center of marble sculpture from the later first century CE.[60] In some cases, however, it can be difficult to know if it is the sculptor or the sculpture that moved.[61] Polynices, for instance, notes that he was from Aphrodisias on third-century CE work found at Aphrodisias itself but also on work found at Rome and Priene.[62] More convincing is the example cited by Russell of a sculptor from Alexandria who signed his name on two statue bases at Gerasa in Jordan; since these objects were carved in local limestone, the sculptor must have been present at the site.[63] If signatures on sculpture can sometimes be ambiguous, other inscriptions provide somewhat clearer evidence for the mobility of artisans. In the early third century, a marble altar records that one Q. Iulius Miletus, a marble worker (μαρμαράριος; *marmararios*), came from Tripolis in Lydia to Rome, apparently to see the games. His visit must have had a wider purpose, however, since while he was there, he also erected a building. He travelled with a team of workers, as his pupil (*alumnus*) Q. Iulius Faentius also erected a smaller altar honoring Miletus (*IGRR* I 168; *IGUR* IV 1567; *CIL* VI 10091).[64] In the fourth century CE, another μαρμαράριος (*marmararios*), Aurelius Agathias Syros, came to Rome, presumably from Syria (*IGUR* 1860).[65] Nabatean craftsmen appear to have been present at Puteoli in Italy in the early first century CE, carving Aramaic inscriptions on Italian Carrara marble.[66]

Nicomedia, a center of the marble trade, also seems to have exported both stone and stoneworkers to other parts of the Roman world.[67] There was, for example, an association (*synodos*) of Nicomedian stonecarvers (λιθοξόοι) at Nicopolis-ad-Istrum in Bulgaria; two of its members, Maximus and Neikon, dedicated an altar to Hercules on behalf of the entire association (*IG Bulg.* II, 674).[68] Also at Nicopolis was Gaius Bianoros, a δομοτέκτων (*domotektōn;* a carpenter or builder) from Nicaea, who perhaps followed a similar route to stoneworkers from Nicomedia, given the closeness of the two cities (*IG Bulg.* II 690).[69] At Lepcis Magna in Libya, one Asclepiades, a marble worker (*marmararios*) from Nicomedia, erected a bilingual dedication to Aesculapius, and at Tirgusor in Romania, one Phoebus, signed his name and origin in Nicomedia on a Mithraic relief.[70] Another Asclepiades, a *lithourgos* (λιθουργός) from Nicomedia is recorded at Kefez-Keui (close to the ancient Tavium), several hundred kilometers away in the province of Galatia.[71] As we have already seen, a Nicomedian architect found his way to Olbia in Ukraine.[72]

Nicomedians were found further west in Italy too. At Portus, for example, an epitaph records one Gorgias, a worker in marble (λευκουργὸς; *leukourgos*) from Nicomedia who died aged 54 (*I. Porto* 38).[73] At Rome, a poem was composed in Greek on a small marble stele recording the death of one Maximus who died aged 22, probably sometime in the first century CE (*IGUR* 1263; *SEG* 4.105). He is referred to as a "housebuilder and carpenter," an οἰκοδόμος ξυλοεργός, presumably the Greek equivalent of a *faber tignarius.* He is not described as being from the city of Nicomedia itself but from the Astakian homeland (πατρίδος Ἀστακίης). Potentially this could be Astakos in Greece but is usually taken to refer to Astakos in Bithynia, just across the water from Nicomedia, and although he is not a stone worker specifically, we can suppose that he is part of the world of artisans linked to the city.[74] He is the son of one Dionysius and Karpournia (presumably a Greek transliteration of Calpurnia), who are wretched in their grief at the loss of their son. The presence of this family group in Rome, and his "Roman" name would suggest that he is a second-generation migrant in the city but that his family retained a strong sense of affinity with the father's place of origin. Also from Asia Minor, two brothers, Limnaius and Diomedes, came from Dokimeion, the location of marble quarries, to Iconium, a couple of hundred kilometers away; here they left a dedication to an unknown deity in the first or second century CE describing themselves not only as Dokimeians but also as statue carvers and as carvers of Dokimeian marble specifically (ἀγαλματογλύφοι δοκιματογλύφοι).[75]

On occasion, we get a glimpse of a world of migrant stone workers from outside of the well-known centers of the Greek East. Priscus, for example, a stonemason (*lapidarius*) from among the Carnutes in Northern Gaul, made a vow to the goddess Sulis at her sanctuary in Bath in Southwest England (*RIB* 149). A bundle of tools suitable for stone carving found in a shipwreck off the coast of Corsica offers a somewhat different type of evidence for stoneworkers on the move. At least two of these tools were inscribed with letters, one with a letter L and another with the letters CF, suggesting that they were the personal property of two different stoneworkers.[76] The tools were found alongside a cargo of blocks of Luna marble; perhaps here we have evidence for stone and stone workers moving together.

Teams of itinerant carvers have sometimes been identified on stylistic grounds also. In Southern Gaul, for example, Kleiner identified a team specializing in the construction and decoration of monumental tower-tombs in local stone in the Augustan period; he argued that this team also produced a number of decorative reliefs found in the region.[77] If Kleiner is correct, they worked within a relatively restricted area and worked in local stone, so presumably were able to move with just their tools. Itinerant individuals are even more difficult to document, but a small marble stele found in Phrygia in the modern region of Afyonkarahisar, not far from the quarries at Dokimeion, could perhaps be the work of an itinerant carver.[78] Two brothers, Telesphorus and Timolaus, erected the stele to commemorate their parents and two siblings, all of whom are depicted in portraiture on the stone. In the pediment the letter-cutter has carved his name (incorrectly) and origin, Menandros the Dokimeian (*Mennadrous Dokimeus*). Ward-Perkins suggests that he was an itinerant craftsman, who travelled with a stock of small slabs of marble, working to commission, although this is not certain.[79]

The Organization

Workers moved because their skills were in demand in different places, but as is so often the case, there is no single model of movement that can be applied to all workers. As in the late Middle Ages and early modern period, we should probably make a distinction between general builders who moved around a relatively local area and may have been more-or-less constantly itinerant, and those more specialized workers who moved over longer distances, either permanently or temporarily. Some will have travelled to take up specific individual commissions, some independently in search of work, while contractors, agents, or associations—such as the *synodos* of Nicomedian stoneworkers at Nicopolis-ad-Istrum or the large *collegium* of the *fabri tignarii* in Rome, which had well over 100 members in the late second century CE—may have organized the movement of others, either as individuals or in groups.[80] The monumental altar relief attributed to the *fabri tignarii* at Rome, examined in detail by Rogers in this volume, is evidence of the economic success of the *collegium* and similar guilds. We should not rule out the possibility that occupational associations also played a role in the movement of materials and in the allocation of work once people arrived in a particular place.

Architects in particular will likely have moved for specific commissions, but this is also true of other skilled workers within construction. At the very highest level, there were commissions by the Roman state, going right up to the emperor himself. Presumably having heard of his work in Gaul, Nero summoned Zenodorus to Rome to make his colossus (Plin. *HN* 34.46), and as we have seen, Trajan commissioned Apollodorus of Damascus to design his forum and baths (Cass. Dio 69.4). Famous individuals may have been commissioned directly by cities also or by wealthy individuals. Although outside of our period—and in many ways a special case, given his apparent refusal to be paid for his work—the career of the Hellenistic sculptor Damophon gives us some indication of how this might have worked in practice. A series of second-century BCE honorific decrees relating to Damophon were inscribed on a monumental Doric column in Messene, and these detail ambassadors coming to Messene specifically to commission Damophon to undertake work in their particular cities.[81] This reflects fourth-century BCE evidence that heralds visited other *poleis* in order to recruit the necessary skilled labor for major building projects, offering travel expenses and living allowances. Representatives from Epidauros, for example, let out contracts at a number of different cities, including Corinth, Argos, and Athens, among others.[82] Perhaps similar things were happening in the Roman period, recruiting not only particularly famous architects, sculptors, and the like but also issuing more general calls for skilled workers, a method that may have been more common in smaller urban centers. It is notable that there are no fees for recruitment or wages paid to heralds in the extant Athenian building accounts, possibly indicating that they faced less of a problem in finding skilled labor.[83] Those looking for skilled workers in Rome, including the *redemptores* or contractors who oversaw public building works, may also have had less need to go out searching for workers, although this is by no means certain.[84]

Pliny the Younger's correspondence with Trajan during his tenure as governor of Bithynia-Pontus indicates that there was some state-sponsored movement of skilled workers within the provinces, particularly architects and engineers, but that this was relatively limited and was linked principally to the military. Part of Pliny's brief from Trajan was to inspect the accounts of the towns in the provinces, which he clearly suspected were in disarray (10.18.3), in part due to inter-civic rivalry driving excessive spending on large-scale urban building projects.[85] Pliny was, therefore, concerned with ensuring that these building projects were completed satisfactorily, but he seems to have faced some difficulty in finding the skilled workers that he required. Immediately upon his arrival in Bithynia, he requested a land surveyor (*mensor*: 10.17b.2). Trajan responded by writing that there were scarcely enough land surveyors for the work in progress in Rome and its surroundings, but that reliable surveyors could be found in every province, although he does concede that Pliny would have to take the trouble to look for them (10.18.3).[86] Undeterred, Pliny went on to ask Trajan to send him either a water-engineer (*aquilex*) or an architect (*architectus*) to prevent any further failure in the construction of an aqueduct at Nicomedia (10.37.3), a request that Trajan simply ignored in his response (10.38).[87] Yet again, in the face of two disastrous construction projects at Nicaea—a theater that was already subsiding and a badly planned and poorly constructed gymnasium—and a new bath house at Claudiopolis being built in a hollow at the foot of a mountain, Pliny asked Trajan for an architect (*architectus*: 10.39.6). In this case, Trajan acknowledged the request but once again refused to help, claiming that skilled architects could be found in every province (10.40.3). In fact, he noted dryly, architects usually came to Rome from Greece.

Finally, Pliny asked for an engineer (*librator*) or an architect (*architectus*) to assist with his plan to construct a canal between Lake Sophon and Nicomedia, a distance of around 18 miles or 29 kilometers, with the aim of making it easier and cheaper to transport raw materials to the sea (10.41.3).[88] He noted that while this ambitious project would require a great deal of labor, most of this could easily be recruited locally; it is the *skilled* labor that is lacking. Here, Pliny at long last had some success, with

Trajan telling him to apply to Calpurnius Macer for someone with experience in the sort of survey necessary for this kind of work (10.42; see also 10.61.5). The engineer will come not from Rome but from the wider region, as Calpurnius Macer was legate of Lower Moesia at the time (December 111 to December 112), and Trajan notes that "there is no lack of such experts in the provinces where you are" (*neque provinciae istae his artificibus carent:* 10.62, Loeb translation and note). Trajan must be referring to military engineers here, with Calpurnius Macer being asked to send a skilled soldier to Pliny in Bithynia (just as he had previously sent a legionary centurion to Byzantium: 10.77).

At the time there were most likely three legions based in Lower Moesia (the *Legio I Italica;* the *Legio V Macedonica*; and possibly the *Legio XI Claudia*), in stark contrast to Pliny's limited military strength.[89] Perhaps if there had been more of a military deployment in his province, Pliny would not have faced such difficulties in finding the engineers, architects, and surveyors that he required. What is not clear is if Pliny was expecting Trajan to send him military personnel for the purpose of construction and infrastructure projects—he only directly asks for these in relation to border control in Juliopolis (10.77)—but it seems likely, given the connection between the military and technical specializations in engineering and surveying in particular.[90] Indeed, the army was the largest and most mobile body of skilled workers in the Roman world. The secondment of one Nonius Datus from the *Legio III Augusta*, stationed in Lambaesis in Numidia, to Petronius Celer, governor of the neighboring province of Mauretania Caesarensis in the late 130s, suggests that this was a relatively common practice.[91] Nonius, an engineer and soldier, was sent to help plan the construction of an aqueduct in the town of Saldae.[92]

Although Pliny was rarely successful in his appeals, his repeated requests for skilled workers to assist him with urban building projects suggest that the Roman state could and did redistribute skilled labor in the provinces on occasion, particularly from within the army. Similarly, large civic building projects, and especially the large imperial ones, will have resulted in the movement of construction workers; the Nicomedian stoneworkers in Nicopolis-ad-Istrum and Lepcis Magna could, for example, potentially be linked to Trajanic and Severan building programs, respectively.[93] We do not know, however, whether the state, the relevant civic authorities, or private individuals acting as agents or contractors facilitated such movement, or if it was down to the initiative of the workers themselves.

One thing that we can suppose fairly confidently is a link between the movement of skilled workers and the movement and choice of raw materials for a particular project.[94] Although most stoneworkers will surely have been able to work in a range of materials, they were probably still most comfortable—and most adept—when working with the material that was most familiar to them.[95] At Lepcis Magna, Attic and Proconnesian marble were the white marbles predominantly used in architecture from the mid-second century CE, alongside the green-and-white striped marble of Carystos (*cipollino*) and the red granite of Syene.[96] Ward-Perkins argues that makers' marks cut on finished surfaces of the Pentelic marble architecture appear to have been made after the marble arrived at Lepcis itself, and were most likely done *in situ* by the workmen responsible for their carving.[97] Whenever these makers' marks are extensive enough to allow identification, they appear to represent Greek proper names, and may indicate that workers from Attica were brought in to handle the familiar marble quarried to the north of Athens.[98] Similarly, Ward-Perkins argues that Nicomedian workers handled the Proconnesian marble, which was probably traded through the port city of Nicomedia. The presence of Asclepiades, the Nicomedian *marmararios*, could therefore be linked to the import of Proconnesian marble, although whether he worked the marble himself, was a dealer involved in its supply, or both is not clear.[99] Proconnessian marble was also found at Nicopolis-ad-Istrum, alongside the association of Nicomedian stonecarvers, and it is probably no accident that the Nicomedian architect honored in Olbia in Ukraine was working in a region that also imported predominantly Proconnessian marble.[100] Furthermore, as we have seen, the two brothers from Dokimeion documented in Iconium clearly advertised their skills in Dokimeian marble specifically. As we have already seen, the shipwreck at Porta Nova may offer evidence for stonemasons on the move, taking both their expertise and their materials with them. In such cases, craftsmen may have overseen the supply of materials as well.

We should, however, perhaps not overplay the relationship between materials and mobility. When the Temple of Jupiter Capitolinus was rebuilt following a fire in 80 CE, its pillars were of Pentelic marble. Plutarch (*Poplicola*. 15) notes that when he saw them at Athens, their thickness was perfectly proportioned to their length, but when they were recut in Rome, their proportions were spoiled and they became too slender and thin. Whether this was because the craftsmen in Rome were unfamiliar with the material, the technique, or both is unclear (or indeed, if Plutarch means that the Romans simply did not recognize the "correct" column proportions in the same way as the Greeks), but Walker argues that this highlights a difference in skill levels at the time between Rome and Athens.[101] In this particular case, the workers do not appear to have travelled with the material, despite this being an imperial project sponsored by Domitian. Yet by the time of Hadrian, the presence in Rome of Corinthian capitals carved in Pentelic marble and of a stylistic type typically found in Athens and its immediate surroundings suggest either that there were Athenian craftsmen in the city working their local marble or that Roman craftsmen had honed their skills in the interim.[102]

When movement did happen, it could have been organized in a number of different ways. Some workers may have moved with raw materials in the anticipation that wherever the materials were going, there was likely to be demand for those who could work them. Travelling along established trade routes must also have eased their movement. Others will likely have moved with the promise of definite employment. It may be that it was possible at some quarries to obtain not only raw materials but also the artisans capable of handling those materials.[103] When Dio Chrysostom (*Or.* 40.7), for example, was overseeing the building of a colonnade in Prusa, he appears to have visited a quarry himself in order to select materials and possibly workers.[104] If skilled workers were going out from quarries, it is worth noting that the opposite will also have been true, with quarries attracting workers, as can be seen at Mons Claudianus in Egypt.[105]

Contractors or agents could have supplied workers, either as individuals or as teams, although we know frustratingly little about such people and how they operated. We can suppose that some contractors were based at quarries and others at cities that had long artistic traditions, such as Athens, or at cities that were centers of trade, particularly in stone, such as Nicomedia. We know slightly more about labor contractors for seasonal agricultural labor. An inscription from Mactaris in North Africa, for example, recalls the career of an anonymous seasonal worker who after 12 years as a grain harvester became a contractor with his own team of workers (*CIL* VIII 11824). Vespasian's great grandfather was also reportedly a labor contractor involved in the organization of the annual movement of workers from Umbria to the Sabine district (Suet. *Vesp.* 1.4). Such work is different in nature from construction work, in that the annual seasonal demand for agricultural labor is relatively predictable and the contracts were likely to have been regular and longer term. The work itself was also less skilled, and the workers could to a certain extent be replaced more readily.[106] However, the model of a contractor overseeing the mobility of a group of workers can almost certainly be applied to other sectors. The party of craftsmen (*artifices*) that Germanus apparently met on their way back to Italy after a period of working in Gaul may well have been one such group (see above). The possible team of itinerant carvers identified by Kleiner (see above) may also have moved around in response to commissions, organized by a contractor, either externally or from within the group. Dealing with contractors or agents (and we might add, associations) would have simplified the process of finding skilled workers for particular tasks significantly, lowering the transaction costs for all those involved.[107]

Getting Established

As already noted, architects and sculptors often moved for specific commissions, and in those cases, their reputation will have preceded them. For those who needed to establish a reputation, however, the process will in some ways have been similar to that already described for medical practitioners; they will have emphasized their training and experience and may also have undertaken public demonstrations of their skills (see above).[108]

Working for a contractor or being part of a larger team must have made mobility easier for other artisans, as there was no need for them to prove their skills to a new employer. It is the contractor or leader of a team who must negotiate with a potential employer and reassure them that they and their workers are capable of completing the job to the required standard. It may have been easier for contractors and teams to establish a reputation for skill and competence by pointing to previous work. For construction work in particular it may have helped if they were able to give examples of having gone through successful processes of *probatio*, the final inspection and approval of work that took place at the end of a contract.[109]

If a reputation had yet to be established, claiming a link to a particular region or city might have been a quick way to demonstrate skills and credibility, as with medical practitioners. Certain regions or cities, as we have seen with the Anatolian cities of Aphrodisias and Nicomedia, and the quarries at Dokimeion, were considered particular centers of excellence for sculptors. If this were the case, then including a link to one of these cities in an epitaph, an honorific, a signature, or a maker's mark would not only demonstrate civic pride but could also act as a marker of quality and a guarantee of excellence (although in the case of epitaphs this would, of course, be a moot point).[110] Nevertheless, as with medical practitioners, we might question whether these links were always genuine. Membership of an occupational association could also have acted as a marker of quality and prestige.[111]

Itinerant traders or individual artisans might have made use of letters of recommendation to demonstrate their credentials to prospective employers. It is possible that in some cases, such letters were carried speculatively, but in most cases, they were probably addressed to specific individuals and were relatively limited in their scope. Perhaps unsurprisingly, given the nature of our evidence, most surviving letters recommending individuals for specific jobs relate to government or military posts.[112] However, there is some evidence to suggest that this was a broader phenomenon, with workers carrying letters of introduction that recommended them for particular roles. In early third-century CE Egypt, for example, one Sarapammon wrote to Nepotianus to tell him that he had sent him two tanners, Drakon and Melanos, hired workers of Ambrosios, to produce leather with him (P.Gen. 1^2 75; TM 32145).[113] Although much earlier, there are several examples of letters of recommendation in the third-century BCE Zenon archive. Here, for example, Ptolemaios writes a letter to be carried by a man looking for employment in the office of Philiskos, noting that Phileas and other accountants (Sb 26.16636) recommend him for a role.[114] Agricultural workers could also carry such letters; in first-century CE Oxyrhynchus, for instance, one Harpaesis carried a letter indicating that he was to be a sub-lessee of Themistokles for the sowing season (P.Oxy. 14.1661; TM 21962), while in fifth-century Gaul, Sidonius (*Epist.* IV.7) apparently provided a letter to Simplicius vouching for its anonymous bearer.[115]

Conclusions

The mobility of skilled workers was commonplace in the Roman world, but the nature of that mobility varied. Some workers moved more-or-less constantly over a relatively limited geographic range. We might think here of the eye doctors of northwest Europe, Cicero's itinerant seller of medicine, or a construction worker undertaking general building in a local area. These workers were moving largely out of necessity. They probably had regular clients and were well-known locally, following a well-worn circuit of mobility; they may also have had families located within that circuit, but they and their families leave little trace in the literary or archaeological record. Other skilled people moved over greater distances. Many of the wealthier and more famous medical practitioners moved not so much out of economic necessity but to seek training, to enhance their reputation, or to increase their prestige. The same could be said of many of the famous architects whose names come down to us in literary sources in particular. Highly skilled workers such as stonemasons and sculptors in part moved out of necessity. Those who roughed out work in the quarries themselves, or who completed sculptures or sarcophagi for export as finished products had no need to move, but much architectural and sculptural work was undertaken *in situ* and once such commissions were complete (albeit sometimes after many years), it would be time to move on to the next project, wherever that might be. However, we can suppose that considerations of profit and prestige were often part of the strategic decision-making process of stonemasons and sculptors too.

How then did a doctor, an architect, or a stoneworker find the next opportunity? Some may have chosen to move speculatively to Rome or to other large cities of the Roman empire such as Alexandria or Antioch, in the anticipation that there would have been a large enough market in those places for their skills to be more-or-less constantly in demand. It is likely, however, that most movement of skilled workers was more organized. Although we do not know for certain, we can suppose that the big centers of medical training played a role in the redistribution of doctors around the Roman world. It is also tempting to see a role for occupational associations in the allocation of skilled labor. This is particularly true for the construction industry, where associations are somewhat better-attested and there appears to have been more of a practical need for them in an economic sector that typically relied on people working in groups rather than as individuals. Associations, together with labor contractors, simplified the process of finding groups of skilled workers for particular tasks, lowering the transaction costs for all those involved. Alongside this, the military facilitated the movement of doctors, architects, engineers, and other skilled workers, contributing to the diffusion of medical and technical knowledge across the Roman world.

Tapping into existing networks of knowledge—whether these were grouped around particular centers of expertise in medicine or stone working, were linked to occupational associations or labor contractors, or were simply personal recommendations—will have made it easier to trust in the skills of those employed. Reputations could be established, and training guaranteed, reducing risk in a world without professional licenses or recognized qualifications. Connections and social networks would have been invaluable, and wherever possible it must have been preferred to move to a place where someone trusted could vouch for an individual or group. It would be much more difficult for those outside of these networks to prove their credentials to prospective clients or employers. For medical practitioners, a Greek name or origin, and a professed link (genuine or otherwise) to a particular doctor, medical sect, or training center may have helped. Similarly, for stonemasons or sculptures, a connection to a known and respected artisan or to a particular center of excellence may have gone some way toward demonstrating a certain level of skill. In that way, signatures or makers' marks that included the origin of an artisan may indirectly have helped those who followed in their footsteps; certainly much of the surviving stone work is in itself testament to the high level of skill that could be mobilized in the Roman world.

Notes

1. On the Homer passage specifically, see Kostecka 2019: 34–35; *passim* for the mobility of doctors and seers in particular in late archaic and early classical Greece.
2. See various contributions to Kiriatzi and Knappet 2016, for example Bevan and Bloxam 2016 on Minoan stonemasons. Also Blackwell 2014: 475–484 for the possible presence of Hittite masons at Mycenae. For pre-Roman Italy, see now Armstrong and Cohen 2022.
3. See, for example, Epstein 2004; Reith 2008.
4. Epstein 2004: 254–255.
5. Epstein 2004: 253–254. On the development of this system, see also Reith 2008: 116–117. For the importance of "un-organized" or informal tramping, see Epstein 2004.
6. Reith 2008: 122–123; 126; 128–129.
7. On the mobility of medical practitioners in general, see André and Baslez 1993: 312–315.
8. Kostecka 2019: 40–41. On the importance of mobility for doctors in the Greek world from the sixth century BCE onward, see Harris 2020: 49; 58–62.
9. Nutton 2013: 267.
10. Bond 2023.
11. Israelowich 2015: 13.
12. See Polito 1999; Israelowich 2015: 18–20.
13. Nutton 2013: 199.

14. Noy 2000: 111 gives a longer list, but not all these doctors are certain to have visited Rome. See also Nutton 2013: 261–262; Israelowich 2015: 18–21.
15. Nutton 2013: 266, Fig. 17.6.
16. Noy 2000: 112, with further examples.
17. My thanks to both Ann Kuttner and Consuelo Manetta for alerting me to the example of Patron and his tomb.
18. Bagnani 1953: 104; Tortorella 2009: 271.
19. Nutton 2013: 257, Fig. 17.1.
20. Nutton 2013: 263–264. Sausville in this volume investigates Greek examples of doctors recorded in Asia Minor, where their profession afforded them both wealth and professional solidarities with other practitioners of "Greek" medicine.
21. Bader 2014. On healthcare in the Roman army more broadly, see Israelowich 2015: 87–109.
22. Bader 2014: 52.
23. Lavan 2022.
24. See Palombi 1997, 2007.
25. Nutton 2013: 156 for the examples discussed here. For the location, Pisano Sartorio, *LTUR* III, *s.v.* "Compitum Acilium."
26. For example, Palombi 2007: 62; Nutton, *s.v.* "Archagathus," *BNP*, Accessed online 11.10.2022.
27. Moatti 2013: 85; Israelowich 2015: 21–23.
28. Dig. 27.1.6.2; Nutton 2013: 254–78. For doctors and the Greek *polis* in earlier periods, see Harris 2020: 49. On privileges granted to doctors in general, see Israelowich 2015: 21–30.
29. Verboven 2023 notes the small number of medical associations on record, although see also Sausville in this volume for the collective action of doctors (and teachers) in Ephesos.
30. On the recruitment of army doctors in particular, see Bader 2014.
31. Domergue 1990: 270.
32. On the importance of reputation in the Greek world also in earlier periods, see Harris 2020: 48.
33. On such "signalling devices," see Holleran 2021: 162. For doctors as self-proclaimed, see Israelowich 2015: 12; 40.
34. Massar 2020: 72–74.
35. Massar 2020: 73; 74. On Onasander, see also Harris 2020: 47–48; 57–58.
36. Massar 2020: 76.
37. For example, Vit. *De arch.* 10.16.3 for an architect giving a public demonstration at Rhodes.
38. Nutton 2013: 264; Flemming, forthcoming.

39. For practitioner-owner or inventor, see Nutton 2012: 536. On the content of the stamps, see also Padron-Labonnelie 2014: 241.
40. Boyer et al. 1990; Flemming, forthcoming.
41. The eight with stamps are those numbered 1, 2, 3, 4, 7, 9, 18, and 19 in Boyer et al. 1990: 235–243.
42. Numbers 1, 2, 3, 7, 9, and 19. The fragmentary inscription on 18 is in Latin rather than Greek and may include the Latin name Cornelius: Boyer et al. 1990: 235–243.
43. Boyer et al. 1990: 224–235; Flemming n.d.
44. On increased standardization, see Flemming n.d. See also Bliquez 2014: 56–297, for surgical instruments in the Roman empire; 273–278, for rectangular and cylindrical carrying cases in particular; also see 431–435 (Figs. 79–85). Also Boyer et al. 1990: 227–231.
45. Padron-Labonnelie 2014: 241.
46. As noted also by Nutton 2012: 536; Padron-Labonnelie 2014: 241.
47. Bader 2014: 55.
48. Known in an Arabic version and translated into German by Meyerhof 1929: 83.
49. Nutton 2013: 270–271.
50. Nutton 2013: 245.
51. Apollodorus in Dacia; Anderson 1997: 59.
52. Holleran 2023.
53. Ward-Perkins 1980: 34, n. 7.
54. Randall 1953: 203; Epstein 2010; Shear Jr. 2016: 9–10; Hochscheid 2020: 212–213.
55. On rare occasions, convicts or prisoners were forced to provide unskilled labor on large-scale imperial infrastructure projects, but this does not seem to have been the norm (Joseph. *BJ*. 3.10.10; Suet. *Nero* 31.3; Pearse 1974: 148).
56. For mobility of sculptors in the Greek world, see Harris 2020: 51–54. For the Roman world, see Russell 2015: 190–191.
57. Hawkins 2013: 348.
58. Trans. Alexander Gangoly and Peter Kruschwitz; https://mappola.eu/wp-content/uploads/2021/01/MAPPOLA_HANDOUT.pdf. Accessed 12.10.2022.
59. For inscriptions recording short-term mobility among construction workers in the Roman Near East, see Zerbini 2016: 328–329; 335.
60. On Aphrodisias, see Claridge 2015: 118–120. Also for examples of what Claridge terms "travelling sculptors" from Aphrodisias signing their work.
61. For the difficulty of distinguishing between the mobility of statues and of artisans, see Russell 2013: 333–334. See also 339–344, on Aphrodisians.

Also Russell 2015: 190 and 193–196, for the transport of finished or nearly finished works.

62. Erim and Roueché 1982: 102–103.
63. Russell 2015: 190.
64. Pearse 1974: 146; Noy 2000: 114.
65. Pearse 1974: 146.
66. Terpstra 2013: 81.
67. Ward-Perkins 1980. See also Pearse 1974: 89; Varga and Pázsint 2021: 125.
68. Ward-Perkins 1980: 34, n. 4.
69. Pearse 1974: 89. See also for another δομοτέκτων from Mytilene who was recorded at Abydos on the Hellespont.
70. Ward-Perkins 1980: 34, n. 5 (also *IRT* 2021: 264); n. 6.
71. *BCH* 7 (1883): 27, n. 20: Pearse 1974: 145.
72. Ward-Perkins 1980: 34, n. 7.
73. Noy 2000: 114.
74. Noy 2000: 114 simply describes him as from Nicomedia.
75. Hall and Waelkens 1982; McClean 2002: n. 45; Russell 2013: 332. The provenance of the inscription is unknown, but it was probably from Iconium (Konya). In general, see Pearse 1974: 145 for further examples of mobile stoneworkers (and other artisans).
76. Bernard et al. 1988 (for the initials, see 60 and Figs. 5b and 5c); Russell 2013: 335.
77. Kleiner 1977; Russell 2013: 335.
78. See Calder 1955: 35–36; Plate I b.
79. Ward-Perkins 1980: 35.
80. On the *collegium* of the *fabri tignarii*, see DeLaine 2000: 121.
81. On Damophon and the relevant inscriptions, see Melfi 2016.
82. Burford 1969: 160; 191; 198–206; Shear Jr. 2016: 10; Hochscheid 2020: 212.
83. Burford 1969: 112; Hochscheid 2020: 212.
84. On *redemptores* and building work in Rome, see DeLaine 2000: 121.
85. Levick 1979: 119–120. On how to read the letters between Pliny and Trajan in Book 10, see, for example, Noreña 2007; Woolf 2015; Lavan 2018. Although these letters may have been as carefully constructed as any others in Pliny's collection, particularly as regards the self-representation of the correspondents (see esp. Noreña 2007), they still served as official communication between emperor and provincial governor and give us some sense of the issues involved in the day-to-day running of the province (see esp. Lavan 2018).
86. cf. 10.90, where Pliny has clearly found a surveyor himself to survey the land around Sinope for an aqueduct.

87. For the crossover between architects and engineers, particularly in a military context, see Pearse 1974: 153–155. Also, Anderson 1997: 4.
88. *Librator* is translated as engineer in the Loeb edition of the text, but see Cuomo 2011: 159 for the term probably indicating "specialisation in surveying uneven terrain."
89. On legions in Lower Moesia in this period, see Whately 2016: 26–27; on auxiliaries, 36–39. For Pliny's (small) staff in Bithynia, see Levick 1979: 122.
90. On this connection, see Cuomo 2011: 159; 161. For building and the Roman army in general, see Pearse 1974: 152–168. Also Kuttner in this volume, who notes that at least half of the scenes on Trajan's Column show Roman soldiers engaged in construction of some sort.
91. Although cf. Pearse 1974: 161–163.
92. The story was recorded in an inscription on a *cippus* found in Lambaesis. For the text and a discussion, see Cuomo 2011.
93. Ward-Perkins 1980: 33–34.
94. A connection also noted by Pearse 1974: 89; 145.
95. Walker 1979: 104; Russell 2013: 331–32. Although not to be overplayed, see Claridge 2015: 109; Russell 2015: 198.
96. Ward-Perkins 1993: 88.
97. For a discussion of the movement of the carver or the carving, see Taylor 2003: 238–241. Also, Walker 1979: 127. See n. 64 for the trade in finished sculpture. Also, Russell 2015: 199–202 for the trade in sarcophagi, including finished pieces.
98. Ward-Perkins 1993: 88–89; 98–99; pl. 48a.
99. Ward-Perkins 1980: 33; see also 27; 40–41, for Proconnesian marble being traded through Nicomedia. For carvers from Asia Minor working Proconnesian marble, see also Ward-Perkins 1993: 99. For the difficulties of defining the term *marmorarius/marmararios*, see Russell 2013: 206.
100. Russell 2013: 204.
101. Walker 1979: 128.
102. Walker 1979: 127.
103. Ward-Perkins 1980: 25.
104. Russell 2013: 203.
105. On Mons Claudianus, see Cuvigny 1996.
106. Tietz 2021: 31–33 on agricultural contractors in general.
107. For a similar argument concerning associations of artists who performed at festivals in the fourth century and into the Hellenistic period, see Harris 2020: 38–39. Also, Aneziri 2020.
108. See n. 37.

109. On *probatio*, see Martin 1989: 103–113. Cic. *ad Q. Frat.* 3.1.1–2 appears to describe a (somewhat unsuccessful) *probatio* taking place at an interim stage of building work: Anderson 1997: 72; 356. n. 18.
110. On the possibility of such signatures acting as a trademark, see also Erim and Roueché 1982: 111; on Athenian "signatures," see also Russell 2013: 315; 332–333 (the latter also for makers' marks from other famous cities with a strong artistic tradition, such as Rhodes, Miletos, Dokimeion, and Alexandria). On pride as the motivation for signatures, see Claridge 2015: 120.
111. Holleran 2021: 162–163.
112. For example, Cic. *Ad Fam.* 13.19–27; Pliny, *Ep.* 4.4; Fronto, *Ad M. Caes.* v.37 (52); Holleran 2021: 172. On letters of recommendation in general, see Cotton 1981. Also now Schubert 2021 on business letters in Roman Egypt specifically. For envoys with letters of recommendation, see Chaniotis 2009: 249.
113. https://papyri.info/ddbdp/p.gen;1;75; Schubert 2021: 50.
114. Holleran 2021: 173, with further examples.
115. https://papyri.info/ddbdp/p.oxy;14;1661; Schubert 2021: 51; on Sidonius, Holleran 2021: 172–173.

Bibliography

Anderson, J.C. 1997. *Roman Architecture and Society.* John Hopkins Press.

André, J-M. and M-F. Baslez, 1993. *Voyager dans l'Antiquité.* Fayard.

Aneziri, S. 2020. "Artists of Dionysius: the first professional associations in the ancient Greek world." In Stewart, E. Harris, E. and Lewis, D. eds. *Skilled Labour and Professionalism in Ancient Greece and Rome,* 293–312. Cambridge University Press.

Armstrong, J. and Cohen, S., eds. 2022. *Crafting Connections: Production, Trade, and Community in Pre-Roman Italy, 900–400 BCE.* Routledge.

Bader, P. 2014. "The identity, legal status and origin of the Roman army's medical staff in the imperial age." In Maire, B. ed. *'Greek' and 'Roman' in Latin Medical Texts.* 43–59, Brill.

Bagnani, G. 1953. "The tomb of Patro." *AJA* 57.2: 104.

Bernard, H.J-C. Bessac, P. Mardikian, and M. Feugère. 1988. "L'épave romaine de marbre de Porto Novo." *JRA* 11: 53–81.

Bevan, A. and E. Bloxam, 2016. "Stonemasons and craft mobility in the Bronze Age Eastern Mediterranean." In Kiriatzi, E. and Knappet, C. eds. *Human Mobility and Technological Transfer in the Prehistoric Mediterranean.* 68–93. Cambridge University Press.

Blackwell, N. G. 2014. "Making the lion gate relief at Mycenae: Tool marks and foreign influence." *AJA* 118.3: 451–488.

Bliquez, L. 2014. *The Tools of Asclepius. Surgical Instruments in Greek and Roman Times.* Brill.

Bond, S. E. 2023. '2,000-year-old grave of Roman doctor unearthed in Hungary', *Hyperallergic.com*, May 17, 2023.

Boyer, R. et al. 1990. "Découverte de la tombe d'un oculiste à Lyon (fin due IIe siècle apres J.C.) Instruments et coffret avec collyres." *Gallia* 47: 215–49.

Burford A. 1969. *The Greek Temple Builders at Epidauros.* Liverpool University Press.

Calder, W. M. 1955. "Early-Christian epitaphs from Phyrgia." *Anat.St.* 5: 25–38.

Chaniotis, A. 2009. "Travelling memories in the Hellenistic world." In Hunter, R. and Rutherford, I. eds. *Wandering Poets in Ancient Greek Culture: Travel, Locality, and Pan-Hellenism.* 249–269. Cambridge University Press.

Claridge, A. 2015. "Marble carving techniques, workshops, and artisans." In Friedland, E.A. et al. eds. *The Oxford Handbook of Roman Sculpture.* 107–122. Oxford University Press.

Cotton, H. 1981. *Documentary Letters of Recommendation in Latin from the Roman Empire.* Anton Hain.

Cuomo, S. 2011. "A Roman engineer's tales." *JRS* 101: 143–165.

Cuvigny, H. 1996. "The amount of wages paid to quarry workers at Mons Claudianus." *JRS* 86: 139–145.

DeLaine, J. 2000. "Building the eternal city: the construction industry of imperial Rome." In Coulston, J. and Dodge, H., eds. *Ancient Rome: the Archaeology of the Eternal City.* 119–141. Oxford University Press.

Domergue, C. 1990. *Les mines de la péninsule ibérique dans l'Antiquité romaine.* Ecole Française de Rome.

Epstein, S. 2010. "Attic public construction: Who were the builders?" *Ancient Society* 40: 1–14.

Epstein, S. 2004. "Labour mobility, journeyman organisations and markets in skilled labour in Europe, 14th–18th centuries." In Arnoux, A. and Monnet, P., eds. *Le technicien dans la cite en Europe occidentale 1250–1650.* 251–269. Ecole Française de Rome.

Erim, K. T. and C. M. Roueché, 1982. "Sculptors from Aphrodisias: some new inscriptions." *PBSR* 50: 102–115.

Flemming, R. Forthcoming. *Medicine and Empire in the Roman World.* Cambridge University Press.

Hall, A. and M. Waelkens, 1982. "Two Dokimeian sculptors in Iconium." *Anat. St.* 32: 151–155.

Harris, E. 2020. "Many ancient Greek occupations, but few professions." In Stewart, E. Harris, E. and Lewis, D. eds., *Skilled Labour and Professionalism in Ancient Greece and Rome.* 29–67. Cambridge University Press.

Hawkins, C. 2013. "Labour and employment." In Erdkamp, P., ed. *The Cambridge Companion to Ancient Rome.* 336–351. Cambridge University Press.

Hochscheid, H. 2020. "Professionalism in archaic and classical sculpture in Athens: The price of *technē*." in Stewart, E. Harris, E. and Lewis, D. eds., *Skilled Labour and Professionalism in Ancient Greece and Rome*. 205–229. Cambridge University Press.

Holleran, C. 2023. "Mobility, economic." *The Oxford Classical Dictionary* (*digital edition*). Oxford University Press.

Holleran, C. 2021. "Information asymmetry and the Roman labour market." In Rosillo-López, C. and Morcillo, M.G., eds. *Managing Information in the Roman Economy*. 159–178. Palgrave Macmillan.

Israelowich, I. 2015. *Patients and Healers in the Roman Empire*. John Hopkins University Press.

Kiriatzi, E. and Knappet, C., eds. 2016. *Human Mobility and Technological Transfer in the Prehistoric Mediterranean*. Cambridge University Press.

Kleiner, F. S. 1977. "Artists in the Roman world. An itinerant workshop in Augustan Gaul." *MEFRA* 89.1: 661–696.

Kostecka, K. 2019. "Geographical mobility and the dynamics of the status of élite specialists." *Incidenza dell'Antico* 17: 29–52.

Lavan, L. 2022. "Greek names and freed status in Roman Italy: Why ancient historians can't ignore statistics." *Chiron* 52: 1–29.

Lavan, M. 2018. "Pliny *Epistles* 10 and Imperial correspondence. The empire of letters." In König, A. and Whitton, C.L., eds. *Roman Literature under Nerva, Trajan, and Hadrian: Literary Interactions AD 96–138*. 280–301. Cambridge University Press.

Levick, B. 1979. "Pliny in Bithynia—and what followed." *Greece and Rome* 26.2: 119–131.

Martin, S. D. 1989. *The Roman Jurists and the Organization of Private Building in the Late Republic and Early Empire*. Latomus.

Massar, N. 2020. "Skilled workers in the ancient Greek City: public employment, selection methods, and evaluation." In Stewart, E. Harris, E. and Lewis, D., eds., *Skilled Labour and Professionalism in Ancient Greece and Rome*. 68–93. Cambridge University Press.

McClean, B. H. 2002. *Greek and Latin Inscriptions in the Konya Archaeological Museum* (Regional Epigraphic Catalogues of Asia Minor 4). London.

Melfi, M. 2016. "Damophon of Messene in the Ionian coast of Greece." In Melfi, M and O. Bobou, eds. *Hellenistic Sanctuaries: Between Greece and Rome*. 82–105. Oxford University Press.

Meyerhof, M. 1929. "Autobiographische Bruchstücke Galens aus arabischen Quellen." *Sudhoffs Archiv für Geschichte der Medizin* 22: 72–86.

Moatti, C. 2013. "Immigration and cosmopolization." in Erkamp, P., ed. *The Cambridge Companion to Rome*. 77–92. Cambridge University Press.

Noreña, C. 2007. "The social economy of Pliny's correspondence with Trajan." *AJP* 128.2: 239–277.

Noy, D. 2000. *Foreigners at Rome: Citizens and Strangers*. Duckworth.

Nutton, V. 2013. *Ancient Medicine*, 2nd ed. Routledge.

Nutton, V. 2012. "Galen and Roman medicine; or can a Greek become a Latin?" *European Review* 20.4: 534–542.

Padron-Labonnelie, M. 2014. "Collyrium names attested on stone tablets: The example of the Helvetian corpus." In Maire, B., ed. *'Greek' and 'Roman' in Latin Medical Texts*. 240–255. Brill.

Palombi, D. 2007. "Medici e medicina a Roma tra Carine, Velia, e Sacra Via." In Brandenburg, H., Heid, S., and Markschies, C., eds. *Salute e Guarigione nella Tarda Antichità*. Pontificio Istituto di Archeologia Cristiana.

Palombi, D. 1997. "Compitium Acilium: la scoperta, il monument e la tradizione medica del quartiere." *Atti della Pontificia Accademia romana di archeologia. Rendiconti* 70: 115–135.

Pearse, J. L. D. 1974. *The Organisation of Roman Building during the Late Republic and Early Empire*. PhD thesis, Trinity College Cambridge.

Polito, R. 1999. "On the life of Asclepiades of Bithynia." *JHS* 119: 48–66.

Randall, R. H. 1953. "The Erechtheum Workmen." *AJA* 57.3: 199–210.

Reith, R. 2008. "Circulation of skilled labour in late medieval and early modern Central Europe." In Epstein, S. R., and Prak, M., eds. *Guilds, Innovation, and the European Economy, 1500–1800*. 114–142. Cambridge University Press.

Russell, B. 2015. "Transport and distribution." in Friedland, E.A. et al. eds. *The Oxford Handbook of Roman Sculpture*. 189–206. Oxford University Press.

Russell, B. 2013. *The Economics of the Roman Stone Trade*. Oxford University Press.

Schubert, P. 2021. *The Bearers of Business Letters in Roman Egypt*. Peeters.

Shear Jr., T. L. 2016. *Trophies of Victory: Public Building in Periklean Athens*. Princeton University Press.

Taylor, R. 2003. *Roman Builders: A Study in Architectural Process*. Cambridge University Press.

Terpstra, T. 2013. 'Roman trade with the far east: evidence for Nabataean middlemen in Puteoli', in F. De Romanis and M. Maiuro (eds.), *Across the Ocean: Nine Essays in Indo-Mediterranean Trade* (Brill: Leiden), 73–94.

Tietz, W. 2021. "Seasonal labour and migratory work in the Roman empire." in Lichtenberger, A., and Raja, R., eds. *The Archaeology of Seasonality*. 25–38. Brepols.

Tortorella, S. 2009. "Tomba di Patron sulla via Latina a Roma: frammenti di decorazione pittorica." in La Rocca, E., Ensoli, S., Ensoli, S., Tortorella, S., and Papini, M., eds. *Roma: la pittura di un impero*. 270–271. Skira.

Varga, R. and A-I Pázsint, 2021. 'Labour migration in the Roman world: the case of craftsmen', in V. Cojocaru and A-I. Pázsint (eds.), *Migration and Identity in Eurasia: from Ancient Times to the Middle Ages* (Cluj-Napoca: Editura Mega), 115–138.

Walker, S. 1979. "Corinthian capitals with ringed voids: the work of Athenian craftsmen in the second century AD." *Archäologischer Anzeiger*: 103–129.
Ward-Perkins, J. B. 1980. "Nicomedia and the marble trade." *PBSR* 48: 23–69.
Ward-Perkins, J. B. 1993. *The Severan Buildings of Lepcis Magna: an Architectural Survey*. Society for Libyan Studies.
Whately, C. 2016. *Exercitus Moesiae: The Roman Army in Moesia from Augustus to Severus Alexander*. BAR Publishing.
Woolf, G. 2015. "Pliny/Trajan and the poetics of empire." *CPhil.* 110: 132–151.
Zerbini, A. 2016. 'Human mobility in the Roman near east: patterns and motives', in L. de Ligt and L. R. Tacoma (eds.) *Migration and Mobility in the Early Roman Empire* (Leiden: Brill), 305–344.

CHAPTER 4

Working, Learning, and Living Environments: The View from Dolium Repairs

Caroline Cheung

Introduction

How do the environment and work set-up affect workers' skills and work? How might their working and learning environments affect their livelihood? Recent studies have shown that an open office set-up could increase collaboration and communication across office employees today.[1] Open offices proliferated across the United States, especially in the technology industry, as employers hoped to foster a communal work environment.

I am grateful to Jordan Rogers and Del Maticic for organizing and inviting me to participate in this stimulating panel and edited volume. I would also like to thank the other participants for their helpful questions and comments, and Matthew Santirocco and the NYU Ancient Studies Center for sponsoring this conference.

C. Cheung (✉)
Princeton University, Princeton, NJ, USA
e-mail: caroline.cheung@princeton.edu

D. A. Maticic, J. Rogers (eds.), *Working Lives in Ancient Rome*, The New Antiquity,
https://doi.org/10.1007/978-3-031-61234-3_4

Those spaces, it was thought, could influence and increase the ability and frequency of working together, the creation of new ideas, and interdisciplinary exchange. Yet the open office concept has been contentious and problematic for many, as people noted the lack of privacy (perhaps bordering on surveillance for some), heightened stress, and an increase in workplace distractions.[2] The open office concept has come under scrutiny, as businesses reevaluate their office set-up. The configuration of a workspace matters.[3] It can facilitate communication, spark innovation, and cultivate collaboration. Only a few ancient workspaces are archaeologically attested and can provide that type of detailed view of workspaces, but there are ways to examine and even reconstruct the working, learning, and perhaps even living conditions of ancient workers.[4] This chapter explores ancient working and learning environments around a valuable craft commodity known as the *dolium* (pl. *dolia*) to consider experiences of workers who interacted with these containers.

Dolia, large ceramic storage containers with a distinctive strawberry shape, were useful equipment for agriculture and have been found at many sites of food production and storage in the Mediterranean (Fig. 4.1). They varied in size, capable of holding a couple hundred to more than a thousand liters of wine, olive oil, and other agricultural commodities. Their production and use greatly proliferated from the second century BCE onward as they supported and expanded the lucrative wine and olive oil industries.[5] Because of their heftiness and high value, *dolia* were classified as fixed architectural features that defined wine cellars; hundreds of *dolia* can still be found in-situ in farms, warehouses, and even cemented in specialized ships.[6] People in antiquity regularly maintained and repaired *dolia* to extend the use of these costly investments, patching up damage they might have incurred during wine fermentation or other routine tasks. As I have discussed elsewhere, the many *dolia* and *dolium* fragments in the archaeological record often preserve evidence for their production and maintenance and provide a unique opportunity to follow the "life history" of *dolia* to trace the different workers who interacted with these vessels.[7] This chapter expands on previous studies to show that studying *dolium* repairs closely also allows a reconstruction of these craftsmen's skills and learning and working environments.[8]

Dolia were no ordinary pots. They were the most challenging and time-consuming type of pottery to produce, and their production was the most specialized form of ceramic production; only a few potters today can construct a pot of such a scale.[9] Unlike smaller types of pottery, *dolia* were

Fig. 4.1 A *dolium* lying on its side, House of Stabianus (I.22), Pompeii. By concession of the Ministry of Culture—Archaeological Park of Pompeii. Reproduction or duplication is prohibited

so large, that *dolium* potters could not throw them on a regular potter's wheel, but coil-built them on a slow-turning wheel, a process requiring weeks to form a single vessel.[10] The *dolium* maker would have made a base and then added one or two individual coils on a daily basis, waiting for the coil to have dried enough to support the weight of the next coil, but not too much that the coils would not bond together. Drying the vessels would have taken several weeks before the *dolia* could be kiln-fired over the course of several days.[11] The size, quality, and longevity of a *dolium* could therefore vary widely. As a result, well-made *dolia* (and the necessary skills to produce them) were highly valued.

Evidence on potters from the ancient and pre-modern world combined with ethnographic data suggests that *dolium* potters learned the craft through several progressive stages, starting with smaller pots and other ceramic objects and progressing to larger, more complex vessels such as amphorae that combined skill, precision, and strength.[12] In fact, Plato noted that Socrates made a point about governance in relation to the production of *pithoi* (large storage jars similar to dolia):

> In truth would it not be ridiculous that men should come to such folly that, prior to much private practice, sometimes with indifferent results, sometimes with success, and so getting adequate training in the art, they should, as the saying is, attempt to learn pottery by starting on a *pithos*, and attempt public service themselves and summon others of their like to do so?[13]

Dolia were generally made in *opus doliare* workshops, large heavy terracotta manufactories that produced bricks, tiles, *mortaria*, *dolia*, *amphorae*, and/or other heavy terracotta objects.[14] Clay workers gained mastery over the particular groggy clay (coarse clays high in alumina and silica, such as clays consisting of ground-up fired clay particles, e.g., discarded pottery, bricks, tiles) used for *opus doliare* products as they made progressively larger items.

The incredible skill, massive quantities of material, and the time and equipment led to *dolia*'s high prices and value. Diocletian's *Price Edict*, issued in 301 CE, shows that a *dolium* cost 1000 denarii, about 2500 times more than a ceramic lamp or 500 times more than a common undecorated pot.[15] Agricultural manuals also identified *dolia* as valuable vessels, explaining which regions were reputable for high-quality *dolia* and even advising how to select a vessel.[16] In fact, the fourth-century CE writer Anatolios urged potential *pithos* buyers to go to the workshops and clay beds themselves to evaluate the quality of the materials and to test the pot's integrity: "There are those who are content with the examination of whether a *pithos* is well made, if it gives out a sharp and piercing note when struck. But this is not sufficient. The client must be there at the pottery workshop, must perceive beforehand that the clay is in best condition for working" (*Geoponika* 6.3). Indeed, many of the possible problems and damage that *dolia* could exhibit later often stemmed from production defects. Modern experiments of *dolium*-making and *dolium*-based wine production reveal how precarious this could be: even a seemingly well-made *dolium* filled with wine could leak and lose one-third of the contents because the vessel walls were too porous.[17]

Dolia were also vulnerable to breakage. There are two points when *dolia* could become damaged: during use, which was expected given accidents and wear and tear, and during production. Because different parts of the vessel dried at different rates and clay shrinks as it dries, *dolia* could crack even before their production was complete. Horizontal fractures could form between the coils and vertical cracks, known as dunting, could form on areas of extreme curvature, where the drying was uneven; this occurred most often on the shoulder and rim of the vessel during the firing process. *Dolia* could therefore exhibit serious production flaws and break during the production process, before they were even used.[18] Defective and damaged *dolia* could be recycled in the workshop, for example, as refractory material for other heavy terracotta products, but they were still a serious loss for the workshop given the time, skill, and materials invested in a single vessel. Craftsmen began to form repairs regularly during the production process, before *dolia* were fired to minimize further damage and protect their pots.

Over time, *dolium* producers began to master not only forming larger *dolia* but also reinforcing them and making them more robust based on skills obtained in their working environments. Examples of repaired *dolia* reveal that a large portion of *dolia* were mended in the workshop during the course of their production, using two main techniques. The neatness and precision in their execution ties them to the production-phase in the workshop, where *dolium* makers, another *opus doliare* craftsman, or another specialist in the workshop formed the repairs.[19] Menders used mortise and tenons known as double dovetails, which helped anchor the repair more securely and provided some tensile strength (Fig. 4.2). The double dovetail shape acted as both an anchor and a fill. To execute these regularized repairs, menders cut shallow grooves, about half a centimeter to a centimeter deep, into the dry, but not yet fired, clay surface, commonly applying them to fractures between coils and the *dolium* rim and shoulder. The shallow grooves dissipated the nascent crack, preventing it from worsening. To mend more extensive cracks, *dolium* menders employed multiple double dovetails connected by a channel (Fig. 4.3). Some of these double dovetail tenons covered large portions of the vessel, a process that must have required members of the workshop to work together and maneuver the large heavy pots in order to cut some of these extensive double dovetail tenons. After firing the vessels in the kiln, the craftsmen would then add lead or a lead mixture to fill the cut grooves and any cracks that might have formed as a result of the mending process as well as to strengthen the repairs. Overall, the production-phase repairs were neatly and consistently executed, pointing to shared conventions across multiple workshops in west-central Italy.

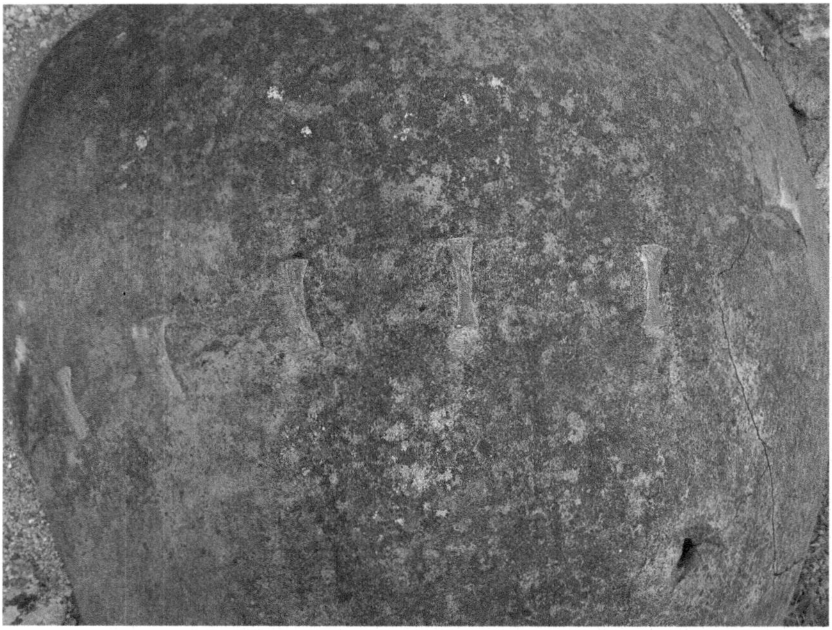

Fig. 4.2 A *dolium* with a row of double dovetail repairs, House of Stabianus (I.22), Pompeii. By concession of the Ministry of Culture—Archaeological Park of Pompeii. Reproduction or duplication is prohibited

The production-phase double dovetail repairs drew on joinery techniques from the architectural realm, reflecting the interactions between building-pottery and architectural objects in *opus doliare* workshops, such as bricks and tiles.[20] *Dolium* makers worked together in workshops for at least several months each year where they shared resources and knowledge and had fixed facilities to practice their craft.[21] Moreover, *dolium* workshops were located near good clay sources for *opus doliare* products, routes of transportation, and might have been in the vicinity of other major workshops, where they could share and exchange space, materials, and equipment. Different craftsmen gathered in these workshops and might have learned to work with new techniques and tools. *Dolium* workshops, especially the larger ones that produced multiple products, would have had many workers with different roles and expertise; some of these workers worked seasonally and might have had jobs in other industries, such as

Fig. 4.3 A *dolium* with a double dovetail tenon, House of Stabianus (I.22), Pompeii. By concession of the Ministry of Culture—Archaeological Park of Pompeii. Reproduction or duplication is prohibited

agriculture or construction, where they saw different joining techniques or even interacted with *dolium* users or repairers who reported their impressions (and complaints) of the vessels and repair techniques. Knowing that *dolia* were exposed to certain types of damage and breakage patterns could help shape a maker's treatment of the *dolium* during its production. *Dolium* producers became better at anticipating damage and identifying points of weakness. A few *dolium* producers known from *dolium* stamps suggest that specializing in *dolium* production could lead to promotions;[22] some enslaved *dolium* makers were later manumitted and managed enslaved *dolium* makers of their own. One figure, Q. Tossius Cimber, was first attested as a slave of Q. Tossius Ingenuus then was freed and became an *officinator*, with two slaves of his own, Redemptus and Euphrastus.[23] A stone funerary altar along the Via Appia in Campania bears the name and occupation of Lucius Aurelius Sabinus, a proud *doliarius* who made the tomb for himself and his household, which could have included enslaved potters.[24] Whether specializing in *dolium* production also meant reinforcing *dolia* is unclear, but becoming a specialist *dolium* maker came with advantages. With *dolia*'s tendency to crack easily, these production-phase repairs were visible signs that *dolium* makers already reinforced the vessel. In fact, many of the *dolia* repaired during the production-phase found at Ostia featured workshop and maker stamps. There was no attempt to hide these reinforcements. Perhaps these were some of the traits of robust *dolia* that Anatolios would have looked for during his visits to the workshops. Archaeological evidence in central Italy shows that many mended *dolia* held up very well and were in use for a long period of time.

Working and Learning Outside the Workshop

Many *dolia* could and did accrue damage during their use, even if the workshop preemptively treated production defects. *Dolia* were commonly damaged because they were often used for the fermentation of wine. With the resulting expansion of gas, if *dolia* were sealed too soon, vessels could crack or even burst. This possibility explains why agronomists advised sealing *dolia* only after the first, most volatile, phase of fermentation was complete.[25] Furthermore, because *dolia* were often partly buried in unroofed courtyards, a loose tile or brick from an adjacent structure could cause serious damage. To avoid such damage, ancient agronomists advise using a two-lid sealing system to seal *dolia* properly: (1) a flat lid (*operculum*) that was usually lined with pitch and placed on top of the *dolium* and (2) an external, raised lid (*tectorium*) that provided an additional buffer. Yet damage could and did often occur, evidenced by the plethora of broken, and occasionally repaired, *dolium* lids (which were made separately from *dolia* and probably replaced more frequently).[26] Other, routine activities could also lead to damage. As Columella cautions, even cleaning and lining the vessels with molten pitch, to prevent the ceramic material from absorbing and adulterating the wine, could burst the *dolium* if the heat source were too close to the vessel.[27] Because *dolia* were large and heavy, these types of damage were often fixed on the spot or at least not far from where the *dolium* was installed. It was probably too cumbersome and expensive to transport a *dolium* back to the workshop and back again, making it unlikely that the original workshop repaired its wares once they were in use.[28]

Repairing *dolia* in these conditions drew on skills different from producing *dolia*.[29] Whereas potters worked with clay, craftsmen mending fired ceramic material had to use different materials and techniques.

Making pottery is an irreversible, chemically transformative process, whereby the fired ceramic material is no longer compatible with clay;[30] to mend a broken pot, then, craftsmen used other materials. Varro and Cato note that people could use organic materials such as rushes or oak wood to bind and mend *dolia*; presumably, menders would have laced the rushes or strips of oak wood through drilled holes on either side of the crack and then tied them to close the gaps. Organic materials, however, would not have survived in the archaeological record, and no trace of these repairs exists today.[31] Juvenal and Cato mention lead as a common material used to bind and repair *dolia*, and the *dolium* repairs in the archaeological record overwhelmingly preserve lead or lead-based mixtures. Lead was a relatively abundant, inexpensive, and malleable metal that was relatively easy to work and shape. A simple flame was enough to bring lead into a workable, moldable liquid state.[32] Craftsmen commonly applied lead and lead mixtures to *dolium* damage, occasionally adding other metals such as tin to strengthen the lead mixture. The metallic elements, coupled with various techniques, could make a cracked jar functional again.

A variety of *dolium* repair techniques for *dolia* damaged while in use is preserved in the archaeological record. *Dolium* menders could simply fill minor cracks or voids with lead to close the void. For more substantial areas, a mender might use more lead or add other materials to conserve lead usage, such as pottery sherds. Both the archaeological record and literary references note that *dolium* repairs were mostly similar to repair techniques found on smaller types of pottery, known as staples and clamps. Forming staples and clamps consisted of drilling holes into and often through the vessel wall on either side of the damage. The mender would then place into the holes lead pins joined by crossbars that would brace the crack, a crossbar on one side of the vessels for a staple and two crossbars for a clamp (Fig. 4.4). This type of repair braced and bound the vessel together and was often applied to more major cracks and damage.

Dolia could break at different points of their lives and, based on the different techniques evidenced in the archaeological record, could have been repaired by a wide variety of menders, including plumbers, farmers, metalworkers, tinkers, and perhaps stoneworkers, among other craftsmen who drew on their own techniques and materials. The archaeological record preserves a range of techniques, executed with varying quality and results: lead fillers, fillers using other materials, staples, clamps, mortise-and-tenon, and hybrid staples or clamps combined with a type of mortise and tenon. These diverse methods reveal the possible range of a given

Fig. 4.4 [L] *Dolium* clamp repairs on vessel shoulder, Garden of the Fugitives, (I.20.2), Pompeii. By concession of the Ministry of Culture—Archaeological Park of Pompeii. Reproduction or duplication is prohibited. [R] Illustration of a *dolium* clamp repair, by Gina Tibbott

repairer's skill sets, as well as the possible variety of materials and tools s/he had on hand; because *dolia* often became damaged during use, *dolium* owners and users would have to find someone locally who was able to mend the vessel, whether it was someone within their own usual staff or an external craftsperson. Access to skilled repairers depended upon location and could vary widely. In the early modern period, generalist tinkers repaired porcelain using tin and other metals to form rivets.[33] Some set-up stands in towns, whereas itinerant tinkers roamed the countryside to repair the high-valued goods. In the Roman world, towns such as Pompeii and Herculaneum had metalworking (and specifically lead) workshops, builders familiar with joining stone and other heavy materials, or general pottery menders' shops where people could find someone to help mend their pot.[34] *Dolium* users on farms and villas in rural areas, however, were typically more limited in their choice of possible menders. In some cases, whether in town or country, *dolium* users might have also tried to fix the damage themselves, as we will see below.

The environment and personnel in workshops likely helped *dolium* makers develop, improve, and standardize their production-phase techniques, but craftsmen mending *dolia* during use did not experience this kind of working and learning environment. By the first century CE, craftspeople in *dolium* workshops began with regularity to identify potential damage and treat it preemptively during the production-phase. These new repairs, which involved no drilling and drew on architectural techniques, seemed effective in rendering the vessels liquid tight and robust and appear on many of the largest, most robust *dolia* in west-central Italy. Yet the new innovative *dolium* repairs, the double dovetails and double dovetail tenons, were not developed by the craftspeople traditionally tasked with repairing in-use *dolia*, that is, the pottery menders, tinkers, and farm hands. Instead, they were developed and refined by those making the vessels in the workshops. This might seem unexpected, or even odd, but not if we consider the context and environment where these repairs developed. Unlike *dolium* makers, pottery menders and tinkers might have worked alone or did not have access to new materials or methods. Several use-life repairs can show how *dolium* menders working in the field, and not in a workshop, would develop their skills and what sorts of opportunities there might have been for them to learn.

There are several examples in Pompeii that suggest *dolium* menders encountered and learned from another *dolium* repair or the repairers themselves. The Villa of the Mysteries produced wine in antiquity, evidenced by the press and *dolia* found on site.[35] Of the four large fermentation *dolia*, three were repaired in antiquity. All three were mended during the production-phase with double dovetails, and two also featured double dovetail tenons. Nonetheless, *dolia* reinforced during production could still become damaged later. In this case, a *dolium* partly buried in the ground exhibits both production-phase and use-life repairs (Fig. 4.5). The *dolium* was mended in the workshop with lead dovetails and double dovetail tenons along the shoulder of the vessel, where curvature was extreme. Additional cracking seemed to have appeared later around the rim, when the vessel was in use, and a craftsperson came to mend it. This cracking was quite severe and repairing the vessel was not an easy job. Working on a fired ceramic surface was different from cutting into a dry, but not yet fired, ceramic surface. Chiseling a double dovetail shape on a fired ceramic surface typically results in ragged and uneven edges, whereas production-phase double dovetails are neat and symmetrical. This repair also goes all the way through the rim and vessel wall (Fig. 4.6). The mender, in this

Fig. 4.5 *Dolium* with various repairs, Villa of the Mysteries, Pompeii. By concession of the Ministry of Culture—Archaeological Park of Pompeii. Reproduction or duplication is prohibited

case, tried to make double dovetails to bind the cracks, removing the ceramic material to shape a double dovetail. But in this case, they were very jagged and uneven, due to the difficulty of working with and cutting into fired ceramics. Unlike the shallowly cut production-phase repairs, these repairs were hybrid repairs; that is, they combined two techniques. A closer look at the repair can reconstruct the repairer's process: on the underside of the repair, the area of the rim where another double dovetail broke off, the repairer combined the dovetail technique with a staple or clamp by drilling through the rim to add two long pins to strengthen the repair. This is a unique repair, where the repairer tried to mimic and adapt effective production-phase double dovetail tenons for use-life damage. Rather than forming a standard staple or clamp, the repairer decided to take the extra step of adding the double dovetail, perhaps because it strengthened the repair or to blend in the use-life repairs with the production-phase repairs. This could have been the handiwork of a specialist in production repairs, who happened to be in the area, using and

Fig. 4.6 [L] Underside of double dovetail hybrid repair, showing pins, Villa of the Mysteries, Pompeii. By concession of the Ministry of Culture—Archaeological Park of Pompeii. Reproduction or duplication is prohibited. [R] Profile view of drilled area for pins of the hybrid repair, Villa of the Mysteries, Pompeii. By concession of the Ministry of Culture—Archaeological Park of Pompeii. Reproduction or duplication is prohibited

adapting the only technique they knew, or of a tinker who tried to imitate the repairs found on the other *dolia*.

Another example in Pompeii shows not only the creative adaptations *dolium* menders made in order to repair damaged *dolia* but also the collaboration necessary to mend such unwieldy vessels. In the Garden of Hercules (II.8.6.) were several *dolia*, including an enormous *dolium* that exhibited extensive repairs on different parts of the vessel (Fig. 4.7).[36] Members of the *opus doliare* workshop placed two lead alloy double dovetails across from one another on the rim to repair dunting cracks during production. *Opus doliare* workers also placed two extensive vertical sets of clamp repairs on the *dolium* body; the quantity of clamps, their neatness (the drill holes show they were made before firing), and their placement (in areas of extreme curvature and hence vulnerability) suggest they were almost certainly made during the production-phase. The series of clamps extended from the middle of the vessel body to the base, terminating in a set of horizontal lead alloy clamps, which individually were arranged in a triangular fashion and collectively straddled an area of weakness between the vessel body and base. The multiple vertical clamps along two sides of the *dolium* and around the base were the work of at least two menders, one of whom had to go into the vessel to form the interior set of clamps. Given the small aperture of the *dolium* (diameter of 44 cm), only petite adults, adolescents, or perhaps even children were able to enter and move

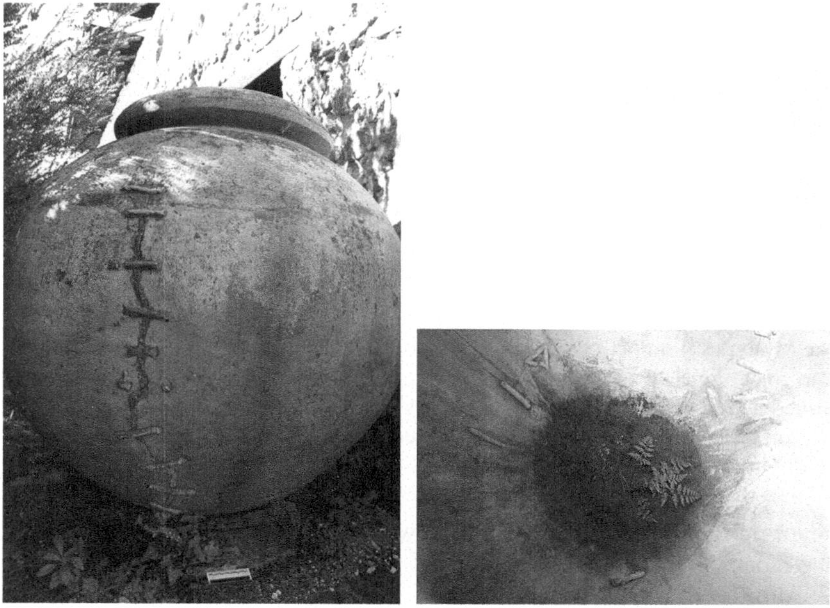

Fig. 4.7 [L] Extensively mended *dolium* in the Garden of Hercules (II.8.6), Pompeii. By concession of the Ministry of Culture—Archaeological Park of Pompeii. Reproduction or duplication is prohibited. [R] Inside the vessel base, with clamp repairs, Garden of Hercules (II.8.6), Pompeii. By concession of the Ministry of Culture—Archaeological Park of Pompeii. Reproduction or duplication is prohibited

within and around the *dolium* to apply the repairs (Fig. 4.7).[37] At some point, the *dolium* user(s) must have felt it necessary to reinforce the production-phase repairs; perhaps the vessel cracked or the production-phase repairs were flimsy. Repairers regularized the emerging vertical cracks, filling them with a lead-based substance; they also formed a few additional use-life clamps and chiseled a double dovetail to strengthen the hybrid clamp repair. By the time Mount Vesuvius erupted in 79 CE, the *dolium* was placed on top of a supportive base to give it a new life as a water container, suggesting that the mended *dolium* ultimately was not liquid-tight enough to store wine.

Traditional pottery menders and tinkers, especially if they were itinerant, probably also repaired a variety of goods beyond pottery and did not develop specialized techniques that worked particularly well for *dolia*.[38] They probably did not have the same opportunities to learn or even attempt new or different repair methods; at places where *dolium* use was low, a tinker might not have ever come across a broken *dolium*.[39] Furthermore, because *dolium* owners and users hired *dolium* repairers directly, repairers might have been restricted in what techniques they could employ. Luigi Pirandello's early twentieth-century work, "La Giara," highlights this potential obstacle.[40] In the story, a wealthy landowner in rural Sicily, the padrone Don Lollò Zirafa, is pleased to acquire a large terracotta jar, similar in size and shape to a *dolium*, for his olive oil production. It was an expensive and anticipated jar, but it cracks after its arrival, and he looks for an itinerant repairman to fix his jar. An itinerant repairman Zi' Dima Licasi carries his kit of tools and materials with him as he travels through the country. After Zi' Dima Licasi inspects the broken vessel and forms his assessment, he proposes using his signature putty-like substance (il mastice), a new type of repair technique he developed himself. Don Lollò Zirafa, however, does not want or trust any experiments and insists the repairer use the traditional metal staple repair (i punti). The repairman begrudgingly follows his wealthy client's wishes. Zi' Dima Licasi carefully drills through the jar's walls and enters the broken pot to attach the clamps properly. Once he has finished mending the pot though, he is stuck inside. The padrone refuses to let him break the jar to get out, and the poor repairman is trapped in the jar he mended until he breaks out late at night after a big party, once everyone is drunk and asleep. This episode, though fictional and anachronous to ancient *dolium* repairs, highlights the uneasy situation *dolium* menders could find themselves in: since they were hired to fix a *dolium*, their client might dictate how to repair the vessel. Maybe the client saw that a neighbor's *dolium* had been successfully patched up a certain way and wanted the same kind of repair for their own vessel. Visibility of and familiarity with certain techniques mattered. That is not to say that repairs made in workshops did not cater to customers either but that the repairs made in the field were probably directly overseen by the *dolium* owner, whereas craftsmen in workshops could develop their techniques together, with their high-quality products convincing customers they were effective.

Other craftsmen might have also been called upon to apply their skills and knowledge to *dolium* damage. The materials of *dolium* repairs, lead and lead mixtures, could have also been the handiwork of metalworkers or even plumbers (*plumbarii*) who worked with lead. Other techniques point to the ironworkers of Pompeii as possible menders, or at least those whose skillsets could have contributed to mending *dolia*.[41] Given the potential urgency in mending a *dolium*, a cracked vessel was a loss of several hundred liters of wine, olive oil, or other food, costing up to thousands of *denarii*, *dolium* users might have resorted to whomever they could find to mend the vessel.[42] Some of the techniques found on mended *dolia* include joinery techniques that have been found in masonry architecture, stone sculpture, or repairs to millstones.[43]

Controlling Human Resources and Workers' Living Conditions

There was also the possibility that use-life repairs were formed not by an outsider craftsman but as a part of the *latifundia*'s essential activities. Agriculture was considered the noblest type of work by the Roman aristocracy, yet the people who performed the labor were not the Republican senators or generals honored in literature. Pliny the Elder comments that, in his day, "but now slaves with fettered ankles, the hands of the condemned with tattooed faces perform those [agricultural tasks]" (*at nunc eadem illa vincti pedes, damnatae manus inscriptique vultus exercent*, *NH* 18.21). Large agricultural estates often employed an expansive workforce, which could encompass a range of skills not only for farm work but also the upkeep of farm equipment. In an extensive and detailed set of instructions in *De Agricultura*, Cato outlines how the farm's enslaved workforce could be productive on a rainy day:

> Ubi tempestates malae erunt, cum opus fieri non poterit, stercus in stercilium egerito, bubile, ovile, cohortem, villam bene purgato; dolia plumbo vincito vel materie quernea vere sicca alligato. Si bene sarseris aut bene allegaveris et in rimas medicamentum indideris beneque picaveris, quodvis dolium vinarium facere poteris. Medicamentum in dolium hoc modo facito: cerae P. I, resinae P. I, sulpuris P. C' C'. Haec omnia in calicem novum indito, eo eddito gypsum contritum, uti crassitudo fiat quasi emplastrum, eo dolia sarcito. Ubi sarseris, qui colorem eundem faciaem cretae crudae partes duas, calcis tertiam conmisceto; inde laterculos facito, coquito in fornace, eum conterito idque inducito.

> When the weather is bad and work cannot be done, clear out dung for the compost heap; clean up the oxen stalls, sheepfolds, courtyard, and farm-

> stead; and fasten dolia with lead, or bind them with thoroughly dried oak wood. If you repair it carefully, or bind it well, closing the cracks with a remedy and pitching it thoroughly, you can make any dolium a wine dolium. Make plaster for a dolium as follows: Take one pound of wax, one pound of resin, and two thirds of a pound of sulphur. Put these all into a new vessel. To this add pulverized gypsum, so that it becomes thick enough like a plaster, and mend dolia with it. To make it the same color after mending, mix together two parts of raw chalk and a third part of lime, then form into small bricks, bake in the kiln, grind, and apply to the dolium. (*De Agricultura* 39)

Cato's directions in the second century BCE for mending *dolia* are in-depth, prescribing how to brace, bind, and even mask damage of *dolia*. As discussed elsewhere, these instructions hint at a "do-it-yourself" approach to *dolium* repair, perhaps before more specialized *dolium* mending emerged in later periods, as seen in the archaeological record. This passage also provides information regarding the personnel behind the repairs and the circumstances under which they were working. First, Cato's agricultural treatise provided instructions for running a farm profitably and assumes an enslaved workforce. Elsewhere in Cato's manual, he discusses supplies and expenditures related to purchasing, feeding, and maintaining the enslaved workforce. Furthermore, this passage was geared specifically toward work during bad weather, including cleaning the barn and animal stalls and preparing the compost heap. Cato's attention and worry were probably focused on a loss of work in the field, a loss of production, and idleness among the enslaved workforce. Control was very much at the center of this work and aligns with this prescription. The detail in the instructions also suggests that the slave owner had considerable authority over not only what the enslaved did but also *how* they did it. The worker was to mend the jar with lead or oak wood and cement the cracks with a particular recipe, while also covering up the mend. Control was at the center of this agricultural treatise, and the enslaved farm workers were constantly expected to perform certain tasks and in a particular way.

Enslaved agricultural workers worked and lived in different conditions compared to free or itinerant craftsmen. The new discoveries of the "slave rooms" in a villa at Civitá Giuliana just outside of Pompeii discovered in 2021 provide a glimpse of the harrowing working and living conditions for the enslaved agricultural workforce. Just next to the space for the luxurious bronze chariot and two rooms down from the horse stables, was a small room where the enslaved workforce not only lived but also worked.

The small room was crammed with a variety of *instrumenta*, from *amphorae* and a chariot shaft, to various tools, all surrounding two adult-length cots and a child-sized cot. Archaeologists have suggested that an enslaved family, or at least two adults and a child, lived and worked in the space. Given this assemblage, there appears to have been no distinction between the different projects they were expected to complete in the small space. Furthermore, they not only lived in these squalid conditions but also sometimes worked in these same spaces, perhaps during rainy days, with their time, resources, work, and knowledge controlled by the enslaver. Although the discoveries at Cività Giuliana are spectacular, they probably represent a common experience for agricultural workers, perhaps even a better alternative to other living arrangements. Other areas thought to be slave quarters were cramped, such as the courtyard of Settefinestre where individual locked rooms around the open courtyard might have confined the enslaved.[44] Even worse were the deep underground pits known as *ergastula*, where the enslaved were chained and detained to work on agricultural estates, especially vineyards;[45] conditions of *ergastula* were so dire that the emperor Hadrian supposedly abolished them.[46] The surveillance the enslaved lived under was not only about control but also ensuring there was no misbehavior or mistakes.

Given that *dolia* were expensive pieces of equipment, accidental breakage or failed repair jobs could have led to punishment for the unlucky enslaved worker. Unfortunately, the common types of use-life repairs had a high likelihood of damaging the vessel further. Forming the staple and clamp repairs commonly found on *dolia* consisted of drilling through the vessel wall on either side of the damage to place lead pins joined by crossbars that would brace the crack. Since *dolium* walls were thick (c. 3.5–6.0 cm), much thicker than a smaller pot, drilling through such a thick wall could crack the vessel further, and several *dolia* and *dolium* fragments exhibit additional damage stemming from this very process. This was problematic also because *dolia* primarily stored liquid goods—wine, olive oil, even garum—and drilling through the vessel walls meant that the vessel was probably no longer entirely liquid tight; even lining a *dolium* with pitch was likely not enough to make a cracked *dolium* water-tight. In addition, the acetic acid of wine was damaging to lead and could break down the lead clamp over time. Sometimes less severe damage would be filled with lead, plaster, or even pot sherds, to plug holes and replace worn areas. These methods could also fail though. It is difficult to know the repercussions of a failed repair job, but the loss of a *dolium* was the loss of hundreds of, if not over a thousand, liters of wine or at least the potential to store and sell wine, a costly loss. A case in the *Digest* shows that a plasterer mending a wine vat could accidentally break the vat and spill the wine; this slip-up would constitute an *actio in factum* because of the lost wine.[47] The Sicilian play "La Giara," mentioned above, provides another interesting view on vessel repair. The repairman is technically a free man and not beholden to the padrone as many agricultural workers or some craftsmen would have been in antiquity. Yet we still see the repairman in a vulnerable position: he is alone and he is on the property of a wealthy and influential man who has a large workforce. The customer was always right or at least could assert one's preferences. Don Lollò Zirafa wanted the traditional staples and that is what Zi' Dima Licasi prepared, eschewing his own tested methods. Ancient craftsmen, especially itinerant or enslaved ones, probably faced similar circumstances, where they were expected to perform certain tasks in a particular way and were at the mercy of the enslaver or *vilicus*.

Yet the archaeological record shows how different *dolium* damage, and hence the possible types of repairs, could be. What might have been someone's reaction if a slave did not follow the instructions? What if the slave was not successful in mending the expensive vessel? Different punishments were possible: being beaten, sexually violated, separated from others, forced to do more hazardous or physically demanding jobs, or sent to another property.[48] Perhaps manumission was off the table, if it was ever a possibility. Pirandello's "La Giara" showed the wealthy padrone's disregard for the itinerant craftsman's well-being. The jar was clearly worth more to him, so he kept Zi' Dima Licasi in the jar. Still, Zi' Dima Licasi was not enslaved, though he was still vulnerable to his customer's whims. Cato's manual placed great emphasis on the monetary value of *instrumenta*, the enslaved included. We can only imagine the repercussions when expensive equipment was destroyed and the potentially profitable wine could not be produced or stored properly. Accidental damage by a specialist craftsman, such as the plasterer, could lead to financial or legal consequences and perhaps more draconian or severe punishment, especially if the craftsman were enslaved. The impetus to experiment with techniques or materials could be stifled out of fear of possible retribution or penalties.

Pottery production was also rife with concerns regarding control over enslaved labor. The stamp evidence found on *dolia*, on other *opus doliare* products, and on pottery shows a preponderance of enslaved workers engaged in these activities. As mentioned before, excelling in *dolium* production might have led to rewards, advantages, or promotions. We do not know much about Roman potters and *doliarii* beyond some of the names that have come down to us in the dolium stamps. The example of David Drake, a nineteenth-century potter enslaved in South Carolina, highlights the possibilities and limitations for a master potter. Although he was incredibly skilled and produced over 40,000 jars, many of which were among the largest and most well-made jars of his time, he was known as "Dave the Slave" or "Dave the Potter" and had passed through the hands of several enslavers, before finally being freed at the conclusion of the Civil War and receiving the name David Drake. Over the course of his enslaved life and work, he worked in at least five pottery production sites, even hired out at times to help at other potteries.[49] He also lost a leg, and he worked as a disabled potter, relying on someone else to turn the wheel. A couple anecdotes recall the accident to his being drunk on the railroad tracks at the wrong time, but some scholars suggest that it was perhaps the result of a hazardous work set-up or some form of punishment.[50] Some even speculate that the clever verses on his pottery, now one of the prized features of his pottery, were the cause of his punishment in a time of explicit legal prohibitions against literacy among the enslaved. His surviving pottery and slivers of other information provide only a glimpse of his life, mostly as an enslaved master potter. Nothing is known about his family line, and one of David Drake's verses even heartbreakingly suggests he was separated from his family: *I wonder where is all my relations/friendship to all—and every nation.*[51] Despite, or because of, his great pottery skills, Dave was moved around, separated from his relations, and forced to work. Yet Dave the Potter's "life seemed reduced to three short words."[52] David Drake and Q. Tossius Cimber are the supposed success stories, craftsmen and laborers whose names survive on their handiwork, but who were forced to work under uncertain, often dangerous, conditions at large-scale potteries in various locations.[53] Enslaved *dolium* potters who were manumitted often continued to work with or for their former enslaver, a reflection of their limited mobility within a web of obligation and duty to their former enslaver.[54]

Conclusion

This chapter has attempted to shed light on the working environments and conditions revolving around *dolia*, one of the most important pieces of farm equipment. From their production to use and maintenance, *dolia* required time, expertise, and resources. Financial incentives and concerns can drive innovation and opportunities for learning and experimentation to a certain degree, as seen among *opus doliare* workshops, but they could also dampen innovation and experimentation. On the one hand, there was an incredible response to production-phase damage on *dolia*, whereby members of the workshop preemptively identified and treated damage before vessels were even fired. Within the *opus doliare* workshops, people were able to learn from and perhaps even practice on the architectural building materials of the workshops by cutting into bricks or tiles. Evidence at *dolium* workshops is sparse though because failed products were likely recycled or reused in some way whether it was slaked down back to groggy clay before it was fired or used as refractory material post-firing; refractory material would have been useful for increasing the durability of *opus doliare* materials. Repairs made in the field, on the other hand, were not in such an environment. In some respects, working alone, or perhaps with one or two other persons on a repair job for objects they were only intermittently commissioned to mend, might have hindered achieving the kind of mastery and specialization seen in the workshops. It must have been extremely challenging for them to work on *dolia* that were damaged during use, especially because they could have been damaged in different ways and required substantial repairs. Each time they came across a broken *dolium*, menders would have had to assess the individual situation, coordinate with and perhaps follow the wishes of the *dolium* owner, and tailor their repairs to the specific damage. Most likely these menders were not specialists of *dolium* repairs, maybe not even of pottery repairs.

Although there are some cases in which craftsmen could advance and improve their social standing through their work, there were surely plenty who suffered under these working conditions. Craftsmen's work, their potential to learn and experiment, and their livelihoods were completely dependent on their environments and their status. Those who were enslaved or indebted to more powerful figures found themselves and their livelihoods at the mercy of others. For many in antiquity, there was no separation between work and life. A single mistake could have meant dire consequences.

Notes

1. For example, Wohlers and Hertel (2017), Haapakangas et al. (2018).
2. Brennan et al. (2002).
3. See chapters by Maticic, Holleran, and Sausville in this volume for importance and impact of environment.
4. For example, Murphy (2015), Van Oyen et al. (2021, 2022), Pallecchi (2008), Peña and McCallum (2009a, 2009b), Van Oyen (2020b).
5. Cheung (2024), Van Oyen (2015, 2020a).
6. For an overview of *dolia* at farms and warehouses, see De Simone (2017). For overview of *dolia* in specialized transport ships, see Brenni (1985), Hesnard et al. (1988), Gianfrotta and Hesnard (1987), Heslin (2011), Rice (2016), Carrato and Cibecchini (2020).
7. Cheung (2021, 2024), Cheung and Tibbott (2020).
8. On object life histories, see Kopytoff (1986), Appadurai (1986), Peña (2007), Skibo (1992).
9. Plato *Gorgias* 514e; see Blitzer (1990) for ethnographic study of *pithoi* production.
10. Peña (2007: 35), Cheung and Tibbott (2020), Cheung (2021), Carroll (2022).
11. See Blitzer (1990), Carroll (2022).
12. Koverman (1998a). Studies of storage jars made by the nineteenth-century enslaved potter, David Drake, show a progression in the storage jars he made until he was capable of producing jars that could hold at least twenty-five gallons (c. 95 liters). Calfas (2018), archaeological work of Pottersville, just outside of Edgefield, SC, uncovered a large, industrial-scale kiln, and large-scale pottery production that was thanks to David Drake.
13. Plato *Gorgias* 514e: οὐ καταγέλαστον ἂν ἦν τῇ ἀληθείᾳ, εἰς τοσοῦτον ἀνοίας ἐλθεῖν ἀνθρώπους, ὥστε, πρὶν ἰδιωτεύοντας πολλὰ μὲν ὅπως ἐτύχομεν ποιῆσαι, πολλὰ δὲ κατορθῶσαι καὶ γυμνάσασθαι ἱκανῶς τὴν τέχνην, τὸ λεγόμενον δὴ τοῦτο ἐν τῷ πίθῳ τὴν κεραμείαν ἐπιχειρεῖν μανθάνειν, καὶ αὐτούς τε δημοσιεύειν ἐπιχειρεῖν καὶ ἄλλους τοιούτους παρακαλεῖν;
14. Steinby (1974/1975, 1981, 1982, 1987, 1993), Cheung (2024).
15. *Price Edict* 15.97–101; Peña (2007: 27–28).
16. For regions where to purchase dolia, see Cato *Agri.* 135; Anatolios *Geoponika* 6.3.
17. Caillaud (2020).
18. Cheung (2021), Peña (2007), Cheung and Tibbott (2020).
19. See Cheung (2021) for more detailed discussion.
20. On different methods of joining masonry, see Adam (2005), Ulrich (2007), DeLaine (1997, 2010), Lancaster (2004).
21. See Goodman (2016), Murphy (2015).

22. See Cheung (2024: ch. 2).
23. See Gregori (1994) for summary of Cimber's career and discussion on a dolium rim bearing two stamps, one of Redemptus and one of Euphrastus, both of which associate the slaves with Cimber. See Giannella in this volume for discussion of the obligation of Cicero's freedmen to him.
24. *CIL* X 403=483; *IG* 14 71; Mandowsky and Mitchell (1963: 118), n. 127, pl. 71a; Zimmer (1982: 201, n. 146). The Greek name of one individual in the inscription suggests that he was enslaved. See Bodel in this volume for the range in the *praefica*'s professionalization and her embeddedness in a family.
25. Varro *de Re Rustica* 1.13.6. According to Cato, *de Agri Cultura*, 25, wine should ferment for at least thirty days. For variations and transformative qualities of wine, see Thurmond (2017), Van Oyen (2020a: 50–53).
26. Taglietti (2015).
27. Columella *de re rustica* 12.18.5–7.
28. See Poehler (2011), on transporting dolia specifically, see Cheung (2024), Carrato (2017: 149–152), Carroll (2022).
29. See Peña (2007), Cheung (2021), Rando (1998), Cheung and Tibbott (2020).
30. Miller (2009: 37–245).
31. Varro *De Latina Lingua* 5.137; Juvenal *Satire* 14.308–310,
32. On pottery repairs, see Peña (2007), Koob (1998), Elston (1990), Guldager Bilde and Handberg (2012), Dooijes and Nieuwenhuyse (2006), Miloglav (2020). On pithos and dolium repairs, see Peña (2007), Cheung (2021), Cheung and Tibbott (2020), Rotroff (2011), Rando (1998), Giardino (2012).
33. Thornton (1998), Albert (2012), Garachon (2010).
34. For iron working in Pompeii, see Gralfs (1988), Gaitzsch (1980), Amarger and Brun (2007), Amarger (2009). For lead workshops in Pompeii, such as VII.5.28, see Monteix and Rosso (2008). Brun et al. (2005: 329–337): lead and lead-tin objects and a crucible were found.
35. On another interesting hybrid repair at the House of Stabianus (I.22), see Cheung (2021), Cheung and Tibbott (2020), Peña and Cheung (2015).
36. For background on this property, which was a flower garden used for the production of perfume, see Jashemski (1979a: 267–288), 1979b, 1993: 138).
37. Perhaps this was a way to train younger members of the workshop; child labor was not uncommon in antiquity, see Laes (2008) for overview.
38. See Holleran in this volume for a case of itinerant workers in Spain.
39. Of course, the experiences and status of itinerant workers probably differed depending on their skillsets and whether they were free, freed, or enslaved.
40. Pirandello (1927).

41. Poehler et al. (2019), Poehler and Crowther (2018).
42. See discussion in Cheung (2021: 184).
43. Wootton et al. (2013), Claridge (1990).
44. Carandini (1985).
45. Columella *Rust.* 1.3.6. Plin. *HN* 18,36; Juv. 14,24; cf. Ov. *Pont.* 1,6,31.
46. SHA *Hadr.* 18.10.
47. *Digest* 9.2.27.35. I thank David Phillips for bringing this to my attention.
48. Vineyard and wine industry work had occupational hazards, see Youakim (2006).
49. Holcombe and Holcombe (1998), Calfas (2018).
50. Koverman (1998a, 1998b). See also papers in Spinozzi (2022).
51. Lm August 16, 1857, at the Greenville County Museum of Art, Greenville, SC. Todd (2008: 239): "In this, Dave's most personal poem, he wonders openly about distant family members. He was apparently separated from this kinfolk three times during his life: in his youth, when he became property of Harvey Drake; in 1836, when Reuben Drake took his other slaves to Louisiana; and in 1847, when Rev. John Landrum's estate was broken up. Here, years after these events, Dave seems to still be burdened by them."
52. Todd (2008: 5), Baldwin (1993: 77).
53. See Calfas (2018) for discussion of the working conditions of an industrial-scale pottery.
54. Giannella in this volume highlights the (limited) range of movement for Cicero's freedmen Tiro and Chrysippus.

Bibliography

Adam, J. P. 2005. *Roman Building: Materials and Techniques*. Routledge.

Albert, K. 2012. "Ceramic Rivet Repair: History, Technology, and Conservation Approaches." *Studies in Conservation* 57 supl: S1–S8.

Amarger, M.P. 2009. "Le meilleur et le pire serviteur de l'humanité.' Fer, forges et forgerons à Pompéi." In Brun, J.-P. ed. *Artisanats antiques d'Italie et de Gaule: Mélanges offerts à Maria Francesca Buonaiuto.* Publications du Centre Jean Bérard.

Amarger, M.P. and Brun, J-P. 2007. "La forge dell'insula I, 6, 1 de Pompéi." *Quaderni di studi pompeiani* 1: 147–68.

Appadurai, A, ed. 1986. *The Social Life of Things: Commodities in Cultural Perspective* Cambridge University Press.

Baldwin, C. 1993. *Great and Noble Jar: Traditional Stoneware of South Carolina.* University of Georgia Press.

Blitzer, H. 1990. "ΚΟΡΩΝΕΪΚΑ: Storage-Jar Production and Trade in the Traditional Aegean." *Hesperia: The Journal of the American School of Classical Studies at Athens* 59.4: 675–711.

Brennan, A., Chugh, J. S. and Kline, T. 2002. "Traditional versus open office design: A longitudinal field study." *Environment and behavior* 34.3: 279–299.

Brenni, G. M. R. 1985. "The *dolia* and the Sea-Borne Commerce of Imperial Rome." Unpublished Master's Thesis, Texas A&M University.

Brun, J.-P., et al. 2005. "Pompéi, Herculanum (Naples) et Saepinum (Molise): recherches sur l'artisanat antique." *Mélanges de l'École française de Rome. Antiquité* 117.5: 317–339.

Caillaud, C. 2020. "Pour une meilleure compréhension des vinifications antiques en dolia: Approches expérimentales et ethnographiques." In Carrato, C. and Cibecchini, F., eds. *Nouvelles recherches sur les dolia: L'exemple de la Méditerranée nord-occidentale à l'époque romaine (Ier s. av. J.-C.–IIIes. ap. J.-C.)*, 141–156. Editions de l'Association de la Revue archéologique de Narbonnaise.

Calfas, G. 2018. "Shifted Perspectives on Dave: Implications of Archaeological Excavation at the Pottersville Kiln Site." In Chaney, M., ed. *Where Is All My Relation? The Poetics of Dave the Potter*. 58–79. Oxford University Press.

Carandini, A., ed. 1985. *Settefinestre. Una villa schiavistica nell'Etruria Romana*. Panini.

Carrato, C. 2017. *Le Dolium, en Gaule Narbonnaise (i[er] s. av. J.-C.–iiie s. ap. J.-C.): contribution à l'histoire socio-économique de la Méditerranée nord-occidentale, Collection mémoires, 46*. Ausonius.

Carrato, C. and Cibecchini, F., eds. 2020. *Nouvelles recherches sur les Dolia: l'exemple de la Méditerranée nord-occidentale à l'époque romaine (i[er] s. av. J.-C.–iiie s. ap. J.-C.); actes de la table ronde tenue à Aspiran les 26 et 27 septembre 2013*. Éditions de l'Association de la Revue archéologique de Narbonnaise.

Carroll, M. 2022. "Viticulture, opus *dolia*re, and the patrimonium Caesaris at the Roman imperial estate at Vagnari (Puglia)." *Journal of Roman Archaeology* 1–26.

Cheung, C. 2021. "Precious Pots: Making and Repairing *Dolia*." in Hochscheid, H. and Russell, B. eds. *The Value of Making: Theory and Practice in Ancient Craft Production*. 171–88. Brepols.

Cheung, C. 2024. *Dolia: The Containers That Made Rome an Empire of Wine*. Princeton University Press.

Cheung, C. and G. Tibbott. 2020. "The *Dolia* of Regio I, Insula 22: Evidence for the Production and Repair of *Dolia*." in Osanna, M and Toniolo, L. eds. *Fecisti Cretaria: Dal frammento al contest; studi sul vasellame ceramic del territorio vesuviano, Studi e ricerche del Parco archeologico di Pompei, 40*. 175–85. 'L'Erma' di Bretschneider.

Claridge, A. 1990. "Ancient Techniques of Making Joins in Marble Statuary." in True, M. and Podany, J. eds. *Marble: Art Historical and Scientific Perspectives on Ancient Sculpture*. 135–62. Paul Getty Museum.

DeLaine, J. 2010. "Structural Experimentation: The Lintel Arch, Corbel and Tie in Western Roman Architecture." *World Archaeology* 21.3: 407–24.
DeLaine, J. 1997. "The Baths of Caracalla: A Study in the Design, Construction, and Economics of Large-Scale Building Projects in Imperial Rome." *Journal of Roman Archaeology Supplementary Series* 25.
De Simone, G. F. 2017. "The agricultural economy of Pompeii: Surplus and Dependence." In Flohr, M. and Wilson, A., eds. *The economy of Pompeii*. 23–51. Oxford University Press.
Dooijes, R. and Nieuwenhuyse, O.P. 2006. "Ancient Repairs: Techniques and Social Meaning." in Bentz, M. and Kästner, U., eds. *Konservieren oder restaurieren: Die Restaurierung griechischer Vasen von der Antike bis heute, Beihefte zum Corpus vasorum antiquorum, 3*. 15–20. Beck.
Elston, M. 1990. "Ancient Repairs of Greek Vases in the J. Paul Getty Museum." *The J. Paul Getty Museum Journal* 18: 53–68.
Gaitzsch, W. 1980. *Eiserne römische Werkzeuge: Studien zur römischen Werkzeugkunke in Italien und den nördlichen Provinzen des Imperium Romanum*. British Archaeological Reports.
Garachon, I. 2010. "Old Repairs of China and Glass." *The Rijksmuseum Bulletin* 58: 34–55.
Gianfrotta, P. A., and Hesnard, A. 1987. "Due Relitti Augustei Carichi di Dolia: Quelli di Ladispoli del Grand Ribaud D." In *El vi a l'antiguitat: Economia, producció i comerç al Mediterrani occidental, I Colloqui d'Arqueologia Romana*, 285–297. Badalona: Museu de Badalona Monogradies Badalonines.
Giardino, C. 2012. "Archaeometric Analyses of Metal, Glass, and Plaster." in Lapadula, E. ed. *The Chora of Metaponto, iv: The Late Roman Farmhouse at San Biagio*. 194–207. University of Texas Press.
Goodman, P. 2016. "Working Together: Clusters of Artisans in the Roman City." in Wilson, A. and Flohr, M., eds. *Urban Craftsmen and Traders in the Roman World, Oxford Studies on the Roman Economy*. 301–33. Oxford University Press.
Gralfs, B. 1988. *Metallverarbeitende Produktionsstätten in Pompeji*. Oxford University Press.
Gregori, G.L. 1994. "Un nuovo bollo *doli*are di Q. Tossius Cimber." *Publications de l'École Française de Rome* 193.1: 547–553.
Guldager-Bilde, P. and Handberg, S. 2012. "Ancient Repairs on Pottery from Olbia Pontica." *American Journal of Archaeology* 116.3: 461–81.
Haapakangas, A., Hongisto, V., Varjo, J., and M. Lahtinen. 2018. "Benefits of quiet workspaces in open-plan offices–Evidence from two office relocations." *Journal of Environmental Psychology* 56: 63–75.
Heslin, K. 2011. "Dolia shipwrecks and the wine trade in the Roman Mediterranean." In Robinson, D. and A. Wilsin, eds. *Maritime Archaeology and Ancient Trade in the Mediterranean*. 157–68. Oxford Centre for Maritime Archaeology, Institute of Archaeology.

Hesnard, A., Carre, M. B., Rival, M., Dangréaux, B., Thinon, M., Blaustein, M., Chéné, A., Foliot, P., and Bernard-Maugiron, H. 1988. "*L'épave romaine* Grand Ribaud D (Hyères, Var)." *Archaeonautica* 8.1: 5–180.

Holcombe, J. and Holcombe, F.E. 1998. "Archaeological Findings." in Koverman. 72–81. University of South Carolina Press.

Jashemski, W. 1979a. *The Gardens of Pompeii, Herculaneum and the Villas Destroyed by Vesuvius, vol. 1.* Caratzas.

Jashemski, W. 1979b. "'The Garden of Hercules at Pompeii' (II.viii.6): The Discovery of a Commercial Flower Garden." *American Journal of Archaeology* 83.4: 403–11.

Koob, S. 1998. "Obsolete Fill Materials Found on Ceramics." *Journal of the American Institute for Conservation* 37: 49–67.

Kopytoff, I. 1986. "The Cultural Biography of Things: Commoditization as Process." In Appadurai, A. ed. *The Social Life of Things: Commodities in Cultural Perspective*. 64–91. Cambridge University Press.

Koverman, J.B. 1998a. *I Made This Jar: The Life and Works of the Enslaved African-American Potter, Dave.* University of South Carolina Press.

Koverman, J.B. 1998b. "Searcing for Messages in Clay: What Do We Really Know About Dave?" In J.B. Koverman (ed.), *I Made This Jar: The Life and Works of the Enslaved African-American Potter, Dave.* 19–38. McKissick Museum, University of South Carolina.

Laes, C. 2008. "Child slaves at work in Roman Antiquity." *Ancient Society* 38: 235–283.

Lancaster, L. C. 2004. *Concrete Vaulted Construction in Imperial Rome: Innovations in Context.* Cambridge University Press.

Mandowsky, E. and Mitchell, C. 1963. *Pirro Ligorio's Roman Antiquities; The Drawings in MS XIII. B. 7 in the National Library in Naples,* Vol. 28. The Warburg Institute.

Miller, H. M.-L. 2009. *Archaeological Approaches to Technology.* Left Coast Press.

Miloglav, I. 2020. "Drills and Holes—Pottery Repairing as Evidence of the Social Meaning of an Object." *Quaternary International* 569–70: 120–27.

Monteix, N. and E. Russo. 2008. "L'artisanat du plomb à Pompéi." *Mélanges de l'Ecole française de Rome-Antiquité* 120: 241–247.

Murphy, E. A. 2015. "Socially Embedded Work Practices and Production Organization: Beyond industry lines." *Journal of Mediterranean Archaeology* 28.2: 221–39.

Pallecchi, S. 2008. "Le fornaci romane di Albinia: identificazione delle unità funzionali e prima ricostruzione delle linee di produzione." In Acconcia, V. and Rizzitelli, C., eds. *Materiali per Populonia 7,* 323–338. Edizioni ETS.

Peña, J. T. 2007. *Roman Pottery in the Archaeological Record.* Cambridge University Press.

Peña, J. T. and Cheung, C. 2015. "The Pompeii Artifact Life History Project: Conceptual Basis and Results of First Three Seasons." in Gambardella, C., ed. *Heritage and Technology: Mind, Knowledge, Experience; Le Vie degli mercanti XIII forum internazionale di studi, Fabbrica della conoscenza, 56.* 2115–23. La scuola di Pitagora.

Peña, J. T. and McCallum, M. 2009a. "The Production and Distribution of Pottery at Pompeii: A Review of the Evidence; Part 1, Production." *American Journal of Archaeology* 113.1: 57–79.

Peña, J. T. and McCallum, M. 2009b. "The Production and Distribution of Pottery at Pompeii: A Review of the Evidence; Part 2, the Material Basis for Production and Distribution." *American Journal of Archaeology* 113.2: 165–201.

Pirandello, L. 1927. *La giara: novelle per un anno.* Mondadori.

Poehler, E. E. 2011. "Where to Park? Carts, Stables and the Economics of Transport in Pompeii." In Laurence, R, and Newsome, D., eds. *Rome, Ostia and Pompeii: Movement and Space.* 194–214. Routledge.

Poehler, E. E. and B. M. Crowther. 2018. "Paving Pompeii: The Archaeology of Stone-Paved Streets." *American Journal of Archaeology* 122.4: 579–609.

Poehler, E. E., van Roggen, J., and Crowther, B.M. 2019. "The Iron Streets of Pompeii." *American Journal of Archaeology* 123.2: 237–62.

Rando, G. 1998. "Le antiche riparazioni in piombo sui *dolia* provenienti dal relitto della nave romana del golfo di Diano Marina." In *XXVIII Convegno 1995: centri di produzione, botteghe e committenza; fonti d'archivio, evidenza archeologica e studi ceramologi; XXIX Convegno 1996; la ceramica nell'iconografia, l'iconografia nella ceramica; rapporti tra ceramica e arte figurativa, Atti dei Convegni Internazionali della Ceramica* All'Insegna del Giglio.

Rice, C. 2016. "Shipwreck cargoes in the western Mediterranean and the organization of Roman maritime trade." *Journal of Roman Archaeology* 29: 165–192.

Rotroff, S. I. 2011. "Mended in Antiquity: Repairs to Ceramics at the Athenian Agora." in Lawall, M.L. and Lund, J., eds. *Pottery in the Archaeological Record: Greece and Beyond.* 117–34. Aarhus University Press.

Skibo, J. 1992. *Pottery Function: Use-Alteration Perspective.* Springer.

Spinozzi, A., ed. 2022. *Hear Me Now: The Black Potters of Old Edgefield, South Carolina.* Metropolitan Museum of Art.

Steinby, E. M. 1993. "Ricerche sull'industria *dolia*re nelle aree di Roma and e Pompei: un possibile modello interpretativo," in Zaccaria, C., ed. *I Laterizi di Età Romana nell'Area Nordadriatica.* 9–14. L'Erma di Bretschneider.

Steinby, E. M. 1987. "Indici complementari ai bolli *dolia*ri urbani (CIL. XV,1)". *Acta Instituti Romani Finlandiae* 11.

Steinby, E. M. 1982. "I Senatori e l'Industria Laterizia Urbana." *Tituli* 4: 227–237.

Steinby, E. M. 1981. "La diffusione dell'opus *dolia*re urbano." In Giardina, A. and Schiavone, A., eds. *Società romana e produzione schiavistica, II.* 237–245. Laterza.

Steinby, E. M. 1974/5. "La cronologia delle figlinae *doli*ari urbane dalla fine dell'età repubblicana fino all'inizio delIII sec." *Bullettino della Commissione Archeologica Comunale di Roma* 84: 7–132.

Taglietti, F. 2015. "*Dolia* e coperchi di *dolia*: problematici assortimenti." in Spanu, M., ed. *Opus doliare Tiberinum: atti delle giornate di studio.* 267–29 Università degli Studi della Tuscia.

Thornton, J. 1998. "A Brief History and Review of the Early Practice and Materials of Gap-Filling in the West." *Journal of the American Institute for Conservation* 37: 3–22.

Thurmond, D.L. 2017. *From Vines to Wines in Classical Rome A Handbook of Viticulture and Oenology in Rome and the Roman West.* Brill.

Todd, L. 2008. *Carolina Clay. The Life and Legend of the Slave Potter Dave.* W.W. Norton & Company.

Ulrich, R. 2007. *Roman Woodworking.* Yale University Press.

Van Oyen, A. 2015. "The moral architecture of villa storage in Italy in the 1st c. BC." *Journal of Roman Archaeology* 28: 97–123.

Van Oyen, A. 2020a. *The socio-economics of Roman storage: agriculture, trade, and family.* Cambridge University Press.

Van Oyen, A. 2020b. "Innovation and investment in the Roman rural economy through the lens of Marzuolo (Tuscany, Italy)." *Past & Present* 248.1: 3–40.

Van Oyen, A., Tol, G.W. & Vennarucci, R.G. 2021. "The missing link. A nucleated rural centre at Podere Marzuolo (Cinigiano – Grosseto)." In Sebastiani, A. and C. Megale, C. eds. *Archaeological Landscapes of Roman Etruria. Research and Field Papers.* 237–250. Brepols.

Van Oyen, A., Tol, G.W., Vennarucci, R.G., Agostini, A. de, Serneels, V., Mercuri, A.M., Rattighieri, E. & Benatti, A. 2022. "Forging the Roman rural economy. A blacksmithing workshop and its toolset at Marzuolo (Tuscany)." *American Journal of Archaeology* 126.1: 53–77.

Wohlers, C. and G. Hertel. 2017. "Choosing where to work at work–towards a theoretical model of benefits and risks of activity-based flexible offices." *Ergonomics* 60.4: 467–486.

Wootton, W., Russell, B., and Rockwell, P. 2013. "Stoneworking Techniques and Processes (Version 1.0)', The Art of Making in Antiquity: Stoneworking in the Roman World." http://www.artofmaking.ac.uk/content/essays/3-stoneworking-techniques-and-processesw-wootton-b-russell-p-rockwell/ [accessed 1 May 2021].

Youakim, S., 2006. "Occupational health risks of wine industry workers." *British Columbia Medical Journal* 48(8): 386–391.

Zimmer, G. 1982. *Römische Berufsdarstellungen.* Gebrüder Mann Verlag.

PART II

Showing Up

CHAPTER 5

Looking at the Laboring: Fictions, "Realities", and a Culture of Competence

Ann Kuttner

Introduction

Why did people look at images of work and workers and discuss exertion by visible means, in the Roman world? What did they get from looking at others' competencies? In this chapter I focus on representational artifacts: images, objects, and monuments, as well as the settings that they charged with meaning and that shaped response to them.[1] I consider avenues of further attention and posit both questions and premises for the importance of "looking at the laboring".[2] Across a host of academic disciplines, and also in non-academic and popular attention to the Roman imperium, there is a palpable fascination with images and things that implicate Roman "work".[3] Already in the third century, rich people in Latium amused themselves with images on luxury artifacts of lowly people working.[4] Into the Roman sphere migrated examples of the Hellenistic fascination to depict the animated bustle behind real performance that was ritual,

A. Kuttner (✉)
University of Pennsylvania, Philadelphia, PA, USA
e-mail: akuttner@sas.upenn.edu

D. A. Maticic, J. Rogers (eds.), *Working Lives in Ancient Rome*, The New Antiquity,
https://doi.org/10.1007/978-3-031-61234-3_5

ceremonious, dramatic, and more, extant in Roman house decorations by the first century BCE, as did mythological images of labor. Think about the megalographic images of the noted red hall of the Villa of the Mysteries at Pompeii, for instance, of ca. 80 BCE:[5] much of the walls' surface shows preparation for religious ritual as well as its enactment. On the long wall where women prepare a ceremony hierarchy seems to play out, with more important/free women assisted by lower-status/slave women. Fitting to my theme is the scene of a young woman having her hair dressed for a bridal ceremony: a female slave does the grooming, while an animated servitor-statue of Cupid holds up the mirror, a pendant divine page watching. Satyr-shepherd and shepherdess tend to goats; a slave-boy assists the ritualists.

But such things did not come into being to fill publications or museum shows on art-and-work: they arose in different contexts, to diverse ends, to provide a spectacle of labors. Repeatedly, printed treatment is positivist: artifacts "illustrate" with what is treated as greater or lesser "fidelity", and images of tools and technology are especially susceptible to this reading. Their visual elements are taxonomized in lean, not ample, ways, in accompaniment to the epigraphic evidence of the funerary monument corpus that, as often used by historians, tells so many of these work stories. Conversely, they are taken as windows into the worker's and businessman's souls, though without always grappling with the materiality of the object. The images, the objects, and structures they animated *only* exist now, both as trace and as cause, because of a broader Roman[6] culture of looking at labor and the laboring. Not all world cultures have made a habit of looking at the laboring by means of images.[7] Why did those who paid for the images want to look at them, and why did they think diverse others would or should look at the images? Those are huge questions, and Greek and Latin ancient texts do not always easily answer them: to some extent, the very objects that pose the queries sketch traces of answers.

The images and artifacts in this chapter are selected from the range between the Late Republic and Late Antiquity for how they bear on a culture of *labor*, *negotium*, and exertion. Not all people within the imperium, at all times, in all possible genres, turned to images of work; our corpus is contingent on classes of artifacts often temporally or spatially confined. One frame I pose is of competency as an esteemed ability, exercised in a society placing extreme value on taking care, on exerting attention and effort toward an end, which I will call *cura*.[8] An esteem for and expectation of labor—*labor* with skill and effort—did indeed cross class lines, even if the master class, being the author class, might derogate the actual worker and profession, as other essays in this volume discuss. Those with the means to labor very little faced, still, heavy social pressure to exert effort, to be competent at something. That esteem for earned and honed competency and its exercise also came by the middle Republic at least to cross the boundary between *negotium* and *otium*, the structuring binary for elite and sub-elite values and practices. The mental, emotional, and physical terrain for images that delineated and denoted *labor* was one both of *negotium* and of *otium*; to take the time to stop and look images over, meditate them, and take satisfaction, challenge, or pleasure from them—was this work, or not-work?[9] At the same time, in the Roman corpus one can sometimes see an intersection of esteem for the products of labor with low esteem of the people involved in its production. This chapter notes a very limited sample of images for the mercantile actors[10] and artisans, a rich source so many have written up, as often to illustrate and document social histories as to examine the artifacts themselves. It also points to the speaking absence of workers' bodies, replaced by their tools and accouterment in some images; and it considers the displacement of human work in human settings onto the not-human, something Roman images intensively do—bodies of beast-men and of children, i.e., satyrs, and Cupids, here (there are more).

For the images in this chapter, makers looked or imagined, for patrons and audiences thought to have wanted to gaze on a spectacle of labor, indeed of any *ars* in action. These makers of a Roman world themselves worked for pay, or as slaves, some with the status of master artificers and even "artists", and others, craftsmen further down the scale. Those represented as laboring sometimes looked too, whether their gaze was intended or discrepant. The lowliest, slave and free, commissioned few images, or none, of themselves, and may have had little or no access to many extant images about themselves; but when they did such picturing could speak of and for the selves of less lowly people who understood themselves to work, whether that might give them bitter thoughts or pleasant ones. When images of workers did occupy the same places where the labor was carried out, it has its own resonance, whether we think of a Roman orator's statue in a space for public speaking, or the image of a shop owner with his staff and wares on the façade of his shop, or for that matter images of slaves in the dwellings where enslaved people lived and worked. As often, what was shown was in a socially and geographically distant place relative to the kind of work depicted, as so often true for images of rural and maritime labor in the heart of cities, for instance, and of peasants inside mansions that no peasant entered. The "city of the dead" in which images spoke to the career and work of the deceased and others' labor for them was ironically removed from the cities, villages, and lands where the spectacle of work was enacted.

No book yet fully discusses the intersection of Roman exertion with art, in this chapter's terms[11]—"Why look?" "Who looks?"—and with its reach across genres, a spread meant to be suggestive even if it has to stay limited.[12] It is true some explore as I do those images which, for master craftsman or professional, manager or contractor, estate owner or commander, gesture to that iconography of the subordinate and the slave worker that compliments the person of superior skill or knowledge or social position. But one should ask for a more sustained review of the imagery of control, command, power, and special knowledge as it affects representational strategies and viewer response. The very tools carved on some funerary monuments were sometimes wielded not by the honorand but by a subordinate. For those surrounding an architect with "tools of the trade", for instance, the square that he might have handled is different to chisel or mallet with which his employees hacked at stones.[13]

Things

This brings up the image of *labor* that is indeed suggested by tools, and implements, and of materials before, during, or at the end of process, that denote the working hand by its very absence, calling on socio-cultural knowledge to fill those gaps, to reimagine hands and persons. That has some pre-Roman Greek precedents, but its great floruit, in monumental and communal art, in habitations, and on objects, is Roman era.[14] There were pre-Roman Greek roots, for instance, in images of arms and armament piled, hung, or abstractly arrayed, a much-studied genre in which Roman public and private art took great interest from the later Republic on; armies and commanders defeated or (when Roman) triumphant could be marshaled metonymically as their equipment, in trophy art of many kinds. The kind of image I have just noted with regard to the funerary corpus, in which objects are arbitrarily distributed on a blank ground, is especially a Roman taste, and it crosses into what art historians talk about as emblem and symbol. Stressed here is the way in which actors' and wearers' bodies and their actions are intimated by those assemblages, because a period viewer could not un-know what they saw. It is not a bad rhetorical gesture to start with these pressingly absent bodies, to introduce themes of interest to images where represented people work and supervise work.

This mode is common on religious buildings and on altars for depictions of implements of ritual, and elements of costume worn by ritualists,[15] just as in funerary art of artisans and artists, merchants and businesspeople, it is common to show the tools, materials, products, armatures of making, even of selling. This tendency follows up on the Roman conviction that piety needs work, with the *labor* of *religio* in mirror relation to what Rogers in his chapter in this volume calls the religion of labor. In these domains of imagery, social structures can further be embedded. Histories of Roman technology, equipment, politics, "religion", society, and sociability depend broadly and deeply on the representational practice of showing such stuff with enormous precision and verisimilitude. When depicted people interact with these things, their postures and gestures also suggest verisimilitude, to the point that people trust such Roman images to show them how-it-was-done. While some compositions passed into a pattern-book culture, at least at the outset one artist has to have gone and actually looked. This seeming mimetic fidelity was important to projects of bearing witness to lived history, meant to engross at least momentarily the passing gaze upon commemoratives. That has to have been generated by an assumption that how-it-is-done could interest the viewer, whether or not those seeing the visual display would have been able to or cared to penetrate the spaces of the work itself. The presence of the tool, the equipment, and accouterment promise there is an *ars*, a skill, that demands their wielding, and in some assemblages, an *ars* of management and oversight: a competence of some kind. What are in English often called still-lives, in which things are disposed pictorially as if in a plausible physical world, speak to the world of *labor*, of craft, of *negotium* in similar ways, evoking persons, users, actions, and settings up and down the social scale of physical and mental skill or exertion.

Think, for instance, of the assemblages of writing equipment and documentary media and even money bags, in the painted celebrations of good and profitable businesses surviving from some elite spaces at Pompeii.[16] They could evoke the single assiduous and talented man (or woman); they could also evoke the assiduous owner and manager of slaves and freedpeople. A huge world of work and expertise that ran from field, sea, and forest into markets and kitchens was encoded in the "still-life" genre that scholars call *xenia*, showing animalia and other things that will end up being eaten. The tag comes from Vitruvius' Augustan-era *On Architecture*

(6.7.4), a confused pronouncement that ancient Greek dinner hosts gave guests cooking ingredients to take home after dinner, but they might, in lieu of the real thing, give pictures of the stuff. The actual images extant that correspond to Vitruvius' text are proleptic of a meal, not retrospective. Whatever their lost Hellenistic prototypes (if there were any) they developed and recurred from the first century BCE into Late Antiquity, in, e.g., domestic (and some commercial) wall painting, domestic floor mosaic, and fine vessels for the table. Always, produce, animals, birds, and fish have been at least partly processed (gathered, cut, trussed, hung), on their way to being manipulated by (servile) cooks' cunning to be brought (by slaves) to table for consumption. This feast for the eye signals workers: hands have grown, reaped, gathered, pastured, fished, trapped and hunted, they have baled and trussed and carted, they have trafficked, purchased, carried; working hands will wash and chop and kill (when we see live animals and birds), clean, and cook.

Empires of extraction and commerce, labor and skill are imaged in the *xenia* genre. The game of images is to make appealing pictures out of what (like dead fish) one would not actually use to decorate a space of representation, showing things that the patron class might not ever handle or process. But patron competency, like that of a good cook, knows the taste of things, even though the producers and handlers of foodstuffs might have seldom or never been able to afford to eat what they touched. Work is at once evoked and erased, in these visually appealing pictures that take one into pantry and kitchen to promise a loaded table.[17] For the people who commissioned images, the work imaged is not the work they do. When it comes to fine houses and villas, many in an intended audience might seldom or never enter a working kitchen. It is, instead, the work they command, exploit, and own.

Art about Roman religious ritual recurs to "thing art" too, from at least the first century onward.[18] All over Rome, Latium, and eventually around the imperium (especially in the west) emerge small stone altars, for instance, onto which are carved a patera, and a jug for filling it. These are funerary, votive, communal. They indicate a free person leading the sacrificial libation with that patera in hand and also the kin or slave who handled the jug to fill the patera held out to them by the ritualist. A slave, too, is to be construed as carrying the vessels for their ritualist master to the place of observance. Thus, users and viewers of the altar will respond differently, with potentially diverse visual, bodily, and emotional memories. The very late Republican or Augustan friezes (late first century BCE to early first century CE) sometimes associated with the Portico of Octavia, in Rome,[19] make the first extant example of a durable genre for the entablatures of sanctuary structures that displayed things to celebrate and denote grand official ceremonies. They are pendant to, and represent an alternative mode to, actual representations of people in ceremony—that, also a large Roman monumental genre, which makes a large proportion of the so-called historical reliefs that fronted a range of structures, sacred and political.

Here, side by side are, for instance, an aristocratic officiant's *lituus*, and another's *flamen*'s cap, and beside them are the whisk and killing tools (axe and knife) wielded by the state slaves at the sacrifice, the incense box and jug those attendants held, the fine towel one carried, the ladle another would bring, a patera for a noble priest's hand. All the objects matter. The box and jug and patera are beautiful, ornamented objects whose decoration adds *venustas* to the decoration of the splendid building which the frieze decorated, in proximity, it seems, to a temple. A working staff, and at least partly a slave staff, spring to mind: the anticipated elite viewer sees what they might hold and also what they will likely never at all touch. But it is the ritualist who knows what must happen, what to do, and what to say. Just so in fleshed-out images of ritual processions and performances on so many Roman public monuments, a free elite that moves to perform piety is often side by side with assistant slaves who do the work of managing and killing animal victims and manage the deployment of offerings of liquids, foods, and incense, while a staff of slave or paid musician(s) supplies appropriate sounds.

It is striking, indeed, that a good bit of Roman religious-political art in the late Republic and empire gives emphatic visual space to these lowly but indispensable workers, with bodies in interesting and even elegant postures. Sometimes, their bodies were even aesthetically appealing. So we see athletically muscled torsos and fine displays of strength by the *victimarii* with their naked upper bodies who handle the animal slaying and animal handling on the so-called Villa Medici reliefs, which come from an early Julio-Claudian monumental structure at Rome.[20] That the sight of worker bodies and slave bodies bared, in Roman arts, and in the live spectacle of labor, could be an occasion to celebrate appealing nudity bears thought. Such *victimarii* are like displaced signs of the virility and strength of the bodies under the clothing of the aristocrats for whom they are shown to work. Older boys and adolescents, slaves who served the free protagonists at altar rituals, *camilli*, are in commemorative art tagged as fine-looking boys: as they adorned a rite, so they adorned, also, images of rite, at once working person and a human object of ritual technology. That role is clear, for instance, for the miniaturized long-haired (so, "lovely") *ministri* who flank and handle, as if tending, a flaming candelabrum, in what work as ornamental spacer bars to separate the panel reliefs of imperial prowess on the façades of Trajan's Arch at Beneventum.[21] They are analogues in official art, with veristic reference to actual liveried *camilli*, to the (in)famous beautiful boys and adolescents, costumed in nakedness, who, in costly bronze, decorated the spaces of eating and drinking in the houses of well-to-do Romans as human-furniture hybrids carrying trays and lamp-holders.[22]

Desirable Things and Their Making

I turn to one of the monuments that first preoccupied me with thinking about the Romans' art of *ars*, the compulsion to detail seemingly real process, that co-existed with a tendency toward outright fantasy. That is the frieze of the emperor Domitian's "imperial forum" precinct at Rome, the so-called Forum Transitorium (almost completed by 96 CE), or, named for the successor of the assassinated Domitian who claimed to complete the temple portion and (re)dicated it in 97 CE, Forum of Nerva. Minerva's temple presided—the emperor's avowed patron deity, goddess of Rome, empire, war, and all *artes*. The elongated precinct took over the footprint of an existing wide boulevard, the Argiletum that connected the Forum Romanum with the Subura and its bustling shops, as well as the street-life of the middling classes with the more lowly.[23] There was no room for the full colonnades that lined the broader piazzas of earlier imperial fora—Forum Julium, for Venus Genetrix, and, flanking Domitian's piazza, the Forum Augustum, for Mars Ultor; and the Templum Pacis for the goddess Peace set up by Domitian's father Vespasian. Instead, the inner wall format of some temples lines this space, with columns on spur plinths making reticulated bays, an entablature carrying a figural frieze, under bays which showcased reliefs of the personified peoples of empire—female bodies, depicted as dutiful subjects.

Visual praise of *ars* and labor is woven into the making of the imperium. One full bay is left, with a bit of spur-wall, and of another bay: the frieze hails Minerva and making. A women's workshop for textile production, busy with looms and wool workers, is the setting for the myth of weaver Arachne who centers the bay, fallen to her knees—Minerva is about to strike her and make her into a spider. The scenario is strongly suggestive of Ovid's *Metamorphoses* (7.1–146), explored by Formisano in this volume, and by Domitian's day, a beloved classic. Read in *otium*, images inspired by it here graced both strollers' leisure and the business of forum and imperium—and *religio*. For those who recalled Ovid, compelling art was being made and in their mind would be more images, those of the contest Formisano here discusses: Arachne's web, telling the lust of male gods for females, human, supernatural, and divine (stories of the gods' rapes were indeed wildly popular in texts and sometimes art); Minerva's web with her victory on the Athenian Acropolis over Neptune to claim the role of Athens' divine governor, and Juno's punishments of hubristic challengers. The sculptors, at the behest of whatever programmatic director (Domitian will surely have had the program explained to him, and perhaps tweaked it), wove light and shadow, form and void, a ribbon banding this space that was once bright with color into their own web of Minerva's triumph. The extant bay suggests the Forum Transitorium had more myths of the goddess' spheres of command; perhaps one can imagine other myths of making too, even without Minerva in the narrative.

For people who look at Roman images of work, this case is repeatedly evoked[24] and often seen as the sole extant "imperial" monument of non-military "work" in a dynast's monument. Its ideological freight has been much meditated.[25] Domitian, like Augustus before him, wished to perform the role of moral rector of social values; here were the lives of women put on show, performing the tasks of wool-working and weaving central to the image of the virtuous, and virtuously industrious, Roman free woman in the spaces of her home. We can note that a slave or a hired textile worker accumulated no such virtue: she did what she had to do, although a *domina* overseeing a household's textile workers still could be thought both admirably careful and appropriately engaged in so doing.

What interests this chapter is all the visual detail in this bay—the work, bustle, equipment, etc. The story needs only Minerva, Arachne, and a loom. Instead, we get profusion—a detailed view of stuff women do with wool, staged for the crowds of all classes using this Forum-avenue. As in Ovid the story's setting is a workshop, here imagined as a modern professional one of several textile producers,[26] in their midst an ancient weaver. This could speak to any in the crowd. Elite men and women could think these carved women producers, like Arachne, of the luxury textiles people craved, beautifully patterned and colorful, for couches, hanging, or garments; sub-elites, as well as those more powerful might, have their own slave staffs of textile workers. Even the lower classes were textile buyers, or wished to be; some might be merchants and producers small and large, dealing in wool and dye and cloth, owning textile workshops (and managing women). The expanse of detail, as if looking at labor could be fun, is significant: the crowd in the Forum gets to see a bit of manufacture just as if walking Rome's streets of workshops and businesses.[27]

Making an artistic spectacle of how-something-is-done as at the Forum Transitorium is not alone in the second half of the first century CE (or before); it happens in domestic contexts also, put on show by people engaged in *negotium* as business. It is well worth asking if imperial art is impacted by the art of the employed and employers, from grand tombs to *collegium* displays, as Rogers in this volume closely examines them also: that is, trickle-up rather than trickle-down. His exemplum is the monument of the guild of fine carpenters, makers of elegant wooden furnishings, the *tignarii*, where Minerva as self or statue looks at the busy artisans (Fig. 8.1 at p. 229 and Fig. 8.2 at p. 232). For the Forum Transitorium's depicted workshop, the obvious comparison is to the House of the Vettii, rich brothers and likely freedpeople, at Pompeii, in the home's painting program of the later 60s CE: a prominent reception room (q) domesticates the urban workshop scene, evokes a ramble through a town by means of images of Cupids (and sometimes Psyches) laboring and vending, and Psyches buying. Famous in Roman art histories, the eye-catching miniaturist frieze is well placed for the gaze of seated guests; remains of similar wall paintings from the Vesuvian zone testify there was a recognized genre of multiple worker-workshop-Cupids in miniaturist panels. The ring of scenes in *oecus* q which takes one past shop and workshop fronts into busy interiors is interesting to compare, at Pompeii, to the illusionistic prospect of a fantasized forum in a frieze from the hotel (*praedia*) of Julia Felix (D'Ambra 2021); here, outdoors commerce, shopping, and strolling people of various classes animate fine portico colonnades, with commemorative statues looming overhead.[28]

This stuff is famous in Roman art history and social history. It mapped for the privileged inhabitants, scholarship notes, the labor exploited to make their own clothes, perfumes, garlands, and vessels, with a distancing that gave them satisfaction in their own relatively high status.[29] Here and in comparable spaces, by means of both miniaturization and the apparently effortless working motions, "the harsh reality of work is thus suppressed in favor of a romantical, almost whimsical version of it".[30]

That is true: but it does not explain away the proliferation of detail, of process expounded, that is still one among the pictorial pleasures in this genre at the House of the Vettii and several other domestic spaces at Pompeii and Herculaneum. Surely, Rome housed such spaces also. It does not explain the indulged wish to peer inside even the noisiest and dirtiest working quarters of shops in art. A habit of curiosity and a taste for the spectacle of production ask for analysis at such houses. At Pompeii, shop-fronts and the customer spaces of businesses from tavern to *fullonica* (textile-cleaning business) might put veristic laboring and vending on show, sometimes with owner presiding:[31] in the *domus* the experience is of "art". In scenes of fields and workshops, bodies that might be sweaty, stinking, unlovely (or by converse dauntingly muscular), turn into cute child bodies, making the visual visit even more appealing, even comic. The genre must have spoken with point to a caste of people—the owners' caste, male and female—who invested in such businesses, worked with labor guilds, and occasionally looked into a shop themselves. House slaves could see other slaves and compare their lot. Happy laborers immune to fatigue could soothe the subjectivities of the patron class, cast potentially resentful or unzealous workers as personifications of affectionate *fides*, or infantilize slaves and workmen as master classes of other slave societies have sometimes done. So too it is actual children who offer guests care and refreshment in the atrium paintings of the same house. In these readings we are in the world of Mitchell's rich 2018 thesis on Cupids acting out in public and private art; she discusses how this huge corpus, in which Cupids often replace (slave) laborers and house- and body-slaves in domestic painting, mosaic, etc., could help a master class think away the disquieting proximities to its own person of subject bodies.

That the Vettii brothers were interested to map worlds of work on their house walls, or at least that their painters were concerned to do it for them, is borne out by how one of the noted rooms here with a triad of mythological scenarios evokes, twice, master craftsmen and their workshop production, in ways that push on the social tensions of bespoke artisanry. The Ixion room depicts on one side Daedalus in his atelier, wearing a workman's one-shouldered tunic, a slave busy at work in the corner; he is showing off to queen Pasiphae a magically real, wheeled heifer simulacrum he has made, to answer her demand he help her mate with her husband Minos' prize bull. Into this cow-machine she can insert herself to lure the bull into copulation. The centerpiece panel that gives the room its name shows Juno gazing (perhaps intrigued?) at the mechanism made to punish her would-be rapist Ixion. A big wooden wheel to spin forever in the heavens, Ixion already bound to it, is wheeled before her by Mercury like a master mechanic.

It is disturbing how these images of mythic females looking at terrible engines made for them resonate with *oecus* q's Psyches, who sit in shops to look at what workshops made for them. The brothers who, most think, owned the house were perhaps freedpeople, and certainly prosperous, which is to say, invested in their town, perhaps beyond it. On the understanding they were freed slaves, their house decor is often discussed as shedding light on ex-slaves' psyches and even the aesthetic preferences of freedpeople. I have issues with that reading: but the meditation on kinds of *negotium*, *otium*, constraint, and freedom is unquestionably a leitmotif in the house. How it spoke to the people performing physical labor in the house—its own slaves—is a complex issue; whether or not by design, the program in aggregate could impact those working with their hands at this compound, enforcing the master's controlling gaze and power to victimize and harm.[32] Yet it is, also, a house where how-to-make-things is celebrated as a competence and an interesting sight—with the making of money a competency also.[33]

The Cupid rooms offer, then, a fine chance to see the class that managed labor and produced luxury objects convey the interesting details of facture and production while putting themselves at the head of actual or implied workforces. Direct from the producer comes the earlier, huge "Baker's Tomb", monument of a late first-century BCE owner, Marcus Vergilius Eurysaces, of an evidently huge baking combine.[34] The Greek cognomen might tag him as a freedperson, though *libertus* is conspicuously absent from the inscription. Not only the scale of his now-famous monument, which alludes to bread processing in its form, and the content of its decoration denote his hard-headed success; his inscription calls him not only baker but also contractor and a man engaged with the city magistracy. In his visual *res gestae*, like the career inscriptions of the aristocracy (and, eventually Augustus) at their tombs and on their public portraits, it is Eurysaces, with some administrative staff, who at a couple of points oversees process, dressed well in the toga that prohibits manual labor. He commands his multitudes; he inspirits; he exercises his competent knowledge of every manufacturing stage. The monument offers to the interested—assumes indeed the interested—an extended visual description of how-it-is-done with glimpses into multiple places of production. A distilled version of such auto-celebration on a small scale is offered by the funerary relief once embedded in a larger structure for a silversmith, of a decorator of luxury silver (a toreutic artist), "Publius Curtilius Agatus, freedman of Publius, silverwork artisan (*faber argentarius*)", unprovenanced but almost certainly from the area of Rome.[35] His high artisanal status is claimed by several things. He is swathed in polite costume (a *himation* or even toga), not a workman's tunic, only the hands visible. He is not bent in toil, nor does he make large motions of brute force: he is seated at a table (it can be construed) to work firmly and delicately on the ornament of a silver vessel (a prized object), with chasing tool in one hand and little mallet in the other for tapping it. The relief purports to place us as visitors to his working quarters, eager to commission from him, perhaps watching what we have already bespoke. He is at the apex of a production chain: out of sight are the workmen tending the forge and hauling its fuel to melt silver bar, casting it or beating it into sheets, and fashioning the body of the vessel so that he can be an artist of ornament and figure. Now a Roman citizen, his face is rendered, as are those of freedpeople on many Republican and early Imperial tomb reliefs in Rome and its region, with Republican-style verism: his visage is marked by lines of middle age hinting at long-practiced skill.

For elite people to look at images of work in the sense it often takes in Romanist studies—lower classes' physical labors—of course entangled with the chances of authors and audiences to watch the working. A range of texts indicate the habits of the flâneur and shopper to poke a nose into workshops. They also show the owner class wanting to hang out with great artificers. Cicero, for instance, vividly depicts the obsessed collector Verres, a corrupt governor of Sicily, assembling artisans in precious metalwork in a huge *officina* in his governor's residence in Syracuse, where he would sit when he could get away to watch the work. Such a man was entranced by what Gell called the "technology of enchantment".[36] Towns afforded the spectacle of work easily; habits of leasing out to shops and workshops the street front *tabernae* of even pretty nice houses, as Pompeii and Herculaneum document, meant free inhabitants of some means lived not only with the working staff within the house, but passed by work spaces in daily movement in and out of the house and not only in districts that were much more frequented for commercial and utilitarian ends. The great *fora* of Roman towns housed market activity, as well as the work of notaries and bankers, served by genres of architecture like the basilica and the market piazza. Evidence fortuitously extant from first-century CE Pompeii shows commercial façades painted to celebrate owner and worker and guild. It would be wonderful to know if other towns and cities showed similar images.

To say that under Trajan the Temple of Venus Genetrix in the nearby Forum Julium, rededicated by him in 113 CE, was given a lavish frieze of bustling workers is to discuss the next generations after the Forum Transitorium (ca. 90–96 CE) and House of the Vettii (60s CE). In this restoration of the Caesarian temple, Cupids worked at their mother's house, impersonating both lowly temple staff and the servants of a household. In the entablature frieze over the interior colonnade, Amores shift and haul objects into place, as furnishings (e.g., a shield of Venus' lover Mars, and the love-gods' quiver), and bring water to a fine basin for Venus' toilette, as if the entablature ledge were the floor of the goddess' sprawling palace, an enlargement of the *cella* in which her statue stood, being readied for celebration. The objects gloss also the accumulation of nice votive things meant to aggregate at the temple.[37] These little divine working bodies salute the labor, *cura*, of the prince who restored the temple.

Competence, Effort, and Power

Of great interest for understanding elite reception of images of how-to-do-it is the phenomenon of how, once upper-crust Romans of the Late Republic and after decided being author was a good thing, they professed competence to estimate work, like Varro in the huge *De Re Rustica* in the first century BCE telling you how to pack fruit in straw and feed pigs, not labors he ever performed. The "treatise habit" invites inquiries into how texts of many kinds, for elite readers, acknowledged and described competencies of many kinds. Others in this volume discuss the anxiety of elites who employed skilled staff to show themselves essential to the results of collaboration: so, an air or actuality of competence was much desired. One kind of competence could be a figure, a cipher, for other kinds of competencies, and those included the earning of cultural capital and socio-political power. *Negotium/otium*, the cognitive and practical binary of Roman life, raises the issue of how "labor" elides with socio-political effort. To be a person of status, a person of power, afforded leisure, and it also demanded effort: care in looking after the family interests, one's own holdings and lands, one's public offices, and even doing cultural work to be a learned and discerning audience for literature and performance. In the highest spheres, exertion was hugely prized, its lack discouraged.[38]

Many centuries' worth of Roman male funerary, domestic, and commemorative portrait sculpture, from the fourth century BCE into Late Antiquity, put on show the lined faces of warlord, magistrate, or man of property. Visible in busy public places, these men looked marked by a career of laudable *cura*. No one's body is paunchy with age: virtuous physical exercise has kept torsos tight, as we see in those portrait statues that bare them. Strong bodies, for the powerful, proved virtuous masculinity because they were the result of voluntary exertion (exercise routines, riding, hunting, walking); these images existed in counterpoint to paid and constrained exertions of the working world around.[39] Lined faces, when they do sometimes occur, demonstrated not just the *gravitas* of the mature and the aged but also laudable *cura* to the point of weariness and beyond. These visual forms were in dialogue with the inscription of career on commemorative statues' bases.[40] Emperors' portraits were sometimes unmarked by age, from Augustus on, but even their faces were sometimes strongly lined, as for many images of Vespasian, Marcus Aurelius, and the third-century rulers, and some portraits of Constantine.[41] Like the very popular images of weary Hercules, worn but not defeated by his own Labors and wanderings,[42] such portraits invited any hard-working subject to feel empathic regard for a great man who worked on their behalf.

To think about the variable coding of labor that depends on the contrast between the voluntary and the coerced or employed, consider the art of the rustic hunt. It was a popular sport for aristocrats from the Late Republic on, when they sojourned at country villas. Hadrian even turned *virtus* at the hunt into a metaphor for imperial defense and conquest when he set up the lost monument from which the well-known reliefs of the imperial hunt now on the Arch of Constantine were extracted. Hunts decorated the sarcophagi, floor mosaics, luxury silver, and other decors of the male elite class of the High and Late Empire, signing elite male *virtus* and providing worthy visual excitement. But a great deal of hunting was not carried out alone by a noble self: paid and enslaved experts and servitors looked after hunting horses and hounds, set out nets and acted as beaters to drive game, handled the butchering of game and its portation back to a residence, and brought along food and drink for a long day's hunt, among others. That entourage in fact sometimes figures in art about the admirable hunter. He voluntarily chooses a sport taking cunning, courage, and exercise, cognate to military exertion, and so, virtuous; those hunt assistants are, simply, doing a job.

Spectacles of Ownership

To turn further to service, in the last decades, a harsh spotlight on Roman private abuse of slave bodies has illuminated such gracile monuments as the eponymous image of the House of the Ephebe at Pompeii, an acquiescent lamp-holder, glossing perhaps the owner-class' sexual predation. Such poised bodies exhibit training, in fact, from exercise to sculpt their muscles to implied instruction on how to stand and serve. If they delight the owner, they also gesture to his competency in running a slave household of well-behaved "pages". In a strange, darker vein, from the same house emerged a box in which were stored a set of four matched bronze statuettes for the table, each bearing a silver tray and gesturing with the other hand at the chin, to dress a table with, perhaps, a pinch of salt or pepper. This gang of slaves acts in unison; they are savagely comic (to some Roman tastes), debasing of nakedness, for the men are gaunt and hunched, with huge lank dangling penises. Their pointed beards (not normally worn by Romans of the first century CE) and bowl of slightly long hair make them look like barbarians taken captive. Neither image is a "truth" of the house's staff naked at work. What did the range of house slaves make of these objects?[43]

The well-selected, well-trained slave entourage is a compliment to the slave owner, even if that *dominus* or *domina* works through a trusted intermediary. Such an entourage was meant to please the sight of guests, too, and in the arts might even be marshaled to give that guest hospitality: thus, at the House of the Vettii at Pompeii, the visitor on entering the atrium was met by the sight of children in matching gowns, manipulating vessels to offer him or her a drink, painted around the walls.[44] A consistent habit of staging the elite self in a frame of real contemporary workers, of entourage, in important rooms, is a fascinating emphasis in later Roman art in particular; a noted 2003 essay by Katherine Dunbabin discusses "the waiting servant" in late Roman representation, especially in wall painting, of houses, collegium halls, and tombs. One can add domestic mosaics and images on luxury objects that assisted female grooming. Extending the employer self as constituted by the company it keeps, the servants even dress and groom their owner-employers. For women, images empire-wide of having servants dress their hair, and bring a jewelry box, date back to the Late Republic. The entourage as attribute did not speak only, though, to an elite person's complacency or competency at managing others' labor; it has to have touched also on deep anxieties and not just in competition with others to see who could afford the most enslaved. One should wonder about its intersection with such persons' keeping company on others, whether attending peers in the performance of *amicitia* or clustering officially and unofficially around superiors in a range of hierarchies from the subtle to the overt. The late Roman representational turn to the "waiting servant" is pendant to late Roman images of the emperor with his courtiers, officers, and officials waiting on the dynast's majesty.[45]

Building a World

A good case to grasp the high esteem for competency as it regarded the management of others' labor is that of building at scale. One cannot do a piece on Roman images of work without the building images, increasingly studied. Here I bring them into what I am calling the culture of competence of the elites whose work was often voluntary, the patron class for architecture and urban projects. We even have extant two treatises of what will have been a much larger literature: Vitruvius' *De architectura* on design and engineering of houses, public works, and civic and religious monuments, by a man of skill who had worked on military engines for Caesar, now with some public commissions, and hoping for more; and the work *On Aqueducts* by a noble of the supervisory class, Frontinus, dedicated public servant.

Aristocrats by birth joined what was in effect a moneyed aristocracy. The mercantile, commercial, and landed high elites, from city and town worthies around the imperium to the very grand equestrians with widespread sources of wealth, often expected of themselves and were expected by others to build. During the Republic, the senatorial aristocracy of Rome built roads, aqueducts, basilicas, warehouse compounds, bridges, port facilities, sanctuaries, theaters, and amphitheaters and, from the second century BCE onward at least, put their names to what they oversaw with an inscription on a building. They also engaged in restoration of existing structures. There is in the Republic, in effect, no "state architecture": individuals saw even to official buildings, even when licensed or commissioned by the Senate. Such projects demanded skill at the selection and management of architects, builders, contractors, and the flow of materials, while the success of the splendors of architecture was imputed to the aristocrat even if he delegated it all to a subordinate. By the end of the reign of the first emperor, Augustus, at the capital city only members of the imperial house signed off on important architectural projects, apart from monuments like arches awarded by the SPQR, which may sometimes have been overseen by a senator or senators, absent though their individual names may have been. But the aristocracy as administrators, and city patrons, all around the empire, even outside Rome, might still do some construction and restoration.

This urge to build and to know how to get it done was nurtured by army service: the aristocracy serving their terms as officers and commanders interacted with the armies' *fabri*, the corps of army engineers and architects, who saw to a range of temporary and permanent structures. By the end of the Republic, art started to show commanders (maybe) and emperors as generals overseeing scenes of construction, on some extant small mold-made terracotta plaques. The general-emperor who built the Roman world is famously embodied on Trajan's Column in his Forum at Rome (dedicated, 113 CE), whose spiraling narrative told a story of the Dacian Wars: at least half of the scenes show Roman soldiers busied at works of construction, from felling trees to getting forts put up, and the entire cycle starts with the army crossing a then unparalleled technowonder, the largest pontoon bridge ever made, designed by Apollodorus to bridge the Danube. Trajan inspirits his soldiers in a military sense and tells them his master strategy, in the reliefs (in which he never actually fights) where he orates before and after battle to soldiers and gives audience to returning officers and legionaries: he also is to be understood as overseeing efficient and effective construction, just as the emperor steers Roman hands to build the imperium.[46]

The urge to build applied also to great townhouses and to villas, both in the sense of working estates and as refined residences. And here, we have Roman voices: texts. When his beloved brother Quintus was serving in the provinces for Caesar, Cicero saw to the construction and elaboration of new villas at his brother's properties, in addition to advising further on estates; and he wrote Quintus about this at length.[47] These letters of course boast of the high status of the brothers from Arpinum, as men who own many villas. We read/see, with Quintus, Cicero managing hired labor from masons to contractors to proud architects, visiting the building sites, trying to goad the dilatory, and complaining when stuff is not done right. He can judge results, find the reliable, has a grasp of the intricacies of managing a big project. He (or Atticus) published these letters thinking they would amuse and interest elite readers. The narratives of building the workforce and working with the architect and work teams at the villa site, go beyond the necessarily informative to entertain Quintus, as it were, to make him feel he could be right there, as well as show off his brother's devoted care, his *cura*, in correcting this or that error in construction. It was a new genre of appealing and impressive epistolary ecphrasis, this quite extended treatment of how-to-do, appraisal of the results of labor, utilitarian and elegant design appraisal alike, even if it would have had roots in the working correspondence of estate-owning and house-owning families. Even the ivy arrangements of Quintus' master gardener get a report—they already nicely trail between columns and wreath statues of Greek men-of-mind. The skill at villa-making takes in the much-cited letters in which Cicero corresponds with Atticus about the purchase of statuary for his own villas, with reference to this or that finely designed section of the edifice where the artifacts are meant to go. And laconic but telling is his exchange with Atticus about impressive public works they are respectively overseeing for the warlords Pompey and Caesar; Atticus helped Pompey with his temple-theater-garden complex for Venus Victrix (*Letters to Atticus* 85 (4.9)), while Cicero, in a period of *amicitia* with Caesar, oversaw building at the huge complex of the Saepta Julia (*Letters to Atticus* 89 (4.16)), with precise details of what "we will make a most glorious thing". Fiction responded to these scenarios: Virgil, in the *Aeneid* (I.419–438), has Aeneas fascinated by his first glimpse of Carthage, described as a colony under construction, full of busy workmen—even a theater is going up. This is a key psychological moment when Aeneas grasps what it would be to find a new home for his refugee people (1.437: "O fortunate people, those whose walls already rise!"). Part of his dalliance with Dido, in fact, is that he takes to overseeing the construction, at which Mercury, sent by Jupiter to force Aeneas to leave for Italy, finds him and upbraids him (*Aen.* 4.259–67).

In such texts, competency is highly extolled; the elite patron may have to depend on a skilled architect and, of course, on many skills of labor, but one is still superior in the sense of understanding, choosing, making-it-all-happen. Hand-in-hand go the praises of the wonderful new buildings that emperors had erected, sung by poets starting in the Augustan period like Ovid and Propertius; Statius and Martial would later celebrate Domitian's works. It is instructive to read Vitruvius, an architect with a background in army engineering, and wishful of patronage by the emperor Augustus to whom *On Architecture* is addressed, praised for his own building projects (Preface, 1–3). The treatise is aimed at other practitioners but also imagines a patron class might read it for some instruction and out of curiosity, and that Augustus, at least, might dip into it. From the professional's point of view, relations with the patron class are negotiated in the preface, often discussed as the text of a man trying to elevate the status of architect to that of esteemed profession (I.1.1–18). So, he promises that a good architect understands a whole host of estimable intelligent *artes*, can draw for you, and converse with you—and be read by you, the elites of the patron class whom at the very end he calls, simply, "those interested in knowledge", *sapientes*. One thinks of Cicero! For the ideology of the *fides* of employed to employer, the moral virtue in being a good and honest employee, the Vitruvian formulations are of interest.

Such discourses had far-reaching reverberations down the centuries. For the emperor Justinian, Procopius (*On Buildings* 1.1.23–79) will first eagerly detail the forms and impact of decoration at the new church of Hagia Sophia (dedicated in 537 CE), expanding on the process by which its astounding dome was designed by Justinian's brilliant architects. But the emperor still knows best: Procopius praises his brilliance (*nous*) in knowing which God-given architects to patronize (1.1.23–4) and retails that, when the grand dome's construction ran into problems, Justinian could tell the architects how to fix the problem! (See 1.1.69–70, announcing Justinian built Hagia Sophia not just with money but also with thought, *dianoia*, and the *aretē*, excellent strength, of his *psychē*—and also 1.1.50, handing credit for the dome to Justinian along with Anthemius and Isidore.)

The visual arts contribute to this kind of celebration of building, actual and mythical, that is inspirited by the grand person. Funerary celebration extols the master-contractor at the Flavian or Trajanic Tomb of the Haterii at Rome; here, a much-celebrated relief that has a wide popular as well as scholarly building shows Haterius overseeing the construction of a towering mausoleum, proleptically shown complete and richly decorated with sculpture, his diminutive workforce operating a lofty crane which is rendered with precision in every detail, down to the form of the pullies. (Another relief at his compound shows labeled public works—Colosseum, temple, arch—at Rome for which, we think, Haterius can have been the contractor; if not, why show them, is the reasoning.)[48] The Late Roman arts keep up what must have been a flourishing tradition: in the Vatican Virgil (MS Vat. lat. 3225), a fourth-century-painted codex, a large illustration shows (folio 13R) Aeneas at that fateful first glimpse of Carthage under construction just described (*Aeneid* I.419–438) from his lofty vantage point, his extended right hand making a speaking gesture to show he is announcing his excited reaction to his companion Achates. Below, and across from him, are queen Dido's workforce for her colony: supervisor figures attend and instruct smiths and masons in their work at rising structures, marble column shafts and blocks lie waiting for attention, and the now-familiar crane makes an appearance.[49] Putting Aeneas in the compositional position of the inspiring patron of one's own project, the image bears out the description of Aeneas' reaction—that it inspired him, in his duty to found a new city in Italy. Still in the sixth century, art celebrated imperial and noble builders, in the company of crowds of zealous and skilled workmen: they are translated into busy Cupids, Erotes, on the frontispiece page (fol. 6v) of the Vienna Dioscurides (Codex Vindobonensis med. gr. 1), in the spandrels of the eight-pointed star frame for the enthroned portrait of Anicia Juliana, daughter of the short-reigned western emperor Anicius Olybrius.[50]

Made ca. 512–15 CE, the richly illustrated codex of Dioscurides' medical herbal was given to her as a token of gratitude by the people of the district of Honoratae at Constantinople for building them a church: the portrait page is from a series of frontispieces, which include Dioscurides himself being taught scientific lore by "Discovery", and working with a painter to produce botanical images (fol. 4v, 5v). On 6v Anicia[51] scatters gold coins, benefaction, onto an open book held up to her by an Eros-servant, "The Desire of Building", and Sophrosyne (Wise Prudence) and Megalopsychia (Greatness of Soul, Magnanimity) are the entourage-like ladies of her court.[52] The building-builder image genre's long life in time[53] across genres and media indicates the frequency of lost examples. The authorial, inspiriting body of the elite patron needs the crowd of skilled workers to make an idea a reality, such that the workforce, in the visual arts, is something like an attribute, not just a narrative device, especially when it is made tiny relative to the mentally competent authorial body. In public monuments of this kind, though, a discrepant gaze by workers could see their own hands as responsible for the edifice of power and of empire.

Is It a Peasant?

Not only the Roman working farm but also the villas that included elegant quarters (*villa urbana*) had work on show, if the master class cared to look: sometimes it was made visible, even if other times screened. Besides the servile labor for household duties, which house art sometimes addressed, those with estates could watch their field-hands and, when it came to the vintage, even join the workers as a form of sport in addition to watching them as a kind of entertainment. That is what is suggested by a letter the young Marcus Aurelius wrote to his tutor Fronto from an imperial villa in Anagni,[54] and the wide popularity of Roman art showing vintaging peasants and, as their proxies, Cupids and satyrs, suggests many other landholders made a kind of festival of watching also. At what may be the very villa from which Marcus wrote, the site of Villa Magna, excavators even uncovered a dining installation that had gleamed with colored marbles constructed to let the diners watch laborers tread the grapes in a press installation, and wine-storage *dolia* were sunk into the compound as in any villa's utilitarian *cella vinaria*. There are parallels, at aristocratic/imperial villas.[55]

Marcus Aurelius describes the pleasure at hearing his laboring vintagers bantering boisterously—but how freely, under such surveillance, one must query. The figure of the happy-go-lucky peasant, free or slave, is a master's fantasy that repeats in later slave societies, including those of antebellum America. Telling too is art that replaces the body of the landworker with that of a half-beast or a silly child in popular vintage scenes, that is, with a satyr, or with an Amor, a Cupid, typically at least two figures cooperating, sometimes many more. The vintaging Cupid stays popular in Late Antique arts as in townhouse and villa mosaics. Satyr-vintagers were popular for, for instance, mold-made Campana reliefs, and terracotta decorative plaques for fine houses' walls, in the first centuries BCE/CE, with different stages of (supervised) "process": satyrs picking the grapes, treading and pressing them, drinking from a fountain of wine.[56]

Images showing rural workers and fishers offer a fascinating case also of the actualities of work being elided or deferred, even though the work is, in the abstract, suggested, and this has to do with isolating the worker's body, even though for the more powerful workers performed in teams, or at least in coordinated gathering (as for fishery supplies for the garum industry). Much of this art is domestic, made for the spaces of leisure as enjoyed by people very far removed from the lowly laborers their fine art depicted. The isolated figure of a farmer, herdsman, or fisherman starts in Roman images in painting and relief by the first century BCE. So do expressive statues of landworkers (shepherd, shepherdess) and fishers, very old, lined and ugly with exertion, often minimally clothed, that are said often to be based on a Hellenistic Greek prototype and persist into Late Antiquity. Imperial and Late Antique table silver and mosaic detail such figures also. They make the worker, for the supervisory class, at once an aesthetic object (as in bucolic and pastoral poetry) and an abject human: to cultivated people in moments of *otium* they showed bodies that were often marred, not made beautiful, by exertion. Do these function as Stoic-style reminders that all must fulfill their duties?

Occasionally landwork occurs on funerary monuments—but not those of the lowliest laborers shown. Such monuments were typically paid for by people at least several steps removed from the plow themselves, and not enslaved, while some of these tombs were for extremely highly placed local elites.[57] Not until the later Empire, second or third century into the fourth century CE, do relevant images in fine homes much proliferate (in some regions) that are more directly referential to the productive extraction of plant and animal resources on a scale greater than that of a single humble household. To see real peasants doing peasanty things on the land one can look to art that connects with an imaginary that even town dwellers might share: the cycle of the rustic calendar, interspersing agricultural activities with urban festivals (including those of Rome) in wall painting and floor mosaic, especially in the Western empire.[58] Their work is shown to found and constrain Roman time. In country villas, fieldwork was close to hand, the town festival further off; in urban dwellings, these cycles acted in anxieties shared by all about good harvests and explained the produce coming into the house, from olive oil and wine to the vegetables in the market.

But the relevant mosaic grids are little ideograms of activity. There was an alternate tradition, of a calendar made of panoramas of seasonal work,[59] to travel by eye in space and time, as shown by a wall painting from a Late Antique Gallic urban *domus* in Tongres/Tongeren (Belgium).[60] It is from Roman North Africa, from the later empire (ca. 200 CE onward) in one of the great agricultural economic zones of the imperium, that art paying attention to human activities in landscapes of extraction especially surfaces, in the domestic floor mosaics of wealthy elites in townhouses and villas.[61]

A very striking large floor at Cherchel (Iol Caesarea) monumentalized the body of the contemporary peasant with the highest quality of pictorial illusionism, verism, and force. In a series of four registers within a border of lush acanthus scrollwork, the men sow and plow, and tend a vineyard with staked vines, with an overseer (*vilicus*) watching at lower left.[62] To lavish pictorial artifice, beauty of any kind, might be said to celebrate its object, though here that object may be the earth's fertility, the spectacle of plenty in the making, human skill, rather than elevating the actual peasant/rural slave who never would have trod this floor.

To what end are these scenarios offered, as very good art, to elite viewers? To simply say they people the originary patron's own lands is too positivist a conclusion, even if it might be true; a contextual reading needs to take in the possibility that the patron, like many viewers, was removed from the direct economy of production. The North African grain trade was important, enormously so in the late Roman period, and viticulture mattered as well. Any guest would know that; any viewer might compare their own *negotium* to the steady work of the good peasant. How might domestic servitors react to views of rural field-hands? It would depend on the arduousness and rank of their own labor, surely. Some will have been relieved to be spared hot and dirty manual labor outdoors; a sweeper or scullery slave might think they would be happier out of the owner's house.

It is interesting to contrast to the Cherchel floor (in high Roman pictorial style in an urbane *domus*) the "Saturn stelai" with agrarian scenes from around the towns and rural hinterland of Roman North Africa, cut in local limestones by craftsmen working in regional, not-classical styles. Noted is the so-called Boglio stele of Cuttinus, third and fourth centuries CE: in the lower registers are peasants hard at work in the grain fields—plowing, harvesting, and bringing in the sheaves on carts to the landowner. Above them their master Cuttinus and his wife happily sacrifice their beasts and produce and thank Saturn for their prosperity.[63] It is very direct about hierarchies of hard labor, whether by slaves or by hired seasonal workers. If it glosses the cycle of life,[64] then it is very clear whose life has been well worth living and whose has been a hard bargain. Much prettier, on the face of it, is the visual map of a fine and prosperous villa economy, much reproduced, from an urban mansion at Carthage: inscribed for a "*dominus Julius*", it takes that name.[65] The mosaic panel comes from a very large floor, placed before an apse that would house a *stibadium* (curved couch) for banquet, at which diners could consume the produce of the land. Zealous male and female producers on a big estate, its pictured villa centering the image actually and conceptually, show their labor's results—from flowers to animals—to male and female masters ensconced among the estate's groves and gardens and orchards. Peasants pick olives and, in a fenced orchard, fruit; a shepherd sits with a flock before his hut and stockade. At lower right the *dominus* receives a tablet, a tally(?) from a peasant carrying ducks; across from him a female body-slave brings jewel box to a *domina* in a rose garden; at the center, the mounted *dominus* heads, with his retainers with hound and net, to the hunt. All is well in this ordered microcosm of the elite villa, a place of competently supervised work and, for its owners, of pleasures, where the peasants are skilled, happy, and deferential.[66]

Running the Roman World

From the villa, back to the urbane. To close this chapter: what of the laboring at infrastructure of socio-political institutions, both in the elite voluntary *cursus* and in paid public service at many ranks? Such images need a comprehensive review. Magistrates' monuments of the Late Republic acclaimed that service, we know from the large statuary base sometimes miscalled the Altar of Domitius Ahenobarbus, what for neutrality one can call the Paris-Munich base. Its reliefs, of the later second or early first century BCE, come from the area of the Circus Flaminius at Rome and emerged and were separated in the early modern period. In Munich are the reliefs of one long and two short sides, showing a marine *thiasos* of tame sea beasts, sea-nymphs, and Amores riding in festival among the waves around the marital chariot of Neptune and Amphitrite, drawn by Tritons; these are Greek Hellenistic reliefs re-used. The long side in the Louvre shows the exercise of Roman institutional power: a ritual at the Altar of Mars in the Campus Martius, by a censor or censors, performing the *lustratio* at the end of censorial office marked by the actual taking of the census at Rome. At a different moment to the sacrifice and in a different spot, figures of cavalry, of equestrian rank, and men of legionary rank, cluster and then approach the bureaucrats who check/inscribe their documentation of rank in the pile of massive tablet sets at far left, records hauled into the open air from a repository.[67] This monument helps mark the onset of a genre of monuments about institutional function; in dynastic art, later, emperors and their ministers are attended by the scribes and administrators present at the distribution of largesse, the burning of tax records, and so forth. The largest depicted crowd of clerkdom extant is the scene of imperial largesse on the Arch of Constantine, of ca. 315 CE, recycled from a monument of Diocletian.[68] Gifts come from the emperor, it proclaims: in a two-storied portico space or hall sits Diocletian/Constantine, his right arm out showering coins from a largesse-paddle into the folds of toga an eager recipient holds up to him from below, acclaiming senators massed around the podium and crowded in the loggia space behind the emperor, squeezed in among his lictors. Left and right cluster the plebs and their children, down the long sides of the space (it is butterflied out in the composition), while, in repeated small groups up and down the second-story gallery, a crowd of bureaucrats, scrolls and tablets in evidence, sees to the registration of a benefaction to men of this crowd of people approaching one by one. This panel intimates something like the real scale of managing a city and, so, an empire. It is not likely the emperor personally showered gold coin from his hand, but he takes the role, and the implement, of the attendant for largesse in other images.

There is not enough space here for the monuments of the professional *scribae*, the adept clerks for public and official business, but there is good work on them, as on the status and iconicity of writing, and writing tools, in the Roman world. Instead, I close with the Late Antique diptych of Probianus,[69] ca. 400 CE (Theodosian), a little window onto a kind of occasion and workforce centuries old—the operation of justice by its judge and the lawyers with him, an object that transforms earlier tribunal scenes into a new idiom, at once "political", "public" in its origins, "private" in its usage, to be shown to intimates of rank in the fine *domus*.

Large ivory diptychs, finely carved on the exterior with figural and ornamental relief, are a distinctive Late Antique luxury artifact of very prestigious character, many of them part of both formal and informal gift economy among the highest nobility and the leading magistrates and commanders. This one celebrated Probianus' service as imperially appointed *vicarius* of the city of Rome. The titulus spells that title out. Fourth- to sixth-century CE ivory diptychs of this general class—celebrating a high official protagonist—concentrate on senators who have just started on their consulship and are giving games for their inauguration; this man is a different kind of appointee, bringing imperial power to bear, in an image of the workings of imperial administration. The consular ones seem to have been made, in multiples, as gifts by the consul to peers and *amici*: to whom Probianus meant to gift this specimen is not clear. Exemplar of the mobile governing class of the imperium, Probianus, with the aristocratic highest rank as *vir clarissimus* (inscription), presides at judicial hearings. On the front leaf he wears an official's fine tunic and *chlamys*, hearing out non-senatorial litigants; on the back leaf he wears the senatorial toga, hearing out senatorial speakers. Judgment takes place in Rome's law courts and administrative halls, the schematic richly curtained architectural backdrop stipulates. Probianus holds a pen on the back, left leaf over an unfolding scroll with the emperor's greeting/codicil visible, enlarged ("may you flourish, Probianus"). Two of his *scribae* flank him in both scenes, with open tablets and pens, recording the proceedings. Beside his judgment seat is a Late Antique official stand with the portraits of the current emperors (Arcadius and Honorius). The imperial portrait's presence was a prerequisite for valid judicial proceedings; here it signals also "personal connection to the emperor".[70]

The image makes clear the *vicarius* is the brilliant agent of the emperor, ultimate upholder of Roman law. The two lawyers below, holding their scripts, arguing heatedly as their speaking gestures show, flank a table that holds a pen and ink dish: only the material text makes judicial proceedings and administration valid. Hierarchy of scale makes Probianus largest, the lawyers (even those of senatorial rank) half his size; his *scribae* are smaller still. Yet, though more lowly than the litigants, they accrue dignity by sharing the upper register with Probianus and, as highly skilled indispensable recorders, functioning as his proxy memory. To treat the snapshot of bureaucratic and legal procedure and functionaries as a compelling, even lovely image, of the finest facture, would make sense to the man who commissioned the Paris-Munich Reliefs base. This tablet marks a good close to what is, also, an exercise in the written word.

Notes

1. I thank our seminar, conference, and volume organizers and editors Jordan Rogers and Del Maticic for the extraordinarily generative intellectual experience they have given me by asking me into the Working Lives project. I also thank Matthew Santirocco for lending his auspices to it. I benefitted greatly from the explorations of all my fellow panelists, the editors included, and from our audiences. I have benefited before, too, from Jordan Rogers' probing assessments of Roman art! Foolishness in this chapter is my own fault. It gives me enormous pleasure that I work for two people who represent, at this time of writing, the very newest generation of Romanists, who are braving a highly problematic job market in an academy where pernicious reliance on precarious and unacknowledged labor has always been pervasive and is becoming more so.
2. This chapter radically, selectively compresses a huge body of material. Bibliography here must be very greatly selective also. Those who know comparisons should take those forward, whether for object classes or for theoretical methods and models for interpretation hinted at in the text, and more. It is clear I hold objects and images as things never transparent, actors as well as things acted upon, and that object theory in the hands of

people like Gosden and Hodder informs the ways in which I seek to cope with ancient things, people, and the textual artifact as well. The other chapters in this volume can suggest generative ways in which to use the material on which I touch in regard to Roman work and workers.

3. Illustration is limited. All I discuss is accessible to view on the open web, in addition to cited publications. I have given museum and archive database urls as well, for good images of their holdings. I am hostile to the often predatory charges and lumbering bureaucracy of some museums and archaeological authorities and archives when it comes to purchase of digital images and permissions for inserting, in scholarly publication, visual images those bodies have themselves often given to the open web. In academia those burdens lie especially heavily on graduate students, junior academics, and those in precarious positions.
4. For the Praenestine *cista* in Brussels (Musées Royaux d'Art et d'Histoire, inv. A 1159) on which cooks prepare fish and meat, their Latin vocalizations inscribed: Bordenache Battaglia 1979: 70–72, n. I 2, pl. 80; Bonfante 1986: Fig. VIII.43, small reproduction of Bordenache Battaglia's drawing. (Philological literature on the Old Latin here is extensive.) In a kitchen, hierarchy is shown—master cook gives orders to his (servile) staff. The effect is a peek behind the scenes of a rich person's banquet, possibly influenced by comic forms of drama; the box's rich owner is not likely to have spent time in kitchens.
5. Bibliography for the room is huge, contentious; what I say here is not controversial. In brief: Clarke 1991: 98–110; Gazda 2000; Gazda 2021; this work as "spectacle", Kuttner 1999: 107–9; on the slave-child reading out ritual words from a scroll for owners, see Beckmann 2023. On the Amor-slave figure in Roman arts, broadly, see Mitchell 2018; see below, on the House of the Vettii and Temple of Venus Genetrix.
6. What is "Roman", besides images at Rome and in its larger region? In the larger imperium, "Roman" art takes in the expressions of many different populations; things and images in that proto-global sphere enjoyed both very wide circulation and more local kinds of production. What is a "Roman artist"? That question plagues Roman studies. In the Late Republic and after, Greeks of the south and east Mediterranean world both emigrated north and west and shipped art for market from their home bases; Greek-speaking artists (who may have been of diverse ethnicities) dominated especially in some sections of the imperium (some of Italy, the East, Egypt, and Northern Africa). But even the images and artifacts that arose from this situation were, as art historian and archeologists increasingly recognize, impacted by Roman needs and wishes. Much I cite from around the empire certainly had no "Greek" artist.

7. For a glimpse at some that do, see, e.g., Ehmer and Lis 2009. (They brought studies on art and on literature together with historical and economic ones.) Global, cross-cultural discussions on this subject are desirable.
8. I say *cura* for what could also be called *diligentia* (diligence), for instance, and attention to *officium* (duty), displaying *providentia* (foresight) and *prudentia* (good judgment), in service to city and to empire, as well as to productive exertion and its supervision of all kinds in *otium* as in *negotium*.
9. See, e.g., Meredith 2023, which posits Late Antique and Early Medieval images of work-in-progress—unfinished work—serve to trope and command viewers' work at viewing, directed to important meanings. In this chapter also are images of work-in-progress. Compare Geue in this volume on the labor of making a poem as it intersects with artful poetry about low labor (the *Moretum* with its hungry peasant making pesto, aided by his African enslaved woman servant), and the labor of careful expert reading.
10. Mercantile actors in Roman art are typically adduced in socio-economic histories of them. With an eye to how monuments helped promise a merchant's good reputation (vital to his/her economic survival) within their social network of peers, rivals, and customers, see, for instance, Sancinito 2018 and Sancinito 2024, which can be contextualized by her essay in this volume.
11. Ferris' 2020 book surveys monuments set up by and about workers, categorized as people of middling and slightly lower status than that, often funerary, with attention to the workers' pride in identities. D'Ambra and Métraux 2006 is a good project idea but very small collection; it looks principally at the art of freedpeople of varying social ranks (Leach 2006, George 2006). Genre-specific studies of kinds of worker/producer often make use of images, especially for documentary ends, e.g., Benton 2020 for bakers, and Flohr 2013 for fullers. Handy for images of labor, domestic, commercial, and funerary, is Clarke 2003, on mostly Italian material, even if his category, "ordinary Romans", has been critiqued for vague spread between what were in fact low, middling, and high elites in the Roman town. As stimulating and problematic is Mayer's 2012 discussion of the Roman "middle classes", analyzed especially under the heading of the "aesthetic": see Chap. 4 on commemoratives of artisans and businessmen. Compare Wolfthal 2023, as a polemic project to address Medieval images of working-class laborers and artisans.
12. In Lytle's edited 2019 volume on a cultural history of work in Greco-Roman antiquity, there is indeed a dedicated chapter (as in our volume) on images, "Picturing Work", Sapirstein 2019—but much is sixth- to fifth-century BCE Athenian vase painting. A briefer section on Roman material has some of this essay's spread, but its premise is that (47) "the highest strata of Roman society avoided images of work". That postulate depends

on a narrower definition than mine of who is working, in what images and settings, and in regard to whose *cura*. Other articles in that volume exemplify the practice to use Roman images of labor to illustrate aspects of work and document workers, e.g., Verboven 2018.

13. Ferris 2020: 39, for a Late Roman sarcophagus for an architect at Rome (with square, ruler, compasses, chisel, hammer), and one from Arles, second to third century BCE, for Quintus Candidus Benignus (square, axe), acclaimed for his penetrating *knowledge* of multiple aspects of building and engineering. See pl. 99, the funerary altar at Aquileia of L. Alfius Statius, early first century CE, and pg. 36–37, on one of the painted images in the fourth-century CE Tomb or Hypogeum of Trebius Justus at Rome (Sapirstein 2019: 47–48). Here, before a large structure (a villa of his own?), Trebius Justus holds the measuring rod of an architect or builder, beside a man labeled "Magister Generosus" who has a short working rule and holds a trowel—master-builder/architect and a foreman who can or does also lay brick. Another image here indeed shows a number of brick-masons making a brick structure. Cf. Meredith 2023: n. 49 contrasting the image of Justus' son in another part of the tomb, seated framed by his books, a *capsa* box for scrolls, and stylus holders.
14. The discussion here of images stressing the object develops some thoughts in the short essay on Greek and Roman relations to objects, Kuttner 2021.
15. See especially La Follette 2011/2.
16. Meyer 2009, for instance, at 570–7, on the "still-lifes", and the assemblage painted with Vestorius Priscus in his "atrium" at his tomb compound in Pompeii, with reference to the domain of *negotium*.
17. Cf. the telling comments of Barkan 2021: 205–13, who stresses the intimation of kitchen activity, things seen (209) "in the context of cuisine rather than that of nature—in other words, as stages *in the labor of the kitchen* and the pleasures of the table" (emphasis mine). People who comment on Hellenistic and Roman regimes of taste bring these pictures in to illustrate Roman passions for "Good Food". The *xenia* participate in what Gowers explored in her 1997 *The Loaded Table*, but are not identical to those texts. For these and other images of foodstuffs cf. Dunbabin 2003a.
18. Earliest at Rome may be the so-called San Omobono Base reliefs, for a monumental statuary base for a victorious commander: center point to a ring of arms and trophies, a decorated votive shield is garlanded by animated Victory statues that replace temple attendants, framed either side by incense stands. Often dated to the early first century BCE, it may be as early as the second century; see, e.g., Kleiner 1992: Chap. 1, sv Figs. 34 and 35 (online version) and Kuttner 2013: 248–67 and Fig. 8.22 for this slab.

19. Now Palazzo Nuovo, Museo Capitolino, fragments of a frieze in Luna marble depicting artifacts and costume items of religious performance and also warship elements. Images, https://arachne.dainst.org/entity/1076169, https://arachne.dainst.org/entity/1076171, https://arachne.dainst.org/entity/1076173, https://arachne.dainst.org/entity/1076174, https://arachne.dainst.org/entity/1076170, https://arachne.dainst.org/entity/1076172. La Follette 2011/2: 25–7, Figs. 10 and 11, two of the slabs, as also Kuttner 2021: Fig. 8.1. For the "sacred still-life" she stresses that some ritual implements should not be thought on all monuments to summon thought of a person, as when a *lituus* (for an adult augur) appears on a child's sarcophagus, or jug and patera manifest on funerary altars. But I argue that in many representational contexts an implement does recall a hand.
20. Known in studies of historical relief and of temples as the Temple of Mars Ultor relief (with bull-slaying) and the Temple of Cybele relief (with procession of bull) once thought erroneously to belong to an Ara Pietatis: casts made for the Museo del civiltà romana (Rome) and the Ara Pacis Museum juxtapose portions immured in the early modern period at the Villa Medici in Rome. Zanker 1988: Fig. 86 (Mars Ultor); Pollini 2012: 335–6, Fig. VII.20, (Cybele), VII.21, II.23a–b. American Academy in Rome, Fototeca Unione, accessible at the AAR's Digital Humanities Center site, https://dhc.aarome.org/: search FU.Roma.ARAPI.7 for the temple of Cybele relief and FU.Roma.ARAPI.8 for the Temple of Mars Ultor relief. Earlier is the Augustan ot Tiberian Boscoreale Cup with Tiberius' sacrifice that echoes a lost monument's reliefs, with the victim-slaying group urgently active, already flattened in the Villa Medici relief (the composition persisted for centuries); Kuttner 1995; Pollini 2012: 85–8 and Fig. II.18b. On a cup, one could finger these impressive bodies.
21. At either end of the panels, similar adolescents bear shields. A large ornamental vase closes each side, dwarfing the servants and the candelabrum, in a typically Roman play with relative scale. See Kleiner 1992: Figs. 188–9 for the façades, and Fig. 191 for the sacrifice panel, sv "The Arch of Trajan at Benevento" (online version); Mitchell 2018: 330. Note that other façade panels on this arch show Victories, not human butchers, killing bulls. In the passage's grand sacrifice relief Trajan and his entourage, including young *camilli*, are joined by a miniaturized group of the *victimarii* at bull-slaying: this miniaturization of laborers relative to a supervisor class occurs often in the Roman corpus.
22. Classic is Lenski 2013. See below 132, n. 22 and n. 43.
23. Kleiner 1992: Figs. 160–61, sv "The Forum Transitorium" (online version); Andrews 2015: 184–237; a book version of the thesis, on the Subura, is in preparation (Dec. 2023). She sees it aimed not as visual sua-

sion to induce moral transformation of the immoral population of prostitutes so much, we think, associated with the Subura, the workshop district for which this "forum" channeled movement to and from the Forum Romanum. For copious images under various light conditions, search "Forum Nerva frieze" and "Le Colonacce" on the open web. Detail of Arachne and Minerva: https://arachne.dainst.org/entity/1216077.

24. Rogers, in this volume puts it in dialogue with his core monument of the *fabri tignarii*, at pp. 142–3.
25. D'Ambra 1993 was seminal. See also Andrews 2015. For Ovid's Arachne, see in this volume Formisano.
26. Lovén 2013 for evidence for Roman women as well as men in stages of cloth production outside the house as well as producing within it, whether for sale or not, and for specialized skills among female slaves. On the case at Pompeii and elsewhere, Caldwell 2021 treats textile work for pay by free women in the *domus*, the employment of house slaves in this competency for economic gain, sometimes in sizable teams such as a rich viewer of our frieze can have owned, dye-works in wealthy houses, etc. "Ordinary" people's daughters can have been earning a *peculium* for home work in the textile business, such a parent could have in mind, seeing this myth.
27. Mayer 2014: 39–77, is a quick reference for the "commercial cityscape", outside and within the *domus*; for the dense urban occupation in Italian suburbs by shops, workshops, and prestige houses alike, and tombs, creating traffic and encouraging attention, Emmerson 2020: 125–62.
28. Clarke 1991: 214.
29. Clarke 1991: 208–36, reviewing the house; the Cupids' room, also Clarke 2003: 98–105, and Ferris 2020: 153–5. See De Angelis 2011: 67–8 for a more recent state of discussion. Positing dramatization of opposing relations between *otium* and *negotium* by the interspersal of scenes with Cupids and Psyches at play, he points out how in the atrium the visitor had already seen miniatures of Cupids and Psyches doing playful or festive things as well as a bit of labor. For other *domus* at Pompeii and Herculaneum with Cupids in action, including at "work", from the early first century CE on, Ferris 2020: 155, Clarke 2003: 105, and De Angelis 2011: 68–70.
30. De Angelis 2011: 71; the house thus obeys rules of *decorum* to imply a *domus* is an exclusive space of *otium*, in his conclusion (73). But *labor* also, always implied by its opposite, was good to think with at home in a culture which approved and urged masculine exertion and being not-idle.
31. As at the Shop of Verecundus, IX.7.5–7, with, right of the door, scenes of textile processing and a large Verecundus presents some cloth to the viewer; left, a woman sells textiles (wife? employee?), Clarke 2003: 105–12. The *fullonica* at VI.8.20 with its well-decorated courtyard had some piers painted with figures; one showed the owner's workforce in action, and a

female customer dropping off some cloth to be cleaned. Clarke 2003: 112–18, seeing in the fine decorations the owner's wish to show pride in his workers, "put a face… on his little industrial operation", give the customer a pleasant surprise matching painted people to the real workers, and give his laborers pride in their work (esp. 117–18) by elevating worker and tool. Flohr 2013 discusses images of *fullones* in his book on their work and its social contexts.

32. So Severy Hoven 2012, analyzing scopic regimes not only of sexual predation but also of coerced service with the *paterfamilias*' power to punish imminent, at this *domus* as exemplar of the Roman "power house".
33. Thus the Priapus painting in the atrium by the vestibule: this frequently occurring guardian god in household art is uniquely shown here balancing a money-changer's or a merchant's scale on which he weighs his huge penis against a sack of coin.
34. Briefly, e.g., George 2006: 23–24; Mayer 2014: 112–14. Fundamental remain Petersen 2003, 2006, with Benton 2020: 176–87 and passim in that chapter (6). Benton sets it in a western Roman tradition of (funerary) depictions of the chaîne operatoire of the baking industry (grain processing, bread making, and bread selling), promising good quality bread with depicted activities and implements. Add Jones 2018, on its character of "encyclopedism" and Emmerson 2020: 79, 134–8, 161. *CIL* I.2 1203–1205, *CIL* VI 1958: "This is the monument of Marcus Virgilius Eurysaces, *pistor* and *redemptor* and public servant" (transl. Petersen).
35. His former master will have apprenticed him to this trade, profited from his skills, perhaps helped set him up in business once he was freed. His Greek-derived eponym (from *agathos*, good) is auspicious for an artisan/artist and may have been given him or been taken by him for just that reason. The decoration is Dionysiac (a dancing satyr), popular iconography for tablewares, J. Paul Getty Museum 96.AA.40, https://www.getty.edu/art/collection/object/104034. Lapatin and Wight 2010: 146; Lapatin 2015: 38–9. Contexts for the dignifying style and iconography of freedpeople's tomb reliefs, George 2006.
36. Cicero, *In Verrem* 2.4.54–55, 70 BCE, describing what Verres ordered done with the wonderful *emblemata*—that is, the detachable repoussé ornament and figuration of gold and silver banquet ware—from the treasures he seized from private citizens all over Sicily: "After he had amassed so many *emblemata* that not even one was left to anyone else he set up an *officina*, an enormous one, in the palace at Syracuse [i.e. his residence as governor]. He ordered publicly that all *artifices—caelatores, vascularii*—should be brought together there; also, he had many on his own staff. He sequestered them, an enormous multitude of men. He gave them enough work to keep them busy 8 weeks without a break, and he ordered every

vessel to be of gold. The ornamental work that he had torn from dishes and censers he now had incorporated within gold cups, and applied to gold basins, so neatly you would say the ornaments to have been made for those settings from the start. And the praetor himself, who said that it is by his diligent attention (*diligentia*) Sicily is peaceful, used to sit in this *officina* much of the day, in dark tunic and the *pallium* [Greek mantle]." (Trans. author, adapting the Loeb version.)

37. On these remains, see recently Mitchell 2018: 325–8, assembling critical bibliography, for these and other busy Cupids (with garlands, at sacrifice, etc.) at this temple; Kuttner 2021: Fig. 8.5. Busy Cupids figured also at the Forum of Trajan, feeding griffins.
38. See, at length, for instance, the work of Catharina Lis, and Hugo Soly, in a long diachronic perspective: Lis 2009; Lis and Soly 2012; Lis and Soly 2016, with reference also to monuments of "productive" work in Roman funerary art and West-European medieval comparanda. Lis' introductory term is *ponos*, with reference to pre-Roman Athens. She refers, as do many commenting on Greek and Roman work, to tenets of the Stoics.
39. It is interesting to think of the no doubt splendidly limned bodies of emperors and benefactors that were put up by a range of professional associations, as sampled in this volume by Sausville at pp. 207–15.
40. On the face lined by aging as a badge of *virtus* (virtue) taken up by the Roman middling classes and craftsmen starting in the Late Republic to signal a successful professional life, Mayer 2012: 114–20.
41. Classic of imperial honorific inscriptions are, for instance, in Tunisia *CIL* VIII 25943 (Aïn-el-Djemal) and 26416 (Aïn-Wassel), relating to the *Lex Hadriana de rudibus agris* for African provinces: "Speech of the procurators of the emperor Caesar Hadrian Augustus: Because our Caesar [in keeping with] his tireless care (*infatigabili cura*) because of which he is assiduously vigilant for the interests of humankind…."
42. The mobile professionals Holleran discusses in this volume might have thought of the laboring heroic wanderer, at some point.
43. Noel Lenski's 2013 essay on these finely made human furnitures remains authoritative, looking at lamp-holder and tray-holder statues, some adapting "high" statuary types; for those see also Mattusch 2017. House of the Ephebe, Pompeii I.7.10–12: the eponymous statue (Naples, Museo Archeologico Nazionale inv. 143753, height 59 in.), Lenski 2013: 137, Fig. 5.6; Mattusch 2017: Fig. 8.3 and section "The Ephebe"; the traybearers, (Naples, Museo Archeologico Nazionale inv. 143760), Lenski 2013: 145 (he thinks they are singing) and Fig. 5.13.
44. Clarke 1991, and see n.29.

45. A genre exemplified in some of the wall paintings of the imperial cult "chapel" inserted into the sanctuary of Amon at Luxor, made into a fine fort under Diocletian, see McFadden in Jones and McFadden 2015.
46. Thill 2010, and cf. 2018 on the Column of Marcus Aurelius, in dialogue with that of Trajan.
47. *In Qu. Fratr.* 2.2, and 2.5, to Quintus in Sardinia; 3.1, to Quintus in Gaul. See 3.1 for the ivy at the statues of the *palliati.*
48. For example, Ferris 2020: 31–42, on the rich dossier of building scenes in Roman funerary, commemorative and domestic art, and n. 53. Tomb of the Haterii: briefly, Kleiner 1992: Fig. 166, building the tomb and crane; Fig. 165, for Flavian monuments; s.v. "The Tomb of the Haterii", in Chap. 4 (online version); Leach 2006; Trimble 2018.
49. Wright 1993: fol. 13r: https://digi.vatlib.it/view/MSS_Vat.lat.3225; and cf. fol. 35v, the very damaged image of when Mercury finds Aeneas as he oversees construction at Carthage (*Aeneid* 4.259–67). The right side of the miniature preserves the now quite substantially completed town, with two little masons carving stone before the walls.
50. One is reminded of the Late Roman gold glass bowl medallion, Musei Vaticani inv. 60788 (MV.6088.2.1), a cemetery on the Via Salaria at Rome, in which a well-to-do shipwright named Dedalus, like the mythic craftsman, standing in tunic and chlamys with scroll and rod of authority, is surrounded by small figures of men working wood for a ship. Minerva instructs one worker at upper right; the small figure of a bearded craftsman before a stylized ship's prow should be Daedalus himself. See Rogers in this volume, pp. 231–2; Meredith 2023 15, Figs. 8 and 9, and n. 45; https://catalogo.museivaticani.va/index.php/Detail/objects/MV.60788.2.1.
51. Fol. 4v, https://digital.onb.ac.at/rep/osd/?10CD7B1E *Euresis* shows the seated doctor a mandrake root; on fol. 5v, https://onb.digital/result/10CD7B27 Dioskourides at the right before a magnificent architectural backdrop reads in a codex at his desk, while on the left an artist paints the mandrake root on a page pinned to an easel, looking over his shoulder at the actual root held up to him by *Epinoia*, Thinking-about, Thinking-on.
52. Fol. 6v, https://onb.digital/result/10CD7AEF. Kiilerich 2001; Brubaker 2002; Nathan 2011; Angelova 2015: 225–8; Ferris 2020: 155–6. Among other details, note here the poem inscribed around the inner border of the interlace in which the parish of Honoratae praises Anicia's raising a high and beautiful temple of the Lord; the personification performing proskynesis at Anicia's feet is "Gratitude of the Arts", the Eros with book is "The Desire to Build/The Desire of the Building-loving Woman" (*philoktistou*). The framing Erotes' activities as masons, carpenters, and builders are badly faded but were once more visible; Kiilerich 2001: 172; Nathan 2011:

100–1. For her other church, of St. Polyeuktos, she wrote poems that extolled this work of building, and had one of them carved in relief as interior decoration: briefly, Angelova 2015: 229–33 and 353, n. 64; Harrison 1989. The composition compares Anicia (an emperor's daughter, descendant of Theodosius the Great) to an empress.

53. For instance, Ferris 2020: 156 after discussing Anicia's portrait looks ahead to the eighth-century paintings of 32 building-workers in one vault of the baths of the Ummayad country palace at Qsayr Amra. Much wall painting here draws on the Roman legacy; for the compound, e.g., Fowden 2004; with reference to Roman-era images, Ali and Guidetti 2017; Taragan 2008. Many of the expert hands behind palaces and paintings had been, until the Islamic conquests, people of Roman Syria. For the Late Antique mosaic of the building the Tower of Babel in a synagogue mosaic at Huqoq in Israel, where busy workmen with contemporary tools and processes make more real the moral warning, Meredith 2023: 10–14. Noted in Late Antique and Byzantine studies is the so-called Trier Ivory, a plaque (13.1 × 26.1 cm, Treasury of Trier Cathedral) of unknown use, perhaps for a reliquary box: on it a reliquary is transported by clergy, led by an emperor, to where his empress stands before a church of her own building where the relics will be deposited and on whose roof little craftsmen still crawl. Sometimes called fifth century (Ferris 2020: 35, Fig. 3), it is ninth to tenth century; see now Chatterjee 2018, with 33–4 on antecedent building scenes.

54. Fronto, *Epistles* 4.6, (141 CE): from Marcus Aurelius—"we are well… we set ourselves to the task of picking grapes; we sweated and rejoiced, and, as the author says, 'we left high-hanging grapes surviving' [= Novius; from his Atellan play]. At the 6th hour we returned home… Having bathed, we therefore dined in the pressing room (= *torcular*) (we didn't bathe in the pressing room but, having washed, we ate there) and we happily heard the peasants bantering (*rustici cavallantes*)."

55. Fentress and Maiuro 2011 and Fentress et al. 2016 propose the aestheticized *cella vinaria* served the emperor's celebration of the *Vinalia*, in a country-echo of the great *Vinalia* festival at Rome. For the similarly splendid *cella vinaria* at the Villa of the Quintilii at Rome (at this date an imperial possession?), see Dodd et al. 2023; Feige 2021 also discusses uses of decoration to highlight areas of wine and oil processing at villa sites.

56. Cf. Rauch 1999: 106–13; von Rohden and Winnefeld 1911: 63–9. For satyrs treading grapes, cf. Louvre inv. Cp 4026, 33 × 42 cm (ca. 50 BCE–50 CE), where a young satyr plays the flute to mark the treaders' time and a Silenus carries grapes to them, https://collections.louvre.fr/ark:/53355/cl010251983 and the similar Cp 4032, https://collections.louvre.fr/ark:/53355/cl010288166, and, from Frascati, the background painted

blue in the nineteenth century Cp 3888, https://collections.louvre.fr/ark:/53355/cl010288153. Satyrs crouch under a vine tree's branches picking grapes on British Museum 1805,0703.350, 15.7 × 31.1 cm, https://www.britishmuseum.org/collection/object/G_1805-0703-350 with reference to other BM versions of this type. Satyrs lean over a basin of wine, under a lion-head spout, Louvre Cp 3868, 36 × 25.5 cm, https://collections.louvre.fr/en/ark:/53355/cl010288145 and Cp 3869, https://collections.louvre.fr/en/ark:/53355/cl010251981. Multiple satyr and vintage types were found in the Villas at the Via Gabina near Rome, in its first-century phases. See Painter 2002.

57. For indigene elites celebrating agriculture and husbandry on their tombs (often discussed for Gaul), look for instance to the third-century CE tombs of Ghirza in Libya. These reliefs in local style share space with scenes of chiefly authority and other motifs on lavish tombs which adapt Roman prestige architecture, their Libyan patrons named in Latin inscriptions. The labor is that of peasants working for the clans that put up the mausolea. Mattingly 2014: 246–68; Nikolaus 2016, contextualizing the Roman-era mausolea of Tripolitania (over 140 known) as made by local Libyan elites, whose wealth tended to be in landholding, at 208–11 on the agricultural scenes at multiple sites.
58. For pictorializations of the Roman calendar of months imaged as scenes of activity, including rural ones, cf. Salzmann 1991 to contextualize a noted fourth-century CE codex with month images made for a senatorial-rank noble at Rome (the Codex Calendar of 354); it has, like calendar mosaic floors, also urban festival activities. See especially 25–34, 91–115, and 269–72 (App. 2, calendar cycles from the Roman west); mosaic floors receive much attention. Looking back into the Roman-era calendar art tradition from the point of view of the rustic and seasonal images of the ceiling of the eight-century great hall at Umayyad Qusayr' Amra (cf. n. 53 above), celebrating Caliphal felicity, Ali and Guidetti 2017: 181–209. Behind the Four Seasons floors widely popular around the imperium from the first century CE on, and the second to fourth century urban elites' Seasons sarcophagi, lie rural labors apparent in the Seasons' attributes; on sarcophagi the Seasons sometimes act like peasants, holding produce and edible *animalia*.
59. Welcome would be comparison with European Medieval images of the "Labors of the Months", which are, and are not, like Roman ones, especially in so often showing settings; cf. Jaritz 2009 on Central European examples, and Thomas in the same volume at 333–35.
60. The little-discussed wall painting of a "rustic calendar" from a town *domus*, from the lower wall of a large room: preserved is a section for August (inscr. AUG). In the foreground is a grain field, an empty wheeled cart

beside it, and, across the middle ground, the view of a farmstead with its *villa rustica* at left, set within an enclosure made of stout wooden stakes and beams, with a large flat garden area or field within its right-hand section. A peasant, seen from behind, perhaps carrying something, walks into the stockade's gate before the farm building; another leans at the fence from within. Conveyed is that the grain is now to be harvested ("the return from the harvest"), a traditional August activity. To be in the room was to be surrounded by vistas of the changing year, transported from the city and a fine house into a landscape to be construed as that of rural Gaul with its peasant population. Ferdière 2011: section 251 ("Le calendrier et le temps qui passe…"), para. 57–60, with color photo.

61. Dunbabin 1978; Sarnowski 1978; Wilson 2018: 273–6, and cf. 277–9 on Oued-Athménia's mosaics; cf. Novello 2007 and Novello and Salvadori 2004, with Nevett 2010: 120–41, framing the Dominus Julius mosaic. Are the workers on the land in the mosaics discussed below slaves or free tenants, *coloni*? That is a vexed question. Recently see, e.g., Lenski 2017: 127–36. Slave forces still existed in the fifth century and after, but the picture is one of increasing numbers of *coloni* with severely constricted status. The third-century CE Cherchel mosaic could have been seen by its first owner to depict free *coloni*, energetic tenants, but by the fifth century can have seemed instead to show people who, more constrained in status, were much more one with the soil they were shown working.
62. From a house at Cherchel (Iol Caesarea; Maison des Travaux champêtres) in Mauretania Caesariensis, 5.25 × 3.50 m, second-third c. CE. Musée de Cherchel. Elsner 1998: 100, Fig. 66. He sees the overseer figure as inscribing the scenes in the context of villa agriculture. "These servants, however realistic, are visualized in the perfumed atmosphere of a rural idyll—the pastoral fantasy of the landowner about those who sustain his standard of living" (repeated, Elsner 2018: 33, Fig. 66). I disagree: visual emphasis is on urgent motions by sturdy bodies, and any aroma is one of perspiration. Are they, or are they not, as abject as Geue's *moretum*-maker and his slave in this volume? More sources: Dunbabin 1999: 117–8, Fig. 121 and, in her survey of North African mosaics, looking to those about life on the land, Dunbabin 1978: 119 for Cherchel; Ferdi 2005: 113–22, no. 94–8 and pl. 87–94. In a study of agricultural implements in the Roman world, the mosaic has a star turn in White 2010: viii, x–xi, 138, 201–2, Figs. 4 and 12 (App. C, cat. I 5). Cf. Shaw 2012 for broad context, adducing this mosaic at 303 (and cf. 336, n. 189) as drawing on a repertoire of images that trace grain from sowing to reaping in an arc that in funerary art can represent the course of life.

63. Shaw 2012: 43–46, Fig. 1.13–14; now in the Bardo Museum, this is one of the most striking of the Saturn stelai of North Africa with images tied to the grain harvest.
64. Shaw 2012: 167–8; cf. 239. On the Saturn stelai, including agrarian ones, local workshop production, and cultic traditions, see McCarty 2016.
65. Nevett 2010: 120–41; Dunbabin 1978. Ca. 380–400 CE, now in the Bardo Museum in Tunis. Search "dominus Julius" for color images online. Argument about the plausibility of the villa's forms generate much of the commentary, by scholars interested in villa architecture and its images. What counts here is that it is a grand building, from which the owner family have emerged, into their gardens and dependencies, cultivated and uncultivated, for pleasure and profit, the human beehive of estate personnel swarming to them. Cf. Novello and Salvadori 2004. Those people are the human technology for the environmental extraction that founds the wealth that built villas. See Lenski 2017 on the binding of tenants, *coloni*, to their estate of *origo* and coerced status in North Africa in the fourth century and after, n. 60 above.
66. Dunbabin 1978: 112–13, another elegant late Roman North African dining room, at Tabarka, has in its triconch apse mosaics views of farmsteads and villas in which humans almost entirely lack, but where animals and birds, like the foliage, trees, and staked vines, speak to landscapes both of elite pleasure and of farmed production.
67. Kleiner 1992, particularly the section "The 'Altar of Domitius Ahenobarbus' (Paris-Munich Reliefs)", Figs. 30 and 31 in Chap. 1 (online version); Maschek 2018 wishes this to be a colony *deductio*, but my point about the relief's fascination with administrative process can still stand. Louvre Ma 975, 84 × 566 cm https://collections.louvre.fr/ark:/53355/cl010304645, with bibliography; https://arachne.dainst.org/entity/1083915.
68. See, for this reuse, Rose 2021 with extensive bibliography for the arch.
69. Staatsbibliothek, Preussischer Kulturbesitz, Berlin, Ms. theol.lat.fol.323. https://digital.staatsbibliothek-berlin.de/werkansicht?PPN=PPN863341861&PHYSID=PHYS_0001, with superb zoomable and downloadable color images. (Select "Scan -Druckseite" 1 and 2.) Each leaf, 31.8 × 13 cm. (They were mounted into the covers of a medieval Life of St. Liudger in Germany.) Volbach 1976: 54–6, n. 62, pl. 34; Weitzmann 1979: 55–6, cat. 53; Gabelmann 1984: 205–6, pl. 38; Rollinger 2019: 54 and Fig. 2.1 (color).
70. So Rollinger 2019: 54. The formula of the large, enthroned superior, and smaller officials and entourage below evolved in the imperial panegyric tradition: compare the paintings in the Diocletianic chapel at Luxor, n. 46 above.

Bibliography

Ali, N. and Guidetti, M. 2017. "Umayyad Palace Iconography: On the Practical Aspects of Artistic Creation." In George, A. and Marsham, A. eds. *Power, Patronage, and Memory in Early Islam: Perspectives on Umayyad Elites.* Oxford University Press.

Andrews, M. 2015. *Matron, Meretrix, Madonna: Archaeology and Urban History of the Cispian Hill in Rome from the Republic through the Early Middle Ages.* Ph.D. dissertation, University of Pennsylvania.

Angelova, D. 2015. *Sacred Founders: Women, Men, and Gods in the Discourse of Imperial Founding, Rome Through Early Byzantium.* University of California Press.

Barkan, L. 2021. *The Hungry Eye: Eating, Drinking, and European Culture from Rome to the Renaissance.* Princeton University Press.

Beckmann, S. 2023. "The Naked Reader: Child Enslavement in the Villa of the Mysteries Fresco". *AJA* 32: 293–316.

Benton, J. 2020. *The Bread Makers: The Social and Professional Lives of Bakers in the Western Roman Empire.* Palgrave Macmillan.

Bonfante, L. 1986. "Daily Life and Afterlife." In Bonfante, L. ed., *Etruscan Life and Afterlife: A Handbook of Etruscan Studies.* 232–78. Wayne State University Press.

Brubaker, L. 2002. "The Vienna Dioskorides and Anicia Juliana." In Littlewoood, A., Maguire, H. and Wolschke-Buhlman, J. eds. *Byzantine Garden Culture.* 189–214. Dumbarton Oaks Research Library and Collection.

Caldwell, L. 2021. "From Household to Workshop: Women, Weaving and the *Peculium*." In Longfellow, B. and Swetnam-Burlands, M., eds. *Women's Lives, Women's Voices.* 51–66. University of Texas Press.

Chatterjee, P. 2018. "Iconoclasm's Legacy: Interpreting the Trier Ivory." *Art Bulletin* 100: 28–47.

Clarke, J. 2003. *Art in the Lives of Ordinary Romans: Visual Representation and Non-Elite Viewers in Italy, 100 B.C.–A.D. 315.* University of California Press.

Clarke, J. 1991. *The Houses of Roman Italy, 100 B.C–A.D. 250: Ritual, Space, and Decoration.* University of California Press.

D'Ambra, E. 2021. "Real Estate for Profit: Julia Felix's Property and the Forum Frieze." In Longfellow and Swetnam-Burland: 85–108.

D'Ambra, E. 1993. *Private Lives, Imperial Virtues: The Frieze of the Forum Transitorium in Rome.* Princeton University Press.

D'Ambra, E. and Métraux, G. eds. 2006. *The Art of Citizens, Soldiers and Freedmen in the Roman World.* BAR International Series 1526. BAR Publishing.

De Angelis, F. 2011. "Playful Workers: The Cupids Frieze in the House of the Vettii." In Poehler, E., Flohr, M., and Cole, K. eds. *Pompeii: Art, Industry and Infrastructure.* 62–73. Oxbow Books.

Dodd, E., Galli, G. and Frontoni, R. 2023. "The Spectacle of Production: A Roman Imperial Winery at the Villa of the Quintilii, Rome." *Antiquity* 97.392: 436–53.

Dunbabin, K. 1999. *Mosaics of the Greek and Roman World.* Cambridge University Press.

Dunbabin, K. 1978. *The Mosaics of Roman North Africa: Studies in Iconography and Patronage.* Oxford University Press.

Dunbabin, K. 2003a. *The Roman Banquet: Images of Conviviality.* Cambridge University Press.

Dunbabin, K. 2003b. "The Waiting Servant in Later Roman Art." *American Journal of Philology* 3: 443–68.

Ehmer, J. and Lis, C. eds. 2009. *The Idea of Work in Europe from Antiquity to Modern Times.* Routledge.

Elsner, J. 2018. *The Art of the Roman Empire AD 100–450.* Oxford University Press.

Elsner, J. 1998. *Imperial Rome and Christian Triumph: The Art of the Roman Empire AD 100–450.* Oxford University Press.

Emmerson, A. 2020. *Life and Death in the Roman Suburb.* Oxford University Press.

Feige, M. 2021. "Decorative Features and Social Practices in Spaces for Agricultural Production in Roman Villas." In Haug, A. and Lauritsen, M. T. eds. *Principles of Decoration in the Roman World.* 33–52. De Gruyter.

Fentress, E. and Maiuro, M. 2011. "Villa Magna near Anagni: The Emperor, His Winery, and the Wine of Signia." *JRA* 24: 333–69.

Fentress et al. eds. 2016. *Villa Magna: An Imperial Estate and its Legacies: Excavations 2006–10.* Archaeological Monographs of the British School at Rome 23.

Ferdi, S. 2005. *Corpus des mosaïques de Cherchel.* Études d'antiquités Africaines. CNRS Editions.

Ferdière, A. 2011. "Voyage à travers la Gaule profonde—XV." *Revue archéologique du centre de la France [RACF]* 50: 569–96, http://racf.revues.org/1712.

Ferris, I. 2020 *The Dignity of Labour: Image, Work and Identity in the Roman World.* Amberley Publishing.

Flohr, M. 2013. *The World of the Fullo: Work, Economy, and Society in Roman Italy.* Oxford University Press.

Fowden, G. 2004. *Qusayr ʿAmra: Art and the Ummayad Elite in Late Antique Syria.* University of California Press.

Gabelmann, H. 1984. *Antike Audienz- und Tribunalszenen.* Wissenschaftliche Buchgesellschaft.

Gazda, E. 2021. "Portraits and Patrons: The Women of the Villa of the Mysteries in Their Social Context." In Longfellow and Swetnam Burland: 133–50.

Gazda, E., ed. 2000. *The Villa of the Mysteries in Pompeii: Ancient Ritual, Modern Muse.* Kelsey Museum of Archaeology and the University of Michigan Museum of Art.

George, M. 2006. "Social Identity and the Dignity of Work in Freedmen's Reliefs." in D'Ambra, E. and Métraux, G. eds. *The Art of Citizens, Soldiers and Freedmen in the Roman World*. 19–29. BAR Publishing.

Harrison, R. M. 1989. A *Temple for Byzantium: The Discovery and Excavation of Anicia Juliana's Palace-Church in Istanbul*. University of Texas Press.

Jaritz, G. 2009. "The Visual Representation of Late Medieval Work: Patterns of Context, People, and Action." In Ehmer and Lis: 125–48.

Jones, N. 2018. "Exemplarity and Encyclopedism at the Tomb of Eurysaces." *Classical Antiquity* 37: 63–107.

Jones, M. and McFadden, S. eds. 2015. *Art of Empire: The Roman Frescoes and Imperial Cult Chamber in Luxor Temple*. Yale University Press.

Kiilerich, B. 2001. "The Image of Anicia Juliana in the Vienna Dioscurides: Flattery or Appropriation of Imperial Imagery?" *Symbolae Osloenses* 76: 169–90.

Kleiner, D. 1992. *Roman Sculpture*. Yale University Press.

Kuttner, A. 2021. "Object Worlds." In Osborne, R. ed. *A Cultural History of Objects in Antiquity*. 185–214. Bloomsbury Academic.

Kuttner, A. 2013. "Representing Hellenistic Numidia, in Africa and at Rome." In Quinn, J. and Prag, J. eds. *The Hellenistic West*. 216–72. Cambridge University Press.

Kuttner, A. 1999. "Hellenistic Images of Spectacle, from Alexander to Augustus." In Bergmann, B. and Kondoleon, C. eds. *The Art of Ancient Spectacle. Studies in the History of Art* vol. 56: 97–122.

Kuttner, A. 1995. *Dynasty and Empire in the Age of Augustus: The Case of the Boscoreale Cups*. University of California Press. http://ark.cdlib.org/ark:/13030/ft309nb1mw/.

La Follette, L. 2011. "Parsing piety: the sacred still life in Roman relief sculpture." *Memoirs of the American Academy in Rome* 56–57: 15–35.

Lapatin, K. 2015. *Luxus: The Sumptuous Arts of Greece and Rome*. The J. Paul Getty Museum. Lapatin, K. and Wight, K. eds. 2010. *The J. Paul Getty Handbook of the Antiquities Collection*. The J. Paul Getty Museum.

Lapatin, K. and Wight, K. eds. 2010. *The J. Paul Getty Handbook of the Antiquities Collection*. The J. Paul Getty Museum.

Leach, E. W. 2006. "Freedmen and immortality in the tomb of the Haterii". In d'Ambra and Métraux eds.: 1–18.

Lenski, N. 2013. "Working Models: Functional Art and Roman Conceptions of Slavery." In George, M. ed. *Roman Slavery and Roman Material Culture*. 129–57. University of Toronto Press.

Lenski, N. 2017. "Peasant and Slave in Late Antique North Africa." In Lizzi Testa, R. ed., *Late Antiquity in Contemporary Debate*. 113–55. Cambridge Scholars Publishing.

Lis, C. 2009. "Perceptions of Work in Classical Antiquity." In Ehmer and Lis: 33–68.

Lis, C. and Soly, H. 2016. "Work, identity and self-representation in the Roman Empire and the West-European Middle Ages: Different interplays between the social and the cultural." In Verboven and Laes 2017: 262–289.

Lis, C. and Soly, H. 2012. *Worthy Efforts: Attitudes to Work and Workers in Pre-Industrial Europe*. Brill.

Lovén, L. L. 2013: "Female Work and Identity in Roman Textile Production and Trade: A Methodological Discussion." In Gleba, M. and Pásztókai-Szeöke, J. eds. *Making Textiles in Pre-roman and Roman Times: People, Places, Identities*. 109–25. Oxbow Books.

Maschek, D. 2018. "Not *census* but *deductio*: reconsidering the Ara of Domitius Ahenobarbus." *The Journal of Roman Studies* 108: 27–52.

Mattingly, D. 2014. *Imperialism, Power, and Identity: Experiencing the Roman Empire*. Princeton University Press.

Mattusch, C. 2017. "When a Statue is Not a Statue." In Daehner, J., Lapatin, K., and Spinelli, A. eds. *Artistry in Bronze: The Greeks and Their Legacy*. J. Paul Getty Museum Conservation Institute: https://www.getty.edu/publications/artistryinbronze/.

Mayer, E. 2012. *The Ancient Middle Classes: Urban Life and Aesthetics in the Roman Empire, 100 BCE–250 CE*. Harvard University Press.

Mayer, E. 2014. *The Ancient Middle Classes: Urban Life and Aesthetics in the Roman Empire, 100 BCE–250 CE*. Harvard University Press.

McCarty, M. 2016. "Gods, Masks, and *Monstra*: Situational Syncretisms in Roman Africa." In Alcock, S., Egri, M., and Frakes, J. eds. *Beyond Boundaries: Connecting Visual Cultures in the Provinces of Ancient Rome*. 266–80. Getty Publications.

Meredith, H. 2023. "Shaping Viewer Experience through Images of Unfinished Work: A Visual History of Making in the Fourth to Eighth-Century CE Eastern Mediterranean." *Different Visions: New Perspectives on Medieval Art* 10: 1–41. https://differentvisions.org/shaping-viewer-experience/.

Meyer, E. A. 2009. "Writing Paraphernalia, Tablets, and Muses in Campanian Wall Painting." *American Journal of Archaeology* 113: 569–97.

Mitchell, E. 2018. *The Other Classical Body: Cupids as Mediators in Roman Visual Culture*. Doctoral dissertation, Harvard University.

Nathan, G. 2011. "The Vienna Dioscorides' dedication to Anicia Juliana: A Usurpation of Imperial Patronage?" In Mathan, G. and Garland, L. eds. *Basileia. Essays on Imperium and Culture in Honour of E.M. and M.J. Jeffreys*. 95–102. Centre for Early Christian Studies, Australian Catholic University.

Nevett, L. 2010. *Domestic Space in Classical Antiquity*. Cambridge University Press.

Nikolaus, J. 2016. "Beyond Ghirza: Roman-period Mausolea in Tripolitania." In Mugnai, N., Nikolaus, J., and Ray, N. eds. *De Africa Romaque: Merging Cultures Across North Africa*. 199–214. The Society for Libyan Studies.

Novello, M. 2007. *Scelte tematiche e committenza nelle abitazioni dell' Africa Proconsolare*. F. Serra.

Novello, M. and Salvadori, M. 2004. "Natura umanizzata e natura selvaggia nei mosaici dell' Africa romana: dallo spazio del giardino ai limiti esterni della tenuta." In Khanoussi, M., Ruggeri, P., and Vismara, C. eds. *L'Africa romana. Ai confini dell'impero: contratti, scambi, conflitti. Atti dell' XV Convegno di studio, Tozeur, 11–15 dicembre 2002* vol. 3. 853–75. Carocci Editore.

Painter, K. 2002. "Campana Reliefs." In Widrig, W. ed. *The Via Gabina Villas, Sites 10, 11 and 13.* http://viagabina.rice.edu/campana/index.html.

Petersen, L. H. 2006. *The freedman in Roman art and art history.* Cambridge University Press.

Petersen, L. H. 2003. "The Baker, His Wife, and Her Breadbasket: The Monument of Eurysaces in Rome." *Art Bulletin* 85: 230–57.

Pollini, J. 2012. *From Republic to Empire: Rhetoric, Religion and Power in the Visual Culture of Ancient Rome.* University of Oklahoma Press.

Rauch, M. 1999. *Bacchische Themen und Nilbilder auf Campanareliefs.* Verlag Marie Leidorf.

von Rohden, H., and Winnefeld, H. 1911. *Die Antiken Terrakotten im Auftrag des Archaeologischen Instituts des Deutschen Reichs.* Verlag Von W. Spemann.

Rollinger, C. 2019. "The Importance of Being Splendid: Competition, Ceremonial, and the Semiotics of Status at the Court of the Late Roman Emperors (4th–6th Centuries)." In Choda, K. C., Sterk de Leeuw, M., and Schulz, F. eds. *Gaining and Losing Imperial Favour in Late Antiquity: Representation and Reality.* (*Impact of Empire*, Vol. 36.) 36–72. Brill.

Rose, C. B. 2021. "Reconsidering the Frieze on the Arch of Constantine." *Journal of Roman Archaeology*: 175–210.

Salzmann, M. 1991. *On Roman Time: The Codex Calendar of 354 and the Rhythms of Urban Life in Late Antiquity.* University of California Press.

Sancinito, J. 2018. *Merchants in the Later Roman Empire.* Ph.D. dissertation, University of Pennsylvania. https://repository.upenn.edu/edissertations/2703/.

Sapirstein, P. 2019. "Picturing Work." In Lyttle, E. ed. *A Cultural History of Work in Antiquity.* 33–56. Bloomsbury Academic.

Sarnowski, T. 1978. *Les répresentations de villas sur les mosaïques africaines tardives.* Zaklad Narodowy.

Severy Hoven, B. 2012. "Master Narratives, and the Wall Painting of the House of the Vettii, Pompeii." *Gender & History* 24: 540–80.

Shaw, B. 2012. *Bringing in the Sheaves: Economy and Metaphor in the Roman World.* University of Toronto Press.

Taragan, H. 2008. "Constructing a Visual Rhetoric: Images of Craftsmen and Builders in the Umayyad Palace at Qusayr 'Amra." *Al-Masaq. Islam and the Medieval Mediterranean* 20: 141–60.

Thill, E. W. 2010. "Civilization Under Construction: Depictions of Architecture on the Column of Trajan." *American Journal of Archaeology* 114: 27–43.

Trimble, J. 2018. "Figure and ornament, death and Transformation in the Tomb of the Haterii." In Doetrich, N. and Squire, M. eds. *Ornament and Figure in Graeco-Roman Art: Visual Ontologies in Classical Antiquity.* 327–52. De Gruyter.

Verboven, K. 2018. "Workplace Cultures." In Lyttle, E. ed. *A Cultural History of Work in Antiquity.* 73–94. Bloomsbury Academic.

Volbach, W. 1976. *Elfenbeinarbeiten der Spätantike und des frühen Mittelalters.* Von Zabern.

Weitzmann, K., ed. 1979. *Age of Spirituality. Late Antique and Early Christian Art, Third to Seventh Century.* Metropolitan Museum of Art, in association with Princeton University Press. [Freely available from MetPublications, https://www.metmuseum.org/art/metpublications/Age_of_Spirituality_Late_Antique_and_Early_Christian_Art_Third_to_Seventh_Century.

White, K. D. 2010. *Agricultural Implements of the Roman World.* Cambridge University Press.

Wilson R. J. A. 2018. "Roman Villas in North Africa." In Marzano, A. and Métraux, G. eds. *The Roman Villa in the Mediterranean Basin: Late Republic to Late Antiquity.* 266–307. Cambridge University Press.

Wolfthal, D. ed. 2023. *Toward a Visual History of the Working Class. Different Visions: New Perspectives on Medieval Art 10.* Accessed 7.19.2024.

Wright, D. 1993. *The Vatican Vergil: A Masterpiece of Late Antique Art.* University of California Press.

Zanker, P. 1988. *The Power of Images in the Age of Augustus.* University of Michigan Press.

CHAPTER 6

Rapacious and Chatty, Deceitful and Memorable: Finding Non-elite Stereotypes of Roman Merchants

Jane Sancinito

Introduction

Two *topoi* dominate representations of professions in ancient literature: the honest farmer and the greedy merchant. In every way, these figures are opposites, and they exist, not on a spectrum, but as a binary categorization into which characters may be fitted without any expectation of nuance. The farmer was honest by default and, though his circumstances could be alternately comfortable or humble, working the land granted him the wisdom and strength to overcome any obstacle in an honorable and praiseworthy way. The merchant, by contrast, was greedy and disreputable, not only willing to abandon any moral standard, to lie or to cheat if it were profitable, but also content to live and work in base conditions that were, otherwise, only suitable for slaves. The greedy merchant's sensibilities

J. Sancinito (✉)
University of Massachusetts Lowell, Lowell, MA, USA
e-mail: jane_sancinito@uml.edu

D. A. Maticic, J. Rogers (eds.), *Working Lives in Ancient Rome*, The New Antiquity,
https://doi.org/10.1007/978-3-031-61234-3_6

were "other" than those of "normal" Romans and could not be offended by the dirt or stink that would adversely affect any other kind of man.

For literary purposes, the appearance of either or both of these characters established an immediately legible, or, in the case of the theater, visible, shorthand. The farmer, ever a protagonist, and the merchant, the perpetual adversary, gave the reader an entry point into the author's narrative or didactic purpose. While they did not always appear together, each character had a long pedigree in ancient literature and therefore enjoyed both an immediate cultural relevance for the reader and a longer intertextual history dating back to Homer and Hesiod for the author to exploit.[1] They were useful *topoi* for writers, who not only displayed their erudition through their appearance but also used the characters as a starting point for broader discussions about morality and justice or as a satirical commentary on their contemporary world.

While scholars of ancient literature recognize the skill with which these types are rendered and recycled, ancient historians have had more trouble with them, not because these types can be recognized as valid representations of a historical reality, but rather because they are so clearly unreal. Intertextuality has made the historical analysis of sources discussing farming and retail trade especially challenging, as it is difficult, if not impossible, to determine what elements might be inherited from specific or general allusions and what might represent the thought or practice of a particular culture or era. It is unclear whether a given example might contain a kernel of truth or whether every appearance of an honest farmer or greedy merchant merely reiterated the same set of preconceptions and cultural beliefs as those that came before. Furthermore, when compared with the historical consensus about the social and economic positions of farmers, merchants, and even the authors of the texts themselves, these *topoi* create a seemingly insurmountable gulf between what the literary evidence claims and what we believe to be true about daily life based on other sources.

Following the groundbreaking work of John D'Arms, historians have mostly focused on the hypocrisy of ancient, and especially Roman, authors, whose praise of the small-scale farmer and disdain for the greedy, often foreign, merchant is directly contradicted by their personal economic choices.[2] Andrea Giardina, in an attempt to analyze the cultural position of the merchant, itself a capacious category that can include everything from retail and wholesale trade to artisanal work, services, and transportation, in Roman society, identified a distinction between retail trade and the sale of one's own produce (or the produce of one's own land).[3] He argued that this divide created an ideological exception for the mercantile activities of Roman elites. Their work on this front was excepted from accusations of greed or baseness because it could be interpreted as being more like the labor of the farmer than that of the merchant.[4] It is a sophistic distinction, a thin line that cannot be maintained in the face of the historical evidence of elite trading. Wealthy Romans diversified their interests. They sponsored and profited from commercial ventures, including those that did not involve the sale of the produce of their villas. They also frequently squeezed out small landowners as they expanded their own holdings.[5] Though they used their writings to advocate for the honor of the small farmer and to denigrate the work of retailers, artisans, and service providers, their actions show that they practiced something rather different than what they preached.

Recent work has pressed this issue still further, making the argument that not only can these *topoi* not be used as a source for the history of the Roman economy, but also these literary tropes may have been unknown to the wider Roman public and therefore cannot be used as evidence for cultural bias in favor of farmers and against merchants. Emmanuel Mayer has lately argued that these ideas were essentially quarantined within an echo chamber of elite thought that never reached the people who worked in these professions, let alone a majority of Roman society.[6] Mayer has made this case for merchants, especially, whom he believes were mostly ignorant of the disdain and hatred that was commonly directed toward them in literature. Instead, he argues that merchants developed their own systems of self- and peer-assessment that operated in isolation from the *topos*.[7] While the extent to which it was possible for Roman tradesmen to have missed the treatment of their professions in famous epics or publicly performed drama might be debated, the real issue at stake in this argument is whether the values that are presented in the writings of elite members of Roman society were in any way representative of the feelings of the culture at large.

This matter may be subdivided into two further lines of questioning: first, to what extent may these recurrent literary *topoi* be equated with practical kinds of prejudice and stereotypes in the real world, and second, do the views of elites in this matter bear any similarity to the views of non-elites? Were these views widespread and, if so, can we determine if one group's views influenced the other, or if stereotypes about merchants developed independently among different sectors of Roman society?

Though there has been growing interest among scholars in the former question, especially as it relates to Roman law, the latter issues have not yet been closely examined in relation to commercial actors.[8]

In the following, I review the *topoi* of the honest farmer and greedy merchant, with the goal of assessing how commercial workers "show up" in our evidence for literary and historical prejudice against merchants in the Roman world. These *topoi* were deeply interconnected with Roman stereotypes, in that both not only served to simplify, categorize, and characterize professional groups that were, in actuality, quite diverse in their composition, but also justified specific actions toward members of those groups, leading, especially, to discriminatory legislation against merchants. In following the merchant *topos*, in particular, it is clear that retailers, artisans, and service providers were highly aware of the cultural bias they faced, in large part because it was present in their day-to-day life, as stereotypes existed, albeit in slightly different forms, among the general, non-elite acquaintance of merchants. While non-elite stereotypes can be difficult to access given the sources that have been preserved from the Roman period, there is nevertheless a range of informal writings, such as jokes, fables, and graffiti, that can be used to assemble a picture of how merchants were viewed by their social equals and inferiors. In contrast to elite views, non-elites had a nuanced understanding of merchant professions, and, while the overall picture generally remains one of distrust, frustration, and dislike, these feelings are frequently tinged with amusement and fondness, if not true respect and affection. As a result, though there are similarities between elite and non-elite stereotypes, they arise from different sources, with elite stereotypes growing out of concerns about social mobility and panic over a perceived decline in morality and non-elite stereotypes deriving from competition and the emotions that came from day-to-day experiences.

The *Topoi*

To understand the differences and similarities between elite and non-elite stereotypes of retailers and artisans, it will be beneficial to examine the literary *topoi* first. Though these types appear early and often in ancient literature, both separately and together, Philostratus' *Heroicus* offers perhaps the most succinct version possible. The core of the types appears in the earliest lines of the work and the interlocutors of the dialogue represent the *topoi* in themselves. As the narrative begins, a Phoenician merchant—a representative of two common stereotypes, one ethnic and one professional—waits for a favorable wind. He is approached by a vinedresser, a specialized agriculturalist of some skill, and a man, as it turns out, with peculiarly detailed knowledge about Homeric heroism. The two quickly fall into conversation. Almost immediately, the vinedresser offers the merchant a strange, back-handed compliment, one that neatly summarizes the most common stereotype leveled against traders:

> ἀμπελουργός: σοφοί γε, ὦ ξένε, τὰ ναυτικὰ ὄντες: ὑμεῖς γάρ που καὶ τὴν ἑτέραν ἄρκτον ἐνεσημήνασθε τῷ οὐρανῷ καὶ πρὸς αὐτὴν πλεῖτε. ὥσπερ δὲ τὰς ναυτιλίας τιλίας ἐπαινεῖσθε, οὕτω τὰς ἐμπορίας διαβέβλησθε ὡς φιλοχρήματοί τε καὶ τρῶκται.
>
> Φοῖνιξ: σὺ δὲ οὐ φιλοχρήματος, ἀμπελουργέ, ζῶν ἐν ταύταις ταῖς ἀμπέλοις καὶ ζητῶν ἴσως ὅστις μὲν ὀπωριεῖ καταβαλών σοι δραχμὴν τῶν βοτρύων, ὅτῳ δὲ ἀποδώσῃ τὸ γλεῦκος ἢ ὅτῳ τὸν ἀνθοσμίαν; ὅν, οἶμαι, καὶ κατορωρυγμένον φῂς ἔχειν ὥσπερ ὁ Μάρων.
>
> ...
>
> ἀμπελουργός: ... τοὐμὸν δὲ πολλῷ ἐπιεικέστερον: οὐ γὰρ ξυμβάλλω ἐμπόροις, οὐδὲ τὴν δραχμὴν ὅ τι ἐστί, γιγνώσκω, ἀλλὰ βοῦν σίτου καὶ οἴνου τράγον καὶ τοιαῦτα τοιούτων ἢ ὠνοῦμαι ἢ αὐτὸς ἀποδίδομαι σμικρὰ εἰπών τε καὶ ἀκούσας.
>
> Vinedresser: Stranger, you are at least skilled in nautical affairs, for you have even designated Cynosura as a sign in the sky, and you sail by reference to it. Yet just as you are praised for your sailing skill, in the same way you are stereotyped as money-lovers and greedy rascals because of your business dealings.
>
> Phoenician: But aren't you also money-loving, vinedresser, living among these vines and presumably seeking someone who will gather grapes after paying a drachma for them, and looking for someone to whom you will sell sweet or fragrant wine, which, I think, you will say you have hidden, just like Maron?...[9]
>
> ...
>
> Vinedresser: ... but my way is much more reasonable, since I do not associate with merchants, and I do not know what a drachma is. I trade a bull for grain and a goat for wine and other such exchanges, and I allow only a little haggling.

The Phoenician responds to this comment by asking how, exactly, the vinedresser profits from *his* work, if not through the sale of his produce, and the farmer replies that he barters with his customers, rather than dealing with merchants or money. He presents himself as being without the love of gain or craftiness that were commonly associated with merchants, making his case through an appeal to the ancient notion that barter, and especially silent barter, was a practice that was simpler, more naïve, and more just than the haggling associated with monetized trade.[10] The implicit or explicit association of money and moral corruption dates back to at least Herodotus and is typically recounted in just this way—with virtuous men, usually some variety of farmer, eschewing the vice of greed by distancing themselves from commerce and close association with commercial actors.[11]

Importantly, though money is often used metonymically in these texts to represent trade more generally, the archetypal association of moral corruption and trade is not defined by coined money alone.[12] The practice of trade itself was believed to be a source of the deterioration of moral standards, as the love of gain in any form, monetary or otherwise, created a snowball effect—no amount of profit could ever be identified as enough.[13] Moreover, once a person began to pursue gain, there would be a growing tendency to view all interactions as an opportunity for profit, which transformed all kinds of relationships into competitions for resources.[14]

At some level, of course, competition may be viewed as a healthy aspect of economic activity, but in the Roman world merchants were viewed as lacking a proper sense of moderation, and customers, as a result, understood all economic activity to be essentially a battle ground—a zero-sum game in which there would always be a winner and a loser, rather than a balanced exchange that reflected something close to the true worth of goods or services.[15] Competition arose, not between competing merchants, trying to secure the greatest share of the market by offering better deals or higher quality goods, but between retailers and consumers. Customers believed that they had to fight with merchants to get a just price and that merchants were likely to cheat to secure their own advantage. In some cases, as with the vinedresser, this could be viewed, grudgingly, with an acknowledgment that "winning" in trade required skill, but at other times merchants were believed to be cheaters, deceiving honest men with specialized tricks, or to have a sort of supernatural edge, an unfair advantage that bordered on the occult.[16] Thus, the vinedresser's comment that he only permitted a little haggling is his attempt to communicate that he consciously absented himself from the commercial battlefield and was not, by extension, interested in maximizing his personal profits.[17]

The central conceit of the *topos* of the greedy merchant rests upon this conceptualization of trade and helps to juxtapose that group with the honest farmer, whose energies were spent in production, not competition. Accordingly, farmers and merchants were not only binary opposites, but could also occupy extreme positions along a variety of moral spectra. Whereas the farmer could be expected to be honest, hard-working, and self-sufficient, the merchant would be deceitful, predacious, and dependent upon the production of others for survival. Agricultural workers were grounded, figuratively and literally, in the place where they lived and labored, while merchants were frequently mobile, less connected to specific communities, and therefore open to attack as foreigners or outsiders.[18] In each case, the deliberate naming of a profession by an author was a meaningful, consciously adopted signal that communicated everything that a reader could need to know about the essence of the character. In the case of Philostratus, the implications of both farming and commerce immediately convey that the vinedresser's positions in the dialogue should be considered authoritative and be given primacy over any position adopted by the merchant. The *topoi* direct the reader through the text and reassert the dominance of agriculture, at least morally, over trade.

Of course, this perspective, that bartering associated with agriculture was somehow morally or categorically different from wholesale or retail trade, is out of touch with modern understandings of the economy as a system of production, redistribution, and consumption and of the equal necessity of commerce and agriculture to the provisioning and maintenance of the population at large. Yet, within the Roman cultural context, these *topoi*, and, as we will discuss, the related stereotypes that existed outside the bounds of literature, make sense. Roman conceptions of the work required for agriculture and trade were drastically different, and they were afforded a level of respect that was precisely commensurate with the amount of labor believed to be involved in each.

Of the two, the Romans had a much clearer image of the physical toll and benefits of working the land.[19] They associated land ownership, especially, with personal and national pride, both because of its long, historical association with military service and because of the need for grain in a city that regularly struggled to feed itself—Italian farmers were particularly honored, and the praise of this group frequently took on a romantic or nostalgic cast, which encouraged Romans to overlook the fact that most landowners did little practical labor themselves, either renting their property to small-holders or filling their fields with enslaved laborers and their overseers. The countryside was imagined as a place of honest labor and both the land and its workers were honored in Roman religion, among Roman politicians, and in a wide range of literary contexts.[20]

Trade, by comparison, was much less readily understood. Its variety and specialization made it difficult to assess, as it not only sometimes took on the form of extremely specialized, skilled labor but also could appear as little more than the assignment of prices to goods that had been labored upon by others. While, as we will discuss, Roman society held different merchants in different degrees of esteem, or rather disdain, there was a widespread belief that prices were kept artificially high by sellers and that goods would be cheaper if customers could buy directly from the source. "Middlemen" trading, and retail, more generally, takes the brunt of the abuse in both literary and documentary sources, and the figures who did this work were believed to cheat both producers and consumers as they bought low and sold high on the goods they transported and vended.[21]

Giardina has argued that retail trade was not even considered to be *labor* in Roman society. It could not be categorized as work, as it was not a generative activity, but rather, at best, adaptive and, at worst, parasitic.[22] Trade was dependent on the *labor* of others, those who grew crops or gathered raw materials, and thus could not create new value in itself. While the work of artisans might physically alter the original materials, making them more valuable through transformation, selling and making goods available in a new market did not change the inherent value of goods. Romans believed, fundamentally, that while it might, at times, be necessary to pay for things to be moved, retailers, neither the makers nor the movers, were essentially extraneous figures clogging up the producer to consumer pipeline. While this point of view might seem impractical, as retail facilitates access to many things that no individual could acquire, create, or experience without a vendor, it was not pointless blustering. At a very deep cultural level, as we will discuss, Romans were convinced that trade was not work and that traders themselves posed a substantial threat to the moral foundations of society. They were making Rome weaker and more inclined to indulge in luxury of all kinds.

Concerns About Commerce

Inherent in these concerns, the moral panic that undergirds much of the logic of the greedy merchant *topos*, were a range of other complicated, interconnected worries, including the threat of both foreignness and effeminacy. Roman authors placed heavy emphasis on self-sufficiency, on using one's own produce rather than acquiring it from others.[23] Buying goods, especially from across the Mediterranean, was an admission that Italy itself did not have the best of everything, and both the real and imagined foreign origins of many merchants were seen as a threat to the homespun, rugged identity that Rome had constructed for itself.[24] Though true self-sufficiency, living only on what one was able to produce for oneself or from one's own lands, required either extreme self-denial or the wealth of an emperor, Romans clung to the ideal and attempted to express, in as many ways as they could, that they limited their involvement with merchants as much as possible, both to display their own autonomy and to limit the influence of decadent foreigners in their lives.[25]

Merchants, of course, were not all foreigners, and few were actually attempting to lure Romans away from the path of *Romanitas*. They came from many places, including Italy, and our historical evidence suggests that most merchants operated in a limited number of local or regional markets. Long-distance trade is prominent in our sources, but likely rarer than the evidence immediately suggests.[26] Nevertheless, merchants were commonly associated with other places, especially with Syria and the greater Levant.[27] This origin, which was often applied to merchants, rather than reflecting their true ethnic identity, tapped into Roman stereotypes about eastern decadence and weakness, which was also commonly elided with femininity.[28] Merchants were seen as the purveyors of temptation and a force that could lead to the enervation of Roman masculinity if it was allowed too much freedom.

Whether they identified the workers as foreigners or Italians, Roman authors comically called upon specialized service providers in their writing as a signal that their society had gone too far. Seneca offers a clear example. In complaining about the loud and irritating cries of the merchants he can hear from his lodgings, he notes, undoubtedly for comedic emphasis, the specialist barber, an *alipilum*, the armpit-hair plucker, who was stationed outside the baths.[29] Not only are Romans no longer shaving themselves, but they will also allow themselves to be primped and fussed over by a specialist, who can only attend to one aspect of their appearance, signaling the vanity and decline of society as a whole. The passage is unusual—Seneca is typically either disinterested in trade or general in his condemnations—but heavily symbolic in Seneca's attempt to hold a mirror up to the growing weakness of Rome and to highlight the unworthy figures who profited and advanced as a result of that degeneration.

All of these conscious and subconscious concerns circulated around merchants and appear regularly in literary discussions of traders and service providers. Retail occupied a prominent place in literature, as vendors, large and small, were especially visible targets for invective. Moreover, Roman authors tended to reduce the complexity of economic activity down to the simple categories of merchant and farmer, including in the former a wide range of actual work that neither fulfilled the same needs economically nor could easily be accused of the same moral failings. Most authors do not acknowledge the unfairness of lumping skilled artisans in with day laborers, though both could, in some circumstances, be construed as merchants, those engaged in *negotium*, but not as farmers.[30]

In general, literary sources produced by elites acknowledge only some limited variation within the category of "merchant." The stereotype or *topos* of the greedy merchant was most readily applicable to retail trade, and so it is in that context that it most often appears. In a famous passage, Cicero notes that this profession was prone to greed and deceit, leaning on the common assumption of the competitive nature of trade: if the only way to secure a profit was by cheating, then the merchant would have to cheat.[31] While by no means the group for which Cicero reserves his greatest disdain, retailers and wholesalers seem to have borne the brunt of many of the most profoundly casual statements about the moral failings of people in commerce. As we will discuss, elite views about retail also bear the strongest similarity to the stereotypes held by non-elites, likely because this was the most commonplace, and commonly experienced, kind of economic activity.

By contrast, artisans and other professions that required specialized training occupied a slightly different position in the elite imagination. Their appearance is often characterized by a grudging respect and even, at times, with complimentary comparisons to the work of philosophers, orators, or legal thinkers.[32] Unlike retailers, they were recognized as at least semi-skilled laborers, though many were nevertheless viewed as sordid due to their proximity to dirt of various kinds.[33] Nevertheless, all labor, including the relatively clean work of teaching students or diagnosing patients, was akin to slavery in the imagination of elite authors. Whether blacksmiths or bankers, these workers were obliged to pursue a wage and were therefore "less free" than the idealized version of farmers, who worked for themselves to eat and support their families, but not to sell their surplus or their labor to others. Seneca even goes so far as to state that no training or study that was intended to result in money-making could be considered good or befitting a man of status.[34] He argues that the study itself is wrong-headed because it is founded upon a greedy impulse and inspires a desire for wealth in the student. To Seneca, this was an inevitable consequence of merely being exposed to someone who taught as a profession. They were ignoble and so too must anything that they attempted to instill in their student. Seneca is somewhat unusual in his condemnation of instructors and seemingly takes a broad view of the category, including master craftsmen together with experts in more technical or specialized fields.[35] Still, he is by no means alone in distrusting this group. Many authors tacitly or explicitly warn against the pursuit of careers in professional or artisanal work, since even the most skilled doctor nevertheless received payment for his work and would, consequently, be a servant to his employer.[36]

Wage labor of any kind was denigrated, believed to be not only a form of dependence on others and likely to result in subservience to them, but also a direct expression of greed, since no amount of payment would ever seem like enough recompense for putting oneself in a position of subordination to others.[37] Receipt of any kind of payment would make the worker eager for more, whereas seeing the result of one's labor in the fields was believed to inspire more wholesome feelings of accomplishment, fulfillment, and joy in the gifts of the gods.[38]

Beyond wage labor were professions that were perceived as being especially shameful, that warranted *infamia* or equivalent social stigma. Cicero refers to these as professions that "cater to sensual pleasure" and seemingly includes everything from prostitutes and perfumers to cooks and barbers.[39] The services provided by these workers were believed to pander to the laziness and baser impulses of men. If someone else could be paid to perform a task, then there was no reason for a Roman to learn to do it, and in the Roman view, choosing to outsource services to others was an admission of weakness or inability. Accordingly, those who were perceived as facilitating a decline in the strength and ability of the Roman people were to be "hate[d] and despise[d]" by all good men.[40] Cicero's category is broad and somewhat ill-defined, but his sentiment is clear: Roman society needed to ostracize or outlaw these figures if it wished to retain its admirable qualities—the same ones that were embodied in the honest farmer.[41]

Topoi, *Infamia*, and Stereotypes

The *topos* of the greedy merchant summarized all of the complicated feelings that were applied to all of these different sub-groups of workers, while the *topos* of the honest farmer reassured Romans of the strength of their *mores*. Neither trope, however, was strictly confined to literature alone. Outside of texts, Roman legal and cultural norms, sharing similar views, reinforced stereotypes and informed both legislative decisions and social relationships. Legal norms, and especially the category of *infamia*, have been studied extensively by Roman historians.[42] *Infamia* was both a legal and a social category, assigned to certain professions that were associated with negative traits in the Roman imagination. The merchants, artisans, and performers who found themselves labeled *infamis* were barred from full participation in public life because of these negative associations.

As Sarah Bond, Catherine Edwards, Jack Lennon, and others have argued, the trades that found themselves most extensively regulated and separated from society were believed to be either literally or figuratively unclean.[43] Thus "smelly" jobs like tanners, "dirty" jobs like grave diggers, and "scandalous" jobs like sex workers or actors were forced into a legal category that ostracized them, at times literally, but mostly socially, from mainstream Roman culture.[44] Though these professions were often no "dirtier" than others, workers could be prevented from holding public office, be denied some kinds of legal protection, or constrained in terms of where they could live and work.

Other, seemingly less objectionable, professions were not legally denied the rights of citizenship, but they were nevertheless considered taboo, unclean, or unacceptable professions to be taken up by good and honest men. Often these workers were held to different standards and subjected to punishments that were not used for members of the general population. Thus, while there were long-standing legal prohibitions, for example, against theft and aiding thieves in the Roman world, the jurist Ulpian argued that additional punishments should be applied to innkeepers who betrayed their guests to robbers:

> … *nisi hoc esset statutum, materia daretur cum furibus adversus eos quos recipiunt coeundi, cum ne nunc quidem abstineant huiusmodi fraudibus.*
>
> …unless this provision were laid down, the means would be given [to innkeepers] for conspiring with thieves against those whom they receive, since even now they do not refrain from this kind of mischief.[45]

This kind of legislation, though unlikely to be relevant, even for innkeepers, on a daily basis, leaned heavily on the "common knowledge" that merchants deserved such treatment—that their likely bad behavior warranted special punishment. In one reading of the text, this may have been because the profession was believed to require a higher degree of trust. Innkeepers were expected to protect their guests from harm and for a longer period of time than most other service providers.[46] Another reading, however, suggests that innkeepers were actually more likely to be tempted to crime than other professionals and that they should consequently be threatened with greater punishments than their peers in other fields. Bias against innkeepers, equating them with thieves, certainly colors the passage, and Ulpian evidently believed that his point of view would be widely accepted, as he does not elaborate further on why he believes innkeepers will join forces with robbers—he believes that his audience will already understand why that would be so, since "even now," he can, without evidence, claim that this kind of betrayal happened regularly.

Ulpian's logic demonstrates that legal and social norms were often complementary, at least in their rough outlines, and that one could often be used to reinforce the other. We also see this in instances of legal conflict, when cultural biases were utilized to strengthen the case of a plaintiff. The case of Ptolemaios son of Diodorus, who lived in Egypt in the second century CE, offers a good example. In addition to his case of assault, which ought to have been a clear-cut legal matter, Ptolemaios takes the time to describe his assailant, also, confusingly, named Ptolemaios, not only as a "violent and nasty man," but also as a greedy moneylender who charged his clients extortionate rates of interest.[47] This information was of material use to Ptolemaios' case, informing the magistrate of the kind of person who was being accused and swaying him to act in accordance with his own prejudices against moneylenders. Ptolemaios believed, probably rightly, that his personal views about people in this profession were likely to align with those of the magistrate and that their shared stereotypes would ultimately help him win his case. If, ultimately, this common dislike manifested as further legal restrictions on the work of moneylenders, so much the better.

Bond has argued that, at a higher level, these kinds of restrictions and punishments were tailored to maintain the social and economic status quo.[48] This is supported by the frequently noted prohibition against commercial work by Roman senators, which was, in turn, commonly reinforced by literary anecdotes. Philostratus, once again, offers an instructive case, when his protagonist Apollonius of Tyana passionately attempts to dissuade a young Spartan noble from pursuing a career in trade. Apollonius argues that such an action would bring shame upon the good name of the man's family and that it was wholly unfitting for an inheritor of the legacy of Lycurgus and Iphitus to "hide himself away in the hold of a ship."[49] Both legally and culturally, becoming a merchant involved the loss of respectability and permanent damage to one's reputation. Not only were elites to be kept away from the corrupting influence of trade, but tradesmen were trapped within their social and economic roles, prevented, even in the face of success, from escaping their social position. While this group might become wealthy, they could never become respectable, so long as they kept buying and selling. Naturally, the lived reality of elite involvement in industry and trade was far more complex, as Sausville demonstrates in this volume, through the example of elite benefactors offering public support to tradesmen in Asia Minor.

Literarily, at least, there was only one exception to this rule that appeared in one set of circumstances: a merchant could potentially escape the shame of his profession by selling out, buying land, and taking up the respectable work of a farmer. Practically, it is clear that this did not actually remove the taint of trade: the ancestral closets of famous Romans are clogged with the skeletons of family members who once worked as tradesmen and whose infamy managed to taint even their respectable, landowning descendants.[50] Yet, the promise that farming could be, and was, a respectable line of work made it clear that it was not work itself that was disreputable, just the work of merchants.

Whether officially or socially codified, *infamia* was merely one manifestation of the common, cultural stereotypes that circulated about Roman merchants. Stereotypes are exaggerated opinions about certain categories of people that are used to justify behavior toward them.[51] Stereotypes stand apart from *topoi*, as they are not confined to the specific circumstances in which stock characters are useful. Moreover, *topoi* can lag behind current stereotypes, preserving even older, more conservative points of view than those in contemporary circulation. Yet stereotypes can also be semi-fossilized and are often reinforced, cyclically, by literary tropes, even as contemporary evidence begins to contradict them. Their long-term stability arises, mainly, from the phenomenon of "confirmation bias," a tendency, even among individuals who are aware of their bias, to accept more readily information that agrees with their preconceived ideas and to ignore, reject, or dismiss information that contradicts their opinions.[52] As a result, no matter how exaggerated or faulty the reasoning behind a stereotype, most people are unable, in the heat of the moment, to sense any injustice or notice any inconsistency in their positions. Contradictory evidence is typically treated as anomalous, and, in the case of Roman merchants, any excessive haggling, cut corners, or exaggeration about quality was useful evidence of merchant greediness, deception, and cheating. Over time, these stereotypes became more and more deeply entrenched in Roman culture and were passed down through many generations.

Consequently, the similarities of literary, legal, and stereotypical depictions of merchants should not be surprising. For one thing, there was a substantial overlap between legal and literary writers, and both groups shared a similar social and cultural milieu, but in general, stereotypes tend to be widely held in any given society. They gain strength from a collective understanding of how groups can be categorized and, accordingly, how they should be treated. While individuals may hold their own, personal prejudices, these do not rise to the level of a stereotype until their feelings are shared by a majority of the population. At that point, individuals and groups feel justified to act in accordance with the beliefs they hold, and the stereotypes become largely self-sustaining, preventing their subjects from escaping the role that society has created for them.

For merchants, the result of these stereotypes was that they were regularly denied any benefit of the doubt and they were painted with the same, broad brush as all their peers. The distaste of Roman society, writ large, was inescapable; merchants were aware not only of the legal restrictions placed upon them, but of the widespread belief in their dishonesty, greed, and shamelessness. Considering the diversity of professions encapsulated by the Roman idea of commercial work, a category that was mostly defined as "everything but agriculture," this was undoubtedly a frustrating oversimplification of reality for merchants, who not only sought to stand out from their immediate peers, but were also eager to differentiate their profession from those that they, themselves, often viewed as disreputable.[53]

Merchant Awareness of, and Responses to, Stereotypes

Merchants were highly aware of negative stereotypes about their profession. Even in the absence of a large, literate body of tradesmen reading the libelous claims of authors with a philosophical axe to grind, there is plenty of evidence to suggest that stereotypical treatments of merchants manifested themselves in daily life and that merchants had to address them. As with other kinds of prejudice, anti-commercialism was both actively and passively expressed, and it influenced all aspects of trade, from interpersonal relationships to the legal frameworks of exchange itself.

Consequently, even at the end of their lives, when merchants took the time to carefully articulate their successes and present them for posterity, they regularly displayed hints of anxiety that these stereotypes would functionally erase all their accomplishments. Funerary inscriptions are full of efforts to anticipate accusations of greed or deceit, either with denials or with statements emphasizing the merchant's virtues instead.

These strategies were keyed to the outlines of the stereotypes we have already discussed, especially to that of the greedy, deceitful merchant. In both public and funerary contexts, merchant claims often specifically respond to accusations of greed in their attempt to use examples of personal or professional generosity as an antidote. This strategy appears often in the work of merchant associations, which used the combined resources of many workers to make large, public displays of community-mindedness, especially in the form of monuments or honors to public figures.[54] The latter, as Sausville discusses in this volume, was a strategy founded on professional solidarity, alliances of workers designed to provide specific aid and to overcome anti-merchant bias. In many cases, even personal inscriptions adopt this language of generosity, attempting to elevate smaller-scale acts of beneficence to a level that warranted public notice.[55]

So regular was the need to assure readers of a merchant's good character that, over time, the most common tactics began to develop into epigraphic *formulae*, appearing in multiple examples and all around the empire:

in hoc tumulo iacet corpus exanimis
cuius spiritus inter deos receptus est.
sic enim meruit, L. Statius Onesimus
viae Appiae multorum annorum negotia(n)s,
homo super omnes fidelissimus,
cuius fama in aeterno nota est,
qui vixit sine macula an(nos) p(lus) m(inusve) LXVIII
Statia Crescentina co(n)iu(n)x
marito dignissimo et merito
cum quo vixit cum bona concordia

sine alteritrum animi lesionem
bene merenti fecit.

In this tomb lies the body of the lifeless man, whose spirit has been welcomed among the gods. For thus he, Lucius Statius Onesimus, deserved. Selling for many years on the Appian Way, he was an exceptionally honest man beyond all others, whose reputation is known in perpetuity, who lived without a stain for roughly sixty-eight years.

Statia Crescentina, his wife, made this for a most worthy and deserving man, lived with him with good harmony without any exchanged hurt feelings because he was deserving.[56]

The inscription of Lucius Statius Onesimus provides a good example of some common *formulae*, including not only numerous superlatives, including the descriptor *fidelissimus* (very trustworthy), the natural antonym of *perfidus* (deceitful) but also a common *formula*: a denial established by the use of *sine* and followed by a specific vice. In Onesimus' case, this is *sine macula*, literally without mark or stain, but, more literarily, without shame or disgrace.[57] The dirtiness associated with certain commercial professions is being evoked, and denied, in this line, just as other merchants use the same phrasing to reject *fraus* (trickery) and *crimen* (wrongdoing).[58] Though separated by time, space, and profession, each worker responded to an aspect of the same, multi-pronged problem: the stereotype that threatened to taint their memory beyond the grave.

In life, merchants seem to have had a different set of strategies for confronting this bias. Some, like Aulus Umbricius Scaurus, the garum magnate of Pompeii, chose to face it boldly, decorating his home with images of the fish sauce he produced.[59] The mosaics in his atrium greeted every guest, whether they arrived for business or personal reasons, and the images of garum jars (*urcei*) immediately reminded everyone of the source of Scaurus' wealth and status. He used both, it seems, to promote his son (or perhaps his grandson) for public office, though we cannot know the emotions that may have accompanied the choice to watch later generations move away from the family business.[60]

Like Scaurus, it is not uncommon to see merchants expressing pride in their profession. In some cases, their expressions of gratitude for their work and public personae as workers is all that we have preserved of their lives. Despite the stereotypes, many embraced their professions, even when their displays could be overblown or distasteful to others.[61] Some, however, were cowed, or even apologetic in the face of the disapprobation of Roman society. The denials we have already examined represent one form of this tactic, but the funerary inscription of the slave-boy Vitalis goes a step further, concluding with a direct apology for his business practices, which seemingly conformed with the common stereotypes about merchant deceit and greed:

> Vitalis C. Lavi Fausti
> ser(vus), idem filius, verna domo
> natus, hic situs est, vixit
> annos XVI, institor tabernas
> aprianas a populo acceptus
> idem ad dibus ereptus. Rogo
> vos viatores si quid minus
> dedi me(n)sura ut patri mero adicere
> ignoscatis, rogo per superos
> et infernos ut patrem et matre(m)
> commendatos (h)abeatis
> et vale
>
> Here lies Vitalis, slave of Gaius Lavus Faustus and son of the same man, born a slave to the house. He lived sixteen years, a manager of the Apriana Tavern, though accepted by the people, he was snatched away by the gods. I ask you, travelers, if I gave you some lesser measure so that I might enrich my father, forgive me. I ask those above and those below that you hold my father and mother in your favor. And so farewell.[62]

Vitalis' justification, or rather the justification that was put into his mouth by his master and father, is that he cut corners on the goods he sold as an act of loyalty to his family. While he is, performatively at least, made to sound apologetic in the inscription, the rhetorical framing suggests that those around Vitalis would have understood the difficult position he was in, caught between running a business honestly and meeting the expectations of his father. The text suggests that he was mostly well-liked in his community, that he was *acceptus* by the people around him, despite his tendency to cheat. The inscription is part preservation of the young man's character, part apology, and part attempt to rehabilitate the public image of Vitalis' father, whose reputation is wrapped up in that of his son. Ultimately, it is, at least in part, an acknowledgment that any defense of a merchant's character was going to be a hard sell in the Roman world. What is essential is that an attempt was made, in this unusual inscription, to do all these things and that merchants were grappling with stereotypes that made all behavior, good and bad alike, difficult to defend and present in a positive light.

Non-elite Stereotypes

It is difficult to deny that merchants were responding to stereotypes, but the question remains: whose stereotypes? Mayer has argued that merchants could not have known what elite authors had written about them and that merchant self-representation was therefore wholly distinct from the *topos* of literary fame. Merchants were aware of and carefully monitored their own systems of categorization and judgment that originated from their peers, not their social superiors, and any overlap between elite rhetoric shaming merchants and merchant expressions of anxiety must be, essentially, coincidental.

To be substantiated, this view requires a deep understanding of the stereotypes and categorizations of non-elite society. Non-elite stereotypes are challenging to study, partly due to the available evidence and partly because close contact between merchants and their social peers seems to have generated nuanced opinions that tend to categorize single types of workers, rather than larger groups of professions. Among non-elite sources, it is difficult to find statements about artisans in general, but it is possible to find, for example, common, specific stereotypes about cobblers, fullers, and goldsmiths. These do not lend themselves to neat summation, and while they share some points of overlap with elite stereotypes, they also deviate from them in critical ways, combining nitpicking critiques of certain professions with a generalized belief that being cheated by merchants was, essentially, inevitable.

Artemidorus' *Oneirocritica*, itself the product of a worker whom Cicero would have identified as a "professional", offers a useful starting point for considering non-elite stereotypes. While it is certainly a polished creation of a literate and careful author who likely enjoyed above-average wealth, it is full of casual references to members of many professions, and the meanings that are attributed to them suggest that Artemidorus and his sources understood commercial and artisanal work at a deeper level than many other contemporary authors.[63] In one telling example, he relates that courtesans and charlatans are represented in dreams by marine birds that "grab and gobble down whatever they can get" because both the birds and the people are "rapacious and foolish."[64] The choice to associate sex workers and swindlers in the same category is one that reflects a broader, non-elite stereotype that aligns prostitution not only with greed, but also with deception.[65] An Italian brothel-keeper, evidently engaging with this stereotype specifically, asserted that she established and operated her business *sine fraude*, without deception, but rather built her career from her own resources and those of her freedwoman colleague.[66]

Artemidorus' interpretations of merchants are often similarly pejorative and specific in their reasoning.[67] He states that vultures are a good sign when they appear in the dreams of tanners, as both are shunned by society because of their association with dead things, but that they signify disaster for doctors for the same reason.[68] Once again, Artemidorus' logic echoes common stereotypes about the trade. Aesop's *Fabulae* preserves at least two stories about tanners, both relating to the stink of the work and the frustration of neighbors with the shame a tannery brought to a neighborhood.[69] Despite these associations, it is difficult to determine whether Artemidorus meant this to be an exclusively negative interpretation. Vultures were famously a good omen in Roman culture, seen by Romulus and Remus at the founding of the city, and generally were believed to bring good fortune to a marching army.[70]

In other passages, Artemidorus is even positive about professions, likening them to mothers and stating that if a merchant dreams of having sex with his mother, his business will thrive.[71] While he is never totally even-handed, professions are a casual part of the world that Artemidorus describes, and he takes the time, in many cases, to interpret the dreams had by specific professionals, as he believes that a given dream is subjectively dependent upon the circumstances of the dreamer.[72] In each reference to retailers, artisans, and service providers, we can see a deeper, more specific understanding of the differences that existed among different kinds of work. Artemidorus is clearly doing a more detailed analysis than a simple calculation of relative skill or cleanliness.

Less literarily, non-elites found many ways to share their opinions about merchants. Often their comments are designed to shame and accuse the workers they encountered in their daily lives and to generalize their personal experiences into broader stereotypes. Pompeian graffiti offer numerous examples of customers and neighbors accusing inn- and bar-keepers of deceitful and miserly conduct. One example accuses a shopkeeper (*copo*) of serving his customers watered-down wine while saving the good stuff for himself.[73] The scribbler accuses the man of lying and wishes that he would experience the disappointment and frustration he inflicts upon his customers. The accusation is undoubtedly the result of either a single instance or repeated bad service, but there is also a repetition of the old accusation of greed and its regular counterpart, deceit (*mendacia*) manifesting itself in the complaint. The practice of watering down wine was commonplace throughout the Roman world, but evidently this vendor had crossed the line, saving himself money and cheating his customers in the process.

Graffiti commonly target a specific merchant, rather than expressing generalities about the group. Nevertheless, they regularly align with broader stereotypes, suggesting that either merchant practices were actually objectionable or that customers, perhaps primed by these common stereotypes, were inclined to think the worst of retailers and apt to consider a single, bad experience as emblematic of the character of everyone who practiced that trade. In terms of innkeepers, Horace's *Satires* preserve a strikingly similar accusation that his host served his guests meager portions, presumably without any kind of discount.[74] While Horace's poetry was not necessarily circulating widely along the streets of Pompeii, the overlap of elite and non-elite views in this case suggests a widespread cultural distaste for and distrust of the profession that likely colored the perceptions of future patrons.[75]

Even without graffiti, some professions were clearly the target of more specific kinds of stereotyping among non-elites. Aesop's *Fabulae* preserves numerous texts that seemingly attribute to butchers a baseline of gullibility as they are regularly robbed by boys and dogs, but also careful attention to their work through narratives where they systematically slaughter animals for market.[76] While these are seemingly inconclusive, a mixture of bad and good that suggests nuance was possible and perhaps easier to find when considering tradesmen who were regular features in the daily lives of non-elites, the stereotype of the deceitful cobbler is much more consistent. Whether in their own work or in cases where cobblers stray from their profession to dabble in that of others, they not only are inveterate liars, but also swindlers who cheat their customers of their due.[77] The best example is the narrative of *Hermes and the Cobblers*, which claims that the god, as he was distributing a measure of deceit into every profession, concluded with the cobblers and poured not only the same amount into cobblers as the rest, but also all the excess, leaving them the most prolific liars of the bunch.[78] Cobblers, who were encountered less frequently than butchers in the day-to-day shopping of non-elites, may have suffered from their lack of familiarity or just from the greater cost associated with repairing or replacing leather goods.

Perhaps the best-documented case of all is that of barbers, who are known from a wide range of sources to have been stereotyped as inveterate gossips who were indiscreet and not to be trusted with any sensitive information.[79] Gossip was distrusted and shamed in Roman society. Gossiping was believed to be, at best, an idle practice that benefited no one and, at worst, a malicious hobby that did real harm to the innocent subjects of speculation and rumor.[80] There has been a strong push in recent scholarship to rehabilitate gossip as a necessary tool that spread information through social networks and benefitted many.[81] There is substantial evidence that gossip corresponded to and enhanced bonds of trust among friends and colleagues, even in antiquity, but gossip was nevertheless believed to be deceptive, shameless, and harmful to the subject and the morals of both the speaker and the listener. Even if, as others have argued, barbershops in antiquity acted, as they do today, as hubs for social contact in which news was received, analyzed, and spread, barbers were nevertheless a popular target for mockery and were, at least on a superficial level, to be avoided.[82]

Ancient mockery and shame tactics are preserved for us today in texts like the *Philogelos*, a fourth-century CE collection of jokes that provides many examples of the ways that non-elites seem to have used humor to distance themselves from merchants.[83] For barbers, this collection preserves:

> When a talkative barber asked, "How should I cut your hair?" A witty man replied, "Silently."[84]

The joke is one of many about barbers, and indeed humor seems to have been one of the few positive things associated with the profession. A now-lost collection of jokes, likely titled, "At the Barbershop," made barbers not the butt of the joke but used their shops as the setting.[85] These jokes, regardless of target, had long lives. Plutarch implies that this particular joke had roots in the late fifth century BCE, as he shared a version in which the witty customer was King Archelaus of Macedon.[86] In that version, as in the *Philogelos*, the implication is that the customer is wise not to engage with the barber, not only to avoid the annoyance of idle chatter, but also to protect himself from the natural tendency of all barbers to know (or say) too much.

Whoever delivers the punchline, the joke mocks the barber as an annoyance and a chatterbox. A similar joke, also from the *Philogelos*, mocks a clothes-mender in a similar way, with a frustrated and grumpy man demanding that the merchant take his tunic and mend it in silence.[87] Evidently, shutting merchants up was a fantasy many customers entertained, and many merchants were inclined to gossip, either to invite intimacy with their clients or simply to pass the time.[88] Being talkative is a fairly innocuous vice, compared with lying or greed, but it is likely that the complaints we see about merchant gossip mask a more serious concern. Barbers, especially, enjoyed an unusual level of intimacy with their clients that was repeated on a regular basis over many years, if the barber was good at his job. Proximity and familiarity might tempt a customer to be more open with their barber than was wise, sharing information that was potentially sensitive.[89] Even worse, a barber held a recognizable weapon in his hand as he plied his trade. All men were potentially vulnerable under the barber's blade, and, anecdotally, at least, we learn that some elite customers were uncomfortable giving their barber this kind of access to their person.[90]

Some barbers evidently used their proximity to important people to become wealthy and set up fine shops, to the point that, as Ammianus relates, the Emperor Julian decided that barbers had risen too high and were encouraging his court to indulge in luxury. He ultimately exiled them to forcibly remove the temptation they posed.[91] The uppermost echelon of these workers threatened elite ideals of self-sufficiency, purveying Cicero's feared "sensual pleasure" and leading to the slow degeneration of the moral fiber of society. Nevertheless, even specialty barbers seem to have been commonplace in the city, providing a vital service, as Romans regularly complain of the difficulty in keeping a blade sharp enough to shave themselves safely.[92]

Despite the belief that, at some level at least, barbers could not be totally trusted, it is clear that non-elites nevertheless flocked to barbershops seeking out the day's news and conversation. These spaces were semi-public and regularly hosted gatherings that were convivial and friendly.[93] This was commonplace across many different professions. In art, retail shops are regularly depicted with a range of customers and onlookers present, while in both elite and non-elite contexts, we hear of shops functioning as landmarks, gathering places, and the sites of (local) historical significance.[94]

The latter, especially, marks a serious departure from elite stereotypes about merchants. Within the regular contours of the *topos*, workshops were depicted as the dirty places where dirty merchants spent their days, but when faced with the potential destruction of a blacksmith's forge, the people of Prusa railed against Dio Chrysostom's casual belief that the place was unimportant. Though we only have Dio's own words on the subject, we see his confusion at the response of the local people, whom he expected to be grateful to have a clean, new portico replacing the filthy squalor of the workshop.[95] Instead, the population rose up to shame Dio as a "destroyer of cities" and to defend the smith's forge, which they say was the site of "happy memories." Evidently, the workshop was a community center of some kind, and the blacksmith, even if he worked in a "dirty" profession, was nevertheless an important member of the neighborhood, whose presence *improved*, rather than detracted from, the area.[96]

Dio is indignant about his treatment, by the implication that anyone in society might prefer the space and company of a blacksmith to his efforts at beautification, to the extent that he brings it up multiple times across his writing.[97] He attempts to downplay the significance of the blacksmith and his forge, claiming the inappropriateness of the locals' attachment, by asserting that it was not as if he had torn down a great monument like the Propylaea. Dio's confusion is predicated on the fundamental difference between elite and non-elite stereotypes. In the former, there is no room for exceptions to the rule. All merchants, artisans, and service providers are greedy, deceitful, cheats whose work hurt Roman society more than it helped. Commercial work was shameful and dirty and no amount of personal virtue could excuse a merchant who did not attempt to work his or her way out of that trade and into a respectable, literal field. In the latter, however, there was room for an individual to be more than the stereotype, to be like Vitalis, a cheater who was nevertheless *acceptus*, accepted and welcome among his peers.

Elite stereotypes existed at a remove from trade itself, not cut off from it entirely, but operating in an un-reality, where authors and wealthy men sent proxies to deal with the details of exchange itself. Non-elite stereotypes, by contrast, grew up at the heart of the competitive atmosphere, the zero-sum *game*, of trade. Like a game, a certain amount of cheerful cheating could be expected and tolerated, and it ultimately did no harm to the underlying relationships that naturally developed between neighbors and friends. Both "good" and "bad" merchants played the game and carved out their place in the community. The blacksmith is given very little description, not even a name, by Dio, who refers to him throughout as "So-and-so" but whether he was a saintly figure who did no wrong or an inveterate liar, he nevertheless held a position in his neighborhood that allowed him to be part of, and an exception to, common stereotypes, at once typical and special to the people who knew him and willingly rose to his defense when his livelihood was threatened by an outsider.[98]

Conclusion

The response of the people of Prusa to the blacksmith "So-and-so" takes us a long way from Philostratus' merchant and vinedresser, but the juxtaposition of these two cases illuminates both the differences between elite and non-elite stereotypes and the effects those stereotypes had upon merchants fighting against the current to make a living in Ancient Rome. While elites could bring themselves, at times, to admit grudgingly that trade was necessary—always with the caveat that it was a necessary evil—their writings do not reflect the way that non-elites could both mock and coexist peaceably with merchants, artisans, and service providers.

Elite stereotypes were generalized and ossified, changing little from the Homeric canon to late antiquity and, at best, they were able to recognize that there might be some distinction between the character of a doctor and a tanner. Their stereotypes were pervasive and, despite their origin, at times influential among merchants themselves. Many merchants, especially those who achieved substantial wealth, were aware of and felt pressured by elite stereotypes. We see this manifest itself in what they chose to do with the profits of their labor: they worked to ensure that the next generation did not stay in trade, as Aulus Umbricius Scaurus seems to have done for the succeeding generations of his family.

Among non-elites, however, stereotypes had a different character and a different impact. Merchants were still viewed as rogues who willingly gave themselves over to greed and miserliness, but they could also, at times, be understood as the rascals who offered you a laugh or a piece of juicy gossip while taking your last *nummus*. Moreover, non-elite stereotypes about merchants and artisans were specific, tailored to particular trades, and based on personal, but commonplace, experiences: feeling cheated by a disappointing night of drinking, regretting a secret shared, or finding that the dealer who was just so pleasant or friendly had given you far less than you paid for. These were relatable experiences to most who lived and worked among merchants themselves, people who did their own shopping and needed to patronize businesses directly. Merchants understood that the views of their neighbors and friends were tinged by negative stereotypes, and many of them responded by attempting to stand out in positive ways: by being generous, helping the community, and giving over their workspace so that the neighbors could form happy memories. Rather than leave their profession behind, merchants responded to non-elite stereotypes by embracing their work, warts and all, and reminding everyone of the place they held in the community, both despite and because of the work they did, day-in, day-out.

Whether preserved for us today as literary *topoi*, stereotypical bias in legislation, or the casual accusation and banter of graffiti and jokes, work and workers were a regular topic of debate and discussion in the Roman world. Ancient attitudes toward merchants, especially, have posed a serious challenge to historians of the period, but they are illuminated when we are able to identify why, when, and among what audiences these tropes were useful. Through this study, we have been able to see how different groups employed stereotypes to constrain merchants and to pressure them, more generally, into conduct that was deemed acceptable within their contemporary context. "Acceptable" merchant conduct was, naturally, socially contingent, and variable among elite and non-elite audiences, but in analyzing the nuance and variety of non-elite stereotypes we can steadily improve our understanding of the many roles of work in Roman society.

Notes

1. For example, Homer *Odyssey* 8.158–164; Hesiod *Works and Days* 625–8. The latter offers perhaps the earliest possible neutral depiction of merchant work, but even in this case Hesiod is clear that Perses' trading is subordinate to his more honorable agricultural labor.
2. D'Arms (1981).
3. Giardina (1993) chose not to include craftsmen in his discussion, on the grounds that such people were set apart by their skill, though the physical evidence of workshops in Pompeii and Dura Europos demonstrates that artisans sold their wares directly to consumers as well as through middlemen. The category "merchant" is an imprecise one, but it is meant, throughout this chapter, to encapsulate the many varieties of non-agricultural work that the Romans saw as less reputable than farming.
4. Giardina (1993: 260).
5. Roman objections, whether performative or sincere, to *latifundia* are regularly associated with language that praises small farms or laments their decline; see, e.g., Pliny *Natural History* 18.7.
6. Mayer (2020: 111).

7. A variation on this idea appears in Lennon (2022), e.g., 64–65, who argues that the denigration of certain professions by elites was essentially performative for an audience of elite peers, not for the workers at hand.
8. More has been done on stereotypes surrounding race and ethnicity, see, e.g., Dueck (2021), and also art, where issues of elite fashion and non-elite emulation have been more commonly debated.
9. Philostratus *Heroicus* 1.3–4.
10. Philostratus *Heroicus* 1.5–7, the vinedresser himself comments that this is a golden age fantasy at 2.2; Giardina (1993: 248–9).
11. Herodotus 4.196; Kurke (1999), especially the introduction and chapter 1, investigate the "imaginary" history of money and metals as developed in Herodotus.
12. Publilius Syrus *Sententiae* 75, *Bona opinio hominum tutior pecunia est*, suggests rather the opposite, that money is a poor metric for both moral worth and personal security.
13. The greed of merchants was both proverbial and constantly referred to, e.g., Chariton, *Chaereas and Callirhoe* 1.11–12, *Disticha Catonis* 1.29, 2.19. In many cases it is tied to a specific profession, see, e.g., Strong (2016, ch. 1) on the greed of prostitutes.
14. Of course, this was present, historically, in the economic aspects of *amicitia*, see, e.g., Verboven (2002). Coffee (2017) follows this thread to perhaps a more literal social-historical interpretation of changing economic practices than the evidence can bear. In either case, here, the belief among Romans that this was the case is what is essential.
15. See discussion in Sancinito (2024), of, e.g., Publilius Syrus *Sententiae* 337: "Profits in trade can only be made by another's loss."
16. *Edict on Maximum Prices* Preface, lines 71–77.
17. There is a tendency among Roman authors to offer similar excuses for historical or literary figures who had at one time worked as merchants. In many cases, authors try to say that these individuals did not actually pursue profit for themselves, but rather used trade to provide useful goods or to experience other cultures. Plutarch *Life of Solon* 2, mentions several famous Greek philosophers and scientists who worked in trade to fund their travel and/or work. Philostratus *Lives of the Sophists* Life 21, chapter 603, discusses Proclus of Naucratis, who reportedly did not even seek profit, just covered his costs to provide useful goods to others.
18. Both Cheung and Holleran (this volume) address the itinerancy of workers and the challenges of building reputation and trust while on the move. On the stereotypical "foreignness" of merchants, see the discussion below.
19. Kolendo (1993).
20. Cato *De Agricultura* preface 2–4 is the *locus classicus* of the type, though many authors and genres contribute to a general idealization of the

countryside and country living. In the same passage Cato also clearly expresses a softened version of the common attitude toward traders.

21. *IG* II-III (II3) 1103/Oliver 1989 #77. See discussion by Silver (2011) of this law of Hadrian, limiting middlemen in the fishing industry.
22. Giardina (1993: 246).
23. This seems to have been a Mediterranean-wide preference and can be traced in the Rabbinic material. Rabbi Elezar says: "Any man who does not have his own land is not a man," and the later Rabbi Papa says: "sow, do not buy, even if the cost is the same." T.B. Yeb. 63a.
24. Hence Juvenal *Satires* 3.62 on the "pollution" of Syrian influence in Rome.
25. Petronius' Trimalchio (*Satyricon* 26–78) offers a mockery of the ideal, since he is clearly a figure to be ridiculed and yet he, of all people, can survive entirely on the produce of his own land.
26. Horden and Purcell (2000: 365ff), D'Arms (1981: 85–87), and Hopkins (1983: 85) all argue that, while difficult to quantify, most trade must have taken place locally.
27. A trend that is visible from the late Republic, e.g., Lucilius 540–1 Warmington, to late antiquity, e.g., Apollinaris, *Letters* 1.8.2. Giardina (1993: 248) notes that in Byzantine records it was westerners who were considered greedy, so it is foreignness, rather than geography, that determines the direction of this stereotype.
28. On the Eastern and the threat of effeminacy: Corbeill (1996: Ch. 4), Edwards (1993: 80), Richlin (2003: 218).
29. Seneca Minor *Letters* 56.2.
30. There is rarely, a sense that some authors that they know they are being unjust to merchants. Philostratus' Phoenician merchant, for example, gets to push back a little bit against the idea that the farmer was an a-commercial actor, but most authors do not bring nuance to their categories. Cicero, discussed below, offers the most thorough and most famous exception.
31. Cicero *de Officiis* 1.150 (42).
32. Thus, the title "Daedalus of Words" is bestowed upon several ancient thinkers (Ulpian, Theodorus of Byzantium) with the positive implication that each is a master craftsman in his own field.
33. Discussed in Lennon (2022), and Bond (2016: esp. chs. 2 and 3), Cicero *De Officiis* 1.150: *Opificesque omnes in sordida arte versantur.* Sausville (this volume) discusses skilled laborers and the public benefits they could receive.
34. Seneca *Letters* 88.1, *Nullum suspicio, nullum in bonis numero, quod ad aes exit. Meritoria artificia sunt, hactenus utilia, si praeparant ingenium, non detinent.* I consider nothing and count nothing among the good things of life, which leads to money. Such employments are just profit-bringing, useful only if they prepare the mind and do not detain it.

35. Sausville (this volume) highlights the fact that many workers enjoyed the support of local benefactors, which suggests that Seneca's disdain is untypical, both literarily and practically, of elite attitudes, at least toward learned professions.
36. For example, Lucian *The Dream (Somnium sive Vita Luciani)* esp. 1–12.
37. Cicero *de Officiis*, 1.150, *est enim in illis ipsa merces auctoramentum servitutis*. For the wage given to them is a sign of slavery.
38. The prevalence of harvest festival narratives in poetry gives us some insight into how authors imagined the emotions that arose from a successful harvest, e.g., Tibullus 2.1. The lack of "completed craft" poetry is probably not merely an absence of evidence, but a reflection of a lack of cultural awareness that this, too, could generate feelings of pride.
39. Cicero *de Officiis* 1.150.
40. Dio *Orationes* 31.37–38, *ἀλλὰ τοὺς μὲν καπήλους τοὺς ἐν τοῖς μέτροις κακουργοῦντας, οἷς ὁ βίος ἐστὶν αὐτόθεν ἀπὸ αἰσχροκερδείας, μισεῖτε καὶ κολάζετε*.
41. Cicero *de Officiis* 1.151.
42. Bond (2016: 7–11) discusses the perhaps outsized emphasis on legal restriction, which seems to have been most confined to those who sold their bodies. Many professions were disreputable without the specific legal categorization of *infamia*.
43. Lennon (2022), Bond (2016), and Edwards (1997).
44. Tanners are the archetypal example of this, but Bond (2016: ch. 3) has argued that this is not actually reflected in the legal sources for tanners. Mortuary workers, however, were legally required, in some cases, to live outside the city limits; see Bond (2016, ch. 2), and Lennon (2013, ch. 4).
45. Ulpian *Digest* 4.9.1.1.
46. Bogen (1992) provides much of the legal material on the burdens placed on innkeepers; he argues that much of the evidence has been wrongly read through the lens of later British common law.
47. SB XX 14401, "From Ptolemaios son of Diodorus, also known as Diskoros… Ptolemaios, son of a certain Pappos, the former gymnasiarch… a violent and nasty man by nature, and who lives the life of a moneylender and does every sort of forbidden, foul thing, asking for a stater of interest on account of his power in the *nome*.…"
48. Bond (2016), see esp. introduction.
49. Philostratus *Life of Apollonius of Tyana* 4.32.3.
50. For example, Suetonius *Life of Augustus* 4.2, reports that the emperor had a great-grandfather who ran a perfume shop and grandfathers who were a baker and a moneychanger; Aulus Gellius, *Attic Nights* 15.4, describes the former muleteer who became consul and was publicly ridiculed by the Roman people.

51. Most modern definitions of stereotypes, including this one, draw their inspiration from Allport (1954: 191). Stangor and Schaller (1996: 22), argue that stereotypes are, themselves, invested in maintaining the status quo and defend their position through appeals to emotion, even when the evidence is not supportive of their case.
52. See, e.g., Skowronski and Carlston (1992).
53. Stereotyping of merchants by merchants occured, mostly between professions, rather than within them. This is hardly surprising, as there is no reason why two unrelated fields should not share in prejudices that were common in the general population.
54. On associations, see originally Van Nijf (1997). Holleran (this volume) also discusses the collaboration of professionals to secure work and distribute reputable workers.
55. The provision of burial places for others was an especially common practice. The formula of *libertis libertabvsqve* became standard, even in cases where it is unclear that the deceased could have afforded to have freedmen or women dependents.
56. *CIL* VI 9663, Rome.
57. *Ibid.*, line 7.
58. *CIL* IX 2029, the funerary inscription of Vibia Chresta, and *CIL* V 7647, the funerary relief of Quintus Minicius Faber, a cartwright.
59. Scaurus' home in Pompeii, Regio VII 16.15/16, is north of the Porta Marina and has never been fully published. The best record is that of Mau (1902: ch. 36).
60. Campbell (2010) has discussed the inscription on the tomb of Scaurus' descendent, including the debate about the exact relationship between the elder and younger Scauri. The text gives no obvious indication of the fate of the business.
61. The reason that the hyperbolic Trimalchio has received such consistent attention from historians is that there seem to be a number of non-fictional figures who share characteristics with him. The tomb of Eurysaces the baker offers one visual comparison; see Petersen (2003). The funerary inscription of Lucius Nerusius Mithres, *CIL* IX 4796, is another example.
62. *ILS* 7479, Macedonia.
63. Harris-McCoy (2012: 30) provides a brief discussion of Artemidorus' autobiography and discusses his competition and engagement with others in his field.
64. Artemidorus *Oneiracritica* 2.17: *ἑταίρας σημαίνει και μαχίμους γυναῖκας ἤ ἄνδρας γόντας ἁρπακτικούς... ὅ τι γὰρ ἂν λάβωσι, τοῦτο καταπίνουσιν.*
65. Discussed in both Strong (2016), and Pomeroy (1995).
66. *CIL* IX 2029, funerary inscription of Vibia Chresta and Vibia Calybenis.

67. *Pace* Sausville (this volume), who is right to say that Artemidorus is rarely direct in his condemnations and never attacks paid labor specifically, rather, it is his comparisons that are often unflattering and echo common stereotypes about "dirty" professions.
68. Artemidorus *Oneirocritica* 2.20.
69. Aesop *Fabulae* 543, 544.
70. Livy *Ab Urbe Condita* 1.7.
71. Artemidorus *Oneirocritica* 1.79. The implication is that sex is antithetical to idleness, so "getting busy with" one's mother is akin to having a prosperous business.
72. For example, Artemidorus *Oneirocritica* 3.52, on dreams about dunghills, which are good for those who work with crowds and in dirty occupations (*τοῖς τὰς ῥυπώδεις ἐργασίας ἐργαζομένοις*) but becomes a bad omen for other professions or when dung is being thrown about.
73. CIL IV 3948. *Talia te fallant utinam mendacia, copo. Tu vendis aquam, et bibes ipse merum.*
74. Horace *Satires* 1.5.71–74.
75. Milnor (2014) also argues for a much deeper engagement with poetry among non-elites than previously believed.
76. On gullibility: Aesop *Fabulae* 540 and 598; on systematic work: Aesop *Fabulae* 58 and 446.
77. Aesop *Fabulae* 588.
78. Aesop *Fabulae* 519. Interestingly, other versions of the narrative, see Chambry (1927: 111), substitute tanners for cobblers, which is likely indicative of the oral culture in which these fables circulated, picking up new punchlines and getting shortened or lengthened, depending on the circumstances.
79. Toner (2015), Lewis (1995), and Nicolson (1891) have all studied barbers closely. Ancient testimony for the gossiping of barbers is plentiful; see, e.g., Plutarch *de Garrulitate* 13 or *Moralia* 509a.
80. For example, Theophrastus *Characters* 3, "Idle Chatter" suggests that the major harm done is wasting the time of the unwilling listener, but also provides a window into the nature of this kind of conversation.
81. Wickham (1998) provides a good summary of the social benefits of gossip. See also Emler (1992), Guastella (2017), and Gluckman (1963).
82. On gossip and hubs of knowledge see: Wickham (1998); on the association with barbers, see: Toner (2015).
83. While joke books also target groups like "Sidonians" and "eggheads," non-elite sources do not regularly lambast entire professional groups. No comparable jokes exist, for example, targeting farmers.
84. *Philogelos* 148.
85. Suda *Phi* 364.

86. Plutarch *Sayings of Kings and Commanders* Archelaus.
87. *Philogelos* 190.
88. Seneca Minor *Letters* 56.2, to Lucilius complains of the noise near the baths. Another loud, annoying merchant is a milk seller in Calpurnius Siculus *Eclogue* 4.25–26
89. Plutarch *De Garrulitate* 13, recounts an Athenian barber who learned, in advance of the Ekklesia, of the defeat of Athens in Sicily. He was unable to report from whom he had heard the story and was tortured for spreading "misinformation."
90. *Ibid.*, also relates that the tyrant Dionysius of Syracuse killed his barber after the man joked that he held a blade to the tyrant's neck every week. There was some cause for real-world concern; see: Digest 9.2.11.pr for a discussion of a case where a slave was accidentally killed by a barber.
91. Ammianus *Res Gestae* XXII.4.
92. Nicholson (1891) discusses the difficulty of maintaining razors and provides a thorough analysis of the relevant evidence and vocabulary of barbering.
93. Plutarch *Quaestiones Convivales* V.5.2 records Theophrastus calling barbershops "wineless symposia" because the patrons sit around and chat.
94. For the visuals, see Clarke (2003). In funerary inscriptions, shops are regularly referred to as part of a landscape dotted with landmarks (e.g., *CIL* VI 9671 and 9822). More specifically, the scene of Acts 19:24–27 depicts the silversmiths of Ephesus seemingly gathering at the workshop of Demetrius to discuss the threat posed by Paul.
95. Dio Chrysostom *Orationes* 47.10–11, 17, 19–20.
96. Rogers (this volume) also notes the importance of labor to its local communities in his discussion of the *fabri tignarii* relief.
97. The same smithy is also mentioned in Dio Chrysostom *Orationes* 40.8–9.
98. Dio Chrysostom *Orationes* 47.11. Throughout it is: *τὸ χαλκεῖον τὸ τοῦ δεῖνος*, the smithy of So-and-so.

Bibliography

Allport, G. W. 1954. *The Nature of Prejudice*. Basic Books.

Bogen, D. 1992. "Ignoring History: The Liability of Ships' Masters, Innkeepers, and Stablekeepers under Roman Law." *The American Journal of Legal History* 36.3: 326–360.

Bond, S. E. 2016. *Trade and Taboo: Disreputable Professions in the Roman Mediterranean*. University of Michigan Press.

Campbell, V. L. 2010. "The Epitaph of Aulus Umbricius Scaurus (CIL X 1024): A Reconsideration." *Zeitschrift für Papyrologie und Epigraphik* 174: 229–236.

Chambry, E. 1927. *Fables d'Ésope*. Société d'édition "*Les Belles Lettres*".

Clarke, J. 2003. *Art in the Lives of Ordinary Romans: Visual Representation and Non-Elite Viewers in Italy, 100 B.C.–A.D. 315.* University of California Press.

Coffee, N. 2017. *Gift and Gain: How Money Transformed Ancient Rome.* Oxford University Press.

Corbeill, A. 1996. *Controlling Laughter: Political Humor in the Late Roman Republic.* Princeton University Press.

D'Arms, J. H. 1981. *Commerce and Social Standing in Ancient Rome.* Harvard University Press.

Dueck, D. 2021. "Ethnic Stereotypes in Ancient Latin Idioms." In J. J. Price, M. Finkelberg, and Y. Shaher, eds. *Rome: An Empire of Many Nations; New Perspectives on Ethnic Diversity and Cultural Identity*, 43–57. Cambridge University Press.

Edwards, C. 1997. "Unspeakable Professions: Public Performance and Prostitution in Ancient Rome." In Hallett, J.P. and Skinner, M.B., eds. *Roman Sexualities.* 66–98. Princeton University Press.

Edwards, C. 1993. *The Politics of Immorality in Ancient Rome.* Cambridge University Press.

Emler, N. 1992. "The Truth about Gossip." *Social Psychology Section Newsletter* 27: 23–37.

Giardina, A. 1993. "The Merchant." In Giardina, A., ed. *The Romans.* 245–271. University of Chicago Press.

Gluckman, M. 1963. "Papers in Honor of Melville J. Herskovits: Gossip and Scandal." *Current Anthropology* 4, no. 3: 307–316.

Guastella, G. 2017. *Word of Mouth: Fama and Its Personifications in Art and Literature from Ancient Rome to the Middle Ages.* Oxford University Press.

Harris-McCoy, D.E. 2012. *Artemidorus' Oneirocritica: Text, Translation, and Commentary.* Oxford University Press.

Hopkins, K. 1983. "Models, Ships and Staples." In Garnsey, P. and Whittaker, C.R., eds. *Trade and Famine in Classical Antiquity.* 84–109. Cambridge Philological Society.

Horden, P. and Purcell, N. 2000. *The Corrupting Sea: A Study of Mediterranean History.* Wiley-Blackwell.

Kolendo, J. 1993. "The Peasant." In Giardina, A. *The Romans.* 199–213. University of Chicago Press.

Kurke, L. 1999. *Coins, Bodies, Games, and Gold: The Politics of Meaning in Archaic Greece.* Princeton University Press.

Lennon, J. 2013. *Pollution and Religion in Ancient Rome.* Cambridge University Press.

Lennon, J.. 2022. *Dirt and Denigration: Stigma and Marginalisation in Ancient Rome.* Approaches to Ancient History 1. Mohr Siebeck.

Lewis, S. 1995. "Barber's shops and perfume shops: Symposia without wine." in Powell, A., ed. *The Greek World.* 432–441. Routledge.

Mau, A. 1902. *Pompeii: Its Life and Art*. Macmillan.
Mayer, E. 2020. "Money Making, 'Avarice', and Elite Strategies of Distinction in the Roman World." In Stewart, Harris, and Lewis 2020. 94–126.
Milnor, K. 2014. Graffiti and the Literary Landscape in Roman Pompeii. Oxford University Press.
Nicolson, F. W. 1891. "Greek and Roman Barbers." *Harvard Studies in Classical Philology* 2: 41–56.
van Nijf, O. 1997. *The Civic World of Professional Associations in the Roman East*. Brill.
Petersen, L. H. 2003. "The Baker, His Wife, and Her Breadbasket: The Monument of Eurysaces in Rome." *Art Bulletin* 85: 230–57.
Pomeroy, S. B. 1995. *Goddesses, Whores, Wives, and Slaves: Women in Classical Antiquity*. Schocken Books.
Richlin, A. 2003. "Gender and Rhetoric: Producing Manhood in the Schools." In Golden, M and Toohey, P. eds. *Sex and Difference in Ancient Greece and Rome*: 202–20. Edinburgh University Press.
Sancinito, J. 2024. *The Reputation of the Roman Merchant*. University of Michigan Press.
Silver, M. 2011. "In Dubious Battle: An Economic Analysis of Emperor Hadrian's Fish and Olive Oil Laws." *Roman Legal Tradition* 7: 1–15.
Skowronski, J. J. and Carlston, D.E. 1992. "Caught in the Act: When Impressions Based on Highly Diagnostic Behaviours Are Resistant to Contradiction." *European Journal of Social Psychology* 22, no. 5: 435–452.
Stangor, C., and Schaller, M. 1996. "Stereotypes as Individual and Collective Representations." In Macrae, C., Stangor, C., and Hewstone, M., eds. *Stereotypes and Stereotyping*, 3–40. The Guilford Press.
Strong, A. K. 2016. *Prostitutes and Matrons in the Roman World*. Cambridge University Press.
Toner, J. P. 2015. "Barbers, Barbershops and Searching for Roman Popular Culture." *Papers of the British School at Rome* 83: 91–109.
Verboven, K. 2002. *The Economy of Friends: Economic Aspects of Amicitia and Patronage in the Late Republic*. Latomus.
Wickham, C. 1998. "Gossip and Resistance among the Medieval Peasantry." *Past & Present* 160: 3–24.

CHAPTER 7

Working Relationships in Roman Asia Minor

Rebecca Sausville

Two doctors who died in the second century CE orient this chapter on professional and social solidarity in Roman Asia Minor. The physician Apollonios died at age 63 in Saittai, a small city in northeastern Lydia, a place long associated with the textile trade. A white marble stele, adorned with a sculpted wreath, was raised upon his death—around 109–110 CE—by his wife Ammion and their son Diomedes.[1] By all accounts, it is no different than the other Greek epitaphs published in the same cohort of inscriptions, the grave markers of "common people" (*kleine Leute*), per the editors' description; the stele only noted that biographical information.[2] Meanwhile, around the same time, a chattier posthumous *curriculum vitae* from rugged Aperlai, some 280 miles south, in Lycia, commemorated a different sort of doctor. There, at some point in the second century, the Aperlite high priestess Erpidase Sarpedonis raised a monument in honor of her great-grandfather. Lysandros, she reported, had been among the city's "pre-eminent men, of powerful ancestors."[3] He dispatched all his duties for his fatherland and served among the

R. Sausville (✉)
The Graduate School, Princeton University, Princeton, NJ, USA
e-mail: rsausville@princeton.edu

D. A. Maticic, J. Rogers (eds.), *Working Lives in Ancient Rome*, The New Antiquity,
https://doi.org/10.1007/978-3-031-61234-3_7

decemprimi, the municipal authorities of Aperlai. And, on top of that, he had been a splendid doctor.[4]

Separated by distinctions, opportunities, money, and distance, the two men shared medicine as an occupation, albeit with different stakes. The career that was for Apollonios most certainly a livelihood was for Lysandros another outlet for public prestige. In this chapter, I aim to put the *kleine Leute* in conversance with those who, in the words of the alt-rock band Pulp, "never do what common people do."[5] I do so through an exploration of professional and social solidarity in the Roman east. These instances of accord between workers and elite members of their communities, especially as represented in epigraphic sources, evince dynamic interpersonal relationships suggestive of their shared civic and commercial interests. I examine in this chapter two preliminary arenas in which professional solidarity might be observed: first, by considering the official and unofficial groupings of "learned" professions that were shared by elite and sub-elite figures alike, and then by evaluating working professionals as actors in the euergetic infrastructure that underlay civic life in the Roman east.

Holleran's chapter examined the broad geographical sweep of skilled itinerant laborers such as doctors and architects in the Roman world. This chapter focuses on Asia Minor during the early-through-high Roman empire (first to fourth centuries CE), since this area furnishes the best evidence for socio-economic relationships among professionals such as our doctors. This is due to the preponderance of epigraphic evidence testifying to the system of euergetic exchange and illustrative of the lively participation of professional associations in civic life. Euergetism—the nineteenth-century neologism referring to the obligatory system of public benefactions (both tangible and intangible) taken up by elite citizens, largely in the Hellenophone world—played a central role in the infrastructural and cultural functioning of cities throughout Asia Minor. The corresponding swaths of honorific inscriptions that were raised to commemorate elite individuals and their actions attest to the participation of sub-elite groups in the conferral of public recognition.[6] The regional variations evident in the epigraphic materials, moreover, provide a compelling alternative to the largely negative valuations of remunerated labor that one distills from contemporary elite authors.[7] Regional distinctions matter when it came to labor appreciation and estimation. This is true whether one considers positive valuation or negative opinion. In the latter camp, for instance, are the linen weavers of Tarsos, whose spotty reputation Dio Chrysostom described in his *Oration* 34: while some considered them a part of the city, others viewed them as annoying causes of civil unrest (*Or.* 34.21–23). But industrial labor was an integral part of certain towns in Asia Minor, and local inscriptions from towns such as Hierapolis reflect the heightened appreciation for all those who contributed to the textile trade that did not only exist in the city, but which *made* the city.

What I aim to do in this chapter is identify points of overlapping interests between remunerated workers and elite non-workers. These overlapping interests can best be explored under a lexical framework of solidarity as it is deployed in classical sociology. The word choice, with its modern connotations of "a sense of unity in industrial or political action," warrants explication.[8] In the context of imperial Rome, solidarity of the social variety is most evident, an outgrowth from familial solidarity that allowed for the emergence of a patrician elite in the archaic period.[9] In the postclassical Hellenophone east, Roman expansion and entrenchment was successful (in part) due to the enfolding of indigenous and Greek elites into an imperial superstructure, a solidary union founded on like-recognizing-like in cultural and social fora. The existence and maintenance of a social hierarchy rooted in wealth and birth (*eugeneia*, in a broad sense) was not inherently different whether one lived in Ionia or in Cappadocia. The possibility for laborers—skilled or otherwise—to play roles within the upper echelons of that society had hard limits.

Ancient solidarity lacks a key feature of the connotation we give it today wherein collective organization leads (ideally) to improvement in working conditions in a material sense. Employing the term in a classical sociological sense, solidarity is shorthand for the modes and structures by which individuals integrate into groups.[10] The categories of interest are: (1) professional, with individuals sharing the same *profession*, despite variability in social status; and (2) productive, with individuals sharing the same *goals*, despite variability in social status. Working at the interface of professional solidarity and productive solidarity opens a new channel for thinking about the relationships between workers and non-workers in cities of the Roman east. These interactions operated at the level of an "alternative infrastructure," as Michael Mann deemed the relationships existing between economically empowered artisans and traders excluded from the official channels of communication under the Roman empire.[11] Here I employ the phrasing in passing to situate our laborers on the rung below a broad band of elites to illustrate the lives of people who possessed economic resources but were not incorporated into formal positions of influence, reserved for those with political and military power. Sub-elite workers in Asia Minor benefited from their relationships with powerful benefactors and *vice versa*.

Choosing a Learned Profession

The practitioners of certain "learned professions" occupied, as in the case of our doctors above, a variety of social statuses from enslaved to blue-blood.[12] This is true for doctors, architects, and teachers.[13] Part of the social acceptability attached to these varieties of occupation came from successful advertising of the inherently beneficial nature of the work, which was undertaken collectively by groups of practitioners.

Healing, building, and teaching, when done appropriately, were sources of prestige to their non-remunerated elite practitioners (and to their families and cities). For the workers who performed those activities in exchange for money, the oft-cited hierarchies espoused by Cicero, Seneca, and Posidonius deem them not the most maligned of all possible occupations.[14] That one's occupation (learned or otherwise) was a source of personal pride is obvious from ornate tombstones raised by craftsmen of every stripe.[15] Literary evidence from the Hellenophone east, rather than casting wholesale aspersion on wage labor, addressed the person for whom paid work was a necessity but there existed a range of choices—the sort of person who might have ended up pursuing a learned profession. Dio Chrysostom promised, toward the end of his lengthy *Euboikos* (*Or.* 7)—a fantastical rendering of a visit he supposedly took to a desolated version of Euboea—that he was going to answer the question of what someone who *had* to work ought to look for in a job. However, the oration as it came down to us only includes the bad types of jobs—comic actor and brothel owner furnishing the prime examples—before breaking off. But we can extrapolate from that section (112–113) the attributes of good jobs: the ones that did not contribute to any depravity of soul or body and that provided consistent work and a living to those who performed them zealously and industriously. In exchange, the jobholder would, to his or her credit, always have work and livelihood. Moreover, we can envision the types of jobs that would be acceptable to Dio, who advised workers (114–115) to ignore occupational critiques directed at them individually or at their parents. There ought to be no shame, he declared, in having a mother who worked as a paid servant (ἔριθος), a grape-harvester (τρυγήτρια), or a paid wet-nurse (μισθοῦ τιτθεύσῃ παῖδα), or a father who taught letters, or tutored children (διδάξῃ γράμματα ἤ παιδαγωγήσῃ). The quality of the paid work was subject to moral censure, but the general status was not.[16]

The anti-work sentiment is not directly obvious in Artemidoros' *Oneirokritika*, an interpretive guide to dreams that hints at subaltern quotidian concerns in the imperial East.[17] Throughout, Artemidoros did not offer much in the way of career advice, but he tended not to condemn equivocally any paid occupation on moral grounds. Tax-collectors (τελῶναι) alone earned his outright disdain (1.25).[18] Indeed, dreams about descents to hell were bad not for nightmarish reasons but instead for what they meant about one's occupational life—stress dreams, as it were: "To dream of going down into Hades and seeing all that is traditionally said to be there, signifies inactivity and harm for successful people who live a life of their own choosing."[19]

The qualifier of "choosing" is notable. It calls to mind people for whom work was necessary but who enjoyed some range of choices. This was the sort of life decision, for example, that the satirist Lucian described as necessitating a debate among his father and his friends in *The Dream* (or *Somnium*). Among the career aspects to be considered were ease, suitability, cost of outfitting, and lucrativeness (*Somn.* 2). Lucian quickly rejected the sculpting track that won the initial debate, opting instead for a life of *Paideia*, who appeared to him in a dream as an alluring figure promising prestige (*Somn.* 9–15). His choice prompts a further consideration to be kept in mind: How does an interpreter today distinguish work from hobby (an anachronistic shorthand for one's πάρεργον) amid the cerebral popular culture that dominates in imperial Greek literature? The question of work versus hobby is most relevant in the medical sphere, as medicine was a prong of *paideia* and pitched as a civic boon from the Hellenistic period onward.[20] Plutarch counted medicine as a study "inferior to none as to elegance, excellence, and satisfaction, and it bestows upon its eager students a great perk—well-being and health."[21] But he was likely talking about the sort of polymath aristocrats and medical hobbyists who populate his *Moralia*.

Removing financial concerns, how did one choose their vocational path? The fact that both Dio Chrysostom and Artemidoros mention choice indicates that something such as family precedent was not the primary determinant of occupation. It is common but ultimately of limited value to assume that ancient physicians passed down their craft from father to son.[22] Instead, we might consider the experience of Galen, avowedly not a physician-for-hire, who recounted a sort of vocational awakening by proxy that happened to him as a youth. In *On Prognosis*, he wrote that a philosophically minded patient named Eudemos "heard that when my father [Nikon] was introducing me to philosophy, he had been commanded by unambiguous dreams to educate me thoroughly in medicine, not just as a hobby."[23] Nikon's distinct dreams were what led him to switch Galen's "vocation" from philosopher to doctor, but not only as a πάρεργον, or "hobby, secondary occupation." It was not the money to be had from doctoring that led Galen's land-rich architect father (whose ambitions we will discuss later) to make this unilateral decision, and Galen's assiduous output over the course of his career make it difficult to speak about him as anything other than a doctor. Yet he shared this generic title with scores of fellow doctors whose status was more likely to be the comfortable *media plebs*, judging by the lively epigraphic record that testifies to the civic participation and status of people in the Roman East.[24] Doctors of the Galenic ilk are recognizable through epigraphic attestations for people such as the Lycian Lysandros, whom we met above—people whose medical prowess was accompanied by recollections of magistracies and *paideia*, all emblematic of a spirit of civic beneficence.[25]

Motives for choosing a vocation were also often linked to ethical considerations, and non-remunerated professionals grounded their pursuits with literary and philosophical foundations in which mastery of the arts evinced overall excellence. Herakleitos of Rhodiapolis, for instance, the "Homer of medical poetry" and an Epicurean philosopher, functioned as a conventional benefactor-builder who further benefited his communities by sending his entire textual oeuvre to Athens, Alexandria, and Rhodes.[26] A schematic rendering that Galen envisioned in the *Protreptikos* (V, 2 Boudon = 1.6–7K) is germane: doctors took their rightful places in the circle of practitioners of arts "nearest the god," alongside geometers, mathematicians, philosophers, astronomers, and scholars. Galen's implicit correlation of professional excellence with eugenic moral excellence is another manifestation of the legitimizing language employed on contemporaneous honorific monuments. Highlighted in these inscriptions were the civic and ethical excellence of honorands: their pursuit of public honor (φιλοτιμία), magnanimity (μεγαλοψυχία), piety (εὐσέβεια), and assorted φιλόπατρις and φιλόκαισαρ gestures articulated that the honorands naturally belonged in their seats of civic and economic eminence.[27]

Architects, too, showcased this tendency. Like doctors, architects were of varying social status in the Greek east,[28] and it was uncommon for anyone's name to be associated with a building beyond the person who sponsored it.[29] The textual record of Galen offered several admiring characterizations of his father as an exemplar of the erudite philosophically minded citizen, but not as an architect. The only direct evidence of Galen's family profession for generations was that found in the *Suda* (*s.v.* Galen,

Γ32), where it was reported that Galen was the son of the geometer and architect Nikon (υἱὸς Νίκωνος γεωμέτρου καὶ ἀρχιτέκτονος), as John Tzetzes seconded (*Chil.* 12.1.8–10). But it was not until the 2007 rediscovery of Galen's *Peri alupias* (*Avoiding Distress/de Indolentia*) that there was explicit confirmation of his father's professional activity in Galen's own works.[30]

For a long time, Aelius Nikon-father-of-Galen has been associated with a small group of Pergamene isopsephic inscriptions[31]—mathematical texts in which the numerical value of each letter is totaled, and the sum of certain words or lines is equal throughout the poem and used to highlight meaningful connections and, seemingly above all in this setting, to highlight the playful erudition of the inscriber. Among the people who contributed to this microcorpus were Aelius Nikon and another architect, named Iulius Nikodemos, aka "new" Nikon. Nikodemos, likely a protégé of Aelius Nikon, paid homage to his teacher both by employing his name and by "composing" this dedication of a portico he completed in Pergamon (*I.Pergamon* II 33):

Architect [=2,186] to the gods, ever sacred artisans, I. Nikodemos the good, and at the same time the young Nikon, [=2,186] entirely secured and adorned the colonnaded office of the *agoranomos* with his own love of honor. In life only one goal is noble: beneficence [=2,186].	ἀρχιτέκτων ͵βρπς´ θίοις ἀὶ τεχνείταις ἱεροῖς Ἰ. Νεικόδημος ἀγαθός, ἅμα δὴ ὁ καὶ Νείκων νέος, ͵βρπς´ ἠσφαλίσατο καὶ κόσμησε ἅπασι ἀγορανόμιον · περίπατον ἰδίῃ φιλοτειμίηι ἐν βίῳ δὲ καλὸν ἔργον ἓν · μόνον · εὐποιία βρπς´

Nikodemos was here represented as a divine craftsman motivated purely by the euergetic values of *philotimia* and *eupoiia*. Incidentally, such values were, as Galen reported elsewhere in his corpus, the desired byproduct of every area of study: his fellow students attributed Galen's superior intellect to his father's public interests—"Because of your father's *philotimia*, you have made use of your surpassing nature and an excellent education." Elsewhere, Galen claimed that the outcome of any intensive study ought to be *euergesia*, or literal do-gooding.[32] In both medicine and architecture, then, the proffering of one's services as a gesture of *philotimia* is what elevated the activity from work to ministration. *Philotimia* was at the root of the vocation for people of Galen's ilk and what distinguished it from paid labor.

Perks for Learned Practitioners

Amid such environs, one's intellectually inflected "profession" itself served as a benefaction along with one's financial, temporal, and built contributions to the functioning of a city. This is evident from contemporary honorary inscriptions recognizing the achievements of philosophers, doctors, lawyers, sophists, orators, teachers, and architects as supplementary benefactions to more conventional munificence in the form of magistracy-holding and building construction.[33]

But beyond feathers in caps and personal prestige, what was the upshot of these public-facing intellectual activities? Individual practitioners could enjoy various types of exemptions and bonuses, which could be grouped under three headings: localized, generalized, and *ad hoc*. The first two categories tended to include *groups* of doctors and teachers, seemingly regardless of social status and including sub-elite practitioners. Their status as beneficiaries of local and imperial privileges speaks to their generic civic value and utility. Localized "perks" include those which elites provided to people of their choosing when making other benefactions. This was not a common practice in Asia Minor.[34] Looking beyond the self-imposed temporal and geographical bounds of Roman Anatolia, though, furnishes a few examples of individuals favoring local lettered laborers. As professional groups, doctors appeared in documents such as a first-century BCE decree from a portico wall in Priene. The decree was in honor of the benefactor Krates, who offered distributions of meat (κρεαδοσία) to Dionysiac *technitai*, masseuses, and trainers in addition to doctors, presumably of the athletic variety (*I.Priene* 111, ll. 174–176). Teachers were the recipients of money and food (γλυκεισμοὺς καὶ ἄριστα) in a late Hellenistic honorific decree for the *paidonomos* (supervisor of education) Chrysippos in Mylasa, in Caria, who included in his official distributions students (*paides*) and their instructors (*paideutai*) (*I.Mylasa* 909, l. 12). We see teachers and doctors recognized side by side in the most outsized fashion in Istros, in Thrace: the gymnasiarch Aba, upon the start of her year in office, bestowed two *denarii* each upon an array of civic personages: members of the assembly (*bouletai*), the senate (*gerousia*), the Istrian worshippers of Poseidon called *Taureastai*, and doctors and teachers, which "before her no other woman had done" (*I.Histria* 57, ll. 20–30). She went on to extend distributions of wine to other associations, but clearly these groupings of doctors and teachers held pride of place and were, in Aba's eyes, worthy of outsized public recognition. There is, as I said, relative scarcity when it comes to associative inclusion in other commensal settings. But the breadcrumbs we find in the individual choices of Krates, Chrysippos, and Aba are suggestive, I contend, of a wider tendency toward local expressions of thanks to, and enhanced valuations of, teachers and doctors—another aberrance from the views of elite authors explored by Sancinito in this volume.

Generalized exemptions and perks were extended to lettered laborers and members of specific professions through imperial initiatives. A well-known copy of a group of *senatus consulta* from 42 or 32 BCE, reinscribed under Trajan or Hadrian and found around the Marienkirche in Ephesos, exempted teachers, sophists, and doctors from taxes.[35] Elsewhere in the *senatus consulta*, the same professionals were exempted from import and export taxes. The underlying impetus could be related to the freedom of movement encouraged for lettered people in Rome by Caesar, who conferred citizenship on all those who practiced medicine and taught liberal arts in Rome in order to encourage other people to do the same.[36] Before the doctors and teachers of Ephesos saw fit to reinscribe the documents, there appeared at Pergamon an edict issued by Vespasian (Oliver, *Greek Constitutions* 38). Under the edict, physicians, teachers, and *iatra*-masseuses were made exempt from taxation and billeting soldiers. They were also granted the right to gather wherever they wanted with asylum.

Legal sources affirm and expand upon the generalized rights offered to those and other professional groups. Freedom from billeting was affirmed in *Dig.* 50, by the fourth-century jurist Arcadius Charisius, who wrote that it had been rescripted by Vespasian and then Hadrian, and benefited orators and philosophers in addition to doctors and teachers. Modestinus, writing in the third century, cataloged a glut of perks for these lettered laborers. In addition to being exempted from tutelage and curatorship and general liturgies, Modestinus (*Dig.* 27.1.6) quoted a constitution that discussed Hadrian's actions on behalf of learned professions: philosophers, orators, grammarians, and doctors were officially exempted from service as gymnasiarchs, as market supervisors (*agoranomoi*), and as civic priests. They did not have to buy grain or oil, and they were released from jury duty and ambassadorial duties. The incentive structures for learned labor seemed to be generalized throughout the Roman east, perhaps in part due to Hadrian's philhellene appreciation for all things erudite. In a conservative revision, Antoninus Pius placed caps (*Dig.* 27.1.6.2) on the number (*arithmos*) of professionals who could enjoy these privileges in the province of Asia based on the size of the granting city. Small cities could have five exempt doctors, three sophists, and the same number of grammarians, while larger cities (*conventus* locales) could exempt seven physicians, four sophists, and four grammarians, and the largest provincial metropolises could thus designate ten doctors, five rhetoricians, and the same number of grammarians. It was the local *boule*, moreover, that determined the make-up of their local *arithmos*. The need to impose limits on these groups is reflective of a saturated field of people taking advantage of existing exemptions to the detriment of the city. The limits also speak to the mobility of those practicing these professions and their ability to find work in more rewarding atmospheres, as Holleran indicated in her chapter. The demand for such limits could have come from cities tired of missing out on the tangible help to be reaped from their rich lettered citizens: erudite instruction did not put grain in the cellar.

A third variety of exemptions and perks was the *ad hoc* recognition requested by lettered citizens on professional grounds, known from legal sources and from the examples of a small group of people known to have received such exemptions. A loophole was provided for those outside the *arithmos* imposed by Antoninus Pius: those who were "especially learned" (ἄγαν ἐπιστήμονες) and "practicing" outside of their home could get exemptions, a genius visa of sorts, which could be obtained by appeal to local governors (*Dig.* 27.1.6.10). Those possessing the most outward knowledge (*epistēmē*) were likely those with the most training and education, who were the most "learned" (*pepaideumenoi*), and thus the most "elite." To forgo liturgies, one would have to admit that one did not seek the recognition attached to them—the voluntary lavishing of benefactions carried far more prestige than did the reluctant fulfilling of required liturgies. The extant examples are well-known. On such grounds did Aelius Aristides try to get out of a series of civic posts (the high priesthood of Asia, a priesthood of Asklepios, tax-collector, and eirenarch, a judicial position), as he reported in the second half of his fourth *Hieros Logos*. Another *ad hoc* request—which will be further discussed in the context of benefactions—is known from an inscribed imperial letter, in which Septimius Severus and Caracalla wrote to the Smyrnans on behalf of the sophist Claudius Rufinus. Among the reasons for such an extra-*arithmos* exemption, the emperors wrote, was his previous dispatching of civic duties as well as his "ever-present concern for *paideia*" (διὰ τὴν προαίρεσιν ἧ σύνεστιν ἐπὶ παιδεία). A final example comes from Roman Egypt, where the doctor Marcus Valerius Gemellus requested an exemption from a supervisory role based on (among other circumstances) his status as someone who practiced medicine and was *dedokimasmenos*. The best suggestion for the meaning of *dedokimasmenos* seems to be that it marked Gemellus as having received exemptions, though his request indicates that he still felt the pressure from some corner to maintain his public duties.[37]

While in the next section I will link the exemptions received by exceptional individuals to their relationships with professional associations, I turn by way of conclusion back to the notion of solidarity. The first two types of privileges were enjoyed by groups of doctors and groups of teachers, so we might consider other venues in which these groups acted collectively.[38] As María Paz de Hoz has argued, there were specific professional (and not solely social or intellectual) benefits to be had through membership in an association of teachers or doctors, ranging from access to students/patients to recognition that could lead to exempt status.[39] Civic recognition and exemption, whether enjoyed individually or by the collective of workers, were facilitated by the promotional efforts of the group. The *senatus consulta* from Ephesos are an example of this possibility. They were not inscribed when they were first issued: the documents were reinscribed under Hadrian or Trajan. It is unclear in Ephesos where exactly the *Mouseion* was located, but it is possible that the 2nd c. CE copies may have been displayed near the physical locale of that building.[40] It was, in effect, an advertisement of the variety of professional acumens present in the *Mouseion*, but also loaded with the symbolic meaning that these professional groups contributed to the livelihood of the city in a way that had earned recognition on multiple levels. Lettered associations offered mechanisms for social and economic advancement given the opportunities they provided and the intermingling of statuses they hosted; they also supported inter-city mobility via recommendations, as Holleran illustrates in this volume through her discussion of architects. But associations also bolstered urban profiles in a period when intellectual and technical achievements supplanted military and territorial successes as spaces for prestige-garnering. The same civic concerns can be traced among associations of non-lettered laborers.

Euergetic Exchange, or Behind the Smokescreen

In the Phrygian city of Hierapolis, known in antiquity and today for its hot springs, a person called Tiberius Claudius Zotikos Boas took on a number of local offices. For his dispatching of these roles, he was recognized in two inscriptions. "The most august guild of purple dyers (ἐργασία τῶν πορφυραβάφων)," one reads, "raised a statue of Tib(erius) Cl(audius) Zotikos [Boas], first *strategos* and honor-loving agonothete and secretary of the temples (of the imperial cult of the province) of Asia, and outstanding ambassador and high priest, benefactor of his fatherland." A second inscription repeats the same career highlights, the key difference being that it was raised by the local guild of wool-washers (ἐργασία τῶν ἐριοπλυτῶν), and gives the names of the people tasked with raising the statue, seemingly recent Roman citizens.[41] The nature of the relationship between Zotikos and the wool-washers and purple dyers is left unstated. But the affirmation by these associations indicates a notable instance of civic discourse across socio-economic bounds—manual laborers as the arbiters of civic honors.

While the associations' use of honorific language is an instance of the integration of sub-elite people into a euergetic structure otherwise closed off to their ilk, it also speaks to Zotikos' possible integration in the commercial structure of Hierapolis. If the laborers were being integrated upward, that is, why not consider Zotikos as being integrated downward? Two points from this guiding example of Zotikos and the textile workers ought to be kept in mind. Their relationship goes beyond civic pleasantries and functions, as noted above, as an example of the "alternate infrastructures" of ideological power which were increasing in prominence during the middle and high empire. It is also emblematic of the variability of esteem accorded to remunerated labor and commercial activities: in Hierapolis, the textile industry was a citywide affair that transcended socio-economic boundaries.

The members of associations in the Roman east were united by at least one combination of shared profession, cult practice, neighborhood, or ethnic background. Membership conferred social and economic privileges while also serving as powerful constituents of individual and occupational identity.[42] Solidarity seems from the outset to have been an integral part of their functions, and the variety of their communal activities in the public sphere are evident from a number of different epigraphic sources. Those activities were, in part, attempts to make meaningful civic spaces for groups excluded from formal political life amid the straitening of opportunities in the Roman period. Through public-facing activities including honorific recognition of local benefactors, associations (and the people they honored) gleaned social capital to be expended in varying modes. Beyond the goals of social integration, though, associations were concerned with the livelihoods of their members, and so competition and exclusion ought not to be overlooked when considering their economic functions.[43]

What particularly stands out about the situation in the Greek east, moreover, are the interpersonal relationships that existed between professional associations and local benefactors. These relationships were characterized by necessary reciprocation and social asymmetry.[44] Here, I want to draw out more explicitly how the relationship between elite benefactor and professional association furnishes an example of an alternative infrastructure. Elite benefactors encountered industrial laborers as consumers, compatriots, civic leaders, and investors. Laborers employed the lexicon of values affiliated with civic munificence to approve of the public-facing activities of local elites while showcasing their own vitality in the civic life of their cities. Associations' affirmation of euergetic actions via honorary monuments provided physical instantiations of the symbolic capital bolstering a given benefactor's individual and familial standing. The honorary monuments, then, both provided sought-for space in the public sphere to laborers and a tangible source of demonstrative euergetism for the benefactor to highlight when seeking respite from further euergetic obligations. And even if monuments were not the spaces to advertise any commercial relationships that existed between benefactor and association, such spaces should nevertheless not be overlooked as potential fora for euergetism.

In keeping with the theme of this volume, I limit my attention here to associations formed around common professions. I do this not because the actions of these sorts of associations differ from those of other associations, but because they are the most suggestive of the lived relationships between worker and benefactor. Such a selection omits evidence from groups with shared ethnic and religious (or both) interests, such as a city's Jewish population or Isis worshippers, although these groups, too, epigraphically advertised their collective actions.[45] Some groups that "count" as occupational ones are, nevertheless, less significant in elucidating the social interface between urban elite and working professional elite: athletes, for instance, undertook public-facing actions collectively, but there was much variability with regard to their social origins and financial and temporal investments in athletics.[46] Neighborhood associations, too, are often mentioned in inscriptions. Sometimes there are clear indications that these groups cohered not only out of geographical proximity, but also due to shared professions, with one perhaps informing the other, as in the case of the individuals "of the Leather-workers Plateia" who honored a benefactor in Apameia Kelainai, in Phrygia.[47] Setting those groups to the side, we are left with hundreds of inscriptions that attest to the fraternization of groups of gardeners, dyers, weavers, fullers, wine-skin dealers, and metalworkers, among others.[48]

The public activities and civic participation of such groups varied from city to city, but a summary will suffice to illustrate the range. Inscriptions attest to associations' involvement in overseeing the funerals of their members, dedicating buildings and statues, consulting oracles, using public spaces for commercial and cultural activities, and proffering honorary monuments. Associations were mentioned in three funerary contexts. First, associations placed epitaphs for deceased coworkers; the most significant source for this is Saittai in Lydia (whence came our doctor Apollonios). Despite never having been systematically excavated, the city has produced the second largest number of graves that reference associations, second only to the major metropolitan area of Ephesos. Most inscriptions are about as laconic as the one for doctor Apollonios, mentioning only the name and the age of the deceased along with the recognition offered by his professional association.[49] Associations also took on the role of caretakers of graves, as designated in inscriptions that name them as the recipients of fines to be levied should the grave or its contents be violated. Under such an arrangement, for instance, the guild (*syntechnia*) of builders (τῶν τεκτόνων) in Aphrodisias would receive 1000 *denarii* if anyone disturbed the sarcophagus under their watch. Further examples of this practice can be found all over Asia Minor.[50] Thirdly, associations could be deemed the presiders over various activities as mandated by the deceased and their family: overseeing the "grave-crowning," burning incense, or maintaining a foundation for events such as wine feasts.[51] The social benefits to be had from association membership during one's lifetime, seemingly, continued into death.[52]

Dedications of statues and buildings furnished various professional organizations with opportunities to showcase their civically minded piety and collective euergetism while also creating infrastructure to further their commercial activities. Perhaps, too, these building projects served to mitigate public distrust of commercial professions, akin to how the merchants discussed by Sancinito attempted to stave off accusations of greed in their funerary inscriptions. In this capacity an association (*synergasia*) of Smyrnan silversmiths and goldsmiths raised a statue to Athena between 14 and 37 CE (*I.Smyrna* 721). Emperors received statuary honors, too, as Hadrian did from the linen-workers of Anazarbos, in Cilicia (*I.Anazarbos*

3), or Caracalla from the same city's guilds of wool-carders and doorkeepers (*I.Anazarbos* 4). The construction and outfitting of buildings occasioned collective action, too. In Ephesos between 54 and 59 CE, using land allotted by the city, the city's fishers and fish-dealers paid to build a tollhouse in its entirety, from its foundations to its ornamentation (*I. Ephesos* 20). Dedicated to Artemis, Neo, Agrippina, Octavia, and the Roman and Ephesian peoples, the tollhouse facilitated the collection of taxes directed to Roman coffers. But in subsidizing the infrastructure of the building, the local fishers and their Roman benefactors, who comprised around 50% of the co-sponsors, could have been showcasing the fishers' exclusive rights to sell fish in the city and creating a space that streamlined the group's commercial activities (unloading and selling fish) and bureaucratic obligations.[53]

Two varieties of inscription are less common but nevertheless illuminating. A near-unicum is the oracular consultation which a group of builders carried out at Didyma in the second century CE (*I.Didyma* 502). Found in the back wall of the theater at Miletos, the inscription testifies to the builders' uncertainty about whether to continue working on the structure's vaults; the god responded with advice to consult someone skilled in building-techniques. But professional concerns are not otherwise among the social, political, and religious concerns remnant from other oracular consultations.[54] More common, especially in late antique urban contexts, were *topos* inscriptions, which attest to the designation of public spaces for the commercial, entertainment, and leisure activities of individuals and groups. Theater seats, for instance, were reserved for professionals including goldsmiths, stonemasons, leatherworkers, and ironsmiths in cities such as Miletos, Aphrodisias, and Assos. Market stalls in Ephesos were assigned to occupational groups that included wine-skin dealers and leatherworkers. Elsewhere in Ephesos, latrines in the Vedius bath-gymnasium were reserved for workers such as linen-weavers, hemp-workers, and basket-makers.[55] These texts are indicators of the elevated prominence of these professional groups, at least locally, given the official approval that was necessary for their inscription.[56]

Of most interest to this chapter is the last category, that of honorary inscriptions raised by professional associations for individual benefactors. An example that has become exemplary is the assortment of professional groups who recognized the benefactor and jurist M. Gnaius Licinius Rufinus from Thyateira (Lydia).[57] Long known as a legal professional from the *Digest*, where his *Regulae* were epitomized and his consultation with the prolific jurist Iul. Paulus was noted, Rufinus' imperial and local career have been elucidated by inscriptions from Thyateira, Beroia (Macedonia), and Thessalonike. In Thyateira, the leatherworkers and the head of the athletic association (τοῦ σύνπαντος <ξυ>στοῦ) honored him as a benefactor and friend of the emperor (*TAM* V,2, 984 and 968). In the most recently found Thyateiran inscription (*SEG* 47-1656), the gardeners there reported that he held five imperial secretarial posts (including *ab epistulis graecis*) and, upon being adlected to the Senate, held at least four senatorial posts, including praetorian governorship of Noricum.

Why did this matter to the gardeners of Thyateira? Their most direct interactions with Rufinus would have been in the context of his local contributions, which were summarized as "the generosity of his provision and his construction of many great works, a benefactor collectively and individually."[58] The short answer is that Rufinus' career mattered to the gardeners because it mattered to everyone else in Thyateira, especially Rufinus, that their local jurist had risen to such heights. The free-flowing *philotimia* and *eunoia* commented on with approbation by these gardeners and leatherworkers, as well as by the dyers, leather cutters, and wool-washers of Lydia and throughout Asia Minor, were part of a calculated exchange. If one had money, one was expected to expend it on the city in a fluid, *philopatris* gesture.

The absence of an explanatory *heneka* or *dia*, or the presence of the formulaic lexicon of euergetic virtues, occludes concrete beneficent actions of the honorand. We are left to hypothesize reasons based on the inscriptions that outlined more explicitly the stakes and relationships between professional association and honorand. What remains is to fill in the *why* that underlay the public recognition of these workers for urban benefactors. The reason was founded, at times, on personal relationships between workers and elites. Besides the very real social capital to be gained by benefactors, *cui bono* were these monuments raised? Was there a commercial or economic relationship between benefactor and association?

While, again, many inscriptions do not offer enough information to spell out a personal relationship, we know that occupational groups recognized individuals who, in their official capacity, served the interests of the group. Those entrusted locally with oversight of the marketplace would have formed relationships with associations by virtue of their shared commercial and public interests. In such a capacity did a group of Bithynians in Prusias ad Hypium honor an administrator of the city who also served as a *logistēs*, or auditor (*I.Prusias* 29, after 212 CE). While holding these offices, he finished the construction of the city's trading station (ἐνπόριον) while also increasing its shared profits. He was honored by "those inhabiting the *enporion*," referring to a group of businesspeople acting as a sort of neighborhood group. By acknowledging the administrator's promotion of the city's trading infrastructure, the businesspeople of Prusias ad Hypium set a bar for future administrators while also providing this administrator with a record of his civic goodwill. Market supervisors (ἀγορανόμοι) appear not infrequently in associations' honorary inscriptions. Given the commercial interests of the occupational groups, it comes as little surprise that they would have had interests in cultivating robust relationships with the people in charge of the marketplace. One elite market supervisor from Thyateira concurrently held the role of grain distributor (*trieutēs*) and was honored by the city's bakers, whose business relied more than a little on grain and the market (*TAM* V,1 966, second to third centuries CE). In one instance, the role was occupied by someone who did business in the very *agora* he managed: the slaver Alexandros was honored by fellow merchants and brokers in the slaver market (*TAM* V,1 932, undated). His four-month stint as *agoranomos* was recognized in an inscription showcasing the success of *one* slaver as an important achievement for *all* slave traders. A similar impetus was behind the recognition by Ephesian physicians for Trajan's *archiatros* T. Statilius Kriton (*I.Ephesos* 719, c. 102–114 CE).

But promotion could come through a variety of channels, and so occupational groups could benefit from knowing the right advocate or person holding a rather flexible posting, such as a *praefectus fabrum*.[59] In the latter instance, after a decree was voted by the city council, the leatherworkers of Kibyra (Phrygia) recognized Tiberius Claudius Polemon, an equestrian asiarch, "in return for his provision in the supervision of public works," ἀνθ' ὧν τῶν δημοσίων ἔργων μετὰ ἐπιμελείας προενοήσατο.[60] These provisions could have taken the form of financial or infrastructural improvements. In the same city, the leather cutters honored T. Fl. Alexandros, who acted as their market-overseer and advocate (*TAM* V,2 1002, late first century CE). Woolworkers in Philadelphia (Lydia) honored the crowd-pleasing elite Aurelius Hermippos, who while high-priest put on a gladiatorial show contributed to the city's wheat fund and gave money to the city's council, *gerousia*, and seven tribes (*TAM* V,3 1490, after 212 CE). The woolworkers referred to themselves as a *phylē*, or tribe, suggesting that they had enjoyed some of the 1000 *denarii* that had been the tribal allotment. Two Latin inscriptions by "those conducting business in the slave-market" of Ephesos honor their own patron, indicating a financial relationship between benefactor and slaver (*I.Ephesos* 3025 and 646, 42–43 and 100 CE). Public postings granted new opportunities to exercise reciprocal relationships between elite benefactors and various associations who benefited from knowing their local officials.

Elite citizens benefited economically from their relationships with workers beyond the social capital that has become the accepted rationale for their generalized euergetic actions. van Nijf argues there is no overt evidence that the honorary recognition of benefactors by associations indicated a "smokescreen" occluding benefactors' commercial and industrial investments. But, as Liu has pointed out, this means little, given the wholesale tendency of landed elites not to advertise their economic activities. Other scholars have invited the likelihood of economic interests underlying associations' honorary practices. Henri Pleket argued that Aurelius Artemagoras, honored by the dyers of Thyateira in *TAM* V,2 945, was an investor in the dying enterprise. Recently, Angela Kalinowski has suggested a commercial relationship between P. Vedius Antoninus and the woolwashers who recognized him. And Peter Thonemann, writing about Hierapolis, noted the prominence with which local wealthy denizens advertised their links to the textile industry.[61] Roman elites were known to have diversified land-based income through industrial investment, and urban incomes were linked not only to spending of landowning elites within those cities, but also to trade and manufacturing supported by the same elites.[62] In cities that had vigorous and lucrative industries and urban infrastructures dedicated to the maintenance of those industries (such as Hierapolis), it seems overly cautious to eliminate the possibility that honorary recognitions were offered to those who made monetary investments in the businesses overseen by associations.

By way of a conclusion to this section and chapter, the case of a group of Egyptian weavers is informative for how professional solidarities could bridge social and economic differences. A petition the weavers submitted indicates that exemption-chasing was not solely an interest among elite individuals. The petition, *P.Phil. 10* (139 CE), records a request from a group of 12 weavers, asking that 4 among them be exempted from their public duties so that they might be able to fulfill a public order of clothing. The petition indicates the weavers' organizational prowess: by releasing members from liturgical obligations, the weavers were freed up to undertake more orders.[63] Their collective action shows one application of

Mann's alternative infrastructure: not exempt because of individual largesse of the kind enjoyed largely by elite people, the group of weavers claimed exemption by virtue of a different kind of public good. Exemptions, it was understood between the elite and sub-elite, were freeing in terms of time, money, and labor. Given that sub-elite workers understood the upsides of exemptions as much as elite benefactors did, it makes sense that such calculations would enter the euergetic considerations of both sides. Solidarity, whether predicated on mutual interests or mutual professions, offers one mode of considering this mutual understanding, however unbalanced it was.

Notes

1. *SEG* 29-1180 = Samama, *Médecins* no. 235 (epigraphic abbreviations conform to those outlined in AIEGL's GrEpiAbbr, version 02).
2. Bakır-Barthel and Müller (1979: 164).
3. *CIG* 4289 = Samama, *Médecins* no. 287: ll. 6–8: ἄνδρα ἐκ τῶν πρωτευσάντων, ἐκ προγόνων ἀρξάντων.
4. ll. 12–13: ἰα[τ]ρὸν ἄριστον γεμόμενον.
5. From Pulp's 1995 "class slumming" alt-rock anthem, "Common People."
6. The two fields—euergetism and private associations—have individually been the focus of much attention over the centuries. For the former, see a recent overview in the volume by Domingo-Gygax and Zuiderhoek (2020); for private associations in Asia Minor, see texts in Harland (2014), a sourcebook that wrangles representative inscriptions from the mass of epigraphic evidence. On the intersection between euergetism and occupational associations in the Roman world, van Nijf (1997), Dittmann-Schöne (2001: 52–81), and Liu (2009: 213–245), are key.
7. "Hackneyed" though elite contempt may be as a starting point for discussions about ancient labor, as Tran (2016: 248) assesses. For further elucidation of these elite perspectives in authors from the Republican period onward, see Maticic and Rogers in this volume, and the paragraphs below for Hellenophone authors.
8. Williams (2015 (1976)), *s.v.* "socialist" (227).
9. Solidarity when construed as consensus was not the only defining feature of these elites in a fiercely competitive culture: pedigree had to be accompanied by active social participation and pursuit of honors. For the interplay between competition and consensus see Hölkeskamp (2010: 99–106).
10. Such, in a nutshell, is the classic view laid out by Émile Durkheim (in Lukes 2013), who further distinguished between mechanical (the hallmark of societies with little individual differentiation) and organic stages of solidar-

ity. Huebner (2013: 9), employs such a definition in her study of familial solidarity in Roman Egypt, and her introduction is fruitful for thinking with the term in a Roman context.

11. Mann (1986: 312). Roman historians have employed Mann's IEMP model (in which power is configured as a synthesis between ideological (I), economic (E), military (M), and political (P) sources) as starting points to explain the aforementioned coalescing of local elites with imperial rule; for its potential applications and its pitfalls see Slootjes (2011).
12. I prefer the slightly more cumbersome term "learned professions" to the oft-unexamined substantive "intellectuals," for precisely the reason of social variation. Following the concerns flagged for the medieval period in Copeland (2001: 24–49), I posit that if intellectuals did exist in the pre-modern world, they were not these kinds of professionals. People who worked for money, no matter how illustrious their training, were almost certainly not *pepaideumenoi*, the class of educated people who were the products of youthful *paideia*.
13. For an overview of *grammatikoi*, see Agusta-Boularot (1994). See Samama (2003: 59–79), on the status of physicians, and Borgia (2012) for the variety of statuses held by construction professionals. On doctors and architects as itinerant laborers, and the role of the military in their mobility and training, see Holleran in this volume.
14. Cic. *Off.* 1.51; Sen. *Ep.* 88.1, with Posidonius' hierarchy of arts (*quattor…atrium genera*) explicated in 88.21.
15. For which see Joshel (1992) and, more in the quotidian realm of personal identity, Tran (2013).
16. While this section is concerned with paid work, Dio expressed—most of all in *Or.* 15—disdain for the institution of enslavement and concern for the well-being of the enslaved. See Ramelli (2016: 74–76), for a brief discussion on how this opinion rendered him an outlier among contemporary writers.
17. For Artemidoros' perceptions of social division and neutral view of work, see Pack (1955) and Thonemann (2020: 177–189). See also the discussion by Sancinito in this volume.
18. Artemidoros equates tax-collectors in the same passage (1.25) with criminals and those who engaged in criminal business practices—cheats (κάπηλοι), robbers (λησταί), and people who use faulty weights and counting (ζυγοκρούσται and παραλογισταί). On the literary perception (including Artemidoros) of tax-collectors, see van Nijf (2008: 281–285).
19. *Oneirokritika* 2.55.1: Εἰς Ἅιδου καταβῆναι δοκεῖν καὶ τὰ ἐν Ἅιδου ὁρᾶν, ὅσα ἐκεῖ εἶναι νενόμισται, τοῖς μὲν εὖ πράττουσι καὶ κατὰ προαίρεσιν ζῶσιν ἀπραξίαν καὶ βλάβην σημαίνει. (tr. Hammond 2020: 126).

20. For the increasing presence of intellectual doctors in high places in the Hellenistic period, see Massar (2005).
21. Plut. *Mor.* 122E (*Precepts of Healthcare*): ἰατρικὴ τὸ μὲν γλαφυρὸν καὶ περιττὸν καὶ ἐπιτερπὲς οὐδεμιᾶς ἐνδεέστερον ἔχει, θεωρικὸν δὲ μέγα τοῖς φιλομαθοῦσι τὴν σωτηρίαν καὶ τὴν ὑγίειαν ἐπιδίδωσιν.
22. A holdover from the notion that medical knowledge was passed down by the Asklepiads, ancestors of Asklepios on Kos. On this tradition, see Nutton (2012: 69–71).
23. Gal. *On Prognosis* 2.12 (14.608K): καὶ γὰρ ἐπέπειστο τοῦ πατρὸς ἐπὶ φιλοσοφίαν ἄγοντός με, προσταχθὲν αὐτῷ δι' ὀνείρων ἐναργῶν, ἐκδιδάξαι καὶ τὰ τῆς ἰατρικῆς, οὐχ ὡς πάρεργόν τι μάθημα τοῦτο (ed. and tr. Nutton 1979).
24. Sixty percent of Roman *archiatroi* in Greek cities might be considered sub-elite, per the assessment in Pleket (1995).
25. For example, Hermogenes the tax-exempt philosopher-doctor from Rhodiapolis (*SEG* 56-1777), or Archelaos of Herakleia Salbake, who dispatched various civic functions and "through his medical art paid much attention to the advantage of the poor" (*MAMA* VI 114 = Samama, *Médecins* no. 245).
26. See İplikçioğlu (2014) for Herakleitos' dossier.
27. This legitimizing discourse is thoroughly sketched out in Zuiderhoek (2009: 113–152), where his interest lies in ascribing political substance to Pierre Bourdieu's "symbolic capital" that is often described as the recompense given to urban benefactors in euergetic exchanges.
28. For a discussion of the employment of architects in the military, see Holleran in this volume.
29. More than uncommon, it was also of questionable legality; see, for instance, *Dig.* 50.10.3.2, in which Macer (third century CE) reported it unlawful for any names other than that of the emperor or the benefactor to appear on public works. Pliny (*HN* 36.42–43 and 36.83), too, emphasized the limitations on whose name could take up epigraphic real estate. There were workarounds, for which see Thomas (2007: 91–92).
30. Gal. *de Indolentia* 59: "But he [Nikon] said that he followed his own father and his grandfather equally, the one as an architect and the other as a land-surveyor" (ἀλλὰ καὶ τὸν ἐκείνου πατέρα καὶ τὸν πάππον ὁμοίως ἔφη <βε>βιωκέναι, τὸν μὲν ἀρχιτέκτονα, τὸν δὲ γεωμέτρην γενόμενον).
31. There are six total, most readily accessible as an appendix in Thomas (2007: 256–258). For a word of caution on making this assumption of Galen's parentage, see Schlange-Schöningen (2003: 45–54) (somewhat tempered by the publication of *Peri alupias*).
32. Paternal *philotimia*: Gal. *The Therapeutic Method* 10.561K; *euergesia*: Gal. *The Best Doctor Is Also a Philosopher* 1.57K.

33. Philosophers: e.g., *I.Ancyra* 103 (C. Aelius Flavianus Sulpicius honored as a philosopher and public official); doctors: see Samama (2003), *passim*, e.g., no. 277 = *TAM* II 663 (praise for the Lycian doctor and prytanis Menophilos); lawyers: e.g., *TAM* V,3.1457 (praise by city institutions for Diogenes and his knowledge of laws); sophists and orators: see *passim* in Puech (2002), including, for instance, *I.Aphrodisias* 2007 12.325 (Puech no. 167), a statue for the sophist and civic functionary M. Fl. Ant. Lysimachos); teachers: e.g., *I.Labraunda* 66 (grammarian Anteros honored by the city of Mylasa); architects: the best example is Aelius Nikon, but see also the funerary inscription for the Mylasan architect Perikles (*I. Mylasa* 468 = *Steinepigramme* I, 01/15/30). All examples date to the second century CE.
34. For differing commensal practices in the western and eastern parts of the empire, see van Nijf (1997: 253–256).
35. *I.Ephesos* 4101, ll. 7–14 and see Laffi (2006) (*SEG* 56-1219) for an updated edition and commentary: he argues, in part, that the dossier includes a *senatus consultum* and a triumviral edict.
36. Suet. *Iul.* 42. For more on the mobility of laborers in the ancient world, see Holleran in this volume.
37. *P.Fay* 106 (c. 140 CE); see Lewis (1965) on *dokimasia*.
38. The evidence from Asia Minor of teachers and doctors acting collectively is almost exclusively from Ephesos. For instance, the "teachers of the *mouseion*" honored a superintendent of torch-races (*I.Ephesos* 3068, 110–120 CE) and the major benefactor P. Vedius Antoninus (*I.Ephesos* 2065, c. 160 CE), while doctors competed in a variety of public contests (*I.Ephesos* 1162, 138–161 CE). Doctors also honored Trajan's physician T. Statilius Kriton (*I.Ephesos* 719, c. 102–114 CE) and tended to the grave of a fellow-physician and his spouse (*I.Ephesos* 2304).
39. Paz de Hoz (2015), she also compares these groups to the Dionysian *technitai*, performers whose associations helped obtain contracts with cities. The performers likewise contributed to the "diffusion of Hellenic education in the East" (103), which adduces another associative boon: the sharing of knowledge within the association in a time before technical schools and accreditations.
40. This is an assumption offered in Laffi (2006: 460–461).
41. *I.Hierapolis Judeich* 41 and 40, 200–250 CE.
42. See n. 1 for condensed bibliography on associations.
43. On associations' economic considerations, see Liu (2016).
44. These characterizations follow those pointed out by van Nijf (1997: 76). I also subscribe to his use of patronage alongside euergetism as models informing these honorary practices (75–81). Euergetic behaviors of the variety recognized by professional associations during the Roman period

were the purview of aristocratic elites. This change over time from a more (if not thoroughly) democratic and less status-connected *philotimia* is visible in, for example, classical Attic honorary inscriptions; on the inversion of *philotimia* see Canevaro (2021).

45. For example, the Judeans in Kyme or Phokaia honored a woman called Tation for building them an *oikos* (*I.Jud. Orientis* II 36), and Bithynian Isis worshippers honored their fellow worshipper Anubion for decking out the trireme used in the annual *Navigium Isidis* that kicked off the sailing season (*I.Kios*22); on each see Harland (2014: no. 106 and 101, respectively).
46. For the social status of athletes and the overall question of the pursuit as a "job," see Pleket (2014) and Mann (2020).
47. *IGR* IV 790. For neighborhood associations' internal organization and role in civic life, see Pont (2013).
48. The variety of professions is well covered in Dittmann-Schöne (2001)and Zimmermann (2002: 191–213) (for craftspeople).
49. For instance, the *synergasia* of linen-weavers (τῶν λεινοργῶν) at Saittai honored Herakleides, who died at 35 (*SEG* 29-1191). For additional examples see Harland (2014: 193–196).
50. *I.Aphrodisias* 2007 13.1111, after 212 CE.
51. "Grave-crowning" was common in the Lykos Valley of Phrygia; in Hierapolis, one sarcophagus stipulated 250 *denarii* for a crowning that was to be overseen by the flax-workers, and if they should fail to provide the money, they would pay double to what seemed to be a gladiatorial fan club ("those who love weapons"). Incense-burning: assigned to the purple-dyers, with the livestock-dealers as their backups in *I.Hierapolis Judeich* 227b. Wine feasts: *I.Ephesos* 2115, feast meant to be thrown for the sawyers. For more examples, see Harland (2014: 170–171).
52. For the value of associations in imparting social differentiation (rather than in offsetting burial costs or substituting for a family unit) and the status one received from having one's tomb under the oversight of a professional association, see van Nijf (1997: 31–69); for a summary of various funerary functions with examples from across Asia Minor see Harland (2014: 411–417).
53. See Horsley (1989) and Lytle (2012) on the economic benefits sought by the group in building the space.
54. See comments in Harland (2014: 287–290).
55. Theater space: *I.Aphrodisias* 2007 10.33; *I.Miletos* 940a-d; *SEG* 63-1010-1012 (Assos). Market stalls: *I.Ephesos* 444–445 and *I.Ephesos* 2076–2082. Latrines: *I.Ephesos* 454.
56. See Roueché (1989: 229–230), for the social and economic implications of commercial designations in formerly public spaces during the high empire into late antiquity.

57. See Millar (1999) for texts and translations of the six inscriptions.
58. *SEG* 47-1656, ll. 15–18: διά τε ἀφθονίαν τροφῶν καὶ ἔργων πολλῶν καὶ μεγάλων κατασκευὰς κοινῇ τε καὶ κατὰ ἕνα εὐεργέτην.
59. See van Nijf (1997: 95–100), on the power of the public broker. On the flexibility of the *praefectus fabrum*, see Buraselis (2000: 69–72) (who discusses the posting in the context of the imperial physician C. Stertinius Xenophon, who held a *praefectura fabrum*). See also Kuttner in this volume on the practice of elites "supervising" labor and how this practice communicated elite competency and *cura*.
60. *I.Kibyra* 63, 150 CE (tr. Harland 2014: 164).
61. van Nijf (1997, 100), Liu (2009: 215–216, and 216n15 for elite commercial involvement), Pleket (1984: 24–28), Kalinowski (2021: 251–259), Thonemann (2011: 185–190).
62. For the diverse spending of Roman elites, see Erdkamp (2001).
63. On the other benefits of organizing, see Liu (2016: 213–214).

Bibliography

Agusta-Boularot, S. 1994. "Les références épigraphiques aux *Grammatici* et *Γραμματικοὶ* de l'Empire romain (1er s. av. J.-C., IVe s. ap. J.-C.)." *MÉFRA* 106 (2): 653–746.

Bakır-Barthel, S. and Müller, H. 1979. "Inschriften aus der Umgebung von Saittai (II)," *ZPE* 36: 163–194.

Borgia, E. 2012. "Attestazioni epigrafiche di mestieri legati alla costruzione nell'Asia Minore romana e proto-bizantina: Specializzazioni e ruolo sociale," in Camporeale, S. et al., eds. *Arqueología de la construccíon III. Los procesos constructivos en el mundo romano: La economía de las obras.* 53–68. Consejo Superior de Investigaciones Científicas.

Buraselis, K. 2000. *Kos Between Hellenism and Rome: Studies on the Political, Institutional and Social History of Kos from ca. the Middle Second Century B.C. Until Late Antiquity.* American Philosophical Society.

Canevaro, M. 2021. "Upside-down hegemony? Ideology and power in ancient Athens," in Zucchetti, E. and Cimino, A. M. eds. *Antonio Gramsci and the Ancient World.* 63–85. Routledge.

Copeland, R. 2001. *Pedagogy, Intellectuals, and Dissent in the Later Middle Ages: Lollardy and Ideas of Learning.* Cambridge University Press.

Dittmann-Schöne, I. 2001. *Die Berufsvereine in den Städten des kaiserzeitlichen Kleinasiens.* S. Roderer.

Domingo Gygax, M. and Zuiderhoek, A., eds. 2020. *Benefactors and the Polis: The Origins and Development of the Public Gift in Greek Cities from the Homeric World to Late Antiquity.* Cambridge University Press.

Erdkamp, P. 2001. "Beyond the Limits of the 'Consumer City': A Model of the Urban and Rural Economy in the Roman World." *Historia* 50 (3): 332–356.

Hammond, M. (tr.). 2020. *Artemidorus: The Interpretation of Dreams.* Oxford University Press.

Harland, P. 2014. *Greco-Roman Associations: Texts, Translations and Commentary,* vol. II: *North Coast of the Black Sea, Asia Minor.* De Gruyter.

Hölkeskamp, K-J. 2010. *Reconstructing the Roman Republic: An Ancient Political Culture and Modern Research.* Translated by Henry Heitmann-Gordon. Princeton University Press.

Horsley, G. 1989. *New Documents Illustrating Early Christianity,* vol. 5. Wm. B. Eerdmans Publishing Co.

Huebner, S. 2013. *The Family in Roman Egypt: A Comparative Approach to Intergenerational Solidarity and Conflict.* Oxford University Press.

İplikçioğlu, B. 2014. "Heraklit von Rhodiapolis, ein gefeierter Arzt der traianischen Zeit," in Fischer, J., ed. *Der Beitrag Kleinasiens zur Kultur- und Geistesgeschichte der griechisch-römischen Antike.* 231–255. Verlag der Österreichischen Akademie der Wissenschaften.

Joshel, S. 1992. *Work, Identity, and Legal Status in Rome: A Study of the Occupational Inscriptions.* University of Oklahoma Press.

Kalinowski, A. 2021. *Memory, Family, and Community in Roman Ephesos.* Cambridge University Press.

Laffi, U. 2006. "L'iscrizione di Efeso sui privilege di insegnanti, sofisti, medici (*I. Ephesos,* 4101)," in Virgilio, B., ed. *Studi Ellenistici,* 19. 453–521. Fabrizio Serra.

Lewis, N. 1965. "Exemption of Physicians from Liturgy." *Bulletin of the American Society of Papyrologists* 2.3: 87–92.

Liu, J. 2009. Collegia Centonariorum: *The Guilds of Textile Dealers in the Roman West.* Brill.

Liu, J. 2016. "Group Membership, Trust Networks, and Social Capital: A Critical Analysis," in Verboven and Laes. 203–226.

Lukes, S., ed. 2013. *The Division of Labour in Society,* by Émile Durkheim. Translated by W. D. Halls. 2nd ed. Free Press.

Lytle, E. 2012. "A Customs House of Our Own: Infrastructure, Duties and a Joint Association of Fishermen and Fishmongers (*IK,* 11.1a-Ephesos, 20)," in Chankowski, V. and Karonis, P., eds. *Tout vendre, tout acheter: Structures et équipements des marchés antiques.* 213–224. Ausonius.

Mann, C. 2020. "Neither Amateurs nor Professionals: The Status of Greek Athletes," in Stewart, E., Harris, E., and Lewis, D., eds. *Skilled Labour and Professionalism in Ancient Greece and Rome.* 313–332. Cambridge University Press.

Mann, M. 1986. *The Sources of Social Power. Vol. 1: A History of Power from the Beginning to A.D. 1760.* Cambridge University Press.

Massar, N. 2005. *Soigner et servir: histoire sociale et culturelle de la médecine grecque à l'époque hellénistique*. De Boccard.
Millar, F. 1999. "The Greek East and Roman Law: The Dossier of M. Cn. Licinius Rufinus." *JRS* 89: 90–108.
Nutton, V. 1979. *Galeni* de Praecognitione. Akademie Verlag.
Nutton, V. 2012. *Ancient Medicine*. 2nd ed. Routledge.
Pack, R. 1955. "Artemidorus and his Waking World." *Transactions of the American Philosophical Society* 86: 280–90.
Paz de Hoz, M. 2015. "Associations of Physicians and Teachers in Asia Minor: Between Private and Public," in Gabrielsen, V. and Thomsen, C.A., eds. *Private Associations and the Public Sphere*. 92–121. The Royal Danish Academy of Sciences and Letters.
Pleket, H. W. 1984. "Urban Elites and the Economy in the Greek Cities of the Roman Empire." *Münstersche Beiträge zur antiken Handelsgeschichte* 3: 3–36.
Pleket, H. W. 1995. "The social status of physicians in the Graeco-Roman world," in Horstmanshoof, M., van der Eijk, P., and Schrijvers, P.H., eds. *Ancient Medicine in Its Socio-Cultural Context, Vol. 1*. 27–34. Brill.
Pleket, H. W. 2014. "On the Sociology of Ancient Sports," in Scanlon, T. F., ed. *Sport in the Greek and Roman Worlds, vol. 2: Greek Athletic Identities and Roman Sports and Spectacle*. 49–89. Oxford University Press.
Pont, A-V. 2013. "Les groupes de voisinage dans les villes d'Asie Mineure occidentale à l'époque impériale," in Fröhlich, P. and Hamon, P., eds. *Groupes et associations dans les cités grecques, IIIe siècle av. J.-C.-IIe siècle apr. J.-C.* 129–156. Librairie Droz.
Puech, B. 2002. *Orateurs et sophistes grecs dans les inscriptions d'époque impériale*. Librairie Philosophique Vrin.
Ramelli, I. E. 2016. *Social Justice and the Legitimacy of Slavery: The Role of Philosophical Asceticism from Ancient Judaism to Late Antiquity*. Oxford University Press.
Roueché, C. 1989. *Aphrodisias in Late Antiquity*. Society for the Promotion of Roman Studies.
Samama, É. 2003. *Les médecins dans le monde grec. Sources épigraphiques sur la naissance d'un corps médical*. Librairie Droz.
Schlange-Schöningen, H. 2003. *Die römische Gesellschaft bei Galen: Biographie und Sozialgeschichte*. De Gruyter.
Slootjes, D. 2011. "Local Elites and Power in the Roman World: Modern Theories and Models." *The Journal of Interdisciplinary History* 42 (2): 235–249.
Thomas, E. 2007. *Monumentality and the Roman Empire: Architecture in the Antonine Age*. Oxford University Press.
Thonemann, P. 2011. *The Maeander Valley: A Historical Geography from Antiquity to Byzantium*. Cambridge University Press.

Thonemann, P. 2020. *An Ancient Dream Manual: Artemidorus'* The Interpretation of Dreams. Oxford University Press.

Tran, N. 2013. Dominus tabernae: *le statut de travail des artisans et des commerçants de l'occident romain (Ier siècle av. J.-C.-IIIe siècle ap. J.-C.)*. École française de Rome.

Tran, N. 2016. "*Ars* and *Doctrina*: The Socioeconomic Identity of Roman Skilled Workers (First Century BC-Third Century AD)," in Verboven & Laes. 246–261.

van Nijf, O. 1997. *The Civic World of Professional Associations in the Roman East*. Brill.

van Nijf, O. M. 2008. "The Social World of Tax Farmers and their Personnel," in Cottier, M. and Corbeille, M. eds. *The Customs Laws of Asia*. 279–311. Oxford.

Verboven, K. and Laes, C., eds. 2016. *Work, Labour, and Profession in the Roman World*. Brill.

Williams, R. 2015 (1976). *Keywords: A Vocabulary of Culture and Society*. Oxford University Press.

Zimmermann, C. 2002. *Handwerkervereine im griechischen Osten des Imperium Romanum*. Gnomon.

Zuiderhoek, A. 2009. *The Politics of Munificence in the Roman Empire*. Cambridge University Press.

CHAPTER 8

Labor as *Religio* in Imperial Rome: The *fabri tignarii* Relief

Jordan Rogers

Opificesque omnes in sordida arte versantur; nec enim quicquam ingenuum habere potest officina….

"All artisans are engaged in filthy craft, for a workshop is incapable of having anything noble about it."
—Cicero, *De officiis* 1.150

I would like to express my sincere gratitude to Ann Kuttner, Brian Rose, Lauren Hackworth Petersen, and Del Maticic for their comments and suggestions on this chapter. Many thanks also go to all of the contributors to the formerly dubbed "Work/Life" project, now "Working Lives," including those in this volume, and those who joined in our discussions during the workshop and conference. With that said, any errors or infelicities of judgment or analysis remaining in this piece are all my own.

J. Rogers (✉)
North Carolina State University, Raleigh, USA
e-mail: jrroger7@ncsu.edu

D. A. Maticic, J. Rogers (eds.), *Working Lives in Ancient Rome*, The New Antiquity,
https://doi.org/10.1007/978-3-031-61234-3_8

πόλις δέ ἐστιν πρᾶγμα ἀνακεκραμένον †πάντων ξυνεργατῶν†·
καθάπερ καὶ ἡ τοῦ σώματος χρεία, πολυμερής τε οὖσα καὶ πολυδεής …
εἰ γὰρ ἐθελήσαι ἕκαστος, ὄκνῳ τοῦ πονεῖν ἀφέμενος τοῦ παράγειν,
ἐπαναχωρεῖν ἐκ τῆς κοινωνίας πρὸς τὴν αὑτοῦ σχολήν, τί κωλύει
διαλυθῆναι τὸ πᾶν καὶ φθαρῆναι;

"A city is composed entirely of fellow workers. It is like the human body, which is composed of many parts of many different kinds … if each participant were to decide from aversion to hard work to give up contributing and to retreat from the partnership into his own private leisure, what is there to stop the whole system from falling apart and going to ruin?"
—Maximus of Tyre, *Oratio* 15.4–5

The glut of recent publications exploring the rich, complex world of Roman conceptions of work has demonstrated that our typical frameworks for analyzing how workers' perceptions of their own labor and its relationship to their lives require revisiting.[1] Numerous studies investigating the assertion of social status through occupational identity, for example, have shown that Cicero's infamous assessment of labor in *de Officiis* was more aristocratic fantasy than ancient reality.[2] On the other hand, the recent interest of historians in reconstructing the productivity of the ancient economy has managed to avoid entirely the interminable problem of Roman status by concentrating on the inputs, the technologies, and the products of labor rather than the individual laborers themselves.[3] Both models—the status model and the economic model—have proven useful in advancing our knowledge of ancient labor. Yet both also commoditize the laboring body, construing it in terms of social or economic capital and effacing the individual and the agency of the laborer entirely.

Concerns of status and economic value, of course, cannot be ignored when discussing Roman conceptions of work. This chapter, however, offers another means of analyzing Roman depictions of labor that avoids reducing their complex communicative vocabulary and multivalence to simple claims of status, identity, or economic value.[4] It does so by taking seriously iconographic expressions of religious piety and proper ritual performance on the so-called *fabri tignarii* relief. These expressions can be interpreted as assertions by laborers of the fundamental importance of work and the laboring body to the maintenance of communal cohesion at Rome.[5] Crucially, this should not be considered a mere "imitation" or replication of elite religious practice by relatively wealthy urban artisans, as some have tended to view similar expressions in the material record,[6] but should rather be interpreted as positing an epistemic alternative to "laboring" and its role in society.[7]

The *fabri tignarii* relief similarly offers an alternative perspective and worldview relating to the self, work, and community, one closer to that articulated in *Oratio* 15 of Maximus of Tyre's *Philosophical Orations* than to Cicero's by now infamous adage in *de Officiis*, the dueling epigraphs of this chapter. In Maximus' fifteenth oration, the speaker imagines an ideal city, in which each individual contributes to society according to their ability. It is the sum of each worker's contribution, laboring in tandem towards the "common good" of the community, that comprises and guarantees a well-ordered society. Without builders building, weavers weaving, or even cooks cooking, the entire system is at risk of collapsing, as if each worker, through the *praxis* of their labor, were simultaneously the keystone in the edifice of communal life—much like Geue's account in this volume of the *Moretum*'s Simulus, whose hands are his workmen and form an essential part of his microcosmos. Naturally, even the rhetoric of labor espoused by Maximus must account for its artificial quality—in the case of the fifteenth oration, it is paired in dialectic with the following oration, which disparages labor along Ciceronian lines. Even so, what is clear in such a picture is that the understanding of the individual and their work could be imagined outside of the hierarchical interpretations of status often used to explain iconographic depictions of labor, tools, or expertise in the Roman world.

The same can be said about the depictions of the so-called *fabri tignarii* relief. The relief is currently housed in the Centrale Montemartini museum in Rome, a poetically appropriate location for the scene of work, placed within the mostly hollowed out shell of Rome's first public power plant. The relief itself is a paramount example of an alternative understanding of work that communicates the importance of the laboring body to the well-being of society. As unique as it is among iconographic depictions of labor, the relief itself has been the subject of remarkably little focused analysis, appearing only infrequently as a *comparandum* for other iconographic representations of workshop or labor scenes outside of its initial publication by Antonio Maria Colini in 1947.[8] Yet there are two clear ways in which value claims are made regarding the relationship between work and life and its importance to communal cohesion. In the first instance, the relief's iconographic content and style bridges the aesthetic worlds of funerary and state monumental art, taking cues from each in its unique representation of labor, its tools, and its products in a public, non-funerary context. In particular, the relief draws upon the genre of still-life so common in funerary depictions of workers' instruments. These depictions share much with the representation of other "tools" of Roman life—namely those involved in religious ritual—including the positioning of the tools themselves and their symbolic meaning. On the other hand, the clear parallels between the *fabri tignarii* relief—monumental in scope and executed with the utmost craftsmanship—and public monumental architecture encourage us to reconsider how the relief manipulates the conventions of state-art for its own ends. Rather than adopting the visual vocabulary of monumental imperial architecture as a mere status claim, the relief's content reformulates that vocabulary entirely to offer an alternative definition of the craftsperson's role in Roman society, focusing in particular on the bodily practices and products of the laborer.[9] In both cases, the religious aspects of the image are to be emphasized rather than ignored as communicating significant meaning for viewers.

From that examination of the relief's content, the essay will then explore just one social and religious moment within which the viewing of the relief itself might have proven meaningful. That moment was the festival *Quinquatria*, celebrated from March 19th to March 23rd in honor of the goddess Minerva in her capacity as patron of crafts and education. Beyond offering individuals an opportunity to react to and interact with the relief, the festival would have provided the necessary contextual framing for understanding its iconography. As art historians have long realized, the cultural, social, or religious setting of the moment of viewing has an indelible effect on the transmission of meaning from object of art to viewer. In the case of the *Quinquatria*, the ritual procession to the *fabri tignarii* relief's altar and the concurrent sacrifices undertaken by members of the associated *collegium fabrum tignariorum* would have activated the religious valence of the relief itself, much as we expect to have taken place in other public religious contexts.[10] By way of a caveat, for the discussions of both the aesthetic and religious contexts of the relief, it is important to clarify that this paper offers only one reconstruction of what would have been, necessarily, many understandings of the monument itself. By their very nature, images such as the *fabri tignarii* relief were capable of communicating different things to different—or even the same—viewers; rather than attempt to capture this full range of meaning, this paper offers but one, small part of that range, concentrating in particular on the religious and communal claims suggested by the relief scene.

The So-called *Fabri Tignarii* Relief

In 1938, a group of six marble architectural blocks were uncovered by the team of Antonio Maria Colini during excavation of the Piazza Montanara, to make way for the new Via del Mare, today the Via del Teatro di Marcello.[11] Two of these blocks preserved figural relief; of the two, the smaller is heavily damaged, its iconographic imagery impossible to discern. The larger block, aside from damage to the deepest parts of the relief, remains reasonably well-preserved and is currently on display in the Centrale Montemartini museum in Rome (Fig. 8.1). In his 1947 publication, Colini hypothesized that, given their proximity to one another in excavation, their corresponding dimensions, and their shared form as cornice blocks, all six blocks belonged to the same monument. In Colini's estimation, the monument was a square altar of approximately 3.8 meters on each side; the appearance of a figure of Minerva at far left on the relief suggested to Colini that the altar was therefore dedicated to the goddess, most likely by the *collegium* of the *fabri tignarii*, whose headquarters (*schola*) historians presume was located in the nearby *forum Boarium*. The

Fig. 8.1 *Fabri Tignarii* relief, on display in Centrale Montemartini, Rome. (Photo: Author's. Reproduced with the permission of the Ministry of Culture—Musei Capitolini)

location of the *schola* in the *forum Boarium* has been hypothesized based principally on the density of inscriptions and dedications related to the *collegium* discovered in that area, including a fragmentary inscription that could be interpreted as referring to the *schola* of the *fabri* itself, though its restoration is not without dispute.[12] Finally, Colini has dated the relief and associated, albeit hypothesized, altar structure to the late first century CE, preferring a Flavian era dating for two reasons. First, the architectural use of a carved attic cornice (*cornice con attico*) on altars begins appearing with some regularity in this period. Second, the style and content of the relief find their closest *comparanda* in the Flavian period, examples of which will be analyzed in closer detail below.

Colini's original conclusions of 1947 are still largely acceptable, even if the particulars remain tentative. To be sure, the size of the blocks, as Colini remarks, would have allowed for a remarkably large altar structure at 3.8 × 3.8 meters, placing the six cornice blocks on par with the cornice blocks of the podium of the Temple of Portunus in the *forum Boarium*, as well as with the cornice blocks of the bases of the monumental Columns of Trajan and Antoninus Pius. This dwarfs the size of the numerous examples of Augustan-era altars dedicated to the *lares Augusti* by neighborhood magistrates throughout the city of Rome, to say nothing of another, vastly smaller, altar dedicated by the *fabri* in Rome in the last decade of the first century BCE, examined below. This would make the hypothesized altar one of the largest of which we are aware existed in Rome.[13] The actual altar structure within Augustus' *ara Pacis* enclosure, for an illustrative comparative example, measures approximately 3x5 meters. Caution is nevertheless warranted. Colini's assumption that the six cornice fragments belonged to the same structure, while reasonably secure given their similarities, is not guaranteed. There is also the possibility that the structure itself was not in fact an altar, but, plausibly, a statue-base.[14] Whether an altar or statue base—perhaps for a cult statue of Minerva—the case could be made that the meaning of the relief and its relationship to viewers would not have been greatly affected. This will become clearer as the content and context of the relief are considered in more detail. Even so, the preponderance of the evidence as marshalled by Colini strongly encourages an identification of the monument to which the six cornice blocks belonged as an altar.

Examining the content of the scene places us on firmer ground. The relief depicts a workshop scene *in medias res*, as the remains of seven laboring bodies can be identified in various stages of work, punctuated by the tools of the *faber tignarius* hanging isolated in the background. Reading from left to right, the scene shows first a laborer hard at work standing on a raised platform. To the right of that figure is a representation of Minerva, her right arm, now lost, outstretched before her, her left arm, also lost, raised; at her left side, our right, is her shield. A bracket saw hangs on the wall between Minerva and another worker to the right; this latter labors at a sawhorse, or perhaps a lathe as some have argued, with a mallet at his foot and a carpenter's square hanging above on the wall. His muscular torso peeks out of his tunic, which drapes only over his left shoulder. Further to the right are two figures engaged in some form of collaborative work—carrying an object, perhaps, given the double-belted tunic of the right-hand worker—unfortunately lost due to damage. A large pair of calipers on the wall separates these two workers from the scene to the right, which depicts one heavily damaged laborer, tunic half-slung over left shoulder, right-shoulder bared, intently laboring on a piece of fine furniture, raised on a platform for easier access. Another figure sits to the right—only the lower body is preserved, but it appears that the worker could be painting or "finishing" a rounded table-top, evidence of which is seen just to our left. The final figure extant in the relief is separated by another, smaller bracket saw, again appended to the wall. This figure faces to the right, likely in visual conversation with a now lost figure from the other piece of the altar. He wears a heavy tunic and holds a flat and round object in his left hand, again perhaps a finished piece of the work performed by the figure to his right, our left.

There remains one part of the scene, however, that raises some questions. At the left of the relief, the figure of Minerva, clearly identified by her aegis and shield, appears slightly to the right and in front of a laboring figure, obscuring the content of the work performed by that individual (Fig. 8.2).[15] In his initial publication of the frieze, Colini had suggested that Minerva's appearance in the scene was epiphanic, thereby explaining the seeming ignorance of the other figures in the scene, whose work continues unabated.[16] In favor of this reading is the larger-than-human height of Minerva, the top of whose head, though damaged, appears to be at the same height as the obscured worker, even though he stands behind the goddess upon a dais. A similar example of Minerva's epiphanic representation in a workshop scene as observed in the third-century CE gold-glass medallion of the *faber navalis* Dedalius would support a similar interpretation of Minerva's appearance in the *fabri tignarii* relief.[17] On that medallion, Minerva appears in apparent epiphany in the background work scene

Fig. 8.2 Detail of *fabri tignarii* relief, showing the *imago* of Minerva and a workman. (Photo: Author's. Reproduced with the permission of the Ministry of Culture—Musei Capitolini)

with hand outstretched, apparently urging the ship-builders to continue their diligent laboring.

A closer examination of the two figures at the far-left of the *fabri tignarii* relief, however, indicates that the depiction of Minerva in this instance is best understood to represent an *imago* of the goddess rather than an epiphany. My own investigation and photographs of the stone in profile suggest that the worker is interacting directly with the figure of Minerva, as what remains of his left-hand rests upon the damaged remnants of the goddess' helmet; this same angle reveals that the two figures are in fact the same height, if we account for Minerva's helmet and the additional height of the dais upon which the worker stands. This latter detail places the artisan in a position to work on the helmet of Minerva's *imago*. Supporting this interpretation is the goddess' pose, which is repeated in other media and iconographic representations of the goddess' cult statues. In one such depiction, on an altar dedicated, in the late first century BCE, to Minerva by six *ministri* of the *collegium fabrum tignariorum*, a statue of the goddess is shown with her left arm raised, holding a spear to her side, and right arm lowered, bearing what appears to be a *patera* (Fig. 8.3). In the so-called *fabri tignarii* relief, a similar pose—the goddess' left arm raised, holding a spear; her right arm lowered, holding an object unfortunately lost to damage—can be observed through the scant but evident remains of the accompanying spear. In front of the shield at Minerva's left side, the remnants of the butt of the goddess' spear can be identified. Tracing the now missing spear shaft at the same angle as the spear butt to the top of

Fig. 8.3 Image of MC Inv. 1909, altar dedicated by six *ministri* of the *collegium fabrum tignariorum*, showing an *imago* of Minerva surrounded by worshippers. (Photo from Ryberg 1955. Reproduced with the permission of the Ministry of Culture—Musei Capitolini)

the relief provides a connection between spear point, arm, and what was likely the connecting point for the other end of the spear to the stone block. Unfortunately, the goddess' right forearm is entirely missing, while the angle of its protrusion is somewhat unclear. In any case, what remains of the right arm, in addition to the subtle turn of the torso, would suggest that the right arm was held at hip level, slightly in front of the body.

What, if anything, Minerva held in that hand can only be a matter of informed speculation, though iconographic comparisons in other media can at least provide some hints. In 1985, Schürmann similarly argued that the depiction of Minerva in the *fabri* relief was a statue. His case rested upon the identification of a new Minerva type, evidenced by the heavily damaged Dresden statuette of Minerva and a passage from Procopius' *Gothic Wars* (5.15.11–12),[18] in which the historian mentions a bronze statue of the goddess standing visibly in the open air close to the supposed location of the *schola* of the *fabri tignarii*.[19] To this growing list of comparanda for a new "type" of cult image for Minerva we can add contemporary numismatic evidence. Several coins minted under Domitian show Minerva on the reverse in a similar pose—her left arm raised holding a spear, her shield propped against her left leg, and her right hand outstretched holding an object. In the Domitianic coins, all of these types show the Goddess holding thunderbolts in her right hand, presumably to emphasize her Jovian origins.[20] Lacking in the numismatic examples is an explicit rendering of the signature *aegis* that links the *fabri* relief with the Dresden statuette. Yet the similarity in pose is a sure sign that the depictions of Minerva on both the coinage and the *fabri* relief were derived from, and meant to evoke, actual statues to be seen in the contemporary landscape.

An immediate issue with this interpretation is raised by the fact that the tools displayed in the relief, as it stands, were utilized in the working of wood rather than stone. By the first century CE, cult statues were typically fabricated in stone or metal given the superior durability of the materials and the ease with which fine details could be reproduced in those media. As a result, in the literary sources wooden statues are consistently referred to as both more ephemeral, due to their tendency to rot, and more crude, given the difficulty with which intricate details could be rendered.[21] Nevertheless, the rusticity of wooden statues could lend either positive or negative associations to the image, particularly in relation to moralizing Roman appeals to their rustic, agrarian past.[22] Aside from this possible archaizing appeal, wooden statues were also imminently more mobile, an important attribute for ritual processions in which statues of the gods, either depicted in miniature and carried in-hand or rendered life-sized and placed upon a litter (*ferculum*), played an integral role.[23]

Two paintings from Pompeii demonstrate what these processions might entail. The image of the carpenter's procession on the façade of a shop (VI. 7, 8–12) provides a detailed representation of several statues displayed atop a *ferculum*, including images of Daedalus, Perdix, and Minerva, whose likeness is barely visible to the far-left of the image. The scene has been interpreted as part of a celebration of the patron deities of the local *collegium fabrum tignariorum* in Pompeii, with images of wood-working, most likely crafted from wood and carved by members of the guild, on proud-display.[24] Another painting, along the Via dell'Abbondanza, shows a ritual procession of a larger than life-sized Cybele seated upon her *ferculum* and attended by litter-carriers, a priest, a *canephoros*, and an audience of nearly a dozen individuals. Given the placement of the *ferculum* on the ground, the scene seems to depict the culmination of Cybele's ritual procession, as the ritual attendants prepare to offer a sacrifice to the goddess in a final act of propitiation.[25] In this instance, too, the size of the cult image and the need to carry it in procession would have necessitated its construction out of wood or a similarly light material. In any case, religious images of the gods rendered in wood came as no surprise to Romans. Several references to the creation of wooden cult statues are implied in textual references to woodworking tools, such as the plane, in the creation of religious images.[26] Tertullian, for example, in a passage describing the failings of pagan cult images, specifies that their creation is undertaken with "axes, planes, and rasps" (*ascia et runcinae et scobinae*) and comments upon the irony—or blasphemy—of doing such material violence to an image of divinity during the very act of its creation (Tert. *Apol.* 12.4).[27]

If we understand the appearance of Minerva in the *fabri tignarii* relief as reflecting the creation of an *imago* rather than as the epiphanic manifestation of the goddess herself, the content of the workshop scene both becomes more visually coherent and strengthens the religious connotations of the iconographic vocabulary of the scene overall. The reconstructed ritual context within which individuals interacted with and viewed the altar relief encouraged a religiously inflected interpretation of its content, which made strong claims regarding the role of skilled work—via the creation of the *imago* of the goddess and the crafts over which Minerva stood as patroness—in the propitiation of the gods and the stability of Roman society.

Religious Content of the Relief

Given the monumentality of its associated altar, the two distinct stylistic traditions upon which the *fabri tignarii* relief draws would seem, at first blush, to appear contradictory. It is nevertheless clear that the relief engages with these traditions in a unifying and coherent manner to assert the importance of the laboring body to the public welfare. Of the two, the most manifest is the celebration of labor and its associated instruments in funerary art, evidenced in abundance at Ostia and Rome but found with regularity throughout the cities of the Roman Mediterranean. These reliefs declare the artisanal affiliations of the deceased through an iconographic reproduction of their tools, of the settings within which the deceased labored, or of both.[28] So numerous are such examples by the end of the first century CE—ranging from the activity of a bustling butcher's block, in one Ostian relief, to the simple if proud display of one's tools, as in the Capponianus relief in the Capitoline Museum in Rome—that their sheer ubiquity has prompted art historians to reconsider whether the harsh attitudes towards work and labor typically associated with Roman culture had drastically softened over the course of the first two centuries CE. To be sure, in combination with Sandra Joshel's study of the occupational inscriptions found at Rome and Paul Veyne's hypothesis of a culturally distinct *plebs media* during the imperial period, also largely through epigraphic evidence, it would be tempting to see in this shift in the commemoration of the dead the crystallization of a shared identity that lauded the harsh realities of a laboring life.[29] Numerous inscriptions communicate this sentiment clearly. "From childhood, harsh work was always by my side, but now it's gone" (*CIL* V 3415: *labor a puero qui mihi semper erat nunc labor omnis* [*abest durus*]), reads one epitaph from Verona; another, from the Alpine city of Aosta, proclaims, "While I lived I strove for more; never did I stop experiencing loss" (*CIL* V 6482: *dum vixi quaesi / cessavi perdere [n]umquam*).[30]

While many sepulchral monuments relied on language alone to communicate this intimate relationship with work, some funerary reliefs were more explicit in visualizing the *labor durus* with which the deceased identified. The well-known marble Altar of L. Cornelius Atimetus, dated to the early second century CE, is one such example. The relief sculpture approaches the stylistic refinement of the *fabri tignarii* relief and echoes many of its elements, including a scene of *labor in medias res* as well as the depiction of the products that such work yielded. Ostia's Isola Sacra necropolis, too, hosts dozens of similar reliefs, many in much more affordable terracotta, revealing laborers' access to these types of images for their economic and ritual consumption. On tomb 29 in the Isola Sacra necropolis, for example, another dual scene displays the production and sale of knives and other tools, much like the altar of Atimetus, and communicates a similar relationship between the dead, their work, its products, and the tools with which those products were created. Even excepting the drastic stylistic differences between examples such as these, of which dozens more exist, the similarities in their content and apparent messaging have received extensive comment. Zimmer, in his 1982 publication and catalog documenting images of work and tools in funerary art, suggested that such scenes were representative, on the one hand, of a formation of occupational identity and, on the other, of an assertion of the same values claimed by the upper classes, though in these instances through the very representation of labor itself.[31] Similar interpretations of the depiction of *labor* in sepulchral art have become the norm, especially in analyses of the occupational art associated with the tombs of freedpeople.[32] All of these interpretations share the reasonable assumption that the depictions of work and tools in grave reliefs are representative of the deceased's real circumstances, if not also their desire to imitate elite forms of status proclamation.

As with the analysis of other iconographic motifs found in funerary art, there should be some degree of hesitance in settling upon a singular meaning in the display of tools or work scenes in Roman iconographic representation.[33] In the case of the carpenter's square, for example, Cuomo has argued for its interpretation as a multivalent symbol, whether of the status and identity of the deceased, of their claims to specialized, esoteric knowledge, or as a simple representation of the realities of the worker's life.[34] Indeed, understanding images of tools as potent and multivalent symbols can help to reveal the range of potential meanings available to ancient viewers, whose own interpretation of the iconography of funerary art was conditioned by the image-saturated world within which they lived. In such a world, images could and did transform, taking on new symbolic meanings that were unintended upon their initial creation. A fine example of this phenomenon is the depiction of the axe (*ascia*) on sepulchral monuments in Roman Gaul. Rather than declaring the occupational identity of the deceased, being buried "under the axe" (*sub ascia*) signaled the completion of proper ritual formulae in the interment process.[35] That the artistic representation of tools in funerary contexts could have both literal and symbolic meanings is also clear in the way in which craftworkers' tools regularly replaced implements of religious ritual on their grave stelae and altars, often appearing in the very same location where the libation bowl (*patera*), augural staff (*lituus*), or ritual jug (*vasa*) are typically observed.[36] This seemingly one-to-one replacement of religious implements with economic ones would seem, at first blush, to indicate the lack of concern among non-elites for traditional ritual or even a simple celebration of the profane among this same demographic. Yet the world of Roman funerary relief is too vast, rich, and complex to make such authoritative proclamations; in the same location where one altar might display the *norma* of the carpenter, a dozen others nearby might display the *vasa*.

To make sense of such substitutions, it is helpful to remember that these funerary altars were not consumed as singular objects, but would have to be understood as being in visual communication with other nearby grave markers, what Matthew Roller has dubbed "intersignification."[37] Interpreting both the laboring and religious tools within a singular iconographic category, therefore, is warranted. The preponderance of Roman "thing-art" explored by Kuttner in this volume—a genre that takes as its subject the display of ritual implements and religious tools in reverent array, on as varied media as funeral altars and public, monumental architecture—would here suggest that the depiction of a craftsperson's tools, too, could operate within a similar range of semantic meanings as religious ones.[38] The presence of religious tools, such as the *patera*, *lituus*, *vasa*, *bukrania*, garlands, and religious "relics," on both funerary and neighborhood altars, draws directly upon the iconographic language of sacred, public art.[39] In such cases, the ritual "thing" takes upon a subjectivity of its own as both tool and agent, declaring a sacrificial act both aspirational and completed.[40] For funerary altars in particular, the proper burial of the deceased could be said to have depended upon the visual presence of these ritual "things," as the presence of the religious tools on the altar communicated, as Laetitia La Follette has hypothesized, proper ritual affordances to both the interred and the viewer.[41] In the notable instances in which such implements appear in public architecture—for example in the frieze reliefs of both the Portico of Octavia and the Temple of Vespasian, as well as the later Arch of the Argentarii—the proper performance of ritual is communicated through the ordering of these religious "things" in abstract space, calling to mind the verbal *formulae* uttered by Rome's priests during sacrificial rites.[42] Importantly, however, the ritual objects depicted in such reliefs were actual ritual objects used in the world—things that were held, that were used, and that offered a certain amount of religious utility to their wielder. Their representation in relief, then, activates these same understandings of ritual objects as things-to-be-used and things-with-purpose, inviting viewers to imagine their own visceral participation in the religious rituals being signified. In other words, depictions of objects, like objects themselves, communicate "what they want" and "how they want" to be interacted with.[43] This level of object agency—in which objects *suggest* a use or an interpretation to the individual or viewer—depends upon a banal reality; that successive generations of viewers enter a world already filled with objects, things, and images, whose intentions have already been established. As a consequence, users and viewers, through their engagement with these objects and images, become participants in the ongoing process of meaning-making inherent in the object's existence and in the iterative interactions of object users and viewers.[44] In the case of the iconographic display of *lituus*, *patera*, and *vasa*, the viewer, too, is invited to participate in a mental recreation of the final sacrifice to the dead, reaffirming a previous life through the recognition of the moment of burial.

The altar dedicated to Minerva by six *ministri* of the second *lustrum* (2 BCE–3 CE) of the *fabri tignarii* is one such example of how the iconographic representation of tools entered into the realm of religious communication (Fig. 8.4).[45] Those interested in the monument have concentrated analysis mostly on two sides of the altar, one depicting a sacrifice at a statue of Minerva and the other the commemoration of a processional statuette of the goddess; each image has afforded historians important information regarding the types of ritual commemoration undertaken by corporate groups.[46] The other sides of the altar, however, are equally revealing even if typically overlooked. On one of the sides appear the ritual implements of the sacrifice—*lituus*, *apex*, garlands, and *culter*—above the tools of the *faber tignarius*—the bracket saw, bow saw, the pick-axe, the axe, and helmets. The erasure of any distinction between religious and secular "things" on the panel is clearly illustrated, as the objects declare their intended use to the viewer in a decidedly religious setting.[47] Suggested in such a collocation is an equation of the work of religious sacrifice with the work of the *faber tignarius*, as the wielding, use, and effect of the *culter* is made equal to that of the *serra*. While overtly religious iconography is mostly absent in the extant remains of the *fabri tignarii* relief, save for the fabrication of the *imago* of Minerva discussed above, the monumental size of the altar and its implied place at the center of ritual nevertheless encourages a similar, religiously inflected reading of its depiction of tools—their display, especially in the context of

Fig. 8.4 Detail of MC Inv. 1909, showing tools of the *faber tignarius* below those of sacrifice. (Photo from Zimmer 1982. Reproduced with the permission of the Ministry of Culture—Musei Capitolini)

the careful creation of a cult image of Minerva herself within the same scene, emphasizes the fundamental role that these tools played in the goddess' worship. Just as with the altar dedicated by the six *ministri*, to say nothing of the other examples examined above, the viewers of the *fabri tignarii* relief, whether or not *tignarii* themselves, are invited to wield the tools under the direct tutelage of the goddess, and to transform the act of making depicted on the altar, as well as the act of "looking upon the laboring," into an active mode of worship.

This blurring of the bounds between the secular act of fabrication and the religious act of worship is further emphasized by the altar's visual connections with the monumental art and architecture of the public "state" religion, with which the *fabri tignarii* relief shares numerous similarities. The spacing and corporeality of the figures in the *fabri* relief is immediately evocative, for instance, of the figural relief of the contemporary frieze on the triumphal Arch of Titus. This frieze depicts a triumphal procession in deep relief, its human figures isolated from one another in a somewhat-atypical rendering of processional scenes for the late first century CE.[48] On the one hand, such space and depth gives the viewer of the arch, from ground level, the advantage of being capable of discerning the visual language of the scene of procession and, as a result, its ritual significance. Conversely, the scene recalls similar depictions of processions that would have been viewed much closer to eye-level, including the processions of the Vestal Virgins represented on the inner altar of the *ara Pacis*.[49] Given the difference in style between the Arch of Titus' frieze and its inner panels—the latter much more indicative of contemporary historical relief, approaching *horror vacui* with its emphasis on representing the depth of the scene through the overlapping of numerous visual elements and the lack of empty space in the lower registers—there is little reason to believe that the processional scene was carved with its visibility as the only concern; rather, it would seem that the desire to clearly communicate the constituent parts of ritual procession, including the presence of sacrificial animals and a *ferculum* bearing the image of a deity, was the primary motivator for the choice. One is reminded of similar scenes on state monuments such as the so-called altar of Domitius Ahenobarbus, the triumphal arch at Piedmont, or the arch of Trajan at Beneventum, in which the primary elements of the ritual procession—animals donning the garb of sacrifice, processional attendants bearing various implements of ritual, fabricated images of the gods, the sacrificial altar—are highlighted to communicate a religious message similar to that explored above vis-à-vis the isolated display of ritual implements. It is tempting to interpret the workshop scene of the *fabri tignarii* relief similarly, as a "procession" of sorts, demonstrating the worship of Minerva "in-process" through craft activities and their products. There is something, too, of an aspirational quality to these scenes, which reproduce the moments just before the deity has been properly propitiated—before the sacrifice of the ox, before the pouring of the libation, before the completion of a table.[50]

The clearest *comparandum* we possess in the public sphere, however, is the depiction of the myth of Arachne and a weaving workshop in the contemporary frieze reliefs of the *forum Transitorium*.[51] The most infamous scene shows Minerva looming aggressively over the figure of Arachne, who shrinks back, falling to one knee as she raises her hand in evident fear; Minerva herself raises one hand, though with the intent to devastate rather than deflect. Several other figures to Minerva's right react in apparent horror. Formisano's chapter in this volume examines the myth of Arachne's transformation from worker into laborer, as told by Ovid and referenced in this relief. Flanking this scene of divine punishment are depictions of numerous women engaged in different stages of wool-working and textile manufacture. The parallels to the *fabri* relief are more due to content, however, than style. The figures of both reliefs are depicted laboring *in medias res*, seemingly oblivious to other elements of the scenes within which they are represented and to the outside world of the viewer, who looks into these workshops as a voyeur gazing upon the laborious mysteries of Minerva's worship. The *forum Transitorium* reliefs in particular demonstrate a mastery over the representation of drapery—appropriate for its theme—that far surpasses the heavily weighted and flat fabrics of the *fabri tignarii* relief, aside from the clear care taken in rendering the folds of Minerva's drapery. It is tempting as well to see in the *forum Transitorium* reliefs a direct temporal connection to the *fabri tignarii* frieze, especially given the apparent monumentality of both; Domitian, who erected the Arch of Titus and broke ground on the *forum Transitorium*, held a particular affinity for Minerva since the goddess was an eminently suitable representation of the religious and moral values the emperor wished to convey to the *populus Romanus*.[52] Further emphasizing the religious elements of the *forum Transitorium* reliefs is, of course, their spatial relationship with the Temple of Minerva itself, which stood at the center of that precinct. This temple was likely the location for Domitian's newly instituted public rites of the long-standing festival *Quinquatrus Maiores*, discussed below. In any case, centering the laboring body in the frieze reliefs of the *forum* communicates an entirely different perspective on the artisan's role within Roman society. No longer, we are to understand, is the state religion the sole domain of the imperial household or the magistrate. Workers and, more importantly, their *working*, is shown to be integral to the public wellbeing, possible only through the specialized knowledge of the weaver, of the mason, or of the carpenter. The depiction of work "in process" in these reliefs hints at the spectacular nature of labor, too, worthy of being looked upon and appreciated for the demonstration of skill, much like the labor of Ovid's Arachne in the *Metamorphoses*.

Though there remains less than half of the scene of the *fabri tignarii* relief, thereby making any absolute statements about its content provisional at best, its monumentality, style, and subject matter all coincide to communicate the religious valence of the artisan's specialized knowledge as maker and creator. The *faber*'s tools, skill, and laboring body produce the intricately designed objects pleasing to the gods and Minerva especially, as well as the images of the gods themselves, all in due reverence to the celestial order and in active maintenance to the terrestrial one. Even so, the religious valence of the relief would be far less apparent to an ancient viewer if not considered in close connection with the contexts within which the relief was viewed.

Religious and Social Context of the Relief

Colini's identification of the *fabri tignarii* relief as one part of a monumental altar structure has remained an accepted hypothesis since its initial publication in 1947. Yet since this identification, the precise context(s) of use have been largely ignored; altars, after all, matter precisely because they were integral parts of the sacrificial rituals that served as the basis of collective Roman religious practice.[53] It is important to remember that the altar to which the *fabri tignarii* relief belonged was also an object designed and constructed for a purpose—namely, to be used and interacted with at certain times within the Roman calendar, as the focal point of ritual sacrifice. In one sense, the materiality of the altar itself compelled viewers and users to perform certain religious, non-negotiable actions.[54] Scenes of laboring on altars are exceedingly rare; aside from our relief, only funerary altar reliefs can be adduced as comparative examples of working scenes on altarpieces. The altar's immense size and location—somewhere in the *forum Boarium*, likely in a publicly visible location—may have also placed it in visual communication with the largest altar in Rome, the *Ara Maxima* of Hercules in the southern part of the *forum Boarium*. In this regard, the labors of the *fabri* depicted on the *fabri tignarii* relief might feasibly be conflated with those of Hercules himself, whose mythical work of atonement was meant to bring harmony between the mortal and divine realms.

While we can be reasonably certain of this much, connecting the altar to a specific deity or a specific festival day will necessarily be an exercise in informed hypothesis; nevertheless, even if such speculation cannot be proven one way or another, it can provide a plausible and instructive example that illustrates the role played by such a monument in the religious life of the *fabri tignarii*, to say nothing of others living in Rome. In other words, while the historical value of this contextualization must remain in question, its heuristic value—as a recreation of a moment of religious representation, ritual, and reception, centered on the altar itself—remains analytically useful.

Two festivals have been marked in the *fasti* of the Late Republican and Early Imperial periods as being dedicated to Minerva and, therefore, offer informative case studies of the religious context within which the *fabri tignarii* relief might have been viewed—the *Quinquatrus Maiores*, in mid-March, and the *Quinquatrus Minores* or *Minusculae*, in mid-June.[55] Though each festival shared a name and was dedicated to Minerva, their character and associated rites were considered discrete. In the case of the *Quinquatrus Minores*, the ancient sources remark that its celebration commemorated the clandestine return of the flute-players (*tibicines*) to Rome in 311 BCE after a period of self-exile.[56] While undoubtedly dedicated to Minerva, the festival also appears to have had strong connections to Marsyas; in his explanation of the festival's etiology, Ovid describes how Minerva, as the original creator of the flute (*tibia*), grew tired of playing it and tossed it into the river, where Marsyas discovered the instrument that would ultimately lead to his punishment at Phoebus' hands. For these mythical and legendary reasons, the festival of the *Quinquatrus Minores* was celebrated annually with a procession of flautists, who donned masks and long gowns while playing the instrument that brought upon Marsyas' ruin and the flautists' own exile.

While the *Quinquatrus Minores* would have undoubtedly offered a fitting opportunity to celebrate Minerva more generally, it would not fully account for her role as patron of the crafts specifically, in the guise of Minerva Ergane. In Ovid's *Fasti*, in fact, Minerva explains the nomenclature of the *Quinquatrus Minores*, stating in the voice of the goddess that "March holds a festival under my great name, and this mob [flute-players] is one of my inventions."[57] More immediately appropriate, therefore, was the original *Quinquatrus*, dubbed the *Maiores*, which celebrated Minerva in her capacity as patroness of crafts from the 19th to the 23rd of March.[58] In his *Fasti*, Ovid describes the festivities and their associated rites:[59]

> On the next day, the rites of Minerva take place,
> Which take their name from their five consecutive days.

> The first day is free of blood, nor is it permitted to contest with sword:
> The reason—Minerva was born on that day.
> The next four days are celebrated upon strewn sand:
> By drawn swords is the bellicose goddess pleased.
> Now, boys and slender girls, pray to Pallas.
> If you placate Pallas you will be learned.
> Once she is pleased, let girls learn to card the wool
> And to unburden the full distaffs.
> The Goddess even teaches how to traverse the upright warp with shuttle,
> and she drives home the loose threads with a comb.
> Worship her, you who remove stains from damaged clothing;
> Worship her, whoever prepares the bronze caldrons for fleeces.
> Should Pallas be unwilling, no man will make shoes well,
> Though he were more skillful than Tychius;
> And though he be considered more dexterous than legendary Epeus,
> If Pallas be angry with him, he will be helpless.
> You too, who banish disease by Phoebus' art,
> From your earnings bring a few gifts to the Goddess.
> Nor you, often by tumult defrauded of your wealth, you teachers,
> Spurn her not; She brings you new students:
> Spurn her not, each who guides the chisel and paints pictures in blazing colors;
> Spurn her not, each who makes stones malleable under their skillful hand.
> She is the Goddess of one thousand works: certainly the Goddess of song She is;
> If I deserve it, may She be a friend in my pursuits.

While the historical origins of the *Quinquatrus Maiores*, often simply called the *Quinquatria*, remain a matter of contentious debate among scholars of Roman religion, by the first century BCE it is clear that the festival was officially recognized as being dedicated solely to Minerva.[60] Epigraphic evidence confirms this hypothesis. Our earliest extant Roman calendar, the first-century BCE *fasti Antiates Maiores*, lists the *Quinquatria Minervae* on March 19th as a public holiday.[61] Similarly, the *fasti Praenestini*, among other Augustan-era calendars, list the festival on March 19th, with an accompanying comment from the grammarian Verius Flaccus that the festival was sacred for artisans.[62] The earliest textual reference to the festival can be found in Plautus' *Miles Gloriosus*, in which the character Periplectomenus bemoans a fictional wife's profligate spending on diviners and fortune-tellers during the festival (Pl. *Mil.* 692–3). In several letters, Cicero remarks that the festival created a tumultuous environment within the city of Rome; in a letter to Q. Cornificius in 43 BCE, he explicitly connects the mid-March festival to Minerva (Cic. *Fam.* 12.25).[63] Of additional interest is a fragment from the Atellan Farce "The Pregnant Virgin" (*Virgo Praegnans*), written by the late first-century BCE dramatist Q. Novius, in which there is what appears to be a connection drawn between cloth-fullers and the *Quinquatrus Maiores* (Non. 508M).[64] By the late first century CE, the festival had even drawn the personal attention of the emperor Domitian, who was so taken with the celebration that, Suetonius remarks, he instituted a private version of the festival at his Alban estate, while also establishing a new priestly college to perform Minerva's rites publicly and to oversee annual games held in her honor in the city of Rome (Suet. *Dom.* 4).[65] Peter Heinrich von Blanckenhagen has even suggested that the *forum Transitorium* precinct was initially designed by Domitian to host the private rites of the *Quinquatrus Maiores*, to be celebrated by all of Rome's *collegia*, though the nature of the festival as *sacra publica*, in which Rome's *pontifices* were required to take part, would caution against such a maximalist reading as this.[66]

Although the festival of *Quinquatrus Maiores* was officially celebrated through public rites, it is also clear from the textual evidence mentioned above that the artisans of Rome participated in their own celebrations, either individually or within their corporate *collegia*, and therefore made dedications in honor of their patron goddess. The painting from the Via dell'Abbondanza in Pompeii, discussed above and treated in detail by John Clarke in his book *Art in the Lives of Ordinary Romans*, is illustrative of what such worship would have entailed.[67] The painting shows four men carrying a *ferculum*, complete with a gabled roof, garlands, and several figures engaged in the work of carpentry. Such litters as depicted here were a typical part of religious processions, as images of the gods, sculpted in wood, would be carried through the streets in route to the appropriate altar or temple.[68] Depicted at right in the image is the legendary figure of Daedalus, towering over his nephew and assistant, Perdix, whom the master carpenter has murdered out of envy.[69] At far left are the scant remains of a depiction of Minerva in her by now familiar pose, shield at her left side, right arm outstretched. Between these two larger figures are three smaller ones engaged in the tedious work of carpentry. The juxtaposition of scenes of mundane labor with both the presence of Minerva and a representation of Daedalus' murderous jealousy is, apparently, strange; but, as John Clark has suggested, the message communicated by the Daedalus and Perdix tableau reinforces the one implicitly communicated by the presence of Minerva, who similarly would not hesitate to exact her revenge upon religiously non-compliant artisans, as the central scene of Arachne's punishment in the *forum Transitorium* reliefs so aptly demonstrates.

In different work settings, it is not difficult to imagine other "craft-heroes" playing similar roles for other *collegia*. In the *Fasti*, Ovid himself suggests that Tychius, the Homeric inventor of shoe-making, or Epeus, who constructed the Trojan horse, might be figures of similar veneration by cobblers or carpenters, respectively (Ov. *Fast.* 3.809–34). In an earlier but similar collocation of the mythical and "everyday" craftsperson, it has been suggested that many of the Republican-era engraved gemstones from Etruria and Central Italy depicting laboring artisans are in fact representing mythical craftsmen, such as Daedalus, Hephaestus, or Argos.[70] In the cases of the gems for which specific identification of the artisan is unclear, the very possibility of it signifying both a legendary craftsperson and an "everyday" one is perhaps the point. Those wearing these gemstones, either as signet rings or in necklaces, could very well have been advertising their inclusion in a *collegium* of artisans, especially if their use was similar to the contemporary wearing of signet rings declaring one's factional affiliation in the increasingly partisan politics of the first century BCE.[71] On the other temporal side of the *fabri* relief, the curious establishment sometime during the imperial period of a festival, also in mid-March, for the legendary Etruscan metalsmith Mamurius Veturius—responsible in Roman myth for fashioning the eleven shields (*ancilia*) to hide the sacred heaven-sent shield (*ancile*), all paraded through the streets of Rome by the Salian priests—provides another tantalizing connection to such "hero" worship among Rome's tradespeople, during the very same period and time of year that saw all Roman artisans celebrating Minerva.[72] In all these depictions of artisans, both iconographic and textual, the slippage between the regular and the mythical craftsperson is fraught with the tension of a mortal laborer playing at the immortality of the divine or the legendary. One might consider himself the equal of Mamurius Veturius, of Epeus, of Tychius, or of Argos, yet it must always be acknowledged that the perfection inherent in the divine is unattainable—Mamurius Veturius merely mimicked the construction of the shield that had fallen from the heavens; Argos fabricated the Argo not of his own volition, but under Minerva's guidance (Apoll. *Argo.* 1.18–20); and Epeus, too, was not solely responsible for building the Trojan horse, given that Homer specifies that he "constructed it with Athena" (Hom. *Od.* 8.493–4: τὸν Ἐπειὸς ἐποίησεν σὺν Ἀθήνῃ), which Vergil would later pick up in his description of the horse as a "gift from Minerva" (Verg. *Aen.* 2.189: *dona Minervae*) built "by the divine skill of Pallas" (Verg. *Aen.* 2.15: *divina Palladis arte*) from the improbable combination of four different types of wood.[73]

This fuzzy boundary between the individual declaration of skill and the acknowledgment that such practical knowledge was only possible due to the guidance of deities such as Minerva can be seen reflected in both the content of the *fabri tignarii* relief—with workers dutifully engaged in laborious worship and even the fabrication of the *imago* of Minerva herself, framed by the tools that made such wor(k)ship attainable—and its use as an altar. In this context, the *fabri tignarii* relief can be interpreted, on the one hand, as a devout expression of thanks for bestowing upon the *fabri* the skills required to craft objects pleasing to Minerva. Unlike Arachne, the nameless workers of the relief labor solemnly, their work a direct representation of their faith. As the final destination of a procession and the focus of the final moments of dedication, the altar itself reminds those undertaking the sacrifice—the *magistri quinquennales*, elected every five years—as well as those looking upon the spectacle to maintain their piety and their humility, even in the face of immense success and public acknowledgement. Beyond this surface reading, such ritual interactions with the altar also emphasized the specialized domain of knowledge available only to the *fabri tignarii* and those like them, as Minerva's worship and appeasement ultimately required this group of artisans whose practical knowledge, embodied through the *labor* on full display on the *fabri tignarii* relief, guaranteed the public welfare. "Worship her," Ovid tells the artisan, the doctor, the teacher; "If Pallas be angry, you shall be helpless."

This expression of proper ritual observance—through an analogy of laboring as worship, of *labor* as *religio*—raises an interesting question about the status of this type of work in the eyes of the wider public. One by-product of the *fabri tignarii* relief's equation of *labor* and *religio* is the elision of the elements of work that Cicero, in the passage from *de Officiis* that stands as one of the two epigrams to this chapter, had described as lending to certain professions an innate "filthyness." "All artisans are engaged in vulgar craft," Cicero states, "for a workshop is incapable of having anything noble about it."[74] The abundantly clear statement of the *fabri tignarii* relief, however, contends that it is the very nature of their *officina* that is of fundamental importance to the worship of Minerva. Without the *officina*, without the artisans, there cannot be benefactions. Rather than being *sordida*, the rhetoric of the relief, in combination with the ritual actions taken as part of the celebration of Minerva, communicates the same piety (*pietas*) that art historians have come to expect on state monuments. One must also recall, too, that such public displays of sacrifice were just that—to be viewed and consumed by a public intent on ordering their world through religious epistemologies. The spectacle of the procession; of the objects in tow; of the sacrifice; all served to reinforce the web of relationships binding together their community and highlighting the work—both religious and physical—performed to maintain that community. Research on similar urban ritual processions in Roman and other societies has outlined how such spectacles served to both evoke and reaffirm the solidarities and hierarchies of their respective societies, the ritual procession itself acting simultaneously as a commemorative reminder of past tradition, an affirmation of the present moment, and a blueprint for future behavior.[75] To be looked upon, both in relief and in ritual procession, by spectators further emphasized the specialized claims to knowledge of the *fabri tignarii* and others like them.[76]

Conclusion

Though it is ultimately impossible to know precisely the social or religious context of the *fabri tignarii* relief, reconstructing a plausible scenario for the altar's use and the relief's viewing is nevertheless a heuristically valuable exercise for understanding the mutual inflection of artistic content and the context of viewing. The latent religious meanings suggested by the display of tools and the arrangement of figures on purely stylistic grounds could have been emphasized and made explicit through the religious context within which the relief's images were viewed, imbuing the instruments and images of *labor* depicted on the relief with symbolic meanings beyond the literal. Ancient viewers, after all, were highly sophisticated consumers and interpreters of iconography and spectacle, their worlds rich with both simple and complex representations and images. In the specific case of the *fabri tignarii* relief, the collocation of *labor* and *religio* indicates a community of laborers advocating for a society far removed from the disgusted musings of a Cicero, or even the crowded ledgers of the proto-capitalist. Rather than retracing and discovering the "lore of ritual" through text—what made something *religio* in the mind of Cicero—the *fabri tignarii* relief suggests that such knowledge is to be found instead in the *praxis* of *labor*.[77] It can therefore be interpreted as a disavowal of both traditional ideas of social status and economic notions of profit, here in an explicitly religious context. While not identifying themselves as perfectly analogous to Rome's public priests (*pontifices*), the *fabri tignarii* nevertheless celebrate their own domain of knowledge, that of making, and its importance, under the guidance of Minerva, to maintaining the public welfare of the *res publica*.

Notes

1. See Maticic and Rogers in this volume for a review of relevant literature.
2. See Bowes and Flohr 2024; Tran 2017; Lis and Soly 2016; building upon Joshel 1992 and Veyne 2000. See also Hawkins 2016; Flohr 2013; Wilson and Flohr 2016; Sancinito 2024; Venticinque 2016; Cuomo 2007.
3. Scheidel et al. 2007; Bowman and Wilson 2009; Temin 2012. For a critique of this approach to the study of the ancient economy, see Verboven 2015 and Bowes 2021 with associated bibliographies.
4. In this approach, I build upon the work of Cuomo 2007, who has argued in the specific case of the depiction of the *libella* (carpenter's square) on funerary monuments that such representations should be understood as "multisemantic," their meaning ranging from a simple declaration of professional identity to acting as a symbol of religious or cultural import.
5. This "third way" of interpreting depictions of craftsmanship and its centrality to communal cohesion is influenced especially by Cuomo 2007: 77–102, and by studies in other periods and societies, most notably Barringer 2005, exploring the intersection of labor, art, and religion in Victorian Britain; and Kendrick 2011, arguing that Thomas Dekker's *The Shoemaker's Holiday* expounded an alternative to aristocratic or mercantile understandings of work in Elizabethan England.
6. For example, Zanker 1975; Meyer 1990; Joshel 1992; Mouritsen 2005, 2011. For other attempts to reconstruct labor art outside of such a paradigm, see Petersen 2006 on the art of freedpeople, and Mayer 2014, who argues for a specifically "middle class" visual culture.
7. Cuomo has articulated the possibility that craftspeople, in particular, were *not* in fact participating in the same discourses of work, labor, productivity, and status espoused by authors of what she calls the "mainstream view" of status and labor. Instead, craftspeople were offering an epistemic alternative to work and its role in society (Cuomo 2007: 101–2). Cuomo concentrates her analysis on a single piece of iconography—the carpenter's square (*libella*)—suggesting that, since the "interpretation of individual technical motifs is still at an embryonic stage," we should be cautious in attempting to "read entire sentences" before understanding the "individual words of which they are composed" (Cuomo 2007: 78). Drawing upon work in the

last two decades exploring similar motifs, this chapter reconstructs the metaphorical sentence, including its syntax and semantics, that Cuomo has warned others to avoid.

8. Beyond Colini 1947, the relief is considered briefly by Schürmann 1985: 58–61, as one example of the "Minerva Ergane" type; by D'Ambra 1987: 84 and 124, strictly as a *comparandum* to the *forum Transitorium* relief and its contents; and by Madigan 2012: 13–5, as an aside during a discussion of processional statuettes and largely following the interpretation of Schürmann 1985.
9. The cultural importance of bodily memory, explored by practice theorists such as Bourdieu 1977 and Wacquant 2004, has been especially fruitful for understanding how the social memory of communities is activated by ritual reenactment. See Connerton 1989.
10. The finest example is the *ara Pacis*, capturing the annual procession and the moment just before sacrifice at the altar of Augustan peace. See Elsner 1995: 209.
11. Colini 1947: 21–28.
12. Colini 1947: 28, n. 28; Bollmann 1998: 250–2; Fabiano 2019: 73. *CIL* VI 9415a, discovered originally in the portico of the church of Santa Maria in Cosmedin in the *forum Boarium* but now lost, has been restored as *[...]SIO SCOLAE | [...FABRUM TIGN?]ARIORUM ET | [...INTES?]INARIORUM | [...] PALATI.* Fabiano 2019, 66, n. 2, cites and agrees with Panciera 1981: 279, n. 26, who restores the second line as [*SCUT*]*ARIORUM*, on the basis of *PALATI* in l.4. As Fabiano points out, the *schola scutariorum* was among the *scholae palatinae* of the late antique period.
13. For example, the Belvedere altar (1.94 m × .72 m × 1 m), the Terme altar in the Museo Nazionale Romano at the Terme di Diocleziano (.44 m × .44 m), the altar of the Vicus Statae Matris (.68 m × .45 m × .3 m), and the Venus Augusta altar found in the *forum Boarium* (.63 m × .52 m × .44 m). See Flower and DiLuzio 2019: 216–7, and Lott 2004 for other examples. Two other altars dedicated by the *fabri tignarii* have also been uncovered. One is an altar dedicated by six *ministri* of the second *lustrum* (2 BCE–3 CE) to Minerva on behalf of the *fabri tignarii* (.9 m × .44 m × .44 m) and found in the *Velabrum*. See Ryberg 1955: 87–8; Schürmann 1985: 58–62; Madigan 2012: 10–5. A second is the altar of the Tempio Collegiale in Ostia, V, XI, 1, which is between 1.5 and 2 meters on each side.
14. The Paris-Munich reliefs have been the subject of a similar typological debate, with some arguing that the reliefs were appended to the "altar of Domitius Ahenobarbus," others that they were part of a statue base for

M. Antonius or another Roman general. For an overview of arguments, see Maschek 2018.

15. There is an aesthetic recursivity in the stone representation of Minerva's aegis. Minerva's transformation of Medusa's hair into coiling, venomous snakes (Ov. *Met.* 753–803), and the latter's ability to transform onlookers into stone through her gaze are on full display. The conquest and control of Medusa's gaze (cf. Keith 2009) by Perseus is, perhaps, echoed here by the artisans' conquest of the stone in their depiction of the aegis, and the resulting control over the gaze of the viewer.
16. Colini 1947: 23.
17. Musei Vaticani, Inv. 60788.
18. οὔ φασι Ῥωμαῖοι εἰδέναι, εἰκόνα δὲ αὐτοῦ λίθῳ τινὶ ἐγκεκολαμμένην δεικνύουσι καὶ ἐς ἐμὲ ἐν τῷ τῆς Τύχης ἱερῷ, οὗ δὴ πρὸ τοῦ χαλκοῦ τῆς Ἀθηνᾶς ἀγάλματος κεῖται, ὅπερ αἴθριον ἐς τὰ πρὸς ἕω τοῦ νεὼ ἵδρυται. "The Romans say they do not know, but they show a copy of it carved into some stone even now in the temple of Fortune, where it stands in front of the bronze statue of Athena, which is set up outside in the eastern part of the temple grounds."
19. Schürmann 1985: 59–60.
20. *RIC* 89, *RIC* 108, *RIC* 109, *RIC* 167 (a), *RIC* 188, *RIC* 277, *RIC* 314, *RIC* 315, *RIC* 321, *RIC* 336, *RIC* 439, *RIC* 447, *RIC* 508, *RIC* 509, *RIC* 519, *RIC* 558, *RIC* 568, *RIC* 580, *RIC* 593, *RIC* 659, *RIC* 669, *RIC* 676, *RIC* 691, *RIC* 697, *RIC* 698, *RIC* 721, *RIC* 726, *RIC* 732, *RIC* 737, *RIC* 741, *RIC* 763, *RIC* 772, *RIC* 778, *RIC* 789.
21. Hunt 2011; Donohue 1988.
22. Plin. *NH.* 34.34 connects the end of wooden statue production at Rome to the introduction of marble and bronze statues from the Hellenistic East.
23. Madigan 2012: 39–66, for a discussion of ceremonial sculptures carried on litters (*fercula*). Schürmann 1985: 54–57, provides several other comparanda for *fercula* and statues, including the wall painting in Room 11 of the House of Venus and Mars in Pompeii (VII 9.47), which shows a miniature temple, a tree, a chair, and unidentified object being carried upon *fercula*; cf. Ryberg 1955: 169. Schürmann suggests that such objects were probably made of paper mâché, though he adduces no evidence for this statement, nor am I aware of any literary references to such a process.
24. Clarke 2003: 85–7, with bibliography.
25. Clarke 2003: 87–94, with bibliography.
26. Ulrich 2007: 278–9.
27. Tert. *Apol.* 12.4: *at in deos vestros per omnia membra … incumbent asciae et runcinae et scobinae.* Cf. Arn. 6.14: *simulacra ista quae vos terrent runcinarum … levigata de planis.*

28. Zimmer 1982 collects ~200 examples of depictions of work scenes and tools, the vast majority of which are connected to funerary contexts. Kampen 1981 analyses the examples from Ostia that contain depictions of women. Cuomo 2007 examines only those displaying the carpenter's square (*libella*).
29. Joshel 1992; Veyne 2000.
30. Veyne 2000: 1186, construes statements of this type as examples of the discourse of merit that was typical of *la plèbe moyenne*.
31. Zimmer 1982: 64.
32. Burford 1972; Reddé 1978; D'Ambra 1988; Joshel 1992; Clarke 2003.
33. For example, Dunbabin 2003: 34–5, demonstrates that the depiction of a reclining banqueter in funerary art could have a range of meanings beyond simply communicating the reality of the deceased's life. In the case of the early second-century CE grave stele at Alt-Kalkar of C. Iulius Primus, who was an auxiliary cavalry member in the Roman army, the image of the reclining banqueter was almost certainly not meant to be evocative of his actual circumstances.
34. Cuomo 2007.
35. Meyer 1990: 91; Hatt 1951: 85–107.
36. Zimmer 1982: 72–3, remarks on this development though he does not interpret it as having a religious valence.
37. Roller 2013.
38. Kuttner 2021 and Kuttner, this volume: 117–61. See also Cuomo 2007.
39. For example, on the Belvedere altar and the altar of Amemptus. See also in this volume, Kuttner: 121.
40. For the idea of object agency, see Gosden 2005, Olsen 2010, and Frankfurter 2017. In this particular case, I understand such "things" as invoking an array of uses and practices known to the viewer through previous experience. The agency of the object, therefore, is to be equated with this range of compulsions that it places upon a viewer or doer. Cf. also Harman 2002, who examines the agency of objects through the philosophy of Heidegger.
41. La Follette 2011/2: 15–35.
42. La Follette 2011/2: 24–5, citing Cic. *Har.* 11.23. The importance of these verbal *formulae* are clear in our extant evidence, including the augural *formula* given by Var. *Ling.* 7.8; the lustral *formulae* given by Cato, *Agr.* 141, as well as the charms described at *Agr.* 160; and the archaic *carmina* of the Salii (Var. *Ling.* 7.26–7) and the Arval Brethren (*CIL* VI 2104). For considerations of the importance of verbal *formulae* in religion and magic, see Graf 2004: 79–100, and Versnel 2012: 105–58.
43. Gosden 2005.
44. Elsner 1991.

45. Placing the date sometime between 2 BCE and 3 CE if we understand Augustus' reorganization of *collegia* in 7 BCE to mark the first *lustrum*.
46. Ryberg 1955: 87–8; Pearse 1975; Schürmann 1985: 58–62; Madigan 2012: 10–5.
47. There is also an interesting parallel here to votives; tools of production were dedicated as votive objects, either the tools themselves—cf. Gleba 2008 on textile tools as votives in archaic Italian sanctuaries—or miniature reproductions of tools—cf. Kiernan 2015 on miniature objects in Iron Age and Roman Western Europe.
48. Colini 1947; Schürmann 1985; Madigan 2012. The frieze procession is often an afterthought in analyses of the Arch of Titus. See Ryberg 1955: 147–8, who likens the style to "popular art," without considering the angle and distance of viewing.
49. Ryberg 1955: 41–3.
50. To what extent these resonances would encourage us to consider the *fabri* relief within the category of that most Roman of pictorial genres, the "historical relief" is an interesting problem worth revisiting.
51. See D'Ambra 1993 for a seminal discussion of the reliefs and their context, as well as complete bibliography.
52. D'Ambra 1993: 3–18; Schürmann 1985: 11–13. Schürmann 1985: 89–90, connects the cult image in the Temple of Minerva in the *forum Transitorium* with the image that proliferates under Domitian in the coinage mentioned above, pp. 233–235, n. 20, as well as in the *congiaria* coinage of the first century CE.
53. Moser 2019, though analyzing Republican altars in Rome and Latium, suggests that altars in particular are evocative of the "material memories" inherent in Roman sacrificial practice, which was, by necessity, undertaken in dialogue with the physical world and its spaces.
54. Moser and Knust 2017 collect a number of essays exploring the materiality of religion.
55. Ovid's *Fasti* references both festivals, as does the *fasti Antiates Maiores*, though Ovid places the festival on the Ides of June while the *fasti Antiates Maiores* merely states that June 19th was dedicated to Minerva. Due to its fragmentary state, the *fasti Praenestini* does not contain any information for the month of June, though it too lists the *Quinquatrus Maiores* in mid-March. Other Augustan/Tiberian-era calendars, including the *fasti Caeretani*, *Maffeiani*, *Vaticani*, and *Farnesiani* all list the *Quinquatrus Maiores* on March 19th. Interestingly, the *Quinquatrus Minores* are not explicitly listed on any of our extant calendars, although a festival to Minerva is marked on June 19th in the *fasti Amiternini* and *Esquilini*, while the the *fasti Maffeiani* and *Venusini* list nothing. What precisely accounts for this discrepancy is unclear.

56. Ov. *Fast.* 6.649–710. Cf. Var. *Ling.* 6.17, Fest. 134L, and Cens. *De die nat.* 12.2. Liv. 9.30.5–10, Plut. *Rom. Quaest.* 55, and Val. Max. 2.5.4 offer other versions of the supposed exile story. López Barja de Quiroga 2018: 143, n. 2, contains a bibliography for the festival.
57. Ov. *Fast.* 6.95–6:
'Martius' inquit 'agit tali mea nomine festa,
estque sub inventis haec quoque turba meis.
58. Cinaglia 2016; Granino-Cecere 2001; Storchi Marino 1979.
59. Ov. *Fast.* 3.809–34:
Una dies media est, et fiunt sacra Minervae,
nomina quae iunctis quinque diebus habent,
sanguine prima vacat, nec fas concurrere ferro:
causa, quod est illa nata Minerva die.
altera tresque super strata celebrantur harena:
ensibus exertis bellica laeta dea est.
Pallada nunc pueri teneraeque orate puellae:
qui bene placarit Pallada, doctus erit.
Pallade placata lanam mollire puellae
discant et plenas exonerare colos.
illa etiam stantis radio percurrere telas
erudit et rarum pectine denset opus.
hanc cole, qui maculas laesis de vestibus aufers,
hanc cole, velleribus quisquis aena paras;
nec quisquam invita faciet bene vincula plantae
Pallade, sit Tychio doctior ille licet;
et licet antiquo manibus conlatus Epeo
sit prior, irata Pallade manens erit.
vos quoque, Phoebea morbos qui pellitis arte,
munera de vestris pauca referte deae:
nec vos, turba fere censu fraudata, magistri,
spernite; discipulos attrahit illa novos:
quique moves caelum, tabulamque coloribus uris,
quique facis docta mollia saxa manu.
mille dea est operum: certe dea carminis illa est;
si mereor, studiis adsit amica meis.
60. Cinaglia 2016 traces the possible development of the festival from an archaic celebration to Mars marking the beginning of the martial calendar to the festival described by Ovid.
61. Rüpke 2011.
62. Rüpke 2011.
63. Cic. *Fam.* 12.25: *Quinquatribus frequenti senatu causam tuam egi non invita Minerva*, "During the *Quinquatria*, I plead your case in a packed

senate, with Minerva not unwilling." Cf. Cic. *Fam.* 2.12: *ita tumultuosae contiones, ita molestae Quinquatrus adferebantur; nam citeriora nondum audieramus*, "the assemblies were made so tumultuous, so bothersome by the *Quinquatria*—indeed we could no longer hear those rather close to us."

64. Non. 508M:
...quánto ego
Plús sapiui, quín fullonem cómpressi quinquátrubus. séquere me!
Púriter uolo fácias: <puro> igni átque aqua uolo húnc accipier.

...how much more I know not to bother the fuller on *Quinquatria*. Follow me!
I want you to behave properly: with pure fire and water do I want this man to be greeted.

65. Suet. *Dom.* 4: *Celebrabat et in Albano quotannis Quinquatria Minervae, cui collegium instituerat, ex quo sorte ducti magisterio fungerentur ederentque eximias venationes et scaenicos ludos superque oratorum ac poetarum certamina.* "In Alba for so many years, he also celebrated the *Quinquatria* of Minerva. For her he had created a college, from which leaders for the magistracy were chosen by lot and sponsored animal hunts, theatrical plays, and above all oratorical and poetic contests." Cf. D'Ambra 1993: 76–7.
66. Von Blanckenhagen 1940: 118–27. Cf. Fest. 284L: *Publica sacra, quae publico sumptu pro populo fiunt, quaeque pro montibus, pagis, curis, sacellis: at privata, quae pro singulis hominibus, familiis, gentibus fiunt.* "Public rites, which are undertaken at public cost and on behalf of the people, in the mountain districts, rural districts, *curiae*, and small shrines; and private rites, which are undertaken on behalf of individual men, families, and clans."
67. Clarke 2003: 85–7. Cf. Abaecherli 1935–6; Felletti Maj 1977: 334–5; Fröhlich 1991: 319–20; van Nijf 1997: 200; Madigan 2012: 55–6.
68. Abaecherli 1935–6; Madigan 2012: 39–66.
69. Ov. *Met.* 8.236–59 describes Perdix' transformation by Minerva into a bird after being pushed to his death by Daedalus.
70. Ambrosini 2014.
71. Yarrow 2018.
72. For the story of Mamurius, see Liv. 1.20, Ov. *Fast.* 3.381–92; Plut. *Num.* 13. Prop. 4.2 states that Mamurius Veturius, thought to be an Etruscan, had sculpted the statue of Vertumnus in the Etruscan neighborhood in Rome.
73. As Hexter 1990 notes, Vergil's specification of four types of wood (fir, pine, maple, and oak) has long been interpreted as a problem by textual critics, who seek to solve this conundrum of carpentry. Yet Vergil's poetic description of the horse's materials, while being a purposely insoluble puzzle of the poet's devising, in Hexter's estimation, is also the perfect representation of Minerva's divine and sublime artisanal skill.

74. Cic. *Off.* 1.150: *Opificesque omnes in sordida arte versantur; nec enim quicquam ingenuum habere potest officina.*
75. Moser 2019; Östenberg et al. 2015.
76. Bergmann and Kondoleon 1999; Barton 2002.
77. A similar claim made by craftsmen in the funerary sphere has been detailed by Serafina Cuomo, with whom this chapter began. She sees in such iconographic practices a repudiation of the "marginalized" status often accorded to artisans in both the ancient and modern sources, Cuomo 2007: 101–2: "They celebrated a form of knowledge which was alternative to other forms of knowledge, and a social role, that of the expert, the skilled maker of things and producer of results, which again, perhaps deliberately, posed itself as an alternative to other social and public roles, such as those determined by birth, connections, or a literary education."

Bibliography

Abaecherli-Boyce, A. L. 1935. "Fercula, carpenta and tensae in the Roman procession." *Bollettino dell'Associazione degli Studi Mediterranei* 6: 1–20.

Ambrosini, L. 2014. "Images of artisans on Etruscan and Italic gems." *Etruscan Studies* 17.2: 172–191.

Barringer, T. 2005. *Men at Work: Art and Labour in Victorian Britain.* Yale University Press.

Barton, C. 2002. "Being in the eyes: shame and sight in ancient Rome." In Fredrick, D. C. ed. *The Roman gaze: vision, power, and the body.* 216–235. Johns Hopkins University Press.

Bergmann, B. and Kondoleon, C. eds. 1999. *The Art of Ancient Spectacle.* National Gallery of Art.

Bollmann, B. 1998. *Römische Vereinshäuser: Untersuchungen zu den Scholae der römischen Berufs-, Kult- und Augustalen-Kollegien in Italien.* Zabern.

Bourdieu, P. 1977. *Outline of a Theory of Practice.* Translated by Richard Nice. Cambridge University Press.

Bowes, K. 2021. "When Kuznets Went to Rome: Roman Economic Well-Being and the Reframing of Roman History." *Capitalism* 2.1: 7–40.

Bowes, K. and Flohr, M. 2024. *Valuing Labour in Greco-Roman Antiquity.* Brill.

Bowman, A. and Wilson, A., eds. 2009. *Quantifying the Roman Economy: Methods and Problems.* Oxford University Press.

Burford A. 1972. *Craftsmen in Greek and Roman society.* Cornell University Press.

Cinaglia, T. 2016. "Le *Quinquatrus*, una festa di Minerva." *Gerión* 34: 145–167.

Clarke, J. 2003. *Art in the Lives of Ordinary Romans: Visual Representation and Non-Elite Viewers in Italy, 100 B.C.–A.D. 315.* University of California Press.

Colini, A. M. 1947. "Officina di fabri tignarii nei frammenti di un ara monumentale rinvenuti fra il Campidoglio e il Tevere." *Capitolium* 22: 21–28.

Connerton, P. 1989. *How Societies Remember*. Cambridge University Press.
Cuomo, S. 2007. *Technology and Culture in Greek and Roman Antiquity*. Cambridge University Press.
D'Ambra, E. 1993. *Private Lives, Imperial Virtues: The Frieze of the Forum Transitorium in Rome*. Princeton University Press.
D'Ambra, E. 1988. "A Myth for a Smith. A Meleager Sarcophagus from a Tomb in Ostia." *American Journal of Archaeology* 92: 85–99.
D'Ambra, E. 1987. *Palladis Artes: The Frieze of the Forum Transitorium in Rome*. Ph.D. Diss. Yale University.
Donohue, A. A. 1988. *Xoana and the origins of Greek sculpture*. Scholars Press.
Dunbabin, K. 2003. *The Roman Banquet. Images of Conviviality*. Cambridge University Press.
Elsner, J. 1995. *Art and the Roman viewer: The Transformation of Art from the Pagan World to Christianity*. Cambridge University Press.
Elsner, J. 1991. "Cult and sculpture: sacrifice in the Ara Pacis Augustae." *The Journal of Roman Studies* 81: 50–61.
Fabiano, J. 2019. "Builders and integrated associations in fourth-century CE Rome: A new interpretation of AE 1941, 68." *Journal of Late Antiquity* 12: 65–87.
Felletti Maj, B. 1977. *La Tradizione Italica Nell'arte Romana*. Bretschneider.
Flohr, M. 2013. *The World of the Fullo: Work, Economy, and Society in Roman Italy*. Oxford University Press.
Flower, H. I. and DiLuzio, M. J. 2019. "The women and the *lares*: a reconsideration of an Augustan altar from the Capitoline in Rome." *American Journal of Archaeology* 123.2: 213–236.
Frankfurter, D. 2017. "Ritual Matters: Afterword." In Moser, C. and Knust, J. eds. *Ritual Matters: Material Remains and Ancient Religions*. 145–150. University of Michigan Press.
Fröhlich, T. 1991. *Lararien- und Fassadenbilder in den Vesuvstädten: Untersuchungen zur "volkstümlichen" pompejanischen Malerei*. Zabern.
Gleba, M. 2008. *Textile Production in Pre-Roman Italy*. Oxbow Books.
Gosden, C. 2005. "What Do Objects Want?" *Journal of Archaeological Method and Theory* 12.3: 193–211.
Graf, F. 2004. "The Power of the Word in the Graeco-Roman World." In Beta, S. *Potenza della parola: destinatari, funzioni, bersagli*. 79–100. Cadmo.
Granino-Cecere, M. G. 2001. "*Quinquatrus*: tradizione popolare e tradizione antiquaria di una festività del calendario romano." *Ziva Antika* 51: 25–38.
Harman, G. 2002. *Tool-Being: Heidegger and the Metaphysics of Objects*. Open Court Press.
Hatt, J.J. 1951. *La tombe gallo-romaine. Recherches sur les inscriptions et les monuments funéraires gallo-romains des trois premiers siècles de notre ère*. PUF.

Hawkins, C. 2016. *Roman Artisans and the Urban Economy.* Cambridge University Press.
Hexter, R. 1990. "What Was the Trojan Horse Made of?: Interpreting Virgil's *Aeneid*." *Yale Journal of Criticism* 3: 109–31.
Hunt, A. 2011. "Priapus as wooden god: confronting manufacture and destruction." *Cambridge Classical Journal* 57: 29–54.
Joshel, S. 1992. *Work, Identity, and Legal Status in Rome: A Study of the Occupational Inscriptions.* University of Oklahoma Press.
Kampen, N. 1981. *Image and status. Roman working women in Ostia.* Mann.
Keith, A.M. 2009. "The Lay of the Land in Ovid's "Perseid" (*Met.* 4.610–5.249)." *Classical World* 102: 259–72.
Kendrick, M. 2011. "'A Shoemaker Sell Flesh and Blood—O Indignity!': The Labouring Body and Community in the Shoemaker's Holiday." *English Studies* 92: 259–273.
Kiernan, P. 2015. "Miniature Objects as Representations of Realia." *World Archaeology* 47: 45–59.
Kuttner, A. 2021. "Object Worlds." In Osborne, R. ed. *A Cultural History of Objects in Antiquity.* 185–214. Bloomsbury Academic.
La Follette, L. 2011. "Parsing piety: the sacred still life in Roman relief sculpture." *Memoirs of the American Academy in Rome* 56–57: 15–35.
Lis, C. and Soly, H. 2016. "Work, identity and self-representation in the Roman Empire and the West-European Middle Ages: Different interplays between the social and the cultural." In Verboven and Laes 2017: 262–289.
López Barja de Quiroga, P. 2018. "The *quinquatrus* of June, Marsyas and *libertas* in the late Roman Republic." *Classical Quarterly* 68: 143–159.
Lott, B. 2004. *The Neighborhoods of Augustan Rome.*
Madigan, B. 2012. *The Ceremonial Sculptures of the Roman Gods.* Brill.
Maschek, D. 2018. "Not *census* but *deductio*: reconsidering the Ara of Domitius Ahenobarbus." *The Journal of Roman Studies* 108: 27–52.
Mayer, E. 2014. *The Ancient Middle Classes: Urban Life and Aesthetics in the Roman Empire, 100 BCE–250 CE.* Harvard University Press.
Meyer, E. A. 1990. "Explaining the epigraphic habit in the Roman Empire: the evidence of epitaphs." *The Journal of Roman Studies* 80: 74–96.
Mouritsen, H. 2011. *The Freedman in the Roman World.* Cambridge University Press.
Mouritsen, H. 2005. "Freedmen and decurions: Epitaphs and social history in imperial Italy." *The Journal of Roman Studies* 95: 38–63.
Moser, C. 2019. *The Altars of Republican Rome and Latium: Sacrifice and the materiality of Roman religion.* Cambridge University Press.
Moser, C. and Knust, J. 2017. *Ritual Matters: Material Remains and Ancient Religion.* University of Michigan Press.

van Nijf, O. 1997. *The Civic World of Professional Associations in the Roman East.* Brill.
Olsen, B. 2010. *In Defense of Things. Archaeology and the Ontology of Objects.* AltaMira Press.
Östenberg, I., Malmberg, S., and Bjørnebye, J. eds. 2015. *The moving city: Processions, passages and promenades in ancient Rome.* Bloomsbury.
Panciera, S. 1981. "Fasti fabrum tignariorum urbis Romae." *Zeitschrift für Papyrologie und Epigraphik* 43: 271–280.
Pearse, L. 1975. "A forgotten altar of the collegium fabrum tignariorum of Rome." *Epigraphica* 37: 100–123.
Petersen, L. H. 2006. *The freedman in Roman art and art history.* Cambridge University Press.
Reddé, M. 1978. "Les scènes de métier dans la sculpture funéraire gallo-romaine." *Gallia* 36: 43–63.
Roller, M. 2013. "On the intersignification of monuments in Augustan Rome." *American Journal of Philology* 134: 119–131.
Rüpke, J. 2011. *The Roman calendar from Numa to Constantine: time, history and the Fasti.* Wiley Blackwell.
Ryberg, S. 1955. *Rites of the State religion in Roman art.* Yale University Press.
Sancinito, J. 2024. *The Reputation of the Roman Merchant.* University of Michigan Press.
Scheidel, W. Morris, I., and Saller, W., eds. 2007. *The Cambridge Economic History of the Greco-Roman World.* Cambridge University Press.
Schürmann, W. 1985. *Typologie und Bedeutung der stadtrömischen Minerva-Kultbilder.* G. Bretschneider.
Storchi Marino, A. 1979. "Artigiani e rituali religiosi nella Roma arcaica." *Rendiconti della Accademia di Archeologia, Lettere e Belle Arti* 54: 333–357.
Temin, P. 2012. *The Roman Market Economy.* Princeton University Press.
Tran, N. 2017. "*Ars* and *Doctrina*: the socioeconomic identity of Roman skilled workers (first century BC-third century AD)." In Verboven and Laes. 246–261.
Ulrich, R. 2007. *Roman Woodworking.* Yale University Press.
Venticinque, P.F. 2016. *Honor Among Thieves: Craftsmen, Merchants, and Associations in Roman and Late Roman Egypt.* University of Michigan Press.
Verboven, K. 2015. "The knights who say NIE: can Neo-Institutional Economics live up to its expectation in ancient history research?." In Erdkamp, P., and Verboven, K. eds. *Structure and performance in the Roman economy: Models, methods and case studies.* 33–57. Latomus.
Versnel, H. S. 2012. "The poetics of the magical charm: An essay in the power of words." In Mirecki, P.A. ed. *Magic and ritual in the ancient world.* 105–158. Brill.
Veyne, P. 2000. "La "plèbe moyenne" sous le Haut-Empire romain." *Annales* 55–6: 1169–99.

Von Blanckenhagen, P. H. 1940. *Flavische Architektur und ihre Dekoration untersucht am Nerva-forum.* De Gruyter.

Wacquant, L. 2004. *Body and Soul: Notebooks of an Apprentice Boxer.* Oxford University Press.

Wilson, A. and Flohr, M., eds. 2016. *Urban Craftsmen and Traders in the Roman World, Oxford Studies on the Roman Economy.* Oxford University Press.

Yarrow, L. 2018. "Markers of Identity for Non-Elite Romans: A Prolegomenon to the Study of Glass Paste Intaglios." *Journal of Ancient History and Archaeology* 5.3: 35–54.

Zanker, P. 1975. "Grabreliefs römischer Freigelassener." *Jahrbuch des Deutschen Archäologischen Instituts XC*: 267–315.

Zimmer, G. 1982. *Römische Berufsdarstellungen.* Gebrüder Mann Verlag.

PART III

Escaping, Commuting, and Passing Out

CHAPTER 9

Two Ex-Slaves of Cicero: Tiro and Chrysippus Beyond Reach

Nicole J. Giannella

In November of 50 BCE, Cicero was traveling back to Italy from his proconsulship in Cilicia. He was also worrying over two missing freedmen. The first was Tiro, who fell ill on the journey back and stayed behind in Patras to recover. The second was Chrysippus, a literary worker who was tasked with looking after Cicero's son, but left the position without letting Cicero know. Cicero's reactions to the missing freedmen were very different; the eight letters from Cicero to Tiro about this particular illness date from November 3 to 27, 50 BCE as preserved in Book 16 of his *Letters to Friends* (*Epistulae ad familiares*). These letters are filled with affection, concern for Tiro's health and journey, and anxiousness for his return. In contrast, there is one letter detailing the situation of Chrysippus, from Cicero to Atticus, dated to around November 25, 50 BCE, and instead of expressions of anxiety, Cicero wants to know what Atticus thinks about trying to re-enslave Chrysippus for having left Marcus Jr. in the lurch.

N. J. Giannella (✉)
Cornell University, Ithaca, NY, USA
e-mail: njg68@cornell.edu

D. A. Maticic, J. Rogers (eds.), *Working Lives in Ancient Rome*, The New Antiquity,
https://doi.org/10.1007/978-3-031-61234-3_9

In this chapter, I argue that these situations should be examined together, as despite these differences, the stories of these missing freedmen are being narrated and processed by the same man at the same time, and both freedmen worked as a part of Cicero's literary production. Here I would like to use Cicero's evidence-rich letters to Tiro from this period as a case-study to inform us about a wider group of elite literary freedmen for whom such evidence is lacking. Book 16 of Cicero's *Letters to Friends* is composed entirely of letters to and about Tiro, Cicero's esteemed enslaved, and later freed, literary worker. As such, Book 16 makes us think that Tiro is unique but that is because of the evidence that we have—it is a product of the archive.[1]

The letters date from 53 BCE, when Tiro was still enslaved, to 44 BCE, with the largest batch of letters dating to this post-manumission period in November 50 BCE.[2] The letters from Cicero to Tiro during this period reveal the difficulties (at least in the mind of Cicero) of safe travel even for a freedman of Tiro's stature. I will proceed first by giving an account of Tiro's situation in November 50 BCE and then one of Chrysippus' situation. This chapter will conclude by considering what aspects of Tiro's story can help paint a fuller picture of the lives of other Ciceronian freedmen and finally briefly suggest how this account of Chrysippus' departure might inform how we think of the narrative of Tiro's perpetual string of illnesses presented in Book 16. In doing so, this chapter considers how we can trace the working lives of these freedmen and their efforts to escape such structures of work.

Tiro's Story

Following manuscript order, the first letter of Book 16 was written during Cicero's journey back to Italy from his time as proconsul of Cilicia in November of 50 BCE. Tiro, who had accompanied him during his term as proconsul, stayed behind in Patras because he was ill. In the letter, Cicero suggests several contacts from whom Tiro might find support:

> From Tullius and Marcus and the Quinti to their nicest and best of Tiros best greetings.
>
> Look at how charming you are! We spent two hours at Thyrreum, and our host Xenomenes is as fond of you as if he had spent his life with you. He has promised everything you need, and I believe he will be as good as his word. I'd like it if he brought you to Leucas when you are stronger, to finish

your convalescence there. You must see what Curius and Lyso and the doctor think. I wanted to send Mario back to you for you to send him to me with a letter when you were a little better, but I reflected that Mario could bring me only one letter, and I expect them one after another. So do what you can, and, if you care for me see that Acastus goes down to the harbour every day. There will be plenty of folk to whom you can safely give a letter and who will be glad to carry it to me. For my part I shall take advantage of every traveler to Patras.

I pin all my hope of your getting proper treatment and attention on Curius. He has the kindest of hearts and the truest affection for me. Put yourself entirely in his hands. I had rather see you fit and well a little later on than weak straight away. So care for nothing except getting well—I shall care for the rest.

Good-bye once again.

Leaving Leucas, 7 November

TULLIUS ET CICERO ET QQ. TIRONI HUMANISSIMO ET OPTIMO S. P. D.

Vide quanta sit in te suavitas. duas horas Thyrrei fuimus: Xenomenes hospes tam te diligit quasi vixerit tecum. is omnia pollicitus est quae tibi essent opus; facturum puto. mihi placebat, si firmior esses, ut te Leucadem deportaret, ut ibi te plane confirmares. videbis quid Curio, quid Lysoni, quid medico placeat. volebam ad te Marionem remittere quem, cum meliuscule tibi esset, ad me mitteres; sed cogitavi unas litteras Marionem adferre posse, me autem crebras exspectare. <quod> poteris igitur; et facies, si me diligis, ut cottidie sit Acastus in portu. multi erunt quibus recte litteras dare possis qui ad me libenter perferant. equidem Patras euntem neminem praetermittam.

Ego omnem spem tui diligenter curandi in Curio habeo. nihil potest illo fieri humanius, nihil nostri amantius. ei te totum trade. malo te paulo post valentem quam statim imbecillum videre. cura igitur nihil aliud nisi ut valeas; cetera ego curabo.

Etiam atque etiam vale.

Leucade proficiscens VII Id. Nov. (MS *Fam.* 16.1; *Fam* 16.5; SB 124)[3]

This letter is appropriately programmatic, bringing out the main themes of Book 16, and while it is the first letter of Book 16, this is not the first letter that Cicero wrote to Tiro that day—he would write three in total on November 7th. Much of the focus in this letter is on the free people that either have affection for Tiro or are enlisted by Cicero to help Tiro.

The letter begins with Cicero teasing Tiro for his charm (*suavitas*), as Xenomenes, who hosted Tiro on a previous journey, was taken enough by him that Cicero thinks he would be a good option to transport Tiro to

Leucas once he was well enough. While Cicero has taken the liberty of making such arrangements for Tiro, Tiro is a freedman at this point and Cicero's language here reflects it: he would like Tiro to consider this plan (*mihi placebat*).[4] Tiro's imminent travel plans to return to Cicero are a major theme in Book 16 and, even in this letter, Cicero ropes more free people into the care of Tiro and caring about Tiro. He tells Tiro to ask not just his doctor, but his host Lyso and potential host Curius about Cicero's new plan for his recovery. As Cicero notes, Curius loves nothing more than Cicero, or rather *nostri*, which perhaps in Cicero's mind with Tiro being his ex-slave, could mean Cicero and Tiro instead of just Cicero. We might wonder why Tiro needs help with travel: is he that ill? Is Cicero fretting over nothing? Or is it because as represented in Book 16, Tiro never quite seems to make it back to Cicero?

Finally, the letter touches on another important theme throughout the book: Cicero would like more letters from Tiro. Here also is a contribution to the narrative of Tiro's uniqueness among enslaved or formerly enslaved people; other enslaved and freed people are visibly instrumentalized in order to facilitate Cicero's relationship with Tiro. The commodification of these other enslaved or formerly enslaved people is never too far removed either. Cicero will spare no expense for Tiro, several times in the letters of Book 16 he tells Tiro not to worry about the finances of his care[5] despite that Tiro the freedman would have had the resources to pay for his doctor himself.[6] Here Cicero is thinking of sending Mario, who is either a slave or a freedman of Cicero,[7] all the way back to Patras to collect a single letter from Tiro in person. He also asks Tiro to send Acastus,[8] an enslaved person who was left behind with Tiro, to go post letters at the port each day if he, Tiro, loves Cicero. Love is quantifiable and money is nothing: Cicero loves Tiro too much to just get one letter; Tiro loves Cicero as many times as he sends letters. The labor of Mario and Acastus is seemingly beside the point.

On other occasions, Cicero asserts that no one who loves Cicero does not care for Tiro. For example, in Letter 16.7 (the second letter in the book following manuscript order), written November 16th—9 days after the first letter with no letter from Tiro in between—Cicero says that they are stuck in Corcyra thanks to the very same winds that, allegedly, prohibit a letter from Tiro to arrive. He and Marcus Jr. are anxious about Tiro's health and look forward to him rejoining them, who love him:

> So look after yourself and get strong, and when your health and the time of year enable you to make the voyage conveniently, rejoin us who love you dearly. Nobody loves us who is not fond of you. Everybody will be glad to see you and looking forward to your return. Take care of your health.
>
> *Cura igitur te et confirma et, cum commode et per valetudinem et per anni tempus navigare poteris, ad nos amantissimos tui veni. nemo nos amat qui te non diligat. carus omnibus exspectatusque venies. cura ut valeas.* (MS *Fam.* 16.2; *Fam* 16.7; SB 126)

Who loves (*amat*) Cicero, cares for (*diligit*) Tiro. *Diligo* does not have quite the same valence as *amo*, though Shackleton Bailey suggests here it is used merely for variation.[9] The context of this letter suggests that the people in question who *diligit* Tiro are the other members of Cicero's family. To Marcus Jr.'s well wishes, we can add Cicero's wife Terentia's (as recounted by Cicero) in a letter from the 27th of November, 20 days after the first letter of Book 16 and 25 days since Cicero has seen Tiro. Cicero briefly recounts their travels up to that point—they had landed in Italy at Hydrus (modern Otranto) on the 23rd and then went to Brundisium the following day. Apparently, Terentia arrived at the same time as Cicero in Brundisium and he reports that she also thinks Tiro is great (*quae te facit plurimi*, MS *Fam.* 16.9; *Fam.* 16.9; SB 127). After this little aside, the letter then moves onto other topics, to which we will return below. This particular marker of affection is odd as Tiro and Terentia knew each other well enough that presumably each one was aware of what the other thought of them without Cicero's interjection, but perhaps this is like "Terentia sends her regards as you are sick."[10]

Outside of Cicero's family, as we saw from the first letter, Xenomenes cares for, *diligit* again, Tiro. And in 16.4, actually written the same day (November 7th) as the first letter, we get a similar declaration that includes Lyso and Curius from that first letter and also the quaestor Mescinius Rufus, to whom we will return in a moment. Cicero writes: "Take my word for it, dear Tiro, nobody loves me who does not love you. Your recovery is most important to you and me, but many others are concerned about it (*Sic habeto, mi Tiro, neminem esse qui me amet quin idem te amet; et cum tua et mea maxime interest te valere, tum multis est curae*, MS *Fam.* 16.6; *Fam.* 16.4; SB 123)." Who *amat* Cicero, *amat* Tiro. And Mescinius Rufus, the quaestor, mentioned in two letters of Book 16, is described as "not uncultured" and also as "having seemed to me to have a regard for you" (*non inhumanus est teque, ut mihi visus est, diligit*, MS *Fam.* 16.6;

Fam. 16.4; SB 123). Mescinius *diligit* Tiro as well. We might wonder why Cicero is sending all of these signs of affection to Tiro. Perhaps it is to send him warm wishes while he is ill. Or perhaps Cicero is suggesting that it is simply not possible to love one without the other. To love Cicero is to love Tiro or "if they love me, they (have to) love you: you are me." Tiro's subjectivity is elided by Cicero through these expressions of love. While these different readings are possible, and none are mutually exclusive, these declarations of other people's affections often come attached to discussions of the practicalities of Tiro's imminent travel back to Cicero. I would suggest that this is to encourage Tiro to rely on these other people outside of Cicero's, and therefore his own, usual social network so he can get better and back to Cicero more quickly.

The Mescinius letters in particular showcase this. The first is 16.4 from November 7th, which starts with general worry over Tiro's illness: *is his doctor good enough?*; his travel: *he should not until he is better*; where he should stay: *Lyso is not looking after Tiro well enough and perhaps he should stay with Curius*; and his treatment: *he should spare no expense.* Cicero then enumerates how indispensable Tiro is to him in all things:

> Your duties for me are beyond count—in my home and out of it, in Rome and abroad, in private affairs and public, in our studies and literary work. You will cap them all if I see you your own man again, as I hope I shall. I think it would be very nice, if all goes well, for you to sail home with Quaestor Mescinius. He is not uncultured, and he seemed to me to have a regard for you. But when you have given every possible attention to your health, then my dear Tiro, attend to sailing arrangements. I don't now want you to hurry in any way. My only concern is for you to get well.
>
> Take my word for it, dear Tiro, that nobody cares for me who does not care for you. Your recovery is most important to you and me, but many others are concerned about it.

Innumerabilia tua sunt in me officia, domestica, forensia, urbana, provincialia, in re privata, in publica, in studiis, in litteris nostris: omnia viceris si, ut spero, te validum videro. ego puto te bellissime, si recte erit, cum quaestore Mescinio decursurum. non inhumanus est teque, ut mihi visus est, diligit. sed cum valetudini tuae diligentissime consulueris, tum, mi Tiro, consulito navigationi. nulla in re iam te festinare volo. nihil laboro nisi ut salvus sis.

Sic habeto, mi Tiro, neminem esse qui me amet quin idem te amet; et cum tua et mea maxime interest te valere, tum multis est curae. (MS *Fam.* 16.6; *Fam.* 16.4; SB 123)

The lines between labor and love are blurred: *officia* in general are obligations or responsibilities borne out of family (or *familia*) ties.[11] The *officia* of Tiro for Cicero are countless and Tiro's own self is again collapsed into Cicero's desire in the fact that his own return to health will be the apex of his *officia* for Cicero. Meanwhile Cicero will labor on nothing (but Tiro's health—*nihil laboro nisi ut salvus sis*). Cicero's use of *officia* puts Tiro's labor in a different affective realm than that of the enslaved and formerly enslaved people Cicero instrumentalizes to get letters to and from Tiro. Nor are these the *operae* that a former owner requires new freedpersons to swear to after manumission; there is no place for contract law in this gushy bit of correspondence.[12]

In letter 16.9, 20 days later on the 27th of November, Cicero tries again to recommend Mescinius as a travel companion. This is the letter that begins with Cicero recounting his own travel and Terentia's regards to Tiro; it also contains news of Tiro, as Cicero has finally gotten a letter from him. Tiro's letter reveals he had gone to a concert to be, in Cicero's words, a well-behaved guest to Lyso, choosing good manners (*pudor*) over his health (*valetudo*).[13] Here we again turn to travel plans:

> The only other thing is to ask and beg you not to take a ship without proper care. Sailors with their money to make are apt to be in a hurry. Take no chances, my dear Tiro. You have a long, difficult voyage ahead. If possible, go with Mescinius—he is not one to take chances with the sea. If not, then with some other honorable man whose authority the skipper will respect. If you take every care about this and render yourself up to me safe and sound, I shall have all I ever want of you.
>
> *Reliquum est ut te hoc rogem et a te petam ne temere naviges (solent nautae festinare quaestus sui causa), cautus sis, mi Tiro; mare magnum et difficile tibi restat. si poteris, cum Mescinio (caute is solet navigare), si minus, cum honesto aliquo homine, cuius auctoritate navicularius moveatur. in hoc omnem diligentiam si adhibueris teque nobis incolumem stiteris, omnia a te habebo.* (MS *Fam.* 16.9; *Fam.* 16.9; SB 127)

Tiro, in Cicero's mind, lacks authority (*auctoritas*) and needs an honorable man to travel with to keep the ship captain in check. What is it about Tiro that would imply to a ship captain that he lacks *auctoritas*? We can understand from this that Cicero's meddling in Tiro's travel plans go further than Cicero's anxiousness to see Tiro and get Tiro back to work, but instead reveal that whatever courtesies were extended to Tiro because of his famous ex-owner, they did not go so far as to protect him on the road.

There is a connection between Cicero telling Tiro that other people beyond the Ciceros like him and Tiro's imminent travel back to Cicero. Cicero is, in a way, recommending these people to Tiro because Tiro needs their services: he will rely on them for his travel. Tiro's role as scholarly worker and editor in Cicero's literary production, as well as his ex-owner's affection for him, places Tiro at the heart of an aristocratic labor and at the heights of an elite Roman household.[14] However, the protestations of admiration show us a limit of Tiro's situation: Tiro's high status in the eyes of Cicero and his circle leave a chasm when it comes to the everyday vulnerabilities of an (ex-)slave.

This precarity is of course all according to Cicero. Tiro lacks social status or some trappings of social status to travel securely where there are few safety nets to help. Hence the turn to a figure like Mescinius, a quaestor, or at least someone that presents as honorable and authoritative. This explanation precludes the idea that Tiro is simply bad at travel, especially as there is nothing to suggest this in everything else we know about Tiro. Cicero's care and other people's care for Tiro instead emphasize his vulnerability—at least as it is perceived by Cicero. Tiro, as represented in the carefully crafted portrait that is Book 16 of Cicero's *Letters to Friends*, is special to Cicero and perhaps even to the Ciceros, but beyond the family that does not seem to be the case. The most famous formerly enslaved person in Roman history needs, on this reading, travel assistance. This has implications then for how we understand Tiro as potentially much different from other formerly enslaved people, especially those who were operating at such high levels, as well as how sincerely we are to take Tiro's inability to return to Cicero.

Chrysippus' Story

Around the 25th of November, toward the end of the batch of letters concerning Tiro and the illness keeping him away, Cicero wrote to Atticus about his displeasure with another of his freedmen. In the letter, Cicero relates that Chrysippus, a literary worker known from other correspondence, has left the position that Cicero had asked him to take up—looking after Marcus Jr.—and tries on his idea of a suitable punishment: re-enslavement. Despite his ire at only one freedman in this letter, there were actually two whose freedom was at stake. A person identified only as an *operarius homo*, a worker, who appears to have left at the same time as Chrysippus, is also at risk of re-enslavement. And while this potential re-enslavement is meant as a punishment, Cicero only appears angry at Chrysippus, as he excuses the behavior of the other man as unsurprising, given he was a mere *operarius*.

Cicero asks Atticus what he thinks of his plan:

> I want to respond to all your letters, but there is no need since I will see you soon. But about Chrysippus (for I am less shocked about the other one, a worker; but still nothing is more dishonest than him)—but truly Chrysippus, whom on account of a little bit of literary work I saw happily and held in high regard, to leave my boy without telling me! I can set aside all the many other things which I hear about, I can set aside the theft, but I can't bear the flight, since to me nothing seems more criminal. So, I have taken up that old idea of Drusus the Praetor in that case where, the story goes, a slave, once free, would not swear the oath for *operae*: I have not made those men free, especially as there was no one present from whom they could rightly be vindicated. So take this as you see fit and I will do as you say.
>
> *Cupio ad omnis tuas epistulas, sed nihil necesse est; iam enim te videbo. illud tamen de Chrysippo (nam de altero illo minus sum admiratus, operario homine; sed tamen ne illo quidem quicquam improbius)—Chrysippum vero, quem ego propter litterularum nescio quid libenter vidi, in honore habui, discedere a puero insciente me! mitto alia quae audio multa, mitto furta; fugam non fero, qua mihi nihil visum est sceleratius. itaque usurpavi vetus illud Drusi, ut ferunt, praetoris in eo qui eadem liber non iuraret, me istos liberos non addixisse, praesertim cum adesset nemo a quo recte vindicarentur. id tu, ut videbitur, ita accipies; ego tibi adsentiar.* (*Att.* 7.2.8; SB 125, my translation)

This letter was written at Brundisium, like *Fam.* 16.9 (dated to the 27th of November). It appears that along with the one letter from Tiro, a packet of letters from Atticus awaited Cicero there.[15] This letter to Atticus was a sort of grab-bag where Cicero is picking and choosing different topics to address, presumably in response to the several letters of Atticus awaiting his reply; it seems clear from the way Chrysippus is introduced that Atticus had queried something about the situation in one of the letters and that this is Cicero's response.

Before turning to the issue of re-enslavement, it is important to understand who Chrysippus, the object of Cicero's anger, was. Aside from being Marcus Jr.'s companion in Cilicia, he was most likely the person who in the fall of 54 BCE was tasked with updating Quintus Cicero's library. We have two letters in quick succession from Cicero to his brother Quintus that, among other things, discuss Quintus' desire to build up his library and Chrysippus' role in fulfilling that desire. The first is from October 24th:

> As regards filling the gaps in your Greek library and exchanging books and acquiring Latin ones, I should very much like all this done, especially as I too stand to benefit. But I have nobody I can employ on such business, not even for myself. Books, at least such as one would like to have, are not on the market and they can't be obtained except through someone skilled and meticulous. However, I'll give an order to Chrysippus and talk to Tyrannio.
>
> *De bibliotheca tua Graeca supplenda, libris commutandis, Latinis comparandis, valde velim ista confici, praesertim cum ad meum quoque usum spectent. sed ego mihi ipsi ista per quem agam non habeo. neque enim venalia sunt, quae quidem placeant, et confici nisi per hominem et peritum et diligentem non possunt. Chrysippo tamen imperabo et cum Tyrannione loquar.* (*QF* 3.4.5; SB 24)

Tyrannio was the grammarian of Amisus in Pontus who was captured and brought to Rome as a slave. He was freed and helped people in Cicero's circle with library matters. Updating Quintus' library would be no easy task. Clearly part of this would be acquisition, but not from the typical book trade, as those were full of errors. So part of the job would be to have clean copies made—whether Chrysippus was involved in the actual copying or was in a more supervisory role, checking over other copyists work, for example, is unclear. As Cicero puts it, they needed an experienced and meticulous man (*homo et peritus et diligens*) to do the job, and for whatever reason—either because he was not *peritus* or not *diligens* enough, or perhaps he was too busy with other tasks—Chrysippus did not quite fit the bill. Nevertheless Cicero orders Chrysippus to step in and asks Tyrannio for assistance as well. We can understand from this that Cicero does trust Chrysippus enough to put him in this role; he is the closest that Cicero can muster in terms of skillset and desired moral characteristics.

Shortly thereafter, around the beginning of November 54 BCE, Cicero wrote another letter in which it appears Cicero had reached out to Tyrannio without much success and, as a result, had placed his hopes solely in Chrysippus:

> As for the books, Tyrannio is a dawdler. I shall speak to Chrysippus. But it is a laborious business and needs somebody who will take a lot of trouble. I know that from my own experience of trying very hard and making no headway. As for the Latin ones, I don't know where to turn, the copies are made

and sold so full of errors. None the less, I shall not neglect to do what can be done.

> *De libris Tyrannio est cessator; Chrysippo dicam. sed res operosa est et hominis perdiligentis. sentio ipse, qui in summo studio nihil adsequor. de Latinis vero quo me vertam nescio; ita mendose et scribuntur et veneunt. sed tamen, quod fieri poterit, non neglegam.* (*QF* 3.5.6; SB 25)

This letter tells us what the issue is with Chrysippus. While he is available and *peritus*, he is not as *perdiligens* as someone ought to be to do this careful copy work. But then, neither is Cicero. Cicero's own admission of difficulty gives us some indication of Chrysippus' competence and his standing as a member of Cicero's *familia*: with respect to the difficulties of textual production and acquisition Cicero here is putting himself (*sentio ipse*) on equal footing with Chrysippus. From this letter it appears that Chrysippus' typical job is not that of copyist or librarian, but that he is stepping into the role. We can conjecture too that Chrysippus was still enslaved at this point; as I discuss below, Chrysippus was most likely manumitted in 51 BCE, explaining the suggestive use of *imperabo* in the first letter to Quintus.

It is with this background that we might imagine Cicero deciding to eventually free Chrysippus and his anger at the events that would occur in November of 50 BCE. As Cicero justifies in his letter to Atticus (*Att.* 7.2.8; SB 125 quoted above), he enjoyed Chrysippus' company and conversation because of his literary efforts (*litterulae*), though after Chrysippus' departure, Cicero downplays the extent of his learning—this is more than a little bit of literary work. The language that Cicero uses to describe their relationship is one of liberality and shows that he truly liked Chrysippus: he saw him a lot (*libenter*) and he thought he was an upright person (he held him *in honore*). And it seems he was a trusted member of the *familia* if his post-manumission role was to be a companion to Marcus Jr.

Cicero's reaction to Chrysippus' departure is extreme and contrasts the language of liberality he used previously to describe him. He fixates on the disappearance, which he calls flight (*fuga*), because, as he explains it, there is nothing more criminal (*nihil sceleratius*). With the use of *fuga*, Cicero has Chrysippus, and the unnamed *operarius* for that matter, play-acting as the quintessential bad slaves, runaways, before their possible re-enslavement. And presumably, in his mind, the punishment then fits the crime.

What about the *operarius homo*? The term *operarius* suggests that he was a worker for hire.[16] Cicero does not bother to name the worker and he is dismissed from his ruminations after a terse "nothing is more dishonest (*improbius*) than him." There is also no reason to think Atticus would know whom he was, unlike Chrysippus who needs no introduction to Atticus. But it is clear that Cicero had a personal opinion on the *operarius*, and he did choose to free him at some earlier point. Whether he is *improbius* in Cicero's eyes because of these actions, some particularity of his personality, or precisely because he is an *operarius* is unclear. It seems unlikely that if he were known to be dishonest that Cicero would manumit him. While there could be reasons that we cannot possibly know, it seems that Cicero here plays on stereotypes and uses the man's title to explain his behavior: this is unsurprising because he is a worker for hire. We can also understand that Chrysippus and the *operarius* are somehow linked, Cicero freed them together and they left together. They could have been brothers or lovers or had some other close connection, but this is not legible before the law, and it is not worth mentioning between Cicero and Atticus. The worker's fate is infelicitously set by his connection to Chrysippus rather than his own actions; Cicero is shocked by the breaking of trust and flight of Chrysippus alone.

Cicero's next move is drastic and reveals the level of his outrage. It is clear he is on dubious ethical and legal ground. His grasping for a relevant precedent makes it clear that what he is suggesting is quite exceptional. The precedent (about a rescinded manumission by Drusus the Praetor) is rather truncated and to be taken with the proverbial grain of salt (*ut ferunt*).[17] Most of the emphasis is on the authority of a long-established (*vetus*) tale of a man from a well-respected family (Drusus the Praetor). The actual story is a mere five words (*qui eadem liber non iuraret*). The text is unclear if the slave was Drusus' or if he was simply the magistrate who oversaw the manumission. The problem is as follows: generally, prior to manumission, a slave would promise via *fas* (because a slave could not swear a legal oath) to undertake *operae*, or a certain amount of work, for their owner once they are freed. After manumission, the former slave is made to take an oath swearing to do this work; this creates a binding legal contract.[18] It appears that the would-be former slave of Drusus' day refused to take the oath (*eadem…non iuraret*) to do the work he promised to do while still enslaved, so Drusus as Praetor revoked his freedom.

The parallel with Cicero's case is not exact. If Chrysippus and the *operarius* (who really seems to be suffering from being in the wrong place at the wrong time) did not swear oaths, the time to make that known would be at the moment of manumission, not some months or years later.[19] Another possibility might be that it was the *opera* of Chrysippus to be with Marcus Jr. in Cilicia. In this scenario, while Chrysippus did swear his oath, he would not be carrying out his duties. However, provided that a freedperson had sworn an oath to perform the *operae*, the patron would have an action to sue for the work—this is well documented in the *Digest of Justinian*, so re-enslavement as a legal remedy seems unnecessary. Turning to *Digest* 38.1, which details the surviving juristic literature on the *operae* of freedpersons, there is no mention of re-enslavement or of *liberti ingrati*, ungrateful freedpersons, which is usually where discussions of this extreme punishment appear.[20]

Cicero tells Atticus that he in fact never freed the two slaves (*me istos liberos non addixisse*) and emphasizes then either the reason why they were not freed or a second reason why (*praesertim*—"especially"): there was no one present from whom they could rightly be vindicated (*praesertim cum adesset nemo a quo recte vindicarentur*). The point he is making is that in a manumission *vindicta* (before a magistrate), three people aside from the slave were generally present: the person claiming liberty on behalf of the slave, the person to claim liberty from, and the magistrate to make it so. Cicero was the only magistrate present, it seems, but as they were his slaves, he also was, as their owner, in the role of the person from whom the slaves were claimed. Cicero's reasoning here is rather suspect; Hendrik Mouritsen refers to this as a "legal fudge."[21] Cicero does not tell us when the manumissions took place (though we might infer that Atticus knew). Susan Treggiari argued that it was most likely that Cicero manumitted them in 51 BCE with his praetorian *imperium*.[22] This seems correct. Alternatives could have been 66 (when he was praetor) or 63 (when he was consul), but that seems too long in the past as the technicalities Cicero is arguing over would have been resolved earlier.

It appears then that the connection between the scenarios of Drusus and Cicero are more loosely connected, that they are both instances of proposed re-enslavement, and that both arguments depend on legal technicalities. The reasoning is also questionable, as evidenced by Cicero asking Atticus to give his opinion on whether he buys the idea or not. We know from a one-liner in a letter dated to mid-December that Atticus seemed to approve of Cicero's plan for Chrysippus.[23] But there does not appear to have been an actual method for re-enslavement in the Republic (and even in the early Empire it remained an *ad hoc* procedure)[24] so in order to hunt these people down as slaves, Cicero needed to void their manumission on this technicality. When the idea of re-enslavement is brought up in the sources, it is generally discussed because of perceived moral failures of freedpersons—such as when Claudius re-enslaved a freedman because he had informed on his patron[25] or the case reported by Tacitus under Nero when a group of former owners sought legislation for re-enslavement of freedpersons who behaved with irreverence.[26]

The desire to re-enslave, then, seems like a reaction to a perceived moral failure that is borne out of a particular relationship between former owner and freedperson more than a failure to perform specific work. This is not a rational act: it is why Cicero describes the disappearance of Chrysippus as a *fuga*—and casts him in the role of the most deplored of slaves, the runaway. And while the line between professional responsibility and personal duty is murky, particularly for enslaved people and freedpersons that were so subjected to another's power, the language of liberality that Cicero once used to describe his relationship with Chrysippus certainly pertains to the social realm more than the professional.[27] This point might be driven home if we consider the case of the *operarius*. We might infer, on the one hand, that Cicero is using the phrase *operarius homo* as a means of explaining the behavior on the part of this freedman. On the other hand, it is certainly not the case that it was the *opera* of the *operarius* to look after Marcus Jr. The *operarius* is not re-enslaved because of a failure to perform his job; he is just collateral damage to the severing of the personal relationship between Chrysippus and Cicero.

It is worth bearing in mind that in terms of legal status there was no difference between Chrysippus and the *operarius*, or Tiro for that matter. They were all freedmen of Cicero, but the register in which Cicero talks about his literary freedmen (and slaves) is very different. All we hear about the *operarius* is that he is *improbius*, and we can assume that whatever he did for Cicero as a freedman was covered under *operae*. We get a fuller picture of Chrysippus: as noted he helped with literary work, he was held *in honore*, and presumably did not hire himself out for work. We might imagine that just as with Tiro, Cicero viewed what Chrysippus did as *officia* and thus the breach stung all the more.[28]

Tiro and Chrysippus

Tiro, even once finally freed (53 BCE), could not escape the world of the Ciceros, and especially not this Tiro of Book 16, who is generated through the Ciceros' epistolary habit. Yet the Tiro of Book 16 is at a distance from the Ciceros and this separation provides room for thinking about social relationships of enslaved and freed people beyond their owner or ex-owner's house. The section on Tiro in this chapter looked at Tiro's relationship and social standing with people beyond Cicero and his immediate family. Cicero's own expressions of love for Tiro are repetitive, and Cicero is careful to point out how much other free people care for Tiro as well. As I argued, I believe this to be an effort to secure Tiro's passage back to Cicero.

Specifically, turning to Tiro may help inform us about Chrysippus (the *operarius* will likely largely remain a mystery). After all, Tiro and Chrysippus were part of the retinue that went with Cicero to Cilicia and it seems clear that as two of Cicero's literary freedmen, they would have been well aware of one another and have potentially shared some responsibilities. In the same letter where Cicero tells Atticus of his re-enslavement efforts, (the letter was, as mentioned, a miscellany of responses of Cicero to a number of letters from Atticus), Cicero takes up the topic of Atticus' and Tiro's recent illnesses toward its beginning:

> I come to your letters, a spate of which reached me simultaneously, each more agreeable than the last—those, that is, which were in your own hand. I liked Alexis' hand because it so nearly resembles your own, but again I didn't like it because it showed you were unwell. Apropos of him, I left Tiro sick at Patras, that learned and meticulous young man, as you know, and you might add, if you want, honest. I never saw anyone better. So I miss him sorely, and though he did not seem to be very bad I am anxious. My chief hope is in M. Curius' care, of which Tiro has written to me and many others have brought me word.
>
> *Venio ad epistulas tuas; quas ego sescentas uno tempore accepi, aliam alia iucundiorem, quae quidem erant tua manu; nam Alexidis manum amabam quod tam prope accedebat ad similitudinem tuae, [litterae manum] non amabam quod indicabat te non valere. cuius quoniam mentio facta est, Tironem Patris aegrum reliqui, adulescentem <doctum et diligentem>, ut nosti, et adde, si quid vis, probum; nihil vidi melius. itaque careo aegre et, quamquam videbatur se non graviter habere, tamen sum sollicitus*

> *maximamque spem habeo in M'. Curi diligentia, de qua ad me scripsit Tiro et multi nuntiarunt.* (*Att.* 7.2.3; SB 125)[29]

This letter then begins with Tiro and Alexis (Atticus' freedman)[30] and ends with Chrysippus and the *operarius*. Perhaps part of Cicero's anxiety about Tiro not returning in this batch of letters is bound up with Chrysippus' departure—he has now lost two trusted freedmen. The opening of the letter, in which Cicero uses Atticus' illness to talk about his anxiety over Tiro's illness, gives us a description of an idealized freedman. Tiro is both professionally skilled and morally correct: he is learned, meticulous, and honest (*doctus*, *diligens*, and *probus*). Tiro's actual age is a matter of debate; Cicero refers to him as a young man (*adulescens*) here and in another letter (*Att.* 6.7; SB 120) but according to the Eusebian Chronicle, Tiro would have been in his 50s at this point. The question of Tiro's age aside, *doctus*, *diligens*, and *probus* sum up the characteristics that Cicero was looking for when he is writing to his brother Quintus about who would help with his library (*diligens*, *peritus*, and *perdiligens*)[31]—the role that falls eventually to Chrysippus.

While people like Tiro are exceptional in the history of enslaved and freed people, part of this exceptionality is because of the nature of our sources. There is no Book 16 for Alexis, Chrysippus, or for that matter, the *operarius*, and there never was one. If Cicero ever wrote *nemo nos amat qui te non diligat* ("no one who loves us does not care for you") to a sick Chrysippus, it does not remain in our literary record. However, in his letters to Atticus, Cicero seems to equate Tiro and Alexis. For example, in a letter from 51 BCE Cicero urges Atticus to have Alexis write to him just as "my Alexis" (*meus Alexis*), that is to say, the freed Tiro, writes to Atticus.[32] In 46 BCE, Cicero refers to Alexis as the likeness of Tiro (*imago Tironis*).[33] While Chrysippus' infamy among Cicero's freedmen makes him appear different from Tiro and Atticus' Alexis, recall that, in the letters about Quintus' library, Cicero himself concedes how hard a task book acquisition was (as he himself has had experience working on such matters and with little luck), but that it is nevertheless a task for Chrysippus.[34] In both the cases of Tiro and Chrysippus, Cicero made use of other enslaved and freed people to get what he wants: a letter from Tiro? Mario only just spared a sea voyage to retrieve a single letter from Tiro and Acastus to spend his time sending letters; the return of Chrysippus? The *operarius* can be re-enslaved as well.

From the account of the so-called crime itself, Cicero describes how he and Chrysippus used to spend time together because of his literary learning and projects (*litterulae*).[35] The other person Cicero shared *litterulae* with was Tiro:

> My—or our—literary projects have been drooping their heads missing you, but they looked up a little at the letter which Acastus brought. Pompeius is staying with me as I write, enjoying himself in cheerful mood. He wanted to hear my compositions, but I told him that in your absence my tongue of authorship is tied completely. You must get ready to restore your services to my Muses. My promise will be performed on the appointed day (I have taught you the derivation of "faith").
>
> *Litterulae meae sive nostrae tui desiderio oblanguerunt; hac tamen epistula quam Acastus attulit oculos paulum sustulerunt. Pompeius erat apud me cum haec scribebam, hilare et libenter. ei cupienti audire nostra dixi sine te omnia mea muta esse. tu Musis nostris para ut operas reddas. nostra ad diem dicta<m> fient; docui enim te fides* ἔτυμον *quod haberet.* (MS *Fam.* 16.12; *Fam.* 16.10; SB 43)

While Cicero is more playful with his use of *litterulae* in this pre-manumission letter to Tiro, he makes literature with both Tiro and Chrysippus; they are his literary partners though with Cicero getting the credit. The difference between Chrysippus and Tiro, in Cicero's mind, is that Chrysippus betrayed him after Cicero had let him into this most privileged space. This in itself is a chilling antidote to any social benefits those involved with literary labor might have had, since they remained subject to the same structures of work and demands of a former owner.

What can we make of this? Given Tiro's difficulties returning to Cicero, can we imagine that Chrysippus' departure and travels would be equally difficult and precarious? Alternatively, we might instead read things the other way: here we have two freedmen, freed a couple years apart, both literarily adept and in charge of large projects for their (ex-)owner. Both are apart from their former owner and he wants them back. Tiro, in theory, is on his way, but perhaps the story of Chrysippus should encourage us to view Book 16 as more of a flight narrative than we think. We might add to this that at several points it is suggested that Tiro is not that sick.[36] While in these letters from 50 BCE Tiro is already freed, feigning illness is a textbook method of what is generally thought of as day-to-day resistance to slavery. In this view, illness is a way of softening the blow, what is at best an awkward situation—the worst is what we see with Chrysippus—a formerly enslaved member of the *familia* navigating the complicated waters of professional duty, social obligation, and personal liberty. An alternative reading of Tiro's inability to get back to Cicero and his infrequent letter writing then is that Tiro is in fact in no hurry to get back to Cicero.

Notes

1. We do not know who edited Cicero's *ad Familiares*, but Tiro has long been a leading contender, on this question see most recently Martelli 2024.
2. Tiro is manumitted in 53 BCE. There are a series of five letters (four before and one after his manumission) that comprise the center of the book, on their placement see Martelli (2024: 42–48).
3. Modern editions of Cicero's *Letters to Friends* do not preserve the manuscript order of the letters so I will demarcate the manuscript order as MS *Fam.* 16.1 and so on, as well as providing the traditional modern citations. *Fam.* = the traditional ordering since the 16th c. (chronological but preserving book divisions). SB = Shackleton Bailey's editions of Cicero's *Letters* which go solely by chronology. On this issue, with particular study of the implications for Book 16, see Beard (2002). Throughout I use Shackleton Bailey's Latin text and translation with modifications unless otherwise specified (Shackleton Bailey 2002).
4. On the use of the imperative in Book 16 and Tiro's status as a former slave see Martelli (2024: 42–44) and Fitzgerald (2000: 6).
5. For example, MS *Fam.* 16.6; *Fam* 16.6; SB 123 and MS *Fam* 16.9; *Fam* 16.9; SB 127.
6. In 44 BCE, Marcus Jr. teases Tiro for a new property investment MS *Fam.* 16. 21; *Fam.* 16.21; SB 337.
7. Mario is also mentioned at MS *Fam.* 16.5; *Fam.* 16.3; SB 122 and MS *Fam.* 16.3; *Fam.* 16.1; SB 120. On Cicero's freedmen, see Treggiari (1969b).
8. Acastus is also mentioned (and called a slave) in *Att.* 6.9.1; SB 123, when he delivers a letter from Atticus to Cicero on October 14, 50 BCE. See Treggiari (1969b: 196).
9. Shackleton Bailey (1977) *ad loc.*
10. See Gunderson (2007) on the relationship between Cicero and Tiro and Cicero and Terentia generally, but especially see 27–29 on the nature of Cicero and Tiro's relationship.
11. On *officia* (in particular in contrast to *beneficia* and *ministeria*) see Sen. *Controv.* 2.5.13 and Sen. *Ben.* 3.18.1 (and on these passages Giannella 2019: 80–82).

12. This is not to say that Cicero never uses *opera* to describe what Tiro does; the theme of longing for Tiro and his work returns in the letters from Cicero to Tiro in January of 49 when Cicero has returned to Rome and wants Tiro back (to work). On January 12th Cicero writes, "Although I long for the benefit of your labor at every point I am pained you are not well more on your account than mine" (*Etsi opportunitatem operae tuae omnibus locis desidero, tamen non tam mea quam tua causa doleo te non valere*, MS *Fam.* 16.10; *Fam.* 16.11; SB 143, my translation) and on the 27th Cicero writes that he has abandoned Rome in the face of Caesar's march. After apprising Tiro of the political situation, Cicero gives another suggestion on how Tiro might get back to Rome (with the help of one A. Varro, see Treggiari 1973: 253) and then counsels Tiro to take care of his health, "Since you could not be with me when I most longed for your labor and fidelity, mind you do not hurry or be so foolish as make the voyage either as an invalid or in winter" (*Tu, quoniam eo tempore mecum esse non potuisti quo ego maxime operam et fidelitatem desideravi tuam, cave festines aut committas ut aut aeger aut hieme naviges*, MS *Fam.* 16.11; *Fam.* 16.12; SB 146). These conflations of labor, love, and longing lead directly into the central manumission letters of the book.
13. On Cicero's clear frustration with the situation, see Gunderson (2007: 38–9).
14. See Habinek (2005a).
15. The details from Cicero's voyage back to Italy can be found in MS *Fam.* 16.9; *Fam.* 16.9.1–2; SB 127.
16. See, e.g., Cato, *Agr.* 4; Varro, *Rust.* 1.17, and in the Edict of Diocletian 7.1. At *Fam.* 8.1.2; SB 77 Caelius Rufus refers to scribes for hire as *operarii.* The precarity of itinerant workers is well-documented in Caroline Cheung's chapter on tinkers and pottery menders. In an evocative analogue from Pindarello's "La Giara," Cheung shows that despite not being an enslaved or formerly enslaved member of the household, an itinerant repairman must obey his client's wishes which leads to him getting stuck in the jar he was repairing. In a parallel that brings murky boundaries and conflations of professional duty, social obligation, and personal liberty back to the literal—here the worker must break the jar to escape in the night—we must think of not only the *operarius homo* or Chrysippus, but the liminal space between enslavement and the freedom of Roman citizenship in which all freedpersons existed.
17. Most likely M. Livius Drusus praetor between 120–115 BCE, see Treggiari (1969a: 22).
18. On *operae* see Gardner (1993: 25–38), Mouritsen (2011: 224–6) and Waldstein (1986).
19. See Treggiari (1969a: 257–8) on this possibility.

20. See Mouritsen (2011: 51–65) on ungrateful freedmen and what they owed to their former owners.
21. Mouritsen (2011: 55).
22. On the manumission issue see Treggiari (1969a: 257–8), Watson (1967: 191–2) and Mouritsen (2011: 55).
23. Writing from Formiae, Cicero tells Atticus that he has again received a number of letters from him and proceeds to reply to various topics. The matter of Chrysippus (no mention of the *operarius* here) is mixed in with a brief mention of Atticus' sister and whether Cicero was going to go to Tusculum, "I am glad you approve of the course I took about Chrysippus" (*de Chrysippo, meum consilium probari tibi non moleste fero*, *Att.* 7.5; SB 128).
24. See Giannella (2024).
25. Suet. *Claud.* 25.1. The informers (*delatores*) are mentioned in *Dig.* 37.14.5pr Marcellus, *Institutes*, book 13. See Gardner (1993: 43–4), who argues that Suetonius is referencing the incident mentioned in *Dig.* 37.14.5pr rather than a general policy.
26. Tac. *Ann.* 13.26.2.
27. This tension between professional responsibility and personal duty may also be seen in John Bodel's contribution to this volume in which he traces the movement of the *praefica* or hired mourner from her original role leading public dirges to the internal role of managing the mourning of household slaves.
28. The story of Tyrannio, another literary freedman of an elite Roman, is notable in thinking about the differences between freedpersons. Plutarch reports in his *Lucullus* that Tyrannio was captured and then sent to Rome by Lucullus. Murena in turn asks for him as his own war spoil, and when Lucullus hands him over, Murena promptly frees Lucullus. Plutarch says Murena made "an illiberal use of the gift which he had received. For Lucullus did not think it meet that a man so esteemed for his learning should first become a slave, and then be set at liberty. To give him a nominal liberty was to rob him of the liberty to which he was born (Μουρήνας δ̓ αὐτὸν ἐξῃτήσατο καὶ λαβὼν ἀπηλευθέρωσεν, ἀνελευθέρως τῇ δωρεᾷ χρησάμενος. οὐ γὰρ ἠξίου Λούκουλλος ἄνδρα διὰ παιδείαν ἐσπουδασμένον δοῦλον γενέσθαι πρότερον, εἶτ᾽ ἀπελεύθερον. ἀφαίρεσις γὰρ ἦν τῆς ὑπαρχούσης ἡ τῆς δοκούσης ἐλευθερίας δόσις, Plut. *Luc.* 19, Perrin 1914 translation)."
29. On textual issues on this passage see Shackleton Bailey (1968) *ad loc.*
30. Alexis has been traditionally regarded to be a freedman because he is Atticus' secretary, but there is no direct evidence that supports this, see Treggiari (1969a: 149). Given that in 50 BCE, Cicero sends Alexis a greeting (via a letter to Atticus, *Att.* 7.7; SB 130) in which he comments on

Alexis going from being a *puer* to an *adulescens*, we should be cautious in assuming his freed status.

31. *QF* 3.4.5; SB 24 and 3.5.6; SB 25, quoted above.
32. Cic. *Att.* 5.20.9; SB 113, "I am obliged to Alexis for so often adding his salutations, but why does he not do it in a letter of his own, as *my* Alexis does to you? (*Alexis quod mihi totiens salutem adscribit est gratum; sed cur non suis litteris idem facit quod meus ad te Alexis facit?*)"
33. Cic. *Att.* 12.10; SB 237, "But let us take care of Tiro's counterpart Alexis (Tiro is unwell, and I am sending him back to Rome)... (*Alexim vero curemus, imaginem Tironis, quem aegrum Romam remisi...*)." It is worth noting how invisible Alexis appears: he is the *imago Tironis* here; and earlier his hand is the *similitudo* of Atticus (*Att.* 7.2.3; SB 125).
34. Cic. *QF.* 3.5.6; SB 25, quoted above.
35. Cic. *Att.* 7.2.8; SB 125, quoted above.
36. See, for example, MS *Fam.* 16.9; *Fam.* 16.9 SB 127 and *Att.* 7.2.3; SB 125.

Bibliography

Beard, M. 2002. "Ciceronian Correspondences: Making a Book out of Letters." In Wiseman, T.P. ed. *Classics in Progress: Essays on Ancient Greece and Rome.* 103–44. Oxford University Press.

Fitzgerald, W. 2000 *Slavery and the Roman Literary Imagination.* Cambridge University Press.

Gardner, J. F. 1993. *Being a Roman Citizen.* Routledge.

Giannella, N. J. 2019. "The Freedom to Give: The Legal Basis of Seneca's Treatment of Slaves in *de Beneficiis.*" *Classical Philology* 114: 79–99.

Giannella, N. J. 2024. "The Cost of Ingratitude." In Bell, S. W., Borbonus, D., and MacLean, R. eds. *Freed Persons in the Roman World.* Cambridge: Cambridge University Press. 141–163.

Gunderson, E. 2007. "S.V.B.; E.V." *Classical Antiquity* 26.1: 1–48.

Habinek, T. N. 2005a. "Slavery and Class." In Harrison, S. ed. *A Companion to Latin Literature.* Oxford: Oxford University Press. 385–93.

Martelli, F. K. A. 2024. *Souvenirs of Cicero: Shaping Memory in the* Epistulae ad Familiares. Oxford: Oxford University Press.

Mouritsen, H. 2011. *The Freedman in the Roman World.* Cambridge University Press.

Perrin, B. 1914. *Plutarch. Lives, Volume II: Themistocles and Camillus. Aristides and Cato Major. Cimon and Lucullus.* Loeb Classical Library 47. Cambridge, MA: Harvard University Press.

Shackleton Bailey, D. R. 1977. *Cicero: Epistulae ad Familiares.* 2 vols. Cambridge: Cambridge University Press.

Shackleton Bailey, D. R. 1968. *Cicero's Letters to Atticus*. Vol. 3. Cambridge: Cambridge University Press.
Shackleton Bailey, D. R. 2002. *Letters to Quintus and Brutus. Letter Fragments. Letter to Octavian. Invectives. Handbook of Electioneering*. Loeb Classical Library 462. Cambridge, MA: Harvard University Press.
Treggiari, S. 1973. "Cicero, Horace, and Mutual Friends: Lamiae and Varrones Murenae". *Phoenix* 27 (3): 245–61.
Treggiari, S. 1969a. *Roman Freedmen during the Late Republic*. Oxford: Oxford University Press.
Treggiari, S. 1969b. "The Freedmen of Cicero." *Greece & Rome* 16.2: 195–204.
Waldstein, W. 1986. *Operae Libertorum. Untersuchungen zur Dienstpflicht freigelassener Sklaven*. Steiner.
Watson, A. 1967. *The Law of Persons in the Later Roman Republic*. Oxford: Oxford University Press.

CHAPTER 10

Arachne, or the Metamorphosis of Labor

Marco Formisano

In our highly professionalized modern world, particularly in academia, people tend noticeably to construct their own identity on the basis of their professions, so that they turn out almost exclusively to be *what they do*. Arguably, this identification with a profession is a consequence of an ever-higher level of specialization in all possible fields and, as such, it has become almost an ethical requirement, and one from which employing institutions undoubtedly derive benefit. To say it more bluntly and to use the academic world as an example: the tendency by which professors think of themselves in fundamental, existential terms *as* professors represents a great advantage for their universities, which can then rely on personnel who fundamentally think of themselves as faculty members and, as such, as well-functioning elements in an academic machinery contributing to its agenda of being *productive*. This mechanism of work/life identification (encouraged, of course, not only by academic institutions but by employers of all kinds) is functional to their economic success and, at the same time, makes their employees docile.

M. Formisano (✉)
Department of Literary Studies, Ghent University, Ghent, Belgium
e-mail: Marco.Formisano@ugent.be

D. A. Maticic, J. Rogers (eds.), *Working Lives in Ancient Rome*, The New Antiquity,
https://doi.org/10.1007/978-3-031-61234-3_10

In this chapter, I make the case that the *Metamorphoses* explores the problems inherent in this identification of work and life. I argue that within the famous Ovidian narrative Arachne's obstinate refusal to be associated with the divine patron of her work, Minerva, reveals a profound interior conflict between personal identity and the web of toil. However much she is a passionate and highly talented artist, she decisively refuses to allow her identity to be trapped within the narrow boundaries of her activity as a weaver. The punishment Minerva inflicts on her ingeniously removes this fundamental discrepancy by annihilating it, reducing Arachne and her very body to the ceaseless activity of weaving: she becomes a spider which constantly produces webs, compelled to do so by bodily necessity. The webs she produces might be meaningless per se, since (unlike Arachne's tapestry) they do not visually represent stories, but they are nonetheless admirable in reason of the insect's skill and ability. As observed by feminist theorist Nancy Miller in her important study, significantly entitled *Arachnologies*, the Ovidian figure is "restricted to spinning outside representation, to a reproduction that turns back on itself."[1] Miller takes up Roland Barthes' suggestion in *The Pleasure of the Text* (1973: 64) to name the theory of text "hyphology" (*hyphos* being the Greek word designating the web produced by a spider) and reads the Ovidian episode as an allegory of the critical move from a "strong or unitary subject to a more ambiguous and fragile identity dependent upon the indeterminacy of the *process*"[2] that emphasizes the act of fabrication over the product itself.

But, as a feminist critic, Miller also contends that Arachne is punished by the goddess precisely for her perspective on divine violence and sexual assault. In other words, Arachne's woven representation, which is eventually undone and destroyed by Minerva, refuses to be aligned to what many readers of Ovid tend to see in it, namely a mise en abyme of Ovid's work itself, i.e., a reproduction rather than an original product. Instead, as I suggest, Minerva's punishment can be read precisely as the opposite: as a spider, Arachne has no choice but to weave ad infinitum, and by doing so she is compelled to fully identify not so much with her work as a final product, but rather with her own skilled labor.[3] Karl Marx in *Capital* (vol.1, ch. 7) observed that work consists of a fundamental tension between the will of the worker and their submission to a law determined by the goal of a final project, and that a key role is played by the mediation between humans and nature represented by the tools humans provide themselves. Arachne's metamorphosis can be read as a subversion and extreme reduction of this situation: as a spider she produces her webs without any tools; the shuttle with which Minerva cruelly beats her head acquires a symbolic function. In Arachne-as-spider, the Marxian distinction between work, nature, and tool collapses, since she is existentially compelled to continuously produce webs deprived of any meaning. Her will is annihilated, and her very body becomes her only tool.

Implications of Arachne's *activity* have not received a great deal of attention from Ovidian critics. As with all Latin poets of this period, a major preoccupation of Ovidian scholars has been to read this famous episode within the specifically Augustan cultural and aesthetic context, by, for instance, seeing an identification of Ovid with Arachne, both of them rebellious artists, and comparing the girl's cruel transformation with the poet's exile.[4] Arachne's tapestry has also been interpreted as an original aesthetic manifesto, attuned with Hellenistic poetic experimentalism, and opposed to the authoritarian aesthetics represented by the "official" qualities of Roman and particularly Augustan epic, such as Vergil's *Aeneid*, exemplarily interpreted by Minerva's tapestry.[5] In short, scholars, exemplifying a major trend in Latin studies, have been attracted by the poetological and political implications of the tapestries woven by Minerva and Arachne, much more than by the opening of the episode and the concluding narrative of transformation, which have been treated almost as nonessential embellishments of the ekphrastic core.[6]

Attention has also been devoted to the gendered implications of this narrative. In particular, Patricia Salzman-Mitchell in her book *A Web of Fantasies: Gaze, Image, and Gender in Ovid's Metamorphoses* emphasizes the visual components of weaving by pointing to the necessity of thinking of weaving "as a means available to women to create visually and to have a gaze on their own."[7] John Heath draws attention to the association in the ancient world between spinning and weaving on the one hand and the telling of mythological stories on the other.[8] Following Rosati, Heath is particularly interested in bringing to light the concreteness of the weaving metaphor, exploring various implications of the verb *deducere*.

But, as is the case for all prominent figures of the Ovidian catalog, it is impossible to exhaust the possibilities of interpretation of Arachne. As has been emphasized recently by Stella Alekou, this episode may even be "intentionally ambiguous" since the human protagonist is sentenced by her divine competitor "for having revealed political ambiguities" confirming the kind of *simulatio* sustained by the Augustan regime.[9]

For my part, I try in the following pages to focus on some aspects of this widely discussed episode through the lens provided by the editors of this volume, interpreting Arachne's story from the particular perspective offered by her activity as a weaver. From this vantage point, how can her transformation into a spider be interpreted? What larger symbolic relevance might this narrative have for the perception of work and labor in ancient Rome and beyond? To anticipate the core of my argument, Arachne can be read as a figure for a worker or artist who does not identify with her own work. To be clear, I do not mean to argue that she does not identify *as a person* with her work (whatever such an argument might mean in the case of a mythic character in a poetic text), but rather that in Ovid's narrative the tapestry bears no traces of its maker: Arachne, who does not depict herself in the tapestry's scenes, succeeds in separating herself from her creation, and more fundamentally refuses to align herself with her profession.[10] Consequently, Minerva's punishment can be seen as an ingenious means of compelling the rebellious girl to do precisely what she so fiercely refuses: joining her mind and body in an eternal but meaningless act of weaving, experienced as raw bodily necessity. In this sense, along with Arachne's body Minerva transforms her very *work*, which is eventually deprived of any meaning, becoming pure *labor*.

This point can be brought home by a comparison with a modern text. In Kafka's *Metamorphosis* (*Die Verwandlung* 1915) the now-legendary and yet highly enigmatic protagonist, Gregor Samsa, before becoming a "monstrous vermin," was a respectable salesman of fabrics who, because of the humble conditions of his family, had been forced to provide for his parents under a strict boss who systematically humiliated him. Without entering the complex discussion on whether Kafka intended (or not) to refer to any particular Ovidian narrative(s),[11] this association between the ancient and the modern figures allows us to identify some aspects of the Ovidian tale that are interesting when observed from the perspective of profession, work, and labor in relationship to personal identity and subjectivity. In her book *Fantastic Metamorphoses*, Marina Warner suggests that the Ovidian figure recalled by Kafka might be Arachne: this modernist tale, Warner writes, gives us the possibility to "follow the fate of the bug *after* the change, as if Ovid had remained with Arachne, attentive to her mental state after Minerva has spell-bound her in the shape of a spider."[12] David Gallagher has also noted that Gregor seems to parallel Arachne, because they both usurp the position of the father in the family by daring to believe, though in different ways, that they are better workers, and because Gregor's attempt to usurp the patriarchal function is punished by his transformation into an insect.[13] As in the case of Arachne, the previous hierarchy is re-established after a humiliating transformation into an insect—with, however, a major difference: while Samsa as insect can no longer carry out his duties, Arachne as a spider is compelled precisely to continue endlessly weaving her webs. In short, Ovid's and Kafka's tales deserve to be considered together because both focus on the instability of personal identity, although under different premises. The widely recognized enigmatic quality of the modern text directs attention to Arachne's fundamentally uninterpretable and deeply ambiguous nature. Her story, above all because of her transformation into a spider, ends up being an allegory of the discrepancy between subjectivity and the alignment required by a professional identity. Drawing on the concepts developed by Arendt, her transformation can therefore be read as the metamorphosis of *work* into *labor*.[14]

In his contribution to this volume, Tom Geue analyzes the poetics of the *Moretum* by contrasting the poem's protagonists, the *vilicus* Simulus and his African female slave Scybale, precisely in terms of a distinction between a work capable of being metaphorized (by Simulus) and a labor that is "condemned to remain in a world without metaphor" (p. 29). Similarly, I suggest that we can read Arachne's metamorphosis into a spider precisely as the transformation of a highly skilled narrative art, represented by the magnificent tapestry created during the contest with the goddess, generating a rich world of metaphors and imaginative pictures, into the *antiquae telae* woven by an industrious spider, that are just what they are without generating any particular meaning. For metaphors seem to be constitutively excluded from a spider's web which can only represent its own intricacies.

Arachne Beyond Ovid

Arachne makes her first appearance in Roman literature in book 6 of Ovid's *Metamorphoses*.[15] In book 4 the first human narrators in the text, the impious Minyades, are shown weaving while they tell stories, and in the second part of book 5 Minerva pays a visit to the Muses, from whom she hears the story of the contest between themselves and the Pierides. In book 6, Minerva is now eager to earn praise for herself by displaying her superiority to a human being, a Maeonian girl named Arachne. Already at the beginning of the tale great attention is devoted to the fact that Arachne's family is humble and positioned at the margins of the Greek *oikoumene*, namely in Lydia. Her wondrous skill in woolworking is enhanced by her poor origins. Her father, Idmon of Colophon, is a worker who dyes wool, while her mother's absence is emphasized by Ovid (6.10: *occiderat mater*). Arachne's fame is great, although her origins are as humble as her hometown of Hypaepa is small (6.13: *orta domo parva parvis habitabat Hypaepis*); her fame is so widespread that even the nymphs would leave their woods and rivers in order to admire not only her final products but also Arachne herself while working: *nec factas solum vestes, spectare iuuabat/tum quoque cum fierent—tantus decus adfuit arti* (6.17–18). At this point Ovid offers a vivid description of Arachne's various skilled movements while working the wool (6.19–23 contains a series of verbs: *glomerabat, subigebat, mollibat, versabat, pingebat*). However, although anyone would realize that she had learned from Pallas, goddess of weaving (*scires a Pallade doctam*, 6.23), Arachne furiously denies this (*quod tamen ipsa negat*, 6.24), taking offense at "a teacher so great" (*tantaque offensa magistra*, 6.24) and thereby denying any relation of apprenticeship, instead challenging the goddess to a contest. Minerva then appears in the form of an old woman who tries to convince her to apologize, but Arachne remains stubborn and, after Minerva reveals herself, the contest between the two famous artists begins. They work simultaneously but separately on their own tapestries (6.53 *constituunt diversis partibus ambae*), so that the one cannot see what the other is representing. And both, the narrator observes in an especially interesting expression, are so intently focused that their eagerness (*studium*) "conceals" the *labor* (6.60 *studio fallente laborem*).[16] This rather strange *certamen* then begins: strange because there will be no winner or loser, and no judge is appointed. Rosati in his commentary points out that the composition of each of the tapestries is directed at the rival, with each of the artists addressing a specific message to the other.[17] But this point, as will be shortly argued, invites qualification, for if it is true that Minerva's intention is indeed to terrorize her gifted mortal rival, Arachne seems to ignore the goddess altogether in her tapestry.[18]

Ovid first describes Minerva's work, then Arachne's, noting that both contain mythical subject matter (6.69: *vetus argumentum*). As has been amply discussed by critics, these two artifacts not only represent very divergent views on the gods; more intriguingly, they display radically different styles of representation. Minerva designs the space of her web following an ordered, closed, and rather conformist strategy, placing Jupiter at the center surrounded by twelve deities and, in the four corners, four smaller scenes representing divine punishments of humans as a warning to

Arachne (6. 83: *ut tamen exemplis intellegat aemula laudis*).[19] Minerva's entire composition is bordered by olive wreaths, her own attribute. The goddess is herself an undisputed protagonist of her own representation, which she inhabits both as a personage inside the narration and as a conscious artist who adds her signature, in the form of the olive wreaths. Pallas seems to wholly identify herself with her work and her activity; after all, she is the tutelar goddess of this art, and it is for this reason that she came to take revenge against the highly talented Maeonian girl.

By contrast, Arachne creates an *opera aperta* (to use Umberto Eco's influential phrase), a series of panels without defined structure or narrative coherence, representing mostly animals, which the observer is invited to interpret as transformed gods who rape human women.[20] Andrew Laird points to the material irrepresentability of the scenes Ovid attributes to Arachne's creativity, and defines this ekphrasis as a "disobedient" one which, as opposed to an "obedient" one, cannot be represented in a visual artifact.[21] And so, while Minerva's *opus* follows as aesthetic criterion an *augusta gravitas* (6. 73), what Minerva considers to be *caelestia crimina* (6.131) as woven by Arachne unveil the artist's anarchic and rebellious spirit, privileging formal disorder and, following Laird's suggestion, irrepresentability as powerful alternatives to her opponent's rigid academic style. In short, Arachne does not enter her own tapestry, she herself is not a figure in the scenes it depicts, nor does she aim to challenge Minerva in her own field of action. She creates ambiguous scenes which need a higher level of cooperation on the part of the observer or reader than Minerva's clear statements.[22] At this point, the goddess, furious with envy, first destroys the *pictae vestes* (6.131)[23] and then beats Arachne on the head with her shuttle. When the girl tries to hang herself, Minerva finally takes mercy (6.135 *pendentem miserata*) and allows her to continue her life, but as a spider whose destiny is to hang for ever: *vive quidem, pende tamen, improba* (6.136).

As can be inferred from this brief description of the episode, Arachne is not only a prolific and original artist but a highly skilled technician (the distinction between "art" and "technique," as is well known, does not find a direct correspondence in the ancient languages). Her abilities in weaving and spinning are closely described: Ovid lingers on these aspects at various moments, emphasizing not only the precision and beauty of the representation but also the way in which Arachne executes her work. She is the daughter of the humble worker Idmon, whose name ("the one who knows") suggests a certain intellectual quality that the father might have transmitted to his talented daughter. It is not a coincidence that Arachne is described with the epithet *Idmonia* in the final scene (6. 132–133), when the enraged Minerva violently strikes her head (*frontem Idmoniae*) with the shuttle, symbol of weaving itself and, significantly, the tool used by both artists.[24]

Arachne, then, has developed her marvelous abilities in a humble domestic and social environment and is characterized exclusively by her skills rather than her humble origins. Ovid emphasizes this disconnect from origins through the interesting detail that Arachne's mother has died. The art of weaving, as is well known, was the female activity *par excellence* and as such transmitted from mother to daughter. The fact that she is a motherless child implicitly presents and emphasizes Arachne's proud autodidacticism, a characteristic of Arachne's personality that strongly marks her relationship to the old woman, Minerva's disguise. The girl vehemently rejects her advice precisely by inviting the old woman to give them to her own daughter (6. 38–39: *audiat istas/si qua tibi nurus est, si qua est tibi filia, voces*). Being deprived of her natural and instinctual teacher, her mother, Arachne develops an approach to representation which might symbolize an intellectual distance (as suggested already by her father's name) from her own composition and perhaps from her profession altogether. Moreover, Arachne's refusal might be also caused by the fear of being indoctrinated by the goddess and what she represents. In this sense, work would become for Arachne another form of labor, i.e., a violation of free will, implied by the submission to law, far before her physical transformation. Finally, in this context it is notable, rather unusually for Ovidian narrative, that nothing is said about her bodily appearance.[25]

At the beginning the nymphs, leaving behind their woods and rivers, come to admire the girl while she is working, and they enjoy precisely her technical grace while she is creating her tapestries. To be sure, Minerva is a highly skilled weaver, so that, as we have seen, the reader is invited to imagine that Arachne is her pupil: *scires a Pallade doctam* (6. 23), but this professional affiliation is precisely what the girl so fiercely denies. Her adamantine trust in her own abilities is the narrative motor of the entire episode: it elicits Minerva's indignant reaction and, as I would like to argue, it also represents the motivation for Arachne's transformation into a spider. By rejecting Minerva, Arachne seems to reject her art and profession altogether, Minerva being precisely the patron goddess of weaving. Not having learned from a mother how to spin wool and use colors in order to create tapestries, she rejects any interference with her talent. By not recognizing Minerva as the tutelar divinity of the very art she practices, Arachne clearly rejects any kind of identification with the profession; it is hard to believe that she might appreciate or even recognize a teacher in *anyone* else. In the scene recalled above, where Minerva beats Arachne's forehead *ter quater*, we can also detect the goddess' intention to remind Arachne that she, precisely as patron goddess, does indeed belong to the same profession, since the shuttle is a tool necessary for any weaver.

Although this denial of her profession is a fundamental aspect of Arachne's personality clearly emphasized in the text, scholarly discussions have largely overlooked it. As previously mentioned, critics have been mainly attracted by the aesthetic and poetological implications of the episode, focusing mostly on the ekphrases as models of the textuality of the *Metamorphoses* itself. Feminist scholars, above all Miller and Salzman-Mitchell, have compellingly described the importance of visuality and the material aspects of the tapestries, emphasizing the differences between, we might say, a *masculine* textuality and a *feminine* visuality.

In a 2004 article which significantly advanced interpretation of the scene, Ellen Oliensis interprets the weaving contest in terms not of opposition but of rivalry between two factors. Following a suggestion by Eleanor Leach, Oliensis sees an important difference between Minerva's and Arachne's tapestry: while the goddess has a clear agenda and her intention is evidently to teach her adversary a lesson (especially through the four panels placed at the corners), Arachne does not offer any such directions for the interpretation of her *opus*. She is a prolific artist and, as Oliensis observes, "the unquenchable fertility of the gods is matched by the *copia* of Arachne's episodic representation (...) as if Arachne had an inexhaustible supply of material at her disposal and were trying to cram in as much as she could before her time was up."[26] Along these lines, Oliensis astutely notices that Arachne not only does not criticize the abusive behavior of the gods she represents, but she even aligns with it. The first lines of Arachne's ekphrasis are exemplary on this point:

> *Maeonis elusam designat imagine tauri*
> *Europam: verum taurum, freta vera putares.* (6. 103–4)

> Arachne pictures Europa cheated by the disguise of the bull: a real bull and real waves you would think them. (Trans. Miller).

Oliensis argues for an identification of Arachne with Jupiter: "Arachne stands with Jove, while the viewers of this tapestry—we readers, and also Minerva—are situated alongside Europa as the victims of a ravishingly potent image."[27] In other words, while Minerva is explicitly interested in sending a clear message to Arachne and, of course, the observers of her tapestry, and then the readers (for whom a message needs to be articulated in words), Arachne is perfectly happy with her sole medium of weaving, which she controls with supreme mastery. And while Minerva needs to emphasize her active participation in the "phallic accomplishments" she is representing, Arachne is simply "enacting her creative potency as she weaves"[28] while she shares with the gods a transformative power. Again, she remains excluded from her own representation. But there is also a difference at another level: while Arachne has a real audience, consisting of the nymphs who admire her technical talents literally *in fieri* (6. 18: *cum fierent*), Minerva creates within her tapestry a fictional audience for herself, consisting of her father Jupiter and the other gods surrounding him. Thus, while Arachne is a real actor exhibiting her skills in the real world outside of her artistic tapestry, Minerva remains trapped by and within her own illusion.[29] In a minor but not insignificant detail, Minerva's approach to her own work enacts a conceptual coincidence with its representations. The verbs used here themselves refer both to the actions of the gods in the image and to Minerva's act of depicting them: the gods *sit* around (6.73: *sedent*), Neptune *stands* (6. 75: *stare*) while she *gives* herself her own attributes, a shield, a spear, and a helmet (6. 78–9: *at sibi dat clipeum, dat acutae cuspidis hastam, / dat galeam capiti*), as if she really inhabits her own tapestry. For her part, Arachne seems to perceive her work from a certain distance. The text emphasizes that she is consciously creating an illusion (6. 104: *verum taurum, freta vera putares*) and that she is *making* her tapestry (6. 108–9: *fecit et Asterien* (…) *fecit* (…) *Ledam*). As Oliensis observes, "Minerva's art lies (because it claims to be the truth), while Arachne's tells the truth (because it flaunts its power to deceive)."[30] Following a study by Eleanor Leach who argues that the anti-Olympian interpretation of Arachne's tapestry is only a hermeneutic possibility that is wholly embraced by Minerva,[31] Oliensis remarks that while Minerva's work is very clearly directed toward her competitor, "there is no comparable announcement regarding Arachne's intention, which thus remains as it were open to variant interpretations."[32]

Along these lines, we can argue with Oliensis that we, readers of Ovid, tend to share Minerva's moral judgment: we also tend to identify ourselves within the Minervan script. To Leach's and Oliensis' observations I would add that Minerva sees herself attacked within Arachne's depiction; i.e., she finds and identifies herself where she is not necessarily even vaguely recalled, while Arachne in her tapestry fully ignores both her competitor and herself. Most recently, Barbara Vinken, not referring to Oliensis' article, compares the Ovidian episode to the story of Emma Bovary in Flaubert's most famous novel, making of Arachne a "wunderschöne Frau" and a heroine of the kind of eroticism she evokes in her tapestry, as opposed to the *virago* Minerva, who "hates everything feminine" ("hasst alles Weibliche").[33] Vinken seems to imply that Arachne shows complacency with the feminine personages she depicts in her work by identifying herself with the subject matter of her art.

Following Vinken's interpretation on the one hand and Oliensis' on the other, both Minerva and Arachne appear as strenuous defenders of their respective pictorial programs, with which they wholly identify. But, as I contend, Arachne and Minerva not only represent two different aesthetic paradigms; they are incompatible in the way they conceive of their own activity as artists, in modern terms, or their own profession.[34] On the other hand, Oliensis, who convincingly identifies a crucial point of the weaving competition as the fundamental epistemic difference between Arachne's and Minerva's conception of their art, still considers this episode more generally within the Ovidian poetics of competition with the emperor's figure and in relationship to the poet's exile, establishing a conceptual equation between Arachne and Ovid himself.

Here, though, I would like to focus more specifically on the way Arachne's job as an artisan is described and conceived. As indicated in my title, Arachne's metamorphosis into a spider plays an important role, since it concretely and in a very demonstrative manner embodies the transformation of her ability to weave, reducing her work to pure labor. In other words, what happens if we consider Arachne precisely as an artist who, contrary to a tenacious and perhaps rather modern common opinion, does not wish to be identified with that aspect of her work which we call labor? And why do we so tenaciously tend to take for granted this sort of identification? Is Arachne really only a fictional *Doppelgänger* of Ovid, or does she show an awareness that her creator himself did actually not have? Inspired by feminist approaches to this episode and their programmatic mission to recover and make visible female agency within ancient male-authored texts, I add a stronger sense of individuality, since I am suggesting that Arachne, in comparison with her competitor Minerva, is such a perfectly realized artist that she refuses to be reduced to her *fictional* work. While we will never know whether Ovid himself would confirm or reject this interpretation (a question I do not find particularly interesting anyway), if observed from this angle Arachne's transformation into a spider becomes that much more significant, the means by which Minerva definitively compels Arachne to introject her activity as a weaver to such an extent that in the end, as a spider, she cannot but weave.[35] As pointed out by some scholars, this particular transformation represents a rather strange punishment, since it actually elevates Arachne's skill to its maximum. Françoise Frontisi-Ducroux, for instance, observes, along with some ancient authors (e.g. Ael. *NA* 1.22), that the spider is a kind of animal that in its characteristic field of activity entirely surpasses human beings.[36]

A Rebel Worker

I would suggest that lurking behind this dilemma is the broader question posed by the editors of this volume, namely, how much of our own concepts of profession, work, and labor do we transfer onto antiquity, in particular in our discussions of the individual identities of artists and other workers? While discussing tombs of technicians, Serafina Cuomo argues for a strong identification between the deceased individuals and their professions. But she emphasizes that "identification through profession was only a possible way of having oneself represented after death, and not everybody chose it,"[37] while many other people "enjoyed multiple or combined identities in a completely unproblematic way."[38] Following Pierre Gros, Courtney Roby observes:

> In the Roman world most types of technical expertise conferred no status in and of themselves. Some types of technical activities seem not to have been stigmatized as intrinsically sordid; so Cicero famously exempts medicine and architecture from his critique of technical trades. These practices require discernment (*prudentia*) and offer utility (*utilitas*), and so are acceptable occupations for those whose class permits participation in paying work. However, Cicero only allows that they are not shameful; no particular status seems to have accrued from expertise in medicine and architecture *per se*.[39]

These observations are particularly relevant for this chapter's argument, since they bring out an aspect of a specifically Roman conception of the relationship between labor per se and an expertise: they seem to have been perceived not as interdependent in the way we tend to conceive them today. Moreover, the kind of identification people nowadays tend to establish with their own profession seems not to have functioned as a paradigm in the ancient world. Such questions of personal identity and subjectivity as related to professional skills have received little attention within current debates on work, skilled labor, and professionalism in the ancient world. On a related question, Edmund Stewart, Edward Harris, and David Lewis insist in a recent volume on the applicability of modern concepts of profession and professionalism to ancient Greek and Roman cultures. In the past the validity of such applicability has been questioned, but the authors convincingly show how certain skills were highly ranked in a manner that enables us to speak justifiably of professional élites in ancient societies.[40]

And yet, there is something irremediably different in the representations of work and labor in the Greek and Roman sources that still puzzles modern observers, no matter how successful we are in reconstructing particular ancient historical and social contexts in which modern concepts of professionalism are applicable. The question of how ancient people conceived of their work in terms of subjectivity is both blurry and destined to remain unanswered, but the case of Ovid's Arachne can perhaps offer one model to think with. Along these lines, the fact that Arachne proved to be a fantastically inventive artist does not redeem her from being an *animal laborans* of humble origins. Her wonderful work, like that of any other talented artist or artisan, was not perceived as an improvement of her social status. An important implication of this point is that many other "professional artists" (to use a term far from ancient sensibilities) might not have seen their identity entirely represented by their work. Although Cuomo marshals persuasive evidence for the relevance of one's profession and specialized knowledge for the construction of social personae, this is mostly a postmortem phenomenon, as the funeral material Cuomo discusses suggests: in other words, when it became necessary more than ever to identify elements to describe and commemorate what a person had been during his or her life. In any case, it is not my intention to argue that Arachne's attitude toward her work represents a widespread standard. On the contrary, Ovid's text indicates that she rebels against social or moral expectations in this regard.

From Work to Labor

How, then, can we interpret Arachne's final transformation into a spider, which, as Frontisi-Ducroux points out, has the effect of emphasizing her wonderful skills as a weaver? Here again it is useful to turn to a modern theorization. In the second chapter of *The Human Condition*, Hannah Arendt considers a difference between *labor* and *work* characteristic of some European languages, yet widely ignored in practice.

> The word labor, understood as a noun, never designates the finished products, the result of laboring, but remains a verbal noun to be classed with the gerund, whereas the product itself is invariably derived from the word for work, even when current usage has followed the actual modern development so closely that the verb form of the word 'work' has become rather obsolete.[41]

Arendt argues that this distinction was ignored in classical antiquity, when other mental schemes were operating and the differentiation between public and private sphere—e.g., between politics and household and between masters and slaves—overshadowed and predetermined all other distinctions. Arendt finds it surprising that the modern age, which has resolutely come to prefer the *animal laborans* to the *animal rationale* and substantially reversed the ancient pattern by putting the *vita activa* and the glorification of labor before contemplative activity, never produced a theory in which *animal laborans* and *homo faber*, "the labor of our body and the work of our hands," are clearly distinguished.[42] She further observes that laboring is an activity which "leaves nothing behind," with the result of its effort remaining invisible and in fact coincident with laboring itself.[43] Arendt suggests that "the laboring activity itself possesses indeed a productivity on its own, no matter how futile or non-durable its products may be." Moreover:

> Unlike the productivity of work, which adds new objects to the human artifice, the productivity of labor power produces objects only incidentally and *is primarily concerned with means of its own reproduction; since its power is not exhausted when its own reproduction has been secured, it can be used for the reproduction of more than one life process, but it never produces anything but life.*[44]

In the section entitled "Labor and Life," Arendt distinguishes between two senses of "life," which are well expressed by the Greek terms *bios* and *zōē*: *bios* is human life in its historical appearance, as it can be described in a narrative such as a biography, while *zōē* designates life in its purely organic essence, as a biological being in the world. Action and speech both belong to the realm of *bios*: "It is only within the human world that nature's cyclical movement manifests itself as growth and decay," whereas nature has no time other than the cyclical and it is represented by repetition.[45] Here Arendt introduces another powerful distinction:

> Unlike working, whose end has come when the object is finished, laboring always moves in the same circle, which is prescribed by the biological process of the living organism and the end of its 'toil and trouble' comes only with the death of this living organism.[46]

In short, to paraphrase contemporary HR jargon, while work and life can be in balance, labor and life are inextricably integrated.

Returning to Ovid, Arachne's story can arguably be read from a new perspective with Arendt's considerations in mind, to which I would like to add some minor but revealing details. After Minerva beats her adversary with the very instrument of weaving—the shuttle—Arachne is mute; she does not react to the goddess' aggression with words, and now seems characterized solely by her actions, in sharp contrast with her initial eloquent tirade against the disguised Minerva. Her tapestry has now replaced her speech. She then tries to hang herself, i.e., in Arendt's terms, to put her *bios* to an end. But Minerva intervenes a last time: *vive quidem, pende tamen, improba* (6. 136: "live on, wicked girl, but keep hanging"). The goddess shows mercy toward Arachne *pendentem* by changing the meaning of her action, ironically reinterpreting the verb *pendere*: while the girl wants to commit suicide, she imposes the more literal meaning of "hanging" by transforming Arachne into a spider. Minerva's punishment is both perfidious and ingenious because it undoes Arachne's will to put her *bios* to an end by exalting her *zōē*. The verb *pendere*, first signifying death, becomes here its opposite, life, although a reduced form of life which only consists precisely of an eternal *hanging*. In this sense, Minerva is successful since she compels her intellectualistic, rebellious adversary to wholly identify, body and mind, with her work.[47]

The profound meaning of this gruesome metamorphosis becomes quite transparent: Arachne's *bios* as a living human being and as an active artist needs to be put to an end; but her *zōē* (Walter Benjamin and, in his steps, Giorgio Agamben and Roberto Esposito would call it *das bloße Leben*, her "bare life") will continue. However, how precisely will this purely organic life continue? By a unique, albeit very appropriate, activity, Arachne—and her offspring—will keep hanging from the thread forever. Ovid adds another revealing detail:

> *Fitque caput minimum, toto quoque corpore parva est.*
> *in latere exiles digiti pro cruribus haerent,*
> *cetera venter habet, de quo tamen illa remittit*
> *stamen et antiquas exercet aranea telas.* (6. 142–5)

> And the head shrank up; her whole body also was small; the slender fingers clung to her sides as legs; the rest was belly. Still from this she ever spins a thread; and now, as a spider, she exercises her old-time weaver-art. (Trans. Miller)

As Rosati observes in his commentary, not only was Minerva born from Jupiter's head but this part of the body best represents her identity.[48] I would add that, by minimizing Arachne's head and disproportionally enhancing her belly, from which comes the very thread that she will be working, without interruption or contributions from her woolworking father, the goddess seems to condemn the girl to an insignificant life (*zōē*) that becomes an exemplarily cruel reduction of her skills. The fact that the thread, the raw material needed for weaving, is produced directly from Arachne's belly implies on the one hand that nothing of the beautiful and complex tapestry will remain in the spider's web, and, on the other, that the thread is no longer a tool for creativity, but becomes a cruel, very bodily necessity. This is emphasized by the absence of the very instrument of weaving, the shuttle with which the enraged Minerva strikes Arachne's head. In the terms of Karl Marx cited above, Minerva annihilates the mediation between the worker and nature: now Arachne produces webs directly from her belly. This metamorphosis into a spider condemns Arachne to transform her previous magnificent *opus* into a worthless and insignificant web and to wholly identify herself with her own relentless activity: the spider is indeed its own web, so that a distinction between labor and work cannot be made anymore.[49] Whereas at the beginning of the contest between Arachne and Minerva an "old story" (6, 69: *vetus argumentum*) stood at the center of the narration, after the metamorphosis of the girl into a spider it is her webs which are "old" (6,145 *antiquas telas*): the meaningful content of the tapestry disappears, leaving room only for the very material itself, now "old" because it repeats itself again and again.

Philosopher Roberto Esposito observes in his pathbreaking book *Bios* that, in considering the concept of biopolitics, the very term *bios* seems to fade away whenever we attempt to define it, especially because of the inherent difficulty of defining "natural life."[50] In fact, what we call "natural life" (*z ōē*, as opposed to *bios*, cultural life), today implies the co-presence of a third element: *techne*, human work, technology. And as Esposito writes, today "the human body appears to be increasingly challenged and also literally traversed by technology."[51] Accordingly, the spider Arachne now seems to embody the complexity of biopolitics since her very existence manifestly articulates the tensions between *bios*, *z ōē*, and *techne*.

In *Epistulae morales* 121, Seneca discusses the instincts of animals, arguing that it belongs to their nature to recognize and distinguish among useful and detrimental factors and to adapt to them. Toward the end of his discussion, he cites the example of the spider:

> Do you not see how the spider weaves a web (*illa aranei textura*) so subtle that man's hand cannot imitate it (*inimitabilis*); and what a task it is to arrange the threads, some directed straight towards the center, for the sake of making the web solid, and others running in circles and lessening in thickness—for the purpose of tangling and catching in a sort of net the smaller insects for whose ruin the spider spreads the web? This art is born, not taught (*nascitur ars ista, non discitur*); and for this reason no animal is more skilled than any other. You will notice that all spider-webs are equally fine (*uidebis araneorum pares telas*), and that the openings in all honeycomb cells are identical in shape. (Seneca, *ep.* 121, 22–23, trans. Gummere, adapted)

On the one hand, the Stoic philosopher praises the work of the spiders as inimitable by humans but, on the other, he points out that their webs cannot be distinguished from each other since all look the same: their *ars* is not something to be learned, since it is innate within the creature—it is its instinct. Denis Feeney is perhaps too quick to conclude that according to Seneca "the spider's work is not art."[52] Their webs are the product of an *ars*, so perfect that it cannot be imitated and reproduced by human beings, yet they are reproducible ad infinitum by individual spiders themselves, who are not more or less skilled than any other spiders (*nullum est animal altero doctius*), just as any bee can build the same kind of honeycomb. The punishment inflicted on Arachne by the goddess seems therefore to contain this cruel additional effect: Arachne as a spider is deprived of the very possibility of competing with any other spider, since her web, no matter how perfectly constructed it might look, is destined to be equal to any other web. Moreover, spiders, like Arachne, are self-taught since they have not learnt their craft from someone else. In this sense, not only is Arachne transformed, but her own art undergoes a perhaps even more cruel metamorphosis: one from work to labor.

Notes

1. Miller (1988: 82).
2. Miller (1988: 79).
3. Oliensis 2023 appeared too late for me to fully integrate it into this article. Oliensis, too, focusses precisely on the final metamorphoses, which has traditionally received less scholarly attention than the contest between Arachne and Minerva and the ecphraseis of their tapestries. To oversimplify Oliensis' sophisticated argument, her critical agenda is to show how Minerva loses control over the transformation of her mortal but divinely talented adversary into a spider: "the punishment Minerva envisioned did not include Arachne returning to the loom (…) it is not thanks to Minerva but *in spite of Minerva* that Arachne the spider weaves" (Oliensis 2023, 10). While Pallas wanted to punish Arachne by turning her into a mother, "stubborn Arachne, diminished though she may be, finds a way to spite Minerva and reassert herself: she returns to the loom, reconstituting herself as the 'mother' of textiles." (24).
4. For a similar correction to scholarship on Vergil's *Georgics*, see Geue (2018).
5. See Glei (1998).
6. For example, Rosati (1999) explores the association between weaving (*deducere*) and writing in Ovid, seeing in this episode "the most complete narrative illustration of the metaphor of *textus*" and "the *aition* of the metaphor itself."
7. Salzman-Mitchell (2005: 118).
8. Heath (2011).
9. Alekou (2021: 188).
10. Alekou (2022: 234) observes that "the numbers of the gods' transformations, arranged in gradual decrescendo (103–126: Jupiter's eight, Neptune's six, Apollo's four and Liber's and Saturn's two—one each), also reflected in the number of verses that describe them (103–115, 115–122, 122–124, 125), seem to imply that this tapestry has been completed; and therefore the rape of Arachne could not be added to this list."

11. Ziolkowski (2005: 79) is particularly eager to reconstruct Kafka's Ovidian affiliation, arguing that the young Franz must have read the *Metamorphoses* while he was a student of the *humanistisches Gymnasium* in his native Prague.
12. Warner (2002: 114).
13. Gallagher (2009).
14. My title is inspired by André Gorz's book *Métamorphoses du travail. Critique de la raison économique*, 1988 (translated into English with the more dry title *Critique of Economic Reason*).
15. As for her subsequent appearances in Latin literature, see Rosati (2004) for a discussion of Arachne in late antique poetry (Claudian and Sidonius Apollinaris). See Ballestra-Puech (2006) for the reception of Ovid's Arachne in Western literature and art.
16. A variation on a familiar Ovidian motif. Cf. Met. 10.252: Pygmalion's "art conceals artistry itself" (*ars adeo latet arte sua).*
17. Rosati (2009: 245).
18. Salzman-Mitchell (2005: 131–132) notices that both Minerva and Arachne, weaving in different parts of the room, cannot see each other's work.
19. Dufallo (2013: 167) astutely observes that the four threatening panels are inhabited by foreign offenders to the Greek order. Since Arachne herself, as is emphasized in the text, comes from Lydia, she can be easily associated with those other outsiders.
20. See Eco (1989).
21. Laird (1993). See Salzman-Mitchell (2005: 125–26) (with a remark in n.27).
22. Recently some critics have insisted on Arachne's identification with her tapestry. See, e.g., Scheidegger Lämmle (2021: 367), who sees in Arachne a "Selbst-Identifikation der Künstlerin mit ihrem Werk." In the same vein Vinken (2020) argues for a direct involvement of Arachne with her erotic stories and depicts her as a "wunderschöne Frau" (120), despite the fact that in the text there is no reference to Arachne's appearance.
23. Oliensis (2004: 295) suggests that the plural (*vestes*) refers to both artifacts.
24. See also the comments by Rosati (2009: 269).
25. We might compare Eurydice in Book 10 of Ovid's *Metamorphoses*: She is nowhere to be seen, but in seeing her, Orpheus kills her.

    As for Arachne, readers are confronted with a brutally detailed description of her body while being transformed into a spider. It is as if the beauty in the art of making previously discussed is in the end disturbingly subverted to introduce the painful transition from work to labor as felt by humans (I thank Stella Alekou for this astute observation).
26. Oliensis (2004: 291).
27. Oliensis (2004: 291).

28. Oliensis (2004: 292).
29. As suggested by Stella Alekou (*per litteras*), the fictional character of her tapestry is suggested by an allusion to a pre-existing contest depicted in Phidias' sculptural work.
30. Oliensis (2004: 294).
31. Leach (1974: 117).
32. Oliensis (2004: 290).
33. Vinken (2020: 120).
34. Vinken (2020: 120–121).
35. Serafina Cuomo suggests *per litteras* that any given spider only ever weaves the same type of web, in different sizes but with the same pattern. It is as if Arachne were being forced to weave the Athena way, following a much more rigid pattern than she would ever have chosen for herself.
36. Frontisi-Ducroux (2003: 269).
37. Cuomo (2007: 92).
38. Cuomo (2007: 93).
39. Roby (2016: 83).
40. Stewart et al. (2020: 20).
41. Arendt (1998: 80–81).
42. Arendt (1998: 85).
43. Arendt (1998: 87).
44. Arendt (1998: 88 (emphasis added)).
45. Arendt (1998: 97).
46. Arendt (1998: 98). Serafina Cuomo (*per litteras*) comments on Arendt's argument that the distinction between the labor of our body and the work of our hands might turn out to be artificial, since "our hands are not disembodied, in fact even 'rational' knowledge is not disembodied." Therefore, she continues, "the distinction between work and labor perhaps is not parallel to mind/body, but it is a social distinction. We should not forget that in ancient work the social dimension was paramount in a very concrete sense and most of the crafts would not have been practiced by one person in isolation. The only ancient 'craftsman' who allegedly works in isolation is perhaps the poet. Everybody else has a team of co-workers, even if they are subordinate. So the *animal laborans* and the *homo faber* are part of the same team, in the same workshop, or building site. While there is a distinction, there cannot be a separation, otherwise the task risks failure."
47. Alekou (2022), who reads the entire episode as a "court-like spectacle" (228) illuminating legal language and implications of the weaving contest, also notices the conceptual interdependence between both protagonists' behavior in this crucial moment: both Arachne's attempted suicide and

Minerva's act of clemency "aim to establish one's sovereignty by being excluded from the juridical order" (241).

48. Rosati (2009: 270).
49. As mentioned above, Cuomo (2007) (chapter 3) discusses funeral art in order to reconstruct some aspects of the important social role of technicians in ancient societies. In doing so she focuses in particular on the occurrence of the *labella*, the carpenter's square, i.e., a tool that metonymically characterizes a certain profession. In the case of Arachne the *radium* ("shuttle") characterizing her activity as a weaver is no longer useful since she as a spider produces the webs by herself using only her own body.
50. On this binary, see also Maticic's chapter in this volume.
51. Esposito (2008: 15).
52. Feeney (1991: 193).

Bibliography

Alekou, S. 2022. "Law in Disguise in the Metamorphoses: The Ambiguous Ecphraseis of Minerva and Arachne." In Ziogas, I. and Bexley, E. eds. *Roman Law and Latin Literature*. 227–248. Bloomsbury.

Alekou, S. 2021. "Underneath the Arachnean and Minervan Veil of Ambiguity: Cultural and Political *Simulatio* in Ovidian Ecphrasis." In Vöhler, M., Fuhrer, T., and Frangoulidis, S., eds. *Strategies of Ambiguity in Ancient Literature*. 175–192. De Gruyter.

Arendt, H. 1998. *The Human Condition*. 2nd edition. The University of Chicago Press.

Ballestra-Puech, S. 2006. *Métamorphoses d'Arachné. L'artiste en araignée dans la littérature occidentale*. Droz.

Cuomo, S. 2007. *Technology and Culture in Greek and Roman Antiquity*. Cambridge University Press.

Dufallo, B. 2013. *The Captor's Image. Greek Culture in Roman Ecphrasis*. Oxford University Press.

Eco, U. 1989. *Opera Operta*. Fabbri.

Esposito, R. 2008. *Bios. Biopolitics and Philosophy*. Translated by T. Campbell. University of Minnesota Press.

Feeney, D. 1991. *The Gods in Epic. Poets and Critics of the Classical Tradition*. Oxford University Press.

Frontisi-Ducroux, F. 2003. *L'homme-cerf et la femme-araignée: Figures grecques de la metamorphose*. Gallimard.

Gallagher, D. 2009. *Transformations of the Body and the Influence of Ovid's Metamorphoses on Germanic Literature of the Nineteenth and Twentieth Centuries*. Rodopi.

Geue, T. 2018. "Soft Hands, Hard Power: Sponging off the Empire of Leisure (Virgil, *Georgics* 4)." *JRS* 108: 115–40.

Glei, R. 1998. "Der interepische poetologische Diskurs: Zum Verhältnis von *Metamorphosen* und *Aeneis.*" In Tristram, H. L. C., ed. *Neue Methoden der Epenforschung.* 85–104. Gunter Narr Verlag.

Heath, J. 2011. "Women's Work: Female Transmission of Mythical Narrative." *Transactions of the American Philological Association* 141: 69–104.

Laird, A. 1993. "Sounding out Ecphrasis: Art and Text in Catullus 64." *The Journal of Roman Studies* 83: 18–30.

Leach, E. 1974. "Ecphrasis and the theme of artistic failure in Ovid's Metamorphoses." *Ramus* 3, 102–142.

Miller, N. 1988. "Arachnologies: The Woman, the Text, and the Critic." Ead., Subject to Change. *Reading Feminist Writing* 77–101. Columbia University Press.

Oliensis, E. 2004. "The Power of Image-Makers: Representation and Revenge in Ovid's *Metamorphoses* 6 and *Tristia 4.*" *Classical Antiquity* 23: 285–32.

Oliensis, E. 2023. "Why is Arachne a Spider? (*Ovid, Metamorphoses* 6.129–45)." *Dictynna* 20: 1–15.

Roby, C. 2016. *Technical Ekphrasis in Ancient Science and Literature: The Written Machine between Alexandria and Rome.* Cambridge University Press.

Rosati, G. 2004. "La strategia del ragno, ovvero la rivincita di Aracne. Fortuna tardo-antica (Sidonio Apollinare, Claudiano) di un mito ovidiano." *Dictynna* 1: 2–13.

Rosati, G. 1999. "Form in Motion: Weaving the Text in the *Metamorphoses.*" In Hardie, P., Barchiesi, A., and Hinds, S., eds. *Ovidian Transformations: Essays on the Metamorphoses and its Reception.* 240–253. Cambridge University Press.

Rosati, G. 2009. *Ovidio. Metamorfosi.* Vol. III, Libri V-VI. Fondazione Lorenzo Valla. Arnoldo Mondadori Editore.

Salzman-Mitchell, P.B. 2005. *A Web of Fantasies: Gaze, Image and Gender in Ovid's Metamorphoses.* Ohio State University Press.

Scheidegger-Lämmle, C. 2021. "Der Künstler und sein Werk: Arachne, Pygmalion, Daedalus, Marsyas, Orpheus." In Möller, M., ed. *Ovid-Handbuch. Leben-Werk-Wirkung.* 263–280. J.B. Metzler.

Stewart, E., Harris, E., and Lewis, D., eds. 2020. *Skilled Labour and Professionalism in Ancient Greece and Rome.* Cambridge University Press.

Vinken, B. 2020. "Arachne: *Eros fatal.* Ovid, Flaubert." Möller, M. ed. *Gegen/Gewalt/Schreiben: De-Konstruktionen von Geschlechts- und Rollenbildern in der Ovid-Rezeption.* 117–138. De Gruyter.

Warner, M. 2002. *Fantastic Metamorphoses, Other Worlds: Ways of Telling the Self.* Oxford University Press.

Ziolkowski, T. 2005. *Ovid and the Moderns.* Cornell University Press.

CHAPTER 11

Libitina's Laborers: *Praeficae* and the Origins of the Roman Funerary Trade

John Bodel

Introduction

No figure in the shadowy history of the Roman funerary trade has attracted more interest than the *praefica*, a woman hired to perform at Roman funerals, and no feature of her work has excited more curiosity than her song, the *nenia*. Notable already to Aristotle, the *praefica* and her *nenia* were obscure and a matter of speculation to Roman antiquarians by the end of the second century BCE. Modern treatments of the fragmentary literary testimony have tended to follow the antiquarian approach of their sources, with the predictable consequence that chronological and historical problems have taken second place to creating a compelling synthesis of the available evidence, pieced together from diverse sources. As a result, a significant moment of historical change has been overlooked, and an important perspective on the development of the political culture of the later Roman Republic may have been missed. My aim in this chapter is to

J. Bodel (✉)
Brown University, Providence, RI, USA
e-mail: john_bodel@brown.edu

D. A. Maticic, J. Rogers (eds.), *Working Lives in Ancient Rome*, The New Antiquity,
https://doi.org/10.1007/978-3-031-61234-3_11

identify the moment and nature of this change, to attempt to explain briefly its causes and consequences and, finally, to suggest some implications of the development of aristocratic funerary practices for the behavior of ordinary Romans.

In the ancient Mediterranean world two fundamental and almost universal principles of funerary behavior obtained: care of the dead was primarily the responsibility of close family members, and conduct of the funerary ritual was gendered, with preparation of the body for burial generally falling to women and curation of the posthumous reputation of the deceased falling mainly to men.[1] The *praefica* seems to violate both norms: she was, first and foremost, a hired woman who sang the praises of the deceased. As such she crossed gender boundaries, performing a role normally reserved for men, and socio-cultural boundaries, in that she neither belonged to the slave *familia* nor was biologically kin to the deceased but was a professional performer hired from outside the household. In what location, where in the ceremony, and what precisely she sang remain uncertain, but the sources make clear that the custom applied only to the funerals of prominent men. The *praefica* also led slave women in a mourning song known as a *nenia*, which in certain respects resembled nursery rhymes and magical incantations. That these two songs were different in origin and nature and belonged to different stages of the funerary ritual is apparent from a close reading of our earliest sources, but the second-century lexicographer Festus (or the Augustan-era grammarian Verrius Flaccus whose dictionary he abridged) and Festus's epitomater at the court of Charlemagne, Paul the Deacon, conflate the two songs, and more than one modern authority has followed them in amalgamating what were originally two distinct aspects of the *praefica*'s role and two phases of the funerary ritual into a single performance.[2]

It is easy to see how the confusion arose when we try to consider the evidence for the *praefica* and her role in chronological order, because in practice that is more easily said than done, since most of our testimony comes at second hand from later sources quoting or interpreting earlier authorities. A verbatim quotation of an earlier writer is usually more trustworthy than a later explanation, and some authorities are notoriously more reliable than others, but any modern interpretation of the refractory evidence must acknowledge the fragility of the foundations on which it is based and the possibility that alternative views are possible. The most that can be asked, and the least that should be expected, of any new proposal is that it provide a coherent account of the role of the performer and the character of her performance, which changed over time. Since the discussion requires some attention to textual minutiae, it is easy to lose sight of the forest for the trees; it may therefore be useful to summarize my view of how the role of the *praefica* evolved over the mid- to late Republican period, for which I will then try to sketch in the evidence, giving due attention to its gaps, contradictions, and ambiguities.

The custom of a *praefica* singing the praises of a dead man outside his home supposedly originated in the same hoary age that Cicero characterized as "many centuries" before the time of Cato, who in his *Origines* recalled a time when individual diners chanted the praises of famous men at banquets.[3] In fact, the practice probably went back no further than to the early fourth century, when many Roman cultural institutions later located in the Forum first seem to have taken shape. The role of the *praefica* in moderating women's lamentation, on the other hand, may have come earlier, to judge from restrictions in the Twelve Tables on the mourning behavior of women. During this period, public life was centered in the homes of the élite, each a hub of wealth and political capital; subsequently, during the later fourth and third centuries, the élite began descending from their homes on the hills surrounding the Forum into the common space among them, thus projecting their personal power into the shared civic space of the Forum, where the parameters of public display were monitored by the collective body of the Senate.[4] In this new arena, the *praefica* found little place. The practice of praise-singing in front of the houses of the élite may have persisted, perhaps being transferred at some point in the third century to the familial *atria* that provided public spaces for élite self-representation around the Forum (Livy 39.44.7), but it had become obsolete by the early years of the Second Punic War, when unprecedently high mortality necessitated wide changes in existing funerary practices. It was then, if not a few years earlier, that funeral orations for deceased aristocratic men first began to be delivered publicly in front of the Rostra in the Roman Forum, often by relatives but sometimes by colleagues acting in a civic capacity. Thereafter the role of the *praefica* as praise-singer fades and her association with a funerary song known as a *nenia* becomes more prominent. During the later Republican and early imperial periods, *praeficae* are associated mainly with instructing slave women in how to mourn and leading the ritual lamentation; by the middle of the second century CE, they seem to have disappeared altogether, having been supplanted, in some cases, even from their role in leading lamentation within the household, by male professionals.

Overall, the arc of the story of the *praefica* over the half millennium between the early-middle Republican and Antonine periods seems to trace a depressing trajectory of decline: a professional woman once entrusted with an important role in preserving cultural memory is over time deprived first of the prerogative of praising deceased aristocratic men and then even of her therapeutic role in leading women in ritual lamentation. Ironically, this narrative runs exactly counter to that of Roman women in general, who over the same period saw steady gains in both public and private autonomy and economic power. But it does conform with a broad trend over the same period toward professionalization in the Roman funerary industry, with new lines of demarcation drawn between professional funerary workers and participating family members under the practical constraints of a growing urban population and consistent popular demand for public ceremonies on the model of the aristocratic spectacles of the late Republican period but at a scale appropriate to Romans of more modest means. Organization of these activities increasingly came within the purview of speculators bidding for municipal contracts to provide the complete array of funerary services (*libitinarii*), who profited at the expense of independent entrepreneurs, as the original *praeficae* appear to have been. In this sense the story of the *praefica* is a typical one in the history of labor, of the consolidation of an industry, the streamlining within it of roles deemed expendable, and the consequent elimination from it of many specialist laborers.

Table Ten

Our earliest reliable evidence for the role of women in Roman funerary ritual comes from the passages from Table Ten of the Twelve Tables preserved in Cicero's *De Legibus* limiting expenditure on funerals and funerary lamentation.[5] Several of the law's prohibitions concern burial and the pyre, but two or possibly three seem to concern expenditure for the funeral itself and the mourning behavior of women:

Table X, 3–4, 6:

> X.3: … <tria recinia>…tunicula purpurea…decem <tibicines>
> X.4: mulieres genas ne radunto neve lessum funeris ergo habento.
> X.6: <homini mortuo murratam potionem ne indato.> (prohibition of *circumpotatio*) <rogum? vino ne plus respargito.>

> "...<three veils>...a little purple tunic...ten <flute players> (X.3)...women shall not mutilate their cheeks or have a *lessus* (or *lessum*) for the sake of a funeral (X.4)...<do not dress a dead man with a perfumed drink> (no drinking party)... <do not sprinkle the pyre (?) with wine.>" (X.6)

Law X.3, reconstructed from various sources, seems to impose limits on the number of garments of different sorts (three square pieces of cloth, possibly veils, one small purple tunic) and musicians (ten flute players) to be used at a funeral. The following clause (X.4) prohibits free women (*mulieres*) from tearing their cheeks or having a *lessus* or *lessum*. Cicero notes that the old interpreters (*veteres*) Sex. Aelius and L. Acilius admitted that they did not understand the term *lessus* or *lessum* but thought that it referred to a funeral garment, whereas L. Aelius suspected that the word identified "a sort of mournful ululation," to which Cicero then adds, "as the word itself indicates," suggesting an onomatopoetic derivation based on a sound like hissing or possibly (if Powell's conjecture *leiium* for *lessum* is correct), wailing.[6] Sex. Aelius (Paetus) was consul in 198; L. Acilius was active around the middle of the second century; L. Aelius Stilo taught both Cicero and Varro and flourished around the turn of the second and first centuries.[7] This suggests that the meaning of the prohibitions recorded in the Twelve Tables, which Cicero and his peers memorized as a *carmen necessarium* as boys (*Leg.* 2.59), had been lost by the beginning of the second century; that commentators of the first half of the century interpreted the enigmatic term *lessus* in the context of the restrictions on garments and musicians detailed in the preceding clause; and that, by the end of the century, a rationalizing, philological, explanation that associated the term with the mourning behavior of women (as indeed the parallel injunctions, *ne radunto neve ... habento*, suggest) had come to prevail. That shift says more about the introduction of scientific thought and critical reasoning into Roman cultural and political life following the Second Punic War than it does about the accuracy of either interpretation, but it marks a change in perception of the prominence (and perhaps the role) of mourning women in the funerary ritual between the beginning and end of the century.[8] Cicero elsewhere (*Tusc.* 2.55) follows Aelius Stilo's interpretation of the term ("wailing," *eiulatus*), which he favors on the specious grounds that Solon's legislation had forbidden the same thing.

Modern interpreters too have generally seen these provisions of the Tenth Table restricting funerary expenditure in the context of archaic Greek funerary laws, and thus under the rubric of sumptuary legislation aimed at limiting public displays of wealth and status in order to maintain equilibrium among rival aristocrats.[9] Aristocratic competition for political glory cannot, however, explain the spread of restrictive funerary laws across the Hellenic world among communities in which aristocracies did not exist.[10] Mark Toher makes a strong case instead for recognizing restrictions on private funerary behavior as generally characteristic of the archaic eras of state formation and the early stages of development of civic institutions, rather than of any particular political system.[11] Just as the ideology of Roman Republicanism differed from that of Athenian democracy, so the course of public funerary behavior followed different paths in the two communities, with collective memorials to the war dead typifying Athenian commemorative practices and lavish familial funerals with parades of ancestral *imagines* characterizing the Roman spectacles so admired by Polybius. Whereas Athenians sought to defuse internal competition by discouraging individual funerary display in favor of collective commemoration, Romans coopted and transformed existing traditions of self-representation in order to regulate the arena of élite competition. Polybius was right to focus on the funeral oration before the people as a distinctive element of the Roman ritual, but he fails to note (and perhaps did not know) how recently that convention had developed and says nothing about the older tradition it replaced, which assigned the formal praising of the deceased to a different location and performer, whose role changed over time and, in one aspect, eventually obsolesced.

The *Praefica*

By the beginning of the second century, the meaning of *lessus* or *lessum* in the Tenth Table had become obscure. Authorities of that era understood it to be a garment, but a generation later learned opinion (as represented by Stilo, active around 120, and his pupil Cicero) inclined more toward some type of funeral dirge, and an etymological explanation (onomatopoeia of some sort) had been supplied. What caused this change of opinion? We first hear of funerary tradesmen in plays by Plautus and Naevius. Plautus twice mentions a *pollinctor* or mortician, who applied cosmetics or dessicants (resins and gypsum) to the corpse in preparation for burial, and both poets link the *praefica*, here directly encountered for the first time, with praising a dead man.[12] Varro and Paul the Deacon cite the same verses of an otherwise unknown play of Naevius called "The Strait" (*Fretum*) that virtually defines *praefica* by gender and performative role:

"*Haec quidem hercle, opinor, praefica est: nam / mortuum collaudat.*" ("This woman, by god, I think is a *praefica*, for she is praising a dead man"). Varro and Nonius adduce consecutive lines of Plautus's *Truculentus* that confirm both details and add the implication that her voice was clear-sounding or sharp or that she was talkative and eloquent—the adjective *argutus* seems to carry both senses already in Plautus and can be applied to both pleasant and unpleasant sounds: "*Sine virtute argutum civem mihi habeam pro praefica, / quae alios conlaudare, eapse sese vero non potest*" ("Without a brave deed, I may have for myself a clear-voiced (or eloquent) citizen in place of a *praefica*, who can praise others (but) is herself truly not able to praise herself").[13] The aspect of shrillness or talkativeness is the premise also of a verse of Plautus's *Frivolaria* in which the speaker (perhaps the title character) claims to "surpass all the *praeficae* in prattling (or talking shrilly)."[14] Eduard Fraenkel, who already in 1922 laid out the early lexical evidence for the *praefica* more clearly than anyone since, thought that *argutari* here referred to the *laudatio* (as he called it) that the *praefica* performed, but that sense is difficult to reconcile with the shrill chattering that the verb elsewhere seems to connote. In any case, as Fraenkel rightly notes, the practice of praise-singing by a *praefica* seems to disappear shortly after the time of Plautus.[15]

According to Varro, Aristotle in his work entitled "Foreign Customs" (*Nomima Barbarica*) noted as distinctive of Roman custom the practice described at the end of the second century by the freedman grammarian and Plautine commentator Aurelius Opellus of hiring a *praefica* from the Grove of Libitina, where funerary services and equipment could be rented, to sing the praises of a dead man in front of his house. The custom, in other words, was established and recognized by the time of Aristotle (ca. 335–325) and could still be remembered in its essential detail by Aurelius Opellus two hundred years later.[16] When next we hear about *praeficae* directly, in a fragment from the 22nd book of Lucilius's satires, probably written around 125, they are engaged in histrionic lamentation in an altogether different location defined by activity (the performative grief of ritual mourning) rather than by place: "*mercede quae conductae flent alieno in funere / praeficae multo et capillos scindunt et clamant magis*" ("*Praeficae*, who, hired for wages, weep at another's funeral, greatly tear their hair and cry out more (than the others))" (954–955 M. ap. Nonius s.v. "praeficae" [212 L.]). The only detail that remains consistent, and is consistently emphasized, is that the women are hired for pay, that is, under a standard *locatio/conductio* contract for services. It remains uncertain whether they still operated as independent entrepreneurs or (perhaps more likely at this date) belonged to a workforce of funerary personnel, possibly of mixed free and slave laborers, employed by an undertaking contractor (*libitinarius*), but it is clear that they worked for pay and were not part either of the biological family or of the *familia* of the men (evidently only men) they praised and lamented.[17]

Subsequent literary testimony emphasizes the propaedeutic role of the *praefica* in teaching slave women, presumably those of the matron of the family, both the manner and the limit of the percussive breast and upper-arm beating that, along with the vocalized lament, marked the distinctive sonic space of Roman ritualized mourning.[18] The grammarian Servius Clodius (Stilo's son-in-law), active in the early decades of the first century, is explicit: "A woman who is 'put in charge' of the slave women (to instruct them) how to lament was called a *praefica*" ("*Quae praeficeretur ancillis, quemadmodum lamentarentur, praefica est dicta*," Funaioli p. 98, ap. Varro, *Ling.* 7.70). Centuries later the Virgilian commentator Servius twice uses the phrase *planctus principes* ("leaders of the ritual striking") to emphasize the association of the *praeficae* with the external signs of mourning rather than with grief itself; similarly, the term *modus* employed by Paul the Deacon, excerpting Festus, in the phrase *modus plangendi* implies both manner and measure, indicating that the *praeficae* regulated the formal lamentation by women that had been a traditional element of Greco-Roman funerary ritual since the time of Homer.[19]

By the time of Lucilius, it seems, *praeficae* were primarily associated with performing and orchestrating female lamentation, and their original function of praising the dead had been nearly lost. A learned grammarian might know of the original practice, but contemporary observers associated *praeficae* with extravagant displays of grief. What had happened? Varro, in Book 4 of his work *On the Life of the Roman People*, as quoted by the encyclopedist Nonius Marcellus sometime (probably) in the early fourth century CE, provides valuable information about the *praefica* not attested elsewhere: she was a woman distinguished by having an excellent voice (*optuma voce*)—a characteristic that does not sit well with the idea of prattling or chattering suggested by the verb *argutor* but suits better the qualities of clarity and shrillness associated with the adjective *argutus*; she sang (*cantare*) to the accompaniment of flutes and strings (*fides*) a song called a *nenia* that was subsequent to and separate from the praising performance—the adverb *dein* makes the temporal distinction clear; and she was formerly called a *praefica* up to the time of the Punic War.[20] The wording of the last clause is peculiar (*vocitata olim praefica*) and ambivalent—it is not entirely clear to which Punic War the phrase *usque ad Poenicum bellum* refers, or whether that detail is owed to Varro or to Nonius, but normally it is assumed that Varro is the source and the war against Hannibal is meant, and that date would agree well with other evidence to be considered presently.

The *Nenia*

The *nenia* itself is mysterious and has prompted much speculation and ingenuity, both ancient and modern. Here the testimony is both more plentiful and more inconsistent than in the case of the *praefica*, but three persistent features stand out: it was a funerary song of some kind; it was sung or chanted or spoken (a variety of verbs is used) to the accompaniment of flutes; and it had features that likened it to a magical incantation or a children's song.[21] According to Paul the Deacon (p. 157 L.) there had been a *sacellum* dedicated to a goddess Nenia outside the Viminal Gate at Rome, at the northern end of the region of the Esquiline where the Grove of Libitina and the association of public flute-players (*conlegium tibicinum Romanorum*) were located. This would place her shrine midway between the shrines of Venus Lubentina and Venus Erycina outside the Esquiline and Colline gates, respectively, in the broad funerary zone that during the early imperial period followed the course of the Servian *agger* along the northeast side of the city.[22] It may have been from here that *praeficae* were hired. In any case, literary testimony makes clear that the *nenia* is distinct from and subsequent to the praising part of the funerary ritual.

Whether or not the features that likened the *nenia* to a magical incantation or nursery rhyme are compatible with the performance remarked by Aristotle remains an open question. That Aristotle noted the work of the *praefica* in his treatise on *Foreign Customs* indicates that the practice of hiring a woman to praise a dead man in front of his house was not one familiar in the Greek world. There, the antiphonal structure of ritualized lament involved a series of individual songs followed by choral refrains that included rhythmical cries and moaning of the sort that does not quite resemble a nursery rhyme but could perhaps evoke the chanting of a spell. Of the three types of ritual lament familiar to Aristotle—the *goos* (the least stylized form, closest to inarticulate moaning), the *threnos* (a mournful monody, perhaps a dirge performed by professional mourners), and the *kommos*, which Aristotle in his *Poetics* (1452b24) defines as "a *threnos* in dialogue form between chorus and actors" (θρῆνος κοινὸς χοροῦ καὶ ἀπὸ σκηνῆς)—the *nenia* in form seems most closely to resemble the *threnos*, but the antiphonal structure of the *kommos* responds best to the instructional role of the *praefica*, as described by Servius Clodius and others.[23] Neither, in any case, involves praising the deceased, the role attributed by Aristotle and Aurelius Opillus to the *praefica*.

For greater insight into the role of the *praefica* in leading the slave women in lament we turn to the groundbreaking work of anthropologist Ernesto de Martino in the 1950s and folklorist Margaret Alexiou in the 1960s, who showed how the set rhythms of movement and sound enacted in gesture and song by professional mourning women in rural Lucania and Greece helped the living to modulate a grief felt so deeply by those closest to the deceased that it threatened to overwhelm them. The function of the ritual lament, repeated at every funeral, is to dehistoricize the particular death by assimilating it to all the deaths that have come before and thereby to help the living to accept death's inevitability and their own return to life.[24] In the classical Greek world, the ritual lament and accompanying gestures of affection for the deceased were led by a mother or wife, whereas praise of the deceased in epigram and elegy grew out of the sympotic and literary practices of men.[25] In the Roman world, where praise of the deceased was performed in public (whether by a *praefica* or by a funerary orator) those being instructed by a *praefica* in the appropriate form of lamentation were slaves and newly manumitted ex-slaves, whose choreographed gestures, to judge from figured representations, were an important element of the performance.[26] Close female kin, such as mothers and sisters, known as *funerae* when in mourning, were by contrast obliged by custom to confine their demonstrations of grief to the house and to exhibit restraint when in public. In glossing the term *funerae*, Servius draws a clear distinction between them and the hired *praeficae*, whom he identifies as leaders of the ritual lamentation (*planctus*) but not the grief (*dolor*).[27]

The final piece to the puzzle of the *praeficae* is provided by Cicero in his prescriptions in *De Legibus* for the conduct of funerals, a subject, as Momigliano noted, in which he took little interest and had even less inclination to interfere with popular custom: "Let the praises of honored men be recounted at a public meeting and let there also follow these praises a song accompanied by a flute, namely a *nenia*, by which term mourning songs are called by the Greeks also" (*honoratorum virorum laudes in contione memorentur, easque etiam <et> cantus ad tibicinem prosequatur, cui* *nomen neniae, quo vocabulo etiam <apud> Graecos cantus lugubres nominantur*, Cic. *Leg.* 2.62).[28] Like Varro, Cicero indicates clearly that the *nenia* was distinct from and followed the praising of "honored men" (those who had won public office), and he adds the gratuitous information that Greeks called their mourning songs by the same name. The praise portion of the ceremony, however, he locates at a public meeting (*in contione*), that is, by implication, in the Roman Forum, rather than in front of the house of the deceased, as Aurelius Opillus (cited by Varro) had specified. The different aims of the two authors explain the discrepancy: Varro's linguistic investigation pointed him toward the original meanings of words and thus to the early phases of the formation of Roman culture; Cicero's political treatise aimed to revise contemporary institutions and so took as its point of departure the status quo. Between the two periods a shift had occurred, not only in who delivered the praise of the deceased but where.

Funerary Orations *Pro rostris*

In accordance with a cultural penchant for retrojecting institutional innovations back to the earliest days of the Republic, later authorities (Romanized Greeks, in the first instance) established the tradition of a division of labor by gender in Roman funerary ceremonies and a fixing of place and time for the commemorative ritual in the first year after the expulsion of the kings, when the consul P. Valerius Publicola was said to have delivered a laudatory funeral oration over the body of his deceased colleague, M. Junius Brutus, in the Forum, and the Roman matrons mourned for a year.[29] The entire construct is a fabrication, as Gabba recognized, likely attributable to the late Republican annalist Valerius Antias, who would have been the source for Dionysius of Halicarnassus, who was himself no doubt the authority for Plutarch's version.[30] The Forum did not become the main stage for aristocratic funerary celebrations before the middle of the third century, and our earliest indication of a regular practice of delivering funerary orations there comes in a speech that Livy puts into the mouth of Lucius Cornelius Scipio following the death of his brother Africanus in 187, in which he complains that his brother had been dishonored by not being publicly praised "in front of the Rostra" after his death.[31] Despite the stories told by annalistic historians of the later Republican period and others subsequently, the earliest attested orations we know to have been delivered in the Roman Forum belong to the early years of the Hannibalic War, and the earliest surviving fragments we have of any

Roman funeral oration come from the eulogy delivered for his son by Q. Fabius Maximus (Cunctator) sometime between 207 and 203.[32] The first public eulogies of women belong to the period around the turn of the second and first centuries, and funerary orations *pro rostris* delivered by non-family members come only in the first century.[33]

Two key dates that may mark the period of transition in funerary exhibitions from private contexts to the public civic arena of the Forum are the funerary games for D. Junius Brutus Pera sponsored by his two sons in 264, when three gladiatorial pairs fought to the death in the Forum Boarium in the first exhibition of gladiatorial combats at Rome, and the games for M. Aemilius Lepidus sponsored by his three sons over three days at the end of the year 216, when twenty-two gladiatorial pairs fought in the Forum. The first has the look of improvisation, the venue being chosen, perhaps, for its marginal location beside the Tiber as much as for its celebrity; the second came a few short months after the disastrous Battle of Cannae, a defeat that sent shock-waves through Rome and resulted in the first intervention by the state into private funerary behavior we know of since the Twelve Tables. Thereafter, for the rest of the Republican period, the Forum became the standard venue both for funerary orations for élite men and for gladiatorial combats, all of which that we know of were offered as funerary games.[34]

The first three years of the Second Punic War caused major disruptions in Roman society. Having regrouped after the defeats at Trebia in 218 and Lake Trasimene in 217, the Romans in 216 assembled their largest troop-force to date of some 80,000 men and put them under the joint command of both consuls to confront Hannibal, who had seized the large supply depot of Cannae in Apulia. Following the disastrous battle, in which some 50,000–60,000 Roman soldiers and allies lost their lives, so many Roman matrons went into mourning that the annual rites of Ceres could not be celebrated. As a result, anticipating future losses, the Senate (according to Livy) or the consul Fabius Maximus (according to Plutarch) reduced the prescribed period of mourning for Roman matrons to thirty days, so that the public *sacra* would not henceforth be neglected, and confined those in mourning to their homes, so that the people would not become demoralized by the sight and sound of widespread lamentation.[35] From this point on, the public behavior of Romans in mourning became a matter not simply of private decorum but of public interest; the conduct of aristocratic funerals was organized more formally; and funerary and commemorative services became more professionalized.

During the three years between 218 and the end of 216, the Roman people suffered higher mortality than they had in any previous triennium, losing some 70,000–80,000 Roman soldiers in warfare and others to disease and natural causes.[36] The scale of these losses is generally recognized as having resulted in needed changes in military recruiting methods and qualifications in order to fill manpower shortages.[37] At the same time, both the number and the types of deaths (of young men in warfare, away from home) necessitated changes in the protocols for disposal of the dead (often, for ordinary soldiers, by collective burial at battle sites) and funerary commemoration at Rome, not only for the élite but for rank and file soldiers, whose more modest funerary and commemorative practices imitated those of their commanders. These changes in recruiting, instituted *ad hoc* during the course of the war in order to meet immediate needs, soon became entrenched: just as manpower needs continued to preoccupy Roman commanders throughout the second and first centuries, so too did the demand for military funerals that could honor absentee fallen soldiers remain high.[38]

Nor was it only soldiers' deaths that put a strain on the suppliers of funerary services at Rome: Livy, in describing outbreaks of disease in 181 and 175, twice employs an idiomatic phrase—*Libitina funeribus vix/non sufficiebat*, "Libitina (the goddess of funerals) was barely/not sufficient for the funerals"—to characterize situations when ordinary funerary capacities were overwhelmed, or nearly so.[39] It is in this context that the traditional practice of the *praefica* praising a dead man in front of his house appears increasingly anachronistic, and the advantages of a custom that entrusted the oral commemoration of a dead man or woman neither to a hired professional nor, necessarily, to a family member but to a fellow citizen, as a civic responsibility, become apparent. Soldiers especially, to judge from inscribed epitaphs of the early imperial period, often relied on fellow-soldiers as heirs to ensure their burial and posthumous commemoration. There is little reason to think that circumstances differed greatly among soldiers fighting far from home during the second and first centuries: it was recording practices, specifically the rise of an epigraphic habit of inscribing tombstones, rather than the funerary ritual per se, that changed between the two eras. The soldier Stratophanes in Plautus's *Truculentus* (produced, probably, in 186) reflects a contemporary but relatively recent reality when he claims, in deprecating the veracity of those who praise deeds not witnessed, that, "even without an act of valor, I might have for myself an eloquent citizen in place of a *praefica*" (*sine virtute argutum civem mihi habeam pro praefica*, 495). It is against this backdrop, of increasingly regular, sometimes absentee, funerals (*funera imaginaria*) at Rome, in which the ceremonies of the cortège and cremation performed for an effigy in cases when the body of the deceased was unavailable, and with eulogies delivered by fellow citizens as a matter of course, that the following reconstruction suggests itself.

Praeficae and the Roman Funeral Oration

It seems that two distinct funerary functions originally fulfilled by a hired woman "put in charge" of the vocalized elements of the funeral of a prominent Roman man evolved in such a way over the course of the late third and early second centuries that one, praise of the deceased, became divorced from her, relocated with respect both to social context (from the commercial to the private familial sphere and thence to the public civic realm) and to gender, whereas the other, ritual lament, became more fully embedded in the world of slaves distinct from the biological family.[40] Even as the social location of the vocalized praise shifted from professional women to private men, the physical location for the performance of praise shifted from the domestic to the civic arena, the better to project the family into the state. Conversely, the latter function, ritualized lament, became increasingly separated temporally, spatially, and sonically from the laudatory oration and fixed socially in the domestic realm of the slave *familia*. If we were to try to pinpoint a time and to identify a proximate cause for this momentous shift we might look again to the aftermath of the disastrous Battle of Cannae in 216, when the consul Fabius Maximus, in order to prevent the frightened populace of Rome from abandoning the city, posted armed guards on the gates and set limits to the time and place for mourning. It was from this occasion, traditionally, that Roman matrons (*matronae*) acquired their conventional *habitus* of demonstrated restraint in public displays of grief as a civic responsibility, which gave them a formal public role in collective mourning.[41]

It is not always easy to distinguish family members from professional funerary workers in visual depictions of funerary scenes from the later Republic and early Empire, but where discrimination is possible, the hired mourning women are physically separated from the free family and are grouped with the slave household.[42] Literary references to the *nenia* in the imperial period confirm the enduring cultural significance of the funerary dirge as a marker of the funeral itself, and the song itself is sometimes later described as an honor to the dead, but praise of the dead is no longer central to its purpose, if it ever was, and during the early imperial period it is increasingly associated with the general din of a Roman funeral and is more often likened to a nursery rhyme or incantation, that is, to inarticulate or nonsensical but rhythmical vocalization, than to the organized account of the family and deeds of the deceased that were essential to the formal *laudatio funebris*.[43]

The one surviving example we have of the form is a parodic poem in anapests from the early imperial Menippean satire on the apotheosis of the emperor Claudius, *Apocolocyntosis* (Sen. *Apoc.* 3). It bears such close structural and thematic similarities to Catullus's celebrated poem on the death of Lesbia's sparrow (Cat. 3), itself a mock funerary lament, that it is possible to extrapolate from their correspondences elements that may have been characteristic of genuine *neniae*.[44] These include repeated calls to mourners to demonstrate grief through specific gestures; repeated announcements of the death; and eulogistic recollection of deeds. All three elements are characteristic also of classical Greek laments, which further provide examples of the types of praise characteristic of the form, which are generic and universalizing, in the form "a good man/woman has died," with the aim of enrolling the deceased into the community of all who have died before.[45] This is very different from the detailed accounting of family heritage and individual accomplishments that mark the Roman funerary oration and which may represent an unusual element in the parodic *nenia* sung at Claudius's funeral.[46] That song, moreover, is sung "by a huge Great Chorus" (*ingenti enim* μεγάλωι χορικῶι *nenia cantabatur*, Sen. *Apoc.* 12.3) that calls for "the Forum" to "resound with mournful din" (*resonet tristi clamore Forum*, Sen. *Apoc.* 12.3 v. 2); nowhere is there mention of a *praefica* or mourning women involved. It is difficult to know to what extent the details of this parody of a Roman imperial funeral might have relevance for the funerals of ordinary Romans, but the second-century satirist Lucian, in mocking the histrionic behavior of "most people" at funerals, invokes the practice among bereaved family members of calling in a (male) "professor of dirges" (τινα θρήνων σοφιστὴν, Lucian, *De Luctu* 20) to instruct the grieving mourners in how to respond antiphonally to his threnodic performance. This is precisely the traditional role of the *praefica*, the professional instructor in collective lamentation, now apparently (in Lucian's vision) entirely ousted from her position, with nothing left of her original performative function in singing the praise of the deceased in front of his house, and with even the conventional role of leading the slave women in ritual lament now usurped by a male professional who performed the same function.

The story of the *praefica*, from one perspective, is one of obsolescence and decline, but the transfer of her primary original function of praising the deceased in front of his house to a relative or fellow citizen delivering a eulogy in the Forum marks an important development in the evolution of the Roman funeral from a private familial rite into a public event. The disappearance from Roman life of the *praefica* and her performance of praise thus coincides with a major expansion of the funerary services industry, with the consolidation at the Grove of Libitina of the props and personnel required for pageants of the sort witnessed by Polybius and the rise of entrepreneurial funerary directors (*libitinarii*) undertaking public contracts from the state.

Epilogue

The *nenia*, as Festus took pains to emphasize (Appendix 4), marked the end, just as this chapter comes near the end of this volume, and the *praefica*'s work came at the end of life. Her job originally was to praise others, and yet, as the soldier Stratophanes in Plautus's *Truculentus* poignantly observes (496), "the *praefica*, who can praise others, is truly not able to praise herself." (Appendix 4). No surviving epitaph commemorates a *praefica*, and no surviving literary source identifies one. Even among enslaved workers, such occupational anonymity is rare. The *praefica* of mythical memory lives for us, as she did for Aristotle, like Arachne the spider, as a woman defined by her commemorative work. Her therapeutic role as leader of the ritual lament that helped to restore the living to their working lives endured, and is barely noticed. Such is the fate of the working *praeficae* of Roman antiquity, whose care for the souls of the living and the bodies of the dead counted less than the preservation of the memory of the men they served.

Appendix

1. Varro, *Ling.* 7.70

In *Truculento* (495): "Sine virtute argutum civem mihi habeam pro praefica.": <Praefica> dicta, ut Aurelius scribit (Funaioli p. 90), mulier ab luco quae conduceretur quae ante domum mortui laudis eius caneret. Hoc factitatum Aristoteles scribit in libro qui inscribitur *Nomima barbarika*, quibus testimonium est, quod <in> *Freto* (?) est Naevii: "Haec quidem hercle, opinor, praefica est: nam mortuum collaudat." Claudius scribit (Funaioli p. 98) "Quae praeficeretur ancillis, quemadmodum lamentarentur, praefica est dicta." Utrimque ostendit a praefectione praeficam dictam.

> In *Truculentus:* 'Without a deed of bravery, I may have for myself a clear voiced (shrill) citizen in place of a *praefica*.' As Aurelius (Opillus) writes, a woman who was hired from the Grove to sing the praises of a dead man in front of his house was called a *praefica*. Aristotle in his book entitled *Foreign Customs* writes that this was regularly done, for which the evidence is in the '*Strait*' (?) of Naevius: 'This woman, by god, I think is a *praefica*, for she is praising a dead man.' (Servius) Claudius writes: 'A woman who is "put in charge" of the slave women (to instruct them) how to lament is called a *praefica*.' Both show that the *praefica* was so called from 'being put in charge'.

2. Paulus (250 L.)

Praeficae dicuntur mulieres ad lamentandum mortuum conductae, quae dant ceteris modum plangendi, quasi in hoc ipsum praefectae. Naevius: "Haec quidem mehercle, opinor, praefica est, quae sic mortuum conlaudat."

> The women hired to lament a dead man are called *praeficae*; they give to others the manner and limit of lamenting, as if they were put in charge for this very thing. Naevius: 'This woman, who praises a dead man in this way, by god, I think is a *praefica*.'

3. Nonius s.v. "Praeficae" (212 L. + 92–93 L.)

Praeficae dicebantur aput veteres quae adhiberi solent funeri, mercede conductae, ut et flerent et fortia facta laudarent. Plautus in *Frivolaria* (84): "superabo omnis argutando praeficas." Idem *Truculento* (496): "praefica, quae alios conlaudare, eapse sese vero non potest." Lucilius lib. XXII (954–955 M.): "mercede quae conductae flent alieno in funere praeficae multo et capillos scindunt et clamant magis." Varro *de Vita Populi Romani* lib. IV: "ibi a muliere, quae optuma voce esset, perquam laudari;

dein neniam cantari solitam ad tibias et fides †eorumque ludistricas cursicassent.†[47] Haec mulier vocitata olim praefica usque ad Poenicum bellum."

Our ancestors called *praeficae* the women hired for pay who were customarily used at funerals both to weep and to praise bold deeds. Plautus in *Frivolaria*: 'I will surpass all the *praeficae* in babbling,' Likewise in *Truculentus* (496) 'a *praefica*, who can praise others, is truly not able to praise herself.' Lucilius, Book 22 (954–955 M.): '*Praeficae*, who, hired for wages, weep at another's funeral, greatly tear their hair and cry out more (than the others).' Varro, *On the Life of the Roman People* Book 4: 'there upon [the dead man] is thoroughly praised by a woman with an excellent voice; then a *nenia* is customarily sung to flutes and strings (?). … This woman was formerly called a *praefica*, up to the (time of the) Punic War.'

4. Festus 154.19 (L.), text and translation after those of North 2008: 130–31

Nenia est [carmen, quod in funere laudandi] / gratia can[tatur ad tibiam. Ita enim ait Afra]/nius in *Materter*[*is*: … inter exse]/quias cantit[abant neniam. Sunt qui finem sig]/nificari credụ[nt, ut cum ait Plautus in *Pseudolo* / [.]bi ego circumvọ[rtor, cado; id fuit nenia ludo';] / Idem: 'Huic homị[ni amanti mea era apud nos neniam] dixit domi'; et ạp[ud ???: '… usque ad ne]/niam esto'. Quosdạm [neniam ideo dicere ait ???] / quod e<i> voci sim[ilior querimonia flentium] / sit. Quidam aiunt nom[en ductum ab extre]/mi intestini vocạ[bulo, ???que testimo]/nio utitur Plauti *B*[*acchidibus*: 'Si tibi est ma]/chae{de}ra, a<t> nobịs [vervinast domi, qua quidem] / te reddam, si tụ me [inritaveris, confossio]/rem soricina nạẹnia'. [Nenia autem extremum est quan]/do efferimus mọrtuụ[um, quod extremum aliquid] / Graeci *neaton* … [appellant; siue quod chor]/dạrụm [ult]ịmạ [*nete* dicta est, vocem extre]/mam cantionis nạẹnịạm [appellamus.]

A *nenia* is a [song,] sung [to the flute at a funeral,] for the purpose of [praise. For Afr]anius [writes thus] in the 'Maternal Aunts': '… they were singing [the *nenia*] at the funeral.' [Some people] think that the meaning [is 'end,' as when Plautus writes in the *Pseudolus*]: 'So when I turn round, [I fall down; that was the *nenia* of the fun']; (Plautus) again: ['My mistress has sung the *nenia*] over this [loving] man [among us] at home.' Also, in ???: 'let it be right to the *nenia*.' [??? says] that some authors [explain the word *nenia* because the wailing of the mourners] is actually rather similar to the sound of the word. Others again say that [the word *nenia* is derived from the word for the lowest part] of the intestine, and ??? uses as evidence ['Two Bacchises'] of Plautus: ['You may well have] a dagger; but I have [a spit at home], with which, if you [provoke me], I can make you fuller of holes than a mouse's *naenia*.' [But in fact the *nenia* is the last stage, when] we are carrying out someone who has died [to burial, because the Greeks call something last the *neaton*; [or else, since the last string is] called the *nete*, we call] the highest note (or 'last word'?) of the singing the *nenia*.

5. Paulus 155.27 (L.)

Nenia est carmen, quod in funere laudandi gratia cantatur ad tibiam. Sunt qui eo verbo finem significari putant. Quidam volunt neniam ideo dici, quod voci similior querimonia flentium sit. Quidam aiunt neniae ductum nomen ab extremi intestini vocabulo; Graeci enim *neaton* extremum dicunt; siue quod cordarum ultima *nete* dicitur, extremam cantionis vocem neniam appellarunt.

A *nenia* is a song which is sung to the flute at a funeral for the purpose of praise. Some think the meaning of the word is 'end.' Some (others) think the nenia is so called because the sound is rather similar to the wailing of the mourners. Others again say that the word *nenia* is derived from the word for the very tip of the intestine; for the Greeks call the very end the *neaton*; or else because the topmost string is called the *nete*, they called the highest note (or 'last word?') of the song the *nenia*.

Notes

1. On gendered roles in Mediterranean funerary rites, see, e.g., Richlin (2001), Alexiou (2002: 102–108), Stears (1998: 143–52), Bachvarova (2008), Chiari (2012: 1 n. 5); Montanini (2009), Corbeill (2004: 68–88), Mustakallio (2013). Dates are BCE except where otherwise indicated.
2. So, e.g., Habinek (2005: 233–46) followed by North (2015). Dutsch (2008: 261) rightly distinguishes between the eulogy sung by the *praefica* and the *neniae* that came after.
3. Cic. *Brut.* 75, *multis saeculis ante suam aetatem*; cf. *Tusc.* 1.3, 4.4; Varro ap. Non. s.v. 'assa voce' 107 L. To this same distant age belong also the specialized horn players known as *siticines*, who played a special kind of

long tuba at the gravesite (*siticen* < *siti* + *cano*) at funerals and commemorative ceremonies for the dead: cf. Nonius 77 L; Gell. *NA* 20.2.3 cit. Cato *Orat.* 8.223 M with Chiari (2012: 14–15).

4. Purcell 2022: 180–184 well characterizes the development of the conceptual pairing of *Domus* and *Forum* during the later fourth and early third centuries.
5. Cic. *Leg.* 2.59, 62–64; Festus 342 L; Nonius 849 L; cf. Varro, *Ling.* 5.132; Serv. ad *Aen.* 1.282; further Crawford (1996: 705–707) (2.40).
6. Cic. *Leg.* 2.59: *hoc veteres interpretes Sex. Aelius L. Acilius non satis se intellegere dixerunt, sed suspicari vestimenti aliquod genus funebris, L. Aelius lessum quasi lugubrem eiulationem, ut vox ipsa significat.* "The old interpreters Sex. Aelius and L. Acilius said that they did not fully understand this, but they suspected it was some kind of funeral garment; L. Aelius suspected that the *lessus* (or *lessum*) was a sort of mournful ululation, as the word itself indicates." Dyck (2003: 405) supports J. G. F. Powell's conjecture on the basis of Stilo's etymology and Cicero's gloss, *ut vox ipsa significat.*
7. Sex. Aelius (Paetus): D'Ippolito (1978: 53–70), L. Acilius: *RE* 1.1 (1893) 252.8–17 (Klebs). L. Aelius Stilo (Praeconinus): Cic. *Brutus* 205–207; Suet. *Gram.* 3.1; MacRae (2013: 49–50, 57–58), cf. Dyck (2003: 399, 405).
8. See, e.g., Rawson (1985: 3–54), Moatti (2005), Wallace-Hadrill (2008), with Volk (2021: 10–13), noting that "rationalization" was not an invention of the late Republic. Moatti (2005: 96–98) attributes the different focus of Acilius's and L. Aelius's explanations to the law having lost its practical function and therefore becoming merely an object of scholarly curiosity (98), but Cicero makes it clear that the term had become obscure already by the beginning of the second century (cf. Moatti 2005: 27 n. 52).
9. For example, Engels (1998). Dyck (2003: 402–403) reviews various interpretations of the alleged influence of Solon's legislation on the Twelve Tables.
10. Sourvinou-Inwood (1995) exposed the inadequacy of the socio-political interpretation alone in accounting for the spread of funerary legislation; in her view, the evidence points to some broad shift in attitudes to death across the Hellenic world. This is too general: it is not attitudes toward death but attitudes toward celebrations of death (i.e., display at funerals) that are targeted.
11. Toher (2005: 282–86).
12. For the *pollinctor*, see Plaut. *Poen.* 63; *Asin.* 910; Var. *Men.* 222, 234; *Dig.* 14.3.5.8 [Labeo]; Mart. 10.97.2, etc.

13. Varro, *Ling.* 7.70; Paulus s.v. "mulieres" 250 L.; Nonius s.v. "praeficae" 212 L.; see the Appendix nos. 1–3.
14. Nonius s.v. "praeficae" 212 L.: Plautus in *Frivolaria* (84): "*superabo omnis argutando praeficas*" (Plautus in *Frivolaria*: "I will surpass all the *praeficae* in prattling.").
15. Fraenkel (1960: 19–20). For *argutor*, cf., e.g., Enn. *Scen.* 204; Nov. *Com.* 26.
16. Varro, *Ling.* 7.70 (Appendix 1).
17. For funerary professionals and the organization of the trade in central Italy, see Bodel (2004).
18. Chiari (2012).
19. Servius ad *Aen.* 6.216 and 9.486 (Appendix 5); Paulus (250 L.) (Appendix 2).
20. Nonius s.v. "Praeficae" (92–93 L. = Appendix 3).
21. See, e.g., among recent views, Habinek (2005), Dutsch (2008), Chiari (2012), North (2015), all citing earlier contributions.
22. See Palombi (1995: 7) for the shrine to Nenia; Bodel (2000: 137–39), on the burial ground outside the Servian *agger*; *CIL* VI 3877 ~ I^2 989 ~ *ILLRP* 775 ~ EDR121646 for the *conlegium tibicinum Romanorum*. See also Habinek (2005: 221–25; 233–47).
23. For classical Greek laments, see briefly Mirto (2015: 72–81) and Alexiou (2002: 102–103).
24. Alexiou (2002), De Martino (1958).
25. Mirto (2015: 73), Alexiou (2002: 104–108).
26. In the earlier of two well-known tomb relief panels depicting Roman funerary scenes, the representation of a cortège from Amiternum datable to the middle of the first century, a pair of hired wailing women with arms raised precedes the bier and a trio of female family members (evidently a mother and two daughters) follows decorously behind. In the later relief scene of a *collocatio* in a house atrium from a tomb beside the via Labicana outside Rome, datable to ca. 110 CE, all the figures, male and female, arrayed around the body of the deceased woman lying in state exhibit stylized gestures of mourning (hands on chest, as if beating breasts), and newly manumitted slaves are distinguished by clothing (the felt caps, *pillei*, of the recently freed) and posture (clasping a knee): see Bodel (1999b: 264–68). Literary sources confirm the importance of slaves and ex-slaves performing at funerals of the early imperial period: cf., e.g., Dion. Hal. *Ant. Rom.* 4.24.6; Pers. 3.105–106; Sen. *Epist.* 12.8; Petr. 72.1.
27. Servius ad *Aen.* 9.486: *Nec te tua funera mater: id est 'funerea': nam apud maiores funeras dicebant eas ad quas funus pertinent, ut sororem matrem:*

nam praeficae, ut et supra (ad 6.216) *diximus, sunt planctus principes, non doloris.* "That is, 'funereal', for our ancestors called those women to whom the funeral pertained, such as a sister or mother, *funerae*: for the *praeficae*, as I said above, are the leaders of the lamentation, not of the grief." Hardie (1994: 163) found the explanation to be "without basis," but the *senatus consultum de Cn. Pisone patre* of 19 CE, first published in 1996, imposes mourning restrictions on a group defined as "the women by whom according to ancestral custom he ought to be mourned" (*a feminis quibus {e}is more maiorum ... lugendus esset; SCPP* 74–75), a phrase that might well refer to *funerae* and in any case recognizes a special category of female relatives with formal funerary obligations: see Bodel (1999a: 45–47), further on the role of family women in Roman funerary ceremonies, Treggiari (1991: 493–98), Boëls-Janssen (1993: 266–68), and Montanini (2009).

28. Momigliano (1984: 207).
29. Dion. Hal. 5.17.2–3; Plut. *Pob.* 9.6–7; Iohan. Lyd. *De magistr.* 1.33; *De vir. ill.* 10: *cuius corpus in foro positum a collega laudatum matronae anno luxerunt.* ("His body, placed in the Forum (and) praised by his colleague the matrons mourned for a year.")
30. Gabba (1996: 26). Publicola himself was the subject of another fictitious funerary etiology, no doubt likewise attributable to Antias, according to which, following his death as consul in 504, the people spontaneously offered to pay for his funeral and burial on the Velian hill, and the women mourned for a year; this provided a model for the public funeral, an honor later awarded by the Senate, and a precedent for a ritual privilege of the Valerii: cf. Plut. *Pob.* 23.2–3; Dion. Hal. *Ant. Rom.* 5.48.3; Livy 2.16; Val. Max. 4.4.1; Amm. Marc. 14.6.11; and the next note.
31. Livy 38.54.8–9: *is morte P. Africani fratris, viri omnium fortissimi clarissimique, eam exortam rogationem est conquestus; parum enim fuisse non laudari pro Rostris P. Africanum post mortem;* "He [Scipio] complained that the proposal had arisen because of the death of his brother, Publius Africanus, a man of the highest bravery and distinction: it was not enough that Publius Africanus was not praised after his death before the Rostra." Kierdorf 1980: 95 believes that public funeral orations might have been delivered in the Forum as early as the late fourth or early third century, and Purcell 2022: 183 suggests that the Forum had become the site for élite funerals already by the early third century, but the earliest explicit evidence we have of the Forum as a site of funeral activity is the exceptional case of C. Fabricius Luscinus, who, following his death sometime after his censorship in 275, was awarded a fictitious cremation there, on the supposed model of the honor of burial on the Velian accorded to Publicola: Plut. *Quaest. Rom.* 79. Other legendary funerals fictitiously set in the Forum

include those of L. Iunius Brutus in 509 (Dion. Hal. *Ant. Rom.* 5.17.2–3; Plut. *Pob.* 9; *De vir. ill.* 10); Appius Claudius, ca. 470 (Dion. Hal. *Ant. Rom.* 9.54.5–6; Livy 2.61.9); and the two politically symbolic virgins, Lucretia (in 509: Livy 1.59; Dion. Hal. *Ant. Rom.* 4.71.2, 4.76.3–4, 77) and Verginia (in 449: Dion. Hal. *Ant. Rom.* 11.39).

32. Fabius Maximus: *ORF*[4] no. 3 frr. 2–4. The earliest attested funeral oration made publicly is that delivered by Q. Caecilius Metellus in 221 for his father Lucius, the pontifex, but the location of the eulogy is not specified: Pliny *HN* 7.139–140 = *ORF*[4] no 6 fr. 2; cf. Kierdorf (1980: 10–21, 106–107).
33. Other early magistrates who died in office and, like Brutus, were supposedly eulogized by their colleagues, include Cn. Manlius Cincinnatus, consul in 480 (Livy 2.47.11) and P. Decius Mus, censor in 304 ([Aurel. Vict.] *De Vir. Ill.* 27.5). As with the tradition of public funeral orations for men, the practice of publicly eulogizing women was given legendary origins (a hundred years later, at the beginning of the fourth century), and a paradigmatic motivation (a collective donation of gold in time of military need), either at the destruction of Veii (Plut. *Cam.* 8) or in relieving the siege of the Gauls (Livy 5.50.7); the first public oration for an historical woman was that delivered by Q. Lutatius Catulus (consul in 102) for his mother (Cic. *De Orat.* 2.44): see Pepe (2015: 21–30).
34. D. Junius Brutus Pera: Val. Max. 2.4.7; Livy, Per. 16. M. Aemilius Lepidus: Livy 23.30.15 with Ville 2014: 42 n. 100 on discrepancies in the identification of sponsors, and 42–45, on gladiatorial combats generally during the Republic. For the development of the Forum as a venue for spectacle during the third century, with the concomitant infusion of private élite practices into the public realm, see Purcell (2022: 182–84). The loss of Livy's record between 264 and 218 may have obscured for us the occasion of an earlier transition to the Forum, but the change was perhaps precipitated precisely by the disaster at Cannae, following which the Romans offered two pairs of human burials in the Forum Boarium in expiation (Livy 22.57.6; cf. Pliny, *NH* 28.2.12; Plut. *Marc.* 3.6) and took other extraordinary measures such as consulting the Sibylline books and sending an envoy to the oracle at Delphi: cf. Plut. *Fab. Max.* 18.3 and below in the text.
35. Livy 22.56.4–5 on the interruption of the *sacrum anniversarium Cereris* (cf. 34.6.15); Plut. *Fab. Max.* 18.1–2; cf. Fest p. 86 L; Val. Max. 1.1.15; with Spaeth (1996: 106–107) and Boëls-Janssen (1993: 238).
36. Troop-strength and casualty figures, both ancient and modern, range widely. Daly 2002 reviews the evidence for numbers on both sides of the Battle at Cannae (26–29) and discusses casualty figures in the aftermath

(45, 198–99). For the total numbers of Roman troops lost in the first three years of the war, modern estimates range from a high of 120,000 (Lazenby 1996: 215) to a low of 50,000 (Brunt 1971: 419–20) with many settling for a middling estimate of 80,000–90,000.

37. See, e.g., Brunt (1971: 402–405, 420).
38. Rosenstein (2004: 107–140) demonstrates the devastating demographic consequences of the conflict in Italy and its aftermath, when, on his estimate, a minimum of some 35–40% of soldiers died in service over the course of the second century; between the years 200 and 168, more than 55,000 military deaths can be counted: see Rosenstein (2004: 109–111, Table 2; 115–18; 191–92).
39. Livy 40.19.4 *Libitina funeribus vix sufficeret* ("Libitina was barely sufficient for the funerals"); 41.21.6 *ne liberorum quidem funeribus Libitina sufficiebat* ("Libitina was insufficient for the funerals even of the free," and the unburied bodies of slaves lay in piles beside the road).
40. Kierdorf (1980: 94–105), following Karl Meuli, recognizes the original role of the *praefica* as director of the ritual lament familiar from other Mediterranean contexts and suggests that this function was replaced by the funerary laudation, but he does not venture any explanation for the change, nor does he address the significance of the *nenia* and its continued association with the *praefica*.
41. Plut. *Fab. Max.* 18.1–2 with Loreaux (1998: 29–34), on the civic role carved out for Roman matrons in mourning, in contrast to the practice in Greek cities.
42. In the funerary relief from Amiternum depicting a cortège, hired mourning women precede the bier along with the professional musicians, whereas female family members follow behind. In the *collocatio* scene depicted on the Tomb of the Haterii, two *praeficae* and one *pollinctor*, it seems, are depicted next to a funerary bed laid out in the atrium and surrounded by slaves and freedmen in postures of mourning: see above, n. 26.
43. Habinek (2005: 243–46) sees the purpose of the *nenia* as keeping dead spirits at bay. For the distinctive sounds of Roman funerary wailing and music, see Chiari (2012).
44. For the structural similarities, see Dutsch (2008: 265–70).
45. Alexiou (2002: 133–34, 139–40) on Lucian's parody at *De Luctu* 13 and the stylized complaints of a bereaved father at Ach. Tat. 1.13; 142–45.
46. Detail of specific accomplishments is absent from Catullus's lament for the *passer*, whose characteristic behavior is remembered (Cat. 3.8–10). This may more closely resemble the praises bestowed on ordinary Romans at their obsequies.
47. *eorum qui ludis Troicas* Scaliger | *cursitassent* ed. princ.

Bibliography

Alexiou, M. 2002. *The Ritual Lament in Greek Tradition*, 2nd ed. revised by D. Yatromanolakis. Lanham.

Bachvarova, M. 2008. "Sumerian Gala Priests and Eastern Mediterranean Returning Gods: Tragic Lamentation in Cross-Cultural Perspective." In Suter, A. ed. *Lament: Studies in the Ancient Mediterranean and Beyond*. 18–52. Oxford University Press.

Bodel, J. 2004. "The Organization of the Funerary Trade at Puteoli and Cumae", in Panciera, S. ed. *Libitina e dintorni*. 149–70. Quasar.

Bodel, J. 2000. "Dealing with the Dead: Undertakers, Executioners, and Potter's Fields in Ancient Rome." In E. Marshall, and Hope, V. eds. *Death and Disease in the Ancient City*. 128–51. Routledge.

Bodel, J. 1999a. "Punishing Piso." *American Journal of Philology* 120: 43–63.

Bodel, J. 1999b. "Death on Display: Looking at Roman Funerals." In Bergmann, B. and Kondoleon, C. eds., *The Art of Ancient Spectacle*. 258–81. National Gallery, Washington.

Boëls-Janssen, N. 1993. *La vie religieuse des matrons dans la Rome archaïque*. École Française de Rome.

Brunt, P.A. 1971. *Italian Manpower 225 BC–AD 14*. Oxford University Press.

Chiari, F. 2012. "*Praeficae* e *musici*. I protagonisti "sonori" delle liturgie di morte alto-imperiale." *Ager Veleias* 7.8: 1–19.

Corbeill, A. 2004. *Nature Embodied. Gesture in Ancient Rome*. Princeton University Press.

Crawford, M.H., ed. 1996. *Roman Statutes* vol. 2. Institute of Classical Studies.

Daly, G. 2002. *Cannae. The Experience of Battle in the Second Punic War*. Routledge.

De Martino, E. 1958. *Morte e pianto rituale nel mondo antico. Dal lamento funebre al pianto di Maria*. Edizioni scientifiche Einaudi.

D'Ippolito, F. 1978. *I giuristi e la città. Ricerche sulla giurisprudenza romana della repubblica*. Naples.

Dutsch, D. 2008. "*Nenia*, Gender, Genre and Lament in Ancient Rome." In Suter: 258–79.

Dyck, A.R. 2003. *A Commentary on Cicero, De Legibus*. University of Michigan Press.

Engels, J. 1998. *Funerum Sepulcrorumque Magnificentia*. Franz Steiner Verlag.

Fraenkel, E. 1960. *Elementi Plautini in Plauto*. La Nuova Italia Editrice.

Gabba, E. 1996. "Dionigi di alicarnasso sull'origine romana del discorso funebre." *Studi Classici e Orientali* 46: 25–27.

Habinek, T.N. 2005. *The World of Roman Song*. Johns Hopkins University Press.

Hardie, P. R. 1994. *Virgil Aeneid Book IX*. Cambridge University Press.

Kierdorf, W. 1980. *Laudatio funebris: Interpretationen und Untersuchungen zur Entwicklung der römischen Leichenrede.* Verlag Anton Hain.

Lazenby, J. F. 1996. "Was Maharbal Right?" In Cornell, T. J., Rankov, N. B., and Sabin, P., eds., *The Second Punic War: A Reappraisal.* 39–48. Institute of Classical Studies.

Loreaux, N. 1998. *Mothers in Mourning.* Trans. C. Pache. Cornell University Press.

MacRae, D. 2013. *Legible Religion. Books, Gods, and Rituals in Roman Culture.* Cambridge University Press.

Mirto, M.S. 2015. *Death in the Greek world from Homer to the Classical Age.* A. M. Osborne, trans. University of Oklahoma Press.

Moatti, C. 2005. *The Birth of Critical Thinking in Republican Rome.* Trans. J. Lloyd. Cambridge University Press.

Momigliano, A. 1984. "The Theological Efforts of the Roman Upper Classes in the First Century BC." *Classical Philology* 79: 199–211.

Montanini, L. 2009. "Le donne romane e la morte." *Ager Veleias* 4.12: 1–23.

Mustakallio, K. 2013. "Grief and Mourning in the Roman Context. The Changing Sphere of Female Lamentation," in Chaniotis, A. and Ducrey, P. eds. *Unveiling Emotions II. Emotions in Greece and Rome: Texts, Images, Material Culture.* 237–50. Fran Steiner Verlag.

North, J. A. 2015. "Roman funeral rituals and the significance of the *naenia*." *Religion in the Roman Empire* 1: 114–133.

Palombi, D. 1995. "Dea Nenia, sacellum." *Lexicon Topographicum Urbis Romae* 2: 7. Quasar.

Pepe, C. 2015. *Morire da donna. Ritratti esemplari di bonae feminae nella laudatio funebris romana.* Edizioni ETS.

Purcell, N. 2022. "Historians in the Forum." In Filippi, D. ed., *Rethinking the Roman City. The Spatial Turn and the Archaeology of Roman Italy.* Routledge.

Rawson, E. 1985. *Intellectual Life in the Late Roman Republic.* Duckworth.

Richlin, A. 2001. "Emotional Work: Lamenting the Dead." in Tylawsky, E. and Weiss, C. eds, *Essays in Honour of Gordon Williams.* 229–48. Henry R. Schwab Publishers.

Rosenstein, N. 2004. *Rome at War. Farms, Families, and Death in the Middle Republic.* University of North Carolina Press.

Sourvinou-Inwood, C. 1995. *Reading Greek Death to the End of the Classical Period.* Clarendon Press.

Stears, K. 1998. "Death Becomes Her. Gender and Athenian Death Ritual." In Blundell, S., and Williamson, M., eds., *The Sacred and the Feminine in Ancient Greece.* 113–127. Routledge.

Spaeth, B.S. 1996. *The Roman Goddess Ceres.* University of Texas Press.

Toher, M. 2005. "The Tenth Table and the Conflict of the Orders." In Raaflaub, K. ed. *Social Struggles in Archaic Rome: New Perspectives on the Conflict of the Orders. Expanded and Updated Edition.* 268–92. Blackwell.

Treggiari, S. 1991. *Roman Marriage. Iusti Coniuges from the Time of Cicero to the Time of Ulpian*. Oxford University Press.

Ville, G. 2014. *La Gladiature en Occident des origines à la mort de Domitien*. Ecole Française de Rome.

Volk, K. 2021. *The Roman Republic of Letters. Scholarship, Philosophy, and Politics in the Age of Cicero and Caesar*. Princeton University Press.

Wallace-Hadrill, A. 2008. *Rome's Cultural Revolution*. Cambridge University Press.

CHAPTER 12

The Vergilian Work of Life

Del A. Maticic

> Enough of this! The great work of life goes on—Death draws near—to be better after death than in life is one's hope & endeavor—to be that through self schooling.
>
> —Mary Shelley[1]

Is the poet's name "Vergil" or "Virgil"?[2] Nowadays, one's answer to this question is probably determined by geography, with Americans preferring the former and academics from other Anglophone countries the latter.[3] But for one Medieval biographer of the poet the choice comes down to etymology:[4]

> *Virgilius a virga laurea, quam mater eius per somnium se peperisse viderat, vocatus est sive, ut alii volunt, ut a vere Vergilius quasi vere gliscens, id est, crescens sit nominatus. Erat enim magnae philosophiae praeclarissimus praeceptor et multiplex, sicut vernalia incrementa.*
>
> He was either called Virgil from the shoot [*virga*] of laurel to which his mother saw herself give birth in a dream, or—as others would like—Vergil,

D. A. Maticic (✉)
Vassar College, Poughkeepsie, NY, USA
e-mail: dmaticic@vassar.edu

D. A. Maticic, J. Rogers (eds.), *Working Lives in Ancient Rome*, The New Antiquity,
https://doi.org/10.1007/978-3-031-61234-3_12

> from the "spring" [*ver*], as if "increasing in spring" [*vere gliscens*], *i.e.*, "growing" [*crescens*]. For, as a teacher of important philosophy, he was widely known and multifaceted, just like vernal growth. (JL trans., adapted)

On the one hand, the poet's own life is compared, through his mother's dream, to that of a laurel tree budding prodigiously with various fruits and flowers. On the other hand, his own works were famous and variegated, growing with the intensity of springtime. The first of these explanations is more static and formal in nature, with the poet being compared to a tree. The other is more processual, likening him to a season of growth.

This chapter takes this comparison between Vergil and plant growth as a cue to consider how characterizations of creative *labores*, from Vergil's own works to modern receptions, persistently tie them to different kinds of living things and ways of being alive. In so doing, it has two primary goals. First, by following a vein of tradition from Vergil's own writing through a selection of ancient and medieval biographical accounts of his life, I argue that Vergilian poetry and literature conceives of literary *labor* as a kind of growth that extends in different kinds of symbiosis with plant, animal, and human lives.[5] As I argue here, the poet's conception of *labor* is one that has particular affinity with that of plant growth, which, according to the *Georgics*, is the *labor* of plants. In making this case, I build on recent studies that have come increasingly to appreciate Vergil as a green poet, whose vision of the world is one pulsing with sympathy and interactions across the worlds of mineral, plant, animal, human, and god.[6] Second, I argue that the figuring of literary labor as vital *labor* also offers writers a way to conceptualize how a literary tradition of Vergilianism can be formulated. In referring to a Vergilian tradition, I deploy a concept fleshed out by Ziolkowski and Putnam to refer to the receptions and responses to Vergil, many of which tend to understand themselves as outgrowths of the poet's own work and participants in a clearly defined literary legacy.[7] It is in these two respects that I conceive of a Vergilian "work of life" as a living tradition of literary work that preserves something of a living flame of the poet for posterity. By tracing this vital thread through the tradition of Vergilian life-writing, I address a question addressed obliquely in a number of contributions in this volume; namely, how are ancient Roman configurations of work/life brought to bear on our own modern working lives as Vergilians, classicists, and anyone else who might be reading this volume?

I begin with the 10th *Eclogue*, which contains Vergil's first recorded use of the word *labor*, and which culminates a sustained engagement with concepts of work and leisure that runs throughout the work. I argue that Vergil imagines his own *labor* as merging with the growth of the plants that densely populate his pastoral landscape. By concluding the poem with a command to "rise" (*surgamus*) like a plant or a shepherd departing from the pastoral shades, Vergil takes into his own life the vegetal vitality that had formerly surrounded him. In the following sections, I consider different scenes from the tradition of Vergilian biographies in which the poet's vital energy is channeled into biographical works, effectively blending *Life* (i.e., the written account of a life) and life (the sheer vitality of the person whose biography is reported and the vitalities of the plants, animals, and other humans that surround them). The first considers the late-antique verse life of Phocas, making the case that the biographer imitates both Vergil and Vergil's parents in their capacity as metaphorical and literal givers of life. I then turn to two depictions of the relationship between Augustus and Vergil, first in a medieval poem ascribed to Augustus that cancels Vergil's will and prevents the *Aeneid's* destruction, and then in an episode from the Renaissance-era *Vita Donati Aucti* that depicts Vergil as a veterinarian in the court of Augustus before he became a poet. In both cases, engagements with the poet's works are tempered by a care for life and a desire to preserve it through the struggles of *labor*.

Leaving Work (*Eclogue* 10)

Consoling those worried that they will not enjoy the *Eclogues* for its pastoral content, the Italian humanist Sicco Polenton assured them that "while it may appear to be a pastoral thing, [it] nevertheless has a great deal of blood and nerves" (*quamvis res pastoritia videatur, habet tamen tantum sanguinis ac nervorum*).[8] In this section, I make a similar argument. But rather than showing signs of animal vitality, I argue that the *Eclogues* is possessed of a vigorous vegetal life. By assimilating plant growth and his own literary *labor*, Vergil imagines himself and his work as growing together with the *silvae* that populate it. In reading the poem like this, I contribute to a long tradition of scholarship that read Vergilian plants as important evidence for literary self-reflexivity.[9] But while most of this scholarship sees trees as *formal* analogies for poetics, I instead consider the vitality of the plants as the salient feature in the poetic schema.[10]

Work overwhelms the Vergilian environment, extending from gods and humans to animals and even plants.[11] Indeed, the poet is perhaps the only Roman author to assign them *labor*. In Book 2 of the *Georgics*, Vergil turns to the problem of winter and advises the tender of groves not to waste their time turning the stiff earth in the cold months (2.315–345). For, as he says, they need the reprieve of spring between the extremes of winter and summer to endure the *labor* of living (2.343–5):[12]

> *nec res hunc tenerae possent perferre laborem,*
> *si non tanta quies iret frigusque caloremque*
> *inter, et exciperet caeli indulgentia terras.*

> The tender things would not be able to complete this work, if such a rest did not intersperse the cold of winter and the heat of summer, and the clemency of the sky would give the earth a break.

The work Vergil's plants engage in is growth made possible by the temperate spring. This is a surprising insight for the student of work/life because, for the ancient botanist, a plant's growth was indistinguishable from its life.[13] Agriculture is thus figured, as it often is, as a collaboration between human and plant.[14]

This is the most direct form of a phenomenon throughout Vergil's works in which *labor* generates life and not simply livelihood. When one is pregnant in Latin, as in English, one goes into *labor*.[15] Much of the work his animals perform in *Georgics* 3 is the "seductive labor" (*blando … labori*, 3.127) of procreation.[16] Georgic work, in a more general sense, is a necessary evil for those trying to feed themselves in the post-Saturnian world.[17] This is, of course, not always successful: the animal amory in Book 3 is ultimately undermined, in Lucretian irony, with the suffering of plague (3.525). Orpheus, in an anticlimactic *envoi* to the work world of the *Georgics*, watches all of his work flow away with the ghost of his love receding into the darkness: *omnis/effusus labor* (4.491–2).

Whether seen as vital or deathly, the emphasis placed on *labor* in the *Georgics* is well known and thoroughly analyzed, as is the scarcity of *labor* in the leisurely haunts of the *Eclogues*.[18] In fact, the word does not appear in the work until the final poem, called the "final labor" of the collection (*extremum … laborem*, 10.1). This marks the beginning of the end of the shepherd's youthful *otium* and the hardship coming after the fall of the generic golden age and the departure from the shade of pastoral *silvae*.[19]

What is more, as I hope to show here, the *Eclogue* traces the evolution of a particularly plantlike form of *labor* that flashes briefly in the final lines of the poem as the poet marks the end of his bucolic jaunt. This process, which culminates in Vergil comparing his love of Gallus to a suckering alder tree (10.73–4), develops across the entire *Eclogue*, as the relationship between poet and plant grows more and more sympathetic across the narrative of Gallus' life after Lycoris.

As David Wray and others have argued, Latin authors exploit the double-meaning of *silvae* as both "woods" and "raw material" to metapoetic effect.[20] In pastoral, it allows the poet to demonstrate the tendency of a given eclogue to echo other works, to inscribe its self-aware writtenness (consider the inner bark of a tree, which was called *liber*), to evoke its connection with *otium* (the shade), and to root the close connection of its characters to the natural world.[21] But these interpretations do not succeed in explaining how plant *growth* fits within their analogy. The fact that plants are living things is essential to their representation in pastoral, and the difference between dead poems and living plants is highlighted as much as their formal qualities. *Eclogue* 10 emphasizes that difference, and slowly effaces it as it imagines a poet's *labor* that channels the plant's vitality.

To see how this works, we must survey the different ways in which plant matter appears in the poem. In *Ecl.* 10, we first encounter trees at the end of the poem, where Vergil remarks that "we do not sing to deaf ears: the forest will reverberate everything" (*non canimus surdis, respondent omnia silvae*, 10.8).[22] This is the so-called pathetic fallacy, a literary device that assigns human actions and emotions to nonhuman nature, which functions to incorporate those entities into the emotional world of the human characters.[23] We see a repetition of this device a few lines later in 10.13–15, where the laurels, myrtles, and pine-bearing Maenalus weep, commiserating Gallus. Thus, the poem starts out with a representation of metaliterary trees that are very far from the nature of plants as living things. Rather, we see them as passive, reactive entities—perhaps more audience than co-author—that are personified and instrumentalized by the poet to serve the emotive ends of the poem.[24]

The second batch of plant materials in the poem is also instrumentalized, but by characters in the poem rather than by the poet himself. They are plucked, worn, and eaten as the accoutrement of Gallus and the various characters who come and visit him. Menalcas drips with acorns soaked in water, which was food for his animals in wintertime (*hiberna* ... *de glande*, 10.20).[25] Silvanus arrives waving flowering fennel and tall lilies evoking youth (*florentes ferulas et grandia lilia quassans*, 10.25).[26] Pan arrives ominously stained with the blood-red juice of berries (*sanguineis ebuli bacis minioque rubentem*, 10.27).[27] Each of these figures thus carries vegetal material that not only symbolizes human death and threats to life (through winter, plucked flowers, and blood); they each also vividly involve the arrested lives of plants themselves, as the fruits, berries, and flowers are destroyed rather than being allowed to grow.

This situation is clarified and developed by Pan's words to Gallus when he encounters the elegist weeping (10.28–30):

> "*ecquis erit modus?*" *inquit.* "*Amor non talia curat:*
> *nec lacrimis crudelis Amor nec gramina rivis*
> *nec cytiso saturantur apes nec fronde capellae.*"
>
> "Will there be any moderation?" He said. "Love does not care about such things. Neither does cruel love grow sated with tears nor the grass with streams nor bees with clover nor goats with leaves."

In Pan's formulation, Love, like plants and animals, is a living thing that requires sustenance. Because they are always growing, these insatiable creatures will always need to find more fuel to consume in order to stay alive. What is more, the passage implies that these entities live in something resembling a great chain of being, with grasses drinking water, bees drinking the clover amid those grasses, the goats eating the leaves that sprout from the vegetation among them, and, implicitly, humans consuming what is produced by the bees and goats. This further enlivens the plants since they are perceived as participating in the growth of the world rather than just being personified forms or decorative attributes.

After this, Gallus responds with his song. At first, he expresses a desire to participate in this pastoral world of consumption. He imagines that, if he stays there, he could become a vintner (*maturae vinitor uvae*, 10.36) and participate in the floral economy of the pastoral world, comparing young loves to flowers and plucking blossoms to give to them (10.38–41). Were Lycoris there with him, instead of off with her soldier in the frozen north, he would gladly live out the rest of his days there in pastoral paradise with her, being himself consumed by age (*hic ipso tecum consumerer aevo*, 10.43). But instead, because he has been abandoned, he must instead flee, departing once again from the *silvae* (*ipsae rursus concedite silvae*, 10.63) as Vergil's pastoral characters so often must.

In leaving this pastoral consumption, Gallus offers up a different kind of relation between poem and plant than has existed before (52–4):

certum est in silvis, inter spelaea ferarum,
malle pati tenerisque meos incidere amores
arboribus: crescent illae, crescetis, amores.

Surely it is better to suffer in the woods, among the haunts of beasts, and to carve my love onto the young trees. They will grow and you, loves, will grow too.

Conte, in his influential reading of this passage, has argued that the image of Gallus carving his love on trees harkens ultimately back to Callimachus' *Aetia* and is thus a symbol for elegiac textuality embedded within the pastoral world of the eclogue.[28] But when we contrast Gallus' vision here with the representation of vegetation earlier in the poem, we realize that what he is doing is not just marking generic blending, but also continuing a trend in the poem of taking plant life more seriously on its own terms. We also see that Gallus is offering up to Pan an answer to his question about *amor* and the fuel it needs to grow. By coopting plant growth, *amor* can survive without consumption. Human and plant *labor* here appear to be synthesized. This is emphasized further at the end of Gallus' song, when he celebrates love's staying power in the wake of his writings: "our labors will not be able to change him" (*non illum nostri possunt mutare labores,* 10.64), whether he goes to frozen Thrace to drink the cold Hebrus or whether the dying bark of elm tree withers on the deserts of Ethiopia (10.64–8). Here, Gallus anticipates the passage of the *Georgics* with which we started, describing plant growth and the seasons. As a result, Gallus' *labor* seems to resemble that of a tree struggling to survive in the extremes of hot and cold, wearing *amores* on his fleshy bark.

Finally, the end of the poem recapitulates this increasing immanence of plant life and brings it to fruition (10.70–5):

haec sat erit, divae, vestrum cecinisse poetam,
dum sedet et gracili fiscellam texit hibisco,
Pierides: vos haec facietis maxima Gallo,
Gallo, cuius amor tantum mihi crescit in horas
quantum vere novo viridis se subicit alnus.
surgamus.

> Divine Pierides, it will be enough for your poet to have sung these things while he sits and weaves a basket from slender hibiscus. You will make these things greatest for Gallus, Gallus for whom my love grows as much by the hour as a green alder propagates itself by suckers when spring is new. Let us rise.

Building on Dyer's insight that *se subicit* should not be translated "casts itself upward" as it has been interpreted from Servius onward, but rather as "grows by suckering" (*i.e.*, what happens when trees reproduce with shoots springing out from the base of a tree) as it used in the arboricultural instruction of the *Georgics*, Henkel argues that the passage makes a claim about Vergil's relationship to Gallus.[29] In particular, Henkel argues, the passage metaphorically compares *Ecl.* 10 to a sucker growing out from, but also perpetually in the shadow of, its source, namely Gallus' *Amores.*[30] And, as the ending of a poem that spends considerable space emulating Gallus, it is a charming *homage*.

Rather than simply contrasting the poetic differences of the respective *oeuvres*, the ending also contrasts their relationship with the natural world. Three different strategies for engaging with the wooden world are introduced. First, the plaiting poet weaving the *hibiscum* marks the oldest strategy. This kind of engagement with plant *materia*, clearly evocative of Theocritus' *Idyll* 1.45–54, involves breaking off the twig of a tree or, if we translate *hibiscum* as "marsh-mallow" instead, the death of an entire plant. Thus, the kinds of instrumentalization and consumption of plants that we saw in the first two parts of *Eclogue* 10 are here encapsulated by the Theocritean reference. As a second strategy, by contrast, the recollection of Gallus' metapoetic engagement with trees figures a poet who is still violent against trees, but not fatally so: just as Gallus' inscribed *amores* grow together with the trees they are written on, so Vergil's love will "grow." And then we have Vergil. Reading on to the alder simile, we encounter a third way of conceptualizing the relationship between *arbores* and *amores*, which emphatically involves *living* trees (72–4). Lines 70–74 set up a complicated contrast between Theocritus (sitting and plaiting, which kills the willow twigs), Gallus (incising), and Vergil (growing).[31] The Hellenistic Greek progenitor of pastoral is recalled in the charming image of the basket of marshmallow reeds, broken off from the plant to contain the cricket and his song. In order to do this, the plants must die and be used as tools against the animal world. Gallus, whom we had just seen interfacing with trees, is recalled as the elegiac incisor of *amores* into *arbores*, which, though violent, are not deadly. And, finally, we have Vergil, who relies neither upon plucking nor upon carving, but instead sprouts arbors from amorous roots in a harmonious cooption of the plants' powers for his own poetic ends.[32] Vergil thus ends this poem with a celebration of the triumph, however delicate and ephemeral it might be, of what we would now call the sustainability of his pastoral potential.

Our key here is Vergil's use of the verb, *surgamus*. Putnam, in the first Anglophone monograph on the *Eclogues*, carefully reads the word in light of the immediately preceding comparison, in which Vergil draws between himself and a tree, as meaning "let us rise [up out from the shade]" but also as "let us grow." Scholars since have read the word flatly as announcing Vergil's triumphant promotion to the loftier genre of didactic.[33] But the significance of this remarkably paradoxical pun—let us grow up like a tree, let us sucker like a tree, let us leave the shade of the tree—creates bumps in that interpretive road with its groundswell of roots. Indeed, when read in the full context of the eclogue's trees, Vergil appears not to announce his departure from the physical world of pastoral poetry, but rather to metamorphose into it. In a sense, then, Vergil ends the *Eclogues* from the point of view not of the humans but of the trees. In making up for the shortcomings of his predecessors, Vergil momentarily attains a synthesis between poem and plant, between work and life. Or, at the very least, he channels the energies of the nonhuman at the exclusion of the shepherds he is sending away from his *silvae*. In drawing on the energy and liveliness of his friend's program and the vegetation that populates his own work, Vergil figures his own literary *labor* as operating the same way as the *labor* of a plant. As such, he imagines himself growing incrementally and vernally just like the *Vergilius* of the biography with whom we opened this chapter.

Stealing Time (Phocas' *Life*)

There are many other places we can look in Vergil's work for this kind of work/life synthesis. But rather than dwelling further on the literary *labores of his lifetime,* the next several sections of this chapter turn to literary biographical works that grow from the roots of Vergil's writing. As I will show, these biographies engage in complex receptions not only of Vergil's own life but also of the lives of the plants, animals, and humans populating his works. In making such an argument, these sections build on recent work advancing our understanding of the relationship between ancient poets and their biographers.[34] Particularly important here is Nora Goldschmidt's *The Afterlives of the Roman Poets*. This inventive and wide-ranging work demonstrates that poets incorporated extensive information about their lives into their verses, and that various receptions of this information, including in biography, engage in sophisticated dialogue with the poets through imaginary life-writing. But while Goldschmidt, by and large, is interested in life as events, actions, and personal qualities, my chapter is concerned with biographical engagements with the sheer vitality of Vergil and the organisms that populate his poetry.

The first text we shall consider is the verse life of the late antique grammarian Phocas, a 131-line poem composed of a 24-line Sapphic hymn to Clio and a 107-line, apparently incomplete hexameter versification of the Suetonian-Donatan *Vita* (*VSD*).[35] Scholars have focused largely on the nature of Phocas' sources and his engagements with them.[36] But as I will show here, the poem undertakes a sophisticated engagement with Vergil as a living thing, effectively enlivening his biography and blurring the distinction between *Life* and life.

After the opening Sapphic hymn, the poem begins its biography with a series of fluid metaphors of fertility and filiation (25–34):[37]

> *Maeonii specimen vatis veneranda Maronem*
> *Mantua Romuleae generavit flumina linguae.*
> *quis facunda tuos toleraret Graecia fastus,*
> *quis tantum eloquii potuisset ferre tumorem,*
> *aemula Vergilium tellus nisi Tusca dedisset?*
> *huic genitor figulus Maro nomine, cultor agelli,*
> *ut referunt alii, tenui mercede locatus,*
> *sed plures figulum. quis non miracula rerum*
> *haec stupeat? dives partus de paupere vena*
> *enituit: figuli suboles nova carmina finxit.*

> Revered Mantua gave birth to a likeness of the Maeonian prophet Maro, a stream of the Romulean tongue. Who could bear your pride, eloquent Greece, who could endure such swollen speech, had not the rival land of Tuscany produced Vergil? His father was a potter named Maro, or the farmer of a modest plot, as others report, hired for a meager salary, but to most a potter. Who would not be astounded at such miraculous things? A rich offspring shone forth from a poor vein. The potter's scion fashioned new songs. (Trans. Ziolkowski and Putnam, adapted)

The opening pairs two different progenitors: one the land of Mantua who gave birth (*generavit*) to a river of Latinity, the other Vergil's *genitor*, here named Maro.[38] It is thus suggested that *Tellus* plays the role of Mother Earth. The way in which these two parents interact with each other is through the profession of Vergil's father. Scholars have noted that in asserting that Maro was more likely a potter than a farmer, Phocas inverts what is said in *VSD*, which says it is more likely he was a cultivator of forests and bees—appropriate trades for the poet's progenitor.[39] McGill suggests that Phocas makes this change in order to achieve the *figuli/finxit* pun in line 34.[40] But something more complicated is at issue, which becomes clear once we take the potter's *materia* into account. Potter's clay was dry soil that was good for growing olive trees (*G.* 2.179–81) but poor for growing vines (Col. 3.11.9). As a parent who molds the raw material of Mother Earth, he is figured as collaborating with her in the creation of the poet. In this way Phocas seems to recall the well-known analogy, recorded in *VSD*, of Vergil's process of composition as like that of a mother bear fashioning (*effingere*, *VSD* 22) her whelps with her tongue.[41] The earthen materiality of the clay is further evoked by the mining metaphor that ends the passage, which compares Vergil to precious ore taken from an otherwise poor mineral vein. That the word could also refer to genealogical "blood" and to waters of inspiration ties the different levels of meaning together, binding father and earth together in generative materiality.[42]

These lines thus evoke an elemental mixture of earth and water that results in the poet, who is composed in a way that evokes representations of his own processes of composition-as-parturition.[43] The marked maternality of this passage anticipates the appearance of the poet's human mother.[44] As in most of the other *Lives*, Phocas introduces her in *labor* and records her prophetic dream of giving birth to a laurel tree that represents the poem.[45] In wording that recalls the generative flowing imagery in the previous section, Phocas says that "she thought that a bough of the Phoeban grove sprung up" (*fudisse*, 40). The effect of emergence from out of the earth is further achieved by a reference, unique to Phocas' *Life*, to the end of *Aeneid* 6, when he characterizes Vergil's mother's dream as the truest thing that could have come from the Gate of Horn (*nil certius umquam/cornea porta tulit*, 41–2). Thus, dreams spring from subterranean channels no differently than water, clay, gold, trees, and Vergil himself.[46]

The connection between parental and literary *labor* is made here, as it was with the potter father, when Phocas writes that through the dream Polla "recognized the craft of her own burden" (*oneris … sui cognoverat artem*, 43), punningly evoking both Vergil's innate *ars* and her own act of labor. This, paired with the reference to Vergil's horoscope (45–6), echoes Anchises' instructions to Aeneas on the *artes* of the Roman, which contrasts imperial rule with the various works of the Greeks, such as breathing seeming life into bronze and marble and tracing the stars (6.847–53). Curiously, then, Polla's connection to Aeneas' father seems to extend the gender-bending association of the fatherly potter molding clay to the mother bear licking her young into shape.[47] In addition to reenacting the male theft of female creative labor like those studied by Geue and Bodel in this chapter, the swapping of procreative roles in these two artistic analogies heightens the sense in which this poem closely affiliates the processes of work and life.

Given the fact that the fathers of Aeneas and Vergil are connected in these verses, it is no surprise that, soon after, mention of Aeneas' mother, Venus, is also included, albeit obliquely. In *VSD* and other biographies, it is noted that the poet Lucretius dies the same day that Vergil is born.[48] In other versions, Lucretius is said to be Vergil's maternal uncle, and he is said not to die but to interpret the dream of the laurel tree.[49] It is notable that Lucretius' death is not mentioned in this poem, given that *de Rerum Natura* is alluded to throughout. Indeed, when Phocas writes that the boy was "brought forth into the living air" (*vitalibus editus auris*, 44), he ironically echoes a Lucretian phrase.[50] This is the first of a series of references to Lucretius in the description of two portents that attend Vergil's birth. Phocas opens the passage with a reference to the astronomic context of Vergil's birth, which takes the place of the "gliding stars" beneath which Venus moves (*subter labentia signa*, *DRN* 1.2). Phocas adds to this Lucretian allusivity in his description of baby Vergil's placability: he "beholds the world with a serene brow" (*fronte serena/conspexit mundum*, 47–8), reflects the "peaceful sky" (*placatum … caelum*, *DRN* 1.9) and the "vernal face of day" (*species … verna diei*, *DRN* 1.10) that attends Venus' arrival, adding further that it was *serenus*, one of Lucretius' favorite words.[51] Phocas' earth "ministered flowers" (*terra ministrauit flores*, 50), while Lucretius' crafty *Tellus* (an appropriate figure to loom in the background of Phocas' account of generative creativity) "submitted flowers" (*summittit flores*, *DRN* 1.8). Spring gives its vernal gifts of soft grasses (*herbida … fulmenta*, 51), echoing the *pabula laeta* in which Lucretius' young herds frolic (*DRN* 1.14). In light of all this, after Phocas describes the bees pouring honey onto Vergil's lip, one cannot help but recall the analogy of poetry on the rim of Lucretius' bitter philosophy (*DRN* 1.936–42, 4.11–7). Through these references, Phocas, as it were, reanimates Lucretius, bringing him to life again through an evocation of his work. The leitmotif of flowing fluid (here in the future participle *fusura*, 54) closes the opening passage in a hydrological ring composition.[52]

The imagery of life-giving flux gets reversed later in the poem. In explaining the cause of Vergil's composition of his first great work and his coming to Rome, Phocas describes the military campaigns of Augustus that resulted in the infamous land resettlements. These soldiers would form a battle line that "would see Philippi doused (*perfusos*, 94) with the blood of its elders" (*caede priorum*, 93). Here, humans pour ancestors back onto the earth, effectively reversing the generative vital flows that are so central to the opening of the poem. Phocas clinches this by incorporating into the account of *VSD* an allusion to *Ecl.* 10 when the flowering countryside of miserable Cremona (*miserae florentia rura Cremona*, 98) is assigned to veteran settlers. He writes that the "whole place was conceded to the soldiers as a reward for their labors" (*totaque militibus pretium concessa laborum/praeda fuit*, 99–100), echoing Vergil's appeal to Arethusa to "grant him the last labor" (*extremum hunc, Arethusa, mihi concede laborem*, 10.1).

All of this becomes relevant to our analysis when we consider how Phocas reflects on the relationship between his own literary labors and these vital forces. If Vergil's parents, the earth, Natura, and political history are all sources of the poet's work/life, so too is Phocas himself. In order to see how the poet himself takes on the galvanizing impulse of Vergil, let's consider one final passage. In a desiccated moment immediately following the opening scenes ringed with flowing imagery, Vergil's father plants a ritual poplar tree in sterile sand, which not only grows but does so much faster than an average tree, growing to full size even though it was only "nurtured for a brief time" (*tempore … nutrita brevi*, 61). By moving this detail from right after the birth, where it comes in *VSD*, Phocas enables a contrast with the scene that follows. Like many other biographers, he begins his account of Vergil's literary career by remarking on an epitaph attributed to him for the thief Ballista, who was stoned to death. Phocas introduces a couplet from this epitaph with a witty joke (69–74):

> *incidit titulum iuvenis, quo pignera vatis*
> *edidit. auspiciis suffecit poena magistri:*
> *"monte sub hoc lapidum tegitur Ballista sepultus:*
> *nocte die tutum carpe viator iter".*
> *nos tamen hoc brevius, si fas simulare Maronem:*
> *"Ballistam sua poena tegit, via tuta per umbras".*

> The youth cut an inscription by which he made known the pledges of the poet he would become. The punishment of the master sufficed for favorable beginnings: "Ballista is covered, buried under this mountain of stones; by night and by day take your route in safety, traveler". We, however, will put this more briefly, if it is right to ape Maro: "His own punishment covers Ballista, the road through the shadows is safe". (Trans. Ziolkowski and Putnam, adapted)

Phocas here presumes to do to Vergil's lines precisely the same thing the latter poet is said to do to his own works, working them steadily down from a longer size to brevity. Of course, this is also the place where *VSD* includes the mother bear analogy already mentioned, providing yet another key moment of work-life fusion that lurks in the background of Phocas' account. The presence of the generative analogy that Phocas takes on, ironic in the context of shortening an epitaph, is further enlivened by an echo of the tree nurtured by a brief time (*tempore … brevi*)—the only other time that the word *brevis* appears in the poem, there also in the middle of the line. The elegiac form of the epitaph perhaps performs this act of temporal thievery by evoking the way in which Cupid purloins a foot from Ovid's would-be epic poetry, turning it into the limping meter.[53] The analogy is also bolstered by the fact that, according to Phocas, Ballista's demise provided guidance to the "rough" young poet and his hesitant tongue (*tum Ballista rudem lingua titubante receptum/instituit primus*, 65–6). *rudis* is a word often used in poetry to describe unworked raw materials.[54] In a complicated progression, then, Vergil is figured as taking life and form from his parents, from Ballista, and from Phocas, who is also a kind of parental thief of work and life.

To conclude then, while Vergil in his *Eclogues* seemingly grafts the growth of plants into his metaliterary representation of the nature of his and his characters' work, Phocas channels Vergil's own life into a similar meditation. All throughout his poem, Phocas blurs the distinction between *ars* and *vita*, between *labor* and life, and ultimately between *Life* (biography) and life (vitality). He molds the memory of the poet's life and reshapes his work in his own image. This activity was indeed announced in the poem's opening Sapphic hymn, when Phocas celebrates the Muse, who "restores the aging titles of the elders with the flower of enduring youth" (*tu senescentes titulus avorum/flore durantis reparas iuventae*, 13–4). Phocas steps into this role, too, operating as a kind of metaliterary Venus enacting the generative power of parent, poet, and poem, manifesting life through his literary.[55] The power of the biographer enables him to reanimate the poet and to channel the vitality of the reanimated being into his own work. In so doing, he succeeds in writing not only the poet's *bios*, but his *zōē*, or bare life, as well.

The Veterinarian and the Prince

The amply theorized concept of bare life, or *zōē*, which was just introduced at the end of the last section, has been useful in each of these sections as it was earlier in this volume for Formisano's reading of Arachne's unwilling labor. In the first section, drawing on vegetal metaphor, we witnessed Vergil connecting life and work through imitation and growth. Phocas produces a similar connection by inviting us to consider the literary *Vita* as embodying some of the same elements of the lived life of the great poet. In this section, we will consider how a different set of biographies figure Vergil's vulnerable body in relation to the power of the main supporter of his work, namely, Augustus. In this sense, we turn to a sense of *zōē* as it is commonly deployed in the context of political thought and apply it to the biographical.

Georgio Agamben, in his account of power of the state over the lives of individuals, regarded the Roman institution of the *homo sacer* as the punishment of having everything stripped away from someone except their bare life, or *zōē*. As Agamben himself notes, Roman elegiac poets described themselves as *sacer* as a way to describe how they are set apart from the norms of the law, subject instead to the laws of *amor*.[56] In a recent monograph, Ziogas has demonstrated this is in fact a complex posturing in which the body of the elegiac *ego* is positioned between "the utter hopelessness of bare life and the absolute power of sovereignty."[57] In this section, I want to consider a few examples of how the Vergilian biographies treat the body of Vergil as caught up in the same tension, as the poet's working life is at the disposal of the *princeps*. It is well known that *VSD* and later biographies make Augustus at least partially complicit in Vergil's death (*VSD* 35–6). Augustus' return to Rome from an eastern campaign supposedly prompted Vergil to come out of retirement in Greece and Asia Minor and follow the emperor back to the city, during which journey he died in Brundisium from exhaustion. Later biographies, though, offer some interesting complications to this picture and consider the ways in which Augustus was engaged in the preservation of Vergil's working body and body of work. Two illustrative examples will suffice.

Firstly, let us consider a late poem ascribed to Augustus that nullified the poet's will in order to save the *Aeneid* from destruction against the poet's wishes. In this pronouncement, Augustus does not presume to revive Vergil, but rather to save the life of his *Aeneid* and of his literary afterlife by taking advantage of the poet's physical death.[58] Death, as Bodel traces in a difference in a different context in this volume, was a job creator. Augustus cannot allow Vergil's work to be destroyed, even at the expense of violating the sacred obligations of testamentary law. His reasoning, curiously, focuses on the working hours that Vergil spent on the clock (20–3):

> *frangatur potius legum reveranda potestas,*
> *quam tot congestos noctesque diesque labores*
> *auferat una dies, supremaque verba parentis*
> *amittant vigilasse suum.*
>
> It is better that the revered power of the law be broken than that one day take away the built-up labors of so many nights and days, and the final word of the parent/poet sent away his own watch. (Trans. Ziolkowski and Putnam, adapted)

This passage summarizes much of its argument. The emphasis on the value of the hours (*horae*) spent working over time (and working overtime) echoes the connection in other biographies to the incremental growth of Vergil's poem. This detail is anticipated by the emphasis in the preceding section on Vergil's georgic accomplishments in teaching the ways of the seasons (*horae*, 10–11) and of agriculture (12–14). The vital aspect of the *labor* is also signaled when Augustus calls Vergil the "parent" of his words.

The poem opens on an ironic note by asking whether "the great Muse of learned Maro will go into the flames and die" (*ergo ibit in ignes/magnaque doctiloqui morietur Musa Maronis*, 2–3). What it means for the Maronian Muse to burn, and the power of the nullification to save a life real or metaphorical, is even more clear in the striking next section of the poem. Burning the *Aeneid*, Augustus argues, would result in a wave of death and destruction (27–32):

> *iterum sentire ruinas*
> *Troia suas, iterum cogetur reddere †voces†?*
> *ardebit miserae narratrix fama Creusae*
> *sentiet appositos Cumana Sibylla vapores?*
> *uretur Tyriae post funera vulnus Elissae*
> *et iurata mori, ne cingula reddat, Amazon?*
>
> Will Troy once again be compelled to feel her own ruin, to again return cries? Will the storied fame of wretched Creusa burn, or the Cumaean Sibyl feel the vapors set around her? Will the wound of Tyrian Elissa ache after her death along with the Amazon sworn to die lest she return her belt? (Trans. Ziolkowski and Putnam, adapted)

To burn the *Aeneid*, in other words, would result in a reliving of all the deaths-by-fire suffered in the poem, and would even condemn the Sibyl herself to burn. Like the poet who can live on in their literary afterlives, so too do these different characters have an almost autonomous life that would be destroyed thanks to Vergil's will. Vergil, as the "parent" of his poem, is also their parent, and book-burning here is figured as filicide on multiple levels.

The *princeps*' solution to this is to invoke the Pierides not as fonts of inspiration but as divine firefighters (35–8):

> *huc huc, Pierides, date flumina cuncta, sorores;*
> *exspirent ignes, vivat Maro ductus ubique*
> *ingratusque sui stuidorumque invidus orbi*
> *et factus post fata nocens.*
>
> Here here, daughters of Pierus, give all your rivers, sisters: let the fires be extinguished, and let Maro live, brought everywhere, unpleasant to himself and begrudging his efforts to the world and having become harmful after death. (Trans. Ziolkowski and Putnam, adapted)

Augustus was known by ancient authors to have increased the number of firefighters, or *vigiles*, in the city of Rome (Cass. Dio 54.2). Here he deploys this power to extinguish the flames of Troy and save Vergil's living work. He stands in as a negation of the forces of time and decay about which the likes of Ovid and Horace worried in their imagining of a literary afterlife.[59] On the other hand, though, he is also doing the opposite and "saving" time from work, since the nullification is expressly motivated by the intention to preserve the time spent working on the poems.

Our second example comes from the Renaissance-era biography known as the *Vita Donati Aucti* and is the record of an exchange between the poet and *princeps* early on in Vergil's service in Rome. Vergil, according to this biography (*VDA* 8–18), first came to Rome from Naples as a wandering worker, like those discussed by Holleran in this volume, to take up a gig not as a poet but as a veterinary expert in curing horses of various diseases (*multos variosque morbos incidentes equis curavit*, 8). Vergil received a ration of bread for his service, and as he solved more and more important equine problems, Augustus increased the man's ration of bread multiple times. This drew Augustus' attention to the newcomer, and eventually he went to visit Vergil to ask whether he, the *princeps*, was in fact the son of Octavian, since Vergil was an expert at recognizing the sires of animals (*quia canum [et] equi naturam parentesque cognorat*, 12). The biographer reports the dialogue and says that when asked about Augustus' parentage Vergil made the startling claim that, "as far as I can tell, you are the son of a baker" (*quantum rem ego intelligere possum, pistoris filius es*, 17). Of course, this upset Augustus, who seems to have thought not of the life-sustaining power of the baker and instead associated the profession with negative stereotypes like those connected to merchant's in Sancinito's study for this volume. Interrupting his thought, Vergil explained that it appeared that way because Vergil was receiving payment in the form of a generous ration of bread, an *officium* perhaps suited to a baker or baker's son. This joke (*facetia*, 18) pleased Augustus, who guaranteed the man that he would receive the gifts not of a baker, but of a magnanimous king.

This exchange captures the relationship between labor and life as it pertains to the work of the Vergilian biographer. By considering the analogical potential between the work of literature and that of other professions tasked with sustaining life—*vigiles*, bakers, veterinarians, even emperors—the biographies foreground the role in which Vergil's *labor* was about preserving and fostering life in literal and not just metaphorical ways. It imagines Augustus—here, perhaps, as a stand-in for the biographer as life-writer—trying to draw on Vergil's own vital expertise in order to better write his own life. In this way Augustus is a mirror of the biographer who draws on another person's life to save their work. Vergil, instead of using his knowledge of *natura*, considers Augustus' own duty (*officium*) and makes the judgment based on his experience thereof. Vergil demonstrates how a person's works can be observed and, through them, sources can be intuited, lineages traced back, and lives imagined. In a very real way, the baker's work sustains him. Just as Vergil and the biographers collaborate across time to create living works and sustain working lives, so too do Augustus and Vergil play together in the stables, imagining alternate realities and imaginary histories. Thus, in contrast with the more unrelenting scenes from *VSD* in which Augustus ultimtely drives the poet to death, this episode stands out as a culmination of the kind of work/life integration celebrated by the poet, even if the disintegrating power of Augustus' *labor* would eventually undo it all. After all, it is Augustus who, like Simulus in the *Moretum*, holds the keys to the grain cabinet of Rome.[60]

Conclusion

In this chapter, I have considered three different ways in which moments in the Vergilian tradition weave together work and life. Metaphors of growth imbue poems with life, and comparison between the jobs of poet, biographer, *princeps*, fire-fighter, and veterinarian all highlight different ways in which these jobs all involve a different but related form of "life-guarding." The participants in the Vergilian tradition, whether Vergil himself, his characters, or the generations of his heirs, are all compelled toward the Shelleyan "work of life," in which the labor of their hands, their brains, their mothers, and the natural world around them all conspire together toward animation and galvanization. Unlike poets like Ovid and Horace, who hoped for an afterlife in their literary remembrances, Vergil seems to demand something more.[61] Through his thoroughgoing effacement of *labor* and life, captured above all by the figure of the growing plant, Vergil seems to set himself up for continued growth in the *silvae* he labored in life to grow. Vergil's own writings do this, as do the biographers' efforts to represent his relationships with sources, patrons, and his own books. To borrow the schema of the biographer quoted at the head of this chapter, it involves reading the poet as vernal Vergil and not just as Virgil the *virga*.

By way of conclusion, we may contrast the work/life integration effected in the Vergilian tradition with another well-known ancient work composed in the wake of a poet's death: the *Lament for Bion*, dubiously attributed to the poet Moschus. Throughout this work, the participation of plants, animals, and elements in the mourning for Bion comes in multiple forms, and there is emphasis throughout the poem on mourning nature failing to behave as it should, with plants, animals, and divinities experiencing disruption in the flow of their natural lives, seemingly stunned with grief over the beloved poet's death. But in contrast to all this, there is a poignant turn at the end of the poem (99–107):[62]

> αἰαῖ ταὶ μαλάχαι μέν, ἐπὰν κατὰ κᾶπον ὄλωνται,
> ἠδὲ τὰ χλωρὰ σέλινα τό τ' εὐθαλὲς οὖλον ἄνηθον
> ὕστερον αὖ ζώοντι καὶ εἰς ἔτος ἄλλο φύοντι·
> ἄμμες δ' οἱ μεγάλοι καὶ καρτεροί, οἱ σοφοὶ ἄνδρες,
> ὁππότε πρᾶτα θάνωμες, ἀνάκοοι ἐν χθονὶ κοίλᾳ
> εὕδομες εὖ μάλα μακρὸν ἀτέρμονα νήγρετον ὕπνον.
> καὶ σὺ μὲν ὧν σιγᾷ πεπυκασμένος ἔσσεαι ἐν γᾷ,
> ταῖς Νύμφαισι δ' ἔδοξεν ἀεὶ τὸν βάτραχον ᾄδειν.
> ταῖς δ' ἐγὼ οὐ φθονέοιμι, τὸ γὰρ μέλος οὐ καλὸν ᾄδει.

> Alas! When garden mallows die back, or green parsley, or the flourishing curly anise, **they live again and grow another year**; but we men, great and strong and wise, as soon as we die, unhearing **in the hollow earth** we sleep a long, an endless, an unwaking sleep. And so you, surrounded by silence, will be in the earth, while the Nymphs deem it right for the frog to croak forever. But I feel no envy: that song is not a good one. (Trans. Hopkinson, adapted)

Here, in the poem's closing lines, a distinction is drawn between the singer and the natural world that mourns for him. Contrary to the common reading of this poem as a hallmark example of the pathetic fallacy at work, human life and human song are not projected onto insensate nature.[63] In fact, after so much emphasis on the effects of Bion's death on the world, this turn in the poem emphasizes the fact that all this mourning would ultimately be temporary. Though plants and animals will continue to live and grow (ὕστερον αὖ ζώοντι καὶ εἰς ἔτος ἄλλο φύοντι), albeit, perhaps, silent without Bion or at least productive of a less worthy song, the human is consigned to die and, lying beneath the earth, also be silent (ὧν σιγᾷ πεπυκασμένος ἔσσεαι ἐν γᾷ). Rather than simply incorporating the natural world into sadness for the dead, the lament ultimately reifies the futility and impermanence of lament as it echoes amid the trees. Our poet's Bion fails even to achieve the cyclical, quasi-vegetal return of Adonis, which the historical Bion nodded to at the end of *Lament for Adonis*.[64] Even if his song is successfully sung in hell, it would not be heard on the world above by the plants that quietly continue to grow or the frogs that croak loudly amid them.

Without accents and lower-case letters, there is no difference in a Greek phrase like Βίων τέθνακεν ὁ βουκόλος (11) between the present active participle βιῶν (living) and the name Βίων (Bion). In this way, the poet's work and life grow together like the name of Vergilius "*vere gliscens*" Maro. But unlike Bion, Vergil in his afterlife does not suffer the silent indifference of nature. His work continues to expand with it and draw in its energy. It is indeed appropriate in contemporary physics that the technical term "work" refers to any "transfer of energy that takes place from a microscopic to celestial scale."[65] Work, in this sense of energy transferal, is essential to life lived, as it has to be, in the presence of other lives. "To work," to quote James Suzman's recent deep history of work, "is to live." This is true from microbes, frogs, ancient Romans, medieval biographers, and modern philologists, all of whom are brought together in the vibrant ecosystem of Vergilian *labor*.

Notes

1. Shelley in Feldman and Scott-Kilvert (1987: 559).
2. Many thanks to Talitha Kearey, Jordan Rogers, and Ben Nikota for reading drafts of this piece and providing very helpful feedback. Thanks also to Patrick Penso, who was my research assistant in the 2022–2023 academic year at Vassar College, and who helped me with bibliography and copyediting.
3. On the debate, see Flickinger (1930).
4. Ziolkowski and Putnam (2008: 237) call this life the *Periochae Bernenses II*. It was formally called the *Argumentum Bernense*. See Ziolkowski and Putnam (2008: 237–242) for the text and translation. Biographical speculation over Vergil's name goes back to the earliest biographies (cf. *VSD* 3, for instance).
5. I am not the first to observe this. On the connection between Vergilian work and plant growth, see, e.g., Armstrong (2019: 41–9) and Putnam (1970: 387–9).
6. See, e.g., Armstrong (2019: 15–8), Apostol (2015), and Saunders (2008) for different approaches to applying so-called ecocritical theory to Vergil. For more broadly on ecocritical classics, see Schliephake (2022). For a moral general introduction to this body of theory, see Garrad (2012) and the foundational Rueckert (1996).
7. Ziolkowski and Putnam (2008: xxxiii–xxxvi).

8. From the so-called *Sicco Polenton I*. Zioklowski and Putnam (2008: 326).
9. For recent work on metapoetic trees, see Scarborough (2020) and Henkel (2014), with bibliography. This is rooted in a tradition of readings of pastoral landscapes as idealized "landscapes of the mind," or "Muse's gardens" that reflect imaginary rather than real, living nature. See Berg (1974), Leach (1974), and Snell (1953). For the roots of this idea in German philology, see Schmidt (2008). For different approach to the plantlike nature of georgic labor, see Gowers (2016) on ways in which the presence of intoxicating plants adds a dynamic of Dionysiac waywardness to the mix.
10. Claudia Zatta has recently explored how Ovid engages with archaic Greek theories of plant and animal life. See Zatta (2016) as well as Zatta (2019) on Presocratic fragments.
11. Various authors in this volume have situated work in different spaces and environments—this is, it turns out, essential to the work of *Working Lives*. For work in domestic contexts, see Geue and Bodel; in urban settings, see Rogers and Sausville; for itinerant movement between cities, see Holleran; and for the learning environments of Roman craftsmen, see Cheung.
12. Cf. also *Geo*. 2.371–2. Text of the *Eclogues* is the OCT. Translations are my own unless otherwise indicated.
13. See, e.g., Theophr., *Enquiry into Plants* 1.1.4: "[A] plant has the power of growth in all its parts, inasmuch as it has life in all its parts (πανταχῇ γὰρ βλαστητικὸν ἅτε καὶ πανταχῇ ζῶν)" (trans. Hort). Cf. also [Arist.] *On Plants* 1 816a2–3, on the plant as ζῶν but not a ζῷον.
14. Though, as I will discuss below, this collaboration is often mediated through violence and power imbalance.
15. On the English word, see *OED* 8. On *labor* as birth pains, see *TLL* s.v. 1B. See, e.g., Plaut. *Amphy*. 488, V. *Geo*. 4.340, Sen. *Phoen*. 536, Gell. 12.1.4, and Claud. *DRP* 1.193.
16. Geue in this volume accounts for a more protracted erotics of *labor* in the *Moretum*.
17. Cf. esp. 1.145–6: *labor omnia uicit/improbus*.
18. For various readings of *labor* in Vergil, see, e.g., Geue (2018) (a Marxist critique), Gale (2000: 143–195) (on the influence of Lucretius), and Jenkyns (1993) (on optimistic vs. pessimistic readings).
19. On the elite associations of *otium*, see Kuttner in this volume.
20. See Wray (2007) and Henkel (2014).
21. On this play on "wood" and "woods" in Statius' *Silvae*, see Wray (2007).
22. Of course, this line also "echoes" the openings of *Ecl*. 1, the song of Mopsus in *Ecl*. 5.28–44, and the complex soundscapes of *Ecl*. 6.10–15.
23. On the pathetic fallacy, see Buller (1981).

24. In recent years, philosophers and anthropologists have become increasingly interested in plant cognition and communication. See, e.g., Kohn (2013) and Marder (2013). Relatedly, Sheldrake 2020 elegantly discusses mycelial networks and their role in information sharing among plants.
25. On the collection of acorns for winter fodder, see also *Geo.* 1.305.
26. See, e.g., *Ecl.* 2 and *Aen.* 6.883–6 for the common motif of using flowers to symbolize youth in Vergil. On the roots of this link between vegetal imagery and youth in archaic Greek lyric, see Brockliss (2018).
27. See also *Ecl.* 6.20–22 with Clausen (1994): *ad loc.* on the painting of Pan with the juice of berries.
28. Conte ([1986] 2008: 237). See Callim. fr. 73 Pf. For other attestations of this motif, see Clausen (1994): *ad loc.* 53–4. The tree-writing scenes have been frequently studied in literature, with most scholars arriving at similar metapoetic conclusions. See Buckler and Haye (2018) with earlier bibliography.
29. Dyer (1969). See *Geo.* 2.18–9 *etiam Parnasia Laurus/parua sub ingenti matris se subicit umbra.*
30. Henkel (2014: 40–1). See also Henkel (2009: 159–61).
31. It is possible that even a fourth method of engaging with *materia* is suggested too. The plaiting scene in *Idyll* 1 takes place in an *ekphrastic* description of an image engraved into a wooden bowl.
32. On this pun of *arbor* and *ardor*, see Prop. 1.18.19. For similar wordplay in English, see Nabokov's *Ada, or Ardor* [1969] 1990: 159: "Last night I tried to make a poem about it for you, but I can't write verse; it begins, it only begins: Ada, our ardors and arbors—but the rest is all fog, try to fancy the rest."
33. Putnam (1970: 388). For interpretations of *surgamus* as departure, see, e.g., Jenkyns (1989: 35) and Berg (1974: 189).
34. See, e.g., Goldschmidt (2019), Powell and Hardie (2017), and Fletcher and Hanink (2016). Graziosi (2002) was an important milestone in the development of this work, as was Lefkowitz (1981), which was one of the earliest studies of ancient biographies of poets as an inventive fictionalizing genre. In contrast to this approach, see Horsfall (1995), which critiques the lives of Vergil as useful sources on the historical poet. Most recently, Kearey (2019) has engaged in cutting edge works on the ancient depiction of Vergil as a poet at work.
35. For the text, see Ziolkowski and Putnam (2008: 206–9).
36. On this poem, see Harrison (2017), McGill (2010, 2017), Ziolkowski and Putnam (2008: 205–6), Vidal (1991, 2002), Brugnoli (1984, 1988).
37. For the Latin text of the biographies, I cite from Brugnoli and Stok (1997).
38. It is tempting to speculate that line 25 may contain a verbal echo to the description of Maeonian Arachne in Ov. *Met.* 6.103 (*Maeonis elusam …*).

Arachne's mother is said by Ovid to have died and her father supplied her dyed wool. On this section, see Formisano in this volume.

39. Cf. *VSD* 1.
40. McGill (2017: 98).
41. See *VSD* 22.
42. As Harrison (2017: 78) notes, the vein metaphor reworks Ov. *Ex Pont.* 2.5.21, where Ovid uses it to refer to waters of inspiration.
43. On the four elements in Vergil, see Hardie (1986: 325–329).
44. Recent theory has explored the implications of childbirth being a kind of labor. McKinnon (2020), for instance, sketches a scheme that she calls "maternal work," which is the productive work of childbirth that takes place in an assemblage of different human and nonhuman agents, including the mother herself, her midwife, possibly her partner, and the baby.
45. See, e.g., *VSD* 3.
46. A reference, of course, to *Aen.* 6.893–898. For connections between paths to the underworld and subterranean waterways, see Connors and Clendenon (2016).
47. On the connection between materiality and maternality in Latin literature, see McAuley (2016: 117). Kearey (2019) looks to this image of poet as mother bear as exemplary of how later Romans depict Vergil as a poet who exerted careful diligence to his poetic compositions.
48. *VSD* 6, *Vita Philargyrii I* 176.1, *Vita Noricensis II* 240.5, *VDA* 7.
49. *Vita Gudiana I* 213.17 *Vita Monacensis* 225.9, *Vita Noricensis I* 237.12, *Vita Vossiana* 266.3.
50. See *DRN* 3.577 (*uitalis sucipit auras*) and 5.857 (*uesci uitalibus auris*). On this allusion, see Harrison (2017: 80–1).
51. For *serenus* in Lucretius, see 1.142, 2.8, 2.150, 2.1094, 2.1100, 3.293, 4.135, 4.212, 6.99, and 6.247. See esp. 4.136–8.
52. This perhaps evokes the epic *ekphraseis* of the world encircled by rivers or Ocean—a fitting frame for a description of the *Maeonii specimen vatis.*
53. See Ov. *Am.* 1.1.3–4.
54. Cf., e.g., *Met.* 1.7.
55. And thus, as Talitha Kearey points out *per litteras*, he presumes to oust not only Vergil but also Lucretius as well!
56. Agamben (1998: 86), qtd. in Ziogas (2021: 56).
57. Ziogas (2021: 49).
58. See Ziolkowski and Putnam (2008: 282–89). The *Life* is known as *Vita Vaticana II.* The poem is also published as *AL* 1.2.145–8, no. 672.
59. See, e.g., Hor. *Od.* 3.30 and *Met.* 15.871–2.
60. See *Mor.*14–5.
61. Cf. Hor. *Od.* 3.30 and Ov. *Met.* 15.871–9.
62. The text is taken from Gow's OCT of the Greek Bucolic poets.

63. Nature in the poem is subject to "humanization" (*Vermenschlichung*) and "ensouling" (*Enseelung*). Mumprecht (1964: 110).
64. 98: "you will weep again in a year" (πάλιν εἰς ἔτος ἄλλο δακρῦσαι).
65. On this definition of work, see Suzman (2021, Chapter 1).

Bibliography

Agamben, G. 1998. Homo Sacer: *Sovereign Power and Bare Life*. D. Heller-Roazen, Trans. Stanford University Press.

Apostol, R. 2015. "*Urbanus es, Corydon*: ecocritiquing town and country in *Eclogue* 2." *Vergilius* 61: 3–28.

Armstrong, R. 2019. *Vergil's Green Thoughts: Plants, Humans, and the Divine*. Oxford University Press.

Berg, W. 1974. *Early Vergil*. Athlone Press.

Brockliss, W. 2018. *Homeric Imagery and the Natural Environment*. Harvard University Press.

Brugnoli, G. 1988. "Osservazioni sulla Vita Vergilii di Foca." *Maia* 40: 153–7.

Brugnoli, G. 1984. *Foca: Vita di Virgilio*. ETS.

Brugnoli, G. and Stok, F, eds. 1997. *Vitae Vergilianae antiquae*. Officina Typographica.

Buller, J. 1981. "The Pathetic Fallacy in Hellenistic Pastoral." *Ramus* 10: 35–52.

Clausen, W, ed. 1994. *Virgil:* Eclogues. Oxford University Press.

Connors, C. and Clendenon, C. 2016. "Mapping Tartaros: Observation, Inference, and Belief in Ancient Greek and Roman Accounts of Karst Terrain." *Classical Antiquity* 35: 147–188.

Conte, G. B. 2008. [1980] "An Interpretation of the Tenth Eclogue." In Volk, K. ed. *Vergil's Eclogues*. 216–244. Oxford University Press.

Dyer, R. R. 1969. "Vergil Eclogue 10.73–74 and the suckering habit of the white alder." *Classical Philology*, 64: 233–234.

Feldman, P. R. and Scott-Kilvert, D., eds. 1987. *The Journals of Mary Shelley, 1814–1844, Vol. 1: 1814–1822*. Oxford University Press.

Fletcher, R. and Hanink, J., eds. 2016. *Creative Lives in Classical Antiquity: Poets, Artists, Biographers*. Cambridge University Press.

Flickinger, R. C. 1930. "Vergil or Virgil?" *CJ* 25: 658–660.

Gale, M. 2000. *Virgil on the Nature of Things: The Georgics, Lucretius and the Didactic Tradition*. Cambridge University Press.

Garrad, G. 2012. Ecocriticism. Routledge.

Geue, T. 2018. "Soft Hands, Hard Power: Sponging off the Empire of Leisure (Virgil, *Georgics* 4)." *JRS* 108: 115–40.

Goldschmidt, N. 2019. *Afterlives of the Roman Poets: Biofiction and the Reception of Latin Poetry*. Cambridge University Press.

Gowers, E. 2016. "Under the Influence: Maecenas and Bacchus in Georgics 2." In Hardie, P. ed. *Augustan Poetry and the Irrational.* 134–155. Oxford University Press.

Graziosi, B. 2002. *Inventing Homer: The Early Reception of Epic.* Cambridge University Press.

Hardie, P. R. 1986. *Vergil's* Aeneid*: Cosmos and Imperium.* Oxford University Press.

Harrison, S. 2017. "The *Vita Phocae*: literary contexts and texture." In Powell and Hardie: 73–91.

Henkel, J. 2009. *Writing Poems on Trees: Genre and Metapoetics in Vergil's* Eclogues *and* Georgics. Ph.D. Dissertation: UNC Chapel Hill.

Henkel, J. 2014. "Vergil Talks Technique: Metapoetic Arboriculture in *Georgics* 2." *Vergilius* 60: 33–66.

Horsfall, N. 1995. "Virgil: His Life and Times." In Horsfall, N., ed. *A Companion to the Study of Virgil.* 1-25. Brill.

Jenkyns, R. 1993. "*Labor improbus.*" *Classical Quarterly* 43: 243–8.

Jenkyns, R. 1989. "Virgil and Arcadia." *JRS* 79: 26–39.

Kearey, T. E. Z. 2019. *The Poet at Work: Concepts of Authorship in the Ancient Reception of Virgil.* PhD Dissertation. Cambridge University.

Kohn, E. 2013. *How Forests Think: Toward an Anthropology Beyond the Human.* University of California Press.

Leach, E. W. 1974. *Vergil's* Eclogues: *Landscapes of Experience.* Cornell University Press.

Lefkowitz, M. 1981. *The Lives of the Greek Poets.* Johns Hopkins University Press.

Marder, M. 2013. *Plant-Thinking: A Philosophy of Vegetal Life.* Columbia University Press.

McAuley, M. 2016. *Reproducing Rome: Motherhood in Virgil, Ovid, Seneca, and Statius.* Oxford: Oxford University Press.

McGill, S. 2017. "Larger than life: The elevation of Virgil in Phocas' *Vita Vergiliana.*" In Powell and Hardie: 93–114.

McGill, S. 2010. "Another man's miracles: Recasting Aelius Donatus in Phocas' Life of Virgil." In McGill, S, and Watts, E., eds. *From the Tetrarchs to the Theodosians: Later Roman history and culture, 284–450 CE.* 153–170. Cambridge University Press.

McKinnon, K. 2020. *Birthing Work: The Collective Labour of Childbirth.* Palgrave.

Mumprecht, V., ed. 1964. *Epitaphios Bionos.* Juris Verlag.

Powell, A. and Hardie, P. R., eds. 2017. *The Ancient Lives of Virgil: Literary and Historical Studies.* Classical Press of Wales.

Putnam, M. C. J. 1970. *Virgil's Pastoral Art: Studies in the Eclogues.* Princeton University Press.

Rueckert, W. 1996. "Literature and Ecology: An Experiment in Ecocriticism." In Glotfelty, C. and Fromm, H., eds. *The Ecocriticism Reader.* The University of Georgia Press. 105–123.

Saunders, T. 2008. *Bucolic Ecology: Virgil's Eclogues and the Environmental Literary Tradition*. Duckworth.

Scarborough, J. 2020. "*Silva Sonans: The Metapoetic Pastoral Landscape in Vergil's Georgics*." *Vergilius* 66: 3–34.

Schliephake, C. 2022. "Profile: Ecocriticism and Ancient Environments." *Classical Review* 72.2: 393–6.

Schmidt, E. A. 2008. "The German Rediscovery of Vergil in the Early 20th Century (1900–1938)." *Vergilius* 54: 124–149.

Sheldrake, M. 2020. *Entangled Life: How Fungi Make our Worlds, Change our Minds and Shape our Futures*. Random House.

Snell, B. 1953. "Arcadia: The Discovery of a Spiritual Landscape." In *The Discovery of the Mind*. 281–309. Rosenmeyer, T. Trans. Harvard University Press.

Suzman, J. 2021. *Work: A Deep History, from the Stone Age to the Age of Robots*. Penguin.

Vidal, J. L. 2002. "Intención de autor y estilo de la época en la composición de la *vita Vergilii* de Focas." In Walz, D., ed. *Scripturus Vitam: Lateinische Biographie von der Antike bis in die Gegenwart: Festgabe für Walter Berschin zum 65. Geburtstag*. 663–72. Heidelberg.

Vidal, J. L. 1991"La Vita Vergiliana de Focas: Biograpfia y poesía de escuela." *ExcPhilol*. I: 801–12.

Wray, D. 2007. "Wood: Statius's *Silvae* and the Poetics of Genius." *Arethusa* 40(2): 127–143.

Zatta, C. 2019. *Interconnectedness: The Living World of the Early Greek Philosophers*. Academia Verlag.

Zatta, C. 2016. "Plants' Interconnected Lives: From Ovid's Myths to Presocratic Thought and Beyond." *Arion* 24.2: 101–126.

Ziogas, I. 2021. *Law and Love in Ovid: Courting Justice in the Age of Augustus*. Oxford University Press.

Ziolkowski, J. and Putnam, M. C. J., eds. 2008. *The Virgilian Tradition: The First Fifteen-Hundred Years*. Yale University Press.

Bibliography

Abaecherli-Boyce, A. L. 1935–6. "Fercula, carpenta and tensae in the Roman procession." *Bollettino dell'Associazione degli Studi Mediterranei* 6: 1–20.

Adam, J. P. 2005. *Roman Building: Materials and Techniques*. Routledge.

Adams, Z. 2020. *Labour and the Wage: A Critical Perspective.* Oxford University Press.

Agamben, G. 1998. Homo Sacer: *Sovereign Power and Bare Life.* D. Heller-Roazen, Trans. Stanford University Press.

Agusta-Boularot, S. 1994. "Les références épigraphiques aux *Grammatici* et *Γραμ ματικοὶ* de l'Empire romain (1er s. av. J.-C., Ive s. ap. J.-C.)." *MÉFRA* 106 (2): 653–746.

Albert, K. 2012. "Ceramic Rivet Repair: History, Technology, and Conservation Approaches." *Studies in Conservation* 57, sup1: S1–S8.

Alekou, S. 2022. "Law in Disguise in the Metamorphoses: The Ambiguous Ecphraseis of Minerva and Arachne." In Ziogas, I. and Bexley, E. eds. *Roman Law and Latin Literature.* 227–248. Bloomsbury.

Alekou, S. 2021. "Underneath the Arachnean and Minervan Veil of Ambiguity: Cultural and Political *Simulatio* in Ovidian Ecphrasis." In Vöhler, M., Fuhrer, T., and Frangoulidis, S., eds. *Strategies of Ambiguity in Ancient Literature.* 175–192. De Gruyter.

Alexiou, M. 2002. *The Ritual Lament in Greek Tradition*, 2nd ed. revised by D. Yatromanolakis. Lanham.

D. A. Maticic, J. Rogers (eds.), *Working Lives in Ancient Rome*, The New Antiquity,
https://doi.org/10.1007/978-3-031-61234-3

Ali, N. and Guidetti, M. 2017. "Umayyad Palace Iconography: On the Practical Aspects of Artistic Creation." In George, A. and Marsham, A. eds. *Power, Patronage, and Memory in Early Islam: Perspectives on Umayyad Elites.* Oxford University Press.

Allen, A. 2010. "Virgil's Acquisitive Bees." *Classical Quarterly* 60.1: 258–61.

Amarger, M.P. 2009. "Le meilleur et le pire serviteur de l'humanité.' Fer, forges et forgerons à Pompéi." In Brun, J.-P. ed. *Artisanats antiques d'Italie et de Gaule: Mélanges offerts à Maria Francesca Buonaiuto.* Publications du Centre Jean Bérard.

Amarger, M.P. and Brun, J-P. 2007. "La forge dell'insula I, 6, 1 de Pompéi." *Quaderni di studi pompeiani* 1: 147–68.

Ambrosini, L. 2014. "Images of artisans on Etruscan and Italic gems." *Etruscan Studies* 17.2: 172–191.

Anderson, J.C. 1997. *Roman Architecture and Society.* John Hopkins Press.

André, J-M. and M-F. Baslez, 1993. *Voyager dans l'Antiquité.* Fayard.

Andrews, M. 2015. *Matron, Meretrix, Madonna: Archaeology and Urban History of the Cispian Hill in Rome from the Republic through the Early Middle Ages.* Ph.D. dissertation, University of Pennsylvania.

Aneziri, S. 2020. "Artists of Dionysius: the first professional associations in the ancient Greek world." In Stewart, Harris, and Lewis, eds. *Skilled Labour and Professionalism in Ancient Greece and Rome,* 293–312. Cambridge University Press

Angelova, D. 2015. *Sacred Founders: Women, Men, and Gods in the Discourse of Imperial Founding, Rome Through Early Byzantium.* University of California Press.

Apostol, R. 2015. "*Urbanus es, Corydon*: ecocritiquing town and country in *Eclogue* 2." *Vergilius* 61: 3–28.

Appadurai, A, ed. 1986. *The Social Life of Things: Commodities in Cultural Perspective* Cambridge University Press.

Arendt, H. 1998. *The Human Condition, 2nd edition.* The University of Chicago Press.

Arendt, H. 1958. *The Human Condition.* University of Chicago Press.

Armstrong, J. and Cohen, S., eds. 2022. *Crafting Connections: Production, Trade, and Community in Pre-Roman Italy, 900–400 BCE.* Routledge.

Armstrong, R. 2019. *Vergil's Green Thoughts: Plants, Humans, and the Divine.* Oxford University Press.

Bachvarova, M. 2008. "Sumerian Gala Priests and Eastern Mediterranean Returning Gods: Tragic Lamentation in Cross-Cultural Perspective." In Suter, A. ed. *Lament: Studies in the Ancient Mediterranean and Beyond.* 18–52. Oxford University Press.

Bader, P. 2014. "The identity, legal status and origin of the Roman army's medical staff in the imperial age." in Maire, B. ed. *'Greek' and 'Roman' in Latin Medical Texts.* 43–59, Brill.

Bagnani, G. 1953. "The tomb of Patro." *AJA* 57.2: 104.

Bakır-Barthel, S. and Helmut Müller. 1979. "Inschriften aus der Umgebung von Saittai (II)," *ZPE* 36: 163–194.

Ballestra-Puech, S. 2006. Métamorphoses d'Arachné. L'artiste en araignée dans la littérature occidentale. Droz.

Bang, P. 2009. *The Roman Bazaar: A Comparative Study of Trade and Markets in a Tributary Empire.* Cambridge University Press.

Baldwin, C. 1993. *Great and Noble Jar: Traditional Stoneware of South Carolina.* University of Georgia Press.

Barringer, T. 2005. *Men at Work: Art and Labour in Victorian Britain.* Yale University Press.

Barton, C. 2002. "Being in the eyes: shame and sight in ancient Rome." In Fredrick, D. C. ed. *The Roman gaze: vision, power, and the body.* 216–235. Johns Hopkins University Press.

Beard, M. 2002. "Ciceronian Correspondences: Making a Book out of Letters." In Wiseman, T.P. ed. *Classics in Progress: Essays on Ancient Greece and Rome.* 103–44. Oxford University Press.

Beauvoir, S. 2011. *The Second Sex.* Translated by Constance Borde and Sheila Malovany-Chevallier. Vintage Books.

Bellei, Francesca. Forthcoming. "The Nose at the Crossroads: An Intersectional Reading of the Pseudo-Virgilian Moretum."

Benton, J. 2020. *The Bread Makers: The Social and Professional Lives of Bakers in the Western Roman Empire.* Palgrave Macmillan.

Bentz, M. and Kästner, U., eds. 2006. *Konservieren oder restaurieren: Die Restaurierung griechischer Vasen von der Antike bis heute, Beihefte zum Corpus vasorum antiquorum, 3* Beck.

Berg, W. 1974. *Early Vergil.* Athlone Press.

Bergmann, B. 1994. "The Roman House as Memory Theater: The House of the Tragic Poet in Pompeii." *Art Bulletin* 76: 225–56.

Bergmann, B. and Kondoleon, C. eds. 1999. *The Art of Ancient Spectacle.* National Gallery of Art.

Bernard, H.J-C. Bessac, P. Mardikian, and M. Feugère. 1988. "L'épave romaine de marbre de Porto Novo." *JRA* 11: 53–81.

Bernard, S. 2023. "The Premium for Skilled Labor in the Roman World." *Explorations in Economic History.* https://doi.org/10.1016/j.eeh.2023.101516.

Bevan, A. and E. Bloxam, 2016. "Stonemasons and craft mobility in the Bronze Age Eastern Mediterranean." in Kiriatzi, E. and Knappet, C. eds. *Human Mobility and Technological Transfer in the Prehistoric Mediterranean.* 68–93. Cambridge University Press.

Blackwell, N. G. 2014. "Making the lion gate relief at Mycenae: Tool marks and foreign influence." *AJA* 118.3: 451–488.

Blasi, M. 2012. *Strategie funerarie. Onori funebri pubblici e lotta politica nella Roma medio e tardorepubblicana (230–27 a.C.)* Università La Sapienza.

Bliquez, L. 2014. *The Tools of Asclepius. Surgical Instruments in Greek and Roman Times.* Brill.

Blitzer, H. 1990. "ΚΟΡΩΝΕΪΚΑ: Storage-Jar Production and Trade in the Traditional Aegean." *Hesperia: The Journal of the American School of Classical Studies at Athens* 59.4: 675–711.

Bober, P. and Rubinstein, R. 1986. *Renaissance Artists and Antique Sculpture: A Handbook of Sources.* Harvey Miller.

Bodel, J. 2004. "The Organization of the Funerary Trade at Puteoli and Cumae", in Panciera, S. ed. *Libitina e dintorni.* 149–70. Quasar.

Bodel, J. 2000. "Dealing with the Dead: Undertakers, Executioners, and Potter's Fields in Ancient Rome." In E. Marshall, and Hope, V. eds. *Death and Disease in the Ancient City.* 128–51. Routledge.

Bodel, J. 1999a. "Punishing Piso." *American Journal of Philology* 120: 43–63.

Bodel, J. 1999b. "Death on Display: Looking at Roman Funerals." In Bergmann, B. and Kondoleon, C. eds., *The Art of Ancient Spectacle.* 258–81. NGW Stud Hist Art.

Boëls-Janssen, N. 1993. *La vie religieuse des matrons dans la Rome archaïque.* École Française de Rome.

Bogen, D. 1992. "Ignoring History: The Liability of Ships' Masters, Innkeepers, and Stablekeepers under Roman Law." *The American Journal of Legal History* 36.3: 326–360.

Bollmann, B. 1998. *Römische Vereinshäuser: Untersuchungen zu den Scholae der römischen Berufs-, Kult- und Augustalen-Kollegien in Italien.* Zabern.

Bond, S. E. 2016. *Trade and taboo: Disreputable professions in the Roman Mediterranean.* University of Michigan Press.

Bonfante, L. 1986. "Daily Life and Afterlife." In Bonfante, L. ed., *Etruscan Life and Afterlife: A Handbook of Etruscan Studies.* 232–78. Wayne State University Press.

Bordenache Battaglia, G., and Emiliozzi, A. 1979. *Le ciste prenestine.* Vol. 1. *Corpus.* Consiglio Nazionale Delle Richerche.

Borgia, E. 2012. "Attestazioni epigrafiche di mestieri legati alla costruzione nell'Asia Minore romana e proto-bizantina: Specializzazioni e ruolo sociale." In Camporeale, S. et al., eds. *Arqueología de la construccíon III. Los procesos constructivos en el mundo romano: La economía de las obras.* 53–68. Mérida.

Bourdieu, P. 1977. *Outline of a Theory of Practice.* Translated by Richard Nice. Cambridge University Press.

Bowes, K. 2021a. "When Kuznets Went to Rome: Roman Economic Well-Being and the Reframing of Roman History." *Capitalism* 2.1: 7–40.

Bowes, K.. ed. 2021b. *The Roman Peasant Project 2009–2014: Excavating the Rural Poor.* University of Pennsylvania Press.

Bowes, K.. ed. 2021c. "Tracking Consumption at Pompeii: The Graffiti Lists." *JRA* 34.2: 552–84.

Bowman, A. and Wilson, A., eds. 2009. *Quantifying the Roman Economy: Methods and Problems.* Oxford University Press.

Boyer, R. et al. 1990. "Découverte de la tombe d'un oculiste à Lyon (fin due IIe siècle apres J.C.) Instruments et coffret avec collyres." *Gallia* 47: 215–49.

Brannick, M. T., Levine, E.L., and Morgenson, F. P. 2007. *Job and Work Analysis: Methods, Research, and Applications for Human Resource Management.* Sage Publishing.

Brenni, G. M. R. 1985. "The *dolia* and the Sea-Borne Commerce of Imperial Rome." Unpublished Master's Thesis, Texas A&M University.

Brockliss, W. 2018. *Homeric Imagery and the Natural Environment.* Harvard University Press.

Bryen, A. 2013. *Violence in Roman Egypt: a Study in Legal Interpretation.* University of Pennsylvania Press.

Brubaker, L. 1999. "The Chalke gate, the construction of the past, and the Trier Ivory." *Byzantine and Modern Greek Studies* 23: 258–85.

Brubaker, L. 2002. "The Vienna Dioskorides and Anicia Juliana." In Littlewoood, A., Maguire, H. and Wolschke-Buhlman, J. eds. *Byzantine Garden Culture.* 189–214. Dumbarton Oaks Research Library and Collection.

Brugnoli, G. 1988. "Osservazioni sulla Vita Vergilii di Foca." *Maia* 40: 153–7.

Brugnoli, G. 1984. *Foca: Vita di Virgilio.* ETS.

Brugnoli, G. and Stok, F, eds. 1997. *Vitae Vergilianae antiquae.* Officina Typographica.

Brun, J.-P., et al. 2005. "Pompéi, Herculanum (Naples) et Saepinum (Molise): recherches sur l'artisanat antique." *Mélanges de l'École française de Rome. Antiquité* 117.5: 317–339.

Brunt, P.A. 1971 *Italian Manpower 225 BC–AD 14.* Oxford University Press.

Buckler, D. and Hay, P. 2018. "Dendroepigraphy: Botanical Realities in a Bucolic Motif." *CJ* 114.1: 35–58.

Buller, J. 1981. "The Pathetic Fallacy in Hellenistic Pastoral." *Ramus* 10: 35–52.

Buraselis, K. 2000. *Kos Between Hellenism and Rome: Studies on the Political, Institutional and Social History of Kos from ca. the Middle Second Century B.C. Until Late Antiquity.* American Philosophical Society.

Burford A. 1972. *Craftsmen in Greek and Roman society.* Cornell University Press.

Burford A. 1969. *The Greek Temple Builders at Epidauros.* Liverpool University Press.

Calder, W. M. 1955. "Early-Christian epitaphs from Phyrgia." *Anat.St.* 5: 25–38.

Caldwell, L. 2021. "From Household to Workshop: Women, Weaving and the *Peculium.*" In Longfellow, B. and Swetnam-Burlands, M., eds. *Women's Lives, Women's Voices.* 51–66. University of Texas Press.

Campbell, V. L. 2010. "The Epitaph of Aulus Umbricius Scaurus (CIL X 1024): A Reconsideration." *Zeitschrift für Papyrologie und Epigraphik* 174: 229–236.

Canevaro, M. 2021. "Upside-down hegemony? Ideology and power in ancient Athens," in Zucchetti, E. and Cimino, A.M. eds. *Antonio Gramsci and the Ancient World*. 63–85. Routledge.

Carandini, A., ed. 1985. *Settefinestre. Una villa schiavistica nell'Etruria Romana [Seven Windows: A Slave Villa in Roman Etruria] (Vols 1–3)*. Panini.

Carrato, C. 2017. *Le Dolium, en Gaule Narbonnaise (i^er s. av. J.-C.–iiie s. ap. J.-C.): contribution à l'histoire socio-économique de la Méditerranée nord-occidentale, Collection mémoires, 46*. Ausonius.

Carrato, C. and Cibecchini, F., eds. 2020. *Nouvelles recherches sur les Dolia: l'exemple de la Méditerranée nord-occidentale à l'époque romaine (i^er s. av. J.-C.–iiie s. ap. J.-C.); actes de la table ronde tenue à Aspiran les 26 et 27 septembre 2013*. Éditions de l'Association de la Revue archéologique de Narbonnaise.

Carroll, M. 2022. "Viticulture, opus *dolia*re, and the patrimonium Caesaris at the Roman imperial estate at Vagnari (Puglia)." *Journal of Roman Archaeology* 1–26.

Castagnetti, S. 2012. *Le leges Libitinariae Flegree. Edizione e commento*. Satura editrice.

Cato [Marcus Porcius Cato]. *De agri cultura*. Hooper, W. D. and Ash, H.B. eds and trans. 1934. Marcus Porcius Cato on Agriculture, Marcus Terentius Varro on Agriculture, *Loeb Classical Library, 283*. Harvard University Press.

de Certeau, M. 1984. *The Practice of Everyday Life*. University of California Press.

Chambry, E. 1927. *Fables d'Ésope*. Société d'édition "*Les Belles Lettres*".

Chaniotis, A. 2009. "Travelling memories in the Hellenistic world." in Hunter, R. and Rutherford, I. eds. *Wandering Poets in Ancient Greek Culture: Travel, Locality, and Pan-Hellenism*. 249–269. Cambridge University Press.

Chatterjee, P. 2018. "Iconoclasm's Legacy: Interpreting the Trier Ivory." *Art Bulletin* 100: 28–47.

Chausson, F., ed. 2018. *Claude (Lyon, 10 avant J.-C.—Rome, 54 après J.-C.): Un empereur au destin singulier*. Coédition Liénart.

Cheung, C. Forthcoming. *Dolia: Rome's Wine Storage from Craftsman to Consumer*.

Cheung, C. 2021 (May 22–26, 2018). "Precious Pots: Making and Repairing *Dolia*. [Paper presentation]." 19th International Congress of Classical Archaeology. Cologne/Bonn, Germany.

Cheung, C. and G. Tibbott. 2020. "The *Dolia* of Regio I, Insula 22: Evidence for the Production and Repair of *Dolia*." in Osanna, M and Toniolo, L. eds. *Fecisti Cretaria: Dal frammento al contest; studi sul vasellame ceramic del territorio vesuviano, Studi e ricerche del Parco archeologico di Pompei, 40*. 175–85. 'L'Erma' di Bretschneider.

Chiari, F. 2012. "*Praeficae* e *musici*. I protagonisti "sonori" delle liturgie di morte alto-imperiale." *Ager Veleias* 7.8: 1–19.

Cinaglia, T. 2016. "Le *Quinquatrus*, una festa di Minerva." *Gerión* 34: 145–167.

Claridge, A. 1990. "Ancient Techniques of Making Joins in Marble Statuary." in True, M. and Podany, J. eds. *Marble: Art Historical and Scientific Perspectives on Ancient Sculpture*. 135–62. Paul Getty Museum.

Claridge, A. 2015. "Marble carving techniques, workshops, and artisans." in Friedland, E.A. et al. eds. *The Oxford Handbook of Roman Sculpture*. 107–122. Oxford University Press.

Clarke, J. 2003. *Art in the Lives of Ordinary Romans: Visual Representation and Non-Elite Viewers in Italy, 100 B.C.–A.D. 315*. University of California Press.

Clarke, J. 1991. *The Houses of Roman Italy, 100 B.C–A.D. 250: Ritual, Space, and Decoration*. University of California Press.

Clausen, W, ed. 1994. *Virgil:* Eclogues. Oxford University Press.

Coffee, N. 2017. *Gift and Gain: How Money Transformed Ancient Rome*. Oxford University Press.

Colini, A. M. 1947. "Officina di fabri tignarii nei frammenti di un ara monumentale rinvenuti fra il Campidoglio e il Tevere." *Capitolium* 22: 21–28.

Collins, D., Morduch, J., Rutherford, S. and Ruthven, O. 2009. *Portfolios of the Poor: How the World's Poor Live on $2 a Day*. Princeton University Press.

Connerton, P. 1989. *How Societies Remember*. Cambridge University Press.

Connors, C. and Clendenon, C. 2016. "Mapping Tartaros: Observation, Inference, and Belief in Ancient Greek and Roman Accounts of Karst Terrain." *Classical Antiquity* 35: 147–188.

Conte, G. B. 2008. [1980] "An Interpretation of the Tenth Eclogue." In Volk, K. ed. *Vergil's Eclogues*. 216–244. Oxford University Press.

Cotton, H. 1981. *Documentary Letters of Recommendation in Latin from the Roman Empire*. Anton Hain.

Cooper, F. A. 2008. "Greek Engineering and Construction." in Oleson, J.P., ed. *The Oxford Handbook of Engineering and Technology in the Classical World*. 225–55. Oxford University Press.

Copeland, R. 2001. *Pedagogy, Intellectuals, and Dissent in the Later Middle Ages: Lollardy and Ideas of Learning*. Cambridge University Press.

Corbeill, A. 1996. *Controlling Laughter: Political Humor in the Late Roman Republic*. Princeton University Press.

Courrier, C. and Magalhães de Oliveira, J.C. eds. 2022. *Ancient History from Below: Subaltern Experiences and Actions in Context*. Routledge.

Crawford, M.H., ed. 1996. *Roman Statutes* vol. 2. Institute of Classical Studies.

Cruikshank Dodd, E. 2021. *Byzantine Silver Stamps*. Dumbarton Oaks Institute for Byzantine Studies.

Cuomo, S. 2011. "A Roman engineer's tales." *JRS* 101: 143–165.

Cuomo, S. 2007. *Technology and Culture in Greek and Roman Antiquity*. Cambridge University Press.

Cuvigny, H. 1996. “The amount of wages paid to quarry workers at Mons Claudianus.” *JRS* 86: 139–145.

Dalby, A. 1998. *Cato: On Farming; De agricultura; A Modern Translation with Commentary.* Prospect.

Daly, G. 2002. *Cannae. The Experience of Battle in the Second Punic War.* Routledge.

D’Ambra, E. 2021. “Real Estate for Profit: Julia Felix’s Property and the Forum Frieze.” In Longfellow and Swetnam-Burland: 85–108.

D’Ambra, E. 1993. *Private Lives, Imperial Virtues: The Frieze of the Forum Transitorium in Rome.* Princeton University Press.

D’Ambra, E. 1988. “A Myth for a Smith. A Meleager Sarcophagus from a Tomb in Ostia.” *American Journal of Archaeology* 92: 85–99.

D’Ambra, E. 1987. *Palladis Artes: The Frieze of the Forum Transitorium in Rome.* Ph.D. Diss. Yale University.

D’Ambra, E. and Métraux, G. eds. 2006. *The Art of Citizens, Soldiers and Freedmen in the Roman World.* BAR International Series 1526. BAR Publishing.

D’Arms, J. H. 1981. *Commerce and Social Standing in Ancient Rome.* Harvard University Press.

Davies, P. 2017. *Architecture and Politics in Republican Rome.* Cambridge University Press.

De Angelis, F. 2011. “Playful Workers: The Cupids Frieze in the House of the Vettii.” In Poehler, E., Flohr, M., and Cole, K. eds. *Pompeii: Art, Industry and Infrastructure.* 62–73. Oxbow Books.

DeLaine, J. 2010. “Structural Experimentation: The Lintel Arch, Corbel and Tie in Western Roman Architecture.” *World Archaeology* 21.3: 407–24.

DeLaine, J. 2000. “Building the eternal city: the construction industry of imperial Rome.” in Coulston, J. and Dodge, H., eds. *Ancient Rome: the Archaeology of the Eternal City.* 119–141. Oxford University Press.

DeLaine, J. 1997. “The Baths of Caracalla: A Study in the Design, Construction, and Economics of Large-Scale Building Projects in Imperial Rome.” *Journal of Roman Archaeology Supplementary Series* 25.

De Martino, E. 1958. *Morte e pianto rituale nel mondo antico. Dal lamento funebre al pianto di Maria.* Edizioni scientifiche Einaudi.

D’Ippolito, F. 1978. *I giuristi e la città. Ricerche sulla giurisprudenza romana della repubblica.* Edizioni scientifiche italiane.

Dittmann-Schöne, I. 2001. *Die Berufsvereine in den Städten des kaiserzeitlichen Kleinasiens.* S. Roderer.

Domergue, C. 1990. *Les mines de la péninsule ibérique dans l’Antiquité romaine.* Ecole Française de Rome.

Domingo-Gygax, M. and Zuiderhoek, A., eds. 2020. *Benefactors and the Polis: The Origins and Development of the Public Gift in Greek Cities from the Homeric World to Late Antiquity.* Cambridge University Press.

Donohue, A. A. 1988. *Xoana and the origins of Greek sculpture.* Scholars Press.

Dooijes, R. and Nieuwenhuyse, O.P. 2006. "Ancient Repairs: Techniques and Social Meaning." in Bentz, M. and Kästner, U., eds. *Konservieren oder restaurieren: Die Restaurierung griechischer Vasen von der Antike bis heute, Beihefte zum Corpus vasorum antiquorum, 3.* 15–20. Beck.

Droß-Krüpe, K. 2011. *Wolle—Weber—Wirtschaft: die Textilproduktion der römischen Kaiserzeit im Spiegel der papyrologischen Überlieferung.* Harrassowitz.

Droß-Krüpe, K., Föllinger, S. and Ruffing, K., eds. 2016. *Antike Wirtschaft und ihre kulturelle Prägung—The Cultural Shaping of the Ancient Economy.* Harassowitz.

Dufallo, B. 2013. *The Captor's Image. Greek Culture in Roman Ecphrasis.* Oxford University Press.

Dunbabin, K. 2003a. *The Roman Banquet. Images of Conviviality.* Cambridge University Press.

Dunbabin, K. 2003b. "The Waiting Servant in Later Roman Arts." *American Journal of Philology* 3: 443–68.

Dunbabin, K. 1999. *Mosaics of the Greek and Roman World.* Cambridge University Press.

Dunbabin, K. 1978. *The Mosaics of Roman North Africa: Studies in Iconography and Patronage.* Oxford University Press.

Dutsch, D. 2008. "*Nenia*, Gender, Genre and Lament in Ancient Rome." In Suter: 258–79.

Dyck, A.R. 2003. *A Commentary on Cicero, De Legibus.* University of Michigan Press.

Dyer, R. R. 1969. "Vergil Eclogue 10.73–74 and the suckering habit of the white alder." *Classical Philology*, 64: 233–234.

Eco, U. 1989. *Opera Operta.* Fabbri.

Edwards, C. 1997. "Unspeakable Professions: Public Performance and Prostitution in Ancient Rome." In Hallett, J.P. and Skinner, M.B., eds. *Roman Sexualities.* 66–98. Princeton University Press.

Edwards, C. 1993. *The Politics of Immorality in Ancient Rome.* Cambridge University Press.

Ehmer, J. and Lis, C. eds. 2009. *The Idea of Work in Europe from Antiquity to Modern Times.* Routledge.

Elsner, J. 2018. *The Art of the Roman Empire AD 100–450.* Oxford University Press.

Elsner, J. 1998. *Imperial Rome and Christian Triumph: The Art of the Roman Empire AD 100–450.* Oxford University Press.

Elsner, J. 1995. *Art and the Roman viewer: The Transformation of Art from the Pagan World to Christianity.* Cambridge University Press.

Elsner, J. 1991. "Cult and sculpture: sacrifice in the Ara Pacis Augustae." *The Journal of Roman Studies* 81: 50–61.

Elston, M. 1990. "Ancient Repairs of Greek Vases in the J. Paul Getty Museum." *The J. Paul Getty Museum Journal* 18: 53–68.

Emler, N. 1992. "The Truth about Gossip." *Social Psychology Section Newsletter* 27: 23–37.

Emmerson, A. 2020. *Life and Death in the Roman Suburb.* Oxford University Press.

Engels, J. 1998. *Funerum Sepulcrorumque Magnificentia.* Franz Steiner Verlag.

Epstein, S. 2010. "Attic public construction: Who were the builders?" *Ancient Society* 40: 1–14.

Epstein, S. 2004. "Labour mobility, journeyman organisations and markets in skilled labour in Europe, 14th–18th centuries." in Arnoux, A. and Monnet, P., eds. *Le technicien dans la cite en Europe occidentale 1250–1650.* 251–269. Ecole Française de Rome.

Erdkamp, P. 2001. "Beyond the Limits of the 'Consumer City': A Model of the Urban and Rural Economy in the Roman World." *Historia* 50 (3): 332–356.

Erdkamp, P. and Verboven, K., eds. 2015. *Structure and Performance in the Roman Economy: Models, Methods, and Case Studies.* Latomus.

Erdkamp, P., Verboven, K., and Zuiderhoek, A., eds. 2020. *Capital, Investment, and Innovation in the Roman World.* Oxford University Press.

Erdkamp, P., Verboven, K., and Zuiderhoek, A., eds. 2015. *Ownership and Exploitation of Land and Natural Resources in the Roman World.* Oxford University Press.

Erim, K. T. and C. M. Roueché, 1982. "Sculptors from Aphrodisias: some new inscriptions." *PBSR* 50: 102–115.

Esposito, R. 2008. *Bios. Biopolitics and Philosophy.* Translated by T. Campbell. University of Minnesota Press.

Fabiano, J. 2019. "Builders and integrated associations in fourth-century CE Rome: A new interpretation of AE 1941, 68." *Journal of Late Antiquity* 12: 65–87.

Farrell, J. 2014. "Looking for Empedocles in Latin Poetry: A Skeptical Approach." *Dictynna* 11: np. https://journals.openedition.org/dictynna/1063.

Feeney, D. 1991. *The Gods in Epic. Poets and Critics of the Classical Tradition.* Oxford University Press.

Feige, M. 2021. "Decorative Features and Social Practices in Spaces for Agricultural Production in Roman Villas." In Haug, A. and Lauritsen, M. T. eds. *Principles of Decoration in the Roman World.* 33–52. De Gruyter.

Feldman, P. R. and Scott-Kilvert, D., eds. 1987. *The Journals of Mary Shelley, 1814–1844, Vol. 1: 1814–1822.* Oxford University Press.

Felletti Maj, B. 1977. *La Tradizione Italica Nell'arte Romana.* Bretschneider.

Felski, R. 2015. *The Limits of Critique.* University of Chicago Press.

Ferdi, S. 2005. *Corpus des mosaïques de Cherchel.* CNRS.

Ferdière, A. 2011. "Voyage à travers la Gaule profonde—XV." *Revue archéologique du centre de la France [RACF]* 50: 569–96, http://racf.revues.org/1712.

Ferris, I. 2020 *The Dignity of Labour: Image, Work and Identity in the Roman World*. Amberley Publishing.

Finley, M. 1973. *The Ancient Economy*. University of California Press.

Fitzgerald, W. 2000 *Slavery and the Roman Literary Imagination*. Cambridge University Press.

Fitzgerald, W. 2014. "Labor and Laborer in Latin Poetry: The Case of the *Moretum*." *Arethusa* 29.3: 389–418.

Flemming, R. Forthcoming. *Medicine and Empire in the Roman World*. Cambridge University Press.

Fletcher, R. and Hanink, J., eds. 2016. *Creative Lives in Classical Antiquity: Poets, Artists, Biographers*. Cambridge University Press.

Flickinger, R. C. 1930. "Vergil or Virgil?" *CJ* 25: 658–660.

Flohr, M. 2020. *Urban Space and Urban History in the Roman World*. Routledge.

Flohr, M. 2013. *The World of the Fullo: Work, Economy, and Society in Roman Italy*. Oxford University Press.

Flohr, M. & Bowes, K., eds. Forthcoming. *Valuing Labor in Antiquity*. Brill.

Flohr, M. and Wilson, A. eds. 2017. *The Economy of Pompeii*. Oxford University Press.

Flower, H. I. and DiLuzio, M. J. 2019. "The women and the *lares*: a reconsideration of an Augustan altar from the Capitoline in Rome." *American Journal of Archaeology* 123.2: 213–236.

Fraenkel, E. 1960. *Elementi Plautini in Plauto*. La Nuova Italia Editrice.

Freu, C. 2022. *Les salariés de l'Égypt romano-byzantine. Essai d'histoire économique*. StudPAP 3.

Frier, B. and Kehoe, D. 2007. "Law and Economic Institutions." In Scheidel, W., Morris, I., and Saller, P., eds. *The Cambridge Economic History of the Greco-Roman World*, 113–43.

Fowden, G. 2004. *Qusayr 'Amra: Art and the Ummayad Elite in Late Antique Syria*. University of California Press.

Frankfurter, D. 2017. "Ritual Matters: Afterword." In Moser, C. and Knust, J. eds. *Ritual Matters: Material Remains and Ancient Religions*. 145–150. University of Michigan Press.

Fröhlich, T. 1991. *Lararien- und Fassadenbilder in den Vesuvstädten: Untersuchungen zur "volkstümlichen" pompejanischen Malerei*. Zabern.

Frontisi-Ducroux, F. 2003. L'homme-cerf et la femme-araignée: Figures grecques de la metamorphose. Gallimard.

Gabba, E. 1996. "Dionigi di alicarnasso sull'origine romana del discorso funebre." *SCO* 46: 25–27.

Gaitzsch, W. 1980. *Eiserne römische Werkzeuge: Studien zur römischen Werkzeugkunke in Italien und den nördlichen Provinzen des Imperium Romanum*. British Archaeological Reports.

Gallagher, D. 2009. *Transformations of the Body and the Influence of Ovids' Metamorphoses on Germanic Literature of the Nineteenth and Twentieth Centuries*. Rodopi.

Gale, M. 2000. *Virgil on the Nature of Things: The Georgics, Lucretius and the Didactic Tradition*. Cambridge University Press.

Garachon, I. 2010. "Old Repairs of China and Glass." *The Rijksmuseum Bulletin* 58: 34–55.

Gardner, J. F. 1993. *Being a Roman Citizen*. Routledge.

Garrad, G. 2012. Ecocriticism. Routledge.

Gazda, E. 2021. "Portraits and Patrons: The Women of the Villa of the Mysteries in Their Social Context." In Longfellow and Swetnam Burland: 133–50.

Gazda, E., ed. 2000. *The Villa of the Mysteries in Pompeii: Ancient Ritual, Modern Muse*. Kelsey Museum of Archaeology and the University of Michigan Museum of Art.

Gee, E. 2001. "Cicero's Astronomy," *CQ* 51.2: 520–536.

George, M. 2006. "Social Identity and the Dignity of Work in Freedmen's Reliefs." in D'Ambra, E. and Métraux, G. eds. *The Art of Citizens, Soldiers and Freedmen in the Roman World*. 19–29. BAR Publishing.

Geue, T. 2018. "Soft Hands, Hard Power: Sponging off the Empire of Leisure (Virgil, *Georgics* 4)." *JRS* 108: 115–40.

Gianfrotta, P. A., and Hesnard, A. 1987. "Due Relitti Augustei Carichi di Dolia: Quelli di Ladispoli del Grand Ribaud D." In *El vi a l'antiguitat: Economia, producció i comerç al Mediterrani occidental, I Colloqui d'Arqueologia Romana*, 285–297. Badalona: Museu de Badalona Monogradies Badalonines.

Giannella, N. J. 2024. "The Cost of Ingratitude: Freedmen, Patrons, and Re-enslavement." In MacLean, R., Bell, S., and Borbonus, D. eds. *Freed Persons in the Roman World: Integration, Diversity, and Representation*, eds. R. MacLean, S. Bell, and D. Borbonus. 141–163. Cambridge University Press.

Giannella, N. J. 2019. "The Freedom to Give: The Legal Basis of Seneca's Treatment of Slaves in *de Beneficiis*." *Classical Philology* 114: 79–99.

Giardina, A. 1993. "The Merchant." In Giardina, A., ed. *The Romans*. 245–271. University of Chicago Press.

Giardino, C. 2012. "Archaeometric Analyses of Metal, Glass, and Plaster." in Lapadula, E. ed. *The Chora of Metaponto, iv: The Late Roman Farmhouse at San Biagio*. 194–207. University of Texas Press.

Gibbs, L. (tr.) 2002. *Aesop's Fables. A New Translation*. Oxford University Press.

Giuliano, A., ed. 1979. *Museo Nazionale Romano. Le sculture*. vol. I/1. De Luca Editore.

Gleba, M. 2008. *Textile Production in Pre-Roman Italy*. Oxbow Books.

Glei, R. 1998. "Der interepische poetologische Diskurs: Zum Verhältnis von *Metamorphosen* und *Aeneis*." In Tristram, H. L. C., ed. *Neue Methoden der Epenforschung*. 85–104. Gunter Narr Verlag.

Gluckman, M. 1963. "Papers in Honor of Melville J. Herskovits: Gossip and Scandal." *Current Anthropology* 4, no. 3: 307–316.

Goins, S. E. 1992–3. "Two aspects of Vergil's use of *labor* in the *Aeneid*." *Classical Journal* 88: 375–84.

Goldschmidt, N. 2019. *Afterlives of the Roman Poets: Biofiction and the Reception of Latin Poetry*. Cambridge University Press.

Goodman, P. 2016. "Working Together: Clusters of Artisans in the Roman City." in Wilson, A. and Flohr, M., eds. *Urban Craftsmen and Traders in the Roman World, Oxford Studies on the Roman Economy*. 301–33. Oxford University Press.

Gortz, A. 1988. *Métamorphoses du travail. Critique de la raison économique*. Gallimard.

Gosden, C. 2005. "What Do Objects Want?" *Journal of Archaeological Method and Theory* 12.3: 193–211.

Gowers, E. 2021. "Pun-Fried Concoctions: Wor(l)d-Blending in the Roman Kitchen." In Morales, H., Fantuzzi, M., and Whitmarsh, T. eds. *Reception in the Greco-Roman World: Literary Studies in Theory and Practice*. 241–65. Cambridge University Press. https://doi.org/10.1017/9781108993845.011.

Gowers, E. 2016. "Under the Influence: Maecenas and Bacchus in Georgics 2." In Hardie, P. ed. *Augustan Poetry and the Irrational*. 134–155. Oxford University Press.

Graf, F. 2004. "The Power of the Word in the Graeco-Roman World." In Beta, S. *Potenza della parola: destinatari, funzioni, bersagli*. 79–100. Cadmo.

Gralfs, B. 1988. *Metallverarbeitende Produktionsstätten in Pompeji*. Oxford University Press.

Granino-Cecere, M. G. 2001. "*Quinquatrus*: tradizione popolare e tradizione antiquaria di una festività del calendario romano." *Ziva Antika* 51: 25–38.

Graziosi, B. 2002. *Inventing Homer: The Early Reception of Epic*. Cambridge University Press.

Gregori, G.L. 1994. "Un nuovo bollo *doli*are di Q. Tossius Cimber." *Publications de l'École Française de Rome* 193.1: 547–553.

Greppin, J.A.C. 1987. "Latin *nenia* and the Armenian Galen dictionary." *American Journal of Philology* 108: 487–90.

Grey, C. 2011. *Constructing Communities in the Late Roman Countryside*. Cambridge University Press.

Groen-Vallinga, M. J. 2022. *Work and Labour in the Cities of Roman Italy*. Liverpool University Press.

Guastella, G. 2017. *Word of Mouth: Fama and Its Personifications in Art and Literature from Ancient Rome to the Middle Ages*. Oxford University Press.

Guldager-Bilde, P. and Handberg, S. 2012. "Ancient Repairs on Pottery from Olbia Pontica." *American Journal of Archaeology* 116.3: 461–81.

Gunderson, E. 2007. "S.V.B.; E.V." *Classical Antiquity* 26.1: 1–48.

Güthenke, C. 2020. *Feeling and Classical Philology: Knowing Classical Antiquity in German Scholarship, 1770–1920.* Cambridge University Press.

Habinek, T.N. 2005a. "Slavery and Class." In Harrison, S. ed. *A Companion to Latin Literature.* 385–93. Blackwell.

Habinek, T.N. 2005b. *The World of Roman Song.* Johns Hopkins University Press.

Haley, S. P. 1993. "Black Feminist Thought and Classics: Re-Membering, Re-Claiming, Re-Empowering." In *Feminist Theory and the Classics*, edited by Nancy Sorkin Rabinowitz and Amy Richlin, 23–43. Routledge.

Hall, A. and M. Waelkens, 1982. "Two Dokimeian sculptors in Iconium." *Anat. St.* 32: 151–155.

Hamma, K. and True, M. 1994. *A Passion for Antiquities: Ancient Art from the Collection of Barbara and Lawrence Fleischman.* The J. Paul Getty Museum of Art in association with the Cleveland Museum of Art.

Hammond, M. (tr.). 2020. *Artemidorus: The Interpretation of Dreams.* Oxford University Press.

Hardie, P. R. 1994. *Virgil Aeneid Book IX.* Cambridge University Press.

Hardie, P. R. 1986. *Vergil's* Aeneid*: Cosmos and Imperium.* Oxford University Press.

Harland, P. 2014. *Greco-Roman Associations: Texts, Translations and Commentary,* vol. II: *North Coast of the Black Sea, Asia Minor.* De Gruyter.

Harman, G. 2002. *Tool-Being: Heidegger and the Metaphysics of Objects.* Open Court Press.

Harris, E. 2020. "Many ancient Greek occupations, but few professions." In Stewart, Harris, and Lewis, eds., *Skilled Labour and Professionalism in Ancient Greece and Rome.* 29–67. Cambridge University Press.

Harris, W, ed. 2008. *The Monetary Systems of the Greeks and Romans.* Oxford University Press.

Harris-McCoy, D.E. 2012. *Artemidorus' Oneirocritica: Text, Translation, and Commentary.* Oxford University Press.

Harrison, R. M. 1989. A *Temple for Byzantium: The Discovery and Excavation of Anicia Juliana's Palace-Church in Istanbul.* University of Texas Press.

Harrison, S. 2017. "The *Vita Phocae*: literary contexts and texture." In Powell and Hardie: 73–91.

Hatt, J.J. 1951. *La tombe gallo-romaine. Recherches sur les inscriptions et les monuments funéraires gallo-romains des trois premiers siècles de notre ère.* PUF.

Hawkins, C. 2016. *Roman Artisans and the Urban Economy.* Cambridge University Press.

Hawkins, C. 2013. "Labour and employment." in Erdkamp, P., ed. *The Cambridge Companion to Ancient Rome.* 336–351. Cambridge University Press.

Heath, J. 2011. "Women's Work: Female Transmission of Mythical Narrative." *Transactions of the American Philological Association* 141: 69–104.

Heinze, R. 1960. *Vom Geist Des Römertums.* Teubner.

Heller, J. L. 1943. "*Nenia* παίγνιον." *Transactions of the American Philological Association* 74: 215-68.

Heller, J. L. 1939. "Festus on *nenia.*" *Transactions of the American Philological Association* 70: 357-67.

Henderson, J. 2004. *Hortus: The Roman Book of Gardening.* Routledge.

Henkel, J. 2014. "Vergil Talks Technique: Metapoetic Arboriculture in *Georgics* 2." *Vergilius* 60: 33–66.

Henkel, J. 2009. *Writing Poems on Trees: Genre and Metapoetics in Vergil's* Eclogues *and* Georgics. Ph.D. Dissertation: UNC Chapel Hill.

Hesnard, A., Carre, M. B., Rival, M., Dangréaux, B., Thinon, M., Blaustein, M., Chéné, A., Foliot, P., and Bernard-Maugiron, H. 1988. "*L'épave romaine* Grand Ribaud D (Hyères, Var)." *Archaeonautica* 8.1: 5–180.

Hexter, R. 1990. "What Was the Trojan Horse Made of?: Interpreting Virgil's *Aeneid.*" *Yale Journal of Criticism* 3: 109–31.

Hinard, F. and Dumoint, J.-C., Eds. 2003. *Libitina. Pompes funèbres et supplices en Campanie à l'époque d'Auguste. Edition. traduction, et commentaire.* De Boccard.

Hobsbawm, E. 1998. *On History.* The New Press.

Hochscheid, H. 2020. "Professionalism in archaic and classical sculpture in Athens: The price of *technē.*" in Stewart, Harris, and Lewis, eds. *Skilled Labour and Professionalism in Ancient Greece and Rome.* 205–229. Cambridge University Press.

Hochscheid, H. & Russell, B., eds. 2021. *The Value of Making.* Brepols.

Holcombe, J. and Holcombe, F.E. 1998. "Archaeological Findings." in Koverman. 72–81. University of South Carolina Press.

Holleran, C. 2022. "Mobility, economic." *The Oxford Classical Dictionary (digital edition).* Oxford University Press.

Holleran, C. 2021. "Information asymmetry and the Roman labour market." in Rosillo-López, C. and Morcillo, M.G., eds. *Managing Information in the Roman Economy.* 159–178. Palgrave Macmillan.

Holliday, P. 2005. "The Rhetoric of "Romanitas": The "Tomb of the Statilii" Frescoes Reconsidered." *Memoirs of the American Academy in Rome* 50: 89–129.

Hölkeskamp, K-J. 2010. *Reconstructing the Roman Republic: An Ancient Political Culture and Modern Research.* Translated by Henry Heitmann-Gordon. Princeton University Press.

Hölscher, T. 1994. "Claudische Staatsdenkmäler in Rom und Italien. Neue Schritte zur Festigung des Principats." In Strocka, V. M. ed. *Die Regierungszeit des Kaisers Claudius (41–54 n.Chr.): Unbruch oder Episode? Internationales interdisziplinäres Symposion aus Anlass jes hundertjährigen Jubiläums des*

Archäologischen Instituts der Universität Freiburg i. Br., Februar 1991. 91–105. Von Zabern.

Hopkins, K. 1983. "Models, Ships and Staples." In Garnsey, P. and Whittaker, C.R., eds. *Trade and Famine in Classical Antiquity.* 84–109. Cambridge Philological Society.

Horden, P. and Purcell, N. 2000. *The Corrupting Sea: A Study of Mediterranean History.* Wiley-Blackwell.

Horsley, G. 1989. *New Documents Illustrating Early Christianity,* vol. 5. Wm. B. Eerdmans Publishing Co.

Höschele, R. 2005. "Moreto-Poetik: Das Moretum Als Intertextuelles Mischgericht." In Holzberg, N., ed. *Die « Appendix Vergiliana »: Pseudepigraphen Im Literarischen Kontext.* 244–69. Narr.

Howley, Joseph. Forthcoming. *Slavery and the Roman Book.* (Geue).

Huebner, S. 2013. *The Family in Roman Egypt: A Comparative Approach to Intergenerational Solidarity and Conflict.* Oxford University Press.

Hunt, A. 2011. "Priapus as wooden god: confronting manufacture and destruction." *Cambridge Classical Journal* 57: 29–54.

İplikçioğlu, B. 2014. "Heraklit von Rhodiapolis, ein gefeierter Arzt der traianischen Zeit," in Fischer, J., ed. *Der Beitrag Kleinasiens zur Kultur- und Geistesgeschichte der griechisch-römischen Antike.* 231–255. Verlag der Österreichischen Akademie der Wissenschaften.

Israelowich, I. 2015. *Patients and Healers in the Roman Empire.* John Hopkins University Press.

Jaritz, G. 2009. "The Visual Representation of Late Medieval Work: Patterns of Context, People, and Action." In Josef Ehmer and Catharina Lis: 125–48.

Jashemski, W. 1993. *The Gardens of Pompeii, Herculaneum and the Villas Destroyed by Vesuvius, vol. 2,* Appendix. Caratzas.

Jashemski, W. 1979a. *The Gardens of Pompeii, Herculaneum and the Villas Destroyed by Vesuvius, vol. 1.* Caratzas.

Jashemski, W. 1979b. "'The Garden of Hercules at Pompeii' (II.viii.6): The Discovery of a Commercial Flower Garden." *American Journal of Archaeology* 83.4: 403–11.

Jameson, F. 2013. *The Antimonies of Realism.* Verso.

Jenkyns, R. 1993. "*Labor improbus.*" *Classical Quarterly* 43: 243–8.

Jenkyns, R. 1989. "Virgil and Arcadia." *JRS* 79: 26–39.

Jobst, W., Erdal, B., and Gurtner, C. 1997. *Istanbul, the Great Palace Mosaic: The Story of its Exploration, Preservation, and Exhibition, 1983–1997.* Austrian Cultural Institute, Arkeoloji ve Sanat Yayinlari.

Jones, N. 2018. "Exemplarity and Encyclopedism at the Tomb of Eurysaces." *Classical Antiquity* 37: 63–107.

Jones, M. and McFadden, S. eds. 2015. *Art of Empire: The Roman Frescoes and Imperial Cult Chamber in Luxor Temple.* Yale University Press.

Joshel, S. 1992. *Work, Identity, and Legal Status in Rome: A Study of the Occupational Inscriptions.* University of Oklahoma Press.

Juvenal [Decimus Iunius Iuvenalis]. *Saturae*: In Ramsay, G. C., ed. and trans. 1995. *Juvenal and Persius, Loeb Classical Library*, 91. Harvard University Press.

Kadue, K. 2021. *Domestic Georgic: Labors of Preservation from Rabelais to Milton.* University of Chicago Press.

Kalinowski, A. 2021. *Memory, Family, and Community in Roman Ephesos.* Cambridge University Press.

Kampen, N. 1981. *Image and status. Roman working women in Ostia*. Mann.

Kearey, T. 2018. *The Poet at Work: Concepts of Authorship in the Ancient Receptions of Virgil.* Ph.D. Dissertation. Clare College, Cambridge.

Keith, A.M. 2009. "The Lay of the Land in Ovid's "Perseid" (*Met.* 4.610–5.249)." *Classical World* 102: 259–72.

Kelly, P. 2020. "Crafting Chaos: Intelligent Design in Ovid, *Metamorphoses* book 1 and Plato's *Timaeus*." *Classical Quarterly* 70: 734–48.

Kendrick, M. 2011. "'A Shoemaker Sell Flesh and Blood—O Indignity!': The Labouring Body and Community in the Shoemaker's Holiday." *English Studies* 92: 259–273.

Kenney, E. J., ed. 1984. *Moretum. The Ploughman's Lunch, a Poem Ascribed to Virgil.* Bristol Classical Press.

Ker, J. 2023. *The Ordered Day: Quotidian Time and Forms of Life in Ancient Rome.* Johns Hopkins University Press.

Kierdorf, W. 1980. *Laudatio funebris: Interpretationen und Untersuchungen zur Entwicklung der römischen Leichenrede.* Verlag Anton Hain.

Kiernan, P. 2015. "Miniature Objects as Representations of Realia." *World Archaeology* 47: 45–59.

Kiilerich, B. 2001. "The Image of Anicia Juliana in the Vienna Dioscurides: Flattery or Appropriation of Imperial Imagery?" *Symbolae Osloenses* 76: 169–90.

Kiriatzi, E. and Knappet, C., eds. 2016. *Human Mobility and Technological Transfer in the Prehistoric Mediterranean.* Cambridge University Press.

Kleiner, D. 1992. *Roman Sculpture.* Yale University Press.

Kleiner, F. S. 1977. "Artists in the Roman world. An itinerant workshop in Augustan Gaul." *MEFRA* 89.1: 661–696.

Kohn, E. 2013. *How Forests Think: Toward an Anthropology Beyond the Human.* University of California Press.

Kolendo, J. 1993. "The Peasant." In Giardina, A. *The Romans.* 199–213. University of Chicago Press.

Koob, S. 1998. "Obsolete Fill Materials Found on Ceramics." *Journal of the American Institute for Conservation* 37: 49–67.

Kopytoff, I. 1986. "The Cultural Biography of Things: Commoditization as Process." In Appadurai, A. ed. *The Social Life of Things: Commodities in Cultural Perspective.* 64–91. Cambridge University Press.

Kostecka, K. 2019. "Geographical mobility and the dynamics of the status of élite specialists." *Incidenza dell'Antico* 17: 29–52.

Koverman, J.B. 1998a. *I Made This Jar: The Life and Works of the Enslaved African-American Potter, Dave.* University of South Carolina Press.

Koverman, J.B. 1998b. "Searching for Messages in Clay: What Do We Really Know About Dave?" In Koverman. 19–38.

Kramnick, J. 2021. "Criticism and Truth." *Critical Inquiry* 48.2: 218–40.

Kroll, W. 1935. "nenia." *RE* 16.2: 2390–2393.

Kronenberg, L. 2010. *Allegories of Farming from Greece and Rome: Philosophical Satire in Xenophon, Varro, and Virgil.* Cambridge University Press.

Kurke, L. 1999. *Coins, Bodies, Games, and Gold: The Politics of Meaning in Archaic Greece.* Princeton University Press.

Kuttner, A. 2021. "Object Worlds." In Osborne, R. ed. *A Cultural History of Objects in Antiquity.* 185–214. Bloomsbury Academic.

Kuttner, A. 2013. "Representing Hellenistic Numidia, in Africa and at Rome." In Quinn, J. and Prag, J. eds. *The Hellenistic West.* 216–72. Cambridge University Press.

Kuttner, A. 1999. "Hellenistic Images of Spectacle, from Alexander to Augustus." In Bergmann, B. and Kondoleon, C. eds. *The Art of Ancient Spectacle. Studies in the History of Art* vol. 56: 97–122.

Kuttner, A. 1995. *Dynasty and Empire in the Age of Augustus: The Case of the Boscoreale Cups.* University of California Press. http://ark.cdlib.org/ark:/13030/ft309nb1mw/.

Laes, C. 2011. *Children in the Roman Empire: Outsiders Within.* Cambridge University Press.

Laes, C. 2008. "Child slaves at work in Roman Antiquity." *Ancient Society* 38: 235–283.

Laffi, U. 2006. "L'iscrizione di Efeso sui privilege di insegnanti, sofisti, medici (*I. Ephesos,* 4101)," in Virgilio, B., ed. *Studi Ellenistici,* 19. 453–521. Studi Ellenistici.

La Follette, L. 2011/2. "Parsing piety: the sacred still life in Roman relief sculpture." *Memoirs of the American Academy in Rome* 56–57: 15–35.

Laird, A. 1993. "Sounding out Ecphrasis: Art and Text in Catullus 64." *The Journal of Roman Studies* 83: 18–30.

Lancaster, L. C. 2012. "A New Vaulting Technique for Early Baths in Sussex: The Anatomy of a Romano-British Invention." *Journal of Roman Archaeology* 25: 419–40.

Lancaster, L. C. 2004. *Concrete Vaulted Construction in Imperial Rome: Innovations in Context.* Cambridge University Press.

Lapadula, E., ed. 2012. *The Chora of Metaponto, iv: The Late Roman Farmhouse at San Biagio.* University of Texas Press.

Lapatin, K. 2015. *Luxus: The Sumptuous Arts of Greece and Rome*. The J. Paul Getty Museum. Lapatin, K. and Wight, K. eds. 2010. *The J. Paul Getty Handbook of the Antiquities Collection*. The J. Paul Getty Museum.

Lavan, L. 2022. "Greek names and freed status in Roman Italy: Why ancient historians can't ignore statistics," *Chiron* 52: 1–29.

Lavan, M. 2018. "Pliny *Epistles* 10 and Imperial correspondence. The empire of letters." in König, A. and Whitton, C.L., eds. *Roman Literature under Nerva, Trajan, and Hadrian: Literary Interactions AD 96–138*. 280–301. Cambridge University Press.

Lavin, I. 1963. "The Hunting Mosaics of Antioch and Their Sources." *Dumbarton Oaks Papers* 17: 181–216.

Lawall, M. L. and Lund, J., eds. 2011. *Pottery in the Archaeological Record: Greece and Beyond; Acts of the International Colloquium Held at the Danish and Canadian Institutes in Athens, June 20–22, 2008*. Aarhus University Press.

Lazenby, J. F. 1996. "Was Maharbal Right?" In Cornell, T. J., Rankov, N. B., and Sabin, P., eds., *The Second Punic War: A Reappraisal*. 39–48. Institute of Classical Studies.

Lazenby, J. F. 2006. "Freedmen and Immortality in the Tomb of the Haterii." in D'Ambra, E. and Métraux, G. eds. *The Art of Citizens, Soldiers and Freedmen in the Roman World*. 1–18. BAR Publishing.

Leach, E.W. 1974a. "Ekphrasis and the Theme of Artistic Failure in Ovid's *Metamorphoses*." *Ramus* 3: 102–142.

Leach, E.W. 1974b. *Vergil's* Eclogues: *Landscapes of Experience*. Cornell University Press.

Leader Newby, R. 2003. *Silver and Society in Late Antiquity*. Routledge.

Lefkowitz, M. 1981. *The Lives of the Greek Poets*. Johns Hopkins University Press.

Lennon, J. 2013. *Pollution and Religion in Ancient Rome*. Cambridge University Press.

Lennon, J.. 2022. *Dirt and Denigration: Stigma and Marginalisation in Ancient Rome*. Approaches to Ancient History 1. Mohr Siebeck.

Lenski, N. 2013. "Working Models: Functional Art and Roman Conceptions of Slavery." In George, M. ed. *Roman Slavery and Roman Material Culture*. 129–57. University of Toronto Press.

Lenski, N. 2017. "Peasant and Slave in Late Antique North Africa." In Lizzi Testa, R. ed., *Late Antiquity in Contemporary Debate*. 113–55. Cambridge Scholars Publishing.

Lerouxel, F. and Zurbach, J. eds. 2020. *Le changement dans les économies antiques*. Ausonius.

Levi, P. 1993. "People in a Landscape: Theokritos." In Green, P. ed. *Hellenistic History and Culture*. University of California Press. http://ark.cdlib.org/ark:/13030/ft0000035f/.

Levick, B. 1979. "Pliny in Bithynia—and what followed." *Greece and Rome* 26.2: 119–131.

Lewis, N. 1965. "Exemption of Physicians from Liturgy." *Bulletin of the American Society of Papyrologists* 2.3: 87–92.

Lewis, S. 1995. "Barber's shops and perfume shops: Symposia without wine." in Powell, A., ed. *The Greek World*. 432–441. Routledge.

de Ligt, L. 1991. "The Roman Peasantry Demand, Supply, Distribution between Town and Countryside II: Supply, Distribution and a Comparative Perspective." *Münstersche Beiträge zur Antiken Handelsgeschichte* 10, no. 1: 33–77.

Lis, C. 2009. "Perceptions of Work in Classical Antiquity." In Ehmer and Lis: 33–68.

Lis, C. and Soly, H. 2016. "Work, identity and self-representation in the Roman Empire and the West-European Middle Ages: Different interplays between the social and the cultural." In Verboven and Laes 2017: 262–289.

Lis, C. and Soly, H. 2012. *Worthy Efforts: Attitudes to Work and Workers in Pre-Industrial Europe*. Brill.

Liu, J. 2016. "Group Membership, Trust Networks, and Social Capital: A Critical Analysis," in Verboven and Laes. 203–226.

Liu, J. 2009. Collegia Centonariorum: *The Guilds of Textile Dealers in the Roman West*. Brill.

Longfellow, B. and Swetnam-Burland, M., eds. 2021. *Women's Lives, Women's Voices: Roman Material Culture and Female Agency in the Bay of Naples*. 133–50. University of Texas Press.

López Barja de Quiroga, P. 2018. "The *quinquatrus* of June, Marsyas and *libertas* in the late Roman Republic." *Classical Quarterly* 68: 143–159.

Loreaux, N. 1998. *Mothers in Mourning*. Trans. C. Pache. Cornell University Press.

Lott, B. 2004. *The Neighborhoods of Augustan Rome*.

Lovén, L. L. 2013: "Female Work and Identity in Roman Textile Production and Trade: A Methodological Discussion." In Gleba, M. and Pásztókai-Szeöke, J. eds. *Making Textiles in Pre-roman and Roman Times: People, Places, Identities*. 109–25. Oxbow Books.

Lukes, S., ed. 2013. *The Division of Labour in Society*, by Émile Durkheim. Translated by W. D. Halls. 2nd ed. Free Press.

Lundgreen, C. 2017. "Norme, loi, règle, coutume, tradition: Terminologie antique et perspectives modernes." In Itgenshorst, T. and Le Doze, P. eds. *La norme sous la République et le Haut-Empire romains: élaboration, diffusion et contournements*. 17–33. Ausonius.

Lytle, E. 2012. "A Customs House of Our Own: Infrastructure, Duties and a Joint Association of Fishermen and Fishmongers (*IK*, 11.1a-Ephesos, 20)." in Chankowski, V. and Karonis, P., eds. *Tout vendre, tout acheter: Structures et équipments des marchés antiques*. 213–224. Ecole française d' Athenes.

MacRae, D. 2013. *Legible Religion. Books, Gods, and Rituals in Roman Culture.* Cambridge University Press.

Madigan, B. 2012. *The Ceremonial Sculptures of the Roman Gods.* Brill.

Mandowsky, E. and Mitchell, C. 1963. *Pirro Ligorio's Roman Antiquities; The Drawings in MS XIII. B. 7 in the National Library in Naples,* Vol. 28. The Warburg Institute.

Mann, C. 2020. "Neither Amateurs nor Professionals: The Status of Greek Athletes," in Stewart, Harris, Lewis. 313–332.

Mann, M. 1986. *The Sources of Social Power. Vol. 1: A History of Power from the Beginning to A.D. 1760.* Cambridge University Press.

Marcone, A., ed. 2016. *Storia del lavoro in Italia. L'età Romana. Liberi, semiliberi e schiavi in una società moderna.* Roma.

Marder, M. 2013. *Plant-Thinking: A Philosophy of Vegetal Life.* Columbia University Press.

Martelli, F. Forthcoming. *Souvenirs of Cicero: Shaping Memory in the Epistulae ad Familiares.* Oxford University Press.

Martin, S. D. 1989. *The Roman Jurists and the Organization of Private Building in the Late Republic and Early Empire.* Latomus.

Maschek, D. 2018. "Not *census* but *deductio*: reconsidering the Ara of Domitius Ahenobarbus." *The Journal of Roman Studies* 108: 27–52.

Massar, N. 2020. "Skilled workers in the ancient Greek City: public employment, selection methods, and evaluation." in Stewart, Harris, and Lewis. 68–93.

Massar, N. 2005. *Soigner et servir: histoire sociale et culturelle de la médecine grecque à l'époque hellénistique.* De Boccard.

Mattusch, C. 2017. "When a Statue is Not a Statue." In Daehner, J., Lapatin, K., and Spinelli, A. eds. *Artistry in Bronze: The Greeks and Their Legacy.* J. Paul Getty Museum Conservation Institute: https://www.getty.edu/publications/artistryinbronze/.

Mau, A. 1902. *Pompeii: Its Life and Art.* Macmillan.

Mayer, E. 2020. "Money Making, 'Avarice', and Elite Strategies of Distinction in the Roman World." In Stewart, Harris, and Lewis 2020. 94–126.

Mayer, E. 2014. *The Ancient Middle Classes: Urban Life and Aesthetics in the Roman Empire, 100 BCE–250 CE.* Harvard University Press.

McCallum, M. 2010. "The Supply of Stone to the City of Rome: A Case Study of the Transport of Anician Building Stone and Millstone from the Santa Trinità Quarry (Orvieto.)" in White, C. and Dillian, C, eds. *Trade and Exchange: Archaeological Studies from History and Prehistory.* 75–94. Springer.

McCarty, M. 2016. "Gods, Masks, and *Monstra*: Situational Syncretisms in Roman Africa." In Alcock, S., Egri, M., and Frakes, J. eds. *Beyond Boundaries: Connecting Visual Cultures in the Provinces of Ancient Rome.* 266–80. Getty Publications.

McGill, S. 2017. "Larger than life: The elevation of Virgil in Phocas' *Vita Vergiliana.*" In Powell and Hardie: 93–114.

McGill, S. 2010. "Another man's miracles: Recasting Aelius Donatus in Phocas' Life of Virgil." In McGill, S, and Watts, E., eds. *From the Tetrarchs to the Theodosians: Later Roman history and culture, 284–450 CE.* 153–170. Cambridge University Press.

McLean, B. H. 2002. *Greek and Latin Inscriptions in the Konya Archaeological Museum.* British Institute at Ankara.

Melfi, M. 2016. "Damophon of Messene in the Ionian coast of Greece." in Melfi, M and O. Bobou, eds. *Hellenistic Sanctuaries: Between Greece and Rome.* 82–105. Oxford University Press.

Meredith, H. 2023. "Shaping Viewer Experience through Images of Unfinished Work: A Visual History of Making in the Fourth to Eighth-Century CE Eastern Mediterranean." *Different Visions: New Perspectives on Medieval Art* 10: 1–41. https://differentvisions.org/shaping-viewer-experience/.

Meyer, E. A. 1990. "Explaining the epigraphic habit in the Roman Empire: the evidence of epitaphs." *The Journal of Roman Studies* 80: 74–96.

Meyer, E. A. 2009. "Writing Paraphernalia, Tablets, and Muses in Campanian Wall Painting." *American Journal of Archaeology* 113: 569–97.

Meyerhof, M. 1929. "Autobiographische Bruchstücke Galens aus arabischen Quellen." *Sudhoffs Archiv für Geschichte der Medizin* 22: 72–86.

Millar, F. 1999. "The Greek East and Roman Law: The Dossier of M. Cn. Licinius Rufinus." *JRS* 89: 90–108.

Miller, H. M.-L. 2009. *Archaeological Approaches to Technology.* Left Coast Press.

Miller, N. K. 1988. "Arachnologies. The Woman, the Text, and the Critic." in Miller, N. *Subject to Change. Reading Feminist Writing.* Columbia University Press.

Milnor, K. 2014. Graffiti and the Literary Landscape in Roman Pompeii. Oxford University Press.

Miloglav, I. 2020. "Drills and Holes—Pottery Repairing as Evidence of the Social Meaning of an Object." *Quaternary International* 569–70: 120–27.

Moatti, C. 2013. "Immigration and cosmopolization." in Erkamp, P., ed. *The Cambridge Companion to Rome.* 77–92. Cambridge University Press.

Moatti, C. 2005. *The Birth of Critical Thinking in Republican Rome*, transl. by J. Lloyd. Cambridge University Press.

Momigliano, A. 1984. "The Theological Efforts of the Roman Upper Classes in the First Century BC." *Classical Philology* 79: 199–211.

Moormann, E. 2015. "Images of Statues in Other Media." In Friedland, E., Grunow-Sobocinski, M., and Gazda, E. eds. *The Oxford Handbook of Roman Sculpture.* 638–52. Oxford University Press.

Montanini, L. 2009. "Le donne romane e la morte." *Ager Veleias* 4.12: 1–23.

Monteix, N. 2017. "Urban Production and the Pompeian Economy." In Wilson, A. and Bowman, A., eds. *The Economy of Pompeii.* 209–242. Oxford University Press.

Monteix, N. 2016. "Perceptions of technical culture among Pompeian élites, considering the Cupids frieze of the Casa dei Vettii." In Droß-Krüpe, K., Föllinger, S., and Ruffing, K., eds. *Antike Wirtschaft und ihre kulturelle Prägung (2000 v.Chr.–500 n.Chr.)—The cultural shaping of the Ancient economy.* 199–221. Philippika.

Monteix, N. 2010. *Les lieux de métier: boutiques et ateliers d'Herculanum. Collection du Centre Jean Bérard, 34.* École française de Rome.

Monteix, N. and Russo, E. 2008. "L'artisanat du plomb à Pompéi." *MEFRA* 120: 241–247.

Monteix, N. and Tran, N. eds. 2020. *Les savoirs professionnels des gens de métier: études sur le monde du travail dans les sociétés urbaines de l'Empire romain.* Centre Jean Bérard.

Morel, J.-P. 1993. "The Craftsman." In Giardina, A. *The Romans.* 214–244. University of Chicago Press.

Mouritsen, H. 2011. *The Freedman in the Roman World.* Cambridge University Press.

Mouritsen, H. 2005. "Freedmen and decurions: Epitaphs and social history in imperial Italy." *The Journal of Roman Studies* 95: 38–63.

Moser, C. 2019. *The Altars of Republican Rome and Latium: Sacrifice and the materiality of Roman religion.* Cambridge University Press.

Moser, C. and Knust, J. 2017. *Ritual Matters: Material Remains and Ancient Religion.* University of Michigan Press.

Mumprecht, V., ed. 1964. *Epitaphios Bionos.* Juris Verlag.

Murphy, E. A. Forthcoming. *Crafting Community: Potters of the Roman East.*

Murphy, E. A. 2015. "Socially Embedded Work Practices and Production Organization: Beyond industry lines." *Journal of Mediterranean Archaeology* 28.2: 221–39.

Mustakallio, K. 2013. "Grief and Mourning in the Roman Context. The Changing Sphere of Female Lamentation," in Chaniotis, A. and Ducrey, P. eds. *Unveiling Emotions II. Emotions in Greece and Rome: Texts, Images, Material Culture.* 237–50. Fran Steiner Verlag.

Nabokov, V. [1969] 1990. *Ada, or Ardor: A Family Chronicle.* Vintage.

Nathan, G. 2011. "The Vienna Dioscorides' dedication to Anicia Juliana: A Usurpation of Imperial Patronage?" In Mathan, G. and Garland, L. eds. *Basileia. Essays on Imperium and Culture in Honour of E.M. and M.J. Jeffreys.* 95–102. Centre for Early Christian Studies, Australian Catholic University.

Nevett, L. 2010. *Domestic Space in Classical Antiquity.* Cambridge University Press.

Nicolson, F.W. 1891. "Greek and Roman Barbers." *Harvard Studies in Classical Philology* 2: 41–56.

van Nijf, O. 1997. *The Civic World of Professional Associations in the Roman East*. Brill.

Nikolaus, J. 2016. "Beyond Ghirza: Roman-period Mausolea in Tripolitania." In Mugnai, N., Nikolaus, J., and Ray, N. eds. *De Africa Romaque: Merging Cultures Across North Africa*. 199–214. The Society for Libyan Studies.

Noreña, C. 2022. "From Wigwams to Worlds: on the Work of Keith Hopkins." *JRA* 35.1: 524–39.

Noreña, C. 2007. "The social economy of Pliny's correspondence with Trajan." *AJP* 128.2: 239–277.

North, J. A. 2015. "Roman funeral rituals and the significance of the *naenia*." *Religion in the Roman Empire* 1: 114–133.

Novello, M. 2007. *Scelte tematiche e committenza nelle abitazioni dell' Africa Proconsolare*. F. Serra.

Novello, M. and Salvadori, M. 2004. "Natura umanizzata e natura selvaggia nei mosaici dell' Africa romana: dallo spazio del giardino ai limiti esterni della tenuta." In Khanoussi, M., Ruggeri, P., and Vismara, C. eds. *L'Africa romana. Ai confini dell'impero: contratti, scambi, conflitti. Atti dell' XV Convegno di studio, Tozeur, 11–15 dicembre 2002* vol. 3. 853–75. Carocci Editore.

Noy, D. 2000. *Foreigners at Rome: Citizens and Strangers*. Duckworth.

Nutton, V. 2013. *Ancient Medicine*, 2nd ed. Routledge.

Nutton, V. 2012. "Galen and Roman medicine; or can a Greek become a Latin?" *European Review* 20.4: 534–542.

Nutton, V. 1979. *Galeni de Praecognitione*. Akademie Verlag.

Oliensis, E. 2004. "The Power of Image-Makers: Representation and Revenge in Ovid's *Metamorphoses 6* and *Tristia 4*." *Classical Antiquity* 23: 285–32.

Olsen, B. 2010. *In Defense of Things. Archaeology and the Ontology of Objects*. AltaMira Press.

Östenberg, I., Malmberg, S., and Bjørnebye, J. eds. 2015. *The moving city: Processions, passages and promenades in ancient Rome*. Bloomsbury.

Pack, R. 1955. "Artemidorus and his Waking World." *Transactions of the American Philosophical Society* 86: 280–90.

Padron-Labonnelie, M. 2014. "Collyrium names attested on stone tablets: The example of the Helvetian corpus." in Maire, B., ed. *'Greek' and 'Roman' in Latin Medical Texts*. 240–255. Brill.

Painter, K. 2002. "Campana Reliefs." In Widrig, W. ed. *The Via Gabina Villas, Sites 10, 11 and 13*. http://viagabina.rice.edu/campana/index.html.

Pallecchi, S. 2008. "Le fornaci romane di Albinia: identificazione delle unità funzionali e prima ricostruzione delle linee di produzione." In Acconcia, V. and Rizzitelli, C., eds. *Materiali per Populonia 7*, 323–338. Edizioni ETS.

Palombi, D. 2007. "Medici e medicina a Roma tra Carine, Velia, e Sacra Via." in Brandenburg, H., Heid, S., and Markschies, C., eds. *Salute e Guarigione nella Tarda Antichità*. Pontificio Istituto di Archeologia Cristiana.

Palombi, D. 1997. "Compitium Acilium: la scoperta, il monument e la tradizione medica del quartiere." *Atti della Pontificia Accademia romana di archeologia. Rendiconti* 70: 115–135.

Palombi, D. 1995. "Dea Nenia, sacellum." *Lexicon Topographicum Urbis Romae* 2. Quasar.

Panciera, S. 1981. "Fasti fabrum tignariorum urbis Romae." *Zeitschrift für Papyrologie und Epigraphik* 43: 271–280.

Papadopoulos, J. and Urton, G., eds. 2012. *The Construction of Value in the Ancient World*. Cotsen Institute of Archaeology Press.

Panciera, S. Ed. 2004. *Libitina e dintorni*. Quasar.

Paz de Hoz, M. 2015. "Associations of Physicians and Teachers in Asia Minor: Between Private and Public," in Gabrielsen, V. and Thomsen, C.A., eds. *Private Associations and the Public Sphere*. 92–121. The Royal Danish Academy of Sciences and Letters.

Pearse, L. 1975. "A forgotten altar of the collegium fabrum tignariorum of Rome." *Epigraphica* 37: 100–123.

Pearse, J. L. D. 1974. *The Organisation of Roman Building during the Late Republic and Early Empire*. PhD thesis, Trinity College Cambridge.

Peña, J. T. 2007. *Roman Pottery in the Archaeological Record*. Cambridge University Press.

Peña, J. T. and Cheung, C. 2015. "The Pompeii Artifact Life History Project: Conceptual Basis and Results of First Three Seasons." in Gambardella, C., ed. *Heritage and Technology: Mind, Knowledge, Experience; Le Vie degli mercanti XIII forum internazionale di studi, Fabbrica della conoscenza, 56*. 2115–23. La scuola di Pitagora.

Peña, J. T. and McCallum, M. 2009a. "The Production and Distribution of Pottery at Pompeii: A Review of the Evidence; Part 1, Production." *American Journal of Archaeology* 113.1: 57–79.

Peña, J. T. and McCallum, M. 2009b. "The Production and Distribution of Pottery at Pompeii: A Review of the Evidence; Part 2, the Material Basis for Production and Distribution." *American Journal of Archaeology* 113.2: 165–201.

Pepe, C. 2015. *Morire da donna. Ritratti esemplari di bonae feminae nella laudatio funebris romana*. Edizioni ETS.

Perrin, B. 1914. *Plutarch: Lives, Volume II: Themistocles and Camillus. Aristides and Cato Major. Cimon and Lucullus*. Loeb Classical Library 47. Harvard University Press.

Petersen, L. H. 2006. *The freedman in Roman art and art history*. Cambridge University Press.

Petersen, L. H. 2003. "The Baker, His Wife, and Her Breadbasket: The Monument of Eurysaces in Rome." *Art Bulletin* 85: 230–57.

Pirandello, L. 1927. *La giara: novelle per un anno*. Mondadori.

Pleket, H. W. 2014. "On the sociology of ancient sport," in Scanlon, T.F., ed. *Sport in the Greek and Roman Worlds, Vol. 2: Greek Athletic Identities and Roman Sports and Spectacle*. 29–81. Oxford University Press.

Pleket, H. W. 1995. "The social status of physicians in the Graeco-Roman world." in Horstmanshoof, M., van der Eijk, P., and Schrijvers, P.H., eds. *Ancient Medicine in Its Socio-Cultural Context, Vol. 1*. 27–34. Brill.

Pleket, H. W. 1984. "Urban Elites and the Economy in the Greek Cities of the Roman Empire." *Münstersche Beiträge zur antiken Handelsgeschichte* 3: 3–36.

Poehler, E. E. 2011. "Where to Park? Carts, Stables and the Economics of Transport in Pompeii." in Laurence, R. and Newsome, D., eds. *Rome, Ostia and Pompeii: Movement and Space*. 194–214. Routledge.

Poehler, E. E. and Crowther, B.M. 2018. "Paving Pompeii: The Archaeology of Stone-Paved Streets." *American Journal of Archaeology* 122.4: 579–609.

Poehler, E. E., van Roggen, J., and Crowther, B.M. 2019. "The Iron Streets of Pompeii." *American Journal of Archaeology* 123.2: 237–62.

Polito, R. 1999. "On the life of Asclepiades of Bithynia." *JHS* 119: 48–66.

Pollini, J. 2012. *From Republic to Empire: Rhetoric, Religion and Power in the Visual Culture of Ancient Rome*. University of Oklahoma Press.

Pomeroy, S. B. 1995. *Goddesses, Whores, Wives, and Slaves: Women in Classical Antiquity*. Schocken Books.

Pont, A-V. 2013. "Les groupes de voisinage dans les villes d'Asie Mineure occidentale à l'époque impériale." in Fröhlich, P. and Hamon, P., eds. *Groupes et associations dans les cités grecques, IIIe siècle av. J.-C.-IIe siècle apr. J.-C.* 129–156. EPHE.

Powell, A. and Hardie, P. R., eds. 2017. *The Ancient Lives of Virgil: Literary and Historical Studies*. Classical Press of Wales.

Puech, B. 2002. *Orateurs et sophistes grecs dans les inscriptions d'époque impériale*. Librairie Philosophique Vrin.

Purcell, N. 2022. "Historians in the Forum." In Filippi, D. ed., *Rethinking the Roman City. The Spatial Turn and the Archaeology of Roman Italy*. Routledge.

Putnam, M. C. J. 1970. *Virgil's Pastoral Art: Studies in the Eclogues*. Princeton University Press.

Ramelli, I.E. 2016. *Social Justice and the Legitimacy of Slavery: The Role of Philosophical Asceticism from Ancient Judaism to Late Antiquity*. Oxford University Press.

Randall, R. H. 1953. "The Erechtheum Workmen." *AJA* 57.3: 199–210.

Rando, G. 1998. "Le antiche riparazioni in piombo sui *dolia* provenienti dal relitto della nave romana del golfo di Diano Marina." In *XXVIII Convegno 1995: centri di produzione, botteghe e committenza; fonti d'archivio, evidenza archeologica e studi ceramologi; XXIX Convegno 1996; la ceramica nell'iconografia, l'iconografia nella ceramica; rapporti tra ceramica e arte figurativa, Atti dei Convegni Internazionali della Ceramica* All'Insegna del Giglio.

Rauch, M. 1999. *Bacchische Themen und Nilbilder auf Campanareliefs.* Verlag Marie Leidorf.

Raud, R. 2016. *Meaning in Action: Outline of an Integral Theory of Culture.* Polity Press.

Rawson, E. 1985. *Intellectual Life in the Late Roman Republic.* Duckworth.

Reay, B. 2005. "Agriculture, Writing, and Cato's Aristocratic Self-Fashioning." *ClAnt* 24.2: 331–61.

Reddé, M. 1978. "Les scènes de métier dans la sculpture funéraire gallo-romaine." *Gallia* 36: 43–63.

Reith, R. 2008. "Circulation of skilled labour in late medieval and early modern Central Europe." in Epstein, S. R., and Prak, M., eds. *Guilds, Innovation, and the European Economy, 1500–1800.* 114–142. Cambridge University Press.

Richlin, A. 2003. "Gender and Rhetoric: Producing Manhood in the Schools." In Golden, M and Toohey, P. eds. *Sex and Difference in Ancient Greece and Rome*: 202–20. Edinburgh University Press.

Richlin, A. 2001. "Emotional Work: Lamenting the Dead." in Tylawsky, E. and Weiss, C. eds, *Essays in Honour of Gordon Williams.* 229–48. Henry R. Schwab Publishers.

Ridgway, B. 2000. *Hellenistic Sculpture: The Styles of ca. 200–100 B.C.* University of Wisconsin Press.

von Rohden, H., and Winnefeld, H. 1911. *Die Antiken Terrakotten im Auftrag des Archaeologischen Instituts des Deutschen Reichs.* Verlag Von W. Spemann.

Roller, M. 2013. "On the intersignification of monuments in Augustan Rome." *American Journal of Philology* 134: 119–131.

Rollinger, C. 2019. "The Importance of Being Splendid: Competition, Ceremonial, and the Semiotics of Status at the Court of the Late Roman Emperors (4th–6th Centuries)." In Choda, K. C., Sterk de Leeuw, M., and Schulz, F. eds. *Gaining and Losing Imperial Favour in Late Antiquity: Representation and Reality.* (*Impact of Empire,* Vol. 36.) 36–72. Brill.

Roby, C. 2016. *Technical Ekphrasis in Ancient Science and Literature: The Written Machine between Alexandria and Rome.* Cambridge University Press.

Rosati, G. 2004. "La strategia del ragno, ovvero la rivincita di Aracne. Fortuna tardo-antica (Sidonio Apollinare, Claudiano) di un mito ovidiano." *Dictynna* 1: 2–13.

Rosati, G. 1999. "Form in Motion: Weaving the Text in the *Metamorphoses.*" In Hardie, P., Barchiesi, A., and Hinds, S., eds. *Ovidian Transformations: Essays on the Metamorphoses and its Reception.* 240–253. Cambridge University Press.

Rose, C. B. 2021. "Reconsidering the Frieze on the Arch of Constantine." *Journal of Roman Archaeology*: 175–210.

Rosenstein, N. 2004. *Rome at War. Farms, Families, and Death in the Middle Republic.* University of North Carolina Press.

Ross, D. O. 1975. "The Culex and Moretum as Post-Augustan Literary Parodies." *Harvard Studies in Classical Philology* LXXIX: 235–63.

Rotroff, S. I. 2011. "Mended in Antiquity: Repairs to Ceramics at the Athenian Agora." in Lawall, M.L. and Lund, J., eds. *Pottery in the Archaeological Record: Greece and Beyond.* 117–34. Aarhus University Press.

Roueché, C. 1989. *Aphrodisias in Late Antiquity.* Society for the Promotion of Roman Studies.

Ruffing, K. 2008. *Die berufliche Spezialisierung in Handel und Handwerk: Untersuchungen zu ihrer Entwicklung und zu ihren Bedingungen in der römischen Kaiserzeit im östlichen Mittelmeerraum auf der Grundlage griechischer Inschriften und Papyri.* Leidorf.

Rüpke, J. 2011. *The Roman calendar from Numa to Constantine: time, history and the Fasti.* Wiley Blackwell.

Russell, B. 2015. "Transport and distribution." in Friedland, E.A. et al. eds. *The Oxford Handbook of Roman Sculpture.* 189–206. Oxford University Press.

Russell, B. 2013. *The Economics of the Roman Stone Trade.* Oxford University Press.

Rutherford, I. 2008. "'When You Go to the Meadow…': The Lament of the *Taptara*-Women in the Hittite Sallis Wastais Ritual." In Suter: 53–69.

Ryberg, S. 1955. *Rites of the State religion in Roman art.* Yale University Press.

Salido Domínguez, J. 2017. 'Los *dolia* en Hispana: caracterización, funcionalidad y tipología', Fernández Ochoa, C., Morillo, A., and Zarzalejos, M., eds. *Manual de cerámica romana, iii: Cerámicas romanas de epoca altoimperial, iii: Cerámica común de mesa, cocina e almacenaje, imitaciones hispanas de series romanas, otras producciones, Cursos de formación permanente para arqueólogos.* 239–309. Museo arqueológico regional.

Salzmann, M. 1991. *On Roman Time: The Codex Calendar of 354 and the Rhythms of Urban Life in Late Antiquity.* University of California Press.

Salzman-Mitchell, P.B. 2005. *A Web of Fantasies: Gaze, Image and Gender in Ovid's Metamorphoses.* Ohio State University Press.

Samama, É. 2003. *Les médecins dans le monde grec. Sources épigraphiques sur la naissance d'un corps médical.* Librairie Droz.

Sancinito, J. 2024. *The Reputation of the Roman Merchant.* University of Michigan Press.

Sancinito, J. 2018. *Merchants in the Later Roman Empire.* Ph.D. dissertation, University of Pennsylvania. https://repository.upenn.edu/edissertations/2703/.

Sarnowski, T. 1978. *Les répresentations de villas sur les mosaïques africaines tardives.* Zaklad Narodowy.

Saunders, T. 2008. *Bucolic Ecology: Virgil's Eclogues and the Environmental Literary Tradition.* Duckworth.

Scarborough, J. 2020. "*Silva Sonans: The Metapoetic Pastoral Landscape in Vergil's Georgics.*" *Vergilius* 66: 3–34.

Scheidegger-Lämmle, C. 2021. "Der Künstler und sein Werk: Arachne, Pygmalion, Daedalus, Marsyas, Orpheus." In Möller, M., ed. *Ovid-Handbuch. Leben-Werk-Wirkung*. 263–280. J.B. Metzler.

Scheidel, W. Morris, I., and Saller, W., eds. 2007. *The Cambridge Economic History of the Greco-Roman World*. Cambridge University Press.

Schiffer, M. 1972. "Archaeological Context and Systemic Context." *American Anthropologist* 37: 156–65.

Schiffer, M. 1996. *Formation Processes of the Archaeological Record*. University of Utah Press.

Schlange-Schöningen, H. 2003. *Die römische Gesellschaft bei Galen: Biographie und Sozialgeschichte*. De Gruyter.

Schliephake, C. 2022. "Profile: Ecocriticism and Ancient Environments." *Classical Review* 72.2: 393–6.

Schmidt, E. A. 2008. "The German Rediscovery of Vergil in the Early 20th Century (1900–1938)." *Vergilius* 54: 124–149.

Schubert, P. 2021. *The Bearers of Business Letters in Roman Egypt*. Peeters.

Schürmann, W. 1985. *Typologie und Bedeutung der stadtrömischen Minerva-Kultbilder*. G. Bretschneider.

Seaman, K. 2020. *Rhetoric and Imitation in Hellenistic Art*. Cambridge University Press.

Sedley, D. 2008. *Creationism and its Critics in Antiquity*. University of California Press.

Severy Hoven, B. 2012. "Master Narratives, and the Wall Painting of the House of the Vettii, Pompeii." *Gender & History* 24: 540–80.

Shackleton Bailey, D. R. 2002. *Cicero: Letters to Quintus and Brutus; Letter Fragments; Letter to Octavian; Invectives; Handbook of Electioneering*. Loeb Classical Library 432. Cambridge, MA: Harvard University Press.

Shackleton Bailey, D. R. 2001. *Cicero: Letters to Friends*. Vol. 2. Loeb Classical Library 216. Cambridge, MA: Harvard University Press.

Shackleton Bailey, D. R. 1980. *Cicero: Epistulae ad Quintum Fratrem et M. Brutum*. Cambridge: Cambridge University Press.

Shackleton Bailey, D. R. 1977. *Cicero: Epistulae ad Familiares*. 2 vols. Cambridge: Cambridge University Press.

Shackleton Bailey, D. R. 1968. *Cicero's Letters to Atticus*. Vol. 3. Cambridge: Cambridge University Press.

Shaw, B. 2012. *Bringing in the Sheaves: Economy and Metaphor in the Roman World*. University of Toronto Press.

Shear Jr., T. L. 2016. *Trophies of Victory: Public Building in Periklean Athens*. Princeton University Press.

Sheldrake, M. 2020. *Entangled Life: How Fungi Make our Worlds, Change our Minds and Shape our Futures*. Random House.

Silver, M. 2011. "In Dubious Battle: An Economic Analysis of Emperor Hadrian's Fish and Olive Oil Laws." *Roman Legal Tradition* 7: 1–15.

Skibo, J. 1992. *Pottery Function: Use-Alteration Perspective*. Springer.

Skowronski, J. J. and Carlston, D.E. 1992. "Caught in the Act: When Impressions Based on Highly Diagnostic Behaviours Are Resistant to Contradiction." *European Journal of Social Psychology* 22, no. 5: 435–452.

Slootjes, D. 2011. "Local Elites and Power in the Roman World: Modern Theories and Models." *The Journal of Interdisciplinary History* 42 (2): 235–249.

Snell, B. 1953. "Arcadia: The Discovery of a Spiritual Landscape." In *The Discovery of the Mind*. 281–309. Rosenmeyer, T. Trans. Harvard University Press.

Snow, C. E. 1986. "The Affecter Amphora: A Case Study in the History of Greek Vase Restoration." *The Journal of the Walters Art Gallery* 44: 2–7.

Sourvinou-Inwood, C. 1995. *Reading Greek Death to the End of the Classical Period*. Clarendon Press.

Spaeth, B.S. 1996. *The Roman Goddess Ceres*. University of Texas Press.

Stachniw, J. M. 1973–4. "*Labor* as key to the *Aeneid*." *Classical Bulletin* L: 49–53.

Stangor, C., and Schaller, M. 1996. "Stereotypes as Individual and Collective Representations." In Macrae, C., Stangor, C., and Hewstone, M., eds. *Stereotypes and Stereotyping*, 3–40. The Guilford Press.

Stears K. 1998. "Death Becomes Her. Gender and Athenian Death Ritual." In Blundell, S. and Williamson, M. eds. *The Sacred and the Feminine in Ancient Greece*. 113–27. University of Chicago Press.

Steinby, E. M. 1993. "Ricerche sull'industria *dolia*re nelle aree di Roma and e Pompei: un possibile modello interpretativo," in Zaccaria, C., ed. *I Laterizi di Età Romana nell'Area Nordadriatica*. 9–14. L'Erma di Bretschneider.

Steinby, E. M. 1987. "Indici complementari ai bolli *dolia*ri urbani (CIL. XV,1)". *Acta Instituti Romani Finlandiae* 11.

Steinby, E. M. 1982. "I Senatori e l'Industria Laterizia Urbana." *Tituli* 4: 227–237.

Steinby, E. M. 1981. "La diffusione dell'opus *dolia*re urbano." In Giardina, A. and Schiavone, A., eds. *Società romana e produzione schiavistica, II*. 237–245. Laterza.

Steinby, E. M. 1974/5. "La cronologia delle figlinae *dolia*ri urbane dalla fine dell'età repubblicana fino all'inizio delIII sec." *Bullettino della Commissione Archeologica Comunale di Roma* 84: 7–132.

Stewart, E., Harris, E., and Lewis, D., eds. 2020. *Skilled Labour and Professionalism in Ancient Greece and Rome*. Cambridge University Press.

Storchi Marino, A. 1979. "Artigiani e rituali religiosi nella Roma arcaica." *Rendiconti della Accademia di Archeologia, Lettere e Belle Arti* 54: 333–357.

Strong, A. K. 2016. *Prostitutes and Matrons in the Roman World*. Cambridge University Press.

Strong, D. 1988. *Roman Art*. Yale University Press.

Suter, A., ed. 2008. *Lament: Studies in the Ancient Mediterranean and Beyond*. Oxford University Press.

Taglietti, F. 2015. "*Dolia* e coperchi di *dolia*: problematici assortimenti." in Spanu, M., ed. *Opus doliare Tiberinum: atti delle giornate di studio*. 267–29 Università degli Studi della Tuscia.

Taragan, H. 2008. "Constructing a Visual Rhetoric: Images of Craftsmen and Builders in the Umayyad Palace at Qusayr 'Amra." *Al-Masaq. Islam and the Medieval Mediterranean* 20: 141–60.

Taylor, R. 2003. *Roman Builders: A Study in Architectural Process*. Cambridge University Press.

Temin, P. 2012. *The Roman Market Economy*. Princeton University Press.

Terkel, S. 1974. *Working: People Talk about What They Do All Day and How They Feel about What They Do*. Ballantine Books.

Thill, E. W. 2010. "Civilization Under Construction: Depictions of Architecture on the Column of Trajan." *American Journal of Archaeology* 114: 27–43.

Thill, E. W. 2018. "Setting War in Stone: Architectural Depictions on the Column of Marcus Aurelius." *American Journal of Archaeology* 122: 277–308.

Thomas, E. 2007. *Monumentality and the Roman Empire: Architecture in the Antonine Age*. Oxford University Press.

Thomas, K. 2009. "Representations of Labour in Visual Images and Literary Texts: Comments on Gergard Jaritz, Ilja M. Veldman and Cynthia J. Koepp." In Ehmer, J., and Lis, C. *The Idea of Work in Europe from Antiquity to Modern Times*. 331–48. Routledge.

Thompson, E. P. 1993. *Customs in Common: Studies in Traditional Popular Culture*. The New Press.

Thompson, E. P. 1963. *The Making of the English Working Class*. Victor Gollancz.

Thonemann, P. 2011. *The Maeander Valley: A Historical Geography from Antiquity to Byzantium*. Cambridge University Press.

Thonemann, P. 2020. *An Ancient Dream Manual: Artemidorus'*The Interpretation of Dreams. Oxford University Press.

Thornton, J. 1998. "A Brief History and Review of the Early Practice and Materials of Gap-Filling in the West." *Journal of the American Institute for Conservation* 37: 3–22.

Thurmond, D.L. 2006. *A handbook of food processing in classical Rome. For her bounty no winter*. Brill.

Thurmond, D.L. 2017. *From Vines to Wines in Classical Rome A Handbook of Viticulture and Oenology in Rome and the Roman West*. Brill.

Tietz, W. 2021. "Seasonal labour and migratory work in the Roman empire." in Lichtenberger, A., and Raja, R., eds. *The Archaeology of Seasonality*. 25–38. Brepols.

Todd, L. 2008. *Carolina Clay. The Life and Legend of the Slave Potter Dave*. W.W. Norton & Company.

Toher, M. 2005. "The Tenth Table and the Conflict of the Orders." In Raaflaub, K. ed. *Social Struggles in Archaic Rome: New Perspectives on the Conflict of the Orders. Expanded and Updated Edition.* 268–92. Blackwell.

Toner, J. P. 2015. "Barbers, Barbershops and Searching for Roman Popular Culture." *Papers of the British School at Rome* 83: 91–109.

Tortorella, S. 2009. "Tomba di Patron sulla via Latina a Roma: frammenti di decorazione pittorica." in La Rocca, E., Ensoli, S., Ensoli, S., Tortorella, S., and Papini, M., eds. *Roma: la pittura di un impero.* 270–271. Skira.

Tran, N. 2013. Dominus tabernae: *le statut de travail des artisans et des commerçants de l'occident romain (Ier siècle av. J.-C.-IIIe siècle ap. J.-C.).* Ecole Francaise de Rome.

Tran, N. 2017. "*Ars* and *Doctrina*: the socioeconomic identity of Roman skilled workers (first century BC-third century AD)." In Verboven and Laes. 246–261.

Treggiari, S. 1991. *Roman Marriage. Iusti Coniuges from the Time of Cicero to the Time of Ulpian.* Oxford University Press.

Treggiari, S. 1973. "Cicero, Horace, and Mutual Friends: Lamiae and Varrones Murenae". *Phoenix* 27 (3): 245–61.

Treggiari, S. 1969a. *Roman Freedmen during the Late Republic.* Oxford: Oxford University Press.

Treggiari, S. 1969b. "The Freedmen of Cicero." *Greece & Rome* 16.2: 195–204.

Trimble, J. 2018. "Figure and ornament, death and Transformation in the Tomb of the Haterii." In Doetrich, N. and Squire, M. eds. *Ornament and Figure in Graeco-Roman Art: Visual Ontologies in Classical Antiquity.* 327–52. De Gruyter.

True, M. and Podany, J., eds. 1991. *Marble: Art Historical and Scientific Perspectives on Ancient Sculpture.* J. Paul Getty Press.

Ulrich, R. 2007. *Roman Woodworking.* Yale University Press.

Vanhaegendoren, K. 2007. "Travail et loisir en Grèce ancienne: à propos de la complémentarité des activités du citoyen." *Ancient Society* 37: 1–35.

Van Nijf, O. M. 2008. "The Social World of Tax Farmers and their Personnel." In Cottier, M. and Corbeille, M. eds. *The Customs Laws of Asia.* 279–311. Oxford.

Van Nijf, O. M. 1997. *The civic world of professional associations in the Roman East.* Gieben.

Van Oyen, A. 2020a. *The socio-economics of Roman storage: Agriculture, trade, and family.* Cambridge University Press.

Van Oyen, A. 2020b. "Innovation and investment in the Roman rural economy through the lens of Marzuolo (Tuscany, Italy)." *Past & Present* 248.1: 3–40.

Van Oyen, A. 2015. "The moral architecture of villa storage in Italy in the 1st c. BC." *Journal of Roman Archaeology* 28: 97–123.

Van Oyen, A., Tol, G.W., Vennarucci, R.G., Agostini, A., Serneels, V., Mercury, A.M., Rattighieri, E. and Benatti, A. 2022. "Forging the Roman rural economy: A blacksmithing workshop and its toolset at Marzuolo (Tuscany)." *American Journal of Archaeology* 126.1: 53–77.

Varro [Marcus Terentius Varro]. De lingua Latina: Kent, R. G. (ed. and trans.). 1951–1958. *On the Latin Language, Loeb Classical Library*, 333–34, 2 vols. Harvard University Press. (Cheung)

Venticinque, P.F. 2016. *Honor Among Thieves: Craftsmen, Merchants, and Associations in Roman and Late Roman Egypt.* University of Michigan Press.

Verboven, K. 2015. "The knights who say NIE: can Neo-Institutional Economics live up to its expectation in ancient history research?." In Erdkamp, P., and Verboven, K. eds. *Structure and performance in the Roman economy: Models, methods and case studies.* 33–57. Latomus.

Verboven, K. 2002. *The Economy of Friends: Economic Aspects of Amicitia and Patronage in the Late Republic.* Latomus.

Verboven, K. 2016. "Guilds and gods. Religious profiles of occupational *collegia* and the problem of the *dendrophori.*" In Trentacoste, A., Ray, N., and Wilson A., eds. *The Economics of Roman Religion.* Oxford University Press.

Verboven, K. and Laes, C. 2017a. "Work, Labour, Professions. What's in a Name?" In Verboven and Laes. 1–19.

Verboven, K. and Laes, C., eds. 2017. *Work, Labour, and Professions in the Roman World. Impact of Empire, 23.* Brill.

Versnel, H. S. 2012. "The poetics of the magical charm: An essay in the power of words." In Mirecki, P.A. ed. *Magic and ritual in the ancient world.* 105–158. Brill.

Veyne, P. 2000. "La "plèbe moyenne" sous le Haut-Empire romain." *Annales* 55–6: 1169–99.

Vidal, J. L. 2002. "Intención de autor y estilo de la época en la composición de la *vita Vergilii* de Focas." In Walz, D., ed. *Scripturus Vitam: Lateinische Biographie von der Antike bis in die Gegenwart: Festgabe für Walter Berschin zum 65. Geburtstag.* 663–72. Heidelberg.

Vidal, J. L. 1991"La Vita Vergiliana de Focas: Biograpfia y poesía de escuela." *ExcPhilol.* I: 801–12.

Ville, G. 2014. *La Gladiature en Occident des origines à la mort de Domitien.* Ecole Française de Rome.

Vinken, B. 2020. "Arachne: *Eros fatal.* Ovid, Flaubert." Möller, M. ed. *Gegen/Gewalt/Schreiben: De-Konstruktionen von Geschlechts- und Rollenbildern in der Ovid-Rezeption.* 117–138. De Gruyter.

Volbach, W. 1976. *Elfenbeinarbeiten der Spätantike und des frühen Mittelalters.* Von Zabern.

Volk, K. 2021. *The Roman Republic of Letters. Scholarship, Philosophy, and Politics in the Age of Cicero and Caesar.* Princeton University Press.

Von Blanckenhagen, P. H. 1940. *Flavische Architektur und ihre Dekoration untersucht am Nerva-forum.* De Gruyter.

Wacquant, L. 2004. *Body and Soul: Notebooks of an Apprentice Boxer.* Oxford University Press.

Wagner-Hasel, B. and Nosch, M., eds. 2019. *Gaben, Waren und Tribute: Stoffkreisläufe und antike Textilökonomie: Akten eines Symposiums (9./10. Juni 2016 in Hannover).* Steiner.

Waldstein, W. 1986. *Operae Libertorum. Untersuchungen zur Dienstpflicht freigelassener Sklaven.* Steiner.

Wallace-Hadrill, A. 2008. *Rome's Cultural Revolution.* Cambridge University Press.

Walker, S. 1979. "Corinthian capitals with ringed voids: the work of Athenian craftsmen in the second century AD." *Archäologischer Anzeiger*: 103–129.

Ward-Perkins, J. B. 1980. "Nicomedia and the marble trade." *PBSR* 48: 23–69.

Ward-Perkins, J. B. 1993. *The Severan Buildings of Lepcis Magna: an Architectural Survey.* Society for Libyan Studies.

Warner, M. 2002. *Fantastic Metamorphoses, Other Worlds: Ways of Telling the Self.* Oxford University Press.

Watson, A. 1967. *The Law of Persons in the Later Roman Republic.* Oxford: Oxford University Press.

Weitzmann, K., ed. 1979. *Age of Spirituality. Late Antique and Early Christian Art, Third to Seventh Century.* Metropolitan Museum of Art, in association with Princeton University Press. [Freely available from MetPublications, https://www.metmuseum.org/art/metpublications/Age_of_Spirituality_Late_Antique_and_Early_Christian_Art_Third_to_Seventh_Century.

Whately, C. 2016. *Exercitus Moesiae: The Roman Army in Moesia from Augustus to Severus Alexander.* BAR Publishing.

White, K. D. 2010. *Agricultural Implements of the Roman World.* Cambridge University Press.

Wickham, C. 1998. "Gossip and Resistance among the Medieval Peasantry." *Past & Present* 160: 3–24.

Williams, R. 2015 (1976). *Keywords: A Vocabulary of Culture and Society.* Oxford University Press.

Wilson, A. and Flohr, M., eds. 2016. *Urban Craftsmen and Traders in the Roman World, Oxford Studies on the Roman Economy.* Oxford University Press.

Wilson, A. and Bowman, A. eds. 2018. *Trade, Commerce, and the State in the Roman World.* Oxford University Press.

Wilson R. J. A. 2018. "Roman Villas in North Africa." In Marzano, A. and Métraux, G. eds. *The Roman Villa in the Mediterranean Basin: Late Republic to Late Antiquity.* 266–307. Cambridge University Press.

Wolfthal, D., ed. 2023. *Toward a Visual History of the Working Class. Different Visions: New Perspectives on Medieval Art.* https://differentvisions.org/issue-ten/.

Wootton, W., Russell, B., and Rockwell, P. 2013. "Stoneworking Techniques and Processes (Version 1.0)', The Art of Making in Antiquity: Stoneworking in the RomanWorld."http://www.artofmaking.ac.uk/content/essays/3-stoneworking-techniques-and-processesw-wootton-b-russell-p-rockwell/ [accessed 1 May 2021].

Woolf, G. 2015. "Pliny/Trajan and the poetics of empire." *CPhil.* 110: 132–151.

Wray, D. 2007. "Wood: Statius's *Silvae* and the Poetics of Genius." *Arethusa* 40(2): 127–143.

Yarrow, L. 2018. "Markers of Identity for Non-Elite Romans: A Prolegomenon to the Study of Glass Paste Intaglios." *Journal of Ancient History and Archaeology* 5.3: 35–54.

Youakim, S., 2006. "Occupational health risks of wine industry workers." *British Columbia Medical Journal* 48(8): 386–391.

Zanker, P. 1975. "Grabreliefs römischer Freigelassener." *Jahrbuch des Deutschen Archäologischen Instituts XC*: 267–315.

Zanker, P. 1988. *The Power of Images in the Age of Augustus.* University of Michigan Press.

Zatta, C. 2019. *Interconnectedness: The Living World of the Early Greek Philosophers.* Academia Verlag.

Zatta, C. 2016. "Plants' Interconnected Lives: From Ovid's Myths to Presocratic Thought and Beyond." *Arion* 24.2: 101–126.

Zimmer, G. 1982. *Römische Berufsdarstellungen.* Gebrüder Mann Verlag.

Zimmermann, C. 2002. *Handwerkervereine im griechischen Osten des Imperium Romanum.* Gnomon.

Ziogas, I. 2021. *Law and Love in Ovid: Courting Justice in the Age of Augustus.* Oxford University Press.

Ziolkowski, T. 2005. *Ovid and the Moderns.* Cornell University Press.

Ziolkowski, J. and Putnam, M. C. J., eds. 2008. *The Virgilian Tradition: The First Fifteen-Hundred Years.* Yale University Press.

Zuiderhoek, A. 2009. *The Politics of Munificence in the Roman Empire.* Cambridge University Press.

Index[1]

[1] Note: Page numbers followed by 'n' refer to notes.

D. A. Maticic, J. Rogers (eds.), *Working Lives in Ancient Rome*, The New Antiquity,
https://doi.org/10.1007/978-3-031-61234-3

SPRINGER NATURE

GPSR Compliance

The European Union's (EU) General Product Safety Regulation (GPSR) is a set of rules that requires consumer products to be safe and our obligations to ensure this.

If you have any concerns about our products, you can contact us on ProductSafety@springernature.com

In case Publisher is established outside the EU, the EU authorized representative is:

Springer Nature Customer Service Center GmbH
Europaplatz 3
69115 Heidelberg, Germany

The manufacturer's authorised representative in the EU is Springer Nature Customer Service Centre GmbH, Europaplatz 3, 69115 Heidelberg, Germany. If you have any concerns regarding our products, please contact ProductSafety@springernature.com

Printed and bound by CPI Group (UK) Ltd, Croydon, CR0 4YY
01/10/2026
02225903-0017